Why Do You Need This New Edition?

If you're wondering why you should buy this new edition of _The Writer's World_, here are 10 good reasons!

❶ **New "Visualizing [the mode]" Feature:** Chapters 4 to 12 now include a new feature that illustratively represents each of the nine patterns/modes so you can visually grasp how they are used in everyday writing situations! "Visualizing [the mode]" helps you "see" how to use each of the nine modes/patterns.

❷ **New Annotated "At Work" Paragraphs:** In Chapters 4 to 12, each "At Work" paragraph pattern includes real-world examples and now contains callouts and annotations pointing out the paragraph's key elements: the topic sentence, the supporting ideas, and the concluding sentence.

❸ **New Grammar Chapters:** New to this edition, the Fragments and Run-On chapter has been split into two separate chapters. Chapter 24, Past Participles, now features a section called "Past Participle as an Adjective." Chapter 25, Other Verb Forms, has a new section on Gerunds and Infinitives.

❹ **New Photos:** New opening photos and photo writing prompts appear throughout the book. Each grammar chapter has an opening photo that helps to show the thematic content.

❺ **New Media Writing Activities:** Every paragraph pattern chapter now ends with a newly modified Media Writing activity. You are asked to view a television program, film, or online video and use the content as writing prompts that will help you sharpen your overall writing skills.

❻ **Getting Motivated:** Cooperative Learning Teaching Tips appear throughout the book and can be used by your instructor to promote peer-to-peer interaction, share knowledge, solve a problem, negotiate, and reflect. These activities will help prepare you for the workplace!

❼ **Your World:** You spend your day texting friends and family, checking Facebook and Twitter, and listening to music on your iPod. New teaching suggestions help your instructors to incorporate more activities that include these cutting edge devices. For example, in Chapter 4, you are invited to list the most useful apps and features on your cell phone, and in Chapter 5, you can look on Facebook and narrate what happened recently to a friend.

❽ **New MLA Updates:** Chapter 15, Enhancing Your Writing with Research, contains updated information from the Seventh Edition of the _MLA Handbook_. Material in the chapter has been streamlined and revised with topical examples and references. The final student essay about cell phones and health has a detailed Works Cited page, and the chapter ends with a practice related to the sample essay.

❾ **New Readings:** The first 12 chapters include a wide selection of new paragraph examples. Chapter 14 contains four new essays, including two written by students about their personal experiences. New essay topics include homophobia, the purpose of pets, and guy chores. In Chapter 38, From Reading to Writing, there are six fascinating new readings including "Musicophilia" by Oliver Sachs and "Gone with the Windows" by Dorothy Nixon.

❿ **Chapter Objectives & MyWritingLab:** Each chapter in _The Writer's World: Paragraphs and Essays_ now opens with a list of chapter objectives and ties them into the most powerful online writing tool on the planet with Pearson's **MyWritingLab** (www .mywritinglab.com). Now you can truly grasp chapter content and test your understanding of that content with MyWritingLab in a more meaningful way!

MyWritingLab™ has helped students like you from all over the country.

MyWritingLab™ can help you become a better writer and help you get a better grade.

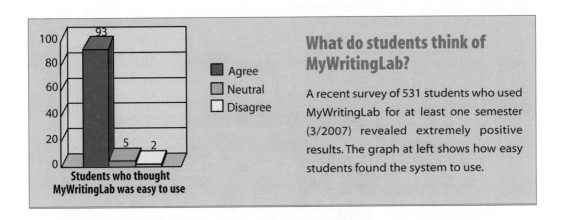

What do students think of MyWritingLab?

A recent survey of 531 students who used MyWritingLab for at least one semester (3/2007) revealed extremely positive results. The graph at left shows how easy students found the system to use.

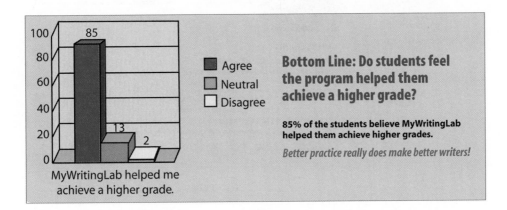

Bottom Line: Do students feel the program helped them achieve a higher grade?

85% of the students believe MyWritingLab helped them achieve higher grades.

Better practice really does make better writers!

Registering for MyWritingLab™ . . .

It is easy to get started! Simply follow these steps to get into your MyWritingLab course.

1. **Find Your Access Code** (it is either packaged with your textbook, or you purchased it separately). You will need this access code and your course ID to join your MyWritingLab course. Your instructor has your course ID number, so make sure you have that before logging in.

2. **Click on "Students"** under "First-Time Users." Here you will be prompted to enter your access code, enter your e-mail address, and choose your own Login Name and Password. After you register, you can **click on "Returning Users"** to use your new login name and password every time you go back into your course in MyWritingLab.

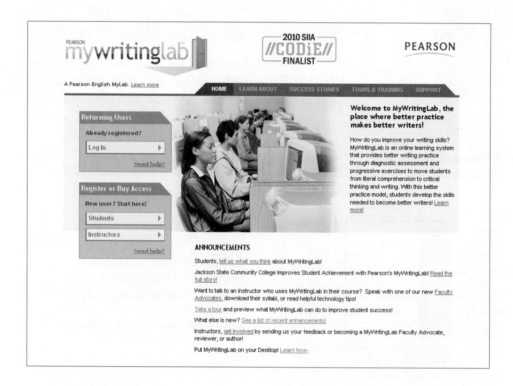

After logging in, you will see all the ways MyWritingLab can help you become a better writer.

www.mywritinglab.com

The Homepage . . .

Here is your MyWritingLab HomePage.
You get a bird's eye view of where you are in your course every time you log in.

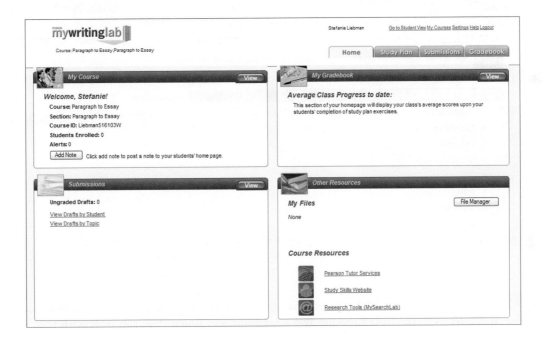

Your **Course** box shows your class details.

Your **Study Plan** box shows what you last completed and what is next on your **To Do** list.

Your **Gradebook** box shows you a snapshot of how you are doing in the class.

Your **Other Resources** box supplies you with amazing tools such as:

- **Pearson Tutor Services**—click here to see how you can get help on your papers by qualified tutors . . . before handing them in!

- **Research Navigator**—click here to see how this resembles your library with access to online journals for research paper assignments.

- **Study Skills**—extra help that includes tips and quizzes on how to improve your study skills

- **Pearson e-Text**—click here to read and reference the e-text version of your textbook!

Now, let's start practicing to become better writers. Click on the Study Plan tab. This is where you will do all your course work.

www.mywritinglab.com

The Study Plan . . .

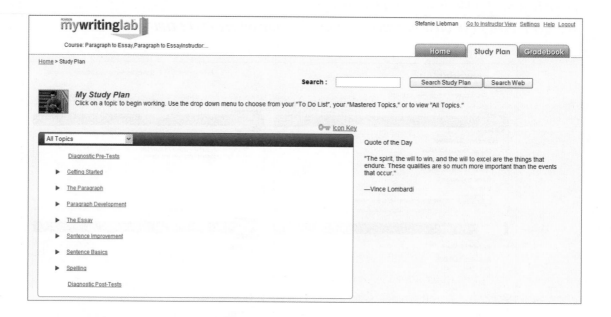

MyWritingLab provides you with a simple Study Plan of the writing skills that you need to master. You start from the top of the list and work your way down. You can start with the Diagnostic Pre-Tests.

The Diagnostic Pre-Tests . . .

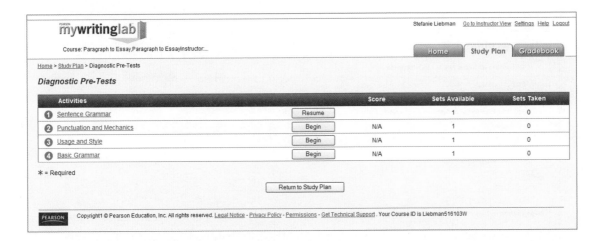

MyWritingLab's Diagnostic Pre-Tests are divided into four parts and cover all the major grammar, punctuation, and usage topics. After you complete these diagnostic tests, MyWritingLab will generate a personalized Study Plan for you, showing all the topics you have mastered and listing all the topics yet unmastered.

www.mywritinglab.com

The Diagnostic Pre-Tests . . .

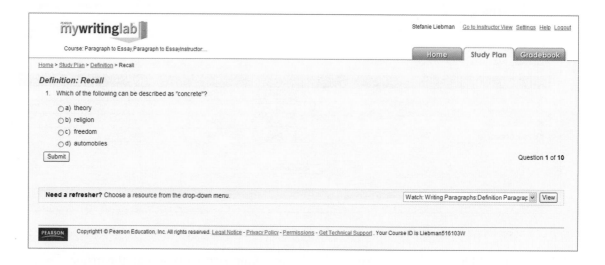

The Diagnostic Pre-Tests contain five exercises on each of the grammar, punctuation, and usage topics. You can achieve mastery of the topic in the Diagnostic Pre-Test by getting four of five or five of five correct within each topic.

After completing the Diagnostic Pre-Test, you can return to your Study Plan and enter any of the topics you have yet to master.

www.mywritinglab.com

Watch, Recall, Apply, Write . . .

Here is an example of a MyWritinglab Activity set that you will see once you enter into a topic. Take the time to briefly read the introductory paragraph, and then **watch** the engaging video clip by clicking on "Watch: Tense."

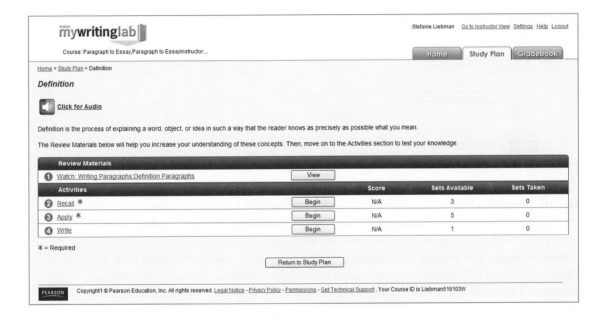

The video clip provides you with a helpful review.
Now you are ready to start the exercises. There are three types:

- Recall—activities that help you *recall* the rules of grammar

- Apply—activities that help you *apply* these rules to brief paragraphs or essays

- Write—activities that ask you to demonstrate these rules of grammar in your own writing

www.mywritinglab.com

Watch, Recall, Apply, Write . . .

Recall questions help you recall the rules of grammar and writing when you complete multiple-choice questions, usually with four possible answers. You get feedback after answering each question, so you can learn as you go!

There are many sets available for lots of practice. As soon as you are finished with a set of activities, you will receive a score sheet with helpful feedback, including the correct answers. This score sheet will be kept in your own gradebook, so you can always go back and review.

Watch, Recall, Apply, Write . . .

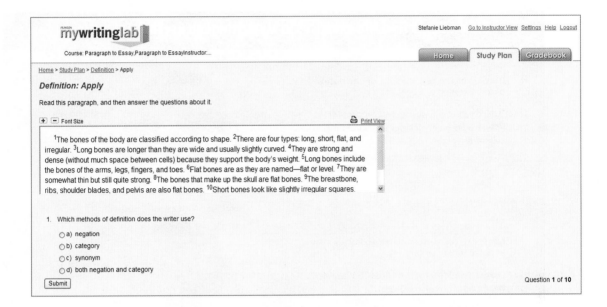

Apply exercises help you apply writing and grammar rules to brief paragraphs or essays. Sometimes these are multiple-choice questions, and other times you will be asked to identify and correct mistakes in existing paragraphs and essays.

Your instructor may also assign **Write exercises**, which allow you to demonstrate writing and grammar rules in your own writing.

www.mywritinglab.com

Helping Students Succeed . . .

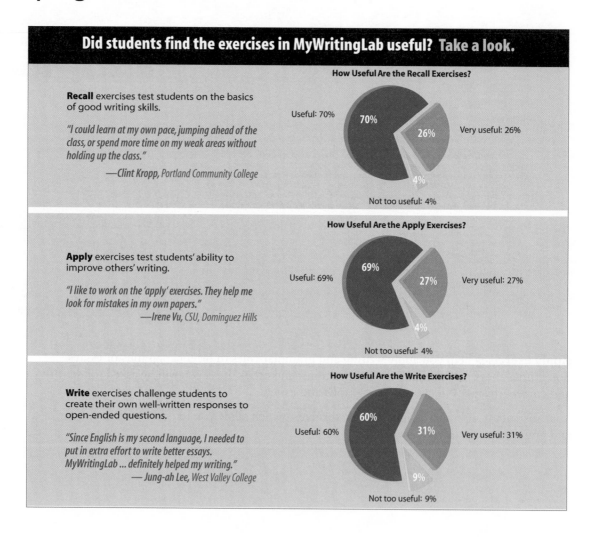
Students just like you are finding MyWritingLab's Recall, Apply, and Write exercises useful in their learning.

The Gradebook . . .

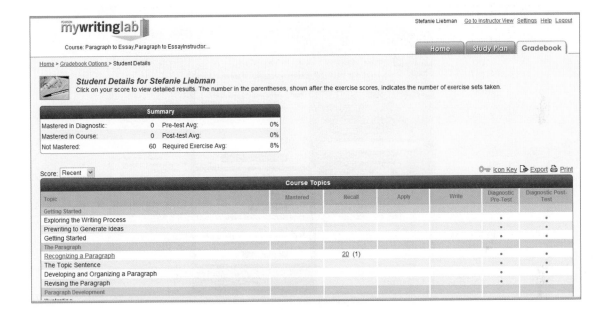

Let's look at how your own on-line gradebook will help you track your progress.

Click on the "Gradebook" tab and then the "Student Detail" report.

Here you are able to see how you are doing in each area. If you feel you need to go back and review, simply click on any score and your score sheet will appear.

You also have a Diagnostic Detail report so you can go back and review your diagnostic Pre-Test and see how much MyWritingLab has helped you improve!

www.mywritinglab.com

Here to Help You . . .

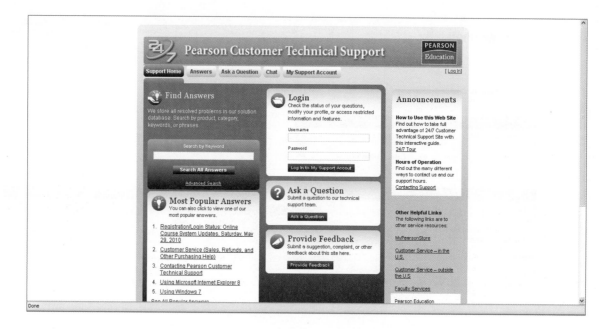

Our goal is to provide answers to your MyWritingLab questions as quickly as possible and deliver the highest level of support. By visiting www.mywritinglab.com/help.html, many questions can be resolved in just a few minutes. Here you will find help on the following:

- System Requirements
- How to Register for MyWritingLab
- How to Use MyWritingLab

For student support, we also invite you to contact Pearson Customer Technical Support (shown above). In addition, you can reach our Support Representatives online at http://247.pearsoned.com. Here you can do the following:

- Search Frequently Asked Questions About MyWritingLab
- E-mail a Question to Our Support Team
- Chat with a Support Representative

www.mywritinglab.com

LYNNE GAETZ
Lionel Groulx College

SUNEETI PHADKE
St. Jerome College

The Writer's World

Paragraphs and Essays

THIRD EDITION

Prentice Hall

Boston   Columbus   Indianapolis   New York   San Francisco   Upper Saddle River
Amsterdam   Cape Town   Dubai   London   Madrid   Milan   Munich   Paris   Montreal
Toronto   Delhi   Mexico City   Sao Paulo   Sydney   Hong Kong   Seoul   Singapore   Taipei   Tokyo

Senior Acquisitions Editor: Matthew Wright
Senior Development Editor: Katharine Glynn
Senior Marketing Manager: Thomas DeMarco
Senior Supplements Editor: Donna Campion
Senior Media Producer: Stefanie Liebman
Project Coordination, Text Design, and Electronic Page Makeup: Laserwords Maine
Art Director: Anne Nieglos
Cover Designer: Ximena Tamvakopolous
Cover Illustration: Sunglasses, Thorsten Rust/Shutterstock Images; left image, © MBI/Alamy; right image, © Jack Hollingsworth/
   Corbis Premium/Alamy
Photo Researcher: Katharine S. Cebik
Image Permissions: Lee Scher
Senior Manufacturing Buyer: Mary Ann Gloriande
Printer and Binder: Courier Corporation
Cover Printer: Lehigh-Phoenix Color Corporation

For permission to use copyrighted material, grateful acknowledgment is made to the copyright holders on pages 595–596, which are hereby made part of this copyright page.

2 3 4 5 6 7 8 9 10—CRK—14 13 12 11

Student Edition ISBN-13: 978-0-205-78175-1
Student Edition ISBN-10: 0-205-78175-6
Annotated Instructor s Edition ISBN-13: 978-0-205-78177-5
Annotated Instructor s Edition ISBN-10: 0-205-78177-2

Prentice Hall
is an imprint of

www.pearsonhighered.com

Brief Table of Contents

Contents

Inside Front Cover
Paragraph and Essay Checklists

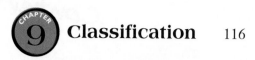
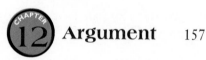

PART III — The Essay 174

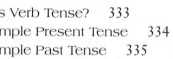

Appendices

Preface

Welcome to the Third Edition of *The Writer's World: Paragraphs and Essays*

Thank you for making the second edition of *The Writer's World* a resounding success. We are delighted that the book has been able to help so many students across the country. This third edition, too, can help your students produce writing that is technically correct and richly detailed whether your classes are filled with students who have varying skill levels, whether students are native or nonnative speakers of English, or whether they learn better through the use of visuals. When we started the first edition, we set out to develop practical and pedagogically sound approaches to these challenges, and we are pleased to hear that the book is helping students succeed in their writing courses.

For those new to the book, here is some background information to give a more complete picture.

A Research-Based Approach

We began with the idea that this project should be a collaboration with other developmental writing teachers. So we met with more than forty-five instructors from around the country, asking for their opinions and insights regarding (1) the challenges posed by the course, (2) the needs of today's ever-changing student population, and (3) the ideas and features we were proposing in order to provide them and you with a more effective teaching and learning tool. Prentice Hall also commissioned dozens of detailed manuscript reviews from instructors, asking them to analyze and evaluate each draft of the manuscript. These reviewers identified numerous ways in which we could refine and enhance our key features. Their invaluable feedback was incorporated throughout *The Writer's World*. The text you are seeing is truly the product of a successful partnership between the authors, publisher, and well over one hundred developmental writing instructors.

How We Organized *The Writer's World*

The Writer's World is separated into five parts for ease of use, convenience, and ultimate flexibility.

Part I: The Writing Process teaches students (1) how to formulate ideas (Exploring); (2) how to expand, organize, and present those ideas in a piece of writing (Developing); and (3) how to polish writing so that they convey their message as clearly as possible (Revising and Editing). The result is that writing a paragraph or an essay becomes far less daunting because students have specific steps to follow.

Part II: Paragraph Patterns gives students a solid overview of the patterns of development. Using the same easy-to-understand process (Exploring, Developing, and Revising and Editing), each chapter in this section explains how to convey ideas using one or more writing patterns. As they work through the practices and write their own paragraphs and essays, students begin to see how using a writing pattern can help them fulfill their purpose for writing.

Part III: The Essay covers the parts of the essay and explains how students can apply the nine patterns of development to essay writing. This section also discusses the role research plays in writing and explains some ways that students can incorporate research in their essays.

Part IV: The Editing Handbook is a thematic grammar handbook. In each chapter, the examples correspond to a theme, such as popular culture, college life, and work. As students work through the chapters, they hone their grammar and editing skills while gaining knowledge about a variety of topics. In addition to helping build interest in the grammar practices, the thematic material provides a spark that ignites new ideas that students can apply to their writing.

Part V: Reading Strategies and Selections offers tips, readings, and follow-up questions. Students learn how to write by observing and dissecting what they read. The readings relate to the themes found in Part IV: The Editing Handbook, thereby providing more fodder for generating writing ideas.

How *The Writer's World* Meets Students' Diverse Needs

We created *The Writer's World* to meet your students' diverse needs. To accomplish this, we asked both the instructors in our focus groups and the reviewers at every stage not only to critique our ideas but to offer their suggestions and recommendations for features that would enhance the learning process of their students. The result has been the integration of many elements that are not found in other textbooks, including our **visual program, coverage of nonnative speaker material, and strategies for addressing the varying skill levels students bring to the course.**

The Visual Program

A stimulating, full-color book with more than 80 photos, *The Writer's World* recognizes that today's world is a visual one, and it encourages students to become better communicators by responding to images. Chapter-opening visuals in Parts I, II, and III help students to think about the chapter's key concept in a new way. For example, in the Chapter 9 opener, a photograph of children's toys sets the stage for classification. Toys are grouped by type, which helps students understand the premise of classification. In Part IV, chapter-opening photos help illustrate the theme of the examples and exercises. These visual aids can also serve as sources for writing prompts.

Each **At Work** box in the Part II chapters features multi-colored highlighting and annotations, along with content on how that particular pattern of development is used on the job.

The visuals in Part II provide students with another set of opportunities to write in response to images, with Photo Writing and Media Writing activities that encourage them to respond using particular paragraph and essay patterns.

Throughout *The Writer's World*, words and images work together to encourage students to explore, develop, and revise their writing.

Seamless Coverage for Nonnative Speakers

Instructors in our focus groups noted the growing number of nonnative/ESL speakers enrolling in developmental writing courses. Although some of these students have special needs relating to the writing process, many of you still have a large portion of native speakers in your courses whose more traditional needs must also be satisfied. In order to meet the challenge of this rapidly changing dynamic, we have carefully implemented and integrated content throughout to assist these students. *The Writer's World* does not have separate ESL boxes, ESL chapters, or tacked-on ESL appendices. Instead, information that traditionally poses a challenge to nonnative speakers is woven seamlessly throughout the book. In our extensive experience teaching writing to both native and nonnative speakers of English, we have learned that both groups learn best when they are not distracted by ESL labels. With the seamless approach, nonnative speakers do not feel self-conscious and segregated, and native speakers do not tune out detailed explanations that may also benefit them. Many of these traditional problem areas receive more coverage than you would find in other textbooks, arming the instructor with the material to effectively meet the needs of nonnative speakers. Moreover, the Annotated Instructor's Edition provides over seventy-five ESL Teaching Tips designed specifically to help instructors better meet the needs of their nonnative speaking students.

Issue-Focused Thematic Grammar

In surveys, many of you indicated that one of the primary challenges in teaching your course is finding materials that are engaging to students in a contemporary context. This is especially true in grammar instruction. **Students come to the course with varying skill levels**, and many students are simply not interested in grammar. To address this challenge, we have introduced **issue-focused thematic grammar** into *The Writer's World*.

Each chapter centers on a theme that is carried out in examples and activities. These themes include topics related to popular culture, psychology, espionage, college life, inventions and discoveries, health care, the legal world, and the workplace. The thematic approach enables students to broaden their awareness of subjects important to American life, such as understanding advertising and consumerism and thinking about health care issues and alternative medicine. The thematic approach makes reading about grammar more engaging. And the more engaging grammar is, the more likely students will retain key concepts—raising their skill level in these important building blocks of writing.

We also think that it is important to teach grammar in the context of the writing process. Students should not think that grammar is an isolated exercise. Therefore, **each grammar chapter includes a warm up writing activity**. Students write and edit their paragraphs, paying particular attention to the grammar point covered in the chapter. The end of each grammar section also contains paragraph and essay writing topics that are related to the theme of the section and that follow different writing patterns. Suggestions are given for readings in these chapters in Part V that relate to the grammar themes.

What Tools Can Help Students Get the Most from *The Writer's World*?

Overwhelmingly, focus group participants and reviewers asked that both a larger number and a greater diversity of exercises and activities be incorporated into *The Writer's World*. In response, we have developed and tested the following learning aids in *The Writer's World*. We are confident they will help your students become better writers.

Hints
In each chapter, **Hint** boxes highlight important writing and grammar points. Hints are useful for all students, but many will be particularly helpful for nonnative speakers. For example, in Chapter 12, one Hint encourages students to state an argument directly and a second Hint points out the need to avoid circular reasoning. In Chapter 22, a Hint discusses checking for consistent voice in compound sentences. Hints include brief discussions and examples so that students will see both concept and application.

Hint   Spelling, Grammar, and Vocabulary Logs

- **Keep a spelling and grammar log.** You probably repeat, over and over, the same types of grammar and spelling errors. You will find it very useful to record your repeated grammar mistakes in a spelling and grammar log. You can refer to your list of spelling and grammar mistakes when you revise and edit your writing.
- **Keep a vocabulary log.** Expanding your vocabulary will be of enormous benefit to you as a writer. In a vocabulary log, you can make a list of unfamiliar words and their definitions.

See Appendix 7 for more information about spelling, grammar, and vocabulary logs.

Vocabulary Boost
Throughout Part II of *The Writer's World*, Vocabulary Boost boxes give students tips to improve their use of language and to revise and edit their word choices. For example, a Vocabulary Boost in Chapter 4 asks students to replace repeated words with synonyms, and the one in Chapter 5 gives specific directions for how to vary sentence openings. These lessons give students concrete strategies and specific advice for improving their diction.

---

vo•cab•u•lar•y BOOST

Using Varied Language

1. Underline the opening word of every sentence in your first draft. Check to see if some are repeated.
2. Replace repeated opening words with adverbs, such as *usually*, *generally*, or *fortunately*, or a prepositional phrase such as *On the side* or *Under the circumstances*. You can also begin the sentences with a modifier such as *Leaving the door open*. In other words, avoid beginning too many sentences with a noun or transitional word.

Repeated First Words

We opened the door of the abandoned house. We looked nervously at the rotting floorboards. We thought the floor might collapse. We decided to enter. We walked carefully across the kitchen floor to the bedroom, one by one.

Variety

My cousins and I opened the door of the abandoned house. Nervously, we looked at the rotting floorboards. Thinking the floor might collapse, we decided to enter. One by one, we walked across the kitchen floor to the bedroom.

The Writer's Desk
Parts I, II, and III include **The Writer's Desk** exercises that help students get used to practicing all stages and steps of the writing process. As the chapter progresses, students warm up with a prewriting activity, and then use specific methods for developing, organizing (using paragraph and essay plans), drafting, and finally, revising and editing to create a final draft.

The Writer's Desk **Write a Paragraph Plan**

Choose one of the topic sentences that you wrote for the previous Writer's Desk. Write a paragraph plan using some of the supporting ideas that you have generated. Include details for each supporting idea.

Topic
sentence: _____

_____

Support 1: _____

Details: _____

_____

Support 2: _____

Details: _____

_____

Support 3: _____

Details: _____

_____

Paragraph Patterns at Work To help students appreciate the relevance of their writing tasks, Chapters 4–12 highlight an authentic writing sample from work contexts. Titled **Illustration at Work, Narration at Work,** and so on, this feature offers a glimpse of how people use writing patterns in different workplace settings.

Illustration at Work
Patti Guzman is a registered nurse at a large hospital. She was invited to speak to nursing students in a local university. In the following excerpt from her speech, she gives examples to explain why a nurse must be in good physical health.

Physically, the job of a nurse is demanding. On a daily basis, we must lift patients and move them. When patients are bedridden for prolonged periods, we must change their positions on their beds. When new patients arrive, we transfer them from stretchers to beds or from beds to wheelchairs. If patients fall, we must be able to help them stand up. If patients have difficulty walking, we must assist them. Patients who have suffered paralysis or stroke need to be lifted and supported when they are bathed and dressed. Keep in mind that some patients may be quite heavy, so the job requires a good level of physical strength.

Reflect On It Each **Reflect On It** is a chapter review exercise. Questions prompt students to recall and review what they have learned in the chapter.

REFLECT ON IT

Think about what you have learned in this chapter. If you do not know an answer, review that topic.

1. What are four things that you should look for when revising?

   _____ _____

   _____ _____

2. Circle the best answer(s). A paragraph is unified if
   a. there are no irrelevant supporting details.
   b. there are many facts and statistics.
   c. all details support the topic sentence.

3. Circle the best answer: Transitional words are _____ that help ideas flow in a logical manner.
   a. links   b. sentences   c. verbs

The Writer's Room The **Writer's Room** contains writing activities that correspond to general, college, and workplace topics. Some prompts are brief to allow students to freely form ideas while others are expanded to give students more direction.

There is something for every student writer in this end-of-chapter feature. Students who respond well to visual cues will appreciate the photo writing exercises in **The Writer's Room** in Part II: Paragraph Patterns. Students who learn best by hearing through collaboration will appreciate the discussion and group work prompts in **The Writers' Circle** section of selected **The Writer's Rooms.** In Part III: The Essay, students can respond to thought-

provoking quotations. To help students see how grammar is not isolated from the writing process, there are also **The Writer's Room** activities at the end of sections 1–8 in Part IV: The Editing Handbook.

The Writer's Room

Writing Activity I: Topics

Choose any of the following topics, or choose your own topic. Then write an illustration paragraph.

General Topics

1. activities that relieve stress
2. great things in life that are free
3. mistakes parents make
4. items you have lost
5. positive personality traits

College and Work-Related Topics

6. pressures faced by college students
7. qualities that help you succeed
8. claustrophobic work environments
9. qualities of a good instructor
10. tools or equipment needed for your job

Writing Activity 2: Photo Writing

In the photo, a woman has the annoying habit of biting her nails. Write a paragraph about things that annoy you. Provide many examples.

The Writer's World e-Text Accessed through MyWritingLab (www.mywritinglab.com), students now have the e-text for *The Writer's World* at their fingertips while completing the various exercises and activities within MyWritingLab. Students can highlight important material and add notes to any section for further reflection and/or study throughout the semester.

New to the Third Edition
Visualizing the Mode

Chapters 4–12 cover nine paragraph patterns. To help students visualize how to use each pattern, they complete a practice called "Visualizing." For example, Chapter 4, Visualizing Illustration, includes the topic sentence "Some workers risk their lives daily . . ." Photos of workers, including a high-rise window cleaner, an electrician, a fisherman, and police officers, are shown. Chapter 8 includes the topic statement, "Timeless fashions remain popular and will not go out of style." Students see images of a bobbed haircut, a little black dress, and a classic black suit. These visual examples help students get an overview of the paragraph mode.

Annotated At Work Paragraphs

In Chapters 4–12, each paragraph pattern includes a real-world example. Each "At Work" paragraph now contains callouts pointing out the paragraph's key features: the topic sentence, the supporting ideas, and the concluding sentence.

Narration at Work
Joseph Roth, a boiler and pressure vessel inspector, used narrative writing in a memo he wrote to his supervisor.

As you know, I recently inspected the boiler and pressure vessels in the refinery on Highway 11. I had a few problems that I would like to mention. When I first arrived, the manager of the unit was uncooperative and initially tried to stop me from examining the boiler! After much discussion, I was finally permitted into the boiler room, where I noticed several defects in the operation and condition of the equipment. Immediately, I saw that the low-water fuel cutoff chamber was filled with sludge and could not possibly function properly. Then I realized that the boiler heating surfaces were covered with scale. Finally, I found stress cracks in the tube ends and in tube seats. This is a sure sign of caustic embrittlement, which makes the boiler unsafe to operate and in danger of exploding. I have asked that the boiler be taken out of service immediately. We must follow up to make sure that measures are being taken to replace the boiler.

New Photos

New opening photos and photo writing prompts appear throughout the book. Each grammar chapter has an opening photo that helps to show the thematic content.

Media Writing

Every paragraph pattern chapter now ends with a Media Writing activity. Students are invited to view a television program, film, or online video and to use the content as a writing prompt.

Cooperative Learning Teaching Tips

Are your students sometimes lacking in motivation? Do they seem bored? Distributed throughout the book are cooperative learning teaching tips. Cooperative learning promotes peer interaction, helps students share knowledge, problem solve, negotiate, and reflect. Students are responsible for their contribution to a team effort. For example, Chapter 1 features a jigsaw activity in which groups of students focus on a specific

prewriting strategy and then collaborate. Other tips such as Roundtable Writing, Nonstop Talking, and Pair & Share help make routine lessons far more interesting and enjoyable. These communicative and interactive activities are especially useful for nonnative speakers.

Teaching Tip:

Cooperative Learning (Pair & Share)
The Writers' Exchange activity helps students understand comparison and contrast. Students should work with a partner to share ideas. If you have time, ask the member with the most jewelry to stay seated. The other partners should rotate and share information with their new partner.

Tech Tips

New to this edition are some teaching tips that incorporate everyday technology. Students in this digital age spend their days texting, checking their Facebook page, and listening to music on their iPods. The Tech Tips help students learn while using the technology with which they are familiar. For example, in Chapter 4, students are invited to list the most useful apps and features on their cell phones, and in Chapter 5, students can look on Facebook and narrate what happened recently to a friend.

New ESL and Regular Teaching Tips

Instructors will notice an abundance of updated teaching tips throughout the book. The authors have extensive experience with nonnative speakers, and have included more precise ESL tips to help teachers in the classroom.

Research Chapter Is Revised and MLA Information Is Updated

Chapter 15, Enhancing Your Writing with Research, contains updated information from the Seventh Edition of the *MLA Handbook for Writers of Research Papers*. Material in the chapter has been streamlined and renewed with topical examples and references. The final student essay about cell phones and health has a detailed Works Cited page, and the chapter ends with a practice related to the sample essay.

New Grammar Chapters

New to this edition, the Fragments and Run-On chapter has been split into two separate chapters. Chapter 24, Past Participles, now features a section called "Past Participle as an Adjective." Chapter 25, Other Verb Forms, has a new section on gerunds and infinitives. Many of the thematic grammar exercises have been modified, updated, or completely changed. The section previously called "Espionage" now contains information about political intrigue.

Updated High-Interest Paragraph Models and Practices

Throughout the book you will notice new examples, sample paragraphs, writing practices, Writer's Desk topics, and grammar practices. In fact, to make the content more topical and appealing, roughly 30 percent of the book's content has been updated.

New Readings

The first 12 chapters include a wide selection of new paragraph examples. Chapter 14 contains four new essays, including two written by students about their personal experiences. New essay topics include homophobia, the purpose of pets, and guy chores. In Chapter 38, From Reading to Writing, there are six fascinating new readings including "Musicophilia" by Oliver Sachs and "Gone with the Windows" by Dorothy Nixon.

Acknowledgments

Many people have helped us produce *The Writer's World*. First and foremost, we would like to thank our students for inspiring us and providing us with invaluable feedback. Their words and insights pervade this book.

We also benefited greatly from the insightful comments and suggestions from over two hundred instructors across the nation, all of whom are listed in the opening pages of the Annotated Instructor's Edition. Our colleagues' feedback was invaluable and helped shape *The Writer's World* series content, focus, and organization.

We are indebted to the team of dedicated professionals at Prentice Hall who have helped make this project a reality. They have boosted our spirits and have believed in us every step of the way. Special thanks to Katharine Glynn for her careful job in polishing this book and to Matthew Wright for trusting our instincts and enthusiastically propelling us forward. We owe a deep debt of gratitude to Yolanda de Rooy, whose encouraging words helped ignite this project. Karen Berry's attention to detail in the production process kept us motivated and on task and made *The Writer's World* a much better resource for both instructors and students.

Finally, we would like to dedicate this book to our husbands and children who supported us and who patiently put up with our long hours on the computer. Manu, Octavio, and Natalia continually encouraged us. We especially appreciate the help and sacrifices of Diego, Becky, Kiran, and Meghana.

Lynne Gaetz and Suneeti Phadke

A Note to Students

Your knowledge, ideas, and opinions are important. The ability to clearly communicate those ideas is invaluable in your personal, academic, and professional life. When your writing is error-free, readers will focus on your message, and you will be able to persuade, inform, entertain, or inspire them. *The Writer's World* includes strategies that will help you improve your written communication. Quite simply, when you become a better writer, you become a better communicator. It is our greatest wish for *The Writer's World* to make you excited about writing, communicating, and learning.

Enjoy!

Lynne Gaetz & Suneeti Phadke
writingrewards@pearson.com

Call for Student Writing!

Do you want to be published in *The Writer's World*? Send your paragraphs and essays to us along with your complete contact information. If your work is selected to appear in the next edition of *The Writer's World*, you will receive an honorarium, credit for your work, and a copy of the book!

Lynne Gaetz and Suneeti Phadke
writingrewards@pearson.com

Suneeti Phadke on Salt Spring Island, British Columbia.

Lynne Gaetz in the Rocky Mountains.

PART I

The Writing Process

An Overview

The writing process is a series of steps that most writers follow to get from thinking about a topic to preparing the final draft. Generally, you should follow the process step by step; however, sometimes you may find that your steps overlap. For example, you might do some editing before you revise, or you might think about your main idea while you are prewriting. The important thing is to make sure that you have done all of the steps before preparing your final draft.

Before you begin the chapters that follow, review the steps in the writing process.

Exploring

Step 1: Think about your topic.

Step 2: Think about your audience.

Step 3: Think about your purpose.

Step 4: Try exploring strategies.

Developing

Step 1: Narrow your topic.

Step 2: Express your main idea.

Step 3: Develop your supporting ideas.

Step 4: Make a plan or an outline.

Step 5: Write your first draft.

Revising and Editing

Step 1: Revise for unity.

Step 2: Revise for adequate support.

Step 3: Revise for coherence.

Step 4: Revise for style.

Step 5: Edit for technical errors.

Exploring

CHAPTER 1

LEARNING OBJECTIVES

1. The Paragraph and the Essay (p. 3)
2. What Is Exploring? (p. 4)
3. Topic (p. 5)
4. Audience (p. 5)
5. Purpose (p. 6)
6. Exploring Strategies (p. 8)
7. Journal and Portfolio Writing (p. 12)

Before creating a final image, a pastel artist takes the time to consider what to create. Similarly, before developing a draft, a writer needs to explore the topic.

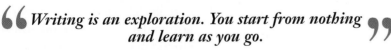

> **Writing is an exploration. You start from nothing and learn as you go.**
>
> —E. L. DOCTOROW
> *American author (b. 1931)*

The Paragraph and the Essay

Most of the writing that we do—e-mail messages, work reports, college papers—is made up of paragraphs and essays. A **paragraph** is a series of sentences that are about one central idea. Paragraphs can stand alone, or they can be part of a longer work such as an essay, a letter, or a report. An **essay** is a series of paragraphs that are about one central idea. Both the paragraph and the essay are divided into three parts.

Characteristics of a Paragraph

- The **topic sentence** introduces the subject of the paragraph and shows the writer's attitude toward the subject.

- The **body** of the paragraph contains details that support the topic sentence.

- The paragraph ends with a **concluding sentence.**

Characteristics of an Essay

- The **introduction** engages the reader's interest and contains the **thesis statement.**

- The **body** paragraphs each support the main idea of the essay.

- The **conclusion** reemphasizes the thesis and restates the main points of the essay. It brings the essay to a satisfactory close.

Look at the relationship between paragraphs and essays. Both examples are about real-life heroes. However, in the essay, each supporting idea is expanded into paragraph form.

The Paragraph

Topic sentence

The public should pay more attention to real-life heroes. First, firefighters risk their lives to save others. Additionally, police officers patrol city streets and help keep citizens safe. When someone is attacked or robbed, police come to the rescue. Of course, medical staff and researchers save lives and cure diseases. Instead of focusing on celebrities, citizens should appreciate the daily heroes in their lives.

Supporting ideas

Concluding sentence

The Essay

Introduction

Asked who his hero is, Andrew Rigget said, "Steve Nash." Most people hold sports figures or celebrities in high esteem. However, the public should pay more attention to real-life heroes.

Thesis statement

Body paragraphs (Each paragraph has a topic sentence that supports the thesis statement)

First, firefighters risk their lives to save others. Last night, a fire in a downtown apartment building could have ravaged a city block, but firefighters brought it under control. Some families were safely evacuated. Firefighter Mel Klein needed to be hospitalized after she risked her life.

Additionally, police officers patrol city streets and help keep citizens safe. People complain about the police, but whom do they call when there is a robbery or an assault? Last month, local police intervened in a street fight in Langley and helped avert further violence. The police help people in their hour of need.

Medical staff and researchers save lives and cure diseases. Often working long hours under difficult circumstances, doctors, nurses, and many other medical personnel labor to cure us. My family doctor worked late last Friday just to give my son an emergency prescription for a severe ear infection.

Concluding paragraph

Our nation is filled with local people who help others for low pay and very little gratitude. Instead of focusing on celebrities, citizens should appreciate the daily heroes in their lives.

All writing begins with ideas. In the next section of this chapter, you will practice ways to explore ideas.

What Is Exploring?

Have you ever been given a writing subject and then stared at the blank page, thinking, "I don't know what to write"? Well, it is not necessary to write a good paragraph or essay immediately. There are certain things that you can do to help you focus on your topic.

Understand Your Assignment

As soon as you are given an assignment, make sure that you understand what your task is. Answer the following questions about the assignment:

- How many words or pages should I write?
- What is the due date for the assignment?
- Are there any special qualities my writing should include?

After you have considered your assignment, follow the four steps in the exploring stage of the writing process.

EXPLORING

STEP 1	➤	**Think about your topic.** Determine what you will write about.
STEP 2	➤	**Think about your audience.** Consider your intended readers and what interests them.
STEP 3	➤	**Think about your purpose.** Ask yourself why you want to write.
STEP 4	➤	**Try exploring strategies.** Experiment with different ways to generate ideas.

ESSAY LINK

When you plan an essay, you should follow the four exploring steps.

Topic

Your **topic**, or **subject**, is what you are writing about. When an instructor gives you a topic for your writing, narrow the topic and find an angle that interests you. For example, if your instructor asks you to write about travel, you can take many approaches to the topic. You might write about the dangers of travel or explain what people can learn when they travel. Try to narrow the topic to suit your interests. When you think about your topic, ask yourself the following questions.

- What special knowledge do I have about the topic?
- What subtopics are most relevant to me?
- What aspect of the topic arouses my emotions?

Audience

Your **audience** is your intended reader. Your audience might be your instructor, your classmates, your boss, your coworkers, and so on. Remember to adapt your language and vocabulary for a specific audience. For example, in a report written for your business class, you might use specialized accounting terms that would not be appropriate in an essay for your English class. When you think about your audience, ask yourself the following questions.

- Who will read my assignment? Will the reader be my instructor, or will other students also read it?
- What does my audience already know about the topic?
- What information will my readers expect?
- Should I use formal or informal language?

 **Instructor as the Audience**

Your instructor represents a general audience. Such an audience will expect you to use correct grammar and to reveal what you have learned or understood about the topic. Your ideas should be presented in a clear and organized manner. Also, do not leave out information because you assume that your instructor is an expert in the field.

Purpose

Your purpose is your reason for writing. Sometimes you may have more than one purpose. When you consider your purpose, ask yourself the following questions.

- Is my goal to **entertain**? Do I tell a personal story or anecdote?
- Is my goal to **persuade**? Do I convince the reader that my point of view is correct?
- Is my goal to **inform**? Do I explain something or present information?

 **General and Specific Purpose**

Your **general purpose** is to entertain, inform, or persuade. Your **specific purpose** is your more precise reason for writing. For example, imagine that you have to write about music. You can have the following general and specific purposes.

General purpose: to inform
Specific purpose: to explain how to become a better musician

PRACTICE I

Read text messages A and B. Then answer the questions that follow.

1. Who is the intended audience for text message A?
   _____ friend   _____ boss
   What language clues helped you determine the audience?
   _____

2. Who is the intended audience for text message B?
   _____ friend   _____ boss
   What language clues helped you determine the audience?
   _____

PRACTICE 2

Read each selection carefully. Underline any words or phrases that help you identify its source, audience, and purpose. Then answer the questions that follow each selection.

EXAMPLE:

I'm totally <u>psyched</u> about learning the drums. It's taken me a while to get used to keeping up a steady beat, but I think I'm getting it. My drum teacher is <u>cool</u>, and he's <u>pretty patient</u> with me. I try to practice, but it bugs the neighbors when I hit the cymbals.

◄ Slang

◄ Slang, informal tone

What is the most likely source of this paragraph?

    a. Web site article   b. textbook   (c.) e-mail

What is its purpose? *To inform*

Who is the audience? *Friend or family member*

1.   Lomax also found a relationship between polyphony, where two or more melodies are sung simultaneously, and a high degree of female participation in food-getting. In societies in which women's work is responsible for at least half of the food, songs are likely to contain more than one simultaneous melody, with the higher tunes usually sung by women.

What is the most likely source of this paragraph?

    a. novel   b. textbook   c. e-mail

What is its purpose?

Who is the audience?

2.   When dealing with club managers, it is imperative that you act professionally. Get all the details of a gig in advance. Doing so will eliminate any confusion or miscommunication that could result in a botched deal. It will also instantly set you apart from the legions of flaky musicians that managers must endure on a daily basis. That's a good thing.

What is the most likely source of this paragraph?

    a. Web site article   b. novel   c. e-mail

What is its purpose?

Who is the audience?

3.   But there was no reason why everyone should not dance. Madame Ratignolle could not, so it was she who gaily consented to play for the others. She played very well, keeping excellent waltz time and infusing an expression into the strains which was indeed inspiring. She was keeping up her music on account of the children, she said, because she and her husband both considered it a means of brightening the home and making it attractive.

What is the most likely source of this paragraph?

    a. novel   b. textbook   c. e-mail

What is its purpose?

Who is the audience?

View the following cartoon. What is the topic? Who is the audience? What is the purpose? Does the cartoon achieve its purpose?

"Oh no, not homework again."

© The New Yorker Collection 1999, Amie Levin from cartoonbank .com. All Rights Reserved.

Exploring Strategies

After you determine your topic, audience, and purpose, try some **exploring strategies**—also known as **prewriting strategies**—to help get your ideas flowing. The four most common strategies are freewriting, brainstorming, questioning, and clustering. It is not necessary to do all of the strategies explained in this chapter. Find the strategy that works best for you.

You can do both general and focused prewriting. If you have writer's block and do not know what to write, use **general prewriting** to come up with possible topics. Then, after you have chosen a topic, use **focused prewriting** to find an angle of the topic that is interesting and that could be developed in your paragraph.

> *Hint* **When to Use Exploring Strategies**
>
> You can use exploring strategies at any stage of the writing process.
>
> • To find a topic
> • To narrow a broad topic
> • To generate ideas about your topic
> • To generate supporting details

Freewriting

Freewriting is writing for a limited period of time without stopping. The point is to record the first thoughts that come to mind. If you have no ideas, you can indicate that in a sentence such as "I don't know what to write." As you write, do not be concerned with your grammar or spelling. If you use a computer, let your ideas flow and do not worry about typing mistakes.

Sandra's Freewriting

College student Sandra Ahumada did freewriting about work. During her freewriting, she wrote everything that came to mind.

> Work. I've only worked in a restaurant. Schedules are good for college students. Can work nights or weekends. Serving people so different from studying. You can relax your brain, go on automatic pilot. But you have to remember people's orders so it can be hard. And some customer are rude, rude, RUDE. In some jobs, you get tips in addition to the salary. Should people always tip servers?

Sandra's Focused Freewriting

After Sandra did her general freewriting, she underlined ideas that she thought could be expanded into a complete paragraph. Then she looked at her underlined ideas to decide which one to write about. Her purpose was to persuade, so she chose a topic that she could defend. She did focused freewriting about tipping.

> People should always tip in restaurants. Why. I dont earn a lot, so the tips are really important. I gotta lot a bills, and can't pay everything with minimum wage. What else? Diners should just consider the tip as a part of the cost of eating out. If they don't wanna tip, they should cook at home. Also, lots of other service people get tips and nobody cares. And bad service. It could be the cook's fault. We need those tips. Sure do.

The Writer's Desk **Freewriting**

Choose one of the following topics and do some freewriting. Remember to write without stopping.

The family   Travel   Sports

Brainstorming

Brainstorming is like freewriting except that you create a list of ideas, and you can take the time to stop and think when you create your list. As you think about the topic, write down words or phrases that come to mind. Do not be concerned about grammar or spelling; the point is to generate ideas.

Jin's Brainstorming

College student Jin Park brainstormed about health issues. He made a list of general ideas.

- lack of health care
- obesity
- fast food
- not enough exercise

Jin's Focused Brainstorming

Jin chose "not enough exercise" as his topic, and then he did focused brainstorming.

- video games, PlayStation
- parents worry about dangers on streets
- sports activities (e.g., football) cost a lot for fees, equipment, etc.
- too much sitting at school
- not enough physical education time
- need more community sports programs

The Writer's Desk Brainstorming

Choose one of the following topics and brainstorm. Create a list of ideas.

Ceremonies   Gossip   Good or bad manners

Questioning

Another way to generate ideas about a topic is to ask yourself a series of questions and write responses to them. The questions can help you define and narrow your topic. One common way to do this is to ask yourself *who, what, when, where, why,* and *how* questions. Like other exploring strategies, questioning can be general or focused.

Clayton's Questioning

College student Clayton Rukavina used a question-and-answer format to generate ideas about binge drinking.

What is binge drinking?	—having too much alcohol in a short time
Who does binge drinking?	—students who are away from home for the first time, or insecure students
Why do students drink too much?	—peer pressure, want to be more relaxed, don't think about consequences
When do students drink too much?	—spring break, weekends, to celebrate legal age
How dangerous is binge drinking?	—may get alcohol poisoning, may choke, and may drink and drive
Where does it happen?	—dorm rooms, house parties, fraternities
Why is it an important topic?	—can die from binge drinking, or drunk driver can kill somebody else

---

The Writer's Desk Questioning

Choose one of the following topics and write questions and answers. Ask *who, what, when, where, why,* and *how* questions.

Beliefs   Patriotism   Health

Clustering

Clustering is like drawing a word map; ideas are arranged in a visual image. To begin, write your topic in the middle of the page and draw a box or a circle around it. That idea will lead to another, so write the second idea and draw a line connecting it to your topic. Keep writing, circling, and connecting ideas until you have groups, or "clusters," of them on your page. You can use clustering to get ideas about a general or a specific topic.

Mahan's Clustering

College student Mahan Zahir used clustering to explore ideas about crime. He identified some main topics.

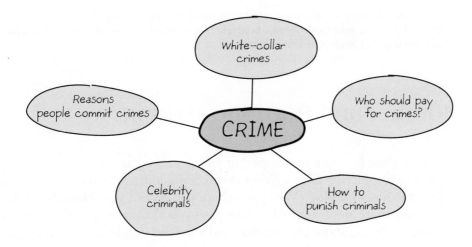

Mahan's Focused Clustering

Mahan decided to write about the reasons that people commit crimes. He added clusters to that topic.

The Writer's Desk **Clustering**

Choose one of the following topics and use clustering to explore it on a separate sheet of paper. Begin by writing the key word in the middle of the space. Then connect related ideas.

Jobs   College   Relationships

 **More About Exploring**

When you explore a topic using any of the listed strategies, keep in mind that a lot of the ideas you generate may not be useful. Later, when you develop your ideas, be prepared to cut irrelevant information.

Journal and Portfolio Writing

Keeping a Journal

You may write for work or school, but you can also practice writing for pleasure. One way to practice your writing is to keep a journal. A **journal** is a book, a computer file, or a blog (Web log) where you record your thoughts, opinions, ideas, and impressions. Journal writing gives you a chance to practice your writing without worrying about your readers and what they might think about it. Journal writing also gives you a source of material when you want to write about a topic of your choice. According to the author Anaïs Nin, "Keeping a diary is a way of making everyday life seem as exciting as fiction."

In your journal, you can write about any topic that appeals to you. Here are some topics for journal writing.

- Anything related to your personal life, such as your feelings about your career goals, personal problems and solutions, opinions about your college courses, reflections about past and future decisions, or feelings about your job
- Your reactions to controversies in the world, in your country, in your state, in your city, or in your college
- Facts that interest you
- Your reflections on the opinions and philosophies of others, including your friends or people that you read about in your courses

Keeping a Portfolio

A **writing portfolio** is a binder or an electronic file folder where you keep samples of all of your writing. The reason to keep a portfolio is to have a record of your writing progress. In your portfolio, keep all drafts of your writing assignments. When you work on new assignments, review your previous work in your portfolio. Identify your main problems, and try not to repeat the same errors.

REFLECT ON IT

Think about what you learned in this chapter. If you do not know an answer, review that topic.

1. Before you write, you should think about your topic, audience, and purpose. Explain what each one is.

   a. topic: _____

   b. audience: _____

   c. purpose: _____

2. Briefly define each of the following exploring styles.

   a. freewriting: _____

   b. brainstorming: _____

   c. questioning: _____

   d. clustering: _____

 The Writer's Room

Writing Activity 1

Choose one of the following topics, or choose your own topic. Then generate ideas about the topic. You may want to try the suggested exploring strategy.

General Topics

1. Try freewriting about a strong childhood memory.

2. Try brainstorming about anger, listing any thoughts that come to mind.

3. Try clustering. First, write "music" in the middle of the page. Then write clusters of ideas that connect to the general topic.

4. Ask and answer some questions about cosmetic surgery.

College and Work-Related Topics

5. Try freewriting about a comfortable place. Include any emotions or other details that come to mind.

6. Try brainstorming about study habits. List any ideas that come to mind.

7. To get ideas, ask and answer questions about famous athletes.

8. Try clustering. First, write "cars" in the middle of the page. Then write clusters of ideas that relate to the general topic.

Writing Activity 2

Look carefully at the poster. First, determine the topic, audience, and purpose. Whom is the poster trying to convince? What is the purpose? Is the purpose fulfilled? Then try exploring the topic. Use questioning as your exploring strategy. Ask and answer *who, what, when, where, why,* and *how* questions.

To check your progress in meeting this chapter's objectives, log in to **www.mywritinglab.com**, go to the **Study Plan** tab, click on **The Writing Process** and choose **Recognizing the Paragraph, Recognizing the Essay, Getting Started, Prewriting, and The Writing Process** from the list of subtopics. Read and view the resources in the **Review Materials** section, and then complete the **Recall, Apply,** and **Write** sets in the **Activities** section.

✔ EXPLORING CHECKLIST

As you explore your topics, ask yourself the following questions.

☐ What is my topic? (Consider what you will write about.)

☐ Who is my audience? (Think about your intended reader.)

☐ What is my purpose? (Determine your reason for writing.)

☐ How can I explore? (You might try freewriting, brainstorming, questioning, or clustering.)

Developing

After finding an idea, an artist begins to define shapes and layer on colors. Like an artist, a writer shapes ideas to create a solid paragraph or essay.

> ❝ *You can only learn to be a better writer by actually writing.* ❞
>
> —DORIS LESSING
> *British author (b. 1919)*

What Is Developing?

In Chapter 1, you learned how to use exploring strategies to formulate ideas. In this chapter, you will focus on the second stage of the writing process: **developing**. There are five key steps in the developing stage.

ESSAY LINK

When you develop an essay, you follow similar steps. For details about essay writing, see Chapter 13.

DEVELOPING

STEP 1	➤	**Narrow your topic.** Focus on some aspect of the topic that interests you.
STEP 2	➤	**Express your main idea.** Write a topic sentence that expresses the main idea of the paragraph (or a thesis statement that expresses the main idea of the essay).
STEP 3	➤	**Develop your supporting ideas.** Find facts, examples, or anecdotes that best support your main idea.
STEP 4	➤	**Make a plan.** Organize your main and supporting ideas, and place your ideas in a plan or an outline.
STEP 5	➤	**Write your first draft.** Communicate your ideas in a single written piece.

Reviewing Paragraph Structure

Before you practice developing your paragraphs, review the paragraph structure. A **paragraph** is a series of related sentences that develop one central idea. Because a paragraph can stand alone or be part of a longer piece of writing, it is the essential writing model. You can apply your paragraph writing skills to longer essays, letters, and reports. A stand-alone paragraph generally has the following characteristics.

- A **topic sentence** states the topic and introduces the idea the writer will develop.
- **Body sentences** support the topic sentence.
- A **concluding sentence** ends the paragraph.

College student Tam Wang wrote the following paragraph. Notice how it is structured.

The topic sentence expresses the main idea. ➤

Greenwashing occurs when companies misleadingly promote themselves as environmentally friendly. Just as whitewashing means "to make something look better than it is," greenwashing is an attempt to look greener than one really is. Some greenwashers spend more money advertising their "green" qualities than actually doing ecological practices. For instance, an electronic device can be advertised as energy-efficient even though it contains hazardous materials. Oil companies promote eco-friendly corn ethanol even though its production is energy-intensive. Finally, some products have misleading labels with images of mountains and trees. Various household cleaners claim to be organic, but they were never tested by an impartial organization. **In short, greenwashers make use of vague and misleading marketing.**

Supporting sentences provide details and examples. ➤

The concluding sentence brings the paragraph to a satisfying close. ➤

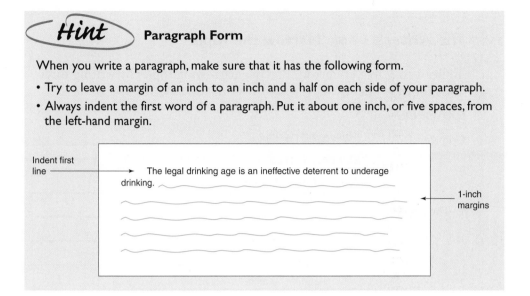

Hint Paragraph Form

When you write a paragraph, make sure that it has the following form.

- Try to leave a margin of an inch to an inch and a half on each side of your paragraph.
- Always indent the first word of a paragraph. Put it about one inch, or five spaces, from the left-hand margin.

Indent first line → The legal drinking age is an ineffective deterrent to underage drinking.

← 1-inch margins

Narrow the Topic

A paragraph has one main idea. If your topic is too broad, you might find it difficult to write only one paragraph about it. When you **narrow** your topic, you make it more specific. To narrow your topic, you can use exploring strategies such as freewriting, brainstorming, and questioning. These strategies are explained in more detail in Chapter 1, "Exploring." Review the following examples of general and narrowed topics.

General Topic

Narrowed Topic

General Topic	**Narrowed Topic**
The job interview	How to dress for a job interview
College	My misconceptions about college life
Rituals	The high school prom

Hint Narrowing the Topic

One way to narrow your topic is to break it down into smaller categories.

Sports

Steroids in sports — Team sports — Dangerous sports

ESSAY LINK

An essay contains several paragraphs and can have a broader topic than a paragraph.

Sandra's Example of Narrowing a Topic

College student Sandra Ahumada practiced narrowing a topic by thinking of ideas about work.

- types of work: paid work, housework, homework
- jobs I have done in the service industry: server, cashier
- reasons to work in a restaurant
- how to find a job
- bad jobs that I have had
- are online job sites useful?

The Writer's Desk **Narrow the Topic**

Topics 1 to 5 are very broad. Practice narrowing topics by writing three ideas for each one.

EXAMPLE:

Crime: *white-collar crime*

  why people steal

  types of punishment

1. The family: _____

   _____

   _____

2. Gossip: _____

   _____

   _____

3. Travel: _____

   _____

   _____

4. Sports: _____

   _____

   _____

5. Jobs: _____

   _____

   _____

ESSAY LINK

Just as a topic sentence expresses the main point of a paragraph, the thesis statement expresses the main point of an essay. Both have a controlling idea.

The Topic Sentence

After you have narrowed the topic of your paragraph, your next step is to write a topic sentence. The **topic sentence** has specific characteristics.

- It introduces the topic of the paragraph.
- It states the paragraph's controlling idea.
- It is the most general sentence in the paragraph.
- It is followed by other sentences that provide supporting facts and examples.

The **controlling idea** makes a point about the topic and expresses the writer's opinion, attitude, or feeling. You can express different controlling ideas about the same topic. For example, the following topic sentences are about youth offenders, but each sentence makes a different point about the topic.

  narrowed topic   controlling idea

Youth offenders should not receive special treatment from the correctional system.

controlling idea   narrowed topic

Rehabilitation and education are the best ways for the state to handle **youth offenders.**

PRACTICE I

Circle the topic and underline the controlling idea in each topic sentence.

EXAMPLE:

(Repair a water heater) with three simple steps.

1. Music education is essential in public schools.
2. There are three types of terrible bosses.
3. My furnished room has everything a student could need.
4. We had many problems during our vacation in Florida.
5. The town library has a very impressive design.
6. A largely misunderstood religion is Islam.
7. The Beatles went through many musical phases.
8. Learning the guitar requires practice, patience, and perseverance.

Identifying the Topic Sentence

Before you write topic sentences, practice finding them in paragraphs by other writers. To find the topic sentence of a paragraph, follow these steps.

- Read the paragraph carefully.
- Look for a sentence that sums up the paragraph's subject. Professional writers may place the topic sentence anywhere in the paragraph.
- After you have chosen a sentence, see if the other sentences in the paragraph provide evidence that supports that sentence.

If you find one sentence that sums up what the paragraph is about and is supported by other sentences in the paragraph, then you have identified the topic sentence.

PRACTICE 2

Underline or highlight the topic sentences in paragraphs A, B, and C. Remember that the topic sentence is not always the first sentence in the paragraph.

EXAMPLE:

Researchers say they have found the remains of a rodent the size of a buffalo in South America. Fossils suggest a 1,545-pound rodent that was a plant eater lived 6 million to 8 million years ago in what was then a lush, swampy forest. Marcelo R. Sanchez-Villagra of the University of Tubingen in Germany described the creature as "a weird guinea pig . . . with a long tail for balancing on its hind legs." The fossils were found in a desert area some 250 miles west of Caracas, Venezuela.

—Lee Krystek, "Strange Science," *Unnatural Museum.com*

A. The idea of controlling music in society has been around for a long time. About 2,400 years ago, the Greek philosopher Plato said that the types of music people listened to should be controlled by the state. During the Middle Ages and the Renaissance, it was the Church that specified how music should be composed and performed. And in later centuries, secular rulers held a virtual monopoly over the music that was allowed in their realm. Often, composers had to submit a work to a committee before it was allowed to be published or performed.

—Jeremy Yudkin, *Understanding Music*

B. Cosmetic surgery is not like fooling around with a bottle of hair dye or getting a set of fake fingernails. The procedures are invasive, the recovery sometimes painful, and mistakes, while not common, can be difficult or impossible to correct. Breast implants may rupture, noses sink inward, and smiles turn unnaturally tight. People who merely wanted fat vacuumed from their thighs have died, while balding men have found themselves sporting new hair in symmetrical rows like tree farms. Stephen Katz, a sociologist at Trent University in Ontario, Canada, says, "To have plastic surgery, you have to think of your body as an object. It's a kind of social madness."

—Patricia Chisholm, "The Body Builders," *MacLean's*

C. Imagine a society without laws. People would not know what to expect from one another (an area controlled by the law of contracts), nor would they be able to plan for the future with any degree of certainty (administrative law); they wouldn't feel safe knowing that the more powerful or better armed could take what they wanted from the less powerful (criminal law); and they might not be able to exercise basic rights which would otherwise be available to them as citizens of a free nation (constitutional law).

—Frank Schmalleger, *Criminal Justice Today*

Writing an Effective Topic Sentence

When you develop your topic sentence, avoid some common errors by asking yourself these three questions.

1. **Is my topic sentence a complete sentence that has a controlling idea?**
   You might state the topic in one word or phrase, but your topic sentence should always reveal a complete thought and have a controlling idea. It should not simply announce the topic.

Incomplete:	Working in a restaurant.
	(This item gives a topic but is *not* a topic sentence. It does not contain both a subject and a verb, and it does not express a complete thought.)
Announcement:	I will write about part-time jobs.
	(This sentence announces the topic but says nothing relevant about it. Do not use expressions such as *My topic is . . .* or *I will write about. . . .*)
Topic sentence:	Part-time jobs help college students build self-esteem.

TECHNOLOGY LINK

If you write your paragraph on a computer, make your topic sentence bold (ctrl B). Then you and your instructor can easily identify it.

2. **Does my topic sentence make a valid and supportable point?**

Your topic sentence should express a valid point that you can support with your evidence. It should not be a vaguely worded statement, and it should not be a highly questionable generalization.

Vague:	Beauty is becoming more important in our culture.
	(Beauty is more important than what?)
Invalid point:	Beauty is more important than it was in the past.
	(Is this really true? Cultures throughout history have been concerned with notions of beauty.)
Topic sentence:	Fashion magazines do not provide readers with enough varied examples of beauty.

3. **Can I support my topic sentence in a single paragraph?**

Your topic sentence should express an idea that you can support in a paragraph. It should not be too broad or too narrow.

Too broad:	Love is important.
	(It would be difficult to write a paragraph about this topic. There are too many things to say.)
Too narrow:	My girlfriend was born on March 2.
	(What more is there to say?)
Topic sentence:	During my first relationship, I learned a lot about being honest.

ESSAY LINK

If you find that your topic is too broad for a paragraph, you might want to save it so you can try using it for an essay.

 **Write a Clear Topic Sentence**

Your topic sentence should not express an obvious or well-known fact. When you clearly indicate your point of view, your topic sentence will capture your readers' attention and make your readers want to continue reading.

Obvious: Money is important in our world.
(Everybody knows this.)

Better: There are several effective ways to save money.

PRACTICE 3

Choose the word from the list that best describes the problem with each topic sentence. Correct the problem by revising each sentence.

Announces	Incomplete	Narrow
Broad	Invalid	Vague

EXAMPLE: This paragraph is about television advertisements.

Problem:	*Announces*
Revised statement:	*Television advertisements should be banned during*
	children's programming.

1. I will write about negative political campaigns.

   Problem: _____

   Revised statement: _____

2. History teaches us lessons.

   Problem: _____

   Revised statement: _____

3. Deciding to go to college.

   Problem: _____

   Revised statement: _____

4. The subject of this paragraph is annoying coworkers.

   Problem: _____

   Revised statement: _____

5. Everybody wants to be famous.

   Problem: _____

   Revised statement: _____

6. The coffee shop walls are painted green.

   Problem: _____

   Revised statement: _____

PRACTICE 4

The following paragraphs do not contain topic sentences. Read the paragraphs carefully and write appropriate topic sentences for each.

1. _____

   _____

   First, take shorter showers. Five minutes is enough time to get clean. Also, do the laundry only when there is a full load. When brushing your teeth, don't leave the water running. Just turn the water off and on as needed. Finally, ask your landlord to install toilets that use very little water. Remember that water is a precious resource.

2. _____

   _____

   For example, a common myth is that autistic children never learn. But many programs can help those with autism, and every child responds differently. Another incorrect belief is that autistic children cannot speak, yet many can communicate quite well. Also, a misconception is that those with autism will never show affection. Although it is difficult for an autistic person to touch and show love, many do learn to show their emotions. The greatest myth is that people with autism cannot have productive lives. In fact, Dr. Temple Grandin has autism, but she is also a highly regarded university professor and author. Autism covers a wide spectrum, so everyone should remember that not all people with autism are alike.

The Writer's Desk **Write Topic Sentences**

Narrow each of the topics in this exercise. Then write a topic sentence
that contains a controlling idea. You could look at the Writer's Desk:
Narrow the Topic on page 18 for ideas.

EXAMPLE: Crime

Narrowed topic: *Why people steal*

Topic sentence: *People steal for several reasons.*

1. The family

   Narrowed topic: _____

   Topic sentence: _____

   _____

2. Gossip

   Narrowed topic: _____

   Topic sentence: _____

   _____

3. Travel

   Narrowed topic: _____

   Topic sentence: _____

   _____

4. Sports

   Narrowed topic: _____

   Topic sentence: _____

   _____

5. Jobs

   Narrowed topic: _____

   Topic sentence: _____

   _____

The Supporting Ideas

Once you have written a clear topic sentence, you can focus on the **supporting
details**—the facts and examples that provide the reader with interesting
information about the subject matter.

Generating Supporting Ideas

You can try an exploring strategy such as brainstorming or freewriting to generate
ideas. Then you can choose the best ideas.

ESSAY LINK

When writing an essay, place
the thesis statement in the
introduction. Then each supporting
idea becomes a distinct paragraph
with its own topic sentence.

An effective paragraph has **unity** when all of its sentences directly relate to and support the topic sentence. Create a unified paragraph by selecting three or four ideas that are most compelling and that clearly support your topic sentence. You may notice that several items in your list are similar; therefore, you can group them together. If some items do not support the topic sentence, remove them.

Mahan's Supporting Ideas

College student Mahan Zahir narrowed his topic and brainstormed a list of supporting ideas. Then he grouped similar ideas together and crossed out two items.

People steal for many reasons.

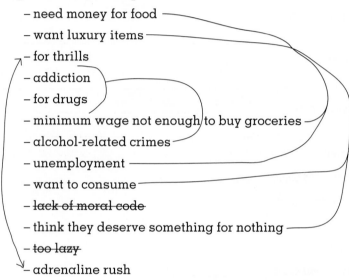

- need money for food
- want luxury items
- for thrills
- addiction
- for drugs
- minimum wage not enough to buy groceries
- alcohol-related crimes
- unemployment
- want to consume
- ~~lack of moral code~~
- think they deserve something for nothing
- ~~too lazy~~
- adrenaline rush

TECHNOLOGY LINK

On a computer, you can cut (ctrl X) and paste (ctrl V) similar ideas together.

 Hint **Identifying the Best Ideas**

There are many ways that you can highlight your best ideas. You can circle the best supporting points and then use arrows to link them with secondary ideas. You can also use highlighter pens or asterisks (*) to identify the best supporting points.

PRACTICE 5

College student Sandra Ahumada brainstormed ideas about tipping. Her purpose was to persuade, so she created a topic sentence that expressed her opinion about the issue.

Underline the three ideas from her list that you think are the most compelling and that most clearly illustrate the point she is making in her topic sentence. Then group together any related ideas under each of the main subheadings. If any ideas do not relate to her topic sentence, cross them out.

TOPIC SENTENCE: <u>Customers should always tip restaurant servers.</u>

- is part of the cost of going to a restaurant
- shows appreciation for the server's work
- servers need tips to have an adequate standard of living
- their salaries are below the standard minimum wage
- some customers are rude
- servers often don't get benefits such as health care
- you tip hairdressers and taxi drivers
- mistakes aren't always the server's fault
- slow service could be the cook's fault
- sometimes there are not enough servers
- some people in the service industry earn good salaries (cooks, I think)

The Writer's Desk Generate Supporting Ideas

Choose two of your topic sentences from the Writer's Desk on page 23. For each topic sentence, develop a list of supporting ideas.

After you have two complete lists, choose the one that you find most interesting. Then group ideas together and cross out any ideas that are not useful.

ESSAY LINK

In an essay, you can use time, space, or emphatic order to organize your ideas.

Organizing Your Ideas

To make your ideas easy for your readers to follow, organize your ideas in a logical manner. You can use one of three common organizational methods: (1) time order, (2) emphatic order, or (3) space order.

Transitional expressions help guide the reader from one idea to another. A complete list of transitional expressions appears on page 40 in Chapter 3.

Time Order

When you organize a paragraph using **time order (chronological order),** you arrange the details according to the sequence in which they have occurred. When you narrate a story, explain how to do something, or describe a historical event, you generally use time order.

first   then   after that

Here are some transitional expressions you can use in time-order paragraphs.

after that	first	later	next
eventually	in the beginning	meanwhile	suddenly
finally	immediately	months after	then

The next paragraph is structured using time order.

> One day, some gentlemen called on my mother, and I felt the shutting of the front door and other sounds that indicated their arrival. Immediately, I ran upstairs before anyone could stop me to put on my idea of formal clothing. Standing before the mirror, as I had seen others do, I anointed my head with oil and covered my face thickly with powder. Then I pinned a veil over my head so that it covered my face and fell in folds down to my shoulders. Finally, I tied an enormous bustle round my small waist, so that it dangled behind, almost meeting the hem of my skirt. Thus attired, I went down to help entertain the company.
>
> —Helen Keller, *The Story of My Life*

Emphatic Order

When you organize the supporting details of a paragraph using **emphatic order,** you arrange them in a logical sequence. For example, you can arrange details from least to most important, from least appealing to most appealing, and so on.

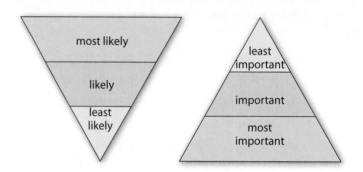

Here are some transitional expressions you can use in emphatic-order paragraphs.

above all	first	moreover	principally
clearly	in particular	most importantly	the least important
especially	last	of course	the most important

The following paragraph uses emphatic order. The writer presents the conditions from bad ones to the worst ones.

> The conditions experienced by the eager young volunteers of the Union and Confederate armies included massive, terrifying, and bloody battles, apparently unending, with no sign of victory in sight. First, soldiers suffered from the uncertainty of supply, which left troops, especially in the South, without uniforms, tents, and sometimes even food. They also endured long marches over muddy, rutted roads while carrying packs weighing fifty or sixty pounds. Most importantly, disease was rampant in their dirty, verminous, and unsanitary camps, and hospitals were so dreadful that more men left them dead than alive.
>
> — Adapted from John Mack Faragher et al., *Out of Many: A History of the American People*

> **Hint**   **Using Emphatic Order**
>
> When you organize details using emphatic order, use your own values and opinions to determine what is most or least important, upsetting, remarkable, and so on. Another writer might organize the same ideas in a different way.

Space Order

When you organize ideas using **space order,** you help the reader visualize what you are describing in a specific space. For example, you can describe something or someone from top to bottom or bottom to top, from left to right or right to left, or from far to near or near to far.

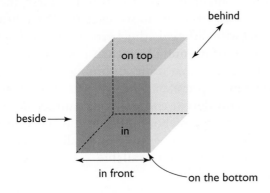

Here are some transitional expressions you can use in space-order paragraphs.

above	beneath	nearby	on top
behind	closer in	on the bottom	toward
below	farther out	on the left	under

In the next paragraph, the writer describes a location beginning at the beach and ending up at the front of the house.

> Their house was even more elaborate than I expected. It was a cheerful red-and-white Georgian Colonial mansion overlooking the bay. The lawn started at the beach and ran toward the front door for a quarter of a mile, jumping over sundials and brick walks and burning gardens. Finally, when it reached the house, drifting up the side in bright vines as though from the momentum of its run. The front was broken by a line of French windows.
>
> —F. Scott Fitzgerald, *The Great Gatsby*

PRACTICE 6

Read each paragraph and underline the topic sentence. Then decide what order the writer used: time, emphatic, or space order. Circle any transitional words or phrases that help you make your choice.

A. After two months of work, I realized that my job selling a health drink was actually a pyramid scheme. In the beginning, I answered an online ad promising great money in sales. I went to the initiation meeting, and there were about twenty job seekers. Enthusiastic speakers spoke to us about the enormous amounts of money we would soon be earning. The next day, after a screening process, the recruiter claimed to choose the best candidates. I now realize that she chose everybody. Then, a week later, we were asked to invest $200 in our initial samples. "Sell your drinks and the money will start rolling in," the recruiter promised. We could also earn income by recruiting more salespeople. I was nervous, but I really needed the job, so I put almost all of my savings into those powered drinks. After two months of unsuccessful sales, I understood that the only people making money were those at the top of the scheme.

—Latonza Hines, student

Order: _____

B. Many factors contribute to racist attitudes. First, there are often higher levels of racist incidents in societies that have historically had very little contact with different ethnic groups. According to the writer and political analyst Gwynne Dyer, such isolated societies may feel threatened when there is an influx of immigrants. Moreover, racist attitudes become more prevalent when various ethnic communities do not intermingle. If different cultural communities do not work and study together, stereotypes about other groups become entrenched. Most importantly, high levels of poverty contribute to racist reactions; immigrants become easy and available scapegoats when there is competition for limited jobs.

—Eliot Mandel, student

Order: _____

C. The tiny interior of the shop was in fact uncomfortably full, but there was almost nothing in it of the slightest value. The floor space was very restricted because all around the walls were stacked innumerable dusty picture-frames. In the window, there were trays of nuts and bolts, worn-out chisels, penknives with broken blades, tarnished watches that did not even pretend to be in going order, and other miscellaneous rubbish. Only on a small table in the corner was there a litter of odds and ends—lacquered snuffboxes, agate brooches, and the like—which looked as though they might include something interesting. As Winston wandered towards the table, his eye was caught by a round, smooth thing that gleamed softly in the lamplight, and he picked it up.

—George Orwell, *1984*

Order: _____

PRACTICE 7

Read the following topic sentences. Decide what type of order you can use to develop the paragraph details. Choose time, emphatic, or space order. (There may be more than one correct organizational method.)

EXAMPLE:

Repair a water heater with three simple steps.   *time*

1. Music education is essential in public schools.   _____

2. There are three types of terrible bosses.   _____

3. My furnished room has everything a student could need.   _____

4. We had many problems during our vacation in Florida.   _____

5. The town library has a very impressive design.   _____

6. A largely misunderstood religion is Islam.   _____

7. The Beatles went through many musical phases.   _____

8. Learning the guitar requires practice, patience, and perseverance.   _____

The Paragraph Plan

A **plan** (or **outline**) of a paragraph is a map showing the paragraph's main and supporting ideas. To make a plan, write your topic sentence and then list supporting points and details. Remember to use time, emphatic, or space order to organize the supporting points. In a more formal outline, you can use letters and numbers to indicate primary and secondary ideas.

Mahan's Paragraph Plan

Mahan completed his paragraph plan. He narrowed his topic, wrote a topic sentence, and thought of several supporting details. Here is his paragraph plan.

TOPIC SENTENCE: People steal for many reasons.
Support 1: Poverty is a primary motivation for people to steal.
Details: —some people are unemployed
—others work at low-paying jobs
—need money for food, rent, clothing
Support 2: Some criminals are greedy.
Details: —want to live a life of luxury
—crave jewels and nice cars
—wish for a larger yacht or faster jet
Support 3: Some people steal due to drug or alcohol addictions.
Details: —addicts steal to buy drugs
—alcohol ruins good judgment
Support 4: Some people steal for the kicks.
Details: —experience the thrill
—receive an adrenaline rush when stealing

ESSAY LINK

Make a plan when you write an essay. In essay plans, each supporting idea becomes a separate paragraph.

 **Adding Specific Details**

When you prepare your paragraph plan, ask yourself if the details clearly support your topic sentence. If not, then you could add details to make your points stronger. For example, when Mahan first brainstormed a list of supporting details (page 24), he did not think of specific details to support his point about greed. In his paragraph plan, however, he added a couple of more details (larger yacht, faster jet) to make that point stronger and more complete.

The Writer's Desk **Write a Paragraph Plan**

Look at the topic sentence and the organized list of supporting ideas that you created for the previous Writer's Desk exercises. Now, in the space provided, make a paragraph plan. Remember to include details for each supporting idea.

Topic
sentence: _____

_____

Support 1: _____

Details: _____

_____

Support 2: _____

Details: _____

_____

Support 3: _____

Details: _____

_____

ESSAY LINK

Essays end with a concluding paragraph. For more information, see pages 191–192.

Writing the Concluding Sentence

A stand-alone paragraph may have a **concluding sentence** that brings it to a satisfactory close. There are several ways to write a concluding sentence.

- Restate the topic sentence in a new, refreshing way.
- Make an interesting final observation.
- End with a prediction, suggestion, or quotation.

 **Problems with Concluding Sentences**

When you write your concluding sentence, do not introduce a contradictory idea or change the focus of the paragraph. For example, in Mahan's paragraph about crime, he should not end with a statement that questions or contradicts his main point.

Weak: But nobody really understands why people break the law.

(This concluding sentence undermines the main point, which is that people steal for many reasons.)

Better: Knowing why people steal may help social services and lawmakers deal with criminals more effectively.

(This prediction brings the paragraph to a satisfactory close.)

PRACTICE 8

The topic sentences in paragraphs A and B are underlined. For each paragraph, circle the letter of the most effective concluding sentence and then explain why the other choice is not as effective.

EXAMPLE:

<u>Picasso painted many different types of people that he saw in the Paris neighborhood of Montmartre.</u> He painted musicians, prostitutes, street vendors, circus performers, and fellow artists, as well as his many lovers. During his blue period, he was drawn to emaciated figures; impoverished mothers and hungry children populated his art.

a. Picasso painted many different types of people.

b. The human body was ultimately the most important and repeated image in his paintings and sculptures.

Why is the other choice not as effective?

Sentence "a" just repeats the topic sentence.

A. <u>Our state should insist that day care centers provide more flexible hours for families.</u> Today, in many families, both parents work outside the home. These parents do not necessarily work from nine to five. For example, nurses and factory employees work in shifts. It is important for these parents to have flexible day care. Also, many parents who are in the service and retail industries work on weekends. For these parents, it is important to have adequate child care facilities during their work hours.

a. The current hours of most day care centers do not meet the needs of a great number of families.

b. However, maybe day care owners do not want to open on nights and weekends.

Why is the other choice not as effective?

B. College students should find part-time jobs that require them to exercise different muscles. If a business student spends hours sitting in front of a computer screen, then he should try to find a job that requires physical activity. If an engineering student has to do advanced calculus, then maybe her part-time job should allow her to rest her brain. Students who do a lot of solitary study could try to find jobs that allow them to interact socially.

    a. Some college students should not take part-time jobs because they need to concentrate on their studies.

    b. Humans need to do a variety of activities to be mentally and physically strong, so college students should keep that in mind when they look for work.

Why is the other choice not as effective?

_____

The First Draft

After making a paragraph plan, you are ready to write your first draft, which is a very important step in the writing process. Your first draft includes your topic sentence, some supporting details, and a concluding sentence. It is okay if your first draft is incomplete or messy. Later, during the revising and editing stages, you can clarify your ideas and modify the organization of your paragraph.

Mahan's First Draft

Here is Mahan Zahir's first draft. You may notice that his paragraph has errors. He will correct these when he gets to the revising and editing stage of the process.

      People steal for many reasons. Poverty is a primary motivation for people to steal. Because some people are unemployed and others may be underemployed. They may not have enough money for food, clothing rent. Stealing money or food may be very tempting. As a means of survival. Criminals do fraud because they are greedy. In fact, some extremely wealthy people steal simply because they want to acquire a larger yacht or a more better jet. Another important reason that people engage in stealing is to pay for their addictions. Finally, people also steal for kicks. Criminals get an adrenaline rush when you outwit the cops.

The Writer's Desk **Write Your First Draft**

In the previous Writer's Desk on page 30, you made a paragraph plan.
Now use the plan's information to type or write your first draft paragraph.

REFLECT ON IT

Think about what you have learned in this chapter. If you do not know an answer, review that topic.

1. What is a topic sentence? _____

_____

2. What is time order? _____

_____

3. What is emphatic order? _____

_____

4. What is space order? _____

_____

Are the following sentences true or false? Circle the best answer.

5. A paragraph has more than one main idea.   True   False

6. A paragraph's details support its topic sentence.   True   False

The Writer's Room

Writing Activity 1

In the Writer's Room in Chapter 1, "Exploring," you used various strategies to find ideas about the following topics. Select one of the topics and write a paragraph. Remember to follow the writing process.

General Topics

1. a childhood memory
2. anger
3. music
4. cosmetic surgery

College and Work-Related Topics

5. a comfortable place
6. study or work habits
7. college life
8. cars

Writing Activity 2

Choose a topic that you feel passionate about, and write a paragraph. Your topic could be an activity (painting, basketball) or an interest (music, politics). Your topic sentence should make a point about the topic.

✔ DEVELOPING CHECKLIST

As you develop your paragraph, ask yourself the following questions.

☐ Have I narrowed my topic?

☐ Does my topic sentence make a valid and supportable point about the topic?

☐ Is my topic sentence interesting?

☐ Does my paragraph focus on one main idea?

☐ Do the details support the topic sentence?

☐ Do the supporting details follow a logical order?

☐ Does my paragraph end in a satisfactory way?

mywritinglab To check your progress in meeting this chapter's objectives, log in to **www.mywritinglab.com**, go to the **Study Plan** tab, click on **The Writing Process** and choose **Developing and Organizing a Paragraph and The Topic Sentence** from the list of subtopics. Read and view the resources in the **Review Materials** section, and then complete the **Recall, Apply,** and **Write** sets in the **Activities** section.

Revising and Editing

The revising and editing stage of the writing process is similar to adding the finishing touches to an artwork. Small improvements can make the work more solid and complete.

> " *Life is trying things to see if they work.* "
> —RAY BRADBURY
> *American author (b. 1920)*

What Are Revising and Editing?

After you have written the first draft of your paragraph, the next step in the writing process is to revise and edit your work. When you **revise,** you modify your writing to make it stronger and more convincing. To revise, read your first draft critically, looking for faulty logic, poor organization, or poor sentence style. Then you reorganize and rewrite your draft, making any necessary changes. When you **edit,** you proofread your final draft for errors in grammar, spelling, punctuation, and mechanics.

There are five key steps to follow during the revising and editing stage.

REVISING AND EDITING

STEP 1	➤	**Revise for unity.** Ensure that all parts of your work relate to the main idea.
STEP 2	➤	**Revise for adequate support.** Determine that your details effectively support the main idea.
STEP 3	➤	**Revise for coherence.** Verify that your ideas flow smoothly and logically.
STEP 4	➤	**Revise for style.** Ensure that your sentences are varied and interesting.
STEP 5	➤	**Edit for technical errors.** Proofread your work, and correct errors in grammar, spelling, mechanics, and punctuation.

Revise for Unity

Unity means that all of the sentences in a paragraph support the topic sentence. If a paragraph lacks unity, then some sentences drift from the main idea that the writer expresses in the topic sentence. To check for unity, ensure that every sentence in the body of the paragraph relates to one main idea.

Paragraph Without Unity

In the next paragraph, the writer drifted away from her main idea. The highlighted sentences do not relate to the topic sentence. When they are removed, the paragraph has unity.

Every idea in a paragraph should move in the same direction just as the vehicles on this bridge need to move in the same direction to reach their destinations. There should be no forks in the road.

The writer took a detour here. ➤

> **During World War II, the status of women changed profoundly.** The military industry needed "manpower" to fight the war, but it also needed womanpower. From 1940 to 1944, about 17 million women joined the workforce. They filled jobs in defense industries, steel mills, shipyards, and aircraft factories. By the end of the war, women had proved that they could be invaluable workers. Today, many women work in these industries, and that isn't considered unusual. In fact, according to Brigid O'Farrell, women make up more than 17 percent of all blue-collar workers in the United States. When men returned home in 1945, most women left the factories; however, women had developed confidence and earning power, and North America's workplace had changed forever.

PRACTICE I

Paragraphs A and B contain problems with unity. In each paragraph, underline the topic sentence and cross out any sentences that do not support the controlling idea.

A. Although parents and teachers often criticize the negative influence of video games on today's youth, such games may actually have a positive impact on young people. First, video games help people acquire important skills, such as problem solving, hand-eye coordination, and memory skills. With "Guitar Hero" or "Wii Sports," players improve these skills because the levels of games vary in difficulty. Also, video games improve players' social skills. Some video games, such as "Lara Croft" and "The Sims," teach players about leadership, friendship, and real-life rules. Lastly, video games are powerful tools to aid children who lack

ESSAY LINK

When revising and editing your essay, check that the body paragraphs support the thesis statement. Also, ensure that each body paragraph has unity.

self-esteem. If a child attains a high level playing the "Tony Hawk's Motion" game, he or she may feel a sense of accomplishment. My friend Joe and I often play video games at the arcade. Yesterday, we played for two hours, and then we went to the park. Thus, parents and teachers should keep a balanced perspective about video games.

B. Orville and Wilbur Wright had an unlikely dream, but they turned it into reality. When the brothers first tried to make a plane fly, they were unsuccessful. In fact, in 1901, a frustrated Wilbur Wright said that humans wouldn't fly for a thousand years. However, just two years later, on December 17, 1903, Wilbur and Orville Wright flew a plane for 105 feet. The brothers were overjoyed; their hard work and planning had finally paid off. Since that time, air travel has changed a lot. Many different types of planes exist today. Jets fly across our skies and can go from London to New York in a few hours. Eventually, the Wright brothers produced nineteen types of aircraft. By sticking with an idea and persevering, the Wright brothers made their dream a reality.

Revise for Adequate Support

A paragraph has **adequate support** when there are enough details and examples to make it strong, convincing, and interesting. The following paragraph attempts to persuade, but it does not have any specific details that make a strong point.

A bridge is built using several well-placed support columns. Like a bridge, a paragraph requires adequate support to help it stand on its own.

Paragraph Without Adequate Support

In the past, the entertainment industry stereotyped women as the weaker sex. However, women are now portrayed as tough and intelligent characters. Most comic books usually depicted males as superheroes. But comic books now embrace super heroines. Recent films have portrayed females as super heroines. Video games are also changing stereotypical gender roles. The image of women as the weaker sex in the entertainment media is definitely being redefined.

> **ESSAY LINK**
>
> When revising your essay, ensure that you have adequately supported the thesis statement. Also ensure that each body paragraph has sufficient supporting details.

PRACTICE 2

When the preceding paragraph about female stereotypes in the entertainment media is expanded with specific details and examples, the paragraph becomes more convincing. Add details on the lines provided. You can do this practice alone or with a partner.

In the past, the entertainment industry stereotyped women as the weaker

sex. However, women are now portrayed as tough and intelligent characters.

Most comic books usually depicted males as superheroes. For example,

_____ and _____ fought creepy

scoundrels. But comic books now embrace super heroines. One of the most famous female comic book heroines is _____. She is beautiful, but she can fight evil as well as any man. Furthermore, recent films have portrayed females as super heroines. In the movie, _____, the actress _____ plays a character with superpowers, defeating a mighty villain. Video games are also changing stereotypical gender roles. For example, _____ is a super sexy heroine who is strong, determined, and intelligent. She can overcome any obstacle in her way. The image of women as the weaker sex in the entertainment industry is definitely being redefined.

Avoiding Circular Reasoning

Circular reasoning means that a paragraph restates its main point in various ways but does not provide supporting details. The main idea goes in circles and never progresses. Avoid using circular reasoning by providing a clear, concise topic sentence and by supporting the topic sentence with facts, examples, statistics, and anecdotes.

CELIA'S PARAGRAPH

Celia Raines, a student, wrote the following paragraph about a popular proverb. In the paragraph, she repeats her main point over and over and does not provide any evidence to support her topic sentence.

Circular reasoning in a paragraph is like a Ferris wheel. The main idea of the paragraph does not seem to progress.

Circular   Those who make the most noise usually get what they want. People sometimes shout and make a fuss, and then others listen to them. Those who are quiet get ignored, and their opinions do not get heard. It is important for people to speak up and express their needs. This attitude is expressed in the proverb "The squeaky wheel gets the grease."

In the second version of this paragraph, Celia added a specific example (an anecdote) that helped illustrate her main point.

Revised Paragraph   Those who make the most noise usually get what they want. Those who are quiet get ignored, and their opinions do not get heard. For example, two years ago, the local government started a passenger train service that helped local commuters get into the city. Many citizens loved commuting by train, but those who live near the train tracks complained about the noise. They made petitions, wrote to newspapers, and lobbied the local government to cancel the train service. Those people were so loud and persistent that they got their wish, and the train service was canceled. The silent majority disagreed with that lobby group, but as the proverb says, "The squeaky wheel gets the grease."

PRACTICE 3

Paragraphs A and B use circular reasoning. Neither has specific evidence to support the topic sentence. List supporting examples for each paragraph. With numbers, indicate where you would place the supporting examples.

EXAMPLE:

American teenagers go through several rites of passage. These rites of passage help the teenager navigate the transition from childhood to *(1)* adulthood. Some rites of passage are shared with the community. *(2)* These rites are an important part of every youth's life.

Examples: *(1) The first date and the first kiss are important. The first job is also a special step.*

(2) During the high school prom, the community members gather together.

A. Police officers have an important function in our society. They provide many useful and necessary services in the community. If there were no police officers, there would be anarchy in the streets. Law-enforcement officers deserve our respect and appreciation.

Examples: _____

_____

_____

_____

B. Having a summer job teaches adolescents some valuable life lessons. There are many situations that students will experience through a summer job that will help them navigate the adult world. So students should try to get some work knowledge before graduating.

Examples: _____

_____

_____

_____

Revise for Coherence

When you drive along a highway and you suddenly hit a pothole, that is an uncomfortable experience. Readers experience similar discomfort if they encounter potholes in a piece of writing. Make your writing as smooth as possible by ensuring that it has **coherence:** the sentences should flow smoothly and logically.

Transitional Expressions

Transitional expressions are linking words or phrases, and they ensure that ideas are connected smoothly. Here are some common transitional expressions.

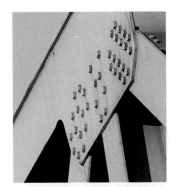

Just as bolts link pieces of a bridge, transitional expressions can link ideas in a paragraph.

ESSAY LINK

To create coherence in an essay, you can place transitional expressions at the beginning of each body paragraph.

Function	Transitional Word or Expression	
Addition	again	in addition
	also	in fact
	besides	last
	finally	moreover
	first (second, third)	next
	for one thing	then
	furthermore	
Concession of a point	certainly	no doubt
	even so	of course
	indeed	to be sure
Comparison and contrast	as well	likewise
	equally	nevertheless
	even so	on the contrary
	however	on the other hand
	in contrast	similarly
	instead	
Effect or result	accordingly	otherwise
	as a result	then
	consequently	therefore
	hence	thus
Example	for example	in particular
	for instance	namely
	in other words	specifically
		to illustrate
Emphasis	above all	least of all
	clearly	most important
	first	most of all
	especially	of course
	in fact	particularly
	in particular	principally
	indeed	
Reason or purpose	for this purpose	the most important reason
	for this reason	
Space	above	near
	behind	nearby
	below	on one side/on the other side
	beneath	on the bottom
	beside	on the left/right
	beyond	on top
	closer in	outside
	farther out	to the north/east/south/west
	inside	under
Summary or conclusion	in conclusion	therefore
	in other words	thus
	in short	to conclude
	generally	to summarize
	on the whole	ultimately
Time	after that	later
	at that time	meanwhile
	at the moment	months after
	currently	now
	earlier	one day
	eventually	presently
	first (second, etc.)	so far
	gradually	subsequently
	immediately	suddenly
	in the beginning	then
	in the future	these days
	in the past	

GRAMMAR LINK

For more practice using transitions in sentences, see Chapter 17, "Compound Sentences," and Chapter 18, "Complex Sentences."

 **Use Transitional Expressions with Complete Sentences**

When you add a transitional expression to a sentence, ensure that your sentence is complete. Your sentence must have a subject and a verb, and it must express a complete thought.

Incomplete:	For example, the rules posted on the wall.
Complete:	For example, the rules <u>were</u> posted on the wall.

PRACTICE 4

The next paragraph contains eight transitional expressions that appear at the beginning of sentences. Underline each expression, and then indicate its purpose. The first one has been done for you.

The McDonaldization of society—the standardization of everyday life—does not refer just to the robot-like assembly of food. <u>Indeed</u>, sociologist George Ritzer points out that this process is occurring throughout society—and it is transforming our lives. First, shopping malls offer one-stop shopping in controlled environments. In addition, travel agencies offer "package" tours. They will transport tourists to ten European capitals in fourteen days. All visitors experience the same hotels, restaurants, and other scheduled sites—and no one need fear meeting a "real" native. Similarly, news agencies **spew** out McNews— short, bland unanalytical pieces that can be digested between gulps of McShake or McBurgers. Moreover, our programmed education will eliminate the need for discussion of social issues. Accordingly, computerized courses will teach the same answers to everyone—the approved, "politically correct" ways to think about social issues. Likewise, mass testing will ensure that students **regurgitate** the programmed responses. Therefore, for good or bad, our lives are being McDonaldized, and the predictability of packaged settings seems to be our social destiny.

—James M. Henslin, *Sociology*

spew:
pour out

regurgitate:
repeat

Transitional Expression	**Function**
1. *Indeed*	*Emphasis*
2. _____	_____
3. _____	_____
4. _____	_____
5. _____	_____
6. _____	_____
7. _____	_____
8. _____	_____

PRACTICE 5

Add appropriate transitional expressions to the following paragraph. Choose from the following list, and use each transitional word once. There may be more than one correct answer for each blank.

consequently   furthermore   on the other hand
for example   first   therefore

Workplace gossip has both positive and negative effects. _____, when two colleagues share secrets about others, that helps build trust and create intimacy. _____, in large organizations, gossip helps form small social groups that provide workplace support systems. _____, overly negative gossip can undermine employee moral. An employee who hears malicious gossip may suspect that he or she is also the subject of office chatter. _____, Latisha Bishop, an employee at CR Industries, says that she felt devastated when she realized that her coworkers were spreading information about her private life. _____, she seriously considered leaving her job. _____, when office workers gossip, they should try to do so without malice.

Just as paint and lighting can make a bridge more beautiful, varied sentence style makes a paragraph more compelling.

Revise for Style

When you revise for sentence **style,** you ensure that your paragraph has concise and appropriate language and sentence variety. You can ask yourself the following questions.

- Have I used a **variety of sentence patterns?** (To practice using sentence variety, see Chapter 19.)
- Have I used **exact language?** (To learn about slang, wordiness, and overused expressions, see Chapter 32.)
- Are my sentences **parallel in structure?** (To practice revising for parallel structure, see Chapter 22.)

MAHAN'S REVISION

On page 32 in Chapter 2, you read the first draft of student Mahan Zahir's paragraph about crime. Look at his revisions for unity, support, coherence, and style.

First, poverty

People steal for many reasons. ~~Poverty~~ is a primary motivation for   ◄ Transition

people to steal. Because some people are unemployed and others may

be underemployed. They may not have enough money for food,

clothing rent. Stealing money or food may be very tempting. As a

Next,   *perpetrate*   ◄ Transition

means of survival. Criminals ~~do~~ fraud because they are greedy. In fact,   ◄ Better word

some extremly wealthy people steal simply because they want to

For example, Bernie Madoff was
found guilty of stealing from clients, he did not lack personal wealth.   ◄ Specific example

acquire a larger yacht or a more better jet. Another important reason

According to the bureau of Justice Statistics, 68 percent of jailed
inmates reported that their substance abuse problems contributed   ◄ Add statistic
to there decisions to commit crimes.

that people engage in stealing is to pay for their addictions. Finally,

people also steal for kicks. Criminals get an adrenaline rush when you

police   ◄ Better word

outwit the ~~cops~~.

Knowing the different reasons that people steal may help social   ◄ Add concluding sentence
workers and lawmakers deal with criminals more effectively.

 **Hint**   **Adding Strong Support**

When you revise, look at the strength of your supporting details. Ask yourself the following questions.

- Are my supporting details interesting, and do they grab the reader's attention? Should I use more vivid words?

- Is my concluding sentence appealing? Could I end the paragraph in a more interesting way?

ESSAY LINK

You should revise your essays for style, ensuring that sentences are varied and parallel. Also, ensure that your language is exact.

PRACTICE 6

In Chapters 1 and 2, you saw examples of Sandra Ahumada's prewriting and planning. Now look at the first draft of Sandra's paragraph, and revise it for unity, support, and coherence. Also, ask yourself what you could do to enhance her writing style.

Customers should always tip restaurant servers. Servers need tips to live. Their salary is very low. They depend on tips to pay for food, housing, and other necessities. They do not get benefits such as health insurance. If you do not like the service, remember that mistakes are not always the server's fault. Poor service could be the cook's fault. Sometimes there are not enough servers. I work as a server in a restaurant, I know how hard it is when customers leave bad tips. Always tip your restaurant server.

GRAMMAR LINK

For more editing practice, see Chapter 37.

TECHNOLOGY LINK

Word processors have spelling and grammar checkers. Do not automatically choose the first suggestion for a correction. Make sure that suggestions are valid before you accept them.

Edit for Errors

When you **edit,** you reread your writing and make sure that it is free of errors. You focus on the language, and you look for mistakes in grammar, punctuation, mechanics, and spelling. There is an editing guide at the back of this book. It contains some common error codes that your teacher may use and provides you with a checklist to proofread your text.

Editing Tips

The following tips will help you proofread your work effectively.

- Put your writing aside for a day or two before you do the editing. Sometimes, when you have been working closely with a text, you might not see the errors.
- Begin your proofreading at any stage of the writing process. For example, if you are not sure of the spelling of a word while writing the first draft, you could either highlight the word to check later or immediately look up the word in the dictionary.
- Keep a list of your common errors in a separate grammar log, such as the one in Appendix 7. When you finish a writing assignment, consult your error list, and make sure that you have not repeated any of those errors. After each assignment has been corrected, you can add new errors to your list.

MAHAN'S EDITED PARAGRAPH

Mahan Zahir edited his paragraph about crime. He corrected errors in spelling, capitalization, punctuation, and grammar.

People steal for many reasons. First, poverty is a primary motivation

for people to steal. Because some people are unemployed and others

                , they

may be underemployed. ~~They~~ may not have enough money for food,

    , and   *as*

clothing rent. Stealing money or food may be very tempting. ~~As~~ a means

of survival. Next, criminals perpetrate fraud because they are greedy.

              extremely

In fact, some ~~extremly~~ wealthy people steal simply because they want

                   faster

to acquire a larger yacht or a ~~more better~~ jet. For example, Bernie

                                 . He

Madoff was found guilty of stealing from clients, ~~he~~ did not lack

personal wealth. Another important reason that people engage in

                                  B

stealing is to pay for their addictions. According to the ~~b~~ureau of

Justice Statistics, 68 percent of jailed inmates reported that their

                    their

substance abuse problems contributed to ~~there~~ decisions to commit

crimes. Finally, people also steal for kicks. Criminals get an adrenaline

       they

rush when ~~you~~ outwit the police. Knowing the different reasons that

people steal may help social workers and lawmakers deal with

criminals more effectively.

The Writer's Desk **Revise and Edit**

Choose a paragraph you wrote for Chapter 2, or choose one that you
have written for another assignment. Carefully revise and edit the
paragraph. You can refer to the Revising and Editing Checklist at the
end of this chapter.

Peer Feedback

After you write a paragraph or essay, it is useful to get peer feedback. Ask another
person, such as a friend, family member, or fellow student, to read your work and
make suggestions for addressing its weaknesses.

Offer Constructive Criticism

When you peer-edit someone else's writing, try to make your comments useful. Phrase your comments in a positive way. Look at these examples.

Instead of saying . . .	**You could say . . .**
Your sentences are boring.	Maybe you could combine some sentences.
Your supporting ideas are weak.	You could add more details here.

You can use the following peer feedback form to evaluate written work.

Peer Feedback Form

Written by: _____   Feedback by: _____

Date: _____

1. What is the main point of the written work?

   _____

2. What details effectively support the topic sentence?

   _____

   _____

3. What, if anything, is unclear or unnecessary?

   _____

   _____

4. Give some suggestions about how the work could be improved.

   _____

   _____

5. What is an interesting or unique feature of this written work?

   _____

   _____

Write the Final Draft

When you have finished making revisions on the first draft of your paragraph, write the final draft. Include all of the changes that you have made during the revision and editing phases. Before you hand in your final draft, proofread it one last time to ensure that you have caught any errors.

The Writer's Desk **Write Your Final Draft**

You have developed, revised, and edited your paragraph. Now write the final draft. Before you offer it to readers, proofread it one last time to ensure that you have found all of your errors.

 **Spelling, Grammar, and Vocabulary Logs**

- **Keep a spelling and grammar log.** You probably repeat, over and over, the same types of grammar and spelling errors. You will find it very useful to record your repeated grammar mistakes in a spelling and grammar log. You can refer to your list of spelling and grammar mistakes when you revise and edit your writing.

- **Keep a vocabulary log.** Expanding your vocabulary will be of enormous benefit to you as a writer. In a vocabulary log, you can make a list of unfamiliar words and their definitions.

See Appendix 7 for more information about spelling, grammar, and vocabulary logs.

REFLECT ON IT

Think about what you have learned in this chapter. If you do not know an answer, review that topic.

1. What are four things that you should look for when revising?

   _____   _____

   _____   _____

2. Circle the best answer(s). A paragraph is unified if

   a. there are no irrelevant supporting details.

   b. there are many facts and statistics.

   c. all details support the topic sentence.

3. Circle the best answer: Transitional words are _____ that help ideas flow in a logical manner.

   a. links   b. sentences   c. verbs

4. The Editing Handbook in Part IV includes information about grammar, spelling, and punctuation errors. In what chapter would you find information about the following topics? Look in the table of contents to find the chapter number.

a. capitalization   _____

b. subject-verb agreement   _____

c. faulty parallel structure   _____

d. commas   _____

e. commonly confused words   _____

The Writer's Room

Writing Activity 1

Choose a paragraph that you have written for your job or for another course. Revise and edit that paragraph, and then write a final draft.

Writing Activity 2

Choose any of the following topics, or choose your own topic. Then write a paragraph. Remember to follow the writing process.

General Topics

1. interesting things about yourself
2. heroes in the media
3. risky adventure
4. bad service

College and Work-Related Topics

5. something you learned in a college course or on campus
6. reasons to change jobs
7. telemarketing
8. an interesting job

✔ REVISING AND EDITING CHECKLIST

When you revise and edit, ask yourself the following questions. (For a more detailed editing checklist, refer to the inside back cover of this book.)

Unity

☐ Is my paragraph unified under a single topic?

☐ Does each sentence relate to the topic sentence?

Support

☐ Does my paragraph have an adequate number of supporting details?

Coherence

☐ Is my paragraph logically organized?

☐ Do I use transitional words or expressions to help the paragraph flow smoothly?

Style

☐ Do I use a variety of sentence styles?

☐ Is my vocabulary concise?

☐ Are my sentences parallel in structure?

Editing

☐ Do my sentences contain correct grammar, spelling, punctuation, and mechanics?

mywritinglab To check your progress in meeting this chapter's objectives, log in to **www.mywritinglab.com**, go to the **Study Plan** tab, click on **The Writing Process** and choose **Revising the Paragraph** from the list of subtopics. Read and view the resources in the **Review Materials** section, and then complete the **Recall, Apply,** and **Write** sets in the **Activities** section.

Paragraph Patterns

What Is a Paragraph Pattern?

A *pattern or mode* is a method used to express one of the three purposes: to inform, to persuade, or to entertain. Once you know your purpose, you will be able to choose which writing pattern or patterns can help you to express it.

Patterns can overlap, and it is possible to use more than one pattern in a single piece of writing. For example, imagine you are writing a paragraph about bullying, and your purpose is to inform the reader. You might use *definition* as your predominant pattern, but in the supporting details, you might use *comparison and contrast* to compare a bully and a victim. You might also use *narration* to highlight an incident in which a bully harassed a victim.

Before you work through the next chapters, review the paragraph patterns.

Illustration
To illustrate or prove a point using specific examples

Narration
To narrate or tell a story about a sequence of events that happened

Process
To inform the reader about how to do something, how something works, or how something happened

Description
To describe using vivid details and images that appeal to the reader's senses

Definition
To define or explain what a term or concept means by providing relevant examples

Classification
To classify or sort a topic's qualities to help readers better understand the topic.

Comparison and contrast
To present information about similarities (compare) or differences (contrast)

Cause and effect
To explain why an event happened (the cause) or what the consequences of the event were (the effects)

Argument*
To argue or to take a position on an issue and offer reasons for your position

*Argument is included as one of the nine patterns, but it is also a purpose in writing.

Illustration

Travel agencies use examples of attractions to sell tour packages. In illustration writing, you give examples to support your point of view.

“ *A wisely chosen illustration is essential to fasten the truth upon the ordinary mind.* ”

—HOWARD CROSBY
American preacher and educator (1826–1891)

Writers' Exchange

Work with a team of two or three other students. List at least five examples of each part of speech. Include only words that begin with the letters *H* or *S*. Do as many as you can in two minutes.

Noun   Verb   Adjective   Pronoun

What Is Illustration?

When you write using **illustration,** you include specific examples to clarify your main point. You illustrate, or give examples, anytime you want to explain, analyze, narrate, or give an opinion about something. As a writer, you can use many different types of examples to help your reader acquire a deeper and clearer understanding of your subject. You can include personal experience or factual information, such as a statistic.

You give examples every day. When telling a friend why you had a good day or a bad day, you might use examples to make your story more interesting. At college, you might give an oral presentation using examples that will help your audience better understand your point. At work, you might give examples to show clients where or how they might market their products.

Illustration at Work

Patti Guzman is a registered nurse at a large hospital. She was invited to speak to nursing students in a local university. In the following excerpt from her speech, she gives examples to explain why a nurse must be in good physical health.

Physically, the job of a nurse is demanding. On a daily basis, we must lift patients and move them. When patients are bedridden for prolonged periods, we must change their positions on their beds. When new patients arrive, we transfer them from stretchers to beds or from beds to wheelchairs. If patients fall, we must be able to help them stand up. If patients have difficulty walking, we must assist them. Patients who have suffered paralysis or stroke need to be lifted and supported when they are bathed and dressed. Keep in mind that some patients may be quite heavy, so the job requires a good level of physical strength.

The topic sentence expresses the main idea.

Supporting sentences provide details and examples.

The concluding sentence brings the paragraph to a satisfying close.

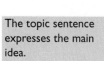
ESSAY LINK

You can develop illustration essays with a series of examples or extended examples.

The Illustration Paragraph

There are two ways to write an illustration paragraph.

- **Use a series of examples** to illustrate your main point. For example, if you are writing a paragraph about an innovative teacher that you had, you might list things that the teacher did such as wear a costume, let students teach parts of the course, and use music to make a point.
- **Use an extended example** to illustrate your main point. The example can be an anecdote or a description. For example, in a paragraph about creativity, you might describe a time when you tried to make a sculpure.

PRACTICE I

Read the next paragraph and answer the questions.

Across the country, lawmakers are coming up with inventive ways to punish criminals. Some judges in New Orleans, for example, treat offenders like unruly children. In 2003, one of the judges ordered a shoplifter in Baton Rouge to stand in front of a Dillard's store holding a sign that says "I will not shoplift anymore," and another judge ordered an offender to write "I will not steal other people's property" 2,500 times. In Florida, a hard-working judge orders drunk drivers to put bumper stickers on their cars that read, "How's my driving? The judge wants to know." The stickers feature a toll-free number. A Kentucky judge sometimes instructs **deadbeat dads** to choose between jail or a **vasectomy.** The best creative sentencing is done by a judge from Santa Fe, New Mexico. Judge Frances Gallegos, arguing that traditional anger management courses are ineffective, sentences violent offenders to tai chi, meditation, and Japanese flower-arranging classes.

deadbeat dad:
a father who avoids paying for his child's upkeep

vasectomy:
medical procedure to sterilize a male

—Rebecca Bloom, student

1. Underline the topic sentence of this paragraph. (The topic sentence expresses the main idea of the paragraph.)

2. What type of illustration paragraph is this? Circle the best answer.
   a. Series of examples   b. Extended example

3. List the examples that the writer gives to illustrate her point.

   _____

   _____

   _____

   _____

PRACTICE 2

Read the next paragraph and answer the questions.

Online chatting is one way that computer viruses can be spread. For example, my friend Chelsea met someone online. She thought her new acquaintance was a polite, well-behaved young man who was a few years older than she was. They exchanged pictures at his request. However, the file he sent via e-mail was actually a virus. He was able to control my friend's computer through his screen. Later, using Chelsea's name, he sent threatening messages to others in chatrooms. He could even open and close my friend's disk drawer through clicking on the Eject button on her screen. Of course, Chelsea was terrified. She was only able to get rid of the virus with the help of a computer specialist.

—Nancy A. Ghaley, student

1. Underline the topic sentence.

2. What does the writer use to present her supporting details? Circle the best answer.
   a. a series of examples   b. an extended example

3. What example(s) does the writer give to illustrate her point?

_____

4. What are the main events in the narrative? List them.

_____

_____

_____

_____

_____

_____

Explore Topics

In the Warm Up, you will try an exploring strategy to generate ideas about different topics.

The Writer's Desk Warm Up

Think about the following questions, and write the first ideas that come to your mind. Try to think of two to three ideas for each topic.

EXAMPLE:

What are some effective ways to market a product?

use colorful packaging

create a funny advertisement

give free samples

1. What are some really silly fads or fashions?

_____

_____

_____

2. What are some traits of an effective leader?

_____

_____

_____

3. What are some qualities that you look for in a mate?

_____

_____

_____

DEVELOPING

The Topic Sentence

The topic sentence of the illustration paragraph is a general statement that expresses both your topic and your controlling idea. To determine your controlling idea, think about what point you want to make.

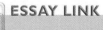

ESSAY LINK

In an illustration essay, the thesis statement expresses the controlling idea.

       topic   controlling idea

Part-time jobs <u>teach students valuable skills.</u>

         controlling idea   topic

<u>Our father became anxious</u> **when my sister started dating.**

The Writer's Desk Write Topic Sentences

Write a topic sentence for each of the following topics. You can look for ideas in the previous Writer's Desk. Remember to narrow your topic. Each topic sentence should contain a general statement that expresses both your topic and your controlling idea.

EXAMPLE:

Topic: Effective marketing strategies

Topic sentence: ___*Advertisers have many clever ways to interest consumers.*___

_____

1. Topic: Silly fads or fashions

   Topic sentence: _____

   _____

2. Topic: Traits of an effective leader

   Topic sentence: _____

   _____

3. Topic: Qualities you look for in a mate

   Topic sentence: _____

   _____

The Supporting Ideas

After you have developed an effective topic sentence, generate supporting ideas. In an illustration paragraph, you can give a series of examples or an extended example.

When you use a series of examples, you can arrange your examples in emphatic order. Emphatic order means that you can place your examples from the most to the least important or from the least to the most important. If you use an extended example, you can arrange your ideas using time order.

Visualizing Illustration

PRACTICE 3

Brainstorm supporting ideas for the following topic sentence. Give examples of how people risk their lives.

TOPIC SENTENCE:

Some workers risk their lives daily.

window washer

electrician

fisher

police officer

_____

_____

The Writer's Desk Generate Supporting Ideas

Generate some supporting examples under each topic. Make sure your examples support the topic sentences that you wrote for the previous Writer's Desk.

EXAMPLE:

Effective marketing strategies

- *use a catchy, memorable jingle*

- *offer free samples*

- *have a contest or sweepstakes*

- *do product placement in TV shows*

2. Traits of an effective leader

_____

_____

_____

1. Silly fads or fashions

_____

_____

_____

_____

3. Qualities you look for in a mate

_____

_____

_____

The Paragraph Plan

A paragraph plan helps you organize your topic sentence and supporting details before you write a first draft. When you write a paragraph plan, make sure that your examples are valid and relate to the topic sentence. Also include details that will help clarify your supporting examples. Organize your ideas in a logical order.

TOPIC SENTENCE: Advertisers have many clever ways to interest consumers.

> **Support 1:**   Relate the product to an interesting character.
>
> **Details:**   —The Pillsbury Dough Boy is cute.
> —Ronald McDonald appeals to children.
>
> **Support 2:**   Give free samples to consumers.
>
> **Details:**   —Junk mail contains free shampoo samples.
> —Perfume samples are passed out on street corners.
>
> **Support 3:**   Put the product in popular movies or television programs.
>
> **Details:**   —*American Idol* judges drink particular brands.
> —Car companies have their products in reality shows.

The Writer's Desk **Write a Paragraph Plan**

Choose one of the topic sentences that you wrote for the previous Writer's Desk. Write a paragraph plan using some of the supporting ideas that you have generated. Include details for each supporting idea.

Topic
sentence: _____

_____

Support 1: _____

Details: _____

_____

Support 2: _____

Details: _____

_____

Support 3: _____

Details: _____

_____

The First Draft

After you outline your ideas in a plan, you are ready to write the first draft. Remember to write complete sentences. You might include transitional words or expressions to help your ideas flow smoothly.

ESSAY LINK

In an illustration essay, place the thesis statement in the introduction. Then, structure the essay so that each supporting idea becomes a distinct paragraph with its own topic sentence.

Transitional Words and Expressions

Transitional expressions can help you introduce an example or show an additional example. The following transitional words are useful in illustration paragraphs.

To Introduce an Example		To Show an Additional Example	
for example	namely	also	in addition
for instance	specifically	first (second, etc.)	in another case
in other words	to illustrate	furthermore	moreover

The Writer's Desk Write the First Draft

For the previous Writer's Desk, you developed a paragraph plan. Now write the first draft of your illustration paragraph. Before you write, carefully review your paragraph plan and make any necessary changes.

REVISING AND EDITING

Revise and Edit an Illustration Paragraph

When you finish writing an illustration paragraph, review your work and revise it to make the example(s) as clear as possible to your readers. Check to make sure that the order of ideas is logical, and remove any irrelevant details. Before you work on your own paragraph, practice revising and editing a student paragraph.

PRACTICE 4

Read the next student paragraph, and answer the questions.

Advertisers have many clever ways to get the consumer's attention. First, to make the product memorable, they can link it with an interesting character. When people see the character, they instantly remember the product. For example, any child will recognize Ronald McDonald, the Energizer Bunny, or the Green Giant. Also, the Pillsbury Dough Boy. Furthermore, free samples help consumers become familiar with the item. Sometimes, when people walk downtown, somebody gives you a snack or a perfume sample. Who can resist getting something for nothing? The most effective advertising method is to place products in popular television shows and movies. On *American Idol*, for instance, the judges promote certain soft drinks. In reality shows such as *Survivor*, the contestants win particular car models, and millions of people hear about the car's features. Apple computers have shown up on *The Office*, *House*, and *24*. Every year, advertisers come up with better and more innovative marketing ideas.

Revising

1. Underline the topic sentence.

2. List the main supporting points.

   _____

   _____

   _____

3. What order does the author use?

   a. time order

   b. space order

   c. emphatic order

Editing

1. Underline a pronoun error. Write your correction in the space below.

   Correction: _____

2. This paragraph contains a fragment, which is an incomplete sentence. Underline the fragment. Then correct it in the space below.

   Correction: _____

GRAMMAR LINK

See the following chapters for more information about these grammar topics:

Pronouns, Chapter 29

Fragments, Chapter 20

Grammar Hint   **Writing Complete Sentences**

A fragment is an incomplete sentence. When you give an example, make sure that your sentence is complete. Avoid fragment errors.

Fragment: For example, too many parties.

Correction: For example, some students go to too many parties.

The Writer's Desk **Revise and Edit Your Paragraph**

Revise and edit the paragraph that you wrote for the previous Writer's Desk. Make sure that your paragraph has unity, adequate support, and coherence. Also, correct any errors in grammar, spelling, punctuation, and mechanics.

---

vo•cab•u•lar•y BOOST

Avoid Repetition

Read through the first draft of your paragraph, and identify some words that you frequently repeat. Replace those words with synonyms.

REFLECT ON IT

Think about what you have learned in this chapter. If you do not know an answer, review that topic.

1. In an illustration paragraph, you _____

2. There are two ways to write illustration paragraphs. Explain each of them.
    a. Using a series of examples: _____
    b. Using an extended example: _____

3. List three transitional expressions that indicate an additional idea.

    _____

The Writer's Room

Writing Activity 1: Topics

Choose any of the following topics, or choose your own topic. Then write an illustration paragraph.

General Topics

1. activities that relieve stress
2. great things in life that are free
3. mistakes parents make
4. items you have lost
5. positive personality traits

College and Work-Related Topics

6. pressures faced by college students
7. qualities that help you succeed
8. claustrophobic work environments
9. qualities of a good instructor
10. tools or equipment needed for your job

Writing Activity 2: Photo Writing

In the photo, a woman has the annoying habit of biting her nails. Write a paragraph about things that annoy you. Provide many examples.

WRITING LINK

More Illustration Writing Topics
Chapter 16, Writer's Room topic 1 (page 272)
Chapter 17, Writer's Room topic 1 (page 284)
Chapter 20, Writer's Room topic 1 (page 316)
Chapter 25, Writer's Room topic 1 (page 370)
Chapter 28, Writer's Room topic 1 (page 408)

READING LINK

More Illustration Readings
"Guy Chores" by Tom Keenan (page 202)
"The Beeps" by Josh Freed (page 562)
"When the Legal Thing Isn't the Right Thing" by Deborah Mead (page 572)

Writing Activity 3: Media Writing

Watch a popular television show or movie that deals with students in a high school or college setting. Examples are the *American Pie* movies, *High School Musical*, or television programs such as *Glee*, *The Hills*, or *Gossip Girl*. You can even go on YouTube and type "peer pressure" into the search bar, and then watch some of the segments. Write a paragraph about the show, movie, or video segment and explain the ways that characters feel peer pressure. Provide several examples.

✔ ILLUSTRATION PARAGRAPH CHECKLIST

After you write your illustration paragraph, review the checklist on the inside front cover. Also ask yourself the following questions.

☐ Does my topic sentence make a point that can be supported with examples?

☐ Does my paragraph contain sufficient examples that clearly support the topic sentence?

☐ Do I use transitions to smoothly connect my examples?

☐ Have I arranged my examples in a logical order?

mywritinglab To check your progress in meeting this chapter's objectives, log in to **www.mywritinglab.com**, go to the **Study Plan** tab, click on **Paragraph Patterns** and choose **Paragraph Development – Illustrating** from the list of subtopics. Read and view the resources in the **Review Materials** section, and then complete the **Recall, Apply,** and **Write** sets in the **Activities** section.

Narration

When investigating a crime scene, a detective must try to find answers to the questions who, what, when, where, why, *and* how. *You answer the same questions when you write a narrative paragraph.*

> *It's all storytelling, you know.*
> *That's what journalism is all about.*
>
> —TOM BROKAW
> *American broadcast journalist (b. 1940)*

Writers' Exchange

Work in a team of at least three students. First, choose a fairy tale to retell in an updated way. Next, one team member begins by saying one sentence. Then, another team member adds a sentence to the tale. Team members continue to take turns until the story is complete.

EXAMPLE: Yesterday, a young woman wearing a red baseball cap decided to visit her grandmother.

EXPLORING

What Is Narration?

When you **narrate,** you tell a story about what happened. You generally explain events in the order in which they occurred, and you include information about when they happened and who was involved in the incidents.

You use narration every day. You may write about the week's events in your personal journal, or you might send a postcard to a friend detailing what you did during your vacation. At college, you may explain what happened during a historical event or what happened in a novel that you have read. At work, you might use narration to explain an incident involving a customer or coworker.

Narration is not only useful on its own; it also enhances other types of writing. For example, Jason must write an argument essay about youth crime. His essay will be more compelling if he includes a personal anecdote about the time a gang of youths attacked him in a subway station. In other words, narration can provide supporting evidence for other paragraph or essay patterns.

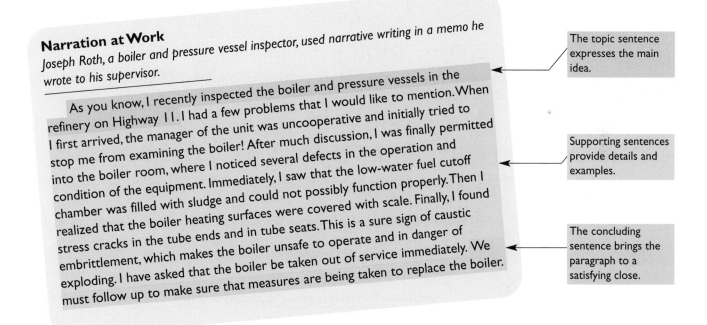

Narration at Work

Joseph Roth, a boiler and pressure vessel inspector, used narrative writing in a memo he wrote to his supervisor.

As you know, I recently inspected the boiler and pressure vessels in the refinery on Highway 11. I had a few problems that I would like to mention. When I first arrived, the manager of the unit was uncooperative and initially tried to stop me from examining the boiler! After much discussion, I was finally permitted into the boiler room, where I noticed several defects in the operation and condition of the equipment. Immediately, I saw that the low-water fuel cutoff chamber was filled with sludge and could not possibly function properly. Then I realized that the boiler heating surfaces were covered with scale. Finally, I found stress cracks in the tube ends and in tube seats. This is a sure sign of caustic embrittlement, which makes the boiler unsafe to operate and in danger of exploding. I have asked that the boiler be taken out of service immediately. We must follow up to make sure that measures are being taken to replace the boiler.

The topic sentence expresses the main idea.

Supporting sentences provide details and examples.

The concluding sentence brings the paragraph to a satisfying close.

The Narrative Paragraph

There are two main types of narrative paragraphs.

1. **Use first-person narration (autobiography).**

   In first-person narration, you describe a personal experience from your point of view. You are directly involved in the story. You use the words *I* (first-person singular) or *we* (first-person plural). For example: "When I was a child, I thought that the world began and ended with me. I didn't know, or care, how other children felt. Thus, when schoolmates ridiculed a shy boy, I gleefully joined in."

ESSAY LINK

In a narrative essay, you can use first- or third-person narration.

2. **Use third-person narration.**

In third-person narration, you do not refer to your own experiences. Instead, you describe what happened to somebody else. The story is told in the third person using *he, she, it,* or *they.* You might tell a story about your mother's childhood, or you might explain what happened during the last election. In this type of narration, you are simply an observer or storyteller; you are not a participant in the action. For example: "The students gathered to protest against the war. One student threw a chair through the window of the student center. Suddenly, people started pushing and shoving."

 **Choose an Interesting Topic**

When you write a narrative paragraph, try to choose a topic that will interest the reader. For example, the reader might not be interested if you write about the act of eating your lunch. However, if you write about a time when your best friend argued with a waiter during a meal, you could create an entertaining narrative paragraph.

Think about a topic that you personally find very interesting, and then share it with your readers. Try to bring your experience to life so that your readers can share it with you.

Explore Topics

In the Warm Up, you will try an exploring strategy to generate ideas about different topics.

The Writer's Desk Warm Up

Think about the following questions, and write down the first ideas that come to your mind. Try to think of two or three ideas for each topic.

EXAMPLE: Can you recount an interesting or funny event that has happened to you, or have family members told you about interesting or funny events that have happened to them?

I got stuck in an elevator. My uncle Donovan taught in Japan for a year.

What else? My sister brought a stray dog home. My brother and his

band members got lost.

I. Think about a time when you did something that took a lot of nerve. Perhaps you resisted peer pressure, or maybe you disagreed with someone's point of view. Write about what happened.

_____

_____

_____

2. What are some memorable parties or celebrations that you have attended?

_____

_____

_____

3. Think about interesting true events that have happened to family members or friends. Are some stories particularly funny, sad, or inspiring? List some ideas.

_____

_____

_____

PRACTICE 1

Read the paragraph and answer the questions.

On the way home, I was more silent than before, and this time there was no effort in it. As soon as we left Martyrs' Square, Mama began craning her neck towards the rear-view mirror. Stopping at the next traffic light, she whispered a prayer to herself. A car stopped so close beside us I could have touched the driver's cheek. Four men dressed in dark safari suits sat looking at us. At first, I didn't recognize them, but then I remembered. I remembered so suddenly I felt my heart jump. They were the same Revolutionary Committee men who had come a week before and taken Ustath Rashid. Mama looked ahead, her back a few centimeters away from the backrest, her fists tight around the steering wheel. She released one hand, brought it to my knee and sternly whispered, "Face forward."

—Hisham Matar, _In the Country of Men_

1. Underline the topic sentence.

2. What type of narration is this paragraph? _____

_____

3. Who is the narrator? _____

_____

4. How did the boy and his mother feel? _____

_____

5. What was happening in the country at the time the paragraph was written?

_____

_____

6. Where did it happen? _____

_____

7. By combining your answers to questions 3–6, write a one-sentence summary of the paragraph. Someone who has never read the paragraph should have a clear idea of the paragraph's content after reading your sentence.

_____

_____

_____

PRACTICE 2

Read the next paragraph and answer the questions.

Isaac Newton
(1643–1727) was an English physicist who described the laws of motion and universal gravitation.

Cambridge:
a famous university in the United Kingdom

betwixt:
between

    Isaac Newton was brilliant beyond measure but capable of the most riveting strangeness. At home, upon swinging his feet out of bed in the morning, he would reportedly sometimes sit for hours, immobilized by the sudden rush of thoughts to his head. In 1667, he returned to **Cambridge** and built his own laboratory. Then he engaged in the most bizarre experiments. Once he inserted a bodkin—a long needle of the sort used for sewing leather—into his eye socket and rubbed it around. "It was **betwixt** my eye and my bone as near to [the] backside of my eye as I could," he wrote. He wanted just to see what would happen. What happened, miraculously, was nothing—at least nothing lasting. After that, on another occasion, he stared at the Sun for as long as he could bear, to determine what effect it would have upon his vision. Again he escaped lasting damage, though he had to spend some days in a darkened room before his eyes forgave him.

—Bill Bryson, *A Short History of Nearly Everything*

1. Who or what is the paragraph about? _____

2. Underline the topic sentence of this paragraph.

3. What point is the author making about Newton?

_____

4. What type of narration is this? _____

_____

5. How does the writer support the topic sentence? List some examples.

_____

_____

_____

_____

6. Do the supporting facts provide adequate support for the topic sentence?

_____

DEVELOPING

The Topic Sentence

When you write a narrative paragraph, it is important to express a main point. Simply describing a list of activities is boring for the reader. To make your paragraph interesting, make sure that your topic sentence has a controlling idea.

ESSAY LINK

In a narrative essay, the thesis statement expresses the controlling idea.

          topic   controlling idea

When somebody broke into my house, I felt totally invaded.

          controlling idea   topic

Jay learned to be responsible **during his first job.**

Make a Point

In a narrative paragraph, the topic sentence should make a point. For help finding the controlling idea, you can ask yourself the following questions.

- What did I learn?
- How did I change?
- How did it make me feel?
- What is important about it?

EXAMPLE:

Topic:	Moving out of the family home
Possible controlling idea:	Becoming more independent

              topic   controlling idea

When I moved out of the family home, I became more independent.

PRACTICE 3

Practice writing topic sentences. Complete the following sentences by adding a controlling idea.

1. When I moved out of the family home, I felt _____

   _____

2. In my first job, I learned _____

   _____

3. When Tara heard the news about _____, she realized

   _____

The Writer's Desk **Write Topic Sentences**

Write a topic sentence for each of the following topics. You can look for ideas in the Writer's Desk Warm Up on pages 64–65. Each topic sentence should mention the topic and express a controlling idea.

EXAMPLE:

Topic: A funny coincidence

Topic sentence: _When Uncle Donovan met a fellow tourist, they turned out to have some strange things in common._

1. Topic: A decision that took nerve

   Topic sentence: _____

   _____

2. Topic: A celebration or party

   Topic sentence: _____

   _____

3. Topic: A story about someone

   Topic sentence: _____

   _____

The Supporting Ideas

A narrative paragraph should contain specific details so that the reader understands what happened. To come up with the details, ask yourself a series of questions. Your paragraph should provide answers to these questions.

- Who is the paragraph about?
- What happened?
- When did it happen?
- Where did it happen?
- Why did it happen?
- How did it happen?

When you recount a story to a friend, you can add details out of order, saying, "I forgot to mention something." When you write a narrative paragraph, however, your sequence of events should be clearly chronological so that your reader can follow your story.

 # Visualizing Narration

PRACTICE 4

Brainstorm supporting ideas for the following topic sentence. Write some descriptive words and phrases.

TOPIC SENTENCE:

Our camping trip exposed us to new experiences.

The Writer's Desk **Develop Supporting Ideas**

Generate supporting ideas for each topic. List what happened.

EXAMPLE: A funny coincidence

Uncle Donovan was working in Japan

went to see some temples

met a stranger

asked where she worked

were colleagues

1. A decision that took nerve

_____

_____

_____

_____

2. A celebration or party

_____

_____

_____

3. A story about someone

_____

_____

_____

The Paragraph Plan

Before you write a narrative paragraph, it is a good idea to make a paragraph plan. Write down events in the order in which they occurred. To make your narration more complete, include details about each event.

ESSAY LINK

In a narrative essay, you place the thesis statement in the introduction. Each event is developed in a supporting paragraph.

TOPIC SENTENCE:	<u>When Uncle Donovan met a fellow tourist, they turned</u> <u>out to have some strange things in common.</u>
Support 1:	My uncle was working in Japan for a year.
	—He went on a tour of some temples.
	—The only other person in the courtyard was a woman.
Support 2:	He started a conversation with the woman.
	—He asked where she was from.
	—She was also American.
	—She was on vacation in Japan.
Support 3:	He asked where she worked.
	—She said, "I teach at Brownfield College."
	—Uncle Donovan said he did also.
	—He asked her which department she taught in.
	—She said the English department.
	—She had been hired while he was away.
	—They were colleagues.

The Writer's Desk **Write a Paragraph Plan**

Choose one of the topic sentences that you wrote for the previous Writer's Desk. Write a paragraph plan using some of the supporting ideas that you have generated. Include details for each supporting idea.

Topic
sentence: _____

_____

Support 1: _____

Details: _____

_____

_____

Support 2: _____

Details: _____

_____

_____

Support 3: _____

Details: _____

_____

_____

The First Draft

After you outline your ideas in a plan, you are ready to write the first draft. Remember to write complete sentences. You might include transitional words or expressions to help your ideas flow smoothly.

Transitional Words and Expressions

Transitions can help you show a sequence of events. The following transitional words are useful in narrative paragraphs.

To Show a Sequence of Events			
afterward	finally	in the end	meanwhile
after that	first	last	next
eventually	in the beginning	later	then

The Writer's Desk **Write the First Draft**

In the previous Writer's Desk, you developed a paragraph plan. Now write the first draft of your narrative paragraph. Before you write, carefully review your paragraph plan and make any necessary changes.

---

vo•cab•u•lar•y BOOST

Using Varied Language

1. Underline the opening word of every sentence in your first draft. Check to see if some are repeated.
2. Replace repeated opening words an adverb like *usually, generally,* or *fortunately* or a prepositional phrase, such as *On the side* or *Under the circumstances.* You can also begin the sentences with a phrase like *Leaving the door open.* In other words, avoid beginning too many sentences with a noun or transitional word.

Repeated First Words

We opened the door of the abandoned house. We looked nervously at the rotting floorboards. We thought the floor might collapse. We decided to enter. We walked carefully across the kitchen floor to the bedroom, one by one.

Variety

My cousins and I opened the door of the abandoned house. Nervously, we looked at the rotting floorboards. Thinking the floor might collapse, we decided to enter. One by one, we walked across the kitchen floor to the bedroom.

REVISING AND EDITING

Revise and Edit a Narrative Paragraph

When you finish writing a narrative paragraph, carefully review your work and revise it to make the events as clear as possible to your readers. Check that you have organized events chronologically, and remove any irrelevant details. Before you revise and edit your own paragraph, practice revising and editing a student paragraph.

PRACTICE 5

Read the next student paragraph and answer the questions.

> When Uncle Donovan met a fellow tourist, they turned out to have some strange things in common. Uncle Donovan was on leave for a year from his teaching job. He was working in Japan. One day, he went to see some Buddhist temples. There was only one other person at the temple, a woman. A few minutes later, he started a conversation with her. He asks her where she was from. Raquel was an American vacationing in Japan. Uncle Donovan then asked her where she worked. She said "I teach at Brownfield College." Astonished, he replied that he worked at the same college. She told him that she worked in the English department. Uncle Donovan was completely dumbstruck. He told her that he also worked in the English department. She had been hired to teach during his absence. They were colleagues. After he returned home, Uncle Donovan told friends and colleagues about how he met Raquel in Japan. Everyone was amazed at the coincidence.

Revising

1. Write down the two parts of the topic sentence.

   topic   +   controlling idea

   _____

2. What type of order do the specific details follow? Circle the best answer.
   a. Space   b. Time
   c. Emphatic   d. No order

3. What are some transitional expressions that the author used?

   _____

4. What type of narration is this paragraph?
   a. First person   b. Third person

Editing

5. This paragraph contains a tense inconsistency. The tense shifts for no apparent reason. Identify the incorrect sentence, and write the correct sentence in the space below.

   _____

6. The direct quotation is incorrectly punctuated. Correct the error.

   _____

GRAMMAR LINK

See the following chapters for more information about these grammar topics:

Tense consistency, Chapter 27
Quotations, Chapter 35

 **Using Quotations**

When you insert a direct quotation into your writing, capitalize the first word of the quotation and put the final punctuation inside the closing quotation marks.

• Place a comma after an introductory phrase.

　　Vladimir screamed, "The kitchen's on fire."

• Place a colon after an introductory sentence.

　　Vladimir watched me coldly: "We have nothing to discuss."

The Writer's Desk Revise and Edit Your Paragraph

Revise and edit the paragraph that you wrote for the previous Writer's Desk. Make sure that your paragraph has unity, adequate support, and coherence. Also, correct any errors in grammar, spelling, punctuation, and mechanics.

REFLECT ON IT

Think about what you have learned in this chapter. If you do not know an answer, review that topic.

1. In narrative writing, you _____

2. What are the differences between the two following types of narration?

　　First person: _____

　　_____

　　Third person: _____

　　_____

3. What are some questions that you should ask yourself when you write a narrative paragraph?

　　_____

4. What organizational method is commonly used in narrative paragraphs? Circle the best answer.

　　a. space order　　　b. time order　　　c. emphatic order

WRITING LINK

More Narrative Writing Topics

Chapter 21, Writer's Room topic 1
(page 323)
Chapter 23, Writer's Room topic 1
(page 346)
Chapter 29, Writer's Room topic 1
(page 426)
Chapter 31, Writer's Room topic 1
(page 450)

READING LINK

More Narrative Readings

"A Lesson in Humility" by Jeff Kemp
(page 207)
"Musicophilia" by Oliver Sachs
(page 551)
"Why I Worked with La Migra" by
Veronica Ortega (page 569)

The Writer's Room

Writing Activity 1: Topics

Choose any of the following topics, or choose your own topic. Then write a narrative paragraph.

General Topics

1. an interesting decade
2. a risky adventure
3. an unforgettable holiday
4. a disturbing news event
5. an unexpected gift

College and Work-Related Topics

6. an embarrassing incident at college or work
7. an inspiring teacher or instructor
8. a positive or negative job interview
9. a difficult coworker
10. a proud moment at work or college

Writing Activity 2: Photo Writing

Have you ever lived through an earthquake, a tornado, a flood, a large storm, an extended power outage, or any other event caused by nature? What happened? What did you do? Write a narrative paragraph about a natural event that you have lived through.

Writing Activity 3: Media Writing

Watch a popular television show or movie that shows a character overcoming a challenge. Examples are the movie *The Soloist* and television programs such as *The Game*, *Harlem Heights*, and *CSI*. You can even go on YouTube and watch some videos about people who have overcome challenges to meet their personal goals. For example, Susan Boyle surprised audiences when she sang on *Britain's Got Talent*. Narrate what happened.

✔ NARRATIVE PARAGRAPH CHECKLIST

As you write your narrative paragraph, review the checklist on the inside front cover. Also ask yourself the following questions.

☐ Does my topic sentence clearly express the topic of the narration?

☐ Does my topic sentence contain a controlling idea that is meaningful and interesting?

☐ Does my paragraph answer most of the following questions: *who, what, when, where, why, how?*

☐ Do I use transitional expressions that help clarify the order of events?

☐ Do I include details to make my narration more interesting?

PEARSON
mywritinglab To check your progress in meeting this chapter's objectives, log in to **www.mywritinglab.com**, go to the **Study Plan** tab, click on **Paragraph Patterns** and choose **Paragraph Development – Narrating** from the list of subtopics. Read and view the resources in the **Review Materials** section, and then complete the **Recall, Apply,** and **Write** sets in the **Activities** section.

Description

When professional photographers prepare for a session, they adjust the lighting, the model, and the camera angle to make a visual impression. In descriptive writing, you use words to create a distinct image.

> ❝ *The beginning of human knowledge is through the senses, and the writer begins where human perception begins.* ❞
>
> —FLANNERY O'CONNOR
> *American author (1925–1964)*

Writers' Exchange

Work with two or three students. First, think about a particular place. It can be a street, a coffee shop, a mall, a park, or any other place in your region. Describe details about that place. Describe sights, sounds, and smells. Speak nonstop about the place for about forty seconds. Your teammates must guess the place that you are describing.

What Is Description?

Description creates vivid images in the reader's mind by portraying people, places, or moments in detail.

You use description every day. At home, you might describe a new friend to your family, or you might describe an object that you bought. At college, you might describe the structure of a cell or the results of a lab experiment. At work, you may describe a new product to a client, or you could describe the qualities of potential clients to your boss.

Description at Work
In this excerpt from an Alba Tours travel brochure, the writer describes the amenities offered at a vacation resort.

With its lavish open-air lobby complete with curving staircase, the gleaming marble columns, and the rich mahogany furniture, Sandals Dunn's River captures the romance of an Italian-style Mediterranean paradise. The centerpiece of this spectacular resort is one of Jamaica's largest swimming pools with its own cascading waterfall and swim-up bar. You can try out the facilities at the open-air fitness center, play some tennis, or shoot a round of golf at the Sandals Golf and Country Club, where greens fees and transfers are included. After that, why not take a complimentary tour of the world-famous Dunn's River Falls or just relax in the Oriental hot and cold plunge pools followed by a soothing sauna?

> The topic sentence expresses the main idea.

> Supporting sentences provide details and examples.

The Descriptive Paragraph

When you write a descriptive paragraph, focus on three main points.

1. **Create a dominant impression.**

   The dominant impression is the overall atmosphere that you wish to convey. It can be a strong feeling, mood, or image. For example, if you are describing a business meeting, you can emphasize the tension in the room.

2. **Express your attitude toward the subject.**

   Do you feel positive, negative, or neutral toward the subject? For example, if you feel positive about your best friend, then the details of your paragraph about him or her should convey the good feelings you have. If you describe a place that you do not like, then your details should express how uncomfortable that place makes you feel. You might write a neutral description of a science lab experiment.

3. **Include concrete details.**

   Details will enable a reader to visualize the person, place, or situation that is being described. You can use active verbs and adjectives so that the reader imagines the scene more clearly. You can also use **imagery,** which is description using the five senses. Review the following examples of imagery.

ESSAY LINK

In descriptive essays, you should also create a dominant impression, express your attitude toward the subject, and include concrete details.

Sight	While talking casually to her husband, Joanna absentmindedly tugs at a hangnail until the skin tears and a tiny droplet of blood appears. —Deborah Tannen, *You're Wearing That?*
Sound	As the glass tinkled onto the cellar floor, he heard a low growl. —Christopher Morley, *The Haunted Bookshop*
Smell	The odor of fresh-sawed pine perfumed the air. —Stewart Edward White, *The Blazed Trail*
Touch	My heart started racing, perspiration dripped down my face causing my glasses to slide, and I had a hard time breathing. —Bebe Moore Campbell, "Dancing with Fear"
Taste	I asked for fresh lemonade, and got it—delicious, and cold, and tangy with real fruit. —Mary Stewart, *My Brother Michael*

PRACTICE I

Read the next paragraph and answer the questions.

I was in Acapulco, Mexico, for a mini-vacation when I was literally swept off my feet. We arrived at the beach early in the morning. As I walked along, sand worked its way into my flip-flop sandals, and I could feel its warmth between my toes. The sun's rays heated up my back, shoulders, and neck. But most of all, I heard the roaring of the waves. How they called to me. A whitecap formed that was about to crash, and I decided that it was mine. With an open-mouthed smile, I ran in its direction with the illusion of breaking the water. With every step I took, the wave grew larger. I realized just how big it truly was as I ducked under it in pure fear. The wave curved over me as it would a surfer, and the world became silent. I imagined that this is how a collision with a truck would feel if the truck were made out of water. My world instantly turned black, and I tumbled and rolled at the mercy of the sea. Water invaded my nose, ears, and eyes. The taste of salty water filled my mouth. Then, just as quickly as it had arrived, the foaming wave receded—leaving me as its footprint. Crawling my way back to dry sand, I coughed up ocean water. I had been chewed up and spat out by the sea.

—Vince Rosas, student

1. Underline the topic sentence.

2. What is the dominant impression that the writer creates?

   _____

   Give two examples that show the dominant impression.

   _____

   _____

3. Give examples of sensory details.

   a. sight   _____

   b. sound   _____

   c. taste   _____

   d. touch   _____

4. What image or impression does the writer bring to life?

_____

Explore Topics

In the Warm Up, you will try an exploring strategy to generate ideas about different topics.

The Writer's Desk **Warm Up**

Think about the following questions, and write down the first ideas that come to your mind. Try to think of two or three ideas for each topic.

EXAMPLE: What are some strong impressions you have had at a workplace?

> *donut shop smells*
>
> *images when I first tried welding*
>
> *the loud banging in the machine shop*

1. What were some very emotional moments in your life? (Think about two or three moments when you felt extreme joy, sadness, excitement, anxiety, or other strong emotions.)

_____

_____

2. Describe your food quirks. What are your unusual tastes or eating habits? Which foods do you really love or hate?

_____

_____

3. What are some very busy places?

_____

_____

_____

ESSAY LINK

In a descriptive essay, the thesis statement expresses the controlling idea.

DEVELOPING

When you write a descriptive paragraph, choose a subject that lends itself to description. In other words, find a subject that appeals to the senses. For example, you can describe the sounds, sights, tastes, and smells in a bakery.

The Topic Sentence

In the topic sentence of a descriptive paragraph, you should convey a dominant impression about the subject. The dominant impression is the overall impression or feeling that the topic inspires.

        topic   controlling idea
The abandoned buildings in our neighborhood <u>are an eyesore.</u>

       topic   controlling idea
When the car skidded, <u>I panicked.</u>

 **How to Create a Dominant Impression**

To create a dominant impression, ask yourself how or why the topic is important.

Poor: The parade was noisy.
             (Why should readers care about this statement?)

                           topic   controlling idea
Better: **The parade participants** <u>loudly celebrated the arrival of the New Year.</u>

The Writer's Desk **Write Topic Sentences**

Write a topic sentence for each of the following topics. You can look for ideas in the previous Writer's Desk. Remember to narrow each topic. Each topic sentence should state what you are describing and contain a controlling idea.

EXAMPLE:

Topic: Impressions at work

Topic sentence: *My first attempt at arc welding filled me with awe.*

1. Topic: An emotional moment

Topic sentence: _____

2. Topic: Food quirks (unusual food habits or foods you love or hate)

Topic sentence: _____

3. Topic: A busy place

Topic sentence: _____

The Supporting Ideas

After you have developed an effective topic sentence, generate supporting details. The details can be placed in space, time, or emphatic order.

Visualizing Description 👓

PRACTICE 2

Brainstorm supporting ideas for the following topic sentence. Write some descriptive words or phrases.

TOPIC SENTENCE:

During my canoe trip, the scenery fascinated me.

_____   _____   _____

_____   _____   _____

_____   _____   _____

Show, Don't Tell

Your audience will find it more interesting to read your written work if you *show* a quality of a place or an action of a person rather than just state it.

Example of Telling: Recently, a snowstorm arrived and was impressive.

Example of Showing: Recently, a blizzard roared off Lake Michigan and blasted our farm. The trees moaned and their branches creaked. Wind-driven snow encased pine needles, heaped into drifts, and sculpted fields. Curtains of snow-draped shrubs created small caverns where sparrows and rabbits hid.

—from "Snow" by Joan Donaldson

PRACTICE 3

Choose one of the following sentences, and write a short description that shows—not tells—the quality of the person, place, thing, or event.

1. The food smelled delicious.

2. It was a hot day.

3. The child's room was messy.

ESSAY LINK

When you plan a descriptive essay, it is useful to list sensory details.

List Sensory Details

To create a dominant impression, think about your topic and make a list of your feelings and impressions. These details can include imagery (images that appeal to sight, sound, touch, taste, and smell).

TOPIC: An abandoned building

Details: —damp floors

—boarded-up windows

—broken glass

—graffiti on the walls

—musty

—gray bricks

—chipping paint

---

vo•cab•u•lar•y BOOST

Using Vivid Language

When you write a descriptive paragraph, try to use **vivid language**. Use specific action verbs and vivid adjectives to create a clear picture of what you are describing.

unpretentious
The wealthy owner was ~~nice~~.
(Use a more vivid, specific adjective.)

howled
The wind ~~blew~~.
(Use a more vivid, specific verb or image.)

Think about other words or expressions that more effectively describe these words:

Hungry: _____

Not friendly: _____

Cry: _____

Speak: _____

The Writer's Desk List Sensory Details

Think about images, impressions, and feelings that the following topics inspire in you. Refer to your topic sentences on page 80, and make a list under each topic.

EXAMPLE: Impressions at work

arc welding

flashing light

burning smell

bright sparks

smell of rust

bending wire

popping sound

1. An emotional moment: _____

2. Food quirks: _____

3. A busy place: _____

The Paragraph Plan

A descriptive paragraph should contain specific details so that the reader can clearly imagine what is being described. When you make a paragraph plan, remember to include concrete details. Also think about the organizational method that you will use.

ESSAY LINK

In a descriptive essay, place the thesis statement in the introduction. Then, develop each supporting idea in a body paragraph.

TOPIC SENTENCE: My first attempt at arc welding filled me with awe.

Support 1:   At first, the flashing lights frightened me.

   Details: —popping and cracking sound

              —like a roaring brush fire

              —bright sparks

Support 2:   The smell of burning newspaper filled the air.

   Details: —oxidized metal

              —odor of a rusty boat hull

Support 3:   I was able to shape the raw metal.

   Details: —red-hot wire

              —bent like licorice

The Writer's Desk **Write a Paragraph Plan**

Choose one of the topic sentences that you wrote for the Writer's Desk on page 80, and write a detailed paragraph plan. You can include some of the sensory details that you have generated in the previous Writer's Desk.

Topic
sentence: _____

_____

Support 1: _____

Details: _____

_____

_____

Support 2: _____

Details: _____

_____

_____

Support 3: _____

Details: _____

_____

_____

The First Draft

After you outline your ideas in a plan, you are ready to write the first draft. Remember to write complete sentences. You might include transitional words or expressions to help your ideas flow smoothly.

Transitional Words and Expressions

You can use space order to describe a person, place, or thing. The following transitions are useful in descriptive paragraphs.

To Show Place or Position			
above	beyond	in the distance	outside
behind	closer in	nearby	over there
below	farther out	on the left/right	under
beside	in front	on top	underneath

The Writer's Desk **Write the First Draft**

In the previous Writer's Desk, you developed a paragraph plan. Now write the first draft of your descriptive paragraph. Before you write, carefully review your paragraph plan and make any necessary changes.

REVISING AND EDITING

Revise and Edit a Descriptive Paragraph

When you finish writing a descriptive paragraph, carefully review your work and revise it to make the description as clear as possible to your readers. Check that you have organized your steps logically, and remove any irrelevant details.

PRACTICE 4

Read the following student paragraph, and answer the questions.

> Eight years ago, my first attempt at arc welding filled me with awe. I was fearful, yet I felt as if I had uncover a great secret. At first, the flashing lights frightened me. They made a popping and crackling noise that sounded like a roaring brush fire. Imagine charging a car battery and accidentally knocking the clamps. Sparks flew, yet I could control and maintain the sparking. An odor like that of burning newspaper filled the air. Also, the oxidized metal. It smelled like a rusty boat hull after a rainfall. I felt so powerful because I could make raw metal take shape. Using a vise, the red-hot steel bent as easily as a piece of licorice.
>
> —Kelly Bruce

Revising

1. Underline the topic sentence.

2. Highlight three vivid images in the paragraph.

3. The paragraph ends abruptly. Add a concluding sentence.

_____

_____

Editing

4. Identify and correct one past participle error.

   Error: _____   Correction: _____

5. A fragment lacks a subject or verb and is an incomplete sentence. Identify and correct one fragment. Write the correction on the line.

_____

GRAMMAR LINK

See the following chapters for more information about these topics:
Past Participles, Chapter 24
Fragments, Chapter 20
Modifiers, Chapter 32

6. The paragraph contains a dangling modifier. Write the correction on the line. (See the Grammar Hint below for more information about modifier errors.)

_____

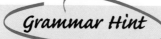 **Grammar Hint** **Using Modifiers**

When you revise your descriptive essay, check that your modifiers are placed near the items they are modifying. Also make sure that the modifier is connected to another part of the sentence and is not dangling.

Incorrect: Gazing at the sky, the pink-colored clouds drifted on the horizon.

Correct: Gazing at the sky, **I noticed** the pink clouds drifting on the horizon.

The Writer's Desk **Revise and Edit Your Paragraph**

Revise and edit the paragraph that you wrote for the previous Writer's Desk. Check that your paragraph has unity, adequate support, and coherence. Also, correct any errors in grammar, spelling, punctuation, and mechanics.

REFLECT ON IT

Think about what you have learned in this chapter. If you do not know an answer, review that topic.

1. What are the main features of a descriptive paragraph? _____

_____

_____

2. Define imagery. _____

3. Look at the familiar words below. Write down at least two more descriptive ways to say each word. Try to find words that are more specific.

a. cute _____   c. sad _____

b. angry _____   d. mean _____

The Writer's Room

Writing Activity 1: Topics

Choose any of the following topics, or choose your own topic. Then write a descriptive paragraph.

General Topics

1. an interesting house or building
2. a useless product or item
3. an evening out
4. a scene from nature
5. an unusual person

College and Work-Related Topics

6. a quiet area on campus
7. an unusual student or coworker
8. a loud place
9. an uncomfortable uniform
10. a place with a good or bad odor

WRITING LINK

More Descriptive Writing Topics

Chapter 20, Writer's Room topic 2 (page 316)

Chapter 22, Writer's Room topic 1 (page 332)

Chapter 23, Writer's Room topic 2 (page 346)

Chapter 27, Writer's Room topic 1 (page 390)

Chapter 36, Writer's Room topic 1 (page 511)

Writing Activity 2: Photo Writing

Visit a public place and take notes about the sights, sounds, and smells. Then, write a paragraph describing that place. Include vivid details.

READING LINK

More Descriptive Readings

"Chicken Hips" by Catherine Pigott (page 211)

"Bound Feet" by Jung Chang (page 528)

"Aunt Tee" by Maya Angelou (page 554)

Writing Activity 3: Media Writing

Watch a popular television show or movie that describes the future or that depicts mysterious places. For example, you can choose the movies *District 9*, *Gamer*, *The Twilight Saga*, and *Star Trek* or television shows such as *Heroes*, *V*, and *True Blood*. In a paragraph, describe the setting or main characters. Use imagery that appeals to the senses.

DESCRIPTIVE PARAGRAPH CHECKLIST

As you write your descriptive paragraph, review the checklist on the inside front cover. Also ask yourself the following questions.

☐ Does my topic sentence clearly show what I will describe?

☐ Does my topic sentence have a controlling idea that makes a point about the topic?

☐ Does my paragraph make a dominant impression?

☐ Does my paragraph contain supporting details that appeal to the reader's senses?

☐ Do I use vivid language?

mywritinglab To check your progress in meeting this chapter's objectives, log in to **www.mywritinglab.com**, go to the **Study Plan** tab, click on **Paragraph Patterns** and choose **Paragraph Development – Describing** from the list of subtopics. Read and view the resources in the **Review Materials** section, and then complete the **Recall, Apply,** and **Write** sets in the **Activities** section.

Process

Dancers learn new steps by following a process. Similarly, in process writing, you describe how to do something.

66 *It is easier to know how to do something than it is to do it.* 99
—CHINESE PROVERB

Writers' Exchange

Choose one of the following topics, and have a group or class discussion. Describe the steps you would take to do that process.

1. How to forgive someone
2. How to ruin a date
3. How to recognize when someone is lying
4. How to bathe your dog

What Is a Process?

A **process** is a series of steps done in chronological order. In process writing, you explain how to do something, how an incident took place, or how something works.

You explain processes every day. At home, you may explain to a family member how to use an electronic appliance, or you may need to give written instructions to a baby-sitter or caregiver. At college, you may explain how to perform a scientific experiment or how a new product was invented. At work, you may explain how to operate a machine or how to do a particular job.

Process at Work

In this memo to fellow employees, Mawlid Abdul Aziz, a network administration assistant, uses process writing to explain how to install antivirus software on a computer.

The topic sentence expresses the main idea.

Supporting sentences provide details and examples.

The concluding sentence brings the paragraph to a satisfying close.

Because of a new security threat circulating on the Internet, the IT department strongly recommends that you update your antivirus software. To do so, double-click on the antivirus icon at the bottom right on your computer screen (system tray). The correct icon should appear at the far left of the row of icons. Then, a window will appear that is called the virus scan console. In this window, there are several items, one of which is labeled "Automatic Update." When you double-click on that button, another window will appear that contains the button "Run Now." Click on it, and after a minute or two, there will be a message box saying "completed." Please do not hesitate to contact the IT department if you encounter any difficulty with this procedure.

ESSAY LINK

Process essays also focus on completing or understanding a process.

The Process Paragraph

There are two main types of process paragraphs.

- **Complete a process.** This type of paragraph contains directions on how to complete a particular task. For example, a writer might explain how to paint a picture, how to repair a leaky faucet, or how to get a job. The reader should be able to follow the directions and complete the task.

- **Understand a process.** This type of paragraph explains how something works or how something happens. In other words, the goal is to help the reader understand a process rather than do a process. For example, a writer might explain how the heart pumps blood to other organs in the body or how a country elects its political leaders.

PRACTICE I

A framed painting hanging on a wall creates its own imaginary world. Understanding and responding to a painting does not have to be difficult. First, get up close. When you approach a picture, step into its universe. Put your nose up close and observe the picture as a physical object. Drink in its visual and physical properties. Next, take a step back and look at the picture as a whole. Look at the arrangement or composition of the picture's elements: background or foreground, implied movement, and dramatic action. Is there a story? Who are the human figures? Are there symbols? What feelings or ideas does it stimulate in you? Then, think and apply what you know. Study the picture in historical context. This knowledge can help identify the style or movement to which a picture belongs. It can tell you the work's patron or something significant about the artist's life and how this work fits into that story. Finally, respond with your own thoughts and feelings. Look at what it shows you and listen to what it says and record that experience for yourself in a journal or notebook. This personal reflection fixes the impression and helps you recall this picture as something you've become acquainted with.

—Philip E. Bishop, *A Beginner's Guide to the Humanities*

1. a. What is the topic of this paragraph? _____

   _____

   b. What is the controlling idea in the topic sentence? _____

   _____

2. List the main steps the author suggests to help you understand a painting.

   _____

   _____

   _____

   _____

PRACTICE 2

Read the next paragraph and answer the questions.

Tsunamis, like the one that occurred in Indonesia in 2004, are caused by shifting layers in the Earth's crust. The plates of hard rock, which fit together like a puzzle, overlap and move slowly over time. As the plates push against each other, pressure builds up. When the plates finally buckle, or if one plate pushes under another, built-up energy is released. When this happens underwater, seawater gets pushed up to the surface. Waves then spread in different directions. The waves can move at over 200 miles per hour in the deep ocean. As they near the shore and get squeezed in inlets, the waves increase in size and can attain 90 feet in height. At the same time, they slow down but can still move at 50 miles per hour, which is faster than a person can run. When the tsunami hits the shore, it strips the sand off beaches, rips away trees and bushes, and pounds buildings.

—Natalia MacDonald, student

1. Underline the topic sentence.

2. What type of process paragraph is this? Circle the best answer.

   a. complete a process   b. understand a process

3. List the steps or stages in the process. The first one has been done for you.

plates push against each other

_____

_____

_____

_____

_____

PRACTICE 3

For each of the following topics, write *C* if it explains how to complete a process, or write *U* if it explains how to understand a process (how something works or how something happens).

1. How to train a pet dog   _____

2. The stages in a child's development   _____

3. How a child learns to read   _____

4. How to avoid being mugged   _____

5. Five steps to keep your motorcycle in top condition   _____

Explore Topics

In the Warm Up, you will try an exploring strategy to generate ideas about different topics.

The Writer's Desk Warm Up

Think about the following questions, and write down the first ideas that come to your mind. Try to think of two or three ideas for each topic.

EXAMPLE: Imagine that you have a new opportunity and want to leave your current job. What are some things that you should do before you quit your job?

- *give supervisor a lot of notice (needs time to hire someone else)*

- *ask for a reference letter (I might need it later)*

- *have a going-away party, and thank co-workers and supervisor*

1. How do you do a particular activity at your workplace?

_____

_____

_____

2. What are some things you should do to succeed in college?

_____

_____

_____

3. Think about a particular holiday or celebration that you enjoy. What are some things you do to prepare for that holiday?

_____

_____

_____

DEVELOPING

ESSAY LINK

In a process essay, the thesis statement expresses the controlling idea.

When you write a process paragraph, choose a process that you can easily cover in a single paragraph. For example, you might be able to explain how to send an e-mail message in a single paragraph; however, you would need much more than a paragraph to explain how to use a particular computer software program.

The Topic Sentence

In a process paragraph, the topic sentence states which process you will be explaining and what readers will be able to do or understand after they have read the paragraph.

topic   controlling idea
To calm your child during a tantrum, follow the next steps.

controlling idea   topic
With inexpensive materials, **you can redecorate a room in your house.**

Make a Point

Your topic sentence should not simply announce the topic. It should make a point about the topic.

Announces: This is how you do speed dating.

                               controlling idea   topic
Correct: It is surprisingly easy and efficient **to meet someone using speed dating.**

The Writer's Desk **Write Topic Sentences**

Write a topic sentence for each of the following topics. You can look for ideas in the previous Writer's Desk. Remember to narrow each topic. Each topic sentence should state the process and should contain a controlling idea.

EXAMPLE:

Topic: How to leave a job

Topic sentence: ___*If you want to leave your job on a positive note, there*___

___*are a few steps that you should consider.*___

1. Topic: How to do an activity at work

   Topic sentence: _____

   _____

2. Topic: How to succeed in college

   Topic sentence: _____

   _____

3. Topic: How to prepare for a holiday or celebration

   Topic sentence: _____

   _____

ESSAY LINK

In an essay, each body paragraph could describe a process. For example, in an essay about how to get rich, one body paragraph could be about buying lottery tickets and another could be about inventing a product.

The Supporting Ideas

A process paragraph contains a series of steps. When you develop supporting ideas for a process paragraph, think about the main steps that are necessary to complete the process. Most process paragraphs use time order.

 **Give Steps, Not Examples**

When you explain how to complete a process, describe each step. Do not simply list examples of the process.

Topic: How to Get Rich

List of Examples	Steps in the Process
write a best seller	do market research
win the lottery	find a specific need
invent a product	invent a product to fulfill that need
inherit money	heavily promote the product

Visualizing Process 👓

PRACTICE 4

Brainstorm supporting ideas for the following topic sentence. List some steps that you should take.

TOPIC SENTENCE:

Putting in contact lenses is not a difficult procedure.

   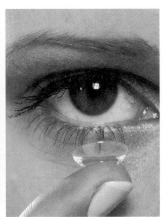

_____ _____ _____ _____

_____ _____ _____ _____

The Writer's Desk List the Main Steps

Think of three or four essential steps in each process. Make a list under each topic.

EXAMPLE: How to leave a job

    explain your reason for going

    give enough notice

    ask for a reference letter

    find out about benefits

    _____

1. How to do an activity at work

    _____

    _____

    _____

    _____

2. How to succeed in college

    _____

    _____

    _____

    _____

3. How to prepare for a holiday or a celebration

    _____

    _____

    _____

    _____

ESSAY LINK

In a process essay, place the thesis statement in the introduction. Then use each body paragraph to explain a step in the process.

The Paragraph Plan

A paragraph plan helps you organize your topic sentence and supporting details before you write a first draft. Decide which steps and which details your reader will really need to know to complete the process or understand it. Write down the steps in chronological order.

TOPIC SENTENCE: If you want to leave your job on a positive note, there are a few steps that you should consider.

Step 1: Explain why you are quitting.
Details: —do not complain about the company
—say you need a new challenge
Step 2: Give employers enough notice.
Details: —the company might need time to hire a replacement
Step 3: Ask for a reference letter.
Details: —may need it in the future
Step 4: Find out about employment benefits.
Details: —might get unused vacation pay

 Include Necessary Tools or Supplies

When you are writing a plan for a process paragraph, remember to include any special tools or supplies a reader will need to complete the process. For example, if you want to explain how to pack for a move, you should mention that the reader will need boxes, felt-tip markers, newsprint, twine, scissors, and tape.

The Writer's Desk Write a Paragraph Plan

Choose one of the topic sentences that you wrote for the Writer's Desk on page 94, and then list the main steps to complete the process. Also add details and examples that will help to explain each step.

Topic
sentence: _____

_____

Supportirng points:

Step 1: _____

Details: _____

_____

Step 2: _____

Details: _____

_____

Step 3: _____

   Details: _____

_____

Step 4: _____

   Details: _____

_____

Step 5: _____

   Details: _____

_____

The First Draft

After you outline your ideas in a plan, you are ready to write the first draft. Remember to write complete sentences. You might include transitional words or expressions to help your ideas flow smoothly.

Transitional Words and Expressions

Most process paragraphs explain a process using time (or chronological) order. The following transitions are useful in process paragraphs.

To Begin a Process	To Continue a Process		To End a Process
(at) first	after that	later	eventually
initially	afterward	meanwhile	finally
the first step	also	second	in the end
	furthermore	then	ultimately
	in addition	third	

The Writer's Desk **Write the First Draft**

In the previous Writer's Desk, you developed a paragraph plan. Now write the first draft of your process paragraph. Before you write, carefully review your paragraph plan and make any necessary changes.

REVISING AND EDITING

Revise and Edit a Process Paragraph

When you finish writing a process paragraph, carefully review your work and revise it to make the process as clear as possible to your readers. Check to make sure that you have organized your steps chronologically and remove any irrelevant details.

PRACTICE 5

Read the following student paragraph and answer the questions.

If you want to leave your job on a positive note, there are a few steps that you should consider. First, remain upbeat as you explain why you are quitting. Instead of complaining about something in the company, you could say that you need a change and want a different challenge. Provide your boss with as much notice as possible, it will leave a favorable impression. It will also give your boss time to find a replacement. If you think you deserve it, ask for a reference letter. Even if you already have a new job, the reference letter could be useful at a future date. Find out if you are entitled to benefits. We may be eligible for back pay or vacation pay. Business consultant Cho Matsu says "The impression you make when you leave a job could have an impact on your future career".

Revising

1. Underline the topic sentence.

2. The author uses *first* to introduce the first step. Subsequent steps would be more clearly recognizable if the writer had used more transitions. Indicate, with a number, where more transitional expressions could be added, and write possible examples on the lines provided.

   _____

   _____

   _____

3. How does the writer conclude the paragraph?
   a. With a prediction   b. With a suggestion   c. With a quotation

Editing

4. This paragraph contains a type of run-on sentence called a comma splice. Two complete sentences are incorrectly connected with a comma. Identify and correct the comma splice.

5. Identify and correct a pronoun shift.

6. This paragraph contains two punctuation errors in the direct quotation. Correct the mistakes directly on the paragraph.

GRAMMAR LINK

See the following chapters for more information about these grammar topics:
   Run-Ons, Chapter 21
   Pronouns, Chapter 29
   Quotations, Chapter 35

 **Pronoun Shifts**

Keep your pronouns consistent. For example, if your process paragraph is addressed to *you*, then do not shift unnecessarily to *we* or *they*.

$$you$$

When you use natural cleaning products, ~~we~~ help the environment.

The Writer's Desk Revise and Edit Your Paragraph

Revise and edit the paragraph that you wrote for the previous Writer's Desk. Ensure that your paragraph has unity, adequate support, and coherence. Also correct any errors in grammar, spelling, punctuation, and mechanics.

---

vo•cab•u•lar•y BOOST

Look at the first draft of your process paragraph. Underline the verb that you use in each step of the process. Then, when possible, come up with a more evocative or interesting verb. Use your thesaurus for this activity.

REFLECT ON IT

Think about what you have learned in this unit. If you do not know an answer, review that topic.

1. What are the two types of process paragraphs? Briefly explain each type.

    a. _____

    _____

    b. _____

    _____

2. What organizational method is generally used in process writing? Circle the best answer.

    a. space order   b. time order   c. emphatic order

3. Why are transitional words important in process writing?

    _____

    _____

WRITING LINK

More Process Writing Topics

Chapter 17, Writer's Room topic 2
(page 284)
Chapter 30, Writer's Room topic 1
(page 441)
Chapter 32, Writer's Room topic 1
(page 461)
Chapter 34, Writer's Room topic 1
(page 491)

READING LINK

More Process Reading

"Steps to Music Success" by Jake
Sibley (page 216)
"How Spies Are Caught" (page 567)
"Control Your Temper" by Elizabeth
Passarella (page 546)

The Writer's Room

Writing Activity 1: Topics

Choose any of the following topics, or choose your own topic. Then write a process paragraph.

General Topics

1. how to make your home safe
2. how to decorate a room with very little money
3. how to be a good roommate
4. how to train a pet
5. how to build or fix something

College and Work-Related Topics

6. how to choose a college
7. how to prepare for a job interview
8. how to get along with your co-workers
9. how to organize your desk or tools
10. how something was discovered

Writing Activity 2: Photo Writing

Pop artist Andy Warhol once said that everyone would be famous for fifteen minutes. Think of some processes related to fame. Some ideas might be how to become famous, how to stay famous, how to lose fame, how to survive fame, or how to meet a celebrity. Then, write a process paragraph.

Writing Activity 3: Media Writing

Watch a reality television show such as *America's Top Model, The Biggest Loser, Hell's Kitchen*, or *Dancing with the Stars*. Describe the process the contestants go through to win the prize.

✔ PROCESS PARAGRAPH CHECKLIST

As you write your process paragraph, review the checklist on the inside front cover. Also ask yourself the following questions.

☐ Does my topic sentence make a point about the process?

☐ Do I include all of the steps in the process?

☐ Do I clearly explain each step so my reader can accomplish the process or understand it?

☐ Do I mention all of the supplies that my reader needs to complete the process?

☐ Do I use transitions to connect all of the steps in the process?

mywritinglab To check your progress in meeting this chapter's objectives, log in to **www.mywritinglab.com**, go to the **Study Plan** tab, click on **Paragraph Patterns** and choose **Paragraph Development – Process** from the list of subtopics. Read and view the resources in the **Review Materials** section, and then complete the **Recall, Apply,** and **Write** sets in the **Activities** section.

Definition

Football has specialized terms—first down, linebacker, wide receiver—that both players and fans must learn. In definition writing, you define what a term means.

> *A successful marriage requires falling in love many times, always with the same person.*
>
> —MIGNON MCLAUGHLIN
> *American journalist (1913–1983)*

Writers' Exchange

Work with a partner or a team of students. Try to define the following terms. Think of some examples that can help define each term.

netiquette   chick flick   carnivore   texting

What Is Definition?

When you **define,** you explain the meaning of a word. Some terms have concrete meanings, and you can define them in a few words. For example, a pebble is "a small stone." Other words, such as *culture, happiness,* or *evil,* are more abstract and require longer definitions. In fact, it is possible to write a paragraph, an essay, or even an entire book on such concepts.

The simplest way to define a term is to look it up in a dictionary. However, many words have nuances that are not necessarily discussed in dictionaries. For example, suppose that your boss calls your work "unsatisfactory." You might need clarification of that term. Do you have poor work habits? Do you miss deadlines? Is your attitude problematic? What does your boss mean by "unsatisfactory"?

The ability to define difficult concepts is always useful. At home, a friend or loved one may ask you to define *commitment.* If you mention that a movie was *great,* you may need to clarify what you mean by that word. In a political science class, you might define *socialism, capitalism,* or *communism.* At work, you might define your company's *winning strategy.*

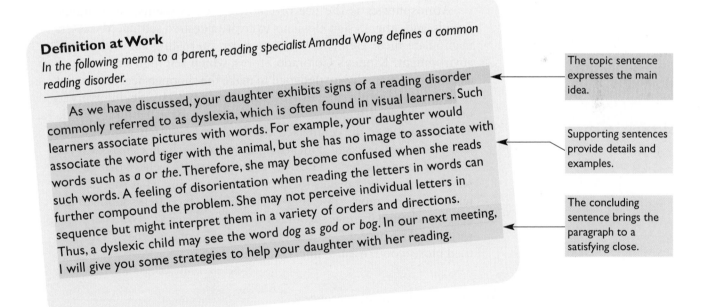

Definition at Work

In the following memo to a parent, reading specialist Amanda Wong defines a common reading disorder.

As we have discussed, your daughter exhibits signs of a reading disorder commonly referred to as dyslexia, which is often found in visual learners. Such learners associate pictures with words. For example, your daughter would associate the word *tiger* with the animal, but she has no image to associate with words such as *a* or *the.* Therefore, she may become confused when she reads such words. A feeling of disorientation when reading the letters in words can further compound the problem. She may not perceive individual letters in sequence but might interpret them in a variety of orders and directions. Thus, a dyslexic child may see the word *dog* as *god* or *bog.* In our next meeting, I will give you some strategies to help your daughter with her reading.

The topic sentence expresses the main idea.

Supporting sentences provide details and examples.

The concluding sentence brings the paragraph to a satisfying close.

The Definition Paragraph

When you write a definition paragraph, try to explain what a term means to you. For example, if someone asks you to define *bravery,* you might tell stories to illustrate the meaning of the word. You may also give examples of acts of bravery. You might even explain what bravery is not.

When you write a definition paragraph, remember the following two points.

- **Choose a term that you know something about.** You need to understand a term in order to say something relevant and interesting about it.
- **Give a clear definition.** In your first sentence, write a definition that is understandable to your reader, and support your definition with examples. Do not simply give a dictionary definition because your readers are capable of looking up the word themselves. Instead, describe what the word means to you.

 **Consider Your Audience**

When you write a definition paragraph, consider your audience. You may have to adjust your tone and vocabulary, depending on who reads the paragraph. For example, if you write a definition paragraph about computer viruses for your English class, you will have to use easily understandable terms. If you write the same paragraph for your computer class, you can use more technical terms.

PRACTICE I

Read the paragraph, and then answer the questions.

Atmospherics is the use of color, lighting, scents, furnishings, sounds, and other design elements to create a desired setting. Marketers manipulate these elements to create a certain feeling about the retail environment. Kinney's Colorado Stores, which sell high-end outdoor clothing, for example, are designed to make the shoppers feel they're out in nature. The stores pipe in New Age background music, interrupted occasionally by the sound of a thunderstorm or a babbling brook. Motion sensors in the ceiling activate displays as a shopper approaches, so a person who walks near an arrangement of beach shoes may hear the sound of waves crashing. The owners of these stores believe that getting people in the mood makes them more likely to buy what they see. To make its stores more appealing to customers, Taco Bell sought to use décor to change its image from cheap fast food to a kind of "Starbucks with a Spanish accent." To attract a wider range of customers, Taco Bell used more wood, natural fibers, and new colors.

—Solomon, Marshall, and Stuart, *Marketing*

1. Underline the topic sentence.

2. What is the writer defining? _____

3. Who is the likely audience for this paragraph? _____

4. What two examples does the author give to develop the definition?

   _____

   _____

5. Think of another example to add to this paragraph.

   _____

   _____

Explore Topics

In the Warm Up, you will try an exploring strategy to generate ideas about different topics.

The Writer's Desk **Warm Up**

Think about the following questions, and write down the first ideas that come to your mind. Try to think of two or three ideas for each topic.

EXAMPLE: What is slang? Think of some examples of slang.

- words people use for effect

- cool, dude, bro

- different cultural groups have their own slang terms

1. What is a white lie? Give some examples of white lies.

_____

_____

_____

2. What is social networking?

_____

_____

_____

3. What are some characteristics of a workaholic?

_____

_____

_____

DEVELOPING

The Topic Sentence

A clear topic sentence for a definition paragraph introduces the term and provides a definition. There are three basic ways to define a term.

- By synonym
- By category
- By negation

ESSAY LINK

In a definition essay, the thesis statement expresses the controlling idea. In the thesis, you can define the term by synonym, category, or negation.

Definition by Synonym

The easiest way to define a term is to supply a synonym (a word that has a similar meaning). This type of definition is useful if the original term is difficult to understand and the synonym is a more familiar word.

term   +   synonym

A pseudonym   is a false name.

I am a procrastinator,   which means I tend to put things off.

Definition by Category

A more effective way to define a term is to give a definition by category (or class). When you define by category, you determine the larger group to which the term belongs. Then you determine what unique characteristics set the term apart from others in that category.

term + category +   detail

Netiquette is proper behavior regarding communication on the
              Internet.

Luddites are people   who are skeptical about new technology.

Definition by Negation

When you define by negation, you explain what a term does not mean. You can then include a sentence explaining what it does mean. Definition by negation is especially useful when your readers have preconceived ideas about something. Your definition explains that the term does not mean what the reader previously thought.

term +   what it is not   +   what it is

Alcoholism is not an invented disease; it is a serious physical
                 dependency.

Hackers   are not playful computer geeks; they are criminals.

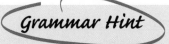 **Using Semicolons**

When you write a definition by negation, you can join the two separate and independent sentences with a semicolon.

Independent clause   ;   independent clause

Feminists are not man haters; they are people who want fairness and equality for women.

PRACTICE 2

A. Write a one-sentence definition by synonym for each of the following terms. Your definition should include the term and a synonym. If necessary, you can look up the terms in the dictionary; however, define each one using your own words.

EXAMPLE:

  To capitulate _*means to give up or surrender.*_____

1. To procrastinate _____

2. A celebrity _____

B. Write a one-sentence definition by category for the following terms. Make sure that your definition includes the term, a category, and details.

EXAMPLE:

Jargon ___*is vocabulary used by specific professions.*_____

3. A knockoff _____

4. Paparazzi _____

C. Write a one-sentence definition by negation for the following terms. Explain what each term is not, followed by what each term is.

EXAMPLE:

A placebo ___*is not a real drug; it is a sugar pill.*_____

_____

5. A television addict _____

_____

6. A vote _____

_____

Use the Right Word

When you write a definition paragraph, it is important to use precise words to define the term. Moreover, when you define a term by category, make sure that the category for your term is correct. For example, look at the following imprecise definitions of insomnia.

Insomnia is the (inability) to sleep well.
(Insomnia is not an ability or an inability.)

Insomnia is (when) you cannot sleep well.
(*When* refers to a time, but insomnia is not a time.)

Insomnia is the (nights) when you do not get enough sleep.
(Insomnia is not days or nights.)

Insomnia is (where) it is hard to fall asleep.
(*Where* refers to a place, but insomnia is not a place.)

Now look at a better definition of insomnia.

                    category
Insomnia is a **sleeping disorder** characterized by the inability to sleep well.

 **Make a Point**

Defining a term by synonym, category or negation is the guideline for writing topic sentences. However, keep in mind that your paragraph will be more interesting if you express an attitude or point of view in your topic sentence.

> **No point:** Anorexia is an eating disorder.
>
> **Point:** Anorexia is a tragic eating disorder that is difficult to cure.

PRACTICE 3

Revise each sentence using precise language.

EXAMPLE:

Tuning out is when you ignore something.

Tuning out is the action of ignoring something.

1. Claustrophobia is the inability to be in a small place.

   _____

2. A bully is the abuse of power over others.

   _____

3. Adolescence is where you are between childhood and adulthood.

   _____

4. Ego surfing is when you surf the Internet to find references to yourself.

   _____

---

vo•cab•u•lar•y BOOST

Using Your Thesaurus

Work with a partner to brainstorm synonyms or expressions that can replace each word listed below. If you have trouble coming up with ideas, use your thesaurus.

1. optimist   _____

2. depressed   _____

3. lazy   _____

4. reckless   _____

Later, when you finish writing your definition paragraph, identify any repeated words and replace them with synonyms.

The Writer's Desk Write Topic Sentences

For each of the following, write a topic sentence in which you define the topic. You can look for ideas in the Warm Up on page 105. Remember to use precise language in your definition.

EXAMPLE:

Topic: Slang

Topic sentence: *Slang is informal language that changes rapidly and*

exists in various forms among different cultural groups.

1. Topic: A white lie

   Topic sentence: _____

   _____

2. Topic: Social networking

   Topic sentence: _____

   _____

3. Topic: A workaholic

   Topic sentence: _____

   _____

The Supporting Ideas

After you have developed an effective topic sentence, generate supporting ideas. In a definition paragraph, you can give examples that clarify your definition.

Think about how you will organize your examples. Most definition paragraphs use emphatic order, which means that examples are placed from the most to the least important or from the least to the most important.

Visualizing Definition

PRACTICE 4

Brainstorm supporting ideas for the following topic sentence. Using words or phrases, describe each example of timeless fashion.

TOPIC SENTENCE:

Timeless fashions remain popular and will not go out of style.

_____   _____   _____

_____   _____   _____

The Writer's Desk **Develop Supporting Ideas**

Choose one of your topic sentences from the Writer's Desk on pages 108–109. List three or four examples that best illustrate the definition.

EXAMPLE:

Topic sentence: *Slang is informal language that changes rapidly and exists in various forms among different cultural groups.*

Supports: *-words change in different eras*

-rappers, punks, goths have own terms

-used like a code between friends

-words show inventive creative thinking

Topic sentence: _____

Supports: _____

_____

_____

_____

_____

ESSAY LINK

In a definition essay, the thesis statement is in the introduction. Each supporting idea is in a distinct body paragraph with its own topic sentence.

The Paragraph Plan

A good definition paragraph includes a complete definition of the term and provides adequate examples to support the central definition. When creating a definition paragraph plan, make sure that your examples provide varied evidence and do not just repeat the definition. Also add details that will help clarify your supporting examples.

TOPIC SENTENCE: Slang is informal language that changes rapidly and exists in various forms among different cultural groups.

Support 1: Slang is a type of code used between friends.

Details: —Punks might call each other emo or poseurs.
—People outside the group might not understand slang.
—Words often help define relationships among group members.

Support 2: Slang words often show very inventive and creative thinking.

Details: —Computer users have come up with a wide variety of net slang terms.
—Some terms are very illustrative and visual.

Support 3: Many slang words come and go quickly.

    Details: —In the 1920s, people used words that have gone out of fashion.

             —In the 1950s, people used words such as hipster or swell.

             —Slang words from the early 2000s, such as homie, are already becoming obsolete.

The Writer's Desk **Write a Paragraph Plan**

Create a detailed paragraph plan using the topic sentence that you wrote for the Writer's Desk on page 110. Arrange the supporting details in a logical order.

Topic sentence: _____

_____

Support 1: _____

   Details: _____

_____

_____

Support 2: _____

   Details: _____

_____

_____

Support 3: _____

   Details: _____

_____

_____

The First Draft

After you outline your ideas in a plan, you are ready to write the first draft. Remember to write complete sentences. You might include transitional words or expressions to help your ideas flow smoothly.

Transitional Words and Expressions

Transitional expressions can show different levels of importance. The following transitions are useful in definition paragraphs.

To Show the Level of Importance	
clearly	next
first	one quality . . . another quality
most of all	second
most important	undoubtedly

The Writer's Desk **Write the First Draft**

In the previous Writer's Desk, you developed a paragraph plan. Now write the first draft of your definition paragraph. Before you write, carefully review your paragraph plan and make any necessary changes.

REVISING AND EDITING

Revise and Edit a Definition Paragraph

When you finish writing a definition paragraph, carefully review your work and revise it to make the definition as clear as possible to your readers. Check that you have organized your steps logically, and remove any irrelevant details.

PRACTICE 5

Read the following student paragraph and answer the questions.

Slang is informal language that changes rapidly and exists in various forms among different cultural groups. It is a type of code used between friends. Punks call each other emo or poseurs. Such words denote a persons status in the group. Often, those outside the group might not understand the group's slang. My grandmother, for example, doesn't know what a gamer is. Soldiers, athletes, musicians, and even wealthy industrialists come up with their own particular jargon. The rich might put down social climbers as wannabes. They might call a spouse a trophy wife or husband. Slang words often show very inventive and creative thinking. Computer users have come up with a wide variety of net slang terms such as blog, flamer, troll, cyberspook, or flamebait. Some terms are very illustrative.

Jerk sounds like a fast movement. Whipped is similar to the sound a whip makes. Most slang words come and go quick, and they change over time. In the 1920s, men would call a woman's legs "gams" and money "clams." In the 1980s, people used words such as bodacious, dweeb, and yuppie, but those words are no longer popular. Even slang words from the early years of the twenty-first century, such as homie and hoser, are already becoming obsolete.

Revising

1. Underline the topic sentence.

2. What type of definition does the topic sentence contain? Circle the best answer.
   a. Definition by synonym   b. Definition by category
   c. Definition by negation

3. This paragraph lacks sentence variety. Revise the paragraph to give it more sentence variety by combining sentences or changing the first word of some sentences. (For more information about combining sentences and sentence variety, see Chapters 17–19.)

4. The paragraph lacks transitions to show the order of ideas. Add some transitional words or expressions.

5. The paragraph needs a concluding sentence. Add a concluding sentence in the lines provided.

   _____

   _____

Editing

6. There is one apostrophe error. Circle and correct the error.

7. There is an error in adverb form. Circle and correct the error.

GRAMMAR LINK

See the following chapters for more information about these grammar topics:
   Apostrophes, Chapter 35
   Adjectives and Adverbs, Chapter 30

The Writer's Desk Revise and Edit Your Paragraph

Revise and edit the paragraph that you wrote for the previous Writer's Desk. Make sure that your paragraph has unity, adequate support, and coherence. Also correct any errors in grammar, spelling, punctuation, and mechanics.

REFLECT ON IT

Think about what you have learned in this chapter. If you do not know an answer, review that topic.

1. In definition writing, what do you do?

   _____

2. Write an example of a definition by synonym.

   _____

3. Write an example of a definition by category.

   _____

4. Write an example of a definition by negation.

   _____

 The Writer's Room

Writing Activity 1: Topics

Choose any of the following topics, or choose your own topic. Then write a definition paragraph.

General Topics

1. a miracle
2. a spoiled child
3. fashion police
4. texting addict
5. mind games

College and Work-Related Topics

6. integrity
7. a headhunter
8. an opportunist
9. the glass ceiling
10. newbie

Writing Activity 2: Photo Writing

Look at the photo, and think of a term that you can define. Examples are *throwaway society*, *planned obsolescence*, *tech trends*, *digital age*, and *tech trash*.

WRITING LINK

More Definition Writing Topics

Chapter 19, Writer's Room topic 1 (page 308)
Chapter 24, Writer's Room topic 1 (page 359)
Chapter 26, Writer's Room topic 1 (page 385)
Chapter 35, Writer's Room topic 1 (page 503)

Writing Activity 3: Media Writing

Watch a television show about people who fight to succeed. Examples are *The Office*, *The Apprentice*, *Parks and Recreation*, or *Survivor*. You could watch a documentary such as *The Corporation* or a movie such as *The Godfather*, *There Will Be Blood*, or *Fame*. You can also watch YouTube videos about people who want to become famous. Define the term "blind ambition," and support your definition with examples or anecdotes from the media.

READING LINK

More Definition Readings

"Homophobia" by Dominic Chartrand (page 221)

"Being a Hyphenated American" by Zaini Arafat (page 530)

"Dancing with Fear" by Bebe Moore Campbell (page 544)

✔ DEFINITION PARAGRAPH CHECKLIST

As you write your definition paragraph, review the checklist on the inside front cover. Also ask yourself the following questions.

☐ Does my topic sentence contain a definition by synonym, negation, or category?

☐ Do all of my supporting sentences relate to the topic sentence?

☐ Do I use concise language in my definition?

☐ Do I include enough examples to help define the term?

mywritinglab To check your progress in meeting this chapter's objectives, log in to **www.mywritinglab.com**, go to the **Study Plan** tab, click on **Paragraph Patterns** and choose **Paragraph Development – Definition** from the list of subtopics. Read and view the resources in the **Review Materials** section, and then complete the **Recall**, **Apply**, and **Write** sets in the **Activities** section.

CHAPTER 9

Classification

Parents often organize their children's toys. In this photo, the toys are divided into animals, trucks, and blocks. In classification writing, you divide a topic into categories to explain it.

" *Inanimate objects are classified scientifically into three major categories: those that don't work, those that break down, and those that get lost.* "

—RUSSELL BAKER
American journalist (b. 1925)

Writers' Exchange

Work with a partner or in a group. Classify the next words into three or four different categories. What are the categories? Why did you choose those categories?

mechanic	fertilizer	kitchen	office
garden	cook	programmer	computer
microwave	landscaper	wrench	garage

What Is Classification?

When you classify, you sort a subject into more understandable categories. The categories must all belong to the subject, yet they must also be distinct from one another. For example, you might write a paragraph about the most common types of pets and sort the subject "pets" into the categories "cats," "dogs," and "birds."

Classification occurs in many situations. At home, you could classify the responsibilities of each person in the family, or you could classify your bills. In a biology course, you might write a paper about the different types of cells, or in a commerce course, you may write about the categories in a financial statement. On the job, you might advertise the different types of products or services that your company sells.

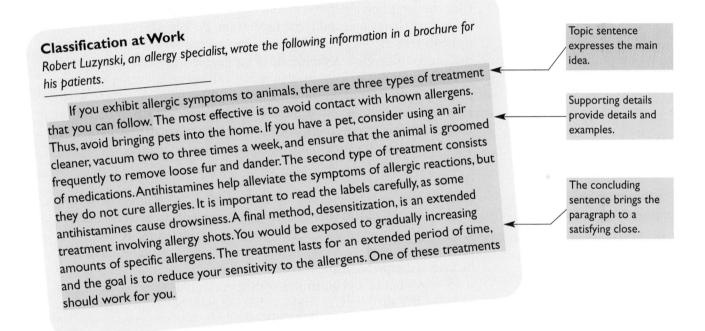

Classification at Work

Robert Luzynski, an allergy specialist, wrote the following information in a brochure for his patients.

If you exhibit allergic symptoms to animals, there are three types of treatment that you can follow. The most effective is to avoid contact with known allergens. Thus, avoid bringing pets into the home. If you have a pet, consider using an air cleaner, vacuum two to three times a week, and ensure that the animal is groomed frequently to remove loose fur and dander. The second type of treatment consists of medications. Antihistamines help alleviate the symptoms of allergic reactions, but they do not cure allergies. It is important to read the labels carefully, as some antihistamines cause drowsiness. A final method, desensitization, is an extended treatment involving allergy shots. You would be exposed to gradually increasing amounts of specific allergens. The treatment lasts for an extended period of time, and the goal is to reduce your sensitivity to the allergens. One of these treatments should work for you.

Topic sentence expresses the main idea.

Supporting details provide details and examples.

The concluding sentence brings the paragraph to a satisfying close.

The Classification Paragraph

To find a topic for a classification paragraph, think of something that can be sorted into different groups, or categories. Also determine a reason for classifying the items. When you are planning your ideas for a classification paragraph, remember these two points.

ESSAY LINK

Classification essays also require a classification principle and distinct categories.

1. **Use a common classification principle. A classification principle** is the overall method that you use to sort the subject into categories. To find the classification principle, think about one common characteristic that unites the different categories. For example, if your subject is "the telephone," your classification principle might be any of the following:

   - types of annoying phone calls
   - reasons that people buy cell phones
   - types of long-distance service
   - types of customer reactions to telephone salespeople

2. **Sort the subject into distinct categories.** A classification paragraph should have two or more categories.

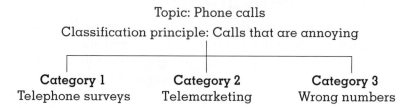

Topic: Phone calls

Classification principle: Calls that are annoying

Category 1	**Category 2**	**Category 3**
Telephone surveys	Telemarketing	Wrong numbers

PRACTICE I

Read the next paragraph and answer the questions.

> There may be no way to rid the world of dishonesty, but researchers have learned a great deal about how to tell when someone is lying. Clues to deception are found in four elements of a performance: words, voice, body language, and facial expression. People who are good liars mentally rehearse their lines, but they cannot always avoid inconsistencies that suggest deception. A simple slip of the tongue—something the person did not mean to say in quite that way—can occur in even a carefully prepared performance. Secondly, voice is also useful to determine when a person is lying. Tone and patterns of speech contain clues to deception because they are hard to control. Especially when trying to hide a powerful emotion, a person cannot easily prevent the voice from trembling or breaking. Or an individual may speak more quickly, suggesting anger, or slowly, suggesting sadness. A "leak," conveyed through body language, may tip off an observer to deception. Body movements, sudden swallowing, or rapid breathing may show that a person is nervous. Because there are forty-three muscles in the face, facial expressions are even more difficult to control than body language. A real smile is usually accompanied by a relaxed expression and lot of "laugh lines" around the eyes; a phony smile seems forced and unnatural, with fewer wrinkles around the mouth and eyes. We all try to fake emotion, but the more powerful the emotion, the more difficult it is to deceive others.
>
> —John J. Macionis, "Spotting Lies: What Are the Clues" in *Sociology*

1. Underline the topic sentence of this paragraph.

2. State the four categories that the author discusses and list some details about each category.

   a. _____

   Details: _____

   _____

   b. _____

   Details: _____

   _____

   c. _____

   Details: _____

   _____

d. _____

   Details: _____

   _____

3. Who is the audience for this paragraph?

   _____

4. What is the purpose of this paragraph? Circle the best answer.

   a. to persuade   b. to inform   c. to entertain

Explore Topics

In the Warm Up, you will try an exploring strategy to generate ideas about different topics.

The Writer's Desk **Warm Up**

Think about the following questions, and write down the first ideas that come to your mind. Try to think of two or three ideas for each topic.

EXAMPLE: What are some challenges college students face?

   Organizational challenges. They are involved in too many activities.

   Emotional challenges. Might become homesick.

   Financial challenges. Might need to work part-time.

1. List some clothing that you own. You might think about old clothing, comfortable clothing, beautiful clothing, and so on.

   _____

   _____

   _____

2. What are some different types of consumers? To get ideas, you might think about some people you know and the way that they shop.

   _____

   _____

   _____

3. List some skills or abilities people need for different jobs. As you brainstorm ideas, consider manual labor as well as professional and office jobs.

   _____

   _____

   _____

Making a Classification Chart

A **classification chart** is a visual representation of the main topic and its categories. Making a classification chart can help you identify the categories more clearly so that you will be able to write more exact topic sentences.

When you classify items, remember to use a single classification principle to sort the items. For example, if you are classifying movies, you might classify them according to their ratings: General Audience, Parental Guidance, and Restricted. You could also classify movies according to their country of origin: British, American, and French, for example. Remember that one classification principle must unite the group.

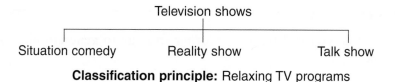

Television shows

Situation comedy   Reality show   Talk show

Classification principle: Relaxing TV programs

Hint ▷ **Categories Should Not Overlap**

When sorting a topic into categories, make sure that the categories do not overlap. For example, you would not classify drivers into careful drivers, aggressive drivers, and bad drivers because aggressive drivers could also be bad drivers. Each category should be distinct.

PRACTICE 2

In the following classification charts, a subject has been broken down into distinct categories. The items in the group should have the same classification principle. Cross out one item in each group that does not belong. Then write down the classification principle that unites the group.

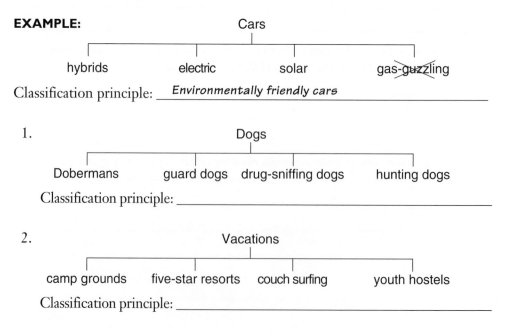

EXAMPLE:

Cars

hybrids   electric   solar   gas-~~guzzling~~

Classification principle: _Environmentally friendly cars_

1. Dogs

Dobermans   guard dogs   drug-sniffing dogs   hunting dogs

Classification principle: _____

2. Vacations

camp grounds   five-star resorts   couch surfing   youth hostels

Classification principle: _____

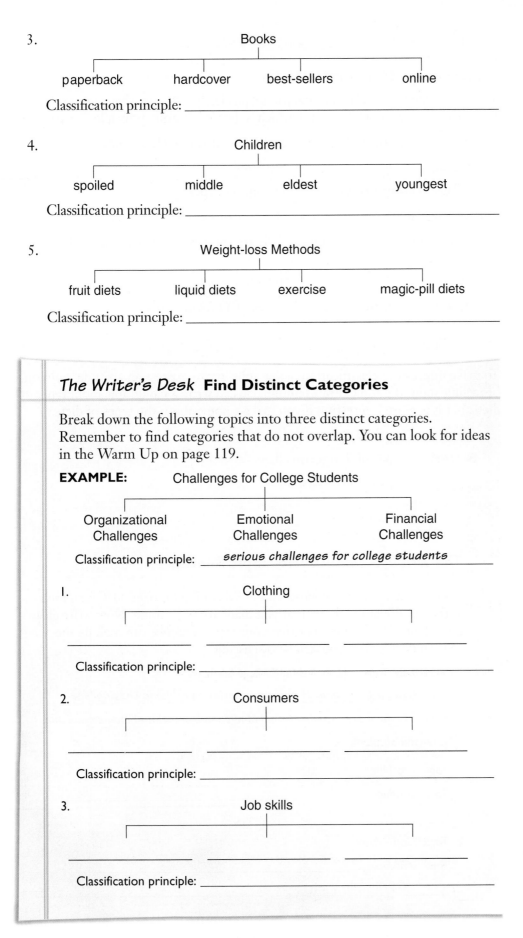

3.
Books

paperback   hardcover   best-sellers   online

Classification principle: _____

4.
Children

spoiled   middle   eldest   youngest

Classification principle: _____

5.
Weight-loss Methods

fruit diets   liquid diets   exercise   magic-pill diets

Classification principle: _____

The Writer's Desk Find Distinct Categories

Break down the following topics into three distinct categories.
Remember to find categories that do not overlap. You can look for ideas
in the Warm Up on page 119.

EXAMPLE: Challenges for College Students

Organizational   Emotional   Financial
Challenges   Challenges   Challenges

Classification principle: *serious challenges for college students*

1.   Clothing

_____   _____   _____

Classification principle: _____

2.   Consumers

_____   _____   _____

Classification principle: _____

3.   Job skills

_____   _____   _____

Classification principle: _____

ESSAY LINK

In a classification essay, the thesis statement expresses the controlling idea, or classification principle.

DEVELOPING

The Topic Sentence

The topic sentence in a classification paragraph clearly indicates what you will classify. It also includes the controlling idea, which is the classification principle that you use.

> Several types of students can completely disrupt a classroom.

> **Topic:**   Students
>
> **Classification principle:**   Disruptive types

You can also mention the types of categories in your topic sentence.

> The most annoying telephone calls are surveys, telemarketing, and wrong numbers.

> **Topic:**   Telephone calls
>
> **Classification principle:**   Types of annoying calls

Make a Point

To make interesting classification paragraphs, try to express an attitude, opinion, or feeling about the topic. For example, you can write a paragraph about types of diets, but it is more interesting if you make a point about the types of diets.

> **Poor:**   Types of diets
>
> **Better:**   Types of **dangerous** diets
>
>   Types of **effective** diets

The Writer's Desk Write Topic Sentences

Look again at what you wrote in the Warm Up on page 119. Also look at the classification charts that you made for each topic. Now write clear topic sentences. Remember that your topic sentence can include the different categories you will be discussing.

EXAMPLE: Topic: Challenges for College Students

Topic Sentence: _Some of the most serious problems that college students face are organizational challenges, emotional challenges, and financial challenges._

1. Topic: Clothing

   Topic sentence: _____

   _____

2. Topic: Consumers

   Topic sentence: _____

   _____

3. Topic: Job skills

Topic sentence: _____

_____

The Supporting Ideas

After you have developed an effective topic sentence, generate supporting ideas. In a classification paragraph, you can list details about each of your categories.

ESSAY LINK

You can make a detailed classification chart when you develop your classification essay. Each supporting idea would become a distinct paragraph.

Visualizing Classification

PRACTICE 3

Brainstorm supporting ideas for the following topic sentence. List unhealthy ingredients in each type of food.

TOPIC SENTENCE:

Junk food can be classified into three main categories.

Salty

_____

_____

Sweet

_____

_____

Fatty

_____

_____

The Paragraph Plan

You can make a standard paragraph plan. You can also create a pie chart to help you visualize the different categories.

Finally, an effective way to visualize your categories and supporting ideas is to make a detailed classification chart. Break down the main topic into several categories, and then give details about each category.

Some of the most serious problems that college students face are organizational challenges, emotional challenges, and financial challenges.

Organizational Challenges	Emotional Challenges	Financial Challenges
- have too many activities - work, social, go to class - overloaded with social activities	- miss friends and family - become homesick - become lonely	- need to work part time - living away from home very expensive

The Writer's Desk **Make a Detailed Classification Chart**

Choose one of the topic sentences that you wrote for the previous Writer's Desk, and make a detailed classification chart. Arrange the supporting details in a logical order. You can refer to the information you generated in the Warm Up.

Topic sentence: _____

_____

 **Use the Chart as a Plan**

Your classification chart can also serve as your paragraph plan. Like a paragraph plan, your chart contains your topic sentence, your supporting ideas (categories), and details about each idea (category).

The First Draft

After you outline your ideas in a classification chart or plan, you are ready to write the first draft. Remember to write complete sentences. You might include transitional words or expressions to help your ideas flow smoothly.

Transitional Words and Expressions

Some classification paragraphs use transitional words and expressions to show which category is most important and to signal a movement from one category to the next. The following transitions are very useful in classification writing.

To Show Importance	To Show Types of Categories
above all	one kind . . . another kind
clearly	the first/second type
the most important	the first/second kind
most of all	the last category
particularly	

The Writer's Desk **Write the First Draft**

Write the first draft of your classification paragraph. Before you write, carefully review your detailed classification chart and make any necessary changes.

---

vo•cab•u•lar•y BOOST

Classifying Parts of Words

A prefix is added to the beginning of a word, and it changes the word's meaning. A suffix is added to the end of a word, and it also changes the word's meaning. Review the list of ten common prefixes and suffixes. Then come up with at least two more words using the listed prefix or suffix.

Prefixes	Example	
anti = against	antiwar	_____
un = not	unable	_____
re = again	redo	_____
bi = two	bilingual	_____
mis = wrong	misspell	_____

Suffixes	Example	
er = doer	teacher	_____
ment = condition	agreement	_____
ly = characteristic of	honestly	_____
ous = full of	courageous	_____
ful = filled with	respectful	_____

REVISING AND EDITING

Revise and Edit a Classification Paragraph

When you finish writing a classification paragraph, carefully review your work and revise it to make sure that the categories do not overlap. Check to make sure that you have organized your paragraph logically, and remove any irrelevant details.

PRACTICE 4

Read the following student paragraph and answer the questions.

> College students often confront many different types of difficulties. But some of the most serious problems that college students face are organizational challenges, emotional challenges, and financial challenges. Many students have difficulty keeping to a strict schedule. Thus, they have difficulty organizing their time. They have to juggle attending classes, working part-time, doing homework, and they socialize. Furthermore, emotional challenges. Some students may feel lonely if they are away from home. They may not like their roommate or their dorm room. Also, students can have financial problems. They may have to work part-time to pay for their education. When students get a scolarship, they may feel extra pressure to keep up their grades.
>
> —Daniel Mirto, college student

Revising

1. What is the classification principle in this paragraph? _____

   _____

2. What are the three categories? _____

   _____

3. Add one more supporting example to the following categories:

   organizational challenges: _____

   _____

   emotional challenges: _____

   _____

   financial challenges: _____

   _____

Editing

1. There is one error in parallel structure. Underline the error and correct it.

2. There is a sentence fragment. Identify and correct the fragment.

3. There is one spelling error. Identify and correct the error.

GRAMMAR LINK

See the following chapters for more information about these grammar topics:

Parallel Structure, Chapter 22
Fragments, Chapter 21
Spelling, Chapter 33

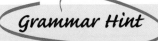 *Grammar Hint*

Use parallel structure when words or phrases are joined in a series.

drug allergies

The three categories of allergies are animal allergies, food allergies, and people who are allergic to medicine.

The Writer's Desk Revise and Edit Your Paragraph

Revise and edit the paragraph that you wrote for the previous Writer's Desk. Make sure that your paragraph has unity, adequate support, and coherence. Also correct any errors in grammar, spelling, punctuation, and mechanics.

REFLECT ON IT

Think about what you have learned in this chapter. If you do not know an answer, review that topic.

1. What is classification? _____

_____

2. What is the classification principle? _____

_____

3. Give examples of various classification principles that you can use to classify the following items.

   EXAMPLE: Cars   *Types of owners, degrees of fuel efficiency, price*

   a. Animals _____

   b. Sports _____

4. Now choose one classification principle for each item in question 3. Write down three possible categories for that item.

   EXAMPLE: Cars

   Classification principle: ___*Types of owners*_____

   Categories: ___*SUV owners, sports car owners, and tiny eco car owners*___

a. Animals

Classification principle: _____

Categories: _____

b. Sports

Classification principle: _____

Categories: _____

5. Why is it useful to make a classification chart? _____

_____

The Writer's Room

Writing Activity 1: Topics

Choose any of the following topics, or choose your own topic. Then write a classification paragraph.

WRITING LINK

More Classification Writing Topics

Chapter 22, Writer's Room topic 2 (page 332)

Chapter 32, Writer's Room topic 2 (page 461)

Chapter 34, Writer's Room topic 2 (page 491)

Chapter 36, Writer's Room topic 2 (page 511)

READING LINK

More Classification Readings

"The Purpose of Pets" by W. Stephen Damron (page 225)

"Fads" by David A. Locher (page 533)

"Advertising Appeals" by Michael R. Solomon, Greg W. Marshall, and Elnora W. Stuart (page 557)

General Topics

Types of . . .

1. problems in a relationship
2. friends
3. tech users
4. games
5. greetings

College and Work-Related Topics

Types of . . .

6. campus fashions
7. housing
8. bosses
9. cheating
10. co-workers

Writing Activity 2: Photo Writing

Examine this photo, and think about some classification topics. For example, you might discuss types of risky behavior, dangerous jobs, or culturally specific entertainment. Then write a classification paragraph based on the photo or your related topic.

Writing Activity 3: Media Writing

Watch a television show or movie about spies. Television shows are *MI5*, *24*, *Chuck*, and *The Unit*, and movies are *Mission Impossible*, *The Good Shepherd*, *Syriana*, or *Duplicity*. You could also watch James Bond or Bourne Identity films. Classify spies into types or describe different types of spying, and use examples to support your ideas.

✔ CLASSIFICATION PARAGRAPH CHECKLIST

As you write your classification paragraph, review the checklist on the inside front cover. Also ask yourself the following questions.

☐ Does my topic sentence explain the categories that will be discussed?

☐ Do I use a common classification principle to unite the various categories?

☐ Do I offer sufficient details to explain each category?

☐ Do I arrange the categories in a logical manner?

☐ Does all of the supporting information relate to the categories that are being discussed?

☐ Do I include categories that do not overlap?

mywritinglab To check your progress in meeting this chapter's objectives, log in to **www.mywritinglab.com**, go to the **Study Plan** tab, click on **Paragraph Patterns** and choose **Paragraph Development – Division / Classification** from the list of subtopics. Read and view the resources in the **Review Materials** section, and then complete the **Recall, Apply,** and **Write** sets in the **Activities** section.

CHAPTER 10

Comparison and Contrast

Shoppers compare prices in order to make an informed decision. In this chapter, you will practice comparing and contrasting.

> *Life is often compared to a marathon, but I think it is more like a sprint; there are long stretches of hard work punctuated by brief moments in which we are given the opportunity to perform at our best.*
>
> —MICHAEL JOHNSON
> *American sprinter (b. 1967)*

Writers' Exchange

Work with a partner. Each of you should discuss your food preferences. Then make a short list showing which food preferences you share and which ones you do not share.

What Is Comparison and Contrast?

When you want to decide between options, you compare and contrast. You **compare** to find similarities and **contrast** to find differences. The exercise of comparing and contrasting can help you make judgments about things. It can also help you better understand familiar things.

You often compare and contrast. At home, when you watch TV, you might compare and contrast different programs. At college, you might compare and contrast different psychological or political theories. On the job, you might need to compare and contrast computer operating systems, shipping services, or sales figures.

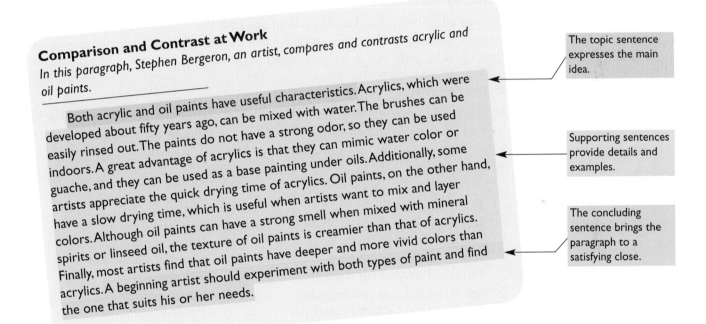

Comparison and Contrast at Work

In this paragraph, Stephen Bergeron, an artist, compares and contrasts acrylic and oil paints.

Both acrylic and oil paints have useful characteristics. Acrylics, which were developed about fifty years ago, can be mixed with water. The brushes can be easily rinsed out. The paints do not have a strong odor, so they can be used indoors. A great advantage of acrylics is that they can mimic water color or guache, and they can be used as a base painting under oils. Additionally, some artists appreciate the quick drying time of acrylics. Oil paints, on the other hand, have a slow drying time, which is useful when artists want to mix and layer colors. Although oil paints can have a strong smell when mixed with mineral spirits or linseed oil, the texture of oil paints is creamier than that of acrylics. Finally, most artists find that oil paints have deeper and more vivid colors than acrylics. A beginning artist should experiment with both types of paint and find the one that suits his or her needs.

The topic sentence expresses the main idea.

Supporting sentences provide details and examples.

The concluding sentence brings the paragraph to a satisfying close.

The Comparison and Contrast Paragraph

In a comparison and contrast paragraph, you can compare and contrast two different subjects, or you can compare and contrast different aspects of a single subject. For example, you might contrast married life and single life, or you might write only about marriage but contrast the expectations people have before they get married to what realistically happens after marriage.

When you write a comparison and contrast paragraph, remember to think about your specific purpose.

- **Your purpose could be to make judgments about two things.** For example, you might compare and contrast two restaurants in order to convince your readers that one is preferable.

- **Your purpose could be to describe or understand two familiar things.** For example, you might compare two stories to help your readers understand their thematic similarities.

Comparison and Contrast Patterns

Comparison and contrast texts follow two common patterns. One pattern is to present the details point by point. Another is to present one topic and then the other topic.

When you are thinking about ideas for writing a comparison and contrast paragraph, you can choose one of two methods to organize your supporting ideas: point by point or topic by topic.

ESSAY LINK

To write a comparison and contrast essay, organize *each paragraph* in point-by-point or topic-by-topic form.

Point by Point

Present one point about Topic A and then one point about Topic B. Keep following this pattern until you have a few points for each topic. You go back and forth from one side to the other like tennis players hitting a ball back and forth across a net.

Topic by Topic

Present all points related to Topic A in the first few sentences, and then present all points related to Topic B in the last few sentences. So, you present one side and then the other side, just as lawyers might in the closing arguments of a court case.

Kyle's Example

Kyle is trying to decide whether he should take a job in another city or stay at his current job in his hometown. His goal is to decide whether he should move or stay where he is. Kyle could organize his information using a point-by-point or topic-by-topic method.

POINT BY POINT		TOPIC BY TOPIC	
Job A	Low salary	Job A	Low salary
Job B	Good salary		Parents nearby
Job A	Parents nearby		Like my colleagues
Job B	Parents far away		
Job A	Like my colleagues	Job B	Better salary
Job B	Don't know colleagues		Parents far away
			Don't know colleagues

PRACTICE 1

Read the next two paragraphs and answer the questions.

A. Fashion is fashion and teen fashion is meant to shock. According to my son, the girls in his school like to wear decorative thongs and let them peek out from over the tops of their low-slung jeans "for all the boys to see in English class." Their *T*-shirts are tiny, about the size of face cloths. Covering up the back is optional. Oddly, it is my son who finds this style of dressing shocking (among other things). It is not a flattering fashion, for sure, but I dare not complain. In high school, I wore a micro miniskirt, and I am sure the boys could see my panties as I climbed the stairs in front of them. I seldom wore a bra (which bothered a friend's father so much, I was not allowed into her house). So, when my son brings home his first near-naked girlfriend, I will not act shocked; I will merely crack a conspiratorial smile.

—Dorothy Nixon, "Teen Fashion"

1. Underline the topic sentence.

2. What aspects of fashion does the author compare? _____

   _____

3. What pattern of comparison does the author follow? Circle the correct answer.

   a. Point by point   b. Topic by topic

4. What does this paragraph focus on? Circle the correct answer.

   a. Similarities   b. Differences

> B. There are some major differences between the supermarket and a traditional marketplace. The cacophony of a traditional market has given way to programmed innocuous music, punctuated by enthusiastically intoned commercials. A stroll through a traditional market offers an array of sensuous aromas; if you are conscious of smelling something in a supermarket, there is a problem. The life and death matter of eating, expressed in traditional markets by the sale of vegetables with stems and roots and by hanging animal carcasses, is purged from the supermarket, where food is processed somewhere else, or at least trimmed out of sight. But the most fundamental difference between a traditional market and the places through which you push your cart is that in a modern retail setting nearly all the selling is done without people. The product is totally dissociated from the personality of any particular person selling it-with the possible exception of those who appear in its advertising. The supermarket purges sociability, which slows down sales.
>
> —Thomas Hine, "What's in a Package?"

5. Underline the topic sentence.

6. What pattern of comparison does the author follow? Circle the best answer.

   a. Point by point   b. Topic by topic

7. What does the author focus on? Circle the best answer.

   a. Similarities   b. Differences

8. Using your own words, list the main differences.

Traditional market	**Supermarket**
_____	_____
_____	_____
_____	_____
_____	_____

vo•cab•u•lar•y BOOST

Brainstorming Opposites

Work with a partner to brainstorm words that have the opposite meaning of the words listed below. Try to come up with as many antonyms (words that have the opposite meaning) as possible.

Example: tiny   *huge, immense, gigantic* _____

shy   _____

happy   _____

run   _____

spicy   _____

Explore Topics

In the Warm Up, you will try an exploring strategy to generate ideas about different topics.

The Writer's Desk Warm Up

Think about the following questions, and write down the first ideas that come to your mind. Try to think of two to three ideas for each topic. Then decide if a good paragraph would be about similarities or differences.

EXAMPLE: What are some key features of two cultural traditions?

My mother's tradition: Diwali	**My father's tradition: Hanukkah**
festival of lights	*festival of lights*
share gifts with siblings	*light the Menorah*
great desserts	*gold-wrapped chocolates*

My paragraph will focus on ____X____ similarities _____ differences

1. What are some stereotypes about your nationality? What is the reality about your nationality?

Stereotypes	**Reality**
_____	_____
_____	_____
_____	_____

This paragraph will focus on _____ similarities _____ differences.

2. What were your goals when you were a child? What are your goals today?

Goals in childhood

_____

_____

_____

This paragraph will focus on _____ similarities _____ differences.

Goals today

_____

_____

_____

3. Write down the names of two famous people. Think about actors, athletes, politicians, and music stars. Choose one who is accomplished and respected, and choose another who is less respected. List some interesting characteristics of each person.

Person 1:

_____

_____

_____

Person 2:

_____

_____

_____

This paragraph will focus on _____ similarities _____ differences.

When you plan your comparison and contrast paragraph, decide whether you want to focus on comparing (looking at similarities), contrasting (looking at differences), or both. In a paragraph, it is usually best to focus on either comparing or contrasting. In a larger essay, you could more easily do both.

DEVELOPING

The Topic Sentence

In a comparison and contrast paragraph, the topic sentence indicates what is being compared and contrasted and expresses a controlling idea.

> Although all dogs make good house pets, large dogs are much more useful than small dogs.

Topic: Large dogs versus small dogs
Controlling idea: One is more useful than the other.

ESSAY LINK

In a comparison and contrast essay, the thesis statement expresses the main point of the essay.

PRACTICE 2

Read each topic sentence, and then answer the questions that follow. State whether the paragraph would focus on similarities or differences.

EXAMPLE:

Before the baby comes, people expect a beautiful world of soft coos and sweet smells, but the reality is quite different.

a. What is being compared? _____Expectation versus reality of life with a baby_____

b. What is the controlling idea? _____Reality not as pleasant as expectation_____

c. What will the paragraph focus on? Circle the correct answer.

Similarities   (Differences)

1. Many media pundits complain about reality television; however, reality shows are just as good as regular scripted shows.

   a. What is being compared? _____

   b. What is the controlling idea? _____

   _____

   c. What will the paragraph focus on? Circle the correct answer.

   Similarities   Differences

2. Women's sports lag behind men's in media attention, prize money, and salaries.

   a. What is being compared? _____

   b. What is the controlling idea? _____

   _____

   c. What does the paragraph focus on? Circle the best answer.

   Similarities   Differences

3. Teenagers are as difficult to raise as toddlers.

   a. What is being compared? _____

   b. What is the controlling idea? _____

   _____

   c. What will the paragraph focus on? Circle the correct answer.

   Similarities   Differences

The Writer's Desk Write Topic Sentences

For each topic, write whether you will focus on similarities or differences. Then, write a topic sentence for each one. Look for ideas in the Writer's Desk Warm Up on pages 134–135. Your topic sentence should include what you are comparing and contrasting, as well as a controlling idea.

EXAMPLE: Topic: Two cultural traditions

Focus: _Similarities_

Topic sentence: _Diwali and Hanukkah have some surprising similarities._

_____

1. Topic: Stereotypes and reality about my nation

   Focus: _____

   Topic sentence: _____

   _____

2. Topic: Goals in childhood and goals in adulthood

   Focus: _____

   Topic sentence: _____

   _____

3. Topic: Two famous people

Focus: _____

Topic sentence: _____

_____

The Supporting Ideas

After you have developed an effective topic sentence, generate supporting ideas. In a comparison and contrast paragraph, think of examples that help clarify the similarities or differences.

ESSAY LINK

In a comparison and contrast essay, place the thesis statement in the introduction. Each supporting idea becomes a distinct paragraph with its own topic sentence.

Visualizing Comparison and Contrast

PRACTICE 3

Brainstorm supporting ideas for the following topic sentence. Compare and contrast the types of heroes.

TOPIC SENTENCE:

My childhood heroes were very different from my current heroes.

Childhood heros   **Current heros**

Make a Venn Diagram

To generate supporting ideas, you might try using a Venn diagram. In this example, you can see how the writer draws two circles to contrast Diwali and Hanukkah. Where the circles overlap, the writer includes similarities. If you are focusing only on similarities or differences, then you can make two separate circles.

Diwali

* candles and oil lamps lit for five days to symbolize the victory of good over evil
* food includes fried sweets and delicacies
* people give each other clothes & jewelry

* people light candles
* place candles near windows
* feasts
* gift giving

Hanukkah

* candles on Menorah are lit each night for eight consecutive nights
* food is fried to symbolize the miraculous oil
* children receive money, clothing, or toys

The Paragraph Plan

Before you write a comparison and contrast paragraph, it is a good idea to make a paragraph plan. Decide which pattern you will follow: point by point or topic by topic. Write "**A**" and "**B**" alongside your topics. Then add supporting details. Make sure that each detail supports the topic sentence.

TOPIC SENTENCE: Diwali and Hanukkah have some surprising similarities.

POINT BY POINT

A/B Both celebrations are festivals of light.
Details: -People light candles.
-They place candles near windows.

A/B Both have traditions of feasts.
Details: -People eat fried sweets for Diwali.
-Everyone loves fried food for Hanukkah.

A/B Both celebrations include gift giving.
Details: -Diwali, people give clothing and jewelry to each other.
-Hanukkah, people give gifts to children.

TOPIC BY TOPIC

A Diwali is a festival of light.
Details: -Oil lamps are lit for five days, symbolizing the victory of good over evil.

A Diwali includes feasts.
Details: -Food includes fried sweets and delicacies.

A During one day of the Diwali festival, people give gifts to each other.
Details: -Clothes and jewelry are given.
-Children get the most gifts.

B Hanukkah is also a festival of light.
Details: -People light Menorah candles.
-Candles lit each night for eight nights.

B People have feasts during Hanukkah.
Details: -Food is fried to symbolize the miraculous oil.

B People give gifts to children during Hanukkah.
Details: -They get money, clothing, or toys.

The Writer's Desk **Write a Paragraph Plan**

Write a detailed paragraph plan in a point-by-point or side-by-side pattern. You can refer to the information you generated in previous Writer's Desk exercises. You can use the letters **A** and **B** to indicate which side you are discussing in your plan. Include details about each supporting idea.

Topic sentence: _____

_____

Support 1: _____

Details: _____

_____

Support 2: _____

Details: _____

_____

Support 3: _____

Details: _____

_____

Support 4: _____

Details: _____

_____

Support 5: _____

Details: _____

_____

Support 6: _____

Details: _____

_____

The First Draft

After you outline your ideas in a plan, you are ready to write the first draft. Remember to write complete sentences. You might include transitional words or expressions to help your ideas flow smoothly.

Transitional Words and Expressions

In comparison and contrast paragraphs, there are some transitional words and expressions that you might use to explain either similarities or differences.

To Show Similarities		To Show Differences	
additionally	in addition	conversely	nevertheless
at the same time	in the same way	however	on the contrary
equally	similarly	in contrast	then again

The Writer's Desk **Write the First Draft**

Write the first draft of your comparison and contrast paragraph. Before you write, carefully review your paragraph plan to see if you have enough support for your points and topics.

REVISING AND EDITING

Revise and Edit a Comparison and Contrast Paragraph

When you finish writing a comparison and contrast paragraph, carefully review your work and revise it to make the comparison or contrast as clear as possible to your readers. Check that you have organized your paragraph logically, and remove any irrelevant details.

PRACTICE 4

Read the following student paragraph and answer the questions.

The Hindu and Jewish faiths have distinct religious celebrations. However, Diwali and Hanukkah have surprising similarities. For Hindus, Diwali is known as the festival of light. For five nights, celebrators are lighting as many small oil lamps as possible to symbolize hope and the victory of good over evil. Similarly, Hanukkah is a festival of lights, and people light candles on a Menorah for eight consecutive nights. The candles celebrate the miracle of an oil lamp found in the Temple, which burned for eight days and nights even though it had only a day's worth of oil in it. Furthermore, both Hindus and Jews place the lights near windows so that people passing by can see them. Another similarity: feasts. People celebrating Diwali and Hanukkah work real hard to create special meals. The Diwali feast includes fried sweets and other desserts.

In the same way, during Hanukkah, people eat food fried in oil, such as potato pancakes and donuts. Finally, both Diwali and Hanukkah involve gift-giving, with children as the major beneficiaries of the generosity. During Diwali, children receive gifts of clothing or jewelry. Hanukkah celebrants give gifts of money, clothing, or toys. Thus, Hindus and Jews celebrate some festivals in a similar way.

Revising

1. What is the writer comparing? _____

2. What does the writer focus on?
   a. similarities   b. differences

3. Number the three main points.

4. Underline six transitional words or expressions that appear at the beginnings of sentences.

Editing

5. Identify and correct one verb-tense error.

6. This paragraph contains one fragment, which is an incomplete sentence. Identify and correct the fragment.

7. Find and correct one error with an adjective or adverb.

GRAMMAR LINK

See the following chapters for more information about these grammer topics:
Verb Tenses, Chapter 25
Fragments, Chapter 20
Adjectives and Adverbs, Chapter 30

Grammar Hint   **Comparing with Adjectives and Adverbs**

When comparing or contrasting two items, ensure that you have correctly written the comparative forms of adjectives and adverbs. For instance, never put *more* with an adjective ending in *-er*.

Living alone is ~~more~~ quieter than living with a roommate.

If you are comparing two actions, remember to use an adverb instead of an adjective.

    more quickly
My roommate cleans ~~quicker~~ than I do.

The Writer's Desk **Revise and Edit Your Paragraph**

Revise and edit the paragraph that you wrote for the previous Writer's Desk. Make sure that your paragraph has unity, adequate support, and coherence. Also correct any errors in grammar, spelling, punctuation, and mechanics.

REFLECT ON IT

Think about what you have learned in this chapter. If you do not know an answer, review that topic.

1. Define the words *comparing* and *contrasting*.

a. Comparing: _____

b. Contrasting: _____

2. Explain the following comparison and contrast patterns.

a. Point by point: _____

_____

b. Topic by topic: _____

_____

The Writer's Room

Writing Activity 1: Topics

Choose any of the following topics, or choose your own topic. Then write a comparison and contrast paragraph.

WRITING LINK

More Comparison and Contrast Writing Topics

Chapter 16, Writer's Room topic 2 (page 272)

Chapter 18, Writer's Room topic 1 (page 296)

Chapter 21, Writer's Room topic 2 (page 323)

Chapter 28, Writer's Room topic 2 (page 408)

General Topics

Compare or contrast . . .

1. two types of music

2. people from two different regions

3. your current home and a home that you lived in before

4. expectations about marriage and the reality of marriage

5. two Web sites

College and Work-Related Topics

Compare or contrast . . .

6. high school and college

7. two career options

8. working indoors and working outdoors

9. leaving a child in day care and leaving a child with a family member

10. working mainly with your hands and working mainly with your head

Writing Activity 2: Photo Writing

Examine the photos on the next page and brainstorm ideas about the similarities or differences between two places that you go to relax. For example, you can compare a park with your bedroom, a campus coffee shop with a bookstore, or two public parks. After developing your ideas, write a comparison and contrast paragraph.

READING LINK

More Comparison and Contrast Readings

"Two Jobs" by Adrianna Gonzalez (page 230)

"Religious Faith Versus Spirituality" by Neil Bissoondath (page 541)

"Gone with the Windows" by Dorothy Nixon (page 564)

Writing Activity 3: Media Writing

Compare another country to the United States. Watch a foreign film such as *Paradise Now* (Palestine), *Close to Home* (Israel), *Volver* (Spain), *The Queen* (Great Britain), *The Kite Runner* (Afghanistan), and *Slumdog Millionaire* (India). You can also watch YouTube videos about foreign places. You can compare the clothing, music, attitudes, and landscapes of the two places.

COMPARISON AND CONTRAST PARAGRAPH CHECKLIST

As you write your comparison and contrast paragraph, review the checklist on the inside front cover. Also ask yourself the following questions.

☐ Does my topic sentence explain what I am comparing and/or contrasting?

☐ Does my topic sentence make a point about the comparison?

☐ Does my paragraph have a point-by-point or topic-by-topic pattern?

☐ Does my paragraph focus on either similarities or differences?

☐ Do all of my supporting examples clearly relate to the topics that I am comparing or contrasting?

mywritinglab To check your progress in meeting this chapter's objectives, log in to **www.mywritinglab.com**, go to the **Study Plan** tab, click on **Paragraph Patterns** and choose **Paragraph Development – Comparing and Contrasting** from the list of subtopics. Read and view the resources in the **Review Materials** section, and then complete the **Recall, Apply,** and **Write** sets in the **Activities** section.

CHAPTER 11
Cause and Effect

Pollution is a major problem in our world. What causes dirty air, water, and soil? What are the results of a contaminated environment? Cause and effect writing helps to explain the answers to these types of questions.

> *Do not go where the path may lead; go instead where there is no path and leave a trail.*
>
> —RALPH WALDO EMERSON
> *American essayist and poet (1803–1882)*

Writers' Exchange

Your instructor will divide the class into two groups. You should work with a partner or a team of students. Your group will discuss one of the following topics.

What are some reasons that students go to college?
What effects does a college education have on a person's life?

EXPLORING

What Is Cause and Effect?

Cause and effect writing explains why an event happened or what the consequences of such an event were. A cause and effect paragraph can focus on causes, effects, or both.

You often analyze the causes or effects of something. At home, you may worry about what causes your siblings or your own children to behave in a certain manner, or you may wonder about the effects of certain foods on your health. In a U.S. history course, you might analyze the causes of the Civil War, or you might write about the effects of industrialization on American society. At work, you may wonder about the causes or effects of a promotion or a pay cut.

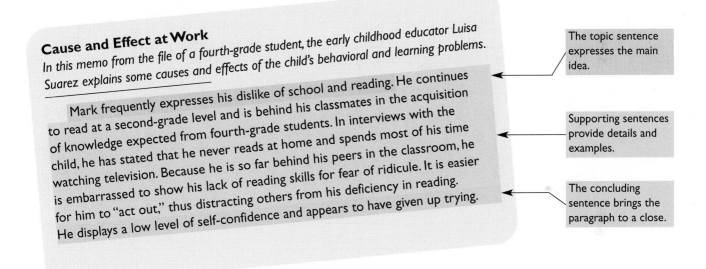

Cause and Effect at Work

In this memo from the file of a fourth-grade student, the early childhood educator Luisa Suarez explains some causes and effects of the child's behavioral and learning problems.

Mark frequently expresses his dislike of school and reading. He continues to read at a second-grade level and is behind his classmates in the acquisition of knowledge expected from fourth-grade students. In interviews with the child, he has stated that he never reads at home and spends most of his time watching television. Because he is so far behind his peers in the classroom, he is embarrassed to show his lack of reading skills for fear of ridicule. It is easier for him to "act out," thus distracting others from his deficiency in reading. He displays a low level of self-confidence and appears to have given up trying.

The topic sentence expresses the main idea.

Supporting sentences provide details and examples.

The concluding sentence brings the paragraph to a close.

The Cause and Effect Paragraph

When you write a cause and effect paragraph, focus on two main points.

1. **Indicate whether you are focusing on causes, effects, or both.** Because a paragraph is not very long, it is often easier to focus on either causes or effects. If you do decide to focus on both causes and effects, make sure that your topic sentence announces your purpose to the reader.

2. **Ensure that your causes and effects are valid.** Determine real causes and effects, and do not simply list things that happened before or after the event. Also verify that your assumptions are logical.

   Illogical: The product does not work because it is inexpensive.

   (This statement is illogical; quality is not always dictated by price.)

   Better: The product does not work because it is constructed with poor-quality materials.

PRACTICE I

Read the following paragraph and answer the questions.

When I played football, I learned to be an animal. Being an animal meant being fanatically aggressive and ruthlessly competitive. If I saw an arm in front of me, I trampled it. Whenever blood was spilled, I nodded approval. Broken bones (not mine of course) were secretly seen as little victories within the bigger struggle. The coaches taught me to "punish the other man," but little did I suspect that I was devastating my own body at the same time. There were broken noses, ribs, fingers, toes and teeth, torn muscles and ligaments, bruises, bad knees, and busted lips, and the gradual pulverizing of my spinal column that, by the time my jock career was long over at age 30, had resulted in seven years of near-constant pain. It was a long road to the surgeon's office.

—Don Sabo, "Pigskin, Patriarch, and Pain"

1. Underline the topic sentence.

2. What does this paragraph mainly focus on? Circle the best answer.
    a. Causes   b. Effects

3. Who is the audience? _____

4. List the supporting details.

    _____

    _____

    _____

    _____

    _____

Explore Topics

In the Warm Up, you will try an exploring strategy to generate ideas about different topics.

Imagine that you had to write a cause and effect paragraph about employee absenteeism. You might brainstorm to come up with as many causes and effects as possible.

Do Not Confuse *Effect* **and** *Affect*

Generally, *affect* is used as a verb, and *effect* is used as a noun. *Affect* (verb) means "to influence or change" and *effect* (noun) means "the result."

> verb
> How will your new job <u>affect</u> your family?

> noun
> What <u>effect</u> will moving to a new city have on your spouse's career?

Effect can also be used as a verb that means "to cause or to bring about." It is generally used in the following phrases: "to effect a change" or "to effect a plan."

> The union members demonstrated to <u>effect</u> changes in their working conditions.

Causes
- Child is sick
- Employee is sick
- Personal problems such as marital strife, depression
- Lack of motivation

Employee absenteeism

Effects
- Other employees do more
- May lose job
- Could get demoted
- Develop financial problems

The Writer's Desk Warm Up

Write some possible causes and effects for the following topics. Then decide if your paragraph will focus on causes or effects.

EXAMPLE: Reduction of violent crime

Causes	Effects
more police on street	*citizens feel sense of security*
reduction in youth population rate	*less cost to taxpayers*
harsher sentences for nonviolent	*public money spent for crime*
crimes	*prevention can be spent on other*
	things

Focus on: *Causes*

1. Cheating

Causes	Effects
_____	_____
_____	_____
_____	_____
_____	_____

Focus on: _____

2. Popularity of fast food

Causes	Effects

Focus on: _____

3. Teenage rebellion

Causes	Effects

Focus on: _____

ESSAY LINK

In a cause and effect essay, the thesis statement expresses whether the essay will focus on causes, effects, or both.

DEVELOPING

The Topic Sentence

The topic sentence in a cause and effect paragraph must clearly demonstrate whether the focus is on causes, effects, or both. Also, make sure that you have clearly indicated your controlling idea. For example, read the topic sentences. Notice that the controlling ideas are underlined.

topic   controlling idea (causes)

The American public is paying high gasoline prices for many reasons.

topic   controlling idea (effects)

High gasoline prices have led Americans to change their driving habits.

topic   controlling idea (causes and effects)

High gasoline prices, which are caused by many factors, have profound consequences for many Americans.

PRACTICE 2

Carefully read the following topic sentences. Decide whether each sentence focuses on causes, effects, or both. Look for key words that give you clues. Circle the best answer.

1. People become homeless because of difficult life circumstances.
   a. Causes   b. Effects   c. Both

2. Homeless people must deal with difficult situations in their day-to-day lives.

   a. Causes   b. Effects   c. Both

3. Because of many problems at the Chernobyl nuclear site, the environment in Ukraine has changed forever.

   a. Causes   b. Effects   c. Both

4. Scientists have proposed many theories that explain the disappearance of the dinosaurs.

   a. Causes   b. Effects   c. Both

The Writer's Desk **Write Topic Sentences**

Write a topic sentence for each of the following topics. You can look for ideas in the Writer's Desk Warm Up on pages 147–148. Determine whether you will focus on causes, effects, or both in your paragraph.

EXAMPLE: Topic: Reduction of violent crime

Topic Sentence: *The number of serious crimes committed in the United States has fallen recently for several reasons.*

1. Topic: Cheating

   Topic sentence: _____

   _____

2. Topic: Popularity of fast food

   Topic sentence: _____

   _____

3. Topic: Teenage rebellion

   Topic sentence: _____

   _____

The Supporting Ideas

After you have developed an effective topic sentence, generate supporting ideas. When planning a cause and effect paragraph, think of examples that clearly show the causes or effects. Then arrange your examples in emphatic order. When you use **emphatic order**, you place your examples from the most to the least important or from the least to the most important.

Visualizing Cause and Effect

PRACTICE 3

Brainstorm supporting ideas for the following topic sentence. Explain how a dam might affect the environment.

TOPIC SENTENCE:

A dam has profound effects on the environment.

_____   _____   _____

_____   _____   _____

 **Do Not Oversimplify**

Avoid attributing a simple or general cause to a complex issue. When you use expressions such as *It appears that* or *A possible cause is,* you show that you are aware of the complex factors involved in the situation.

Oversimplification:	The growing rate of homelessness in the United States is caused by the foreclosure crisis.
	(This is an oversimplification of a complicated problem.)
Better:	A possible cause of the growing rate of homelessness in the United States is that a large number of families have lost their homes through foreclosure.

The Writer's Desk **Generate Supporting Ideas**

Choose one of the topic sentences from the Writer's Desk on page 149. Then list either causes or effects.

EXAMPLE: Topic sentence: _The number of serious crimes committed in_
the United States has fallen recently for several reasons.

Supports: _youth population rates have declined_
different policing tactics
harsher sentences for all types of crimes

Topic sentence: _____

Supports: _____
_____
_____
_____

The Paragraph Plan

In many courses, instructors ask students to write about the causes or effects of a particular subject. Plan your paragraph before you write your final version. Also think about the order of ideas. Arrange the supporting details in a logical order. As you make your plan, ensure that you focus on causes, effects, or both.

ESSAY LINK

In a cause and effect essay, place the thesis statement in the introduction. Then use body paragraphs, each with its own topic sentence, to support the thesis statement.

TOPIC SENTENCE: The number of serious crimes committed in the United States has fallen recently for several reasons.

Support 1: There are fewer people between the ages of fifteen and twenty-four.
Details: —There was a drop of almost 5 percent in youth populations between 1975 and 2000.
Support 2: Police-patrolling tactics have changed.
Details: —Police get to know locals.
—Police check suspicious individuals for hidden weapons.
Support 3: Punishment for criminals has become tougher.
Details: —Nonviolent offenders and drug dealers are given prison terms.
—More criminals are off the street, which reduces the crime rate.

The Writer's Desk **Write a Paragraph Plan**

Refer to the information you generated in previous Writer's Desk exercises and create a paragraph plan. If you think of new details that will explain your point more effectively, include them here.

Topic sentence: _____

_____

Support 1: _____

Details: _____

_____

_____

Support 2: _____

Details: _____

_____

_____

Support 3: _____

Details: _____

_____

_____

vo•cab•u•lar•y BOOST

Using your thesaurus, come up with three synonyms for *cause* and three synonyms for *effect*.

The First Draft

After you outline your ideas in a plan, you are ready to write the first draft. Remember to write complete sentences. You might include transitional words or expressions to help your ideas flow smoothly.

Transitional Words and Expressions

The following transitional expressions are useful for showing causes and effects.

To Show Causes	To Show Effects
for this reason	accordingly
the first cause	as a result
the most important cause	consequently

The Writer's Desk **Write the First Draft**

Write the first draft of your cause and effect paragraph. Before you write, carefully review your paragraph plan and make any necessary changes.

REVISING AND EDITING

Revise and Edit a Cause and Effect Paragraph

When you finish writing a cause and effect paragraph, review your work and revise it to make the examples as clear as possible to your readers. Make sure that your sentences relate to the topic sentence and flow together smoothly.

PRACTICE 4

Read the next student paragraph and answer the questions.

Most people want to stay safe. They add security devices to their homes because they believe that the violent crime rate has risen in recent times. Yet, the number of serious crimes committed in the United States has fallen recently for several reasons. Many journalists have written about violent crime and a lot of news stories on television are about violent crimes. First, experts believe that there are fewer people between the ages of fifteen and twenty-four. This has led to a reduction in crime rates. From 1975 to 2000, the youth population rate droped by almost 5 percent. In addition, police-patrolling tactics have changed. Police officers get to know locals in various neighborhoods. Officers also check suspicious individuals for concealed weapons. Finaly, punishment has become more tougher. People who commit certain nonviolent crimes and drug offenses are given prison terms. Prison populations have increased. More criminals are off the street, which reduces the crime rate. In conclusion, these factors have had a positive affect on the country's crime rate.

Revising

1. Does the paragraph focus on causes, effects, or both? _____

2. List the causes or effects given. _____

   _____

   _____

   _____

3. There is one sentence in the paragraph that does not relate to the topic. Cross it out.

Editing

4. There is one error with the comparative form. Correct the error.

5. This paragraph contains two misspelled words. Identify and correct them.

6. There is one commonly confused word error. Underline the error and replace it with the correct word.

GRAMMAR LINK

See the following chapters for more information about these grammar topics:
   Adjectives and Adverbs, Chapter 30
   Spelling, Chapter 33

The Writer's Desk **Revise and Edit Your Paragraph**

Revise and edit the paragraph that you wrote for the previous Writer's Desk. Make sure that your paragraph has unity, adequate support, and coherence. Also correct any errors in grammar, spelling, punctuation, and mechanics.

REFLECT ON IT

Think about what you have learned in this chapter. If you do not know an answer, review that topic.

1. What is the difference between the words *affect* and *effect*?

   Affect: _____

   Effect: _____

2. Why should oversimplification of causes or effects be avoided?

   _____

   _____

3. List some common transitional words used in a cause and effect paragraph.

   _____

   _____

The Writer's Room

Writing Activity 1: Topics

Choose any of the following topics, or choose your own topic. Then write a cause and effect paragraph.

General Topics

Causes and/or effects of . . .

1. having a close friendship
2. having a caffeine addiction
3. voter apathy
4. having a poor body image
5. spoiling a child

College and Work-Related Topics

Causes and/or effects of . . .

6. having low (or high) marks in college
7. not keeping up with college workload
8. working with a family member
9. working at home
10. getting a promotion

WRITING LINK

More Cause and Effect Writing Topics

Chapter 18, Writer's Room topic 2 (page 296)

Chapter 19, Writer's Room topic 2 (page 308)

Chapter 24, Writer's Room topic 2 (page 359)

Chapter 30, Writer's Room topic 2 (page 441)

Chapter 35, Writer's Room topic 2 (page 503)

Writing Activity 2: Photo Writing

How has the technological world helped or hindered personal relationships?

READING LINK

More Cause and Effect Readings

"Why Small Businesses Fail" by Jim Baek (page 234)

"Don't Worry, Act Happy" by Albert Nerenberg (page 548)

"Job Candidates and Facebook" by Wei Du (page 559)

Writing Activity 3: Media Writing

Watch a television show or movie that deals with falling in love or breaking up. You could watch any television soap opera or romance movies such as *The Proposal, Love Happens,* or *17 Again.* You could also listen to love songs. Describe the causes or effects of falling in love or breaking up and use examples to support your point.

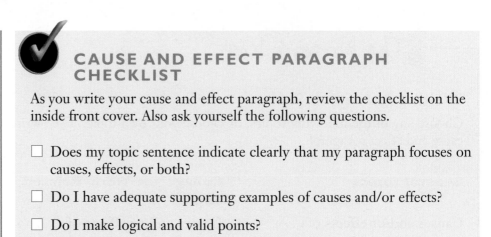

CAUSE AND EFFECT PARAGRAPH CHECKLIST

As you write your cause and effect paragraph, review the checklist on the inside front cover. Also ask yourself the following questions.

- ☐ Does my topic sentence indicate clearly that my paragraph focuses on causes, effects, or both?

- ☐ Do I have adequate supporting examples of causes and/or effects?

- ☐ Do I make logical and valid points?

- ☐ Do I use the terms *effect* and *affect* correctly?

mywritinglab To check your progress in meeting this chapter's objectives, log in to **www.mywritinglab.com**, go to the **Study Plan** tab, click on **Paragraph Patterns** and choose **Paragraph Development – Cause and Effect** from the list of subtopics. Read and view the resources in the **Review Materials** section, and then complete the **Recall, Apply,** and **Write** sets in the **Activities** section.

Argument

LEARNING OBJECTIVES

1. What Is Argument? (p. 158)
2. The Argument Paragraph (p. 158)
3. Explore Topics (p. 160)
4. The Topic Sentence (p. 161)
5. The Supporting Ideas (p. 163)
6. The Paragraph Plan (p. 167)
7. The First Draft (p. 168)
8. Revise and Edit an Argument Paragraph (p. 169)

Teenagers often argue with their parents. In argument writing, you try to convince readers to agree with your point of view.

> *Do not fear to be eccentric in opinion, for every opinion now accepted was once eccentric.*
>
> — BERTRAND RUSSELL
> *British author and philosopher (1872–1970)*

Writers' Exchange

For this activity, you and a partner will take turns debating an issue. To start, choose who will begin speaking. The first speaker chooses one side of any issue listed below, and then argues about that issue, without stopping, for a set amount of time. Your instructor will signal when to switch sides. After the signal, the second speaker talks nonstop about the other side of the debate. If you run out of ideas, you can switch topics when it is your turn to speak.

Possible topics:

Dogs are better than cats.	Cats are better than dogs.
It's better to be married than single.	It's better to be single than married.
Life is easier for men.	Life is easier for women.

EXPLORING

What Is Argument?

When you use **argument,** you take a position on an issue and attempt to defend it. You try to convince somebody that your point of view is the best one.

Argument is both a writing pattern and a purpose for writing. In fact, it is one of the most common aims or purposes in most college and work-related writing. For example, in Chapter 10, there is a paragraph about teen fashion, and the author uses comparison and contrast as the predominant pattern. At the same time, the author uses argument to convince the reader that fashions have not become more shocking over the years. Therefore, in most of your college and work-related writing, your purpose is to persuade the reader that your ideas are compelling and valid.

You use argument every day. At home, you may write a persuasive letter to a newspaper to express your views about public policy. At college, in a sociology class, you might take a position on capital punishment or on gun control. At work, you might have to convince your manager to give you a raise.

Argument at Work

Lawyer Marshal L. Dodge argues on behalf of his client, Wayne Campbell,* a veteran of the first Gulf War, for disability compensation for posttraumatic stress disorder (PTSD).

The topic sentence expresses the main idea.

Supporting sentences provide details and examples.

The concluding sentence brings the paragraph to a satisfying close.

On behalf of my client, I request that the Veterans Claims Board grant Mr. Campbell disability compensation. Campbell, served on active duty during the first Gulf War from September 1990 to January 1991. After his discharge, Mr. Campbell began to experience a nervous condition. He could not sleep, eat, or do other daily activities. The American Psychiatric Association has acknowledged PTSD as a delayed-stress syndrome experienced by combat veterans. My client has provided a list of each stress-related incident he has experienced since returning to civilian life. Mr. Campbell has provided the necessary medical reports from health care professionals. The medical reports indicate that, before serving in the Gulf War, my client functioned very well in his day-to-day activities. Furthermore, my client has responded in a timely manner to all and any requests made by the VA regarding his claim. Therefore, he should receive disability compensation.

*name changed

ESSAY LINK

When you write argument essays, also keep these four points in mind.

The Argument Paragraph

When you write an argument paragraph, remember the following four points.

- **Choose a subject that you know something about.** It would be very difficult to write a good text about space research funds, capital punishment, or conditions in federal prisons, for example, if you have never had experience with, or read about, these issues. On the other hand, if you, or someone close to you, cannot find good day care, then you could likely write a very effective paragraph about the need for better day-care services.

- **Consider your readers.** What do your readers already know about the topic? Are they likely to agree or disagree with you? Do they have specific concerns? Consider what kind of evidence would be most effective with your audience.

- **Know your purpose.** In argument writing, your main purpose is to persuade the reader to agree with you. Your specific purpose is more focused. You may want the reader to take action, you may want to support a viewpoint, you may want to counter somebody else's argument, or you may want to offer a solution to a problem. Ask yourself what your specific purpose is.

- **Take a strong position and provide supporting evidence.** The first thing to do in the body of your paragraph is to prove that there is, indeed, a problem. Then back up your point of view with a combination of facts, statistics, examples, and informed opinions.

 **Be Passionate!**

When you are planning your argument paragraph, try to find a topic that you feel passionate about. If you care about your topic, and if you express your enthusiasm, your audience will be more likely to care about it, too.

PRACTICE I

Read the next paragraph, and answer the questions.

As one solution to global warming, the locavore movement encourages consumers to buy within a 100-mile radius. However, buy-local advice is not especially eco-friendly. First, a 2008 study by researchers at Carnegie Mellon University showed that only 11 percent of greenhouse gases released into the atmosphere come from long-distance transportation of food supplies. Large ships or planes send enormous quantities of produce very efficiently. In 2006, New Zealand researchers at Lincoln University proved that New Zealand lamb transported to Britain consumed less energy than locally-produced British lamb. In addition, local farming methods may be inefficient. The Carnegie-Mellon study showed that almost 83 percent of carbon emissions could be attributed to regional food-production practices. For instance, community-produced crops may require more water, fertilizer, and pesticides than crops from overseas. Large amounts of forest may have to be cleared to ensure that farmers make a profit. In colder climates, food producers often grow and store food in temperature-controlled warehouses. Exotic flowers or fruits cultivated in a tropical climate require less energy than those same flowers and fruit grown in a hothouse in a cold climate. Although reduction of greenhouse gases is a **laudable** goal, consumers should thoroughly inform themselves about the best solutions in fighting climate change.

laudable: praiseworthy

—Kevin Libin, "Rethinking Green: Eat Global, Not Local" (adapted)

1. Underline the topic sentence. Remember that a topic sentence is not necessarily the first sentence in the paragraph.

2. Who is the author's audience? _____

_____

3. What is the author's specific purpose? _____

_____

_____

4. Underline some examples that the author gives to show that there is a problem.

5. Look at the author's supporting evidence, and circle two statistics.

Explore Topics

In the Warm Up, you will try an exploring strategy to generate ideas about different topics.

The Writer's Desk Warm Up

Think about the following questions, and write down the first ideas that come to mind. Try to think of two or three ideas for each topic.

EXAMPLE: Should officials place more speed bumps on city streets?

Yes, I think so. Then speeding cars would have to slow down. Kids often play on the streets. Speeding cars are dangerous for kids. Of course, speed bumps may create traffic jams. But in the long term, I think speed bumps are necessary.

1. Sometimes minors steal, vandalize, go joyriding, and do other illegal acts. Should parents be required to pay for damages when their children break the law?

_____

_____

2. In some countries, all youths must do two years of military service. What do you think about compulsory military service?

_____

_____

3. What are some of the major controversial issues in your neighborhood, at your workplace, at your college, or in the news these days?

_____

_____

_____

The Topic Sentence

In the topic sentence of an argument paragraph, state your position on the issue. In the following topic sentence, notice that the controlling idea has been underlined.

controlling idea   topic

<u>Our government should severely punish</u> **corporate executives who commit fraud.**

Your topic sentence should be a debatable statement. It should not be a fact or a statement of opinion.

Fact: In some public schools, students wear uniforms.

     (This is a fact. It cannot be debated.)

Opinion: I think that it is a good idea for public school students to wear uniforms.

     (This is a statement of opinion. Nobody can deny that you like school uniforms. Therefore, do not use phrases such as *In my opinion, I think,* or *I believe* in your topic sentence.)

Argument: Public school students should wear uniforms.

     (This is a debatable statement.)

PRACTICE 2

Evaluate the following statements. Write *F* for a fact, *O* for an opinion, or *A* for a debatable argument.

1. I think that dieting makes people fat.   _____

2. Most high school graduates take SATs to get accepted into college. _____

3. American businesses should give longer maternity and paternity leave for employees.   _____

4. Since the development of e-mail, many people rarely write traditional letters.   _____

5. In my opinion, teenagers should be at least eighteen years old before they can have a driver's license.   _____

6. High school graduates should be required to work for one year before entering college.   _____

7. Arranged marriages are more successful than courtship marriages. _____

8. I believe that some college students drink too much.   _____

 **Be Direct**

You may be reluctant to state your point of view directly. You may feel that it is impolite to do so. However, in academic writing, it is perfectly acceptable, and even desirable, to state an argument in a direct manner.

In argument writing, you can make your topic debatable by using *should, must,* or *ought to* in the topic sentence or thesis statement.

> Although daily prayer is important for many people in the United States, it **should** not take place in the classroom.

The Writer's Desk Write Topic Sentences

Write a topic sentence for the following topics. You can look for ideas in the previous Writer's Desk Warm Up. Make sure that each topic sentence clearly expresses your position on the issue.

EXAMPLE:

Topic: More speed bumps on city streets

Topic sentence: <u>With the increased traffic flow in the community, speed</u> <u>bumps should be put in place to decrease the number of speeders and</u> <u>increase public safety.</u>

1. Topic: Parents paying for children's crime sprees

   Topic sentence: _____

   _____

2. Topic: Compulsory military service

   Topic sentence: _____

   _____

3. Topic: A controversial issue in your neighborhood, at work, at college, or in the news

   Topic sentence: _____

   _____

The Supporting Ideas

When you write an argument paragraph, it is important to support your point of view with examples, facts, statistics, and informed opinions. It is also effective to think about some answers you can give to counter the opposition's point of view, and you can consider the long-term consequences if something does not occur. Therefore, try to use several types of supporting evidence.

ESSAY LINK

In an argument essay, body paragraphs should contain supporting details such as examples, facts, informed opinions, logical consequences, and answers to the opposition.

- **Examples** are pieces of information that illustrate your main argument. For instance, if you want to argue that there are not enough day-care centers in your area, you can explain that one center has over one hundred children on its waiting list.

    Another type of example is the **anecdote.** To support your main point, you can write about a true event or tell a personal story. For example, if you think that rebellious teenagers hurt their families, you might tell a personal story about your brother's involvement with a gang.

- **Facts** are statements that can be verified in some way. For example, the following statement is a fact: "According to the World Health Organization, secondhand smoke can cause cancer in nonsmokers." **Statistics** are another type of fact. When you use statistics, ensure that the source is reliable, and remember to mention the source. For example, if you want to argue that underage drinking is a problem, you could mention the following statistic from the *Journal of the American Medical Association:* "Underage drinkers consume about 20 percent of all the alcohol imbibed in this country."

- Sometimes experts in a field express an **informed opinion** about an issue. An expert's opinion can give added weight to your argument. For example, if you want to argue that the courts treat youths who commit crimes too harshly or leniently, then you might quote a judge who deals with juvenile criminals. If you want to argue that secondhand smoke is dangerous, then you might quote a lung specialist or a health organization.

- Solutions to problems can carry **logical consequences.** When you plan an argument, think about long-term consequences if something does or does not happen. For example, in response to the terrorist attacks of September 11, 2001, many governments enacted antiterrorism legislation. However, in some cases, the new laws could be used to suppress legitimate dissent or free speech. Also, those new laws could be misused or misinterpreted by future governments.

- In argument writing, try to **answer the opposition.** For example, if you want to argue that drinking laws are ineffective, you might think about the arguments that your opposition might make. Then you might write, "Drinking age laws do a fine job of keeping young people out of clubs and bars; however, these laws do nothing to keep young people from getting access to alcohol from other places." Try to refute some of the strongest arguments of the opposition.

Visualizing Argument

PRACTICE 3

Brainstorm supporting ideas for the following topic sentence. Write a sentence explaining why each activity is dangerous.

TOPIC SENTENCE:

There are several activities you should never do when driving.

Putting on Makeup

Texting

Eating

Hint   **Avoid Circular Reasoning**

When you write an argument paragraph, make sure that your main point is supported with facts, examples, informed opinions, and so on. Do not use circular reasoning. Circular reasoning means that you restate your main point in various ways.

Circular	The abundance of spam is not harmless; in fact, a lot of junk e-mail is offensive. People receive many copies of junk mail and the content offends them. Most people complain when they receive too much junk e-mail, and they feel especially unhappy when the junk e-mail has offensive images.
Not Circular	The abundance of spam is not harmless; in fact, a lot of junk e-mail is offensive. According to Odin Wortman of Internet Working Solutions, about 30 percent of unwanted e-mail is pornographic. Children and adults open such mail hoping for a message from a friend, only to see an offensive picture. Another 30 percent of junk mail advertises fraudulent schemes to get rich quickly or hawks products of questionable value or safety.

PRACTICE 4

You have learned about different methods to support a topic. Read each of the following topic sentences, and think of a supporting reason for each one. Use the type of support suggested in parentheses.

1. Companies should be prevented from marketing to children.

   (Example) _____

   _____

   _____

2. Boys should be encouraged to express their emotions.

   (Logical consequence) _____

   _____

   _____

3. Voting should be mandatory in the United States.

   (Fact) _____

   _____

   _____

4. Teen magazines should not show ads with extremely thin models.

   (Logical consequence) _____

   _____

   _____

5. When a couple goes on a date, the person who earns the most money should always pay the bill.

   (Answer the opposition.) _____

   _____

   _____

 **Using Research**

You can enhance your argument essay with **research** by including information from an informed source. You can look for information in textbooks, newspapers and magazines, and on the Internet.

When you use the Internet for research, make sure that your sources are from legitimate organizations or from reputable magazine, newspaper, or government sites. For example, for information about the spread of AIDS, you might find statistics on the World Health Organization's Web site. You would not go to someone's personal rant or conspiracy theory site.

READING LINK

For more information about avoiding plagiarism and evaluating and documenting sources, refer to Chapter 15, "Enhancing Your Writing with Research."

Consider Both Sides of the Issue

Once you have decided what to write about, try to think about both sides of the issue. Then you can predict arguments that your opponents might make, and you can plan your answer to the opposition.

EXAMPLE: Speed bumps

For	Against
—slows down speeders	—slows down emergency vehicles
—increases safety in residential neighborhoods	—increases noise from braking cars
—children will be able to play freely without being hit by a speeding car	—increases wear and tear on a car
—may reduce traffic accidents	—may increase traffic jams
—may discourage heavy traffic in residential neighborhoods	—may cause some drivers back pain

The Writer's Desk **Consider Both Sides of the Issue**

Write arguments for and against each of the following topics.

1. Parents paying for children's crimes

   For   **Against**

   _____   _____

   _____   _____

   _____   _____

   _____   _____

2. Compulsory military service

   For   **Against**

   _____   _____

   _____   _____

   _____   _____

   _____   _____

3. A controversial issue: _____

   For   **Against**

   _____   _____

   _____   _____

   _____   _____

   _____   _____

Avoid Common Errors

When you write an argument paragraph or essay, avoid the following pitfalls.

Do not make generalizations. If you begin a statement with *Everyone knows* or *It is common knowledge*, then the reader may mistrust what you say. You cannot possibly know what everyone else knows. It is better to refer to specific sources.

Generalization:	Everyone knows that global warming is wrecking havoc on our planet.
Better:	According to the United Nations Panel on Climate Change, governments must take serious steps to reduce greenhouse gas emissions.

Use emotional arguments sparingly. Certainly, the strongest arguments can be emotional ones. Sometimes the most effective way to influence others is to appeal to their sense of justice, humanity, pride, or guilt. However, do not rely on emotional arguments. If you use emotionally charged words (for example, if you call someone *ignorant*) or if you try to appeal to base instincts (for example, if you appeal to people's fear of other ethnic groups), then you will seriously undermine your argument.

Emotional:	Racists believe that illegal immigrants are attacking the American way of life.
Better:	Many sectors of society, including some politicians, students, and activists, believe that illegal immigration hampers the efforts of those who want to immigrate legally.

Do not make exaggerated claims. Make sure that your arguments are plausible.

Exaggerated:	Illegal immigrants are taking everybody's jobs.
Better:	Although illegal immigrants work hard, they continue the demand for cheap labor.

---

vo•cab•u•lar•y BOOST

Looking at Associated Meanings

Some words have neutral, positive, or negative associations. With a partner, try to find the most neutral word in each list. Categorize the other words as positive or negative.

1. macho, jerk, hunk, lout, hottie, man, stud, sweetheart, bully
2. nation, homeland, refuge, kingdom, rogue state, country, motherland, axis of evil
3. freedom fighter, terrorist, anarchist, believer, radical, fanatic, revolutionary, rebel, soldier, activist

---

The Paragraph Plan

Before you write your argument paragraph, make a plan. Think of some supporting arguments, and think about details that can help illustrate each argument. Make sure that every example is valid and that it relates to the topic sentence. Also, arrange your ideas in a logical order.

TOPIC SENTENCE: With the increased traffic flow in Swan Creek, speed bumps should be put in place to decrease the number of speeders and to increase public safety.

Support 1:	By constructing speed bumps, pedestrians will not have to worry about being hit by speeding cars.
Details:	—Often children play sports on streets.
	—Sometimes people cross the street without looking both ways.
Support 2:	Speed bumps can help unify a community.
Details:	—A community can petition the city to put speed bumps on certain streets.
	—Neighbors form friendships based on a common cause.
Support 3:	Speed bumps may reduce traffic accidents.
Details:	—Traffic accidents are often caused by excessive speed.
	—Some drivers have no regard for the speed limits.

The Writer's Desk **Write a Paragraph Plan**

Choose one of the topic sentences that you wrote for the Writer's Desk on page 162, and write a detailed paragraph plan. You can refer to the information you generated in previous Writer's Desk exercises, and if you think of examples that will explain your point more effectively, include them here.

Subject: _____

Topic sentence: _____

_____

Support 1: _____

Details: _____

_____

_____

Support 2: _____

Details: _____

_____

_____

Support 3: _____

Details: _____

_____

_____

The First Draft

After you outline your ideas in a plan, you are ready to write the first draft. Remember to write complete sentences. You might include transitional words or expressions to help your ideas flow smoothly.

Transitional Words and Expressions

The following transitional words and expressions can introduce an answer to the opposition or the support for an argument.

To Answer the Opposition	To Support Your Argument
admittedly	certainly
however	consequently
nevertheless	furthermore
of course	in fact
on one hand/on the other hand	obviously
undoubtedly	of course

The Writer's Desk Write the First Draft

Write the first draft of your argument paragraph. Before you write, carefully review your paragraph plan and make any necessary changes.

REVISING AND EDITING

Revise and Edit an Argument Paragraph

When you finish writing an argument paragraph, carefully review your work and revise it to make the supporting examples as clear as possible to your readers. Check that the order of ideas is logical, and remove any irrelevant details.

PRACTICE 5

College student Craig Susanowitz wrote the following paragraph. Read the paragraph and answer the questions.

> With the increased traffic flow in Swan Creek, speed bumps should be put in place to decrease the number of speeders and to increase public safety. Of course, some people argue that speed bumps increase the wear and tear on a car, cause drivers back pain, and increase traffic jams. But such arguments are idiotic when it comes to public safety. By constructing speed bumps in residential neighborhoods, pedestrians will not have to worry about being hit by speeding cars. Often, in such residential areas, children play sports on the street. As children, my friends and I often played street hockey on roller blades. We wondered why did cars screech to a stop near us. It was a bit scary. In addition, children as well as adults sometimes cross the street without paying attention to the traffic. If a car is going over the speed limit, it may not be able to stop in time if a pedestrian steps into traffic. Next, speed bumps can help unify a community. Neighbors can petition city officials to put speed bumps on certain streets. Being involved in such a worthwhile cause can bring strangers together in a community spirit. Furthermore, speed bumps will prevent car accidents. Traffic accidents are often caused by excessive speed

because drivers do not have enough time to react to surprises on the road. Many guys are in a hurry and have no regard for the posted 25 m.p.h. speed limit. So, in closing, speed bumps should be implemented in Swan Creek to ensure the safety of our community's residents.

Revising

1. Underline the topic sentence.

2. The writer uses an emotionally charged word. Find and replace the word with a more appropriate word.

   Emotionally charged word: _____

   Replacement: _____

3. List three arguments that support the topic sentence.

   _____

   _____

   _____

4. The writer also acknowledges the opposition. List the arguments he acknowledges.

   _____

GRAMMAR LINK

See the following chapters for more information about these grammar topics:
   Slang versus standard English, Chapter 32
   Dangling modifiers, Chapter 31
   Embedded questions, Chapter 18

Editing

5. Find a slang word and substitute it with a standard English word.

   Slang: _____

   Standard English: _____

6. This paragraph contains a dangling modifier. The modifier has no subject. Underline the error, and write the correct sentence below.

   _____

   _____

7. This paragraph contains an embedded question error. Underline the error and write the correct phrase below.

   _____

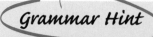 **Using Embedded Questions**

When you embed a question inside a larger sentence, you do not need to use the question word order. Make sure that your embedded questions are correctly written.

why our government doesn't
Some people wonder ~~why doesn't our government~~ strictly regulate the banks.

The Writer's Desk Revise and Edit Your Paragraph

Revise and edit the paragraph that you wrote for the previous Writer's Desk. Make sure that your paragraph has unity, adequate support, and coherence. Also correct any errors in grammar, spelling, punctuation, and mechanics.

REFLECT ON IT

Think about what you have learned in this chapter. If you do not know an answer, review that topic.

1. What is the main purpose of an argument paragraph or essay?

    _____

2. What is the difference between a statement of opinion and a statement of argument?

    _____

    _____

3. What five types of supporting evidence can you use in argument writing?

    _____   _____

    _____   _____

    _____

4. In argument writing, you should avoid circular reasoning. What is circular reasoning?

    _____

    _____

5. Why is it important to avoid using emotionally charged words?

    _____

    _____

The Writer's Room

Writing Activity 1: Topics

Choose any of the following topics, or choose your own topic. Then write an argument paragraph. Remember to narrow your topic and to follow the writing process.

WRITING LINK

More Argument Writing Topics

Chapter 23, Writer's Room topic 2 (page 346)

Chapter 25, Writer's Room topic 2 (page 370)

Chapter 26, Writer's Room topic 2 (page 385)

Chapter 27, Writer's Room topic 2 (page 390)

Chapter 29, Writer's Room topic 2 (page 426)

Chapter 31, Writer's Room topic 2 (page 450)

Chapter 33, Writer's Room topics 1 and 2 (page 478)

READING LINK

More Argument Readings

"The Importance of Music" by Christine Bigras (page 239)

"It's Class, Stupid!" by Richard Rodriguez (page 535)

"The Case for Affirmative Action" by Dave Malcolm (page 538)

General Topics

1. the voting age
2. disciplining children
3. chat room relationships
4. alternative medical therapies
5. home schooling

College and Work-Related Topics

6. drug testing
7. value of a college education
8. compulsory physical education in college
9. longer vacations for workers
10. office relationships

Writing Activity 2: Photo Writing

Examine the photo, and think about arguments that you might make about marriage. For example, you might argue about the high cost of weddings, the best type of wedding, why people should or should not marry, or the benefits of premarital counseling. Then write an argument paragraph.

Writing Activity 3: Media Writing

Watch a television show or movie that deals with health care. You could watch television shows such as *Grey's Anatomy*, *Nurse Jackie*, or *House*. Movies include *Her Sister's Keeper* or *Seven Pounds*. Find a controversial issue in the program or movie, and write an argument paragraph. Give examples to support your ideas.

✓ ARGUMENT PARAGRAPH CHECKLIST

As you write your argument paragraph, review the checklist on the inside front cover. Also ask yourself the following questions.

☐ Does my topic sentence clearly state my position on the issue?

☐ Do I make strong supporting arguments?

☐ Do I include facts, examples, statistics, logical consequences, or answers to the opposition?

☐ Do my supporting arguments provide evidence that directly supports the topic sentence?

mywritinglab To check your progress in meeting this chapter's objectives, log in to **www.mywritinglab.com**, go to the **Study Plan** tab, click on **Paragraph Patterns** and choose **Paragraph Development – Argument** from the list of subtopics. Read and view the resources in the **Review Materials** section, and then complete the **Recall, Apply,** and **Write** sets in the **Activities** section.

The Essay

Each body paragraph begins with a topic sentence.

The introductory paragraph introduces the essay's topic and contains its thesis statement.

The title gives a hint about the essay's topic.

The thesis statement contains the essay's topic and its controlling idea.

What Is an Essay?

An essay is a series of paragraphs that support one main or central idea. Essays differ in length, style, and subject, but the structure of an essay generally consists of an *introductory paragraph,* several *body paragraphs,* and a *concluding paragraph.*

Before you begin reading the following chapters, become familiar with the parts of the common five-paragraph essay.

Kite Boarding

Have you ever had the feeling of total freedom? Have you ever ridden upon deep or shallow water with nothing more than a board at your feet and a kite in your hands? Imagine the muffled sound of the wind, the water squirting on your board, and the rays of the sun shining on you while you are jumping fifteen feet high, totally in control of what you are doing. In fact, of all sports, none is as wonderful as kite boarding.

First, kite boarding is a marvelous sport because it provides an incredible feeling of freedom. Indeed, while riding, a boarder is the only leader; she decides where she goes, how fast she goes, what tricks she does, when she jumps, and how high she jumps. Also, she can decide to go for a short-distance ride or for a long-distance ride, depending on how she feels. For example, this summer, I went to Florida, one of the most wonderful spots ever, and one day, I was in Miami where I learned some new moves. After a while, I decided that I wanted to explore a little bit more. So I crossed the sea and rode to the other side of the bay. The feeling of freedom that I got was so incredible! I was able to go by myself where I wanted for at least five miles.

Furthermore, learning to kite board also helps a person acquire other skills. First, a kite boarder has to be strong enough to manipulate the kite in strong winds. Therefore, most kite boarders have muscle strength. Boarders should also know how to swim well in case they end up in the water. Kite boarders must have a sense of direction. The ocean can be an easy place to get lost, so a boarder always has to keep track of where he is. In addition, it is important for a kite boarder to have some survival skills. He should be able to make rational decisions in difficult situations. For example, if the wind changes direction, becomes too strong, or stops, then the boarder will have to make certain decisions that will ensure his safety.

Finally, kite boarding is an all-season sport. Indeed, it is possible to kite board on the water, on the snow, on the grass, and even on the sand. In the summer, it is possible to ride on the beach with a buggy or in the water with a board. In the winter, almost every type of riding is possible, but the most common ways to ride are with a snowboard or with skis. In autumn, it is possible to ride in the water with a dry suit, or it is possible to ride on the grass with a mountain board.

In conclusion, kite boarding is the most wonderful sport because it provides the rider a deep feeling of freedom, and it costs very little. Furthermore, because it is an all-season sport, addicted riders can practice the sport almost anytime they want to. In fact, with kite boarding, the sky is the limit because, after all, the only thing the rider cannot control is the wind forecast.

—*Genevieve Leonard, student*

The concluding paragraph brings the essay to a satisfactory close.

Each body paragraph contains details that support the thesis statement.

Writing the Essay

CHAPTER 13

Completed in 1973, the Sydney Opera House in Australia has tons of concrete, steel, and glass supporting its structure. In the same way, an essay is a sturdy structure that is supported by a strong thesis statement and solid body paragraphs held together by plenty of facts and examples.

> " *Without words, without writing, and without books there would be no history, and there could be no concept of humanity.* "
>
> —HERMANN HESSE
> *German author (1877–1962)*

EXPLORING

Explore Topics

There are limitless topics for writing essays. Your knowledge and personal experiences will help you find topics and develop ideas when you write your essay.

When you are planning your essay, consider your topic, audience, and purpose. Your **topic** is who or what you are writing about. Your **audience** is your intended reader, and your **purpose** is your reason for writing. Do you hope to entertain, inform, or persuade the reader?

WRITING LINK

For more information about exploring strategies, see Chapter 1.

Narrowing the Topic

Your instructor may assign you a topic for your essay, or you may need to think of your own. In either case, you need to narrow your topic (make it more specific) to ensure that it suits your purpose for writing and fits the size of the assignment. To narrow your topic, you can use some exploring methods such as questioning or brainstorming.

When you narrow your topic, keep in mind that an essay contains several paragraphs; therefore, an essay topic can be broader than a paragraph topic. In the following examples, you will notice that the essay topic is narrow but is slightly larger than the paragraph topic.

Broad Topic	Essay Topic	Paragraph Topic
Job interview	Preparing for the interview	Dressing for the interview
Rituals	Initiation rituals	College orientation week

 **Choosing an Essay Topic**

Paragraphs and essays can also be about the same topic. However, an essay has more details and concrete examples to support its thesis.

Do not make the mistake of choosing an essay topic that is too broad. Essays that try to cover a large topic risk being superficial and overly general. Make sure that your topic is specific enough that you can cover it in an essay.

DAVID NARROWS HIS TOPIC

Student writer David Raby-Pepin used both brainstorming and questioning to narrow his broad topic, "music." His audience was his English instructor, and the purpose of his assignment was to persuade.

- Should street performers be required to have a license?
- downloading music
- difference in earning power between classical and pop musicians
- Why do some rock bands have staying power?
- how to be a successful musician
- What is hip-hop culture?
- the popularity of shows like *American Idol*
- difference between poetry and song lyrics

The Writer's Desk Narrow the Topics

Practice narrowing five broad topics.

EXAMPLE:

Money: – *reasons it doesn't make you happy*

– *teach children about value of money*

– *best ways to be financially successful*

1. Volunteer work: _____

   _____

   _____

2. Environment: _____

   _____

   _____

3. Advertising: _____

   _____

   _____

4. Entertainment: _____

   _____

   _____

DEVELOPING

The Thesis Statement

Once you have narrowed the topic of your essay, develop your thesis statement. The **thesis statement**—like the topic sentence in a paragraph—introduces the topic of the essay and arouses the interest of the reader.

Characteristics of a Good Thesis Statement

A thesis statement has three important characteristics.

- It expresses the main topic of the essay.
- It contains a controlling idea.
- It is a complete sentence that usually appears in the essay's introductory paragraph.

Here is an example of an effective thesis statement.

topic   controlling idea

Marriage has lost its importance for many young people in our society.

Writing an Effective Thesis Statement

When you develop your thesis statement, ask yourself the following questions.

1. **Is my thesis statement a complete statement that has a controlling idea?**
   Your thesis statement should always reveal a complete thought and make a

point about the topic. It should not simply announce the topic or express a widely known fact.

Incomplete:	Gambling problems.
	(This statement is not complete.)
Announcement:	I will write about lotteries.
	(This statement announces the topic but says nothing relevant about the topic. Do not use expressions such as *I will write about . . .* or *My topic is . . .*)
Thesis statement:	Winning the lottery will not necessarily lead to happiness.

2. **Does my thesis statement make a valid and supportable point?** Your thesis statement should express a valid point that you can support with evidence. It should not be a vaguely worded statement, and it should not be a highly questionable generalization.

Vague:	Workplace relationships are harmful.
	(For whom are they harmful?)
Invalid point:	Women earn less money than men.
	(Is this really true for all women in all professions? This generalization might be hard to prove.)
Thesis statement:	Before coworkers become romantically involved, they should carefully consider possible problems.

3. **Can I support my thesis statement in an essay?** Your thesis statement should express an idea that you can support in an essay. It should not be too broad or too narrow.

Too broad:	There are many museums in the world.
	(It would be difficult to write an essay about this topic.)
Too narrow:	The Spy Museum is in Washington.
	(What more is there to say?)
Thesis statement:	Washington's Spy Museum contains fascinating artifacts related to the secret world of espionage.

 **Give Specific Details**

Give enough details to make your thesis statement focused and clear. Your instructor may want you to guide the reader through your main points. To do this, mention both your main point and your supporting points in your thesis statement. In other words, your thesis statement provides a map for the readers to follow.

Weak:	My first job taught me many things.
Better:	My first job taught me about responsibility, organization, and the importance of teamwork.

PRACTICE I

Identify the problem in each thesis statement. Then revise each statement to make it more interesting and complete.

Announces	Invalid	Broad
Incomplete	Vague	Narrow

EXAMPLE:

I will write about human misery on television news.

Problem: _Announces_

Revised statement: _Television news programs should not treat personal tragedies as big news._

1. All teachers have a class favorite.

   Problem: _____

   Revised statement: _____

   _____

2. I think that television influences behavior.

   Problem: _____

   Revised statement: _____

   _____

3. Scientific discoveries have changed the world.

   Problem: _____

   Revised statement: _____

   _____

4. The streets are becoming more dangerous.

   Problem: _____

   Revised statement: _____

   _____

5. How to use a digital camera.

   Problem: _____

   Revised statement: _____

   _____

6. My children know how to count to ten in Spanish.

   Problem: _____

   Revised statement: _____

   _____

The Writer's Desk Write Thesis Statements

For each item, choose a narrowed topic from the Writer's Desk on pages 176–177. Then write an interesting thesis statement. Remember that each thesis statement should contain a controlling idea.

EXAMPLE: Topic: Money

Narrowed topic: *Winning a lottery*

Thesis statement: *Rather than improving your life, winning the lottery can lead to feelings of guilt, paranoia, and boredom.*

1. Topic: Volunteer work

   Narrowed topic: _____

   Thesis statement: _____

   _____

2. Topic: Environment

   Narrowed topic: _____

   Thesis statement: _____

   _____

3. Topic: Advertising

   Narrowed topic: _____

   Thesis statement: _____

   _____

4. Topic: Entertainment

   Narrowed topic: _____

   Thesis statement: _____

   _____

The Supporting Ideas

The thesis statement expresses the main idea of the entire essay. In the following illustration, you can see how the ideas flow in an essay. Topic sentences relate to the thesis statement, and details support the topic sentences; therefore, all the ideas in the essay are unified and support the thesis.

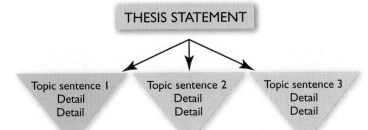

PRACTICE 2

Read the following essay by university student Tami Farr. After you have finished reading, do the following:

1. Create an effective thesis statement. It should sum up the point of the entire essay.

2. Write a topic sentence at the beginning of each body paragraph. The topic sentence should sum up the main point of the paragraph in an interesting way.

Introduction:

   I hear about the Internet everyday. Most of the time, the media report on only the dark side of the Internet. The Internet allows untrustworthy people to have easy access to personal information. The Internet has also been connected to pornography and has raised concerns about minors being targeted by sexual predators. **Thesis Statement:** _____

_____

   Body paragraph 1 topic sentence: _____

_____

Many students use the Internet for school research. The Internet is more accessible than libraries, is quicker than tracking down books, and has a bigger database. Google Advanced Scholar is a wonderful resource where a student can find information on any subject. Encyclopedias can also be accessed on the Internet. Students can also find a tutor for any subject online, which allows them to receive timely help for school success.

   Body paragraph 2 topic sentence: _____

_____

In the past, if we wanted to write to friends, we had to wait for days or weeks for our letter to reach them. Now e-mail helps us to communicate with people in seconds. E-mail is very useful if we want to send the same message to several friends. Instead of having to write multiple letters, we can now just enter in multiple e-mail addresses.

Body paragraph 3 topic sentence: _____

_____

Most companies can now serve the world instead of just communities. Many companies' profits have increased by selling on the Internet. For example, Amazon.com sells products only through the Internet, and it is a very successful business. Consumers can also sell items through the Internet. Companies such as eBay allow both buyer and seller to conduct business easily. More people can work from home and get work done more quickly because of the Internet.

Conclusion:
The Internet has been a wonderful asset to our generation. Even though we see and hear about the negative aspects of the Internet, we need to keep in mind that if we use the Internet wisely, and for the right purposes, it can be a great boon in our lives.

Generating Supporting Ideas

An effective essay has **unity** when the body paragraphs support the thesis statement. When you develop supporting ideas, make sure that they all focus on the central point that you are making in the thesis statement. To generate ideas for body paragraphs, you could use exploring strategies such as brainstorming, clustering, or freewriting.

DAVID'S SUPPORTING IDEAS

David created a list to support his thesis statement. Then he reread his supporting points and removed ideas that he did not want to develop in his essay.

THESIS STATEMENT: Rap and hip-hop artists use their music to share their positive cultural values with others.

- use lyrics to reveal their religious opinions
- Christian lyrics
- ~~hip hop inspired breakdancing~~
- praise Allah
- want to promote peace
- some address issues of violence
- ~~some hip hop artists have been jailed~~
- advise fans about healthy lifestyles
- warn about drugs
- talk about AIDS

The Writer's Desk **List Supporting Ideas**

Choose two of your thesis statements from the previous Writer's Desk on page 180, and create two lists of possible supporting ideas.

Thesis 1: _____   Thesis 2: _____

_____   _____

Support: _____   Support: _____

_____   _____

_____   _____

_____   _____

_____   _____

_____   _____

_____   _____

_____   _____

_____   _____

_____   _____

Organizing Your Ideas

After you have examined your list of supporting ideas, choose three or four that are most compelling and most clearly support your statement. Highlight your favorite ideas, and then group together related ideas. Finally, make your essay as clear and coherent as possible by organizing your ideas in a logical manner using time, space, or emphatic order.

WRITING LINK

For more information about time, space, and emphatic order, see Chapter 2, "Developing."

DAVID'S EXAMPLE

David underlined his three best supporting points, and he grouped related ideas using emphatic order.

3
- use lyrics to reveal their religious opinions
- Christian lyrics
- ~~hip hop inspired breakdancing~~
- praise Allah

1
- want to promote peace
- some address issues of violence
- ~~some hip hop artists have been jailed~~

2
- advise fans about healthy lifestyles
- warn about drugs
- talk about AIDS

The Writer's Desk **Organize Your Ideas**

Look at the list you produced in the previous Writer's Desk, and then follow these steps.

1. Highlight at least three ideas from your list that you think are the most compelling and that most clearly illustrate the point you are making in your thesis statement.

2. Group together any related ideas with the three supporting ideas.

3. Organize your ideas using time, space, or emphatic order.

The Essay Plan

An **essay plan** or an **outline** can help you organize your thesis statement and supporting ideas before you write your first draft. To create an essay plan, follow these steps.

- Look at your list of ideas and identify the best supporting ideas.
- Write topic sentences that express the main supporting ideas.
- Add details under each topic sentence.

In the planning stage, you do not have to develop your introduction and conclusion. It is sufficient to simply write your thesis statement and an idea for your conclusion. Later, when you flesh out your essay, you can develop the introduction and conclusion.

DAVID'S ESSAY PLAN

David wrote topic sentences and supporting examples and organized his ideas into a plan. Notice that he begins with his thesis statement, and he indents his supporting ideas.

THESIS STATEMENT:	Rap and hip-hop artists use their music to share their positive cultural values with others.
Body paragraph 1:	Many musicians shout out a powerful message of nonviolence. —They have broken from the "gansta rap" lyrics. —Encourage listeners to respect themselves and others.
Body paragraph 2:	Some advise fans about responsible and healthy lifestyles. —They discuss the importance of good parenting. —They talk about drug addiction or AIDS.

Body paragraph 3:   These urban musicians use their poetry to
                          reveal their religious beliefs.
                          —Some show their Christian faith through
                            the lyrics.
                          —Others praise Allah.

Concluding sentence: Finally, music is a way for rap musicians to
                          share their personal culture with the world.

Writing a Formal Essay Plan

Most of the time, a basic essay plan is sufficient. However, in some of your courses,
your instructor may ask you to make a formal plan. A formal plan uses Roman
numerals and letters to identify main and supporting ideas.

Thesis statement: _____

I. _____
  A. _____
  B. _____

II. _____
  A. _____
  B. _____

III. _____
  A. _____
  B. _____

Concluding idea: _____

PRACTICE 3

Create an essay plan based on Genevieve Leonard's essay "Kite Boarding" on page 174.

_____

_____

_____

_____

_____

_____

_____

_____

_____

_____

_____

_____

_____

_____

_____

_____

_____

PRACTICE 4

Complete the following essay plan. Add details under each supporting point. Make sure that the details relate to the topic sentence.

Thesis statement: Rather than improving your life, winning the lottery can lead to feelings of guilt, paranoia, and boredom.

I. Feelings of guilt are common in newly rich people.

Details: A. _____

_____

B. _____

_____

C. _____

_____

II. Lottery winners often become paranoid.

Details: A. _____

_____

B. _____

_____

C. _____

_____

III. After lottery winners quit their jobs, they commonly complain of boredom and loneliness.

Details: A. _____

_____

B. _____

_____

C. _____

_____

Concluding idea: _____

_____

_____

The Writer's Desk **Write an Essay Plan**

Write an essay plan using one of your thesis statements and supporting details you came up with in the previous Writer's Desk.

Thesis statement: _____

_____

I. _____

Details: A. _____

B. _____

C. _____

II. _____

Details: A. _____

B. _____

C. _____

III. _____

Details: A. _____

B. _____

C. _____

Concluding idea: _____

_____

The Introduction

After you have made an essay plan, you develop the sections of your essay by creating an effective introduction, linking paragraphs, and writing a conclusion.

The **introductory paragraph** introduces the subject of your essay and contains the thesis statement. A strong introduction will capture the reader's attention and make him or her want to read on. Introductions may have a lead-in, and they can be developed in several different ways.

The Lead-In

You can choose to begin the introduction with an attention-grabbing opening sentence, or lead-in. There are three common types of lead-ins.

- Quotation
- Surprising or provocative statement
- Question

Introduction Styles

You can develop the introduction in several different ways. Experiment with any of these introduction styles.

- **Give general or historical background information.** The general or historical information gradually leads to your thesis. For example, in an essay about winning a lottery, you could begin by giving a brief history of lotteries.

- **Tell an interesting anecdote.** Open your essay with a story that leads to your thesis statement. For example, you might begin your lottery essay by telling the story of a real-life lottery winner.

- **Present a vivid description.** Give a detailed description, and then state your thesis. For example, you might describe the moment when a lottery winner realizes that he or she has won.

- **Present an opposing position.** Open your essay with an idea that contradicts a common belief, and build to your thesis. For instance, if most people want to win the lottery, you could begin your essay by saying that you definitely do not want to be a millionaire.

- **Give a definition.** Define a term, and then state your thesis. For example, in an essay about the lottery, you could begin by defining *happiness*.

Hint **Placement of the Thesis Statement**

Although a paragraph often begins with a topic sentence, an introduction does not begin with a thesis statement. Rather, most introductory paragraphs are shaped like a funnel. The most general statement introduces the topic. The following sentences become more focused and lead to a clear, specific thesis statement. Therefore, the thesis statement is generally the last sentence in the introduction.

PRACTICE 5

In introductions A through E, the thesis statement is underlined. Read each introduction and then answer the questions that follow. Look at David's example for some guidance.

DAVID'S INTRODUCTION

Can hip-hop, with its obscene lyrics and violent culture, have any redeeming qualities? Hip-hop and rap music originated from poor, minority-inhabited neighborhoods located in New York City. Since the residents did not have enough money to buy musical instruments, they began creating beats with their mouths. This raw form of music rapidly became popular within these communities because it gave people a way to express themselves and to develop their creative abilities. <u>Rap and hip-hop artists use their music to share their positive cultural values with others.</u>

1. What type of lead-in does David use? ___*Question*___

2. What introduction style does he use?
   a. Description
   b. Definition
   (c.) Background information
   d. Opposing position

3. What is his essay about?   *The positive message of hip-hop and rap music*

_____

A. "I never saw the blow to my head come from Huck. Bam! And I was on all fours, struggling for my equilibrium." These are the words of Kody Scott, a former member of a Los Angeles street gang. Kody is describing part of the initiation ritual he endured in order to join a local branch (or "set") of the Crips. First, he stole an automobile to demonstrate his "street smarts" and willingness to break the law. Then he allowed himself to be beaten, showing both that he was tough and that he was ready to do whatever the gang required of him. He completed the process by participating in a "military action"—killing a member of a rival gang. Initiations like this are by no means rare in today's street gangs. Kody, by the way, was just eleven years old.

—Linda L. Lindsey and Stephen Beach, "Joining the Crips," *Essentials of Sociology*

1. What type of lead-in does the author use? _____

2. What introduction style does the author use?
   a. Anecdote   b. Definition
   c. Background information   d. Opposing position

3. What is this essay about? _____

B. Why are Westerners getting upset about women wearing burqas? In Spain, the Catalonian assembly almost passed a law to ban women from wearing the burqa in public. In France, politicians want to ban such clothing, and girls cannot wear Muslim head coverings at school. Belgian politicians are also debating this issue. Europeans are very emotional about this subject. But Americans must guard against falling into a similar mindset.

—Amida Jordan, *Student*

4. What type of lead-in does the author use? _____

5. What introduction style does the author use?
   a. Anecdote   b. General background
   c. Description   d. Opposing position

C. High school is a waste of time. In fact, it is a baby-sitting service for teens who are too old to be baby-sat. In England, fifteen-year-olds graduate and can choose technical or university streams of education. They are free to choose what to study, or they can stop schooling and get jobs. In short, they are treated like mature adults. In our country, we prolong the experience of forced schooling much longer than is necessary. We should abolish high schools and introduce a system of technical or pre-university schooling.

—Adelie Zang, student

6. What type of lead-in does the author use? _____

7. What introduction style does the author use?

   a. Anecdote   b. Definition

   c. Background information   d. Opposing position

8. What is this essay about? _____

D. Having been socialized many years in Egypt and identifying with its people, I had regarded it, on one level, to be my home. On another level, however, I had been brought up in a Saudi Arabian family committed in great measure to that country's cultural heritage and the observance of its cultural norms, even while selectively observing certain Egyptian values and practices. Throughout my college days, I had been reminded that I could not do what my Egyptian girlfriends could do because "our" traditions were different and for "us" such behavior was unacceptable.

—Soraya Altorki, "Arab Women in the Field"

9. What introduction style does the author use?

   a. Anecdote   b. Definition

   c. Background information   d. Opposing position

10. What is this essay about? _____

_____

E. The story of how Christianity ultimately conquered the Roman Empire is one of the most remarkable in history. Christianity faced the hostility of the established religious institutions of its native Judea and had to compete not only against the official cults of Rome and the sophisticated philosophies of the educated classes, but also against "mystery" religions like the cults of Mithra, Isis, and Osiris. The Christians also suffered formal persecution, yet Christianity finally became the official religion of the empire.

—Albert M. Craig et al., *The Heritage of World Civilizations*

11. What introduction style does the author use?

   a. Description   b. Definition

   c. Historical information   d. Opposing position

12. What is this essay about? _____

The Writer's Desk Write Three Introductions

In the previous Writer's Desk, you made an essay plan. Now, write three different styles of introductions for your essay. Use the same thesis statement in all three introductions. Later, you can choose the best introduction for your essay.

The Conclusion

A **conclusion** is a final paragraph that rephrases the thesis statement and summarizes the main points in the essay. To make your conclusion more interesting and original, you could close with a prediction, a suggestion, a quotation, or a call to action.

DAVID'S CONCLUSION

David concluded his essay by restating his main points.

> Finally, music is a way for hip-hop and rap musicians to share their personal culture with the world. This cultural facet can be reflected through different values, religious beliefs, and ways of life.

He could then close his essay with one of the following:

Prediction: If you are concerned about hip-hop portraying negative images, don't abandon the music yet. There are many artists who promote and will continue to promote positive values through upbeat lyrics.

Suggestion: Hip-hop fans should encourage musicians to continue to give a positive message through their music.

Call to action: If you are concerned by the negative message of hip-hop music, make your opinions heard by joining the debate on hip-hop blogs and buying CDs from musicians who only write positive lyrics.

Quotation: According to hip-hop artist Doug E. Fresh, "Hip Hop is supposed to uplift and create, to educate people on a larger level, and to make a change."

PRACTICE 6

Read the following conclusions and answer the questions.

A. As soon as smoking is banned in all public places, we will see the benefits. Our hospitals will treat fewer smoking-related illnesses, and this will save money. Non-smokers will be saved from noxious fumes, and smokers, who will be forced to smoke outdoors, might feel a greater desire to give up the habit. In the future, we will have a world where a non-smoker can go through life without having to breathe in someone else's cigarette smoke.

—Jordan Lamott, "Butt Out!"

1. What method does the author use to end the conclusion?
   a. Prediction
   b. Suggestion
   c. Quotation
   d. Call to action

B. So how can nonhuman primates be protected from us? There really are only two major ways: Either human population growth in many places has to be curtailed, or we have to preserve substantial populations of non-human primates in protected parks and zoos.

—Carole R. Ember et al., "Endangered Primates"

2. What method does the author use to end the conclusion?
   a. Prediction
   b. Suggestion
   c. Quotation
   d. Call to action

C. Every once in a while the marketing wizards pay lip service to today's expanding career options for women and give us a Scientist Barbie complete with a tiny chemistry set as an accessory. But heaven forbid should little Johnnie plead for his parents to buy him that Scientist Barbie. After all, it is acceptable for girls to foray, occasionally, into the world of boy-style play, but for boys the opposite "sissified" behavior is taboo. Why is this? One commentator, D. R. Shaffer, says, "The major task for young girls is to learn how not to be babies, whereas young boys must learn how not to be girls."

—Dorothy Nixon, "Put GI Barbie in the Bargain Bin"

3. What method does the author use to end the conclusion?
   a. Prediction
   b. Suggestion
   c. Quotation
   d. Call to action

 **Avoiding Conclusion Problems**

In your conclusion, do not contradict your main point, and do not introduce new or irrelevant information. David initially included the next sentences in his conclusion.

> The rap and hip-hop movement is not restrained only to the musical scene. It influences many other facets of art and urban culture as well. It can be found in dance and fashion, for instance. Thus, it is very versatile.

He revised his conclusion when he realized that some of his ideas were new and irrelevant information. His essay does not discuss dance or fashion.

The Writer's Desk **Write a Conclusion**

In previous Writer's Desks, you wrote an introduction and an essay plan. Now write a conclusion for your essay.

The First Draft

After creating an introduction and conclusion, and after arranging the supporting ideas in a logical order, you are ready to write your first draft. The first draft includes your introduction, several body paragraphs, and your concluding paragraph.

The Writer's Desk **Write the First Draft**

In previous Writer's Desks, you wrote an introduction, a conclusion, and an essay plan. Now write the first draft of your essay.

REVISING AND EDITING

Revising and Editing the Essay

Revising your essay is an extremely important step in the writing process. When you revise your essay, you modify it to make it stronger and more convincing. You do this by reading the essay critically, looking for faulty logic, poor organization, or poor sentence style. Then you reorganize and rewrite it, making any necessary changes.

Editing is the last stage in writing. When you edit, you proofread your writing and make sure that it is free of errors.

Revising for Unity

To revise for **unity,** verify that all of your body paragraphs support the thesis statement. Also look carefully at each body paragraph: make sure that the sentences support the topic sentence.

WRITING LINK

To practice revising for unity and support, see Chapter 3, "Revising and Editing."

 **Avoiding Unity Problems**

Here are two common errors to check for as you revise your body paragraphs.

- **Rambling paragraphs.** The paragraphs in the essay ramble on. Each paragraph has several topics, and there is no clearly identifiable topic sentence.
- **Artifical breaks.** A long paragraph is split into smaller paragraphs arbitrarily, and each smaller paragraph lacks a central focus.

To correct either of these errors, revise each body paragraph until it has *one* main idea that supports the thesis statement.

Revising for Adequate Support

When you revise for adequate **support,** ensure that there are enough details and examples to make your essay strong and convincing. Include examples, statistics, quotations, or anecdotes.

Revising for Coherence

When you revise for **coherence,** ensure that paragraphs flow smoothly and logically. To guide the reader from one idea to the next, or from one paragraph to the next, try using **paragraph links.**

You can develop connections between paragraphs using three methods.

1. **Repeat words or phrases from the thesis statement in each body paragraph.** In the next example, *violent* and *violence* are repeated words.

Thesis statement:	Although some will argue that <u>violent</u> movies are simply a reflection of a <u>violent</u> society, these movies actually cause a lot of the <u>violence</u> around us.
Body paragraph 1:	Action movie heroes train children to solve problems with <u>violence</u>.
Body paragraph 2:	<u>Violent movies</u> are "how to" films for many sick individuals.

2. **Refer to the main idea in the previous paragraph, and link it to your current topic sentence.** In body paragraph 2, the writer reminds the reader of the first point (the newly rich feel useless) and then introduces the next point.

Thesis statement:	A cash windfall may cause more problems than it solves.
Body paragraph 1:	The newly rich often lose their desire to become productive citizens, and they end up <u>feeling useless</u>.
Body paragraph 2:	Apart from <u>feeling useless</u>, many heirs and lottery winners also tend to feel guilty about their wealth.

3. **Use a transitional word or phrase to lead the reader to your next idea.**

Body paragraph 2:	<u>Furthermore</u>, the newly rich often feel guilty about their wealth.

WRITING LINK

Furthermore is a transition. For a list of transitions, see page 40 in Chapter 3.

Revising for Style

Another important step in the revision process is to ensure that you have varied your sentences and that you have used concise wording. When you revise for sentence style, ask yourself the following questions.

- Do I use a variety of sentence patterns? (To practice using sentence variety, see Chapter 19.)
- Do I use exact language? (To learn about slang, wordiness, and overused expressions, see Chapter 32.)
- Are my sentences parallel in structure? (To practice revising for parallel structure, see Chapter 22.)

ESSAY LINK

To practice your editing skills, see Chapter 37, "Editing Paragraphs and Essays."

Editing

When you edit, you proofread your essay and correct any errors in punctuation, spelling, grammar, and mechanics. There is an editing guide on the inside back cover of this book that provides you with a list of things to check for when you proofread your text.

DAVID'S ESSAY

David Raby-Pepin revised and edited this paragraph from his essay about hip-hop culture.

Furthermore, some
~~Some~~ rappers advise fans about responsible and healthy lifestyles.

they are
Several hip-hop artists divulge the fact that ~~their~~ parents and discuss

the importance of good parenting. Others announce their choice of a

and
monogamous lifestyle. ~~They~~ encourage their fans to have respectful

relationships. Some rappers mention past drug addictions and advise

avoid
listeners to ~~be avoiding~~ drugs. Others rap about the dangers of

example,
sexually transmitted diseases. The rapper Ludacris, for ~~example. He~~

warns his fans about AIDS and HIV and advises them to be careful

and to use condoms during sex. Such messages are ~~extremly~~ *extremely*

important since many young people do not take precautions with their

health.

The Writer's Desk Revising and Editing Your Essay

In the previous Writer's Desk, you wrote the first draft of an essay. Now revise and edit your essay. You can refer to the checklist at the end of this chapter.

The Essay Title

It is a good idea to think of a title after you have completed your essay because then you will have a more complete impression of your essay's main point. The most effective titles are brief, depict the topic and purpose of the essay, and attract the reader's attention.

   When you write your title, place it at the top center of your page. Capitalize the first word of your title, and capitalize the main words except for prepositions (*in, at, for, to,* etc.) and articles (*a, an, the*). Double space between the title and the introductory paragraph.

ESSAY LINK

For more information about punctuating titles, see pages 499–500 in Chapter 35.

Descriptive Titles

Descriptive titles are the most common titles in academic essays. They depict the topic of the essay clearly and concisely. Sometimes, the author takes key words from the thesis statement and uses them in the title. Here are some descriptive titles.

   The Importance of Multiculturalism in a Democratic Society
   Why Mothers and Fathers Should Take Parenting Seriously

Titles Related to the Writing Pattern

You can also relate your title directly to the writing pattern of your essay. Here are examples of titles for different writing patterns.

Illustration:	The Problems with Elections
Narration:	My Visit to Las Vegas
Description:	Graduation Day
Process:	How to Dress for an Interview
Definition:	What It Means to Be Brave
Classification:	Three Types of Hackers
Comparison and contrast:	Fast Food versus Gourmet Food
Cause and effect:	Why People Enter Beauty Pageants
Argument:	Barbie Should Have a New Look

> **Hint   Avoiding Title Pitfalls**
>
> When you write your title, watch out for problems.
>
> • Do not view your title as a substitute for a thesis statement.
> • Do not put quotation marks around the title of your essay.
> • Do not write a really long title because it can be confusing.

PRACTICE 7

1. List some possible titles for the essay about the Internet in Practice 2 (pages 181–182).

    _____

    _____

2. List some alternative titles for David's essay about rap and hip-hop music, which appears below.

    _____

    _____

The Final Draft

When you have finished making the revisions on the first draft of your essay, write the final copy. This copy should include all the changes that you have made during the revision phase of your work. You should proofread the final copy of your work to check for grammar, spelling, mechanics, and punctuation errors.

DAVID'S ESSAY

David Raby-Pepin revised and edited his essay about hip-hop culture. This is his final draft.

Positive Messages in Hip-Hop Music

Can hip-hop, with its obscene lyrics and violent culture, have any redeeming qualities? Hip-hop and rap music mainly originated from poor, minority-inhabited neighborhoods located in New York City. Since the residents did not have enough money to buy musical instruments, they began creating beats with their mouths. This raw form of music rapidly became popular within these communities because it gave people a way to express themselves and to develop their creative abilities. The rap and hip-hop artists use their music to share their positive cultural values with others.

Many of these musicians shout out a powerful message of nonviolence. Leading hip-hop and rap artists have broken from the gangsta rap lyrics of the past. Instead, they write lyrics that present a productive way to resolve conflicts. They encourage listeners to respect themselves and others.

Furthermore, some rappers advise fans about responsible and healthy lifestyles. Several hip-hop artists divulge the fact that they are parents and discuss the importance of good parenting. Others announce their choice of a monogamous lifestyle and encourage their fans to have respectful relationships. Some rappers mention past drug addictions and advise listeners to avoid drugs. Others rap about the dangers of sexually transmitted diseases. The rapper Ludacris, for example, warns his fans about AIDS and HIV and advises them to be careful and to use condoms during sex. Such messages are extremely important since many young people do not take precautions with their health.

Moreover, these urban musicians also use their lyrics to reveal their religious beliefs. Some show their Christian faith by including God in their texts. For example, in the song "Tommy" by Mathematics, the lyrics refer to a relationship with God after death. Members of the band Killarmy praise Allah in their lyrics. Hip-hop and rap musicians generally do not criticize other religions through their songs. They use this form of communication to support their own religious opinions. Hip-hop and rap music can be a way for individuals to show their faith or to pass it on to members of their audience.

Finally, music is a way for rap musicians to share their personal culture with the world. This cultural facet can be reflected through different values, religious beliefs, and ways of life. According to hip-hop artist Doug E. Fresh, "Hip Hop is supposed to uplift and create, to educate people on a larger level, and to make a change."

The Writer's Desk Writing Your Final Draft

At this point, you have developed, revised, and edited your essay. Now write the final draft. Before you hand in your essay to your instructor, proofread it one last time to make sure that you have found as many errors as possible.

REFLECT ON IT

Think about what you have learned in this unit. If you do not know an answer, review that topic.

1. What is a thesis statement? _____

_____

2. What are the five different introduction styles?

_____   _____

_____   _____

_____

3. What are the four different ways to end a conclusion?

_____   _____

_____   _____

4. What are the three different ways you can link body paragraphs?

_____

_____

_____

The Writer's Room

Writing Activity 1: Topics

Choose any of the following topics, or choose your own topic. Then write an essay. Remember to follow the writing process.

General Topics

1. communication
2. an unforgettable experience
3. differences between generations
4. advertising
5. peer pressure

College and Work-Related Topics

6. juggling college and family life
7. having a job and going to college
8. long-term career goals
9. a current social controversy
10. an important issue in the workplace

Writing Activity 2: Photo Writing

What ideas come to mind when you examine this photo? You may think about celebrities, culture of excess, culture of entitlement, good or bad role models, big business, and so on. Write an essay based on the photo or your related topic.

✔ REVISING AND EDITING CHECKLIST FOR ESSAYS

Revising

☐ Does my essay have a compelling introduction and conclusion?

☐ Does my introduction have a clear thesis statement?

☐ Does each body paragraph contain a topic sentence?

☐ Does each body paragraph's topic sentence relate to the thesis statement?

☐ Does each body paragraph contain specific details that support the topic sentence?

☐ Do all of the sentences in each body paragraph relate to its topic sentence?

☐ Do I use transitions to smoothly and logically connect ideas?

☐ Do I use a variety of sentence styles?

Editing

☐ Do I have any errors in grammar, spelling, punctuation, and capitalization?

---

mywritinglab To check your progress in meeting this chapter's objectives, log in to **www.mywritinglab.com**, go to the **Study Plan** tab, click on **The Essay** and choose **Thesis Statement, Essay Organization, Essay Introductions, Conclusions, and Titles, and Revising the Essay** from the list of subtopics. Read and view the resources in the **Review Materials** section, and then complete the **Recall, Apply,** and **Write** sets in the **Activities** section.

Essay Patterns

Fashion designers choose fabric patterns that are appropriate for the articles of clothing that they wish to make. In the same way, writers choose essay patterns that best suit their purposes for writing.

> ❝ *The act of writing is the act of discovering what you believe.* ❞
> —DAVID HARE
> *American playright (1947–)*

In Chapters 4 through 12, you read about and practiced using nine different paragraph patterns. In this chapter, you will learn how to apply those patterns when writing essays. Before you begin working through this chapter, take a moment to review the nine writing patterns.

Pattern	Purpose
Illustration	To prove a point using specific examples
Narration	To tell a story about a sequence of events that happened
Description	To portray something using vivid details and images that appeal to the reader's senses
Process	To inform the reader about how to do something, how something works, or how something happened
Definition	To explain what a term or concept means by providing relevant examples
Classification	To sort a topic to help readers understand different qualities about that topic
Comparison and contrast	To present information about similarities (compare) or differences (contrast)
Cause and effect	To explain why an event happened (the cause) or what the consequences of the event were (the effects)
Argument	To take a position on an issue and offer reasons for your position

Most college essay assignments specify one dominating essay pattern. However, you can use several additional essay patterns to fulfill your purpose. For example, imagine that you want to write a cause and effect essay about youth crime and the purpose of the essay is to inform. The supporting paragraphs might include a definition of youth crime and a narrative about an adolescent with a criminal record. You might incorporate different writing patterns, but the dominant pattern would still be cause and effect.

Each time you write an essay, remember to follow the writing process that you learned in Chapter 13, "Writing the Essay."

The Illustration Essay

When writing an illustration essay, you use specific examples to clarify your main point. Illustration writing is a pattern that you frequently use in college essays and exams because you must support your main idea with examples.

> **PARAGRAPH LINK**
>
> For more information about developing ideas with examples, refer to Chapter 4, "Illustration."

The Thesis Statement

The thesis statement in an illustration essay gives the direction of the body paragraphs. It includes the topic and a controlling idea about the topic.

topic   controlling idea

A second language <u>provides students with several important advantages</u>.

The Supporting Ideas

In an illustration essay, the body paragraphs contain examples that support the thesis statement. You can develop the body paragraphs in two different ways. To give your essay variety, you could use both a series of examples and an extended example.

- **Use a series of examples** that support the paragraph's topic sentence. For example, in an essay about bad driving, one body paragraph could be about drivers who do not pay attention to the road. The paragraph could list the things that those drivers do, such as choosing songs on an iPod, using a cell phone, eating, and putting on makeup.
- **Use an extended example** to support the paragraph's topic sentence. The example could be an anecdote or a description of an event. In an essay about bad driving, for example, one paragraph could contain an anecdote about a driver who always wanted to be faster than other drivers.

An Illustration Essay Plan

Read the next essay plan and answer the questions.

Introduction
Thesis statement: New technologies have had a profound impact on self-employed workers.
I. Smart phones help such workers maintain a portable office.
 A. They store e-mails, schedules, phone lists, and more.
 B. Models are lightweight and fit in a pocket.
 C. Instant messaging provides the means to communicate in real time.
II. Laptops provide workers with the ability to do complicated things anywhere.
 A. They can format and design documents using graphs, tables, and art.

      B. They can write, revise, and edit simultaneously.

      C. There is no need to carry large paper files; computers can store hundreds of files.

      D. The self-employed can access the Internet while traveling.

   III. Computer printers have useful features for the self-employed worker.

      A. There are integrated scanners and photocopiers.

      B. Fax machines allow easy sending and receiving of messages.

      C. Laser printers can quickly print out large volumes of documents.

Conclusion: As technologies evolve, more people will work at home.

PRACTICE I

1. Circle the topic and underline the controlling idea in the thesis statement.

2. How does the writer develop each body paragraph? Circle the best answer.

   a. With an extended example   b. With a series of examples

3. Write another topic sentence that could support the writer's thesis statement.

_____

_____

An Illustration Essay

Read the next essay by award-winning science writer Tom Keenan, and answer the questions that follow.

Guy Chores

1   For some reason, hot summer days remind me of my father doing mundane things like changing the oil in the car or washing paintbrushes with turpentine after completing a project around the house. It's far too late to make a difference to him, but experts now say some chemicals we handle doing "guy chores" can be pretty bad for us.

2   The latest is motor oil, which, according to a study in *Arthritis Research & Therapy*, may be linked to a risk of developing rheumatoid arthritis. A Swedish study found men who were exposed to mineral oils had a 30 percent higher risk of developing this disease than a control group. Before people panic and hand their cars over to the pros, it should be noted that the men in this study came into contact with motor or hydraulic oils regularly in the course of their work. The average man is not likely to suffer much from servicing the family car every 3000 miles.

3   Oil-based paint can contain a lot more gunk than just mineral spirits. According to information provided by the city of Phoenix, Arizona, on its very helpful household hazardous materials webpage, "a Johns Hopkins University study found 300 toxic chemicals and 150 carcinogens that may be present in paint." According to that source, the culprit chemicals span several components of oil-based paint and stains. "Pigments that provide the color may contain heavy metals such as cadmium and chromium. Cadmium irritates the respiratory tract while chromium is an eye and skin irritant. Pigments also may be made with zinc oxide, which can cause flu-like symptoms." So if people send their children out to paint the fence, they should make sure the paint is the safe kind.

4   Some guys are getting into gardening. It is relaxing and therapeutic, but some of those pesticides can be as bad as the car stuff in the garage. A study showed a disturbingly high concentration of estradiol—a form of the female sex hormone—in men exposed to pesticides and other agricultural chemicals. One good gardening tip is to avoid watering an area immediately after applying a chemical. Perhaps a better idea would be to get into pesticide-free gardening. That may result in a bit more stooping to get weeds, but the exercise is good for you.

5   Fortunately, I seem to have survived my contact with benzene, transmission fluid, and turpentine. Still, I'd think twice before letting young hobbyists work with dangerous materials. Believing that they are invincible, they may not appreciate the dangers, and they tend to be sloppy. Teenagers love fiddling with cars, and I'm not suggesting they have to switch to pasting stamps in albums. Still, a growing body of research shows common-sense precautions are really important when dealing with that shelf of weird chemicals out in the garage.

PRACTICE 2

1a. Who is the audience for this essay? _____

_____

1b. Why does the writer use vocabulary such as *guys*, *gunk*, and stuff?

_____

_____

2. Underline the thesis statement of the essay.

3. Underline the topic sentence of each body paragraph.

4. What kind of examples does the writer include?
   a. series of examples
   b. extended examples

5. Identify the types of specific examples the writer uses to support his thesis.
   a. statistics   d. expert opinion
   b. research study   e. anecdote
   c. facts

6. What suggestion does the writer make in the conclusion of the essay?

_____

_____

PARAGRAPH LINK

To practice illustration writing, you could develop an essay about one of the topics found in Chapter 4, "Illustration."

The Writer's Room

Writing Activity 1: Topics

Write an illustration essay about one of the following topics.

General Topics

1. important milestones
2. stereotypes on television
3. useless products or inventions
4. activities that relieve stress
5. American symbols

College and Work-Related Topics

6. characteristics of a good boss
7. qualities of an ideal workplace
8. skills that you need for your job
9. temptations that college students face
10. important things to know about doing your job

Writing Activity 2: Quotations

Read the following quotations. Find one that you agree or disagree with, or find one that inspires you in some way. Then write an illustration essay based on the quotation.

> Sports serve society by providing vivid examples of excellence.
>
> —George F. Will, American editor and columnist

> After climbing a great hill, one only finds that there are many more hills to climb.
>
> —Nelson Mandela, former South African president

> Everything has its beauty, but not everyone sees it.
>
> —Confucius, ancient Chinese philosopher and educator

> Everyone I meet is in some way my superior.
>
> —Ralph Waldo Emerson, American author

✔ ILLUSTRATION ESSAY CHECKLIST

As you write your illustration essay, review the essay checklist on the inside front cover. Also ask yourself the following questions.

☐ Does my thesis statement include a topic that I can support with examples?

☐ Does my thesis statement make a point about the topic?

☐ Do my body paragraphs contain sufficient examples that clearly support the thesis statement?

☐ Do I smoothly and logically connect the examples?

The Narrative Essay

When you write a narrative essay, you tell a story about what happened, and you generally explain events in the order in which they occurred.

There are two main types of narrative writing. In **first-person narration,** you describe a personal experience using *I* or *we*. In **third-person narration,** you describe what happened to somebody else, and you use *he, she, it,* or *they*.

PARAGRAPH LINK

For more information about narrative writing, refer to Chapter 5, "Narration."

The Thesis Statement

The thesis statement controls the direction of the body paragraphs. To create a meaningful thesis statement for a narrative essay, you could ask yourself what you learned, how you changed, or how the event is important.

controlling idea   topic
<u>Something wonderful happened</u> **the summer I turned fifteen.**

The Supporting Ideas

Here are some tips to remember as you develop a narrative essay.

- Make sure that your essay has a point. Do not simply recount what happened. Try to indicate why the events are important.

- Organize the events in time order (the order in which they occurred). You could also reverse the order of events by beginning your essay with the outcome of the events and then explaining what happened that led to the outcome.

- Make your narrative essay more interesting by using some descriptive language. For example, you could use images that appeal to the senses.

To be as complete as possible, a good narrative essay should provide answers to most of the following questions.

- *Who* is the essay about?
- *What* happened?
- *When* did it happen?

- *Where* did it happen?
- *Why* did it happen?
- *How* did it happen?

GRAMMAR LINK

For information about punctuating quotations, see Chapter 35.

> *Hint* **Using Quotations**
>
> One effective way to enhance your narrative essay is to use dialogue. Include direct and/or indirect quotations.
>
> A **direct quotation** contains a person's exact words. A direct quotation is set off with quotation marks. When you include the exact words of more than one person, you must start a new paragraph each time the speaker changes.
>
> Sara looked at me sadly: "Why did you betray me?"
>
> "I didn't mean to do it," I answered.
>
> She looked down at her hands and said, "I don't think I can ever forgive you."
>
> An **indirect quotation** keeps the person's meaning but not the person's exact words. An indirect quotation is not set off by quotation marks.
>
> Sara asked why I had betrayed her.

A Narrative Essay Plan

Read the next essay plan, and answer the questions that follow.

Introduction

Thesis statement: The investment manager Bernard Madoff was not a financial genius; he was a conniving scam artist.

I.   It did not take long for charismatic Madoff to establish a positive image of himself as a reputable financier.
  A. He started his business in the 1960s by investing on behalf of family friends who trusted him.
  B. His employees said that Madoff treated them like family.
  C. By the 1990s, Madoff had established himself in New York financial circles.

II. Madoff used his influence to dupe government officials.
  A. In the early 1990s, Madoff became chairman of NASDAQ, a major stock exchange.
  B. Madoff was also on the board of many investment firms in the past twenty years.
  C. By 1999, financial analysts had become suspicious of Madoff's investments but did not investigate.

III. For the past decade, Madoff was luring wealthy clients into his Ponzi scheme through various strategies.
  A. He displayed his wealth through his Manhattan penthouse and private jets.
  B. He was a philanthropist, which added an honorable dimension to his reputation.
  C. His clients were seduced by the high rates of return on their investments.
  D. In 2009, Madoff's fraud was discovered; he had stolen $65 billion of his clients' money.

Conclusion: The financial world is still shocked at how Madoff pulled off such a large fraud.

PRACTICE 3

1. Who is this essay about? _____

_____

2. What happened? _____

_____

3. When and where did this event take place? _____

_____

4. What type of narration is this?
  a. First person   b. Third person

A Narrative Essay

In the next essay, Jeff Kemp recounts what happened during his early years as a professional football player. Read the essay and answer the questions.

A Lesson in Humility

1   We live in an age when, too often, rules are scorned, values are turned upside down, principles are replaced by **expediency,** and character is sacrificed for popularity. Individual athletes are sometimes the worst offenders, but not as often as one might think. In fact, sports teach important moral lessons that athletes can apply on and off the playing field.

expediency:
convenience; self-interest

2   Many people dream of being a professional athlete. For me, the dream seemed to be within reach because my father, Jack Kemp, an outstanding quarterback, played for the American Football League's Buffalo Bills (prior to the AFL's 1970 merger with the National Football League). The trouble was, I was not very good! I was a third-string football player through most of junior high and high school and for two years at Dartmouth College. I was not anyone's idea of a "hot prospect." After graduation, I was passed over by NFL scouts. When I was finally asked to join the Los Angeles Rams in 1981 as a free agent, I was **designated** as a fifth-string quarterback.

designated:
selected

3   It was a 50-to-1 shot that I would survive training camp. Rookies were the only players required to show up for the first week of camp. There were dozens competing for the few spots open on the team. After two days, a young boy approached me as I was walking off the field. He asked if he could carry my helmet to the locker room. It was a long way, but I said, "Sure, I think you can handle that." The next morning, he showed up before practice and offered to carry my helmet and shoulder pads, and he was there again after practice offering the same service. So it went for the rest of the week.

4   On the last day, as we were departing the field, my young assistant said, "Jeff, can I ask you a question?" (We were on a first-name basis by then.)

5   I thought, "This is my first fan! He is going to ask me for an autograph."

6   He then inquired, "When do the good football players come to camp?" Right then and there, I learned a lesson in humility from a seven-year-old boy.

7   In my first three NFL seasons, I was forced to learn the same lesson over and over again. During that time, I threw just 31 passes. Nevertheless, by 1984, I had managed to outlast the five NFL quarterbacks who had been ahead of me. With the Rams' record standing at 1–2, I took over for injured quarterback Vince Ferragamo and earned my first start against the Cincinnati Bengals, eventually leading the Rams to nine more victories and a playoff berth.

8   The next season, I returned to the bench as a backup quarterback. Humility, I was compelled to remind myself, was a good thing. It helped me appreciate what I had and avoid dwelling on what I did not have. It prevented complaining, which drains the spirit and unity of any group. It also led me to persevere and be ready whenever opportunity presented itself.

PRACTICE 4

1. What type of narration is this text? Circle the best answer.

   a. First person   b. Third person

2. Underline the thesis statement of the essay.

3. What introduction style does Kemp use? Circle the best answer.

   a. Definition   c. General information

   b. Anecdote   d. Historical information

4. List the main events that Kemp recounts in his essay.

_____

_____

_____

_____

_____

_____

5. What organizational method does Kemp use? Circle the best answer.
   a. Time order
   b. Space order
   c. Emphatic order

6. Write down one example of an indirect quotation from the essay.

_____

7. Write down one example of a direct quotation from the essay.

_____

8. Narrative writers do more than simply list a series of events. Kemp explains why the events were meaningful. What did Kemp learn?

_____

_____

PARAGRAPH LINK

To practice narrative writing, you could develop an essay about one of the topics found in Chapter 5, "Narration."

 The Writer's Room

Writing Activity 1: Topics

Write a narrative essay about one of the following topics.

General Topics

1. a family legend
2. an illuminating moment
3. a rebellious act
4. an important event in the world
5. when you learned to do something new

College and Work-Related Topics

6. life lessons that college teaches you
7. what your previous job taught you
8. your best or worst job
9. your first job
10. a scandal at work or college

Writing Activity 2: Quotations

Read the following quotations. Find one that you agree or disagree with, or find one that inspires you in some way. Then write a narrative essay based on the quotation.

> The wisest men follow their own direction.
> —Euripides, Greek philosopher

> When your mouth stumbles, it's worse than feet.
> —Oji proverb

> If you tell the truth, then you don't have to remember everything.
> —Mark Twain, American author

> We can draw lessons from the past, but we cannot live in it.
> —Lyndon B. Johnson, former U.S. President

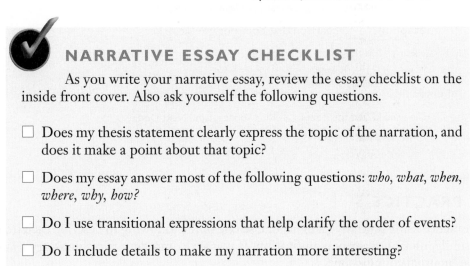

NARRATIVE ESSAY CHECKLIST

As you write your narrative essay, review the essay checklist on the inside front cover. Also ask yourself the following questions.

☐ Does my thesis statement clearly express the topic of the narration, and does it make a point about that topic?

☐ Does my essay answer most of the following questions: *who, what, when, where, why, how?*

☐ Do I use transitional expressions that help clarify the order of events?

☐ Do I include details to make my narration more interesting?

The Descriptive Essay

When writing a descriptive essay, use words to create a vivid impression of a subject. Use details that appeal to the five senses: sight, smell, hearing, taste, and touch. You want your readers to be able to imagine all that you are describing.

PARAGRAPH LINK

For more information about descriptive writing, refer to Chapter 6, "Description."

The Thesis Statement

In a descriptive essay, the thesis statement includes what you are describing and makes a point about the topic.

        topic   controlling idea

The Joshua Tree National Park has an inspirational landscape filled with life.

The Supporting Ideas

When you develop your descriptive essay, make sure it gives a **dominant impression.** The dominant impression is the overall feeling that you wish to convey. For example, the essay could convey an impression of tension, joy, nervousness, or anger.

You can place the details of a descriptive essay in space order, time order, or emphatic order. The order that you use depends on the topic of your essay. For example, if you describe a place, you can use space order, and if you describe a difficult moment, you can use time order.

 **Using Figurative Devices**

When writing a descriptive essay, you can use figurative devices such as simile, metaphor, or personification. These devices use comparisons and images to add vivid details to your writing.

- A **simile** is a comparison using *like* or *as*.

   Just imagine me with no flaws
   like a parking lot with no cars . . .   —Mya, "Movin' On"

   My son's constant whining felt like a jackhammer on my skull.

- A **metaphor** is a comparison that does not use *like* or *as*.

   Jealousy . . . is the green-eyed monster . . .   —William Shakespeare, *Othello*

   The mind is a battlefield.

- **Personification** is the act of attributing human qualities to an inanimate object or animal.

   The wind kicked the leaves.   —Kurt Vonnegut, Jr., "Next Door"

   The sauce hissed on the stove.

PRACTICE 5

Practice using figurative language. Use one of the following to describe each item: simile, metaphor, or personification. If you are comparing two things, try to use an unusual comparison.

EXAMPLE:

Surprising: *Her sudden appearance was as surprising as a 4 a.m. phone call.*
(Simile)

1. Truck: _____

2. Road: _____

3. Crowd: _____

4. Annoying: _____

5. Relaxed: _____

A Descriptive Essay Plan

Read the next essay plan, and answer the questions that follow.

Introduction
Thesis statement: Joshua Tree National Park may appear to be a barren desert, but visitors will notice, upon a closer look, an inspiring landscape filled with life.

I.   The park in the desert is famous for its plant life.
   A. Fan palms offer shade in the hot, arid landscape.

     B. The park derives its name from the Joshua trees, which
        have bizarre shapes.
     C. Beautiful but prickly, many species of cacti sprout among
        the jagged rocks.
  II. Abundant wildlife calls the park home.
     A. The bobcat licks its lips as it devours the unlucky
        jackrabbit.
     B. Visitors often hear coyotes howling at night.
     C. Rattlesnakes slither and shake their tails, making the tell-
        tale rattle sound when they are disturbed.
     D. Roadrunners streak across the brown- and rust-colored
        terrain, looking like speeding toy cars.
 III. With a little rain, the desert glows like a rainbow.
     A. Blue and red wildflowers give off a subtle perfume.
     B. The bladderpod shrub shines with yellow flowers.
     C. The Joshua trees' creamy flowers are graceful and elegant.
Conclusion: Visitors will enjoy an abundance of nature at Joshua
Tree National Park.

PRACTICE 6

1. This essay plan contains imagery that appeals to the senses. Find one
   example of imagery for each sense.
   a. Sight: _____
   b. Sound: _____
   c. Smell: _____
   d. Taste: _____
   e. Touch: _____

2. Which type of imagery is most prevalent? _____

3. What is the dominant impression of this essay? Circle the best answer.
     a. Loathing   b. Sadness   c. Awe   d. Boredom

A Descriptive Essay

Read the following essay by Catherine Pigott, a freelance writer. Pay close
attention to the descriptive details.

Chicken Hips

1   The women of the household clucked disapprovingly when they saw me.
It was the first time I had worn African clothes since my arrival in tiny, dusty
Gambia, and evidently they were not impressed. They adjusted my head-tie
and pulled my *lappa*, the ankle-length fabric I had wrapped around myself,
even tighter. "You're too thin," one of them pronounced. "It's no good." They
nicknamed me "Chicken-hips."

2   I marveled at this accolade, for I had never been called thin in my life. It
was something I longed for. I would have been flattered if those ample-
bosomed women hadn't looked so distressed. It was obvious I fell far short of
their ideal of beauty.

3   I had dressed up for a very special occasion—the baptism of a son. The
women heaped rice into tin basins the size of laundry tubs, shaping it into

mounds with their hands. Five of us sat around one basin, thrusting our fingers into the scalding food. These women ate with such relish, such joy. They pressed the rice into balls in their fists, squeezing until the bright-red palm oil ran down their forearms and dripped off their elbows.

4   I tried desperately, but I could not eat enough to please them. It was hard for me to explain that I come from a culture in which it is almost unseemly for a woman to eat too heartily. It's considered unattractive. It was even harder to explain that to me thin is beautiful, and in my country we deny ourselves food in our pursuit of perfect slenderness.

5   That night, everyone danced to welcome the baby. Women swiveled their broad hips and used their hands to emphasize the roundness of their bodies. One needed to be round and wide to make the dance beautiful. There was no place for thinness here. It made people sad. It reminded them of things they wanted to forget, such as poverty, drought, and starvation. They never knew when the rice was going to run out.

6   I began to believe that Africa's image of the perfect female body was far more realistic than the long-legged leanness I had been conditioned to admire. There, it is beautiful—not shameful—to carry weight on the hips and thighs, to have a round stomach and heavy, swinging breasts. Women do not battle the bulge; they celebrate it. A body is not something to be tamed and molded.

7   The friends who had christened me Chicken-hips made it their mission to fatten me up. It wasn't long before a diet of rice and rich, oily stew twice a day began to change me. Every month, the women would take a stick and measure my backside, noting with pleasure its gradual expansion. "Oh Catherine, your buttocks are getting nice now!" they would say.

8   What was extraordinary was that I, too, believed I was becoming more beautiful. There was no sense of panic, no shame, and no guilt-ridden resolves to go on the miracle grape-and-water diet. One day, I tied my *lappa* tight across my hips and went to the market to buy beer for a wedding. I carried the crate of bottles home on my head, swinging my hips slowly as I walked. I felt transformed.

PRACTICE 7

1. In this essay, what is the author describing? _____

   _____

2. Underline at least five descriptive verbs.

3. What is the dominant impression? Circle the best answer.

   a. homesickness   b. tension   c. admiration

4. The writer appeals to more than one sense. Give an example for each type of imagery.

   a. Sight: _____

   _____

   b. Sound: _____

   _____

   c. Touch: _____

   _____

5. How does the writer change physically and emotionally during her time in Africa?

_____

_____

 The Writer's Room

PARAGRAPH LINK

To practice descriptive writing, you could develop an essay about one of the topics in Chapter 6, "Description."

Writing Activity 1: Topics

Write a descriptive essay about one of the following topics.

General Topics

1. a celebration
2. your ideal house
3. a painting or photograph
4. a physical and psychological self-portrait
5. your hometown

College and Work-Related Topics

6. your first impressions of college
7. a sports event
8. your college or workplace cafeteria or food court
9. a memorable person with whom you have worked
10. a pleasant or unpleasant task

Writing Activity 2: Quotations

Read the following quotations. Find one that you agree or disagree with, or find one that inspires you in some way. Then write a descriptive essay based on the quotation.

The real voyage of discovery consists not in seeking new landscapes but in having new eyes.
—Marcel Proust, French author

I base my fashion taste on what doesn't itch.
—Gilda Radner, comedian

There is no love sincerer than the love of food.
—George Bernard Shaw, English playwright

Iron rusts from disuse, and stagnant water loses its purity and in cold weather becomes frozen; even so does inaction sap the vigor of the mind.
—Leonardo Da Vinci, Italian artist and inventor

✔ **DESCRIPTIVE ESSAY CHECKLIST**

As you write your descriptive essay, review the essay checklist on the inside front cover. Also ask yourself the following questions.

☐ Does my thesis statement clearly show what I will describe in the rest of the essay?

☐ Does my thesis statement make a point about the topic?

☐ Does my essay have a dominant impression?

☐ Does each body paragraph contain supporting details that appeal to the reader's senses?

☐ Do I use figurative language (simile, metaphor, or personification)?

PARAGRAPH LINK

For more information about process writing, refer to Chapter 7, "Process."

The Process Essay

A **process** is a series of steps done in chronological order. When you write a process essay, you explain how to do something, how something happens, or how something works. There are two main types of process essays.

1. **Complete a process.** Explain how to complete a particular task. For example, you might explain how to create a sculpture or how to give first aid to a choking victim. Each step you describe helps the reader complete the process.
2. **Understand a process.** Explain how something works or how something happens. In other words, the goal is to help the reader understand a process rather than do a process. For example, you might explain how a law is passed or explain how a previous war began.

The Thesis Statement

The thesis statement in a process essay includes the process you are describing and a controlling idea. In the introduction of a process essay, you should also mention any tools or supplies that the reader would need to complete the process.

topic   controlling idea
Choosing a college requires some careful thinking and planning.

topic   controlling idea
Pregnancy consists of several stages.

 **List Specific Steps**

You can write a thesis statement that contains a map, or guide, to the details that you will present in your essay. To guide your readers, you could mention the main steps in your thesis statement.

topic   controlling idea
It is possible to quit smoking if you focus on your goal, find alternative relaxing activities, and enlist the support of friends and family.

The Supporting Ideas

The body paragraphs in a process essay should explain the steps in the process. Each body paragraph should include details and examples to explain each step.

   **Using Commands**

When writing an essay to help readers complete a process, you can use commands to explain each step in the process. It is not necessary to write *you should*.

command
First, introduce yourself to your roommate.

command
Ask your roommate about his or her pet peeves.

A Process Essay Plan

Read the next essay plan, and answer the questions that follow.

Introduction
Thesis statement: By introducing yourself, joining groups, and organizing events, you will have a better chance of making friends in a new neighborhood.

I.   Introduce yourself to your neighbors.
    A. Find a good moment.
    B. Explain that you are new to the neighborhood.
    C. Ask a few questions about the area.
II. Have an outdoor party, and invite your neighbors.
    A. Find a pretext (holiday, birthday).
    B. Keep the party casual (the point is to have a relaxing time).
    C. Do not worry if some neighbors turn you down.
    D. Aim to find at least one good friend in your area.
III. Get involved in your community.
    A. Volunteer to work at the library.
    B. Become politically active in local elections.
Conclusion: With a bit of effort, you can make friends in any neighborhood.

PRACTICE 8

1. What kind of process essay is this? Circle the best answer.
   a. Complete a process
   b. Understand a process

2. Add another supporting idea to body paragraph 3.

   _____

   _____

3. What organizational method does the writer use? Circle the best answer.
   a. Time   b. Space   c. Emphatic

A Process Essay

In the following essay, Jake Sibley, a musician who maintains an online music site, explains how to become a successful musician. Read the essay and answer the questions.

Steps to Music Success

1   Before you can achieve anything, you must first imagine it. If you are serious about becoming a successful musician, it will serve you well to look not only at the next step, but also to look down the road to where you ultimately want to be. There is no question that regularly revisiting the fundamentals is critical to success in any long-term **endeavor.** With that in mind, there are some basic things to consider while pursuing your musical dreams.

2   First, setting specific goals and giving them regular attention is **vital** to achieving success at any level in the music business. Goals give direction to your action. Furthermore, achieving goals is a tasty reward that will build your esteem and motivate you to reach even higher. So pick your endpoint, and then write down the steps to get there. If you are just beginning in music, then resolve to take lessons. If you are taking lessons, then resolve to get in a performing band. If you are already performing, then resolve to join a paid project. There is no obstacle that can prevent you from reaching your dream. You just have to plan it and then do it.

3   It is also important to spend time, not money, on your dream. Most likely you have seen rookie musicians with stacks of absurdly expensive gear. Certainly I am guilty of walking into a music store and **ogling** the top-end instruments, convinced that if I could afford that equipment, my sound would improve by leaps and bounds: "If I had that guitar, I would practice *every day.*" If you are not practicing every day already, a new guitar won't change that. The only investment that will improve your success as a musician is *time*—time spent practicing, time spent learning, and time spent pursuing your goals. The lure of expensive gear is a tempting but false road to better musicianship.

4   Furthermore, if you really want to improve, play with others. Music is a form of conversation between human beings. It may well be the oldest language, used for millennia by musically inclined people to jointly convey their own rage, sorrow, hope, and joy to other human beings. Learning music without this community is as futile as learning to play football by yourself. Although hours spent alone with your instrument are certainly necessary for success, engaging in musical conversations and performances is an equally vital element to your progress. A very common weakness among amateur musicians is their inability to make music with other artists—a flaw that can be easily remedied with experience. Even if you are a beginner, get out and play with others and stage a few performances if you can. Without even realizing it, you will begin to assimilate fundamental lessons about listening, interacting, and performing in a live setting that are critical to your future success.

5   Finally, practice, practice, practice! There is simply no other way to ensure your own progress as a musician. Have you been spending hours on

---

endeavor:
attempt

vital:
extremely important

ogling:
staring at with desire

the Internet, combing for information on how to market your music, or cheaply record a CD, or win a music competition? That's great, but have you been spending as least as much time alone with your instrument? If not, you should reconsider your priorities. If you are not practicing several times a week at least, the music you market, or record cheaply, or submit to a competition is not going to get very far. As a musician seeking success at any level, practicing your instrument should be your number-one priority.

6   If you're serious about music, keep focused on your goal. Take the time to learn your craft, and share your gift with others. Do not let anyone else hold you back from what you know you can achieve.

PRACTICE 9

1. Underline the thesis statement of the essay.

2. What type of process essay is this? Circle the best answer.
   a. Complete a process
   b. Understand a process

3. In process essays, the support is generally a series of steps. List the steps to music success.

   _____

   _____

   _____

   _____

   _____

4. What organizational method does the author use?
   a. Time order
   b. Emphatic order
   c. Space order

5. Circle the transitional expressions that Sibley uses to introduce each new paragraph.

6. In which paragraph does Sibley use an anecdote to support his point?

   _____

7. Who is the audience for this essay?

   _____

8. How could this essay have relevance for people who never play music?

   _____

   _____

   _____

   _____

PARAGRAPH LINK

To practice process writing, you could develop an essay about one of the topics in Chapter 7, "Process."

The Writer's Room

Writing Activity 1: Topics

Write a process essay about one of the following topics.

General Topics

1. how to be a good person
2. how to kick a bad habit
3. how someone became famous
4. how something works
5. how to deal with a problematic teenager

College and Work-Related Topics

6. how to manage your time
7. how education changed somebody's life
8. how to do your job
9. how to be a better student
10. how to find satisfaction in your work life

Writing Activity 2: Quotations

Read the following quotations. Find one that you agree or disagree with or one that inspires you in some way. Then write a process essay based on the quotation.

> Treat the earth well. It was not given to you by your parents; it was loaned to you by your children.
>
> —Native American proverb

> The first step to getting the things you want out of life is this: Decide what you want.
>
> —Ben Stein, writer

> Every child is an artist. The problem is how to remain an artist once he [or she] grows up.
>
> —Pablo Picasso, Spanish artist

> If you can spend a perfectly useless afternoon in a perfectly useless manner, you have learned how to live.
>
> —Lin Yutang, Chinese author

✔ PROCESS ESSAY CHECKLIST

As you write your process essay, review the essay checklist on the inside front cover. Also ask yourself the following questions.

☐ Does my thesis statement make a point about the process?

☐ Does my essay explain how to do something, how something works, or how something happened?

☐ Do I include all of the steps in the process?

☐ Do I clearly explain the steps in the process or in the event?

☐ Do I mention the tools or equipment that my readers need to complete or understand the process?

The Definition Essay

A definition tells you what something means. When you write a **definition essay,** you give your personal definition of a term or concept. Although you can define most terms in a few sentences, you may need to offer extended definitions for words that are particularly complex. For example, you could write an essay or even an entire book about the term *love*. The way that you interpret love is unique, and you would bring your own opinions, experiences, and impressions to your definition essay.

PARAGRAPH LINK

For more information about definition writing, refer to Chapter 8, "Definition."

The Thesis Statement

In your thesis statement, indicate what you are defining and include a definition of the term. Look at the three ways you might define a term in your thesis statement.

1. **Definition by synonym.** You could give a synonym for the term.

   term   +   synonym

   Some consumers insist that Frankenfood, or genetically modified food, be labeled.

2. **Definition by category.** Decide what larger group the term belongs to, and then determine the unique characteristics that set the term apart from others in that category.

   term   +   category   +   detail

   A groupie is a fanatical devotee of a musician or band.

3. **Definition by negation.** Explain what the term is not, and then explain what it is.

   term   +   what it is not   +   what it is

   Stalkers are not misguided romantics; they are dangerous predators.

The Supporting Ideas

In a definition essay, you can support your main point using a variety of writing patterns. For example, in a definition essay about democracy, one supporting paragraph could give historical background about democracy, another could include a description of a functioning democracy, and a third paragraph could compare different styles of democracy. The different writing patterns would all support the overriding pattern, which is definition.

 **Enhancing a Definition**

One way to enhance a definition essay is to begin with a provocative statement about the term. Then in the body of your essay, develop your definition more thoroughly. This technique arouses the interest of the readers and makes them want to continue reading. For example, the next statement questions a common belief.

According to Dr. W. Roland, attention deficit disorder is an invented disease.

A Definition Essay Plan

Read the next essay plan, and answer the questions that follow.

Introduction

Thesis statement: Depression is not just the blues; it is a serious health problem.

I. A depressed person cannot just "snap out of it."
   A. Depression is not a sign of self-indulgence.
   B. Some people battle the illness for years and need specific treatment.
   C. Offer the example of Katie Rowen, who has been hospitalized several times.
   D. Include quotations from people suffering from depression: William Styron says, "Nightfall seemed more somber"; Mike Wallace calls it "endless darkness."

II. Symptoms are not always obvious and can be overlooked.
   A. People feel excess fatigue and lack of energy.
   B. They may have unexplained bouts of sadness.
   C. Another symptom is extreme irritability for no obvious reason.
   D. Academic and work performance may suffer.

III. Depression affects a person's physical and emotional life.
   A. A person may neglect nutrition, which can lead to excessive weight gain or weight loss.
   B. He or she may neglect appearance and hygiene.
   C. He or she may alienate family and coworkers.
   D. A depressed person may suffer job loss, which can lead to financial consequences.

Conclusion: Depression is a serious illness that affects many people in our society.

PRACTICE 10

1. What type of definition does the writer use in the thesis statement? Circle the best answer.
   a. Definition by synonym
   b. Definition by category
   c. Definition by negation

2. The writer uses many types of supporting details. Underline a quotation, and circle an anecdote.

3. What organizational strategy does the writer use? Circle the best answer.
   a. Time order
   b. Emphatic order
   c. Space order

A Definition Essay

In the next essay, college student Dominic Chartrand defines homophobia. Read the essay and answer the questions.

Homophobia

1   The status of homosexuality has changed with time in various parts of the world. In Greek mythology, Patroclus was Achilles' lover. Alexander the Great was alleged to have homosexual relationships. Central and South American natives were also known to tolerate homosexuality. When Western religions declared homosexuality a sin, a direct consequence of this edict was homophobia. Homophobia is deplorable feelings of hate and fear toward homosexuals, and it rages on under many forms.

2   Homophobia is a problem that affects people's professional lives. First, some people do not want gays or lesbians to occupy certain jobs, such as teaching, because parents are afraid that teachers may "teach" homosexuality to their children. In the movie *Milk*, Harvey Milk's character asks, "How do you teach homosexuality? Like French?" In addition, people of the opposite sex working in gender-dominated professions are constantly assaulted by homophobic comments. Female plumbers, male hairdressers, or male nurses might be labeled gay. Another common case of homophobia is the debate on gays joining the armed forces. The American military promotes the famous policy of *don't ask, don't tell*. Should people's sexual orientation prevent them from fighting for their country? America has many great gay soldiers, but they have to hide their homosexuality for fear of being discharged from the army.

3   Many discriminatory laws have been passed by people who fear homosexuals. According to *Public Agenda*, a nonpartisan research group, in 2009, homosexuality was still a criminal offense in more than eighty countries. In many Muslim countries, such as Saudi Arabia and Yemen, homosexuality is punishable by death. Some other punishment methods include jail and torture. Some countries prohibit homosexuals from marrying or adopting children. For example, most states in our nation prohibit gay marriage.

4   Homophobia is a social factor destroying people's lives. The Gay, Lesbian and Straight Education Network (GLSEN), an American organization fighting for better tolerance toward homosexuality in schools, has made a very interesting survey about homophobia in public education establishments. The statistics indicate that 86 percent of gay public school students hear homophobic remarks from their peers on a daily basis. Imagine being a fifteen-year-old student and being assaulted and insulted every day just for being gay. In today's society, even parents can be homophobic. I can testify that my relationship with my parents will never be what it was before I came out to them. My emotional bond to my mother and father has been damaged. I am lucky though, because I do not need to flee to another country and leave all the people I care about, like many around the world are forced to do.

5   Homophobia is even a mentality present in the homosexual population. The relatively good situation for the lesbian gay bisexual transgender (LGBT) community in some parts of the world has created another problem: some homosexuals no longer seek shelter and friendship with others like them. They prefer disdaining gay groups, clubs, bars, events, movies, and so on. A new kind of gay youth has emerged. The people in this group do not relate to others like them. Their social anti-gay mentality defines this new gay subculture. Homophobia is even transforming homosexuals!

6   In conclusion, homophobia is a problem present in every sphere of people's lives. It affects individuals on a professional, legal, and personal level. Achieving legal recognition does not annihilate homophobia entirely.

Lots of work still needs to be done to eradicate intolerance completely. However, some progress has been made toward acceptance and tolerance in the last forty years, and homosexuals throughout the world have to keep faith in a brighter future.

PRACTICE 11

1. Who is the audience? _____

2. What is the writer's main purpose? _____

3. Underline the thesis statement of the essay.

4. The author defines the term by
   a. synonym   b. category   c. negation

5. Using your own words, list the main supporting ideas in this essay.

   a. _____

   b. _____

   c. _____

   d. _____

6. What type of introduction style does the writer use?
   a. anecdote   b. contrasting position   c. historical background

7. How does the writer conclude the essay?
   a. prediction   b. suggestion   c. quotation

The Writer's Room

PARAGRAPH LINK

To practice definition writing, you could develop an essay about one of the topics found in Chapter 8, "Definition."

Writing Activity 1: Topics

Write a definition essay about one of the following topics.

General Topics

1. propaganda
2. a pacifist
3. street smarts
4. a control freak
5. our disposable culture

College and Work-Related Topics

6. a McJob
7. a perfectionist
8. a whistle-blower
9. a green-collar job
10. downsizing

Writing Activity 2: Quotations

Read the following quotations. Find one that you agree or disagree with, or find one that inspires you in some way, and use it as the basis for a definition essay.

A cult is a religion with no political power.
—Tom Wolfe, American author

Tact is the ability to describe others as they see themselves.
—Abraham Lincoln, former American president

One of the keys to happiness is a bad memory.
—Rita Mae Brown, American activist

Opportunity is missed by most people because it is dressed in overalls and looks like work.
—Thomas A. Edison, American inventor

✔ DEFINITION ESSAY CHECKLIST

As you write your definition essay, review the essay checklist on the inside front cover. Also ask yourself the following questions.

☐ Does my thesis statement explain what term I am defining?

☐ Does each topic sentence clearly show some aspect of the definition?

☐ Do my supporting paragraphs include examples that help illustrate the definition?

☐ Do I use concise language in my definition?

The Classification Essay

Classifying means to sort a subject into more understandable categories. When you are planning a classification essay, find a topic that you can organize into categories. Each category must be part of a larger group, yet it must also be distinct. For example, if your essay is about types of lawyers, you might sort lawyers into criminal lawyers, divorce lawyers, and corporate lawyers.

PARAGRAPH LINK

For more information about classification writing, refer to Chapter 9, "Classification."

The Thesis Statement

The thesis statement in a classification essay mentions the categories of the subject and contains a controlling idea. In this type of essay, the controlling idea is your classification principle, which is the overall method that you use to sort the items. For example, if your essay topic is "crime," you might sort crime according to types of criminals, categories of violent crimes, or categories of bank-machine crimes.

controlling idea (classification principle)   topic   categories

There are three very effective types of **bank-machine crimes**: no-tech, low-tech, and high-tech.

Hint   **List Specific Categories**

You can guide your reader by listing the specific categories you will cover in your thesis statement.

topic   controlling idea
Children learn gender roles through the family, the school, and the media.

The Supporting Ideas

In a classification essay, each body paragraph covers one category. To organize your categories and supporting details, you can use a classification chart or a more traditional classification essay plan.

A Classification Chart

A classification chart helps you plan your ideas by providing a visual representation of how you wish to classify a subject. In this sample chart, the thesis statement appears at the top, and all of the categories branch from it.

Historically, three types of heterosexual marital unions have been practiced around the world.

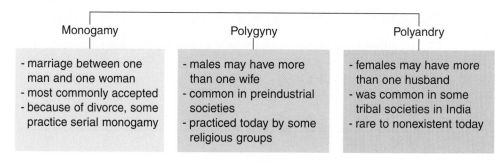

Monogamy	Polygyny	Polyandry
- marriage between one man and one woman - most commonly accepted - because of divorce, some practice serial monogamy	- males may have more than one wife - common in preindustrial societies - practiced today by some religious groups	- females may have more than one husband - was common in some tribal societies in India - rare to nonexistent today

A Classification Essay Plan

A classification essay plan also helps you organize your essay's categories and details. Read the following essay plan and answer the questions.

Introduction

Thesis statement: There are three main types of bad jokes: overused children's jokes, practical jokes, and insulting jokes.

I. Overused children's jokes bore the listener.
    A. Knock-knock jokes are dull.
    B. The "what is it" jokes are overused.
    C. Nobody likes "why did the chicken cross the road" jokes.
    D. Silly riddles are boring.

II. Practical jokes humiliate the victims.
    A. Whoopee cushions can embarrass people.
    B. The plastic wrap on the toilet seat leads to a humiliating mess.
    C. The "paint can over the door" trick can hurt others.
    D. The "kick me" note on a person's back is not funny.

III. Insulting jokes can seriously hurt or offend others.
  A. Jokes about ethnic groups or religious groups can be awful.
  B. Cruel jokes about a person's appearance (big nose jokes, blonde jokes) can be hurtful.
  C. Jokes about a profession (lawyer jokes) can insult professionals.
Conclusion: Let's hope that people come up with better jokes.

PRACTICE 12

1. What is the classification principle? That is, what main principle unifies the three categories?

   _____

2. Why is each type of joke considered bad? Underline the reason in each topic sentence.

3. The author organizes the main ideas in emphatic order. How are they arranged? Circle the best answer.
   a. From most to least offensive
   b. From least to most offensive

4. How does the writer support the main ideas? Circle the best answer.
   a. Examples   b. Anecdotes   c. Statistics

A Classification Essay

This essay first appeared in *Introduction to Animal Science* by W. Stephen Damron. Read the essay and answer the questions that follow.

The Purpose of Pets

1   Pet species provide many practical services to society, and it is clear that some animals are companion animals. Their greatest value is defined by their relationships with the people who share their lives. Once a source of derision, the human–companion animal bond is now recognized for its value as a contributing factor in the physical, mental, emotional, and social health of the owner. However, not all domestic animals qualify as companions. For instance, there are many barn cats across the country whose job in life is just to keep the rats and mice at bay. In fact, many people purchase an animal for the following motives: the animal is ornamental, a status symbol, or a plaything.

Ornamental Pets

2   Ornamental pets serve the same purpose that houseplants serve—they decorate and enhance the atmosphere. Ornamental pets are usually brightly colored birds or fish or some type of animal that adds aesthetic appeal to an environment. It is common to find an aquarium filled with brightly colored or interesting aquatic species in restaurants, professional offices, or homes. Decorators have been known to bring fabric swatches to pet stores in order to pick a bird that matches carpet and draperies. Outdoor environments are often graced by flashy species such as peacocks, pheasants, Sumatra chickens, swans, geese, and ducks. Rarely are these ornamental pets handled, named, or treated in any special way. They are not considered companion animals.

Status Symbols

3   There is strong evidence that at least part of the domestication of the wolf was linked to the status its presence in camp gave the human occupants. A wolf as totem and companion would have conveyed a powerful message to rival clans or tribes. Sometimes we succumb to this same symbolism in modern life. This explains the motives of some people who keep poisonous snakes, piranhas, vicious dogs, big cats, bears, or wolves as pets. The animals are usually admired and well cared for as long as they satisfy the owner's expectations. In a more benign example, the symbolism of animals as totems for ancient people is not so different from that conveyed in modern society by what we generally refer to as "mascots." Status can also be conveyed by a pet kept for another primary reason. Purebred animals generally convey more status than mixed breed animals. Sometimes unusual, rare, and expensive animals are status symbols.

Playthings

4   Pets as playthings may range from living toys given to children, before they are old enough to appreciate the responsibilities, to animals used in sporting events such as hunting or riding. Children are often given a pet as a plaything before they are capable of appreciating it. Some of the people involved in sports and who use animals are only interested in the animal during the competitive season and lose interest and enthusiasm rather quickly at the close of the season. Often, these animals are poorly treated and may be discarded or destroyed by their owners when the animals lose their amusement value.

5   It is clear that some animals are companion animals. Their greatest value is defined by their relationships with the people who share their lives. The Council for Science and Society states, "An animal employed for decoration, status-signaling, recreation, or hobby is being used primarily as an object—the animal equivalent of a work of art, a Rolls Royce, a surfboard, or a collector's item. The companion animal, however, is typically perceived and treated as a subject—as a personality in its own right, irrespective of other considerations. With companion animals it is the relationship itself which is important to the owner."

PRACTICE 13

1. What is the essay's classification principle? _____

   _____

2. What are the three main categories? _____

   _____

3. Underline the topic sentences in body paragraphs 3, 4, and 5.

4. Provide some details about each type of pet. Use your own words.

   Ornamental Pets:

   _____

   _____

   Status Symbols:

   _____

   _____

Playthings:

_____

_____

5. To better understand how the author organizes this essay, make a classification chart. Write the categories on the lines and examples in the boxes. Use your own words to explain each category.

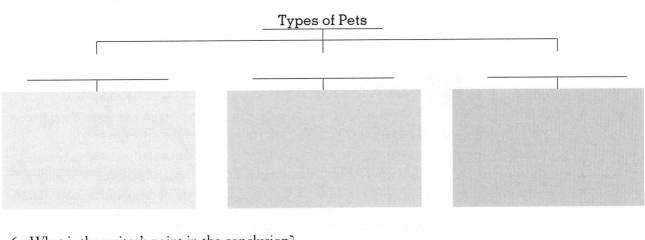

Types of Pets

6. What is the writer's point in the conclusion? _____

_____

_____

The Writer's Room

Writing Activity 1: Topics

Write a classification essay about one of the following topics.

General Topics

1. addictions
2. marriage ceremonies
3. extreme sports
4. things that cause allergic reactions
5. youth subcultures

College and Work-Related Topics

6. annoying customers or clients
7. punishment
8. competition
9. success
10. fashions in the workplace

PARAGRAPH LINK

To practice classification writing, you could develop an essay about one of the topics found in Chapter 9, "Classification."

Writing Activity 2: Quotations

Read the following quotations. Find one that you agree or disagree with, or find one that inspires you in some way. Then write a classification essay based on the quotation.

> Work saves us from three great evils: boredom, vice, and need.
> —Voltaire, French author and philosopher

> There are three kinds of lies: lies, damned lies, and statistics.
>
> —Benjamin Disraeli, former British prime minister

> There appear to be three types of politicians: leaders, lobbyists, and professionals.
>
> —R. Ravimohan, Indian journalist

> Never bear more than one trouble at a time. Some people bear three kinds—all they have had, all they have now, and all they expect to have.
>
> —Edward Everett Hale, American author and clergyman

✓ CLASSIFICATION ESSAY CHECKLIST

As you write your classification essay, review the essay checklist on the inside front cover. Also ask yourself the following questions.

☐ Do I clearly identify which categories I will discuss in my thesis statement?

☐ Do I use a common classification principle to unite the various items?

☐ Do I include categories that do not overlap?

☐ Do I clearly explain one of the categories in each body paragraph?

☐ Do I use sufficient details to explain each category?

☐ Do I arrange the categories in a logical manner?

PARAGRAPH LINK

For more information about this pattern, refer to Chapter 10, "Comparison and Contrast."

The Comparison and Contrast Essay

You **compare** when you want to find similarities and **contrast** when you want to find differences. When writing a comparison and contrast essay, you explain how people, places, things, or ideas are the same or different to prove a specific point.

Before you write, you must make a decision about whether you will focus on similarities, differences, or both. As you explore your topic, make a list of both similarities and differences. Later, you can use some of the ideas in your essay plan.

The Thesis Statement

The thesis statement in a comparison and contrast essay indicates if you are making comparisons, contrasts, or both. When you write a thesis statement, specify what you are comparing or contrasting and the controlling idea.

Although neat people have a very nice environment, messy people are more relaxed.

Topics being contrasted: Neat people and messy people

Controlling idea: Messy people are more relaxed.

Alice's daughter wants to be her own person, but she is basically very similar to her mother.

Topics being compared: Mother and daughter

Controlling idea: Very similar personalities

The Supporting Ideas

In a comparison and contrast essay, you can develop your body paragraphs in two different ways.

1. In a **point-by-point** development, you present *one* point about Topic A and then *one* point about Topic B. You keep following this pattern until you have a few points for each topic.

   Paragraph 1: Topic A, Topic B

   Paragraph 2: Topic A, Topic B

   Paragraph 3: Topic A, Topic B

2. In a **topic-by-topic** development, you discuss one topic in detail, and then you discuss the other topic in detail.

   Paragraphs 1 and 2: All of Topic A

   Paragraphs 3 and 4: All of Topic B

A Comparison and Contrast Essay Plan

Read the next essay plan, and answer the questions that follow.

Introduction

Thesis statement: Soccer is a more exciting, active, and popular sport than baseball.

I. Soccer is fast-paced and thrilling to watch, whereas baseball is boring.
  A. In soccer, fans watch the ball as it gets kicked constantly around the field.
  B. In soccer, there are very few quiet moments; the game has constant action.
  C. In baseball, spectators get bored while watching the pitcher think, consider, and eventually pitch.
  D. Baseball games have very few seconds of excitement because home runs are so rare.
II. Those who play soccer get more exercise than those who play baseball.
  A. During soccer games, players constantly run to cover the opposing player.
  B. After games, soccer players are drenched with sweat.
  C. Baseball players generally stand on bases or in the outfield simply waiting for action.
  D. When baseball players are at bat, they spend most of their time waiting for their turn.
III. The World Cup is more popular than the World Series.
  A. Soccer is the number one sport in South America, Africa, Asia, and Europe.
  B. According to FIFA World Cup organizers, about 26 billion spectators watched the 2010 chamionships.
  C. Baseball is mainly popular in North America and Japan.

D. Only 50 million people watched baseball's World Series in 2009.

Conclusion: Learn about soccer because it is a fantastic sport.

PRACTICE 14

1. The writer compares and contrasts two things in this essay plan. What are they?

   _____

2. Look at the thesis statement. What is the controlling idea?

   _____

3. What will this essay focus on? Circle the best answer.
   a. Similarities   b. Differences

4. What pattern of comparison does the writer use in this essay? Circle the best answer.
   a. Point by point   b. Topic by topic

A Comparison and Contrast Essay

In the next essay, college student Adrianna Gonzalez compares two jobs. Read the essay, and answer the questions that follow.

Two Jobs

1   "I can't believe it's Monday," you say waking up to the alarm clock. It is another Monday morning! The average nine-to-five job may seem like a drag if the person is not fond of the job. Yet there have been instances where one job was better than the other one. My current job as a caregiver is much more fulfilling than my previous job was.

2   My first job was as a receptionist at a church. Although it may sound like an easy job, it wasn't. My tasks were similar to the average receptionist's: take calls, make appointments, and greet visitors. Yet the job was not active. I was the only one present during my shift. I would usually catch the priest every now and then. But my whole shift was quiet, and although you might think "What a peaceful job," it became boring to me. Every day I would just think, "Oh great, another lonely day for me at the office. What will I occupy myself with this time?" Unlike that job, the job I now have is as a caregiver. It is filled with lots of people and diversity. I show up for work eager to pick up the infants I care for. The time passes by so quickly, and all my co-workers are friendly people. I like being active at my job.

3   Furthermore, in my old job, the boss was not organized, and he did not care for the workplace. He did not try to improve or resolve problems that arose. For example, I was alone in the office when two visitors came in for their appointments, and the priest was not there. During such instances, I would have to try to come up with a plausible excuse for why the priest would be thirty minutes late. The priest frequently did not keep the appointments and did not provide me with information to give visitors regarding the cancellations of the meetings. Now in my new job, I am constantly informed of what is happening; memos are sent and meetings take place almost every week. The director and manager want to make the environment as welcoming as possible. Organization is a priority at my new workplace. I now realize that

if there had been just a little bit of organization at my old job, it would have made a big difference.

4   A major reason people hate their jobs is the pay. In my receptionist job, I would try to get as many hours as I could, but it was hopeless. The boss did not allow overtime and did not even want to talk about extra work shifts. I got paid minimum wage. At first this did not bother me because I was young and had never had a previous job, so anything was a lot to me. Because I had so many problems and because I was sick of trying to resolve them for the measly check I received every two weeks, I was angry all the time. With my present job, I did not start at minimum wage and was told that the pay would increase every year. I can get as many as eleven hours in one day; I do that gladly every time it's possible. When I received my check for the first time, I quickly found out that one check at my new job made up for two, maybe even three, at my old job.

5   It is easy to hate a job that is boring and low paying, and it is difficult to deal with a disorganized boss. In such cases, consider looking for a better job. I am happy that I made a change because working as a caregiver is one job that I really enjoy doing.

PRACTICE 15

1. What type of introduction does the writer use?
   a. Opposing position
   b. Definition
   c. General information

2. Underline the thesis statement.

3. What does this essay focus on?
   a. Similarities
   b. Differences

4. What pattern of comparison does the write follow in her essay?
   a. Point by point
   b. Topic by topic

5. Using your own words, list the main points the writer compares in her two jobs.
   a. _____
      _____
   b. _____
      _____
   c. _____
      _____

PARAGRAPH LINK

To practice comparison and contrast writing, you could develop an essay about one of the topics found in Chapter 10, "Comparison and Contrast."

The Writer's Room

Writing Activity 1: Topics

Write a comparison and contrast essay about one of the following topics.

General Topics

Compare and/or contrast . . .

1. expectations about parenthood versus the reality of parenthood
2. two different interpretations of an event
3. living together and getting married
4. male versus female consumers
5. peer pressure versus parental pressure

College and Work-Related Topics

Compare and/or contrast . . .

6. male and female college athletes
7. a good manager and a bad manager
8. a stay-at-home parent and an employed parent
9. student life and professional life
10. expectations about a job and the reality of that job

Writing Activity 2: Quotations

Read the following quotations. Find one that you agree or disagree with, or find one that sparks your imagination. Then write a comparison and contrast essay based on the quotation.

> My grandfather once told me that there are two kinds of people: those who work and those who take the credit. He told me to try to be in the first group; there was less competition there.
>
> —Indira Gandhi, former Indian prime minister

> It seemed the world was divided into good and bad people. The good ones slept better while the bad ones seemed to enjoy the waking hours much more.
>
> —Woody Allen, filmmaker

> Happy families are all alike. Every unhappy family is unhappy in its own way.
>
> —Leo Tolstoy, Russian author

> Imagination is more important than knowledge.
>
> —Albert Einstein, physicist

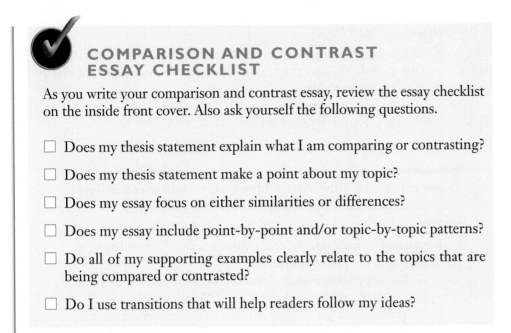

COMPARISON AND CONTRAST ESSAY CHECKLIST

As you write your comparison and contrast essay, review the essay checklist on the inside front cover. Also ask yourself the following questions.

☐ Does my thesis statement explain what I am comparing or contrasting?

☐ Does my thesis statement make a point about my topic?

☐ Does my essay focus on either similarities or differences?

☐ Does my essay include point-by-point and/or topic-by-topic patterns?

☐ Do all of my supporting examples clearly relate to the topics that are being compared or contrasted?

☐ Do I use transitions that will help readers follow my ideas?

The Cause and Effect Essay

When writing a cause and effect essay, you explain why an event happened or what the consequences of such an event were.

PARAGRAPH LINK

For more information about this pattern, refer to Chapter 11, "Cause and Effect."

The Thesis Statement

The thesis statement in a cause and effect essay contains the topic and the controlling idea. The controlling idea indicates whether the essay will focus on causes, effects, or both.

topic   controlling idea (causes)

Chronic insomnia is <u>caused by many factors.</u>

topic   controlling idea (effects)

Chronic insomnia can have <u>a serious impact on a person's health.</u>

topic   controlling idea (causes and effects)

Chronic insomnia, which is <u>caused by many factors,</u> can have <u>a serious impact on a person's health.</u>

 **Thinking About Effects**

If you are writing about the effects of something, you might think about both the short-term and long-term effects. By doing so, you will generate more ideas for the body of your essay. You will also be able to structure your essay more effectively by moving from short-term to long-term effects.

For example, look at the short- and long-term effects of a smoke-free work zone.

Short term: Inside air is cleaner.
                    The smokers get more coffee breaks.

Long term: Fewer smoke-related illnesses occur in nonsmokers.
                    Some smokers might quit smoking.

The Supporting Ideas

The body paragraphs in a cause and effect essay focus on causes, effects, or both. Make sure that each body paragraph contains specific examples that clarify the cause and/or effect relationship.

A Cause and Effect Essay Plan

Read the next essay plan, and answer the questions that follow.

Introduction
Thesis statement: Although the hippie movement was a cultural phenomenon of the 1960s, it has had a lasting impact on contemporary society.

I. In general, Americans' liberal attitude toward sexuality is a legacy of the hippie generation.
    A. The hippies advocated the sexual revolution.
    B. The 1960s welcomed the idea of "free love."
    C. Today, Western society is tolerant of unmarried couples living together.
    D. Rights of homosexuals are openly discussed in the public forum.

II. What used to be peripheral business practices in the 1960s are now mainstream.
    A. Some businesses are profitable cooperatives.
    B. Many food companies offer organic products.
    C. Health foods have become an accepted part of American eating habits.

III. Acceptance of religious and cultural diversity is commonplace.
    A. Vegetarianism is no longer considered strange, and restaurants offer vegetarian-friendly menus.
    B. New Age religion started as a fringe movement in the 1960s, but now enjoys credibility in popular culture.
    C. Social activism has its origins in the 1960s and continues today.

Conclusion: "Old hippies don't die; they just lie low until the laughter stops and their time comes around again." (Joseph Gallivan)

PRACTICE 16

1. In the thesis statement, circle the topic and underline the controlling idea.

2. Does this essay focus on causes or effects? _____

3. Who is the audience for this essay? _____

A Cause and Effect Essay

Read the next essay by student writer Jim Baek, and then answer the questions that follow.

Why Small Businesses Fail

1   Last spring, Pablo Ortiz rented a tiny pizzeria in his neighborhood to turn it into a taco restaurant. Full of enthusiasm, he bought supplies, paid for advertisements, and posted a large menu in the window of his new venture,

called Taco Heaven. Ten months later, Taco Heaven closed, and Ortiz declared bankruptcy. He was not alone. The Small Business Administration Office reports that close to half of all new businesses fail within the first five years. Causes of small business failures are numerous.

2   First, inexperienced business owners often neglect to do market research to find out if community members are interested in the product. In Ortiz's case, he thought that area residents would appreciate the chance to buy hearty chicken or pork tacos. However, there were three other Mexican fast-food restaurants in the area, so Ortiz's competitors took most of the business.

3   Second, inadequate pricing can hurt new businesses. Maggie Stevens, owner of a successful restaurant in Los Angeles, sells stuffed Belgian waffles to an eager clientele. Before pricing her waffles, she calculated the exact cost of each plate, right down to the strawberry that adorned the waffle and the touch of cream next to it. She also considered other costs beyond that of the ingredients, including the cost of labor and food spoilage. Her final price for each dish was 60 percent higher than her base cost. Ortiz, on the other hand, had absolutely no idea what he really spent to make each taco. He ended up underpricing his product and losing money.

4   Additionally, many small business owners have insufficient funds to run their ventures successfully. According to the accountant Louis Polk, most small businesses operate for four years before they break even, let alone actually make money. Therefore, owners need a cash reserve to get through the first slow years. Ortiz, expecting to make a decent profit right away, did not realize that he would have to use up his savings to keep his business afloat.

5   Finally, inexperienced merchants may underestimate the sheer volume of work involved in running a business. Ortiz admits he was very naive about the workload. Taco Heaven had to be open 15 hours a day, 7 days a week. Ortiz also had to shop for ingredients and do the accounting. After months of grueling work and little to no pay, he burned out.

6   People who plan to open small businesses should become informed, especially about potential pitfalls. Inexperience, lack of proper planning, and insufficient funds can combine to create a business failure.

PRACTICE 17

1. Underline the thesis statement of the essay.

2. Does this essay focus on causes, effects, or both? _____

3. Underline a statistic and an anecdote.

4. Using your own words, list the four supporting points.

   _____

   _____

   _____

   _____

PARAGRAPH LINK

To practice cause and effect writing, you could develop an essay about one of the topics found in Chapter 11, "Cause and Effect."

The Writer's Room

Writing Activity 1: Topics

Write a cause and effect essay about one of the following topics.

General Topics

Causes and/or effects of . . .

1. a new law or policy
2. rejecting or adopting a religion
3. patriotism
4. peer pressure
5. leaving your home or homeland

College and Work-Related Topics

Causes and/or effects of . . .

6. being a parent and college student
7. taking time off before college
8. having an office romance
9. gossiping in the office
10. changing jobs or career paths

Writing Activity 2: Quotations

Read the following quotations. Find one that you agree or disagree with or one that inspires you in some way, and use it as the basis for a cause and effect essay.

> Fire and swords are slow engines of destruction, compared to the tongue of a gossip.
>
> —Richard Steele, essayist

> Sometimes when we are generous in barely detectible ways, it can change someone else's life forever.
>
> —Margaret Cho, American comedian

> All human actions have one or more of these seven causes: chance, nature, compulsion, habit, reason, passion, and desire.
>
> —Aristotle, ancient Greek philosopher

> One of the symptoms of an approaching nervous breakdown is the belief that one's work is terribly important.
>
> —Bertrand Russell, British author and philosopher

✔ CAUSE AND EFFECT ESSAY CHECKLIST

As you write your cause and effect essay, review the essay checklist on the inside front cover. Also ask yourself the following questions.

☐ Does my essay clearly focus on causes, effects, or both?

☐ Do I have adequate supporting examples of causes and/or effects?

☐ Do I avoid using faulty logic (a mere asumption that one event causes another or is the result of another)?

☐ Do I use the terms *effect* and *affect* correctly?

The Argument Essay

When you write an **argument essay,** you take a position on an issue, and you try to defend your position. In other words, you try to persuade your readers to accept your point of view.

PARAGRAPH LINK

For more information about argument writing, refer to Chapter 12, "Argument."

The Thesis Statement

The thesis statement in an argument essay mentions the subject and a debatable point of view about the subject. Do not include phrases such as *in my opinion, I think,* or *I am going to talk about* in your thesis statement.

topic   controlling idea

Building a wall on the Mexican border **is an ineffective way to deal with illegal immigration.**

 List Specific Arguments

Your thesis statement can further guide your readers by listing the specific arguments you will make in your essay.

controlling idea   topic   (arguments)
Colleges should implement **work-study programs** to help students acquire

I   2   3

job skills, make professional contacts, and earn money for expenses.

The Supporting Ideas

In the body of your essay, give convincing arguments. Try to use several types of supporting evidence.

PARAGRAPH LINK

For more detailed information about types of evidence, see page 163 in Chapter 12, "Argument."

- **Include anecdotes.** Specific experiences or pieces of information can support your point of view.
- **Add facts.** Facts are statements that can be verified in some way. **Statistics** are a type of fact. When you use a fact, make sure that your source is reliable.
- **Use informed opinions.** Opinions from experts in the field can give weight to your argument.
- **Think about logical consequences.** Consider long-term consequences if something does or does not happen.
- **Answer the opposition.** Think about your opponents' arguments, and provide responses to their arguments.

 Quoting a Respected Source

RESEARCH LINK

For more information about doing research, see Chapter 15, "Enhancing Your Writing with Research."

One way to enhance your essay is to include a quotation from a respected source. Find a quotation from somebody in a field that is directly related to your topic. When you include the quotation as supporting evidence, remember to mention the source.

According to Dr. Tom Houston, co-director of the American Medical Association's SmokeLess States campaign, secondhand smoke "can lead to serious health consequences, ranging from ear infections and pneumonia to asthma."

An Argument Essay Plan

Read the next essay plan, and answer the questions that follow.

Introduction

Thesis statement: Many news-media outlets have lost their reputations as respectable sources of critical news.

I. Reporters lack sensitivity and chase tragic or sensational stories of ordinary people.
    A. Child molestations and tragic accidents figure predominantly in the media.
    B. Reporters hounded the Octomom, the woman who gave birth to octuplets.
    C. Reporters focused on the weeping women belonging to a Texas polygamist cult as authorities took their children away.

II. Television and newspapers often report celebrity scandals to increase their audience.
    A. Around 40 percent of news coverage is about celebrity gossip.
    B. The media gave lurid details when Michael Jackson was accused of pedophilia.
    C. According to Dr. Amin Ghosh, from 2004 to 2009, the major news networks predominantly featured stories of Jackson's court case and ignored the entertainer's other achievements.
    D. Media generates public voyeurism by sensationalizing the deaths of celebrities like Michael Jackson or Anna Nicole Smith.

III. Many media outlets pay individuals to acquire melodramatic stories.
    A. Papparazzi are often offered thousands of dollars to take embarrassing photos of celebrities.
    B. Beyoncé Knowles was offered a lot of money for her wedding photos.
    C. According to *Jossip.com*, NBC paid Nadya Suleman, the Ocotomom, $300,000 for an interview.
    D. Tell anecdote about a major newsmagazine that offered wrongly accused murderer, Chris McEccles, money for an interview about his experience.

Conclusion: Because media outlets focus on sensational stories to increase audience membership, they no longer have outstanding reputations for exposing newsworthy stories.

PRACTICE 18

1. Circle the topic and underline the controlling idea in the thesis statement.

2. The author uses many types of supporting material. Do the following:
    a. underline three anecdotes
    b. circle two informed opinions.

3. Write a few sentences that could appear in the introduction before the thesis statement. (For ideas about how to write an introduction, look in Chapter 13, "Writing the Essay.")

_____

_____

_____

An Argument Essay

The next essay was written by college student Christine Bigras.

The Importance of Music

1   Most parents want their children to receive a well-rounded education. Students study traditional subjects, such as math, science, English, history, geography, and physical education, but many educators and parents have come to believe that school children should also be taught fine arts subjects. Thus, often school boards offer art, dance, and music, if not as core courses, then at least as extracurricular activities. Although the study and practice of all these arts develop sensitivity and creativity in students, learning music is the most beneficial to all-around student success.

2   First, music makes a child smarter. Everybody has already heard about scientists or doctors who are also musicians. A child who studies music may not become a genius; nevertheless, several research findings have shown that music lessons can enhance IQ and develop intelligence. One of the most recent and conclusive studies, "Music Lessons Enhance IQ," was conducted by E. Glenn Schellenberg from the University of Toronto and was published by _American Psychological Society Magazine_ in 2004. This work concluded that there was a link in children between the study of music and academic success because music and schoolwork may develop similar problem-solving skills in children.

3   Furthermore, music education improves a child's physical and psychological health. Playing music is excellent exercise for the heart, especially for those who play a wind instrument. A child will also learn to stand straight and adopt good posture. Playing music also decreases stress and anxiety. Through music, the apprentices will learn concentration and listening skills. Furthermore, high school students who participate in band or orchestra are less interested in the use of all illegal substances (alcohol, tobacco, and drugs) according to the Texas Commission on Drug and Alcohol Abuse Report. The National Data Resource Center states that about 12 percent of students are labeled "disruptive" whereas only 8 percent of students in music programs have that label.

4   Finally, music education helps a child's social development. Playing music may help students connect with one another, particularly through participation in orchestra or a choir. No matter if a child is ugly, poor, big, or shy, he or she is as important as any other musician in the group. Music is the great equalizer. Therefore, musicians learn how to respect each other, how to cooperate, and how to build constructive relationships with others. When Yoko Kiyuka entered my former high school, she was very shy and lonely. The music program changed her life. The connections she made helped her become integrated into the school and feel valued. "Music has the power to unite us. It

proves that by working together, we can create something truly beautiful," said Pinchas Zukerman, Music Director of the National Arts Centre of Canada. Therefore, music may help a child to become a better citizen, another outstanding reason to encourage children to learn music.

5   Many school boards are removing music education from the curriculum. They argue that music is not a necessary or useful course. However, the benefits conveyed by music education are tremendous. By developing a child's brain, body, and feelings, music gives the child a better chance to be confident in life. Parents of elementary or secondary school children can play an active role in the success of their children by encouraging them to learn music. Music can make the difference in a child's life.

PRACTICE 19

1. Underline the thesis statement of the essay.

2. What introductory style opens this essay? Circle the best answer.
   a. Definition   b. Historical information
   c. General information   d. Opposing viewpoint

3. Underline the topic sentence in each body paragraph.

4. In which paragraph does the author address the opposition? _____

5. Find an example in the essay for each of the following types of evidence.
   a. Statistic: _____
      _____
   b. Anecdote: _____
      _____
   c. Quotation from informed source: _____
      _____

6. With what does the writer conclude her essay? Circle the best answer.
   a. Prediction   b. Quotation   c. Suggestion

 The Writer's Room

Writing Activity 1: Topics

Write an argument essay about one of the following topics. Remember to narrow your topic and follow the writing process.

General Topics

1. state-sponsored gambling
2. beauty contests
3. talk shows
4. driving laws
5. the healthcare system

College and Work-Related Topics

6. outsourcing of jobs
7. great reasons to choose your college
8. the cost of a university education
9. student activism
10. dress codes at work

PARAGRAPH LINK

To practice argument writing, you could develop an essay about one of the topics found in Chapter 12, "Argument."

Writing Activity 2: Quotations

Read the following quotations. Find one that you agree or disagree with or one that inspires you in some way, and use it as the basis for an argument essay.

> Advertising is legalized lying.
>
> —H. G. Wells, British author

> Blind belief is dangerous.
>
> —Kenyan proverb

> The thing that impresses me the most about America is the way that parents obey their children.
>
> —King Edward VIII, British monarch

> Choice has always been a privilege of those who could afford to pay for it.
>
> —Ellen Frankfort, American journalist

✔ ARGUMENT ESSAY CHECKLIST

As you write your argument essay, review the essay checklist on the inside front cover. Also ask yourself the following questions.

☐ Does my thesis statement clearly state my position on the issue?

☐ Do I include facts, examples, statistics, logical consequences, or answers to my opponents in my body paragraphs?

☐ Do my supporting arguments provide evidence that directly supports each topic sentence?

☐ Do I use transitions that will help readers follow my ideas?

mywritinglab To check your progress in meeting this chapter's objectives, log in to **www.mywritinglab.com**, go to the **Study Plan** tab, click on **The Essay** and choose **Essay Development – Illustrating, Essay Development – Narrating, Essay Development – Describing, Essay Development – Process, Essay Development – Definition, Essay Development – Division / Classification, Essay Development – Comparing and Contrasting, Essay Development – Cause and Effect, and Essay Development – Argument** from the list of subtopics. Read and view the resources in the **Review Materials** section, and then complete the **Recall, Apply,** and **Write** sets in the **Activities** section.

CHAPTER 15

Enhancing Your Writing with Research

When you want more information about something, you might talk to other people, look for resources in libraries, bookstores, and museums, make phone calls, search the Internet, and so on. You can use the same tools when looking for details to include in your writing.

> *Research is formalized curiosity. It is poking and prying with a purpose.*
> —Zora Neale Hurston
> *American playwright and author (1891–1960)*

What Is Research?

When you **research,** you look for information that will help you better understand a subject. For example, when you plan to see a movie and read movie reviews in the newspaper, you are engaging in research to make an informed decision. At college, you are often asked to quote outside sources in your essays. This chapter gives you some strategies for researching information and effectively adding it to your writing.

Research for Academic Writing

There is a formal type of writing called the research paper. However, many types of academic essays, especially those with the purpose of persuading, can benefit from research. Additional facts, quotations, and statistics can back up your arguments.

Student writer David Raby-Pepin prepared an argument for an essay about rap music. You may have read his essay in Chapter 13. His purpose was to persuade the reader that rap musicians share positive cultural values. The following paragraph is from his essay.

David's Paragraph Without Research

> Many of these musicians shout out a powerful message of nonviolence. Leading hip-hop and rap artists have broken from the gangsta rap lyrics of the past. Instead, they write lyrics that present a productive way to resolve conflicts. They encourage listeners to respect themselves and others.

David's paragraph, although interesting, is not entirely convincing. He mentions that rappers encourage listeners to respect others, but he doesn't give any examples. David decided to do some research to support his points with specific details. He found many Internet sites about his topic that are run by hip-hop fans, but he worried that his readers might be skeptical if he used those sources. He kept searching and found two quotations from reputable sources.

David's Paragraph with Research

> Many of these musicians shout out a powerful message of nonviolence. Leading hip-hop and rap artists have broken from the "gangsta rap" lyrics of the past. Instead, they write lyrics that present a productive way to resolve conflicts. They encourage listeners to respect themselves and others. For instance, the Boston rap group 4Peace has the mission "to sell peace as aggressively as other rappers peddle sex and violence" (Kahn). At a concert in Connecticut, rapper Edo. G said, "You need to respect your parents, respect your teachers, and respect the police. You need to respect yourselves and stop the violence" (qtd. in Macmillan).

David added two quotations from respected publications. He included the authors' last names in parentheses. Because the publications were on Web sites, he did not include page numbers in the parentheses.

Later, at the end of his essay, David also included a "Works Cited" page with the following information. (You will learn more about the Works Cited page later in this chapter.)

Works Cited

Kahn, Joseph P. "The Message." *Boston Globe*. Globe Newspaper
   Company, 10 Oct. 2006. Web. 22 Feb. 2010.
Macmillan, Thomas. "Through Hip Hop, Nonviolence Resonates." *New
   Haven Independent*. New Haven Independent, 7 May 2009. Web. 21
   Feb. 2010.

Gather Information

To find information that will bolster your essay, consult sources in the library or on the Internet.

Using the Library

When you first enter a library, ask the reference librarian to help you locate information using various research tools, such as online catalogs, CD-ROMs, and microforms.

- **Search the library's online catalog.** You can search by keyword, author, title, or subject. When you find a listing that interests you, remember to jot down the title, author, and call number. You will need that information when you search the library shelves.
- **Use online periodical services in libraries.** Your library may have access to *EBSCOhost*® or *INFOtrac*. By typing keywords into EBSCO*host*®, you can search through national or international newspapers, magazines, and reference books. When you find an article that you need, e-mail the link to yourself or paste the document into a word file. Remember to print or copy the publication data because you will need that information when you cite your source.

Using the Internet

The Internet is a valuable research tool. You will be able to find information about almost any topic online. Here are some tips to help you with your online research.

- **Use efficient search engines** such as *Google, Yahoo!*, or *Ixquick*. Those sites can rapidly retrieve thousands of documents from the Internet.
- **Choose your keywords with care.** Narrow your search by putting in very specific keywords. For example, to bolster an essay about binge drinking, you might try to find information about deaths due to alcohol poisoning. By placing quotation marks around your key words, you further limit your search. For example, when you input the term *alcohol poisoning deaths* into Google without quotation marks, you will get more than a million hits. When the same term is enclosed in quotation marks, the number of hits is reduced to about five hundred, and the displayed Web pages are more relevant.
- **Use bookmarks.** When you find information that might be useful, create a folder where you can store the information so that you can easily locate it later. (The bookmark icon appears on the toolbar of your search engine.)

Web Addresses

A Web address (also known as a URL) has the following parts.

Protocol   Host name   Domain name   Document path   Specific topic

http://www.nytimes.com/2008/10/28/technology/28soft.html?ref=business

Sometimes you can determine what type of organization runs the Web site by looking at the domain, shown by the three letters that follow the site name. However, be careful to always evaluate the site's content.

URL ending	Meaning	Example
.com	Company	www.bostonglobe.com
.edu	Educational institution	www.k-state.edu
.gov	Government	www.irs.gov
.org	Organization	www.greenpeace.org

 **Useful Internet Sites**

The following Web sites could be useful when you do research on the Internet.

Statistics

Statistics from more than one hundred government agencies	www.fedstats.gov
Bureau of Labor Statistics	www.stats.bls.gov
U.S. Census Bureau	www.census.gov

News Organizations

Addresses of hundreds of online magazines	newsdirectory.com
Access to newspapers from all over the world	www.newspapers.com
New York Times site for college students	www.nytimes.com/college

Other Sites

Job sites	www.monster.com
	www.jobs.org
Internet Public Library	www.ipl.org/reading
Online encyclopedias	www.encyclopedia.com
	www.britannica.com

Academic Research Sites

Google Scholar	scholar.google.com

Evaluate Sources

Be careful when you use Internet sources. Some sites contain misleading information, and some sites are maintained by people who have very strong and specific biases. Remember that the content of Internet sites is not always verified for accuracy. When you view Web sites, try to determine who benefits from the publication. What is the site's purpose?

 **Evaluating a Source**

When you find a source, ask yourself the following questions:

• Will the information support the point that I want to make?

• Is the information current? When was the site last updated? Ask yourself if the date is appropriate for your topic.

• Is the site reliable and highly regarded? Is it a well-known newspaper, journal, or Web site? Is the English grammatically correct?

• Is the author an expert on the subject? (Many sites provide biographical information about the author.)

• Does the author present a balanced view? Ask yourself if the author has a political or financial interest in the issue.

• Does the author develop key ideas with solid supporting facts and examples? Does the author quote reliable sources?

• Is there advertising on the site? Consider how advertising might influence the site's content.

PRACTICE I

Imagine that you are writing an essay about the dangers of online gambling. Answer the questions by referring to the list of Web sites below.

1. Write the letters of the three sites that you should investigate further. Briefly explain how each site could be useful.

   _____

   _____

   _____

2. Write the letters of three sites that are not useful for your essay. For each site you choose, explain why.

   _____

   _____

   _____

   _____

A. Bill to Ban Gambling Online Gets 4th Chance—washingtonpost.com
   Online poker players will have to fold their hands if a Virginia congressman gets his way. . . .
   www.washingtonpost.com

B. Petition to: Ban Online Gambling In The UK.
   I wish that the Goverment would ban online **gambling** Web sites like JackpotJoy as these online sites a . . .
   petitions.pm.gov.uk/remotegambling/-

C. Gambling.com—Casino Sites
   One of the major benefits of online **gambling** is that it gives the gambler a lot more choice in deciding on where they are going to place their bets. . . .
   www.gambling.com/best/casino-sites.htm

D. The Chronicle: Daily News Blog: Gambling Addiction Blamed as . . .
   A former student at Lehigh University pleaded guilty this morning to a felony charge of robbing a bank in order to finance an online **gambling** addiction, . . .
   chronicle.com/news/article/

E. MedlinePlus Medical Encyclopedia: Pathological gambling
   . . . Like alcohol or drug addiction, pathological **gambling** is a chronic disorder that tends to get worse without treatment. . . .
   www.nlm.nih.gov/medlineplus/ency/article/001520.htm

F. Derek's Rantings and Musings: Poker Archives
   I'm not sure if it's a testament to self-control (and, obviously, the fact that I am not a **gambling** addict *grin*), or if it's simply an indication of how . . .
   blog.megacity.org/archives/cat_poker.php

PRACTICE 2

1. Go to Google, and type *prison reform* in the search bar. How many hits did you get? _____

2. Now put *prison reform* in quotation marks. How many hits did you get? _____

3. Find sites with the following domains.

   .edu _____

   .org _____

   .gov _____

4. On a separate sheet of paper, write a paragraph comparing two Web sites. Choose one site that is not reliable and explain why. Then choose a site that is probably quite reliable and explain why. To evaluate the sites, refer to the questions in the "Evaluating a Source" box.

Keeping Track of Sources

Source information is easy to find in most print publications. It is usually on the second or third page of the book, magazine, or newspaper. On many Internet sites, however, finding the source information can take more investigative work. When you research on the Internet, look for the home page to find the site's title, publication date, and so on. Record as much of the following information from the site as possible.

RESEARCH LINK

To find out more about the MLA and its guidelines, visit the MLA Web site at www.mla.org.

Book, Magazine, Newspaper
Author's full name
Title of article
Title of book, magazine, or newspaper
Publishing information (name of publisher, city, and date of publication)
Pages used

Web Site
Author's full name
Title of article
Title of site
Publisher of site
Date of publication or updating
Date you accessed the site
Complete Web site address

Add a Paraphrase, Summary, or Quotation

To add research to a piece of writing, you can paraphrase it, summarize it, or quote it.

- When you **paraphrase,** you use your own words to present someone's ideas. A paraphrase is about the same length as the original selection.
- When you **summarize,** you briefly state the main ideas of another work. A summary is much shorter than the original selection.
- When you **quote,** you either directly state a person's exact words (with quotation marks) or report them (without quotation marks).

All of these are valid ways to incorporate research in your writing, as long as you give credit to the author or speaker.

Hint — Avoid Plagiarism!

Plagiarism is the act of using someone else's words or ideas without giving that person credit. Plagiarism is a very serious offense and can result in expulsion from college or termination from work.

The following actions are examples of plagiarism.

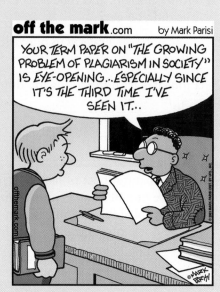

off the mark.com — by Mark Parisi

YOUR *TERM PAPER* ON "*THE GROWING PROBLEM OF PLAGIARISM IN SOCIETY*" IS *EYE-OPENING*...*ESPECIALLY* SINCE IT'S *THE THIRD TIME I'VE SEEN IT*...

- Buying another work and presenting it as your own
- Using another student's work and presenting it as your own
- Failing to use quotation marks or properly set off an author's exact words
- Using ideas from another source without citing that source
- Making slight modifications to an author's sentences but presenting the work as your own
- Copying and pasting text from an Internet source without using quotation marks to set off the author's words

To avoid plagiarism, always cite the source when you borrow words, phrases, or ideas from an author. Include the author's name, the title of the work, and the page number (if it is available).

Paraphrasing and Summarizing

Both paraphrases and summaries present the ideas that you have found in a source. The main difference between a paraphrase and summary is the length. While a paraphrase can be the same length as the original selection, a summary is much shorter.

How to Paraphrase

To paraphrase, do the following:

- Highlight the main ideas in the original text.
- Restate the main ideas using your own words. You can keep specialized words, common words, and names of people or places. However, find synonyms for other words and use your own sentence structure.
- Use a dictionary or thesaurus, if necessary, to find synonyms.
- Acknowledge the source in the paraphrase or place the source information in parentheses after the paraphrase.
- Maintain the original author's ideas and intent.
- After you finish writing, proofread your text.

Remember that a paraphrase is roughly the same length as the original selection.

How to Summarize

When you summarize, you condense a message to its basic elements. Do the following:

- Read the original text carefully because you will need a complete picture before you begin to write.
- Ask yourself *who, what, when, where, why,* and *how* questions to help you identify the central idea of the text.
- Acknowledge the source in your summary, or place the source information in parentheses after the summary.
- Reread your summary. Make sure that you have expressed the essential message in your own words.
- Your summary should be a maximum of 30 percent of the length of the original work.

In written summaries, readers should be able to understand the crucial message. The complete document will contain details and examples, but readers should not require the original to make sense of the central ideas.

Review examples of an original selection followed by a paraphrase and summary.

Original Selection

Glass provides valuable evidence because we come in contact with it so often. If we were to analyze a piece or pieces of glass, we would ask certain questions. . . . For instance, when we observe glass in a fire scene, is the soot baked on? If so, it was most likely a slow moving fire. If the soot is readily wiped off the glass, then we have a fast moving fire and should look for an accelerant.

—Wilson T. Sullivan III, *Crime Scene Analysis*, p. 135

Paraphrase

Investigators are able to determine the speed of a fire, according to Wilson T. Sullivan III. When soot is difficult to remove from glass, the fire probably burned slowly. If the soot can be removed with ease, the fire burned quickly and may have been aided with some type of gasoline or other catalyst.

Summary

According to the book *Crime Scene Analysis*, glass at a fire scene can give clues to a fire's speed, with easily removed soot indicating that a fire may have been intentionally started.

PRACTICE 3

Paraphrase and summarize the following selections.

1. The National Honor Society says that 64 percent of its members— outstanding high school students—are girls. Some colleges give special help to male applicants—yes, that's affirmative action for white males— to avoid skewed sex ratios. A new report just issued by the Center on Education Policy, an independent research organization, confirms that boys have fallen behind in reading in every single state. It found, for

example, that in elementary schools, about 79 percent of girls could read at a level deemed "proficient," compared with 72 percent of boys. Similar gaps were found in middle school and high school.

—Nicholas D. Kristof, "The Boys Have Fallen Behind," *New York Times*

Paraphrase: _____

_____

_____

_____

_____

Summary: _____

_____

_____

2. Unfortunately it turns out that hit men, genocidal maniacs, gang leaders and violent kids often have high self-esteem, not low self-esteem. A recipe for their violence is a mean streak combined with an unwarranted sense of self-worth. When such a boy comes across a girl or parents or schoolmates who communicate to him that he is not all that worthy, he lashes out.

—Martin Seligman, "The American Way of Blame," *APA Monitor Online*

Paraphrase: _____

_____

_____

_____

_____

_____

Summary: _____

_____

_____

GRAMMAR LINK

To find out more about using quotations, see Chapter 35.

Quoting Sources

A **direct quotation** contains the exact words of a source, and the quotation is set off with quotation marks. Use direct quotations to reveal the opinions of an expert or to include ideas that are particularly memorable and important. Quotations should be integrated into sentences, and the source of the quotation should be mentioned either in the introductory phrase or sentence or in parentheses after the quotation. Details about citing sources in the body of your essay appear later in this chapter.

Example: In his book *Sociology*, John E. Farley writes, "Human history abounds with legends of lost or deserted children who were raised by wild animals" (97).

 **Words That Introduce Quotations**

One common way to introduce a quotation is to write *The author says*. However, there are a variety of other verbs that you can use.

admits	comments	explains	mentions	reports	suggests
claims	concludes	maintains	observes	speculates	warns

PRACTICE 4

Read the following selections and try to identify examples of plagiarism. The original selection, written by Bill Bryson, appeared in *A Short History of Nearly Everything*.

Original Selection

Most schoolroom charts show the planets coming one after the other at neighborly intervals, but this is a necessary deceit to get them all on the same piece of paper.... Such are the distances, in fact, that it isn't possible, in any practical terms, to draw the solar system to scale. Even if you added lots of fold-out pages to your textbooks or used a really long sheet of poster paper, you wouldn't come close. On a diagram of the solar system to scale, with Earth reduced to about the diameter of a pea, Jupiter would be over a thousand feet away and Pluto would be a mile and a half distant.

1. **Summary**
   According to Bill Bryson, the solar system's true size is too large to show on a piece of paper, even if you added lots of fold-out pages. If you reduced Earth to the diameter of a pea, Jupiter would be over a thousand feet away.

   Is this plagiarism?   _____ Yes   _____ No

   Why? _____

   _____

2. **Summary**
   Bill Bryson cleverly demonstrates how pictures of the solar system are misleading. In fact, our solar system is so immense that a piece of paper would have to be more than a mile long to show all of the planets.

   Is this plagiarism?   _____ Yes   _____ No

   Why? _____

   _____

3. **Summary**
   Drawings of the solar system are misleading. Actually, the solar system is so immense that it is not possible, in practical terms, to draw the solar system to scale. If the earth were depicted as the size of a pea, Pluto would be over a mile away.

   Is this plagiarism?   _____ Yes   _____ No

   Why? _____

   _____

Cite Sources Using MLA Style

Each time you use another writer's words or ideas, you must **cite the source**, giving complete information about the original document from which you borrowed the material. When quoting, paraphrasing, or summarizing, you can set off the source information using parentheses. These **in-text citations**, also known as **parenthetical citations**, allow you to acknowledge where you obtained the information. You must also cite your sources in an alphabetized list at the end of your essay. The Modern Language Association (MLA) refers to the list as Works Cited.

 **Choose a Documentation Style**

The three most common styles for documenting sources are the Modern Language Association (MLA) format, *Chicago Manual of Style* (CMS) format, and the American Psychological Association (APA) format. Before writing a paper, check with your instructor to see which documentation style you should use and to learn where you can find more information about it.

Citing the Source in the Body of Your Essay

When you paraphrase, summarize, or quote, you must cite the source in the body of the essay. You must also cite the source in a Works Cited page at the end of your essay. See page 254 to view the Works Cited page for the following quotations.

There are two ways to show that you have borrowed an idea or quotation: cite the source in the sentence or cite the source in parentheses.

Source	Source cited in the sentence	Source cited in parentheses
Print	Mention the author's name in the sentence. Include the page number in parentheses.	Put the author's last name and the page number in parentheses.
	In *Business Communications*, Bovee says, "Short, direct messages have a much better chance of being acted on" (149).	One expert says, "Short, direct messages have a much better chance of being acted on" (Bovee 149).
Internet	For online sources, just mention the author's name. No page number is necessary.	For online sources, just put the author's last name in parentheses.
	Rahul Parikh blames popular talk shows for the problem: "Winfrey doesn't try to maintain medical credibility in her shows."	Oprah Winfrey contributes to the problem: "Winfrey doesn't try to maintain medical credibility in her shows" (Parikh).
	If an online source does not provide an author's name, mention the article's title or the Web site title in the sentence.	If the online source does not provide an author's name, write a short form of the title in parentheses.
	According to "Bipolar Support and Self Help," not all people use medications: "Living well with bipolar disorder requires certain adjustments."	Not all people use medications: "Living well with bipolar disorder requires certain adjustments" ("Bipolar").

Grammar Hint   **Quoting from a Secondary Source**

Sometimes you may want to quote from an indirect source. If your source material contains a quotation from someone, then put the abbreviation **qtd. in**—which means *Quoted in*—in the parentheses.

> Dr. Lauren Streicher says, "There are a lot of profit-motivated physicians out there" (qtd. in Parikh).

See Chapter 35 for more information about using quotations.

Preparing a Works Cited Page

The Works Cited page gives details about each source you have used, and it appears at the end of your essay. To prepare a Works Cited list, follow these basic guidelines.

1. Begin the Works Cited section on a new page. Write "Works Cited" at the top of the page and center it. Make sure your last name and page number appear in the upper-right corner.
2. List each source alphabetically, using the author's last name. If no author is mentioned, use the title.
3. Indent the second line and all subsequent lines of each reference.
4. Double space the entire page.

Each Works Cited reference should have the following parts.

Name

Write the author's complete last name followed by the first name.

Title

Add quotation marks around the titles of short works (Web site article, newspaper editorial, book chapter). Italicize the titles of longer works (newspaper, book, magazine, or Web site).

Place of Publication

When using a book as a source, look for the place of publication. Mention the name of the city but not the state.

Publisher's Name

Use a shortened form of the publisher's name. Omit *A*, *An*, or *The* from the beginning, and omit words such as *Co.*, *Corp.*, *Books*, *Press*, and *Publishers*. The short form for University Press is UP. On Internet sites, look at the bottom of the Web page or on the homepage for the publisher's or sponsor's name.

Date of Publication

Add the date that the item was published For online sources, also add the date that you viewed the Web site.

Medium of Publication

Mention the medium in which you found the content. Write *Print* for any paper source such as a book or newspaper. Write *Web* for all content found on the Internet. Other sources might be *CD*, *Performance*, *Television*, or *Film*.

 **Placement and Order of Works Cited**

The Works Cited list should be at the end of the research paper. List sources in alphabetical order of the authors' last names. If there is no author, put the title in the alphabetized list. The example is a Works Cited page for the quotations listed on page 252.

Works Cited

"Bipolar Support and Self Help." *Helpguide.org.* Wise and Healthy Aging, 2009. Web. 25 Feb. 2010.

Bovee, Courtland, and John Thill. *Business Communication Essentials.* 2nd ed. Upper Saddle River: Prentice, 2006. Print.

Parikh, Rahul K. "Oprah's Bad Medicine." *Salon.com.* Salon Media Group, 15 May 2009. Web. 25 Feb. 2010.

Model Entries
Book

Last name, First name. *Title of the Book.* Place of Publication: Publisher, Year. Print.

Book with one author

If the book is a second, third, or subsequent edition, just write the abbreviated form of the edition after the title.

Walker, John R. *Introduction to Hospitality.* 5th ed. Upper Saddle River: Prentice, 2009. Print.

Book with two or three authors

In books with two or three authors, reverse the name of the first author but not the subsequent authors.

Kimmel, Michael, and May Aronson. *Sociology Now.* Boston: Allyn, 2009. Print.

Book with four or more authors

Just give the first author's name, and then write *et al.*, which means "and others."

Goldfield, David, et al. *The American Journey.* Upper Saddle River: Prentice, 2002. Print.

Work in an anthology

For articles or essays taken from an anthology, write *Ed.* and the editor's name after the title.

Budnitz, Judy. "Nadia." *The Best American Nonrequired Reading.* Ed. Dave Eggers. Boston: Houghton, 2006. Print.

Encyclopedia or dictionary

It is unnecessary to mention volume and page numbers. Simply list the edition and year of publication.

"Morocco." *Columbia Encyclopedia.* 6th ed. 2005. Print.

"Democracy." *The New American Webster Handy College Dictionary.* 3rd ed. 1995. Print.

Periodical

> Last name, First name. "Title of Article." *Title of the Magazine or Newspaper*
> Date: Pages. Print.

Newspaper article

> Knight, Heather. "The Final Farewell." *San Francisco Chronicle* 15 Apr.
> 2007: A1. Print.

Magazine article

> Stix, Gary. "Spice Healer." *Scientific American* Feb. 2007: 66–69. Print.

Electronic Source

When using a source published on the Internet, include as much of the following information as you can find. Keep in mind that some sites do not contain complete information. **Generally, do not include the complete Web address unless the site is difficult to find or your teacher requires it.**

Put a comma after the publisher or sponsor, and put periods after all other parts of the citation. If there is no clear publisher or sponsor, write **N.p.** If there is no clear publication date, write **n.d.**

> Last name, First name. "Title of Article." *Title of Site or Online Publication.*
> Publisher or sponsor, Date of publication. Web. Date you accessed the
> site (day, month, and year). <Internet address (optional)>.

Online newspaper article

> Stack, Megan K. "In Hungary, Far Right is Making Gains." *Los Angeles
> Times.* Tribune, 10 Oct. 2009. Web. 24 Apr. 2010.

Online magazine article

> Ehrenreich, Barbara. "Overrated Optimism." *Time.* Time Inc, 10 Oct. 2009.
> Web. 15 May 2010.

Web-only article

> O'Hehir, Andrew. "Confessions of a Home Schooler." *Salon.com.* Salon
> Media Group, 28 Sept. 2009. Web. 14 May 2010.

If the site doesn't list an author's name, begin with the title of the article.

> "Avoid Toxic Plastics." *SimpleSteps.org.* Natural Resources Defense
> Council, 2009. Web. 5 May 2010.

If you think your readers will not be able to find the Web page, add the URL address. Use angle brackets.

> Dewar, Paul. "Ottawa Insight: Dangers Inside Bottled Water." *The
> Canadian.* The Canadian, 2007. Web. 14 May 2010. <http://www
> .agoracosmopolitan.com/home/Frontpage/2008/01/07/02088.html>.

Other Sources

Film, video, or DVD

Include the name of the film, the director, the studio, and the year of release. End with the medium (*film, video,* or *DVD*).

> *Friday Night Lights.* Dir. Peter Berg. Universal Studios, 2004. DVD.

Sound recording

Include the name of the performer or band, the title of the song, the title of the CD, the name of the recording company, and the year of release. End with *CD* or *LP*.

> Charles, Ray. "Fever." *Genius Loves Company*. Hear Music, 2004. CD.

Television or radio program

Include the segment title, the program name, the network, and the broadcast date. End with the medium (*television* or *radio*).

> "Photoshop Gone Wild." *Nightline*. ABC News. 9 Oct. 2009. Television.

PRACTICE 5

Imagine that you are using the following sources in a research paper. Arrange the sources for a Works Cited list using MLA style. You can type your Works Cited list on a separate piece of paper. Double-space each entry, and indent the second line of each entry.

- A quotation is from an online article called "Beyond Gold's Glitter" by Jane Perlez and Kirk Johnson. The article was published on October 24, 2005, on the Web site *The New York Times*. The publisher is The New York Times Company. You accessed the site today.

- A paraphrase is from a magazine article in *National Geographic* called "The Real Price of Gold." The magazine was published in January 2009. The author is Brook Larmer. The article appeared on pages 34 to 61.

- Some quotations are from a book called *Business Ethics*. The author is Richard T. De George. The book was published by Prentice Hall in Upper Saddle River, New Jersey, in 2006.

- A summary is from an online article called "Gold Prices." There is no author. The article appeared on the *Gold Research and Statistics* Web site in 2009. World Gold Council is the publisher. You accessed the site today.

Works Cited

_____

_____

_____

_____

_____

_____

_____

_____

_____

_____

Sample Research Essay Using MLA Style

Read the complete student essay thst follows. Notice how the student integrates paraphrases, summaries, and quotations.

Saumur 1

Stephanie Saumur

Professor Pelaez

English 101

15 April 2010

Cell Phone Safety

These days, it's common to see someone holding a cell phone while walking, driving, or having dinner. The big companies design cell phones to be as small and as practical as possible, and the little gadgets have become essential to our way of life. A lot of research has been done, and it reveals that cell phone microwaves may have an impact on the brain. Cell phones have some benefits, but they may be dangerous for human health.

Cell phone emissions have positive and negative effects on concentration and memory. The positive effect is that cell phone microwaves can help humans memorize things. They keep the short-term memory active. An Australian scientist discovered that cell phone use can temporarily help people "with certain tasks that require a working memory but can also slow reaction time" (Svalavitz). In *Psychology*, Sandra Cicarelli says that "long term memory must be fairly well organized for retrieval to be so quick" (222). Radiation may affect the organization. Henrietta Nittby, a researcher from Lund University, tested the theory on rats. For more than a year, some rats were exposed to cell phone radiation on a weekly basis. On memory tests, the rats that had been exposed to radiation did much worse than the rats that had not been exposed ("Mobile Phones").

Although people worry about getting cancer because of their cell phone–usage, scientists are divided on the cell phone and cancer link. Professor John Moulder, from the Medical College of Wisconsin, does not believe cell phones contribute to brain cancer (Svalavitz). However, some researchers disagree: "In 2006, a Swedish study reported that 85 of 905 brain tumor patients had used mobile phones heavily for 10 years or more, and most of their tumors occurred on the side of their head where they usually held their phones" (Butler 43). Kjell Mild, a professor at the Swedish National Institute for Working Life, says, "If you look at the studies with large numbers of people who used mobiles for ten years or more, all show an increased risk" of cancer (qtd. in Svalavitz).

Finally, there are concerns that cell phone radiation may cause brain damage. A University of Rome study showed that phones affect the cortex, "but no one can yet tell whether the effect is harmful, neutral, or even beneficial" (Szalavitz). Yet Henrietta Nittby's research on rats showed that radiation can cause a protein in the blood to infiltrate the brain, causing

> Double space your name, instructor's name, course title, and date.

> Center the title. Notice that the title is not underlined, boldfaced, or italicized.

> End your introduction with a thesis statement.

> Begin body paragraphs with a topic sentence.

> You can place the author's name in parentheses.

> You can cite the source in your sentence. Include the page number of print sources.

> Acknowledge the source of a paraphrase.

> Acknowledge the source of a summary.

> You can introduce a quotation with a complete sentence followed by a colon.

> Use "qtd. in" when you use a quotation that appeared in the source material.

> You can integrate a quotation into a sentence.

Saumur 2

damage to nerve cells ("Mobile Phones"). Furthermore, research suggests that cell phones can cause tissue damage in humans. A study done at Lund University has shown that cell phone microwaves can cause blood products to seep across the blood–brain barrier. The implications are serious: "Blood contains toxins . . . that can be lethal to brain tissue" (Sage).

Although the research isn't clear and complete enough to conclude that cell phones are dangerous, some researchers are convinced that mobile phone radiation can have significant long-term effects on human health. Those who are worried about health consequences should use hands-free phone equipment and minimize the amount of time spent on a cell phone. Another option is to increase the use of text messaging because the phone is not placed next to the head. Finally, because long-term safety of cell phones is unclear, perhaps children should not be given a cell phone.

Three spaced periods indicate that part of the quotation has been deleted.

Saumur 3

Always put the Works Cited list on a separate page.

Center the "Works Cited" heading.

Works Cited

Butler, Kiera. "This is Your Brain on Cell Phones." *Mother Jones* July–Aug 2008: 43. Print.

Place sources in alphabetical order.

Cicarelli, Saundra K., and Glenn E. Meyer. *Psychology*. Upper Saddle River: Prentice, 2006. Print.

If the source has no author, place the title of the article first.

"Mobile Phones Affect Memory In Laboratory Animals, Swedish Study Finds." *ScienceDaily*. ScienceDaily, 5 Dec. 2008. Web. 6 Feb. 2011.

Sage, Cindy. "Cell Phones and Blood–Brain Barrier." *EMFacts*. EMFacts Consultancy, 11 Nov. 2008. Web. 5 Feb. 2011.

Double space throughout, and indent the second line of each source.

Szalavitz, Maia. "Your Brain on Mobile?" *Psychology Today*. Sussex Publishers, 15 May 2007. Web. 4 Feb. 2011.

REFLECT ON IT

Think about what you have learned in this chapter. If you do not know an answer, review that topic.

1. What are the differences between a paraphrase and a summary?

   Paraphrase   **Summary**

   _____   _____

   _____   _____

   _____   _____

2. What is a Works Cited page?

_____

_____

_____

_____

The Writer's Room

Writing Activity 1

Choose a paragraph or an essay that you have written, and research your topic to get more detailed information. Then insert at least one paraphrase, one summary, and one quotation into your work. Remember to acknowledge your sources.

Writing Activity 2

Write an essay about one of the following topics. Your essay should include research (find at least three sources). Include a Works Cited page at the end of your assignment.

1. Write about a controversial issue that is in the news. In your essay, give your opinion about the issue.

2. Write about your career choice. You could mention job opportunities in your field, and you could include statistical information.

3. Write about the importance of a college education. Does a college education help or hurt a person's career prospects? Find some facts, examples, or statistics to support your view.

mywritinglab To check your progress in meeting this chapter's objectives, log in to **www.mywritinglab.com**, go to the **Study Plan** tab, click on **The Essay** and choose **Research Process and Summary Writing** from the list of subtopics. Read and view the resources in the **Review Materials** section, and then complete the **Recall, Apply,** and **Write** sets in the **Activities** section.

PART IV

The Editing Handbook

Why Is Grammar So Important?

When you speak, you have tools such as tone of voice and body language to help you express your ideas. When you write, however, you have only words and punctuation to get your message across. Naturally, if your writing contains errors in style, grammar, and punctuation, you may distract readers from your message, and they may focus, instead, on your inability to communicate clearly. You increase your chances of succeeding in your academic and professional life when you write in clear standard English.

The chapters in this Editing Handbook can help you understand important grammar concepts and ensure that your writing is grammatically correct.

Simple Sentences

Section Theme **POPULAR CULTURE**

In this chapter, you will read about topics related to advertising and consumerism.

The Writer's Journal

What is your cultural background? How would you identify yourself culturally? Write a paragraph about your cultural identity.

Identify Subjects

A **sentence** contains one or more subjects and verbs, and it expresses a complete thought. Although some sentences can have more than one idea, a **simple sentence** expresses one complete thought. The **subject** tells you who or what the sentence is about. The **verb** expresses an action or state. If a sentence is missing a subject or a verb, it is incomplete.

Singular and Plural Subjects

Subjects may be singular or plural. To determine the subject of a sentence, ask yourself who or what the sentence is about.

A **singular subject** is one person, place, or thing.

> **Oprah Winfrey** is known around the world.

> **Chicago** is her hometown.

A **plural subject** is more than one person, place, or thing.

> Contemporary **marketers** try to reach a mass audience.

> Many **countries** import American products.

Pronouns

A **subject pronoun** (*he, she, it, you, I, we, they*) can act as the subject of a sentence, and it replaces the noun.

> Jeff Bezos sold books. **He** founded Amazon.com.

> Consumers have rights. **They** can complain about unethical advertising.

Gerunds (-*ing* words)

Sometimes a gerund (-*ing* form of the verb) is the subject of a sentence.

> **Advertising** surrounds us.

> **Business planning** is an ongoing process.

Compound Subjects

Many sentences have more than one subject. *Compound* means "multiple." Therefore, a **compound subject** contains two or more subjects.

> **Men** and **women** evaluate products differently.

> The **accountants, designers,** and **managers** will meet to discuss the product launch.

 **Recognizing Simple and Complete Subjects**

In a sentence, the **simple subject** is the noun or pronoun. The complete name of a person, place, or organization is a simple subject.

> he   dancer   Tina Fey   Sony Music Corporation

The **complete subject** is the noun, plus the words that describe the noun. In the next examples, the descriptive words are in italics.

> *new electric* piano   *old, worn-out* shoes   *Anna's green* sofa

In the following sentences, the simple and complete subjects are identified.

> simple subject
> The glossy new **magazine** contained interesting articles.
> complete subject

PRACTICE 1

Underline the complete subject and circle the simple subject(s).

EXAMPLE:

Academic (institutions) teach popular culture.

1. Popular music, films, books, and fashions are the sources of our common culture.
2. Marketing is linked to all types of entertainment.
3. You and your friends and family may see hundreds of ads each day.
4. Jack Nevin and Linda Gorchels study consumer behavior.
5. Traditional marketing methods are losing their impact.
6. Restless and cynical citizens are bored with television, radio, and billboard ads.
7. Creative advertisers constantly look for new ways to seduce the public.
8. Social networking sites are now targeted by marketing firms.
9. Other strategies include buzz marketing and guerilla marketing.
10. Expensive advertising does not always produce results.

Special Subject Problems
Unstated Subjects (Commands)

In a sentence that expresses a command, the subject is unstated, but it is still understood. The unstated subject is *you*.

> Remember to use your coupon.

> Pay the cashier.

here/there

Here and *there* are not subjects. In a sentence that begins with *Here* or *There*, the subject follows the verb.

> There are five **ways** to market a product.

> Here is an interesting **brochure** about cosmetics.

PRACTICE 2

Circle the simple subject(s). If the subject is unstated, then write the subject (*you*) before the verb.

EXAMPLE:

you
To see the announcement, watch carefully.

1. There are many advertisements on the streets of our cities.

2. Look at any bus shelter, billboard, store window, or newspaper.

3. Certainly, some ads appear in surprising places. 4. There are framed announcements on the doors of hotel bathrooms, for example. 5. Furthermore, there are commercials hidden in the middle of the action in movies and television shows. 6. For instance, soft-drink and car companies advertised during the popular reality show *American Idol.* 7. There were soft drinks on the table in front of the show's judges. 8. The show's singers sang a tribute to an American automobile company. 9. View advertising with a critical eye.

Identify Prepositional Phrases

A **preposition** is a word that links nouns, pronouns, or phrases to other words in a sentence. It expresses a relationship based on movement or position. Here are some common prepositions.

Common Prepositions

about	before	during	near	through
above	behind	except	of	to
across	below	for	off	toward
after	beside	from	on	under
against	between	in	onto	until
along	beyond	inside	out	up
among	by	into	outside	with
around	despite	like	over	within
at	down			

A **phrase** is a group of words that is missing a subject, a verb, or both and is not a complete sentence. A **prepositional phrase** is made up of a preposition and its object (a noun or a pronoun). In the following phrases, an object follows the preposition.

Preposition	**+**	**Object**
in		the morning
among		the shadows
over		the rainbow

 **Be Careful**

Because the object of a preposition is a noun, it may look like a subject. However, the object in a prepositional phrase is *never* the subject of the sentence. For example, in the next sentence, the subject is *child*, not *closet.*

subject
In the closet, the **child** found the hidden gift.

Sometimes a prepositional phrase appears before or after the subject. To help you identify the subject, you can put parentheses around prepositional phrases or mark them in some other way. In each of the following sentences, the subject is in boldface type and the prepositional phrase is in parentheses.

(With huge sales,) **Amazon** is an amazing success story.

Jeff Bezos, (with very little money,) launched his Web site.

Sometimes a sentence can contain more than one prepositional phrase.

prepositional phrase   prepositional phrase
(In the mid 1990s,) (inside his Seattle garage,) **Bezos** created his online bookstore.

 **According to . . .**

When a sentence contains *according to,* the noun that immediately follows is *not* the subject of the sentence. In the following sentence, *Jack Solomon* is not the subject.

subject
(According to Jack Solomon,) **consumers** are easily persuaded.

PRACTICE 3

Place parentheses around the prepositional phrase(s) in each sentence. Then circle the simple subject.

EXAMPLE:

(In 1995,) a successful online (company) began.

1. In Pierre Omidyar's living room, an idea took shape.
2. With friend and co-founder Jeff Skoll, Omidyar decided to create an online flea market.
3. For several years, the company expanded.
4. Then, in 1998, a Harvard business graduate was asked to join the company.
5. Meg Whitman, with a team of top managers, helped turn eBay into a billion-dollar business.
6. Buyers and sellers, with a click of a mouse, can enter a virtual marketplace.
7. For a small fee, sellers can list items on the site.
8. Buyers, with only a picture and description to evaluate, then bid on the item.
9. At the end of the auction, an eBay employee contacts the buyer and seller.
10. In spite of some initial problems, the online auction has been tremendously successful.

PRACTICE 4

Look at the underlined word in each sentence. If it is the subject, write *C* (for "correct") beside the sentence. If the underlined word is not the subject, then circle the correct subject(s).

EXAMPLES:

In past <u>eras</u>, bustling (markets) sold consumer goods.   _____

Enclosed shopping <u>malls</u> are a fairly recent development.   _*C*_

1. In Edina, <u>Minnesota</u>, the first indoor mall was built.   _____

2. The world's largest <u>mall</u> has 800 stores.   _____

3. For some <u>consumers</u>, the local dress shop is a dangerous place.   _____

4. On her twenty-second <u>birthday</u>, Amber Wyatt divulged a secret.   _____

5. During the previous four years, <u>she</u> had piled up $60,000 in credit card debts.   _____

6. She acknowledges, with a shrug, her shopping <u>addiction</u>.   _____

7. Today, with a poor credit <u>rating</u>, Amber is unable to get a lease.   _____

8. Her <u>brother</u>, boyfriend, and aunt have lent her money.   _____

9. Her <u>parents</u>, with some reluctance, allowed their daughter to move back home.   _____

10. Many <u>American</u> men and women, according to a recent survey, have a shopping addiction.   _____

Identify Verbs

Every sentence must contain a verb. The **verb** either expresses what the subject does or links the subject to other descriptive words.

Action Verbs

An **action verb** describes an action that a subject performs.

In 2006, China <u>launched</u> an electric car called the Zap Xebra.

Engineers <u>designed</u> the car's energy-efficient engine.

Linking Verbs

A **linking verb** connects a subject with words that describe it, and it does not show an action. The most common linking verb is *be*.

The marketing campaign <u>is</u> expensive.

Some advertisements <u>are</u> very clever.

Other linking verbs refer to the senses and indicate how something appears, smells, tastes, and so on.

The advertising photo <u>looks</u> grainy.

The glossy paper <u>feels</u> smooth.

Common Linking Verbs

appear	feel	smell
be (am, is, are, was, were, etc.)	look	sound
become	seem	taste

Compound Verbs

When a subject performs more than one action, the verbs are called **compound verbs.**

Good advertising <u>informs</u>, <u>persuades</u>, and <u>convinces</u> consumers.

Members of the public either <u>loved</u> or <u>hated</u> the logo.

 **Infinitives Are Not the Main Verb**

Infinitives are verbs preceded by *to* such as *to fly, to speak,* and *to go.* An infinitive is never the main verb in a sentence.

      V   infinitive   V   infinitive

Kraft <u>wants</u> **to compete** in Asia. The company <u>hopes</u> **to sell** millions of products.

PRACTICE 5

Underline one or more main verbs in these sentences. Remember that infinitives such as *to sell* are not part of the main verb.

EXAMPLE:

    Some companies <u>use</u> buzz appeal.

1. Buzz marketers depend on word of mouth to sell products.

2. They entice consumers to talk about a brand.

3. Some companies hire students to chat about a particular brand of clothing in online forums.

4. To promote *America's Next Top Model*, the network gave free party kits to five hundred young girls.

5. The teenage girls were the target audience for the campaign.

6. The network asked the girls to invite four friends to their homes to watch the series.

7. Occasionally, buzz advertising backfires.

8. A car company placed people in chatrooms to discuss a new SUV model.

9. However, people in the chatroom became angry about the SUVs and criticized them.

10. Despite the risks, many companies attempt buzz marketing every year.

Identify Helping Verbs

A verb can have several different forms, depending on the tense that is used. **Verb tense** indicates whether the action occurred in the past, present, or future. In some tenses, there is a **main verb** that expresses what the subject does or links the subject to descriptive words, but there is also a helping verb.

The **helping verb** combines with the main verb to indicate tense, negative structure, or question structure. The most common helping verbs are forms of *be*, *have*, and *do*. **Modal auxiliaries** are another type of helping verb; they indicate ability (*can*), obligation (*must*), possibility (*may, might, could*), advice (*should*), and so on. For example, here are different forms of the verb *open*. The helping verbs are underlined.

<u>is</u> opening	<u>had</u> opened	<u>will</u> open	<u>should have</u> opened
<u>was</u> opened	<u>had been</u> opening	<u>can</u> open	<u>might be</u> open
<u>has been</u> opening	<u>would</u> open	<u>could be</u> opening	<u>could have been</u> opened

The **complete verb** consists of the helping verb and the main verb. In the following examples, the helping verbs are indicated with *HV* and the main verbs with *V*.

                   HV HV   V

American culture <u>has been</u> <u>spreading</u> across the globe for years.

            HV   HV V

You <u>must have</u> <u>seen</u> the news articles.

In **question forms,** the first helping verb usually appears before the subject.

       HV   subject HV   V

<u>Should</u> the coffee chain <u>have</u> <u>expanded</u> so quickly?

     HV   subject   V

<u>Will</u> the coffee and cakes <u>sell</u> in Moscow?

Interrupting words may appear between verbs, but they are *not* part of the verb. Some interrupting words are *easily, actually, not, always, usually, sometimes, frequently, often, never,* and *ever.*

           HV   V

Consumers <u>have</u> often <u>complained</u> about product quality.

              HV   HV   V

The car maker <u>should</u> not <u>have</u> <u>destroyed</u> its electric cars.

PRACTICE 6

Underline the helping verbs once and the main verbs twice. Be careful because some sentences only have main verbs.

EXAMPLE:

The modern consumerism movement <u>has</u> <u>been</u> strong since the 1960s.

1. In 1961, President John F. Kennedy outlined the Consumer Bill of Rights.

2. Products should not be dangerous or defective.

3. A single company should never have a monopoly.

4. Businesses must provide consumers with honest information.

5. Some companies have been sued for defective products.

6. Merck, a pharmaceutical company, was forced to remove the drug Vioxx from the market.

> **GRAMMAR LINK**
>
> For information on the position of mid-sentence adverbs, such as *often, sometimes,* and *never,* see page 431 in Chapter 30.

7. To protect consumers, the Federal Trade Commission has implemented rules to prevent misleading advertising.

8. Some companies have been fined for deceptive marketing methods.

9. In a Volvo ad, a monster truck ran over a row of cars and crushed all but the Volvo station wagon.

10. In fact, the Volvo's structure had been reinforced.

11. Volvo was fined $150,000 for deceptive marketing.

12. How should companies respond to consumer complaints?

PRACTICE 7

Circle the simple subjects and underline the complete verbs. Remember to underline all parts of the verb.

EXAMPLE:

Japanese products have captured the imaginations of children around the world.

1. In 1974, a Japanese greeting card company created a white cat with vacant, staring eyes. The cat was given the name "Hello Kitty." Soon, purses, toasters, cameras, and T-shirts had the image of the little animal. For some reason, the strange cat with a bow on one ear and a missing mouth has become a fashion icon for teenagers worldwide. Almost forty years after its debut, Hello Kitty's popularity remains constant.

2. A self-taught illustrator from Japan has created another cute and creepy character. At first glance, you might not notice the details on Mori Chack's bear. The fuzzy pink toy seems to be sweet and cuddly. However, after a closer look, you will see the long, pointed claws and the drop of blood on the bear's mouth. Like Hello Kitty, Gloomy Bear has become trendy. The versatile illustrator has also created Podolly. The cuddly lamb wears a coat made of wolf fur.

3. Some journalists, including Julia Dault and Kjeld Duits, have written about the trends. They credit Japanese animators with an ability to add

a sinister twist to images of saccharine sweetness. Of course, the characters do not simply appeal to children. Gloomy Bear sells briskly to those in their twenties and thirties.

REFLECT ON IT

Think about what you have learned in this chapter. If you do not know an answer, review that concept.

1. What is a sentence? _____

_____

2. What does the subject of a sentence do? _____

_____

3. What is a verb? _____

_____

4. Write an example of a linking verb and an action verb.

Linking _____   Action _____

Circle the best answers.

5. Can the object of a preposition be the subject of a sentence? No   Yes
6. Can a sentence have more than one subject?   No   Yes
7. Can a sentence have more than one verb?   No   Yes

FINAL REVIEW

Circle the simple subjects, and underline the complete verbs. Underline *all* parts of the verb. Remember that infinitives such as *to go* or *to run* are not part of the main verb.

EXAMPLE:

A good (name) and (logo) <u>are</u> immensely important.

1. In their book *Marketing: Real People, Real Choices*, Michael R. Solomon, Greg Marshall, and Elnora Stuart discuss brands. 2. With a great deal of care, companies must carefully choose the best name for their products. 3. According to the authors, product names should be memorable. 4. Irish Spring, for instance, is a fresh and descriptive name for soap.

5. Occasionally, mistakes are made. 6. The company Toro called its lightweight snow blower a "snow pup." 7. The product did not sell well. 8. Later, the product was renamed "Snow Master" and then "Snow Commander." 9. The sales have improved tremendously since then.

10. Some brands have become the product name in consumers' minds. 11. Everyone knows popular brands such as Kleenex, Jell-O, Scotch Tape, and Kool-Aid. 12. Without a second thought, many consumers will ask for a Kleenex but not for a tissue with another brand name. 13. Therefore, a great name can be linked to the product indefinitely.

14. According to Solomon, Marshall, and Stuart, there are four important elements in a good brand name. 15. It must be easy to say, easy to spell, easy to read, and easy to remember. 16. Apple, Coke, and Dove are examples of great product names. 17. Good names should also have a positive or functional relationship with the product. 18. Drano is a very functional name. 19. On the other hand, Pampers and Luvs suggest good parenting but have no relation to the function of diapers. 20. Ultimately, large and small businesses put a great deal of care into product branding.

The Writer's Room

Write about one of the following topics. After you finish writing, identify your subjects and verbs.

1. Describe an effective advertising campaign. List the elements that make the campaign so successful.

2. Compare two online shopping sites. Describe the positive and negative features of each site.

mywritinglab   To check your progress in meeting this chapter's objectives, log in to **www.mywritinglab.com**, go to the **Study Plan** tab, click on **The Editing Handbook—Section 1: Effective Sentences** and choose **Subjects and Verbs** from the list of subtopics. Read and view the resources in the **Review Materials** section, and then complete the **Recall, Apply,** and **Write** sets in the **Activities** section.

Compound Sentences

Section Theme **POPULAR CULTURE**

LEARNING OBJECTIVES

1. Compare Simple and Compound Sentences (p. 273)
2. Combine Sentences Using Coordinating Conjunctions (p. 274)
3. Combine Sentences Using Semicolons (p. 277)
4. Combine Sentences Using Transitional Expressions (p. 279)

In this chapter, you will read about topics related to fads and fashions.

The Writer's Journal

Do you have body art, such as tattoos and piercings? In a paragraph, explain why you do or do not have body art.

Compare Simple and Compound Sentences

When you use sentences of varying lengths and types, your writing flows more smoothly and appears more interesting. You can vary sentences and create relationships between ideas by combining sentences.

Review the differences between simple and compound sentences.

273

A **simple sentence** is an independent clause. It expresses one complete idea, and it stands alone. Simple sentences can have more than one subject and more than one verb.

One subject and verb:	Tattooing is not a new fashion.
Two subjects:	Tattooing and body piercing are not new fashions.
Two verbs:	Della McMahon speaks and writes about current trends.

A **compound sentence** contains two or more simple sentences. The two complete ideas can be joined in several ways.

	Vera creates handbags. + She also designs shoes.
Add a coordinator:	Vera creates handbags, and she also designs shoes.
Add a semicolon:	Vera creates handbags; she also designs shoes.
Add a semicolon and conjunctive adverb:	Vera creates handbags; moreover, she designs shoes.

Combine Sentences Using Coordinating Conjunctions

A **coordinating conjunction** joins two complete ideas and indicates the connection between them. The most common coordinating conjunctions are *for, and, nor, but, or, yet,* and *so*.

Complete idea,	**coordinating conjunction**	complete idea.

Review the following chart showing coordinating conjunctions and their functions.

Coordinating Conjunction	Function	Example
for	to indicate a reason	Henna tattoos are good options, **for** they are not permanent.
and	to join two ideas	Jay wants a tattoo, **and** he wants to change his hairstyle.
nor	to indicate a negative idea	Cosmetic surgery is not always successful, **nor** is it particularly safe.
but	to contrast two ideas	Tattoos hurt, **but** people get them anyway.
or	to offer an alternative	Jay will dye his hair, **or** he will shave it off.
yet	to introduce a surprising choice	He is good-looking, **yet** he wants to get cosmetic surgery.
so	to indicate a cause and effect relationship	He saved up his money, **so** he will get a large tattoo.

> **Hint** **Recognizing Compound Sentences**
>
> To be sure that a sentence is compound, place your finger over the coordinating conjunction, and then ask yourself whether the two clauses are complete sentences.
>
> **Simple:** The fashion model was tall **but** also very thin.
>
> **Compound:** The fashion model was tall, **but** she was also very thin.

PRACTICE I

Indicate whether the following sentences are simple (*S*) or compound (*C*). Underline the coordinating conjunction in each compound sentence.

EXAMPLE:

There are many ways to alter your appearance.   *S*

1. Many humans permanently alter their bodies, and they do it for a variety of reasons.   _____

2. Body altering is not unique to North America, for people in every culture and in every historical period have found ways to permanently alter their bodies.   _____

3. In past centuries, some babies in South America had boards tied to their heads, and their soft skulls developed a long, high shape.   _____

4. In Africa, Ubangi women used to extend their lower lips with large, plate-sized pieces of wood.   _____

5. In the 1700s, wealthy European men and women ate tiny amounts of arsenic to have very pale complexions.   _____

6. Then, in the next century, European and American women wore extremely tight corsets, and they suffered from respiratory and digestive problems.   _____

7. Today, some people want to improve their physical appearance, so they sculpt their bodies with cosmetic surgery.   _____

8. Body altering can be painful, but people do it anyway.   _____

PRACTICE 2

Read the following passages. Insert an appropriate coordinating conjunction in each blank. Choose from the list below, and try to use a variety of coordinating conjunctions.

for   and   nor   but   or   yet   so

EXAMPLE:

Fashions usually take a while to be accepted, _____*but*_____ fads appear and vanish quickly.

1.   Have you heard of Harajuku culture? Harajuku is the name of a district in Tokyo, _____ it is also a teen subculture. Every Sunday afternoon, hundreds of Japanese teenagers meet on Jinju Bridge, _____ they engage in "cosplay" (costume play). Some young males dress up, _____ most of the Harajuku kids are female. The girls want to be noticed, _____ they wear homemade frilly dresses and carry parasols. Their costumes require a lot of effort. They might dress up as a cute cartoon character, _____ they can choose to dress in dark gothic costumes.

2.   The pop star Gwen Stephani has a perfume brand called "Harajuku," _____ she loves that subculture. Today, the Harajuku district is famous, _____ many visitors go there. Tourists and professional photographers search for the best-dressed youths.

3.   Seventeen-year-old Shoshi lives in Toyko, _____ she visits Jinju Bridge every week. Next Sunday, she might wear a yellow bow in her hair, _____ she may wear a white lace cap. Her costumes are elaborately detailed, _____ she attracts a lot of attention. Tourists stare at her, _____ she is not self-conscious. Shoshi is frequently photographed, _____ she always wears the most eye-catching outfits. She never refuses to pose, _____ do most of her friends.

4.   Curiously, participants love to socialize and make friends, _____ they do not use their real names. The teens choose special names, _____ they tell close friends the name. Harajuku culture will probably remain a unique Japanese lifestyle.

) **Place a Comma Before the Coordinating Conjunction**

Add a comma before a coordinating conjunction if you are certain that it joins two complete sentences. If the conjunction joins two nouns, verbs, or adjectives, then you do not need to add a comma before it.

Comma: The word *fashion* refers to all popular styles, **and** it does not refer only to clothing.

No comma: The word *fashion* refers to all popular styles **and** not only to clothing.

PRACTICE 3

Create compound sentences by adding a coordinating conjunction and another complete sentence to each simple sentence. Remember to add a comma before the conjunction.

EXAMPLE:

Many people deny it ____, *but they worry about their personal style.* _____

1. My hair is too long _____

   _____

2. Today, hairstyles are varied _____

   _____

3. Those shoes look uncomfortable _____

   _____

4. You may be surprised _____

   _____

Combine Sentences Using Semicolons

Another way to form a compound sentence is to join two complete ideas with a semicolon. The semicolon replaces a coordinating conjunction.

Complete idea	;	complete idea.

Advertisers promote new fashions every year; they effectively manipulate consumers.

Use a Semicolon to Join Related Ideas

Do not use a semicolon to join two unrelated sentences. Remember that a semicolon takes the place of a conjunction.

Incorrect:	Some societies have no distinct word for art; people like to dress in bright colors.
	(The second idea has no clear relationship with the first idea.)
Correct:	Some societies have no distinct word for art; art is an intrinsic part of their cultural fabric.
	(The second idea gives further information about the first idea.)

PRACTICE 4

Insert the missing semicolon in each sentence.

EXAMPLE:

Tattoos are applied with needles; ink is inserted under the skin.

1. Primitive tribes used sharp, thin instruments to introduce color into the skin methods of tattooing have not changed much over the years.

2. In 1990, in the Alps, Austrian hikers found a 5,000-year-old man they photographed the frozen, tattooed body.

3. The body had long straight lines tattooed on the ankles other lines appeared on the stomach region.

4. An Austrian professor, Konrad Spindler, has a theory about the tattoos he published his ideas in a journal.

5. Perhaps the ancient man received tattoos to cure an illness he may have had intestinal problems.

6. In the past, some tattoos celebrated war victories others honored religious figures.

7. The warriors of the Marquesas Islands wanted to intimidate their enemies they tattooed a staring eye on the insides of their arms.

8. A tribesman would raise his arm to attack an opponent his enemy would then see the staring eye and feel frightened.

9. In the early twentieth century, in Western cultures, tattoos were not common among college students or business people sailors, soldiers, and criminals would get tattoos.

10. Tattoos have had a strong resurgence in our culture people from gang members to Hollywood actors have gotten them.

PRACTICE 5

Write compound sentences by adding a semicolon and another complete sentence to each simple sentence. Remember that the two sentences must have related ideas.

EXAMPLE:

Last year my sister had her tongue pierced _____*; she regretted her decision.*

1. Youths rebel in many ways _____

   _____

2. Hair dyes can be toxic _____

   _____

3. At age thirteen, I dressed like other teens _____

   _____

4. Running shoes are comfortable _____

   _____

Combine Sentences Using Transitional Expressions

A third way to combine sentences is to join them with a semicolon and a transitional expression. A **transitional expression** can join two complete ideas together and show how they are related. Most transitional expressions are **conjunctive adverbs** such as *however* or *furthermore*.

Transitional Expressions

Addition	Alternative	Contrast	Time	Example or Emphasis	Result or Consequence
additionally	in fact	however	eventually	for example	consequently
also	instead	nevertheless	finally	for instance	hence
besides	on the contrary	nonetheless	later	namely	therefore
furthermore	on the other hand	still	meanwhile	of course	thus
in addition	otherwise		subsequently	undoubtedly	
moreover					

If the second part of a sentence begins with a transitional expression, put a semicolon before it and a comma after it.

Complete idea;   **transitional expression,**   complete idea.

Miriam is not wealthy; **nevertheless,** she always wears the latest fashions.
                      ; however,
                      ; nonetheless,
                      ; still,

PRACTICE 6

Punctuate the following sentences by adding any necessary semicolons and commas.

EXAMPLE:

A bizarre fashion style can become accepted; however, future generations may find the style ridiculous.

1. Often, a popular personality adopts a fashion later others copy the style.

2. King Louis XIV originally disliked wigs however he started to go prematurely bald and changed his mind about the fashion.

3. The king started to wear high, curly wigs subsequently others copied his style.

4. The heavy, elaborate wigs were expensive hence only upper-class Europeans wore them.

5. The wigs required constant care in fact they needed to be cleaned, powdered, and curled.

6. Later, the king's mustache started to go gray therefore he shaved it off.

7. Others noticed the king's bare face consequently all the fashionable men removed their mustaches too.

8. Not all new fashions are frivolous in fact some fashions signal a change in a group's status.

9. In the 1920s, women gained the right to vote meanwhile pants became associated with women's new freedom.

PRACTICE 7

Combine sentences using one of the following transitional expressions. Choose an expression from the following list, and try to use a different expression in each sentence.

in fact	for example	~~however~~	of course
therefore	for instance	nevertheless	thus

EXAMPLE:

Today's parents often complain about their children. Young people today
; however, young
are not more violent and rebellious than those of past generations.

1. Youth rebellion is not new. In each era, teenagers have rebelled.

2. Teenagers distinguish themselves in a variety of ways. They listen to new music, create new dance styles, wear odd fashions, and break established social habits.

3. The most visible way to stand out is to wear outrageous fashions. Teenagers try to create original clothing and hairstyles.

4. In the past fifty years, rebellious teens have done almost everything to their hair, including growing it long, buzzing it short, dyeing it, spiking it, shaving it off, and coloring it blue. It is difficult for today's teenagers to create an original hairstyle.

5. Sometimes a certain group popularizes a style. Hip-hop artists wore baggy clothing in the late 1980s.

6. Many parents hated the baggy, oversized pants. Boys wore them.

7. Before the 1990s, most women pierced just their ears. It is now common to see a pierced eyebrow, tongue, or cheek.

8. "Retro" hair and clothing styles will always be popular. People often look to the past for their inspiration.

 Subordinators versus Conjunctive Adverbs

A **subordinator** is a term such as *when, because, until,* or *although.* Do not confuse subordinators with conjunctive adverbs. When a subordinator is added to a sentence, the clause becomes incomplete. However, when a conjunctive adverb is added to a sentence, the clause is still complete.

Complete:	She wore fur.
Incomplete (with subordinator):	When she wore fur.
Complete (with conjunctive adverb):	Therefore, she wore fur.

When you combine two ideas using a conjunctive adverb, use a semicolon.

No punctuation:	She was criticized <u>when she wore fur.</u>
Semicolon:	It was very cold<u>; therefore, she wore fur.</u>

PRACTICE 8

Create compound sentences by using the next transitional expressions. Try to use a different expression in each sentence.

in fact   however   therefore   furthermore   consequently

EXAMPLE:

I have my own style ____*; therefore, I refuse to spend money following the*____ *latest fad.*

1. Designer clothing is expensive _____

   _____

2. I cannot sew _____

_____

3. Some men shave their heads _____

_____

4. My best friend loves to shop _____

_____

REFLECT ON IT

Think about what you have learned in this unit. If you do not know an answer, review that concept.

1. a. What is a simple sentence? _____

_____

b. Write a simple sentence. _____

_____

2. a. What is a compound sentence? _____

_____

b. Write a compound sentence. _____

_____

3. What are the seven coordinating conjunctions? _____

_____

4. Circle the best answer: When two sentences are joined by a coordinating conjunction such as *but,* should you put a comma before the conjunction?   Yes   No

5. When you join two simple sentences with a transitional expression, how should you punctuate the sentence?

_____

_____

FINAL REVIEW

Read the following essay. Create at least ten compound sentences by adding semicolons, transitional expressions (*however, therefore,* and so on), or coordinating conjunctions (*for, and, not, but, or, yet, so*). You may choose to leave some simple sentences.

EXAMPLE:

; for example, top

The fashion industry does not hire average-sized models. ~~Top~~ models are very tall and thin.

1.   The fashion industry promotes a specific body type. Advertisers also prefer

a particular look. They use tall, skinny models to sell fashion. The average

person does not have the body dimensions of a top model. This type of appearance is unfeasible for most people. A public backlash has developed against the skinny top model image. People on both sides of the controversy have an opinion. They may love the fashion industry. They may hate it.

2. Critics blame the fashion industry for depicting unrealistic body types. First, top models are far too thin. Their Body Mass Index (BMI) is less than 18.5. A healthy woman should have a BMI between 18.5 and 25. The industry pressures models to remain uncommonly lean. Young girls compare themselves with models. They develop negative body images. Skinny women are found in fashion magazines, on billboards, and on television. According to psychologists, such images contribute to eating disorders in adolescents. The images may also lead to yo-yo dieting.

3. Some in the fashion industry have chosen to present more realistic body types. In 2006, one Madrid fashion organizer banned overly skinny models from fashion runways. About 30 percent of the models could not participate in the show. A well-known cosmetics company has launched a regular-women campaign. Dove uses ordinary women to promote a line of body creams. According to a Dove spokesperson, the company wants to encourage debate about body image.

4. However, many in the fashion industry are reacting negatively to the critics' demands. For example, Lucio Guerrero is a reporter for the *Chicago Sun-Times*. He is offended by the Dove regular-women campaign. He does not want to see women with big thighs. Also, the Dove campaign is hypocritical. Dove sells anti-cellulite creams and anti-aging creams. Yet the company tells women to accept their own bodies. Furthermore, according to some critics, clothes look better on thin people. The fashion industry is trying to sell clothes.

5.   Clearly, there will be no immediate end to the body image controversy. Such a debate is important. It may never be resolved. Perhaps consumers will influence the direction of the fashion industry in the future.

The Writer's Room

Write about one of the following topics. Include some compound sentences.

1. Think about some fashions over the last one hundred years. Which fashion trends do you love the most? Give examples.

2. List the steps you take when you make a major purchase. For example, what process do you follow when you decide to buy an appliance, car, computer, or house.

mywritinglab To check your progress in meeting this chapter's objectives, log in to **www.mywritinglab.com**, go to the **Study Plan** tab, click on **The Editing Handbook—Section 1: Effective Sentences** and choose **Combining Sentences** from the list of subtopics. Read and view the resources in the **Review Materials** section, and then complete the **Recall, Apply,** and **Write** sets in the **Activities** section.

Complex Sentences

CHAPTER 18

Section Theme **POPULAR CULTURE**

In this chapter, you will read about topics related to sports and activity fads.

The Writer's Journal

How active are you? Write about some of the physical activities that you do.

What Is a Complex Sentence?

Before you learn about complex sentences, it is important to understand some key terms. A **clause** is a group of words containing a subject and a verb. There are two types of clauses.

An **independent clause** has a subject and a verb and can stand alone because it expresses one complete idea.

> Laban Nkete won the race.

A **dependent clause** has a subject and a verb, but it cannot stand alone. It "depends" on another clause to be complete.

> Although he had injured his heel

A **complex sentence** combines both a dependent and an independent clause.

> dependent clause   independent clause
> Although he had injured his heel, Laban Nkete won the race.

 **More About Complex Sentences**

Complex sentences can have more than two clauses.

> 1
> Although women have played organized football for over a century, their salaries
> 2   3
> are not very high because their games are rarely televised.

You can also combine compound and complex sentences. The next example is a **compound-complex sentence.**

> complex
> Although Kyra is tiny, she plays basketball, and she is a decent player.
> compound

Use Subordinating Conjunctions

An effective way to create complex sentences is to join clauses with a subordinating conjunction. When you add a **subordinating conjunction** to a clause, you make the clause dependent. *Subordinate* means "secondary," so subordinating conjunctions are words that introduce secondary ideas. Here are some common subordinating conjunctions followed by examples of how to use these types of conjunctions.

Common Subordinating Conjunctions

after	as though	if	though	where
although	because	provided that	unless	whereas
as	before	since	until	wherever
as if	even if	so that	when	whether
as long as	even though	that	whenever	while

Main idea   **subordinating conjunction**   secondary idea.

Crowds cheered **whenever** the team won.

Subordinating conjunction   secondary idea,   main idea.

Whenever the team won, crowds cheered.

PRACTICE 1

The following sentences are complex. In each sentence, circle the subordinating conjunction, and then underline the dependent clause.

EXAMPLE:

(Even if) we cannot know for sure, early humans probably played games and sports.

1. When humans shifted from being food gatherers to hunters, sports probably developed in complexity.

2. It would be important to practice cooperative hunting before humans attacked mammoths or other large creatures.

3. Early groups of humans probably also practiced war games so that they could win battles with other tribes.

4. Spectator sports evolved when societies had more leisure time.

5. In many places, spectators watched while young boys passed through their initiation rituals.

6. Whenever early humans played sports or games, they tested their physical, intellectual, and social skills.

Meanings of Subordinating Conjunctions

Subordinating conjunctions create a relationship between the clauses in a sentence.

	Cause or Reason	Condition or Result	Contrast	Place	Time
Conjunctions	as because since so that	as long as even if if provided that only if so that unless	although even though if though whereas unless	where wherever	after before once since until when whenever while
Example	Eric learned karate **because** he wanted to be physically fit.	He will not fight **unless** he feels threatened.	People learn karate **even though** it is difficult to master.	**Wherever** you travel, you will find karate enthusiasts.	**After** he received his black belt, he became a teacher.

PRACTICE 2

In each of the following sentences, underline the dependent clause. Then, indicate the type of relationship between the two parts of the sentence. Choose one of the following relationships.

    condition   contrast   reason   location   time

EXAMPLE:

<u>When Rebeka feels lonely</u>, she goes on her
Facebook page.   *time*

1. After the invention of computers, many new fads
emerged.

2. Social networking sites are popular because people
can stay in touch with their friends.

3. A lot of college students use Facebook or Twitter
whenever they have spare time.

4. Generally students use Facebook whereas
professionals use Twitter.

5. Wherever Rebeka goes, she can check her
Facebook page.

6. Rebeka will continue to use Facebook unless a
better networking site appears.

 **Punctuating Complex Sentences**

If you use a subordinator at the beginning of a sentence, put a comma after the
dependent clause. Generally, if you use a subordinator in the middle of the sentence,
you do not need to use a comma.

Comma: **Even though** he is afraid of heights, Malcolm tried skydiving.

No comma: Malcolm tried skydiving **even though** he is afraid of heights.

PRACTICE 3

Underline the subordinating conjunction in each sentence. Then add eight
missing commas.

EXAMPLE:

<u>Although</u> most sports are quite safe, some sports are extremely hazardous.

1. Each year, many people are killed or maimed when they practice
a sport. Although skydiving and bungee jumping are hazardous
extreme sports like base jumping, free diving, and rodeo events are
even more dangerous.

2. Even though they may get arrested many people try base jumping.
Wherever there are tall structures there may also be base jumpers. The
jumpers wear parachutes and dive off buildings and bridges so that they
can feel an adrenaline rush. Because the parachute can get tangled on
the structure base jumping is an extremely risky sport.

3. Free divers hold their breath until they are as deep as possible underwater. So that they can break existing records some free divers have dived almost 400 feet. If their brains lack oxygen they have to be resuscitated.

4. Although most rodeo sports can be safe bull riding is dangerous. Many bull riders are injured or even killed because the bull throws them off and tramples them.

5. Surprisingly, most sports-related injuries occur when people participate in an innocent-sounding sport. According to the American Academy of Orthopedic Surgeons, almost half a million people are injured each year when they ride bicycles. When playing a sport take precautions to protect yourself.

PRACTICE 4

Add a missing subordinating conjunction to each sentence. Use each subordinating conjunction once.

although	even though	~~when~~	whereas
because	unless	whenever	

EXAMPLE:

_____*When*_____ you refer to a "football" in Europe, Africa, or Asia, most people assume you are talking about a round black-and-white ball.

1. British people will assume you are speaking about soccer
_____ you specifically say "American football."

2. Soccer is the world's most popular sport _____ it is inexpensive to play. _____ someone decides to join a soccer team, he or she does not require expensive padding or equipment.

3. _____ a lot of Americans love to play soccer, there are not many professional teams in the United States. Sports such as basketball, baseball, and football have professional teams and are shown on network television _____ soccer is not widely viewed.

4. _____ soccer has yet to become as popular as other sports in the United States, it is America's fastest-growing sport, according to the American Soccer Federation.

> ## Hint · Put a Subject After the Subordinator
>
> When you form complex sentences, always remember to put a subject after the subordinator.
>
>   *it*
> Wrestling is like theater because involves choreographed maneuvers.
>
>   *they*
> Boxers do not know who will win the round when enter the ring.

PRACTICE 5

Add four missing subjects to the next paragraph.

EXAMPLE:

                                                              it
Bullfighting is popular in Mexico and Spain although is controversial.

Each bullfight is an elaborate ceremony with three parts. In the first part, when the matador enters the arena, is dressed in a fine suit embroidered with gold. Holding a red cape, the matador tries to entice the bull. The spectators cheer when see the bull charging at the cape. In the second part, the banderilleros, or matador's assistants, push short spears into the bull until is tired and angry. In the third part, the matador returns to the ring holding a smaller cape and a sword. After has performed well, the matador kills the bull.

PRACTICE 6

Combine each pair of sentences into a single sentence. Add one of the following subordinating conjunctions. Use each conjunction once.

      ~~although~~   even though   because   after   when   if

EXAMPLE:

I am not athletic. I love football.

   Although I am not athletic, I love football.

1. Professional football players can achieve fame and fortune. Many students want to play the sport.

2. Football is a great sport. It has some drawbacks.

   _____

   _____

3. Linebackers hit other players. They can develop head injuries.

   _____

   _____

4. A player has a concussion. The player should not finish the game.

   _____

   _____

5. Professional football players retire. Some have long-term health problems.

   _____

   _____

Use Relative Pronouns

A **relative pronoun** describes a noun or pronoun. You can form complex sentences by using relative pronouns to introduce dependent clauses. Review the most common relative pronouns.

who   whom   whomever   whose   which   that

That

Use *that* to add information about a thing. Do not use commas to set off clauses that begin with *that*.

In 1947, Jackie Robinson joined a baseball team **that** was located in Brooklyn.

Which

Use *which* to add nonessential information about a thing. Generally, use commas to set off clauses that begin with *which*.

Football, **which** was segregated in 1945, included African-American players the following year.

Who

Use *who* (*whom, whomever, whose*) to add information about a person. When a clause begins with *who*, you may or may not need a comma. Put commas around the clause if it adds nonessential information. If the clause is essential to the meaning of the sentence, do not add commas. To decide if a clause is essential or not, ask yourself if the sentence still makes sense without the *who* clause. If it does, the clause is not essential.

Most women **who** play sports do not earn as much money as their male counterparts.
(The clause is essential. The sentence would not make sense without the *who* clause.)

Tennis player Serena Williams, **who** has won many tournaments, earns millions of dollars in endorsement deals.

(The clause is not essential.)

 **Using *That* or *Which***

Both *which* and *that* refer to things, but *which* refers to nonessential ideas. Also, *which* can imply that you are referring to the complete subject and not just a part of it. Compare the next two sentences.

Local baseball teams that have very little funding can still succeed.
(This sentence suggests that some teams have good funding, but others don't.)

Local baseball teams, **which** have very little funding, can still succeed.
(This sentence suggests that all of the teams have poor funding.)

GRAMMAR LINK

For more information about punctuating relative clauses, refer to Chapter 34, "Commas."

PRACTICE 7

Using a relative pronoun, combine each pair of sentences to form a complex sentence.

EXAMPLE:

The Olympic Games celebrate excellence in sports. They occur once every four years.

The Olympic Games, which occur once every four years, celebrate excellence

in sports.

1. The Olympic Games are very expensive to produce. They bring benefits to host countries.

   _____

   _____

2. In 2008, China presented an amazing opening ceremony. The ceremony attracted more than a billion viewers.

   _____

   _____

3. Michael Phelps is very shy. He won eight gold medals.

   _____

   _____

4. Some Chinese citizens complained about human rights abuses. They were arrested.

   _____

   _____

5. Coal-burning plants produce a lot of pollution. They were closed during the games.

_____

_____

6. The 2008 Olympics demonstrated something. China is a modern and vibrant society.

_____

_____

PRACTICE 8

Add a dependent clause to each sentence. Begin each clause with a relative pronoun (*who*, *which*, or *that*). Add any necessary commas.

EXAMPLE:

Teams ___*that have good leadership*___ often win tournaments.

1. The player _____ might be hired to promote running shoes.

2. An athlete _____ should be suspended for at least one game.

3. Bungee jumping is an activity _____

4. Skydiving _____ is a sport I would like to try.

5. Athletes _____ should be warned about the dangers of steroids.

Use Embedded Questions

It is possible to combine a question with a statement or to combine two questions. An **embedded question** is a question that is set within a larger sentence.

Question:	How old are the Olympic Games?
Embedded question:	The sprinter wonders how old the Olympic Games are.

In questions, there is generally a helping verb before the subject. However, when a question is embedded in a larger sentence, you need to remove the helping verb or place it after the subject. As you read the following examples, pay attention to the word order in the embedded questions.

Combine two questions.

Separate:	Do you know the answer? Why **do** they like bullfighting?
	(The second question includes the helping verb *do*.)
Combined:	Do you know why they like bullfighting?
	(The helping verb *do* is removed from the embedded question.)

CHAPTER 18

Combine a question and a statement.

Separate: I wonder about it. When **should** we go to the arena?

(In the question, the helping verb *should* appears before the subject.)

Combined: I wonder <u>when we should go to the arena</u>.

(In the embedded question, *should* is placed after the subject.)

>  **Use the Correct Word Order**
>
> When you edit your writing, make sure that you have formed your embedded questions properly. Remove question form structures from the embedded questions.
>
> He wonders why ~~do~~ people like bullfighting. I asked him what <u>he thought</u> ~~did he think~~ about the sport.

PRACTICE 9

Correct six embedded question errors, and modify verbs when necessary.

EXAMPLE:

The writer explains how ~~can people~~ *people can* love dangerous sports.

One activity that generates controversy is bullfighting. Some people wonder why should bulls die for entertainment. They question how can bullfighting be so popular. Many call it a brutal activity because the bull is weakened and then slaughtered. For others, bullfighting is a respected tradition.

Spanish matador Mario Carrión wonders why do some people call bullfighting a sport. In sports, the goal is to win points in a confrontation with an opponent. In Carrión's view, a bullfight is not a sport because a human cannot compete against

a thousand-pound beast. He defines bullfighting as "a dramatic dance with death."

Bullfight enthusiasts ask themselves why does bullfighting have a bad reputation. They wonder why is it rejected by so many nations. Do you know what can they do to improve the reputation of bullfighting?

REFLECT ON IT

Think about what you have learned in this chapter. If you do not know an answer, then review that concept.

1. Write six subordinating conjunctions. _____

_____

2. Write a complex sentence. _____

_____

3. List six relative pronouns. _____

4. Correct the error in the following sentence.

Clayton wonders why should he wear a helmet when he goes skateboarding.

FINAL REVIEW

The following paragraphs contain only simple sentences. To give the paragraphs more variety, form at least ten complex sentences by combining pairs of sentences. You will have to add some words and delete others.

EXAMPLE:

When people   *, they*
~~People~~ pierce their tongues. ~~They~~ risk getting an infection.

1.   Many activity fads come and go. Many of these fads are ridiculous. Why do fads become so popular? Nobody knows the answer. There were some unusual fads in the 1950s. College students did phone-booth stuffing. Students entered a phone booth one by one. They tried to stuff as many people as possible into the closed space. Later, hula hoops hit the market. In the 1960s, millions of people bought and used the circular plastic tubes. The hula hoop fad did not last long. It briefly provided people with an innovative way to exercise. People put the hoops around their waists. They would gyrate to keep the hoops spinning.

2.   In the spring of 1974, a streaking fad began. It occurred on college campuses in Florida and California. Young people stripped naked. They may have felt embarrassed. They ran through public places such as

football stadiums and malls. They wanted to shock people. The actor David Niven was presenting at the 1974 Academy Awards. A nude streaker dashed behind him. The streaker made a peace sign. Millions of viewers were watching the show. They saw the streaker.

3. Today, many people want to exercise. They do not want to leave their homes. Luckily, video games no longer encourage lethargy. Companies have produced active games. The games force participants to move vigorously. Children play Dance Dance Revolution. They burn three times more calories than those who use traditional hand-held games. Even adults buy the games. They can play tennis or football in their living rooms. Do you know the answer to the following question? Why do adults love active video games? The reasons are simple. The games are entertaining and provide some exercise.

The Writer's Room

Write about one of the following topics. Include some complex sentences.

1. Think about a sport that you really enjoy and a sport that you dislike. Compare and contrast the two sports.
2. Why do athletes train for events such as the Olympics? What are some of the effects of being an Olympic athlete? You can write about causes and/or effects.

Sentence Variety

Section Theme **POPULAR CULTURE**

In this chapter, you will read about topics related to cultural icons.

The Writer's Journal

Would you like to be famous? What are some problems that could be associated with fame? Write a paragraph about fame.

What Is Sentence Variety?

In Chapters 17 and 18, you learned how to write different types of sentences. This chapter focuses on sentence variety. **Sentence variety** means that your sentences have assorted patterns and lengths. In this chapter, you will learn to vary your sentences by consciously considering the length of sentences, by altering the opening words, and by joining sentences using different methods.

Combine Sentences

A passage filled with simple, short sentences can sound choppy. When you vary the lengths of your sentences, the same passage becomes easier to read and flows more smoothly. For example, read the following two passages about the cultural icon Rosa Parks. In the first paragraph, most of the sentences are short, and the style is repetitive and boring. In the second paragraph, there is a mixture of simple, compound, and complex sentences.

> **GRAMMAR LINK**
>
> If you forget what compound and complex sentences are, refer to Chapters 17 and 18.

Simple Sentences

We know the story. A woman left work. She boarded a bus for home. She was tired. Her feet ached. This was Montgomery, Alabama. It was in December 1955. The bus became crowded. The driver ordered the black woman to give her seat to a white passenger. She remained seated. Her decision was important. It led to the changes in the South. It ushered in a new era.

Simple, Compound, and Complex Sentences

We know the story. One December evening, a woman left work and boarded a bus for home. She was tired; her feet ached. But this was Montgomery, Alabama, in December 1955, and as the bus became crowded, the woman, a black woman, was ordered to give up her seat to a white passenger. When she remained seated, that simple decision eventually led to the disintegration of institutionalized segregation in the South, ushering in a new era of the civil rights movement.

—Rita Dove, "The Torchbearer"

 **Hint** **Be Careful with Long Sentences**

If a sentence is too long, it may be difficult for the reader to understand. If you have any doubts, break up a longer sentence into shorter ones.

Long and complicated:	Elvis Presley is a cultural icon who achieved the American dream by using his musical skills to transform himself from a truck driver into a rock-and-roll legend, yet he did not handle his fame very well, and by the end of his life, he was unhappy and addicted to painkillers.
Better:	Elvis Presley is a cultural icon who achieved the American dream. Using his musical skills, he transformed himself from a truck driver into a rock-and-roll legend. However, he did not handle his fame very well. By the end of his life, he was unhappy and addicted to painkillers.

PRACTICE I

Modify the following paragraph so that it has both long and short sentences. Make sure you write some compound and complex sentences.

A cultural icon can be an object, a person, or a place. Cultural icons

symbolize a belief or a way of life. Each country has its own icons.

They become part of the country's history. For example, Mickey Mouse is more than eighty years old. The cartoon character symbolizes American optimism. The Statue of Liberty is also a potent symbol. It represents America's willingness to welcome immigrants. People can be icons too. Benito Juarez is celebrated in Mexico. Martin Luther King Jr. is idolized in the United States. These icons reflect shared cultural experiences.

Include a Question, a Quotation, or an Exclamation

The most common type of sentence is a statement. A simple but effective way to achieve sentence variety is to do the following:

- Ask and answer a **question.** You could also insert a **rhetorical question,** which does not require an answer but is used for effect.

  Did Elvis really do anything shocking?

- Include the occasional **exclamation** to express surprise. However, do not overuse exclamations, especially in academic writing.

  Elvis's swinging hips were considered obscene!

- Add a **direct quotation,** which includes the exact words that somebody said.

  Elvis said, "I didn't copy my style from anybody."

In the next passage, a question, an exclamation, and a quotation add variety.

> Norma Jeane Baker was born to a mentally unstable mother and an absent father. The shy little girl spent her childhood being shuffled between an orphanage and foster parents. From such inauspicious beginnings, a cultural icon was born. Norma Jeane, who later changed her name to Marilyn Monroe, bleached her hair, had plastic surgery on her nose, and became one of Hollywood's most recognizable figures. **Why is she remembered?** Perhaps her   ◄ Question
> fame is partly due to her untimely death at the age of thirty-six. She is also remembered for her sensuality and her childlike vulnerability. **Even at the height of her fame, she exuded unhappiness and once complained, "Everybody is always tugging   ◄ Quotation
> at you. They'd like a chunk out of you."** Some argue that she was not talented, and others suggest that people will forget her. **But the truth   ◄ Exclamation
> is, even half a century after her death, her image is one of the most recognized in America!**

 **Punctuating Quotations**

If you introduce your quotation with a phrase like "he said," put a comma after the phrase and before the opening quotation marks. Put the final period inside the closing quotation marks.

Marilyn Monroe once complained, "Everybody is always tugging at you."

If the end of the quotation is not the end of the sentence, place a comma inside the final quotation mark.

"They were terribly strict," she once said.

GRAMMAR LINK

For more information about punctuating quotations, refer to Chapter 35.

PRACTICE 2

Read the following passage. Change one sentence to a question, one to an exclamation, and one to a quotation.

EXAMPLE:

Why do most   ?
~~Most~~ people want to be famous⁄
                                 ^

We are living in a celebrity era. Many ordinary people achieve almost

saintly status. In previous centuries, heroes were those who fought bravely

in wars or who rescued others. Today, actors, musicians, politicians, and

athletes are routinely deified. Even criminals such as Al Capone and

Charles Manson become household names. In the words of Daniel J.

Boorstin, celebrity worship and hero worship should not be confused.

However, we confuse them every day.

Vary the Opening Words

An effective way to make your sentences more vivid is to vary the opening words. Instead of beginning each sentence with the subject, you could try the following strategies.

Begin with an Adverb

An **adverb** is a word that modifies a verb, and it often (but not always) ends in -ly. *Slowly, usually,* and *suddenly* are adverbs. Other adverbs include words such as *sometimes, never, however,* and *often.*

<u>Generally</u>, a cultural icon arouses strong feelings in members of that culture.

<u>Often</u>, an extremely gifted and famous person becomes an icon.

Begin with a Prepositional Phrase

A **prepositional phrase** is a group of words made up of a preposition and its object. *Under the chair, in the beginning,* and *after the fall* are prepositional phrases.

> In New York's harbor, the Statue of Liberty welcomes visitors.
>
> At dawn, we photographed the statue.

 **Comma Tip**

Generally, when a sentence begins with an adverb or a prepositional phrase, place a comma after the opening word or phrase.

Cautiously, the reporter asked another question to the volatile star.

Without any warning, she stood up and left the room.

PRACTICE 3

Rewrite the following sentences by placing an adverb or prepositional phrase at the beginning. First, strike out any word or phrase that could be moved. Then, rewrite that word or phrase at the beginning of the sentence. Finally, correctly punctuate your new sentence.

EXAMPLE:

<u>Actually, the</u>_____ ~~The~~ United States' most recognizable symbol was ~~actually~~ made in France.

1. _____ A group of French intellectuals, in 1865, met in a restaurant and discussed the United States.

2. _____ The French artists and thinkers carefully criticized their oppressive emperor, Napoleon III.

3. _____ They then expressed in quiet voices admiration for America's new democratic government.

4. _____ A sculptor suddenly decided to create a gift for the United States.

5. _____ Frederic-Auguste Bartholdi searched for a site to place his sculpture during a visit to the United States.

6. _____ He crafted "Lady Liberty" with the help of many workers.

PRACTICE 4

Add an opening word or phrase to each sentence. Use the type of opening that is indicated in parentheses. Remember to punctuate the sentence properly.

EXAMPLE:

Adverb

Surprisingly, the playwright Naomi Iizuka loves the 50-foot Hollywood sign.

1. (Adverb) _____ the sign is more than just white letters that spell "Hollywood."

2. (Prepositional phrase) _____ the sign is like a beacon to aspiring actors.

3. (Prepositional phrase) _____ thousands of people arrive with dreams of stardom.

4. (Adverb) _____ some people fine acting jobs, but many do not.

5. (Prepositional phrase) _____ the sign is an important American symbol.

Combine Sentences with a Present Participle

You can combine two sentences with a present participle. A **present participle** is a verb that ends in _-ing_, such as _believing_, _having_, and _using_. Combine sentences using an _-ing_ modifier only when the two actions happen at the same time and the sentences have the same subject.

Separate sentences:	He looked across the harbor. He saw the Statue of Liberty.
Combined sentences:	<u>Looking</u> across the harbor, he saw the Statue of Liberty.

PRACTICE 5

Combine the next sentences by converting one of the verbs into an _-ing_ modifier.

EXAMPLE:

Pop artists focused on familiar images. They painted comic strips and supermarket products.

Focusing on familiar images, pop artists painted comic strips and

supermarket products.

Painting comic strips and supermarket products, pop artists focused on

familiar images.

1. Andy Warhol worked as an illustrator. He drew footwear for a shoe company.

_____

_____

2. He desired respect. He wanted his work to be in art galleries.

_____

_____

3. One gallery owner rejected Warhol's art. She wanted original ideas.

_____

_____

4. Warhol felt inspired. He decided to create pop art.

_____

_____

5. Warhol needed an original idea. He focused on his favorite brands.

_____

_____

6. He reproduced soup cans and Coke bottles. He attracted a lot of attention.

_____

_____

Combine Sentences with a Past Participle

Another way to combine sentences is to use a past participle. A **past participle** is a verb that has an *-ed* ending (although there are many irregular past participles, such as *gone, seen, broken,* and *known*).

You can begin a sentence with a past participle. To do this, you must combine two sentences that have the same subject, and one of the sentences must contain a past participle.

GRAMMAR LINK

For a complete list of irregular past participles, see Appendix 2.

Separate sentences:	Jesse Owens was raised in Alabama. He became a famous athlete.
Combined sentences:	Raised in Alabama, Jesse Owens became a famous athlete.

PRACTICE 6

Combine each pair of sentences into one sentence beginning with a past participle.

EXAMPLE:

Jesse Owens was born in 1913. He was the son of sharecroppers and the grandson of slaves.

Born in 1913, Jesse Owens was the son of sharecroppers and the grandson

of slaves.

1. Jesse Owens was invited to the 1936 Olympic Games. He competed in twelve events.

   _____

   _____

2. The 1936 Olympic Games were held in Berlin. They were a showcase for the Nazi party.

   _____

   _____

3. Owens went on to win four gold medals. He was encouraged by his fans.

   _____

   _____

4. Hitler was surprised at Owens's success. He refused to shake the medal winner's hand.

   _____

   _____

5. The athlete was treated like a hero upon his return. He basked in glory for a while.

   _____

   _____

6. Owens was forbidden to ride in the front of a bus. He expressed sadness about the segregation laws in his state.

   _____

   _____

Combine Sentences with an Appositive

An **appositive** is a word or phrase that gives further information about a noun or pronoun. You can combine two sentences by using an appositive. In the example, the italicized phrase could become an appositive because it describes the noun *Bob Marley*.

Two sentences: Bob Marley was *a founding member of The Wailers*. He went on to have a solo career.

You can place the appositive directly before the word that it refers to or directly after that word. Notice that the appositives are set off with commas.

appositive

Combined: A founding member of The Wailers, **Bob Marley** went on to have a successful solo career.

appositive

Combined: **Bob Marley**, a founding member of The Wailers, went on to have a successful solo career.

 **Finding an Appositive**

To find an appositive, look for a word or phrase that describes or renames a noun. The noun could be anywhere in the sentence.

Bob Marley popularized a new fashion trend. He wore dreadlocks.

In the preceding sentences, "dreadlocks" describes the new fashion trend. You could combine the sentences as follows:

appositive

Bob Marley popularized **a new fashion trend,** dreadlocks.

PRACTICE 7

Combine the following pairs of sentences. In each pair, make one of the sentences an appositive. Try to vary the position of the appositive. In some sentences, you could put the appositive at the beginning of the sentence, and in others, you could put the appositive after the word that it describes. The first one has been done for you.

EXAMPLE:

Bob Marley was a Jamaican. He greatly popularized reggae music.

Bob Marley, a Jamaican, greatly popularized reggae music.

_____

1. Bob Marley brought international attention to reggae music. He was a great musician.

_____

_____

2. Marley was biracial. He was born in 1945 in Jamaica.

_____

_____

3. Marley's father was a sailor. His father died when Marley was young.

_____

_____

4. At the age of 14, Marley started jam sessions with Joe Higgs. Higgs was a Rastafarian and reggae musician.

_____

_____

5. Jamaicans loved the reggae sound of Bob Marley and The Wailers. The group was one of the most famous bands in the country.

_____

_____

6. Bob Marley has had a profound influence on contemporary music. Marley is a music icon.

_____

_____

REFLECT ON IT

Think about what you have learned in this unit. If you do not know an answer, review that topic.

1. Why is sentence variety important? _____

   _____

2. Write a sentence that begins with an adverb.

   _____

   _____

3. Write a sentence that begins with a present participle. _____

   _____

4. Write a sentence that begins with a past participle. _____

   _____

5. Write a sentence that begins with an appositive. _____

FINAL REVIEW

The next essay lacks sentence variety. Use the strategies that you have learned in this and in previous chapters to create at least ten varied sentences.

EXAMPLE:

, believing
People are obsessed with fame. ~~Perhaps they believe~~ that fame will make them immortal.

1. Andy Warhol was an artist. He predicted that everyone would be famous for fifteen minutes. Today television is filled with ordinary people. They hope to achieve celebrity status. We wonder why this is happening. Our society elevates celebrities above the common human. Certainly, celebrities often have great talent. The talent includes exceptional musical ability, great athletic prowess, or a flair for acting. However, many celebrities lack moral character. They are models of bad behavior. Celebrities often make poor role models.

2. Some famous people have unhealthy lifestyles. They influence their fans. Amy Winehouse is a singer. She wrote a song called "Rehab." It mentions her drug addiction. Her song is catchy. It sends a negative message. Other stars have driven while intoxicated. Paris Hilton, Busta Rhymes, and Lindsay Lohan were arrested. Kanye West was extremely rude during an awards show. He held a bottle of alcohol. Stars endorse drugs and alcohol. They make substance abuse appear glamorous and rebellious.

3. Other celebrities have promoted violence. This includes Tupac Shakur. Shakur certainly had a difficult childhood. He was raised in Baltimore, Maryland. He was accepted to the prestigious Baltimore School for the Arts. He developed his music and writing skills. He also became involved in gangs. He was arrested on several occasions. His rap music often mentioned the thug life. It told stories of gunfights and gang rivalries. He was gunned down during a trip to Las Vegas, Nevada. The rapper died violently.

4. Impressionable youngsters want to emulate their heroes. They do not think about the dangers of drugs or gang life. Some people do not care what celebrities do. Artists are entitled to make mistakes. However, public figures have a responsibility to their fans. They definitely should not promote bad behavior.

The Writer's Room

Choose one of the following topics and write a paragraph or an essay. When you write, remember to follow the writing process.

1. Define *hero*. What makes a person a hero?

2. Why do so many people crave fame? How does celebrity status affect people? Write about the causes or effects of fame.

The Writers' Circle   **Collaborative Activity**

Get into a group of three or four students. Then think about songs that you have on your iPod or about songs that you really love. Each person in your team should contribute four song titles to the list.

Using the titles as inspiration, write a paragraph. Add words and sentences to make your paragraph complete. Your paragraph should have at least one simple sentence, one compound sentence, and one complex sentence.

READING LINK

Culture

"Bound Feet" by Jung Chang (page 528)

"Being a Hyphenated American" by Zaina Arafat (page 530)

"Fads" by David A. Locher (page 533)

mywritinglab To check your progress in meeting this chapter's objectives, log in to **www.mywritinglab.com**, go to the **Study Plan** tab, click on **The Editing Handbook—Section 1: Effective Sentences** and choose **Varying Sentence Structure and Combining Sentences** from the list of subtopics. Read and view the resources in the **Review Materials** section, and then complete the **Recall, Apply,** and **Write** sets in the **Activities** section.

Fragments

Section Theme **PSYCHOLOGY**

LEARNING OBJECTIVE

1 Fragments (p. 309)

In this chapter, you will read about topics related to psychological profiles.

The Writer's Journal

How do men and women deal with personal problems? Do they use different strategies? Write about problem-solving techniques that men and women use.

Fragments

A **sentence** must have a subject and a verb, and it must express a complete thought. A **fragment** is an incomplete sentence. Either it lacks a subject or verb, or it fails to express a complete thought. You may see fragments in newspaper headlines and advertisements (*Wrinkle-free skin in one month*). However, in college writing, it is unacceptable to write fragments.

Sentence: Sigmund Freud was a famous psychologist.

Fragment: Considered to be the founder of psychoanalysis.

Phrase Fragments

A phrase fragment is missing a subject or a verb. In the following examples, the fragments are underlined.

No verb: <u>First, B. F. Skinner.</u> He did research on human behavior.

No subject: B. F. Skinner wrote a novel about human behavior. <u>Called *Walden Two*.</u>

How to Correct Phrase Fragments

To correct a phrase fragment, either add the missing subject or verb, or join the fragment to another sentence. Here are two ways you can correct the phrase fragments in the previous examples.

Join sentences: First, B. F. Skinner did research on human behavior.

Add words: B. F. Skinner wrote a novel about human behavior. It was called *Walden Two*.

 **Incomplete Verbs**

A sentence must have a subject and a complete verb. If a sentence has an incomplete verb, it is a phrase fragment. The following example contains a subject and part of a verb. However, it is missing a helping verb; therefore, the sentence is incomplete.

Fragment: Many books about psychology written by Carl Jung.

To make this sentence complete, you must add the helping verb.

Sentence: Many books about psychology <u>were</u> written by Carl Jung.

PRACTICE I

Underline and correct six phrase fragments.

EXAMPLE:

<u>A childhood trauma.</u> ~~It~~ can be the source of an irrational fear.

1.   First, superstitions. People sometimes have irrational beliefs. Many compulsive gamblers, for example, think that they can control the spin of slot machine reels by carrying good luck charms. Some carry a four-leaf clover. Or a rabbit's foot. The illusion of control.

2.   Many athletes have rituals or lucky items of clothing. A lucky number on their jersey. The St. Louis Rams running back Marshall Faulk always wears black to the stadium. Another football player, Chris Hale. He believes that dressing in a particular sequence is lucky. Also, Michael Jordan played each game. With blue University of North Carolina at Chapel Hill shorts under his Chicago Bulls uniform.

Fragments with -ing and to

A fragment may begin with a **present participle,** which is the form of the verb that ends in -ing (*running, talking*). It may also begin with an **infinitive,** which is *to* plus the base form of the verb (*to run, to talk*). These fragments generally appear before or after another sentence that contains the subject. In the examples, the fragments are underlined.

-ing fragment:	<u>Thinking about positive outcomes.</u> It helps people cope with stress.
to fragment:	Oprah Winfrey has developed a resilient attitude. <u>To overcome her childhood traumas.</u>

How to Correct -ing and to Fragments

To correct an -ing or to fragment, either add the missing words, or join the fragment to another sentence. Here are two ways to correct the previous examples.

Join sentences:	Thinking about positive outcomes helps people cope with stress.
Add words:	Oprah Winfrey has developed a resilient attitude **because she had** to overcome her childhood traumas.

 **Hint**   **When the -ing Word Is the Subject**

Sometimes a gerund (-ing form of the verb) is the subject of a sentence. In the next example, *listening* is the subject of the sentence.

Correct:	<u>Listening</u> is an important skill.

A sentence fragment occurs when the -ing word is part of an incomplete verb string or when the subject was mentioned in a previous sentence.

Fragment:	Oprah Winfrey has achieved success. <u>Listening to people's problems.</u>

PRACTICE 2

Underline and correct six -ing and to fragments.

EXAMPLE:

<u>Living through a childhood trauma.</u> ~~It~~ can be the source of an irrational fear.

Relating characteristics and physical health. Doctors Myer

Friedman and Ray Rosenman divided people into personality types.

Acting extremely competitive. Type A personalities are workaholics.

They feel a strong pressure. To be busy. Type B personalities tend to

be easygoing. Feeling relaxed and at peace. They can spend hours

lying in the sun. Other researchers identified a Type C personality.

Type C people are usually very pleasant but cannot easily express anger. To avoid conflict. They internalize strong emotions. According to Friedman and Rosenman. The personality type at greatest risk of developing heart disease is Type A. However, researchers at Duke University have found that only extremely hostile Type A profiles are at increased risk of coronary disease.

Explanatory Fragments

An **explanatory fragment** provides an explanation about a previous sentence and is missing a subject, a complete verb, or both. Such fragments are sometimes expressed as an afterthought. These types of fragments begin with one of the following words.

also	especially	for example	including	particularly
as well as	except	for instance	like	such as

In each example, the explanatory fragment is underlined.

Fragment: Carl Jung studied with many prominent psychologists. <u>For instance, Sigmund Freud.</u>

Fragment: Psychologists analyze behavior. <u>Particularly through methods of observation.</u>

How to Correct Explanatory Fragments

To correct explanatory fragments, add the missing words, or join the explanation or example to another sentence. Here are two ways to correct the fragments in the previous examples.

Add words: Carl Jung studied with many prominent psychologists. For instance, **he worked with** Sigmund Freud.

Join sentences: Psychologists analyze behavior, particularly through methods of observation.

PRACTICE 3

Underline and correct six explanatory fragments. You may need to add or remove words.

EXAMPLE:

loyal, especially
Some fans are very loyal. <u>Especially Red Sox fans.</u>

Stephen Dubner wrote *Confessions of a Hero Worshipper*. He describes the personality of sports fans, and his book has interesting anecdotes.

For example, the 1994 World Cup. The saliva of male soccer fans was tested before and after an important match. The chosen fans were from Brazil. As well as Italy. The testosterone levels in the fans of the winning team rose quickly. Particularly during the final minutes of the game. The losing fans' testosterone levels decreased. Researcher Paul Bernhardt was surprised. Especially by the percentages. The fans of the winning team, with a 20 percent increase, had the same level of testosterone as the athletes. The findings may explain aggressive episodes. Such as soccer hooliganism. Immediately after a testosterone surge, some males may act more aggressively. Especially when provoked.

Dependent-Clause Fragments

A **dependent clause** has a subject and a verb, but it cannot stand alone. It *depends* on another clause to be a complete sentence. Dependent clauses may begin with subordinating conjunctions (subordinators) or relative pronouns. The following are some of the most common words that begin dependent clauses.

Common Subordinating Conjunctions				Relative Pronouns
after	before	though	whenever	that
although	even though	unless	where	which
as	if	until	whereas	who(m)
because	since	what	whether	whose

The next two examples contain dependent-clause fragments. In each example, the fragment is underlined.

Fragment: Although I cross my fingers for luck. I know that it is a silly superstition.

Fragment: I will not walk under a ladder. That is leaning against a wall.

How to Correct Dependent-Clause Fragments

To correct dependent-clause fragments, either join the fragment to a complete sentence or add the necessary words to make it a complete idea. You could also delete the subordinating conjunction. Here are two ways to correct the fragments in the previous examples.

Delete the subordinator: I cross my fingers for luck. I know that that is a silly superstition.

Join sentences: Although I cross my fingers for luck, I know that it is a silly superstition.
I will not walk under a ladder that is leaning against a wall.

PRACTICE 4

Underline and correct five dependent-clause fragments.

EXAMPLE:

<u>Whenever they blame themselves.</u> ~~Negative~~ ^{, negative} thinkers make their problems larger.

1. Andrew Shatte is a University of Pennsylvania researcher. Who worked on the Resiliency Project. For the project, graduate psychology students taught seventy children. That they can become more resilient. Children learned the difference between productive and self-defeating thinking. After they looked at their own fears. The children had to test their expectations to see if they were realistic.

2. One child in the program who came from a tough inner-city neighborhood had convinced himself that he would probably end up in a gang. Even though he hated violence. The program taught this boy. That there are other possible outcomes. He learned that he did not have to focus on worst-case scenarios.

REFLECT ON IT

Think about what you have learned in this unit. If you do not know an answer, review that concept.

1. What is a sentence fragment? _____

    _____

2. What are the types of fragments?

    _____

    _____

3. Correct the next fragment.

    According to Freud, people unintentionally repress certain memories. Because they are painful or threatening.

FINAL REVIEW

Correct fifteen fragment errors.

EXAMPLE:

Humans rely on memory. ~~To~~ *to* perform any action.

1.   Have you ever forgotten a telephone number? That you have just looked up. Forgetting an item of information. It happens to all of us. Memory is an intriguing process. Psychologists identify three types of memory. First, sensory memory. It refers to the initial perception of information. The second kind of memory is short-term memory. By rehearsing, we can transfer information from our sensory memory to our short-term memory. Researchers have discovered that we can hold about seven pieces of information in our short-term memory. But only for about 30 seconds. We store information in our long-term memory. Through chemical changes in our brain.

2.   As we age, our memory decays. However, there are techniques that we can attempt. To help our memory. We can remember information more easily. Using mnemonics. One mnemonic device employs rhymes. A familiar example is the rule *i* before *e* except after *c*. Which helps us with our spelling. Another mnemonic technique is the acronym. An acronym uses the first letters of a series of words. Such as FBI (Federal Bureau of Investigation). A third type of mnemonic device is called the peg system. Alphabet books. They generally use the peg system when they teach *A for apple*, *B for ball*, and so on.

3.   A very effective memory device is called the SQ4R. According to psychologists. SQ4R (pronounced "square") is an acronym for a study strategy: Survey, Question, Read, Reflect, Recite, and Review. Researchers believe that this system is very useful for students. Who need to remember large amounts of information. By following the SQ4R method, students may have more success at retaining information. Especially when they study for exams.

4.   Finally, we must practice organizing and rehearsing information. Because we cannot develop a good memory by being passive. We should use mnemonic devices. When we need to remember a phone number or another item of information.

 The Writer's Room

Write about one of the following topics. Check that there are no sentence fragments.

1. Explain why people are superstitious, and give examples to support your point of view.

2. Look again at Practice 2. What personality type are you? Are you Type A, B, or C? Describe your personality.

mywritinglab To check your progress in meeting this chapter's objectives, log in to **www.mywritinglab.com**, go to the **Study Plan** tab, click on **The Editing Handbook—Section 2: Common Sentence Errors** and choose **Fragments** from the list of subtopics. Read and view the resources in the **Review Materials** section, and then complete the **Recall, Apply,** and **Write** sets in the **Activities** section.

Run-Ons

Section Theme **PSYCHOLOGY**

LEARNING OBJECTIVE

1 Run-Ons (p. 317)

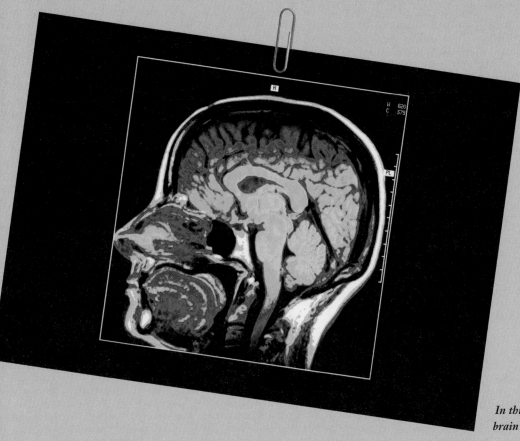

In this chapter, you will read about the brain and personality differences.

The Writer's Journal

Do you have any good habits? Describe your good habits. Why do you think they are positive?

Run-Ons

A **run-on sentence** occurs when two or more complete sentences are incorrectly joined. In other words, the sentence runs on without stopping. There are two types of run-on sentences.

- A **fused sentence** has no punctuation to mark the break between ideas.

  Incorrect: Psychologists describe human behavior they use observational methods.

- A **comma splice** uses a comma incorrectly to connect two complete ideas.

  Incorrect: Wilhelm Wundt was born in 1832, he is often called the founder of modern psychology.

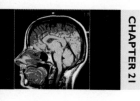

PRACTICE I

Read the following sentences. Write *C* beside correct sentences and *RO* beside run-ons.

EXAMPLE:

Sigmund Freud and Carl Jung were two famous psychologists
they profoundly influenced the field of psychology.   *RO*

1. Psychologists study human behavior, researchers have developed
   many theories on human nature.   _____

2. Instinct theory is one model developed by psychologists it
   proposes that behavior is based on biology.   _____

3. Learning theory suggests that humans learn through experience.   _____

4. Trait theories focus on human characteristics, psychologists
   describe personality types.   _____

5. Freud developed a theory about personality in which he divided
   the mind into three parts.   _____

6. Freud named the parts the *id*, *ego*, and *superego* his theory became
   enormously influential.   _____

7. Psychoanalysis started to lose its popularity by the 1940s, at that
   time other personality theories were developing.   _____

8. One psychologist, William Sheldon, tried to connect personality
   to body shapes.   _____

9. Sheldon's types were mesomorphic, or lean; endomorphic, or fat;
   and ectomorphic, or tall and thin.   _____

10. Human personalities vary greatly it is difficult to categorize them. _____

How to Correct Run-Ons

You can correct run-on sentences in a variety of ways. Read the following run-on
sentence, and then review the four ways to correct it.

Run-On: Thomas Bouchard Jr. studies twins, he is interested in genetic
influences on behavior.

1. Make two separate sentences by adding end punctuation, such as a period.

   Thomas Bouchard Jr. studies twins. **He** is interested in genetic influences
   on behavior.

2. Add a semicolon.

   Thomas Bouchard Jr. studies twins; he is interested in genetic influences
   on behavior.

3. Add a coordinator (*for, and, nor, but, or, yet, so*).

   Thomas Bouchard Jr. is interested in genetic influences on behavior, **so** he
   studies twins.

4. Add a subordinator (*after, although, as, because, before, since, when, while*).

   Thomas Bouchard Jr. studies twins **because** he is interested in genetic
   influences on behavior.

PRACTICE 2

A. Correct each run-on by making two complete sentences.

EXAMPLE:

The twins are identical, *. They* they have brown hair and eyes.

1. Until the 1960s, twins put up for adoption were generally separated they were often adopted by two different families.

2. Psychologists are interested in studying twins raised in different families, they want to determine whether genetics or the environment plays a dominant role in behavior.

3. An amazing case involves Tamara Rabi and Adriana Scott they met each other in 2003.

B. Correct each run-on by joining the two sentences with a semicolon.

EXAMPLE:

The girls are remarkably similar, *;* they both love to dance.

4. Tamara and Adriana were born in Mexico they were separated and raised by different families.

5. The girls were adopted by American families they lived just twenty-five miles apart.

6. Tamara Rabi was raised by a Jewish family in a city Adriana Scott was raised by a Catholic family in a suburb.

C. Correct the next run-ons by joining the two sentences with a coordinator such as *for, and, nor, but, or, yet,* or *so.*

EXAMPLE:

A boy named Justin dated Adriana *, but* there was no mutual attraction.

7. Justin still wanted to find a girlfriend, his friend set him up with another girl.

8. Justin met Tamara he was astounded at her similarity to his previous girlfriend, Adriana.

9. Justin convinced the girls to meet each other, they met in a McDonald's parking lot.

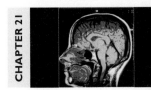

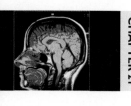

D. Correct the next run-ons by joining the two sentences with a subordinator such as *although*, *because*, *where*, or *when*.

EXAMPLE:

                  because

The girls were happy to meet they each wanted a sister.

10. The twins did not go to the same type of school their families were not in the same income bracket.

11. Their educations differed in quality, they were both B students.

12. The girls flew to Mexico they met their birth mother.

PRACTICE 3

Some sentences are correct and some are run-ons. Write *C* beside each correct sentence and *RO* beside the run-ons. Using a variety of methods, correct each run-on error.

EXAMPLE:

                                and

The origins of fears are complicated, many people live with
unusual fears.   *RO*

1. Maggie Juato, a public relations executive, is afraid of clowns. _____

2. The fear of clowns is known as coulrophobia it can cause panic attacks. _____

3. Professional clowns are aware of the problem they do not approach the fearful. _____

4. There are many theories about the causes of this phobia, none are conclusive. _____

5. Maybe a person becomes afraid because the clown's true emotions are hidden by makeup. _____

6. The fear may have been caused by a past event, an adult may have had a negative experience as a child. _____

7. Perhaps the phobia is caused by clown horror movies. _____

8. In the movie *It*, written by Stephen King, for example, actor Tim Curry plays the evil clown, Pennywise, he smacks his lips every time he is about to murder a child. _____

9. Real clowns are actors and comedians, they entertain children in hospitals and the elderly in nursing homes. _____

10. Certain psychologists can help patients overcome their clown phobias. _____

PRACTICE 4

Correct twelve run-on errors.

EXAMPLE:

About 3 percent of births in the United States are twins ⌃ the percentage is
increasing.

, but

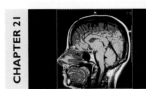

1.   Thomas Bouchard Jr. and some colleagues at the University of
Minnesota began studying twins in 1979. Bouchard had read about twins
who had been raised apart, he contacted them to study their similarities and
differences. By 1990, Bouchard's team had studied seventy-seven sets of
identical twins.

2.   Most of the separated twins had astounding
similarities. For example, two men named Jim had
been separated at birth. They met in 1979 they
found that they were similar in many ways. They
smoked the same brand of cigarettes, they were
both volunteer firefighters. The Jims also enjoyed
carpentry, they built similar white benches.

Jim Lewis and Jim Springer

3.   In the study, one set of twins was unusual.
Japanese-born twins were adopted by different
families in California. They shared some
similarities researchers were puzzled by their differences. One twin had
20/20 vision, the other wore glasses. One was afraid to travel by airplane
the other had no such fear. One twin was quite timid, the other was
easygoing and friendly.

4.   Researchers suspect that the environment may play a role in twin
differences. For example, one twin could be malnourished, the other could
have a healthy diet. The differences in diet could affect the development of
the twins' brains and bodies. Birthing problems may also result in
differences between twins one twin might receive less oxygen during delivery.

5.   The separated-twin studies suggest certain possibilities, for example,
twins raised separately may be more similar than twins raised together.
Twins raised together may emphasize their differences twins raised apart

would have no need to search for their individuality. More research is needed to know how genes influence behavior.

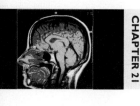

REFLECT ON IT

Think about what you have learned in this unit. If you do not know an answer, review that concept.

1. What is a run-on? _____

_____

2. Define a comma splice. _____

_____

3. Define a fused sentence. _____

_____

4. Explain the four ways to correct a run-on sentence.

a. _____

b. _____

c. _____

d. _____

FINAL REVIEW

Correct fifteen run-on errors.

EXAMPLE:

; it

The brain is an extremely complex organ, ~~it~~ is the center of the human nervous system.

1. The basis of human behavior is the human brain, if it malfunctions, people experience problems. Yet, researchers still have a lot to learn about the human brain.

2. In 1985, Dr. Oliver Sacks wrote a book called *The Man Who Mistook His Wife for a Hat*, he analyzed some interesting cases of patients who had exhibited puzzling behavior. One of Dr. Sacks's patients was a music teacher he had lost his ability to identify objects or people. This condition is known as agnosia, the condition has many possible causes. For example, Anita Kaye was in a car accident. She was hurled out of the car, she

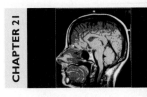

experienced brain trauma. Now she no longer recognizes people, shapes, and objects. She can see a plate placed before her she cannot name it. If she wants something, she describes the object to a family member.

3. Another interesting case concerned Mrs. O'C. She was old, she started to hear Irish music. She became Dr. Sacks's patient she wanted to stop hearing the music. Apparently, she was experiencing small epileptic seizures they triggered her brain to recall music from her childhood. Mrs. O'C was an orphan, the seizures may have released a desire to relive her childhood before her parents' death.

4. A Russian composer had a similar experience. During World War II, a bomb exploded near Dimitry Shostakovich a small piece of metal lodged in his head. Years later, he consulted a Chinese neurologist, the composer wanted to know if the metal should be removed. Whenever he moved his head, the piece of metal shifted, and he would hear music. The doctor recommended leaving the metal in place, the bomb had actually done some good.

5. The brain is a mysterious organ researchers are trying to understand it. According to neurologist Wilder Penfield, the brain is the organ of destiny, it holds secrets that will determine the future of the human race.

The Writer's Room

Write about one of the following topics. Make sure that you have not written any run-ons.

1. Narrate a story about one of your earliest memories.
2. Describe a set of twins. Compare and contrast twins by looking at their similarities and differences. If you don't know any twins, then describe the similarities and differences between siblings (brothers and sisters).

mywritinglab To check your progress in meeting this chapter's objectives, log in to **www.mywritinglab.com**, go to the **Study Plan** tab, click on **The Editing Handbook—Section 2: Common Sentence Errors** and choose **Run-Ons** from the list of subtopics. Read and view the resources in the **Review Materials** section, and then complete the **Recall, Apply,** and **Write** sets in the **Activities** section.

Faulty Parallel Structure

Section Theme **PSYCHOLOGY**

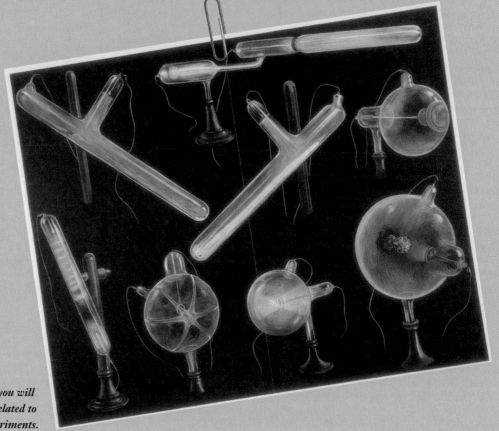

In this chapter, you will read about topics related to psychological experiments.

The Writer's Journal

Write a short paragraph comparing your personality to that of a family member or friend. Describe how your personalities are similar and different.

What Is Parallel Structure?

Parallel structure occurs when pairs or groups of items in a sentence are balanced. In the following sentences, the underlined phrases contain repetitions of grammatical structure but not of ideas. Each sentence has parallel structure.

> Internet sites, magazines, and newspapers published the results of the experiment.
>
> (The nouns are parallel.)

Psychologists <u>observe</u> and <u>predict</u> human behavior.
(The present tense verbs are parallel.)

The experiment was <u>fascinating</u>, <u>groundbreaking</u>, and <u>revolutionary</u>.
(The adjectives are parallel.)

To get to the psychology department, go <u>across the street</u>, <u>into the building</u>, and <u>up the stairs</u>.
(The prepositional phrases are parallel.)

There are some test subjects <u>who develop a rash</u> and some <u>who have no reactions</u>.
(The "who" clauses are parallel.)

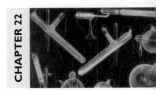

PRACTICE I

All of the following sentences have parallel structures. Underline the parallel items.

EXAMPLE:

Students in my psychology class <u>listened to the instructor</u>, <u>took notes</u>, and <u>asked questions</u>.

1. Professor Stanley Milgram taught at Yale, conducted a famous experiment, and wrote a book about his research.

2. Milgram's experiment was controversial, provocative, and surprising.

3. His experiment tried to understand how humans reacted to authority, how they obeyed authority, and how they felt about authority.

4. For his experiment, Milgram used one actor in a lab coat, one actor with glasses, and one unsuspecting subject in street clothes.

5. The psychologist told the subject to sit at the desk, to watch the "patient" behind the glass, and to listen to the experiment "leader."

6. The leader told the subject when to start electric shocks, when to increase the level of shocks, and when to stop the experiment.

7. Milgram's experiment raised important questions, ended in astonishing results, and gave valuable insight into human behavior.

8. Psychologists continue to perform experiments, give lectures, and debate issues.

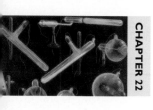

Identify Faulty Parallel Structure

It is important to use parallel structure for a series of words or phrases, paired clauses, a comparison, and a two-part construction.

Series of Words or Phrases

Use parallel structure when words or phrases are joined in a series.

Not parallel:	Students, administrators, and people who teach sometimes volunteer for psychology experiments.
Parallel:	<u>Students</u>, <u>administrators</u>, and <u>teachers</u> sometimes volunteer for psychology experiments. (The nouns are parallel.)
Not parallel:	I plan to study for tests, to attend all classes, and listening to the instructor.
Parallel:	I plan <u>to study</u> for tests, <u>to attend</u> all classes, and <u>to listen</u> to the instructor. (The verbs are parallel.)

Paired Clauses

Use parallel structure when independent clauses are joined by *and*, *but*, or *or*.

Not parallel:	The experimenter placed two probes on her head, and her wrist is where he attached a monitor.
Parallel:	The experimenter placed two probes <u>on her head</u>, and he attached a monitor <u>to her wrist</u>. (The prepositional phrases are parallel.)
Not parallel:	She felt dizzy, and she also had a feeling of fear.
Parallel:	She felt <u>dizzy</u>, and she also felt <u>afraid</u>. (The adjectives are parallel.)

GRAMMAR LINK

To learn more about active and passive voice, see pages 353–356 in Chapter 24.

 **Hint** **Use Consistent Voice**

When a sentence has two independent clauses and is joined by a coordinating conjunction, use a consistent voice. In other words, if one part of the sentence is active, the other should also be active.

Not parallel:	The researcher conducted the experiment, and then a report was written by him.
Parallel:	The researcher <u>conducted the experiment</u>, and then <u>he wrote a report</u>. (Both parts use the active voice.)

PRACTICE 2

Correct the faulty parallel structure in each sentence.

EXAMPLE:

original.

Some psychology experiments are bold, pioneering, and ~~show their~~ ~~originality.~~

1. Ivan Pavlov was a Russian physiologist, a research scientist, and he won a Nobel prize.

2. Pavlov became interested in dog salivation, and digestion also interested him.

3. To get to his lab, Pavlov walked through the door, up the stairs, and the department is where he entered.

4. Pavlov used many sound-making devices to stimulate his dogs, such as metronomes, whistles, and he also used tuning forks.

5. Pavlov noticed that the dogs heard the noise, saw the food dish, and were salivating.

6. Some of the dogs were excited, nervous, and expressed enthusiasm.

7. Western scientists found Pavlov's experiments to be astounding, innovative, and thought they were important.

8. Ivan Pavlov worked quickly and was very efficient.

Comparisons

Use parallel structure in comparisons containing *than* or *as*.

Not parallel:	Creating new experiments is more difficult than to re-create an earlier experiment.
Parallel:	<u>Creating a new experiment</u> is more difficult than <u>re-creating an earlier experiment.</u> (The *-ing* forms are parallel.)
Not parallel:	His home was as messy as the way he kept his laboratory.
Parallel:	His <u>home</u> was as messy as his <u>laboratory</u>. (The nouns are parallel.)

Two-Part Constructions

Use parallel structure for the following paired items.

either . . . or	not . . . but	both . . . and
neither . . . nor	not only . . . but also	rather . . . than

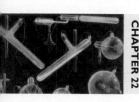

Not parallel:	My psychology class was both informative and a challenge.
Parallel:	My psychology class was both <u>informative</u> and <u>challenging</u>. (The adjectives are parallel.)
Not parallel:	I would rather finish my experiment than leaving early.
Parallel:	I would rather <u>finish</u> my experiment than <u>leave</u> early. (The verbs are parallel.)

PRACTICE 3

Correct ten errors in parallel construction.

EXAMPLE:

Philip Zimbardo is creative and ~~an interesting person.~~ *interesting.*

1. Philip Zimbardo created an experiment that was both unique and startled others. The Stanford Prison Experiment examined how ordinary people react when placed in positions of power or helplessness. He chose twenty-four students who were healthy, stable, and they abided by the law. Each subject would be either a guard or a prisoner for a two-week period.

2. On the first day of the experiment, each guard was told to wear a uniform, carry a baton, and sunglasses were put on. Ordinary people who had committed no crime, who had broken no laws, and had been honest were placed in a cold room. The prisoners were not only arrested but the guards also deloused them.

3. Immediately, the experimenters observed shocking behavior. Some of the guards started to act controlling, sadistic, and they abused the prisoners. On the second day, the prisoners rioted, and the guards attacked. Some prisoners decided that they would rather leave than continuing with the experiment.

4. During the next few days, officials, priests, and teachers observed the experiment. Nobody questioned the morality of the proceedings. Then, on the sixth day, another psychologist arrived. She was appalled and she felt horror when she realized what was happening.

5. Zimbardo realized that his student actors were taking the experiment too seriously. Both the prisoners and the people playing the guards had to stop the experiment. Zimbardo worried that the student actors would be seriously hurt, distressed, and suffer from depression.

PRACTICE 4

Correct nine errors in parallel construction.

EXAMPLE:

interesting.
Information about bystander apathy is surprising and ~~of interest.~~

1. Bystander apathy is the unwillingness of an individual to help another in an emergency. In the 1960s, psychologists started to collect data, investigate behaviors, and proposing theories about bystander apathy. One celebrated instance of bystander apathy is the Kitty Genovese case.

2. On March 13, 1964, Kitty Genovese was on her way to her apartment in Queens, New York. She was walking quietly and her steps were quick. Suddenly, she saw a strange man. He attacked her, and she screamed for help. Kitty Genovese died slowly, violently, and in tragic circumstances.

3. The police investigation was complete, thorough, and done with precision. The results of the investigation were both astounding and nobody expected them. Apparently, thirty-eight people heard the victim screaming, and the attack was watched by some of them, but no one called the police.

4. Many psychologists have studied the phenomenon of bystander apathy, and the results have been published by them. There are many reasons a bystander may not help someone in trouble. Bystanders may not want to risk their own lives, they may not have the skills to help in an emergency, or legal problems could be incurred. In addition, many people do not want to look stupid or be seen as being foolish if there is no real emergency. Psychologists believe that these are only some possible reasons for bystander apathy.

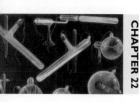

PRACTICE 5

Write sentences using parallel structure with the following grammatical items.

1. Parallel nouns: _____

_____

2. Parallel verbs: _____

_____

3. Parallel adjectives: _____

_____

4. Parallel *who* clauses: _____

_____

REFLECT ON IT

Think about what you have learned in this chapter. If you do not know an answer, review that concept.

1. What is parallel structure? _____

_____

2. Why is parallel structure important? _____

_____

Fill in the blanks of the following sentences. Make sure the grammatical structures are parallel.

1. The college I attend is both _____ and

_____.

2. In my spare time, I _____, _____, and

_____.

FINAL REVIEW

Correct twelve errors in parallel construction.

EXAMPLE:

Psychiatrists, psychologists, and ~~other people who are counselors~~ help
patients deal with their mental health problems.

counselors

1.   Have you ever been in a group discussion where you wanted to offer a

different point of view but did not? Psychologist Irvin Janis was ambitious,

intelligent, and worked hard. In 1972, he studied group dynamics and then

the results were written by him. He called his book *Groupthink*.

2. Groupthink occurs when members of a group feel a strong need to agree with others. These are people who do not criticize a prevailing position, who do not offer alternative strategies, and do not voice any disagreement. Group participants not only suppress common sense, but unpopular opinions are also avoided.

3. Janis presented an interesting example of groupthink in his book. In 1961, CIA operatives, military leaders, and people in American politics wanted to overthrow Fidel Castro. When President John F. Kennedy heard about the plan to invade Cuba, he was both agreeable and full of enthusiasm. Kennedy's group of advisors wanted to be both cooperative and acting patriotic. As a result, all of Kennedy's counselors agreed with the proposal. The invasion was planned blindly, quickly, and without care. As a result, the Bay of Pigs invasion was a failure.

4. In October 1962, the Soviet Union placed nuclear warheads in Cuba. When Kennedy heard about the missiles, he wanted to meet with his advisors. He walked rapidly through the garden, along the corridor, and he went into the Oval Office. At the meeting, Kennedy employed strategies to avoid groupthink. His advisors were encouraged to discuss, to debate, and they could disagree. Therefore, the men could either challenge bad ideas or good ideas could be analyzed. Using diplomacy, the President solved the crisis. The Soviets promptly removed the nuclear weapons from Cuba.

5. Janis's book has shown how groupthink can have negative consequences in government, in academics, and for people who work in business.

The Writer's Room

Choose one of the following topics and write a paragraph or an essay. When you write, remember to follow the writing process.

1. What makes you happy? Describe some situations or events that make you happy.

2. What are some different ways that people deal with their fears? Classify their responses to fear into three categories.

The Writers' Circle   **Collaborative Activity**

When you apply for a job, the employer often asks you what your strengths and weaknesses are. Work with a team of students to do the following activity.

STEP 1   Think of a successful person. You could choose a person from any of the next categories.

| A business tycoon | A politician | A movie star |
| A musician | An athlete | A writer or artist |

STEP 2   Brainstorm one list of that person's strengths and another list of that person's weaknesses.

STEP 3   Write a short paragraph about that successful person, discussing the person's strengths and weaknesses.

STEP 4   Exchange paragraphs with another team. Proofread the other team's paragraph, checking especially for fragments, run-ons, and parallel structure.

READING LINK

Psychology

"Religious Faith Versus Spirituality" by Neil Bissondath (page 541)

"Dancing with Fear" by Bebe Moore Campbell (page 544)

"Control Your Temper" by Elizabeth Passarella (page 546)

"Don't Worry, Act Happy" by Albert Nerenberg (page 548)

"Musicophilia" by Oliver Sachs (page 551)

mywritinglab To check your progress in meeting this chapter's objectives, log in to **www.mywritinglab.com**, go to the **Study Plan** tab, click on **The Editing Handbook—Section 2: Common Sentence Errors** and choose **Parallelism** from the list of subtopics. Read and view the resources in the **Review Materials** section, and then complete the **Recall, Apply,** and **Write** sets in the **Activities** section.

Present and Past Tenses

Section Theme **POLITICAL INTRIGUE**

LEARNING OBJECTIVES

1. What Is Verb Tense? (p. 333)
2. The Simple Present Tense (p. 334)
3. The Simple Past Tense (p. 335)
4. Avoid Double Negatives (p. 344)

In this chapter, you will read about spy tools and equipment.

The Writer's Journal

Write a short paragraph describing the last spy or suspense movie that you have seen. Describe what happened in the movie.

What Is Verb Tense?

A verb shows an action or a state of being. A **verb tense** indicates when an action occurred. Review the various tenses of the verb *work*.

Present:	She <u>works</u> alone.
Past:	The agent <u>worked</u> in Monaco last summer.
Future:	She <u>will work</u> in the Middle East next year.

Use Standard Verb Forms

Nonstandard English is used in everyday conversation, and it may differ according to the region in which you live. **Standard American English** is the common language generally used and expected in schools, businesses, and government institutions in the United States. Most of your instructors will want you to write using Standard American English.

Nonstandard:	He <u>don't</u> have <u>no</u> time.	She <u>be</u> busy.
Standard:	He <u>does not</u> have <u>any</u> time.	She <u>is</u> busy.

The Simple Present Tense

In English there are two forms of the present tense. The **simple present tense** indicates that an action is a general fact or habitual activity.

Fact: The Spy Museum <u>contains</u> many interesting spy artifacts.

Habitual activity: The undercover agent <u>meets</u> her superiors once a month.

Habitual Activity: The undercover agent <u>meets</u> her superiors once a month.

(past)	JANUARY	FEBRUARY	MARCH	APRIL	(future)
	▼	▼	▼	▼	
	They meet.	They meet.	They meet.	They meet.	

> *Hint*   **The Present Progressive**
>
> The **present progressive tense** indicates that an action is in progress at this moment. In this chapter, you will focus on the simple present form.
>
> present progressive tense
> Right now, the agent <u>is taking</u> pictures with her spy camera.

Forms of the Simple Present Tense

Simple present tense verbs (except *be*) have two forms. *Be* has three forms: *is, am, are.*

- **Base form:** When the subject is *I, you, we,* or *they,* or the equivalent (*women, the Rocky Mountains*), do not add an ending to the verb.

   Nations <u>rely</u> on spies to gather secret information.

GRAMMAR LINK

For more information about progressive forms, see pages 360–362 in Chapter 25.

- **Third-person singular form:** When the subject is *he, she, it,* or the equivalent (*Mark, Carol, Miami*), add an *-s* or *-es* ending to the verb. Remember that *have* is an irregular verb. The third-person singular form is *has.*

   That woman <u>works</u> as a spy.

Look at the singular and plural forms of the verb *work.*

Present Tense of *Work*	Singular	Plural
First person:	I work.	We work.
Second person:	You work.	You work.
Third person:	He works.	They work.
	She works.	
	It works.	

PRACTICE 1

Circle the correct present tense form of the verbs in parentheses.

EXAMPLE:

Spying (seem, (seems)) like an exciting job.

1. According to Christopher Andrew, co-author of *The Sword and the Shield*, the acronym *mice* (sum, sums) up the reasons why a person may become a traitor.

2. *Mice* (stand, stands) for "money, ideology, compromise, and ego."

3. According to Andrew, the most popular reason (is, are) money.

4. Some agents (receive, receives) millions in cash, jewelry, and so on.

5. Another reason (is, are) ideology.

6. Sometimes people (believe, believes) that another country's way of life is better.

7. Some men and women (become, becomes) spies because they are ashamed of something that they have done.

8. For example, if a government bureaucrat (steal, steals) money and another person (find, finds) out, the bureaucrat can be blackmailed to become a spy.

9. Finally, many people (think, thinks) that spying (is, are) an exciting profession.

10. Andrew (say, says) that "an interesting minority want to be secret celebrities" in their own little world of espionage.

The Simple Past Tense

The **simple past tense** indicates that an action occurred at a specific past time. In the past tense, there are regular and irregular verbs. **Regular verbs** end in *-d* or *-ed* (*talked, ended, watched*). **Irregular verbs** do not follow a regular pattern and do not end in any specific letter (*knew, saw, met*).

Yesterday morning, the spy satellite **passed** over my home.

CHAPTER 23

Yesterday morning, the spy satellite **passed** over my home.

YESTERDAY MORNING   TODAY

The satellite **passed** over my home.

 **The Past Progressive**

The **past progressive tense** indicates that an action was in progress at a particular past moment. In this chapter, you will focus on the simple past.

past progressive tense

While the detectives <u>were watching</u> the house, the suspect escaped.

Regular Past Tense Verbs

Regular past tense verbs have a standard *-d* or *-ed* ending. Use the same form for both singular and plural past tense verbs.

Singular subject: The agent **learned** to speak six languages.

Plural subject: During the war, spies **used** code names.

Spell Regular Past Tense Verbs Correctly

Most regular past tense verbs are formed by adding *-ed* to the base form of the verb.

walk<u>ed</u>   question<u>ed</u>

However, there are some exceptions.

- When the regular verb ends in *-e*, just add *-d*.

  realize<u>d</u>   appreciate<u>d</u>

- When the regular verb ends in consonant + *-y*, change the *y* to *i* and add *-ed*.

  reply–repl<u>ied</u>   try–tr<u>ied</u>

- When the regular verb ends in the vowel + *-y*, just add *-ed*.

  play<u>ed</u>   employ<u>ed</u>

- When the regular verb ends in a consonant–vowel–consonant combination, double the last consonant and add *-ed*.

  tap–tap<u>ped</u>   plan–plan<u>ned</u>

- When verbs of two or more syllables end in a stressed consonant-vowel-consonant combination, double the last letter and add *-ed*. But if the final syllable is not stressed, just add *-ed*.

  Final stressed syllable: refer–refer<u>red</u>   omit–omit<u>ted</u>

  Final unstressed syllable: open–open<u>ed</u>   develop–develop<u>ed</u>

 **Do Not Confuse *Past* and *Passed***

Some people confuse *past* and *passed*. *Past* is a noun that means "in a previous time" or "before now."

> She has many secrets in her <u>past</u>.

Passed is the past tense of the verb *pass*, which has many meanings.

> Many days <u>passed</u> as we waited for her arrival.
> (*Passed* means "went by.")

> I <u>passed</u> you the butter a moment ago.
> (*Passed* means "took something and gave it to someone.")

> He <u>passed</u> the entrance test.
> (*Passed* means "successfully completed.")

GRAMMAR LINK

See Chapter 33, "Spelling and Commonly Confused Words," for information about the spelling of verbs.

PRACTICE 2

Write the simple past form of each verb in parentheses. Make sure you spell the past tense verb correctly.

EXAMPLE:

The United States (launch) ___*launched*___ a spy satellite in 1960.

1.   The Central Intelligence Agency (use) _____ a series of spy satellites during the 1960s and 1970s. Officials (name) _____ each satellite with a code word. They (call) _____ the operation "Corona." The satellites (pass) _____ over sensitive locations in the former Soviet Union.

2.   Each Corona spy satellite (contain) _____ a powerful camera and regular film. When the camera (finish) _____ filming, it ejected from the satellite inside a special capsule. Then back on earth, experts (study) _____ the images and (learn) _____ about the military secrets of other nations. During the 1960s, the Corona satellites (drop) _____ at least three hundred capsules. Parachutes (open) _____ and the capsules (float) _____ down. Then Air Force pilots (recover) _____ the capsules.

3.   In the 1970s, the numbers of satellites (multiply) _____ dramatically. Last year, thousands of satellites (provide) _____ nations with high-resolution images of everything from shifting ice masses to traffic conditions in Los Angeles.

GRAMMAR LINK

See Appendix 2 for a complete list of irregular verbs.

Irregular Past Tense Verbs

Irregular verbs change internally. Because their spellings change from the present to the past tense, these verbs can be challenging to remember.

> The prisoner <u>wrote</u> with invisible ink.
> (wrote = past tense of *write*)

> The guards <u>sent</u> the letter.
> (sent = past tense of *send*)

PRACTICE 3

Write the correct past form of each verb in parentheses. Some verbs are regular, and some are irregular. If you do not know the past form of an irregular verb, consult Appendix 2.

EXAMPLE:

During the American revolution, soldiers (find) _____*found*_____ new ways to communicate.

1. In 1775, an American soldier named Benjamin Thompson (combine) _____ ferrous sulphate and water to create invisible ink. Then he (write) _____ a letter using the mixture. A few weeks later, the reader of the letter (hold) _____ it over a candle flame, and the ink (become) _____ brown. The lines with the invisible ink (appear) _____ between the lines of the regular letter.

2. During World War II, a mysterious person (send) _____ a postcard to Jacob Rosenblum, a resident of Bucharest. The postcard, dated August 20, 1943, (come) _____ from a concentration camp. In German, the letter (say) _____, "My darling, I remember you with love" and was signed "Lola." In invisible ink, the writer (speak) _____ of "starvation, degradation, killing by gas," and "an agonizing hell." The letter (end) _____ with the mysterious words "K is fulfilling his mission. We will do what we have to do." Many years later, researchers (read) _____ the letter and (see) _____ the hidden message. They (think) _____ it provided proof that resistance movements existed in some concentration camps.

3. During World War II, people (have) _____ to be creative. Many prisoners of war (make) _____ invisible ink out of acidic liquids such as lemon juice or vinegar. Some even (write) _____ secret messages using their own sweat and saliva.

be (*was or were*)

Past tense verbs generally have one form that you can use with all subjects. However, the verb *be* has two past forms: *was* and *were*.

Past Tense of *Be*	Singular	Plural
First person:	I was	We were
Second person:	You were	You were
Third person:	He was	They were
	She was	
	It was	

PRACTICE 4

Write *was* or *were* in each space provided.

EXAMPLE:

Robert Barron _____*was*_____ not an ordinary artist.

1. During the 1970s, Robert Barron worked for the Pentagon. He _____ not happy with his parking spot because he always had to walk a long way to get to his office. One day, when he _____ alone, he created a perfect fake parking permit. Some other employees _____ aware of what Barron had done, and they told their superior officers about it. Barron had to pay a fine. As it happened, some CIA agents _____ curious about Barron's artistic talents.

2. Soon, Barron joined the graphic arts department at the CIA. He became an expert at creating disguises for secret agents, and he _____ happy with his new job. Barron and other artists _____ very creative, and they made false noses, foreheads, and chins so that agents could look completely different. Some artists _____ experts at creating false mustaches, beards, wigs, and teeth. The disguises _____ important because defectors needed to pass army checkpoints and borders.

Problems with *be, have,* and *do*

Some students find it particularly difficult to remember how to use the irregular verbs *be, have,* and *do* in the past tense. Here are some helpful guidelines.

Avoiding Common Errors with *be*

- Use *were* in the past tense when the subject is plural. Do not use *was*.

  were
  The spies ~~was~~ arrested in 1995.

- Use the standard form of the verb (*is* or *was*), not *be*.

  is
  The camera ~~be~~ small enough to fit in a pen.

Avoiding Common Errors with *have*

- Use the past form of the verb (*had*), not the present form (*have* or *has*), when speaking about a past event.

  had
  During the war, the agent ~~has~~ several passports.

Avoiding Common Errors with *do*

- Use *done* only when it is preceded by a helping verb (*was done, is done,* and so on).

  did
  In 2002, Valerie Plame ~~done~~ undercover work.

PRACTICE 5

Correct ten verb errors. If the verb is incorrectly formed, or if the verb is in the wrong tense, write the correct form above it.

EXAMPLE:

have
Some people ~~has~~ very little respect for pigeons.

1.   Most city dwellers believes that pigeons are nuisances. For example, at my apartment building, the owner done many things last year to keep pigeons off the balconies. However, people undervalue pigeons. During past wars, the homing pigeon has an important role in international espionage.

2.   During the Napoleonic wars, homing pigeons gived officials a crucial way to communicate. The small birds carried and delivered secret messages because they was able to fly over enemy territories. Those pigeons be able to transmit messages faster than soldiers on horses, and they haved legendary endurance.

3. According to Richard Platt's book *Spy*, the Roman emperor Julius Caesar also used birds to send messages. Pigeons be valued for their speed, size, and reliability. Additionally, more than half a million pigeons taked messages to soldiers during World War I, and some soldiers actually hided pigeons in their pockets and cared for them on battlefields. We should appreciate pigeons because they played an important role in previous wars.

Negative and Question Forms

In the present and past tenses, you must add a helping verb (*do*, *does*, or *did*) to question and negative forms. In the present tense, use the helping verb *do*, or use *does* when the subject is third-person singular. Use *did* in the past tense.

Questions:	**Do** you know about the Spy Museum in Washington?
	Does the museum open on weekends?
	Did you visit the spy museum last summer?
Negatives:	We **do** not live in Washington.
	The museum **does** not open on holidays.
	We **did** not visit the spy museum last summer.

When the main verb is *be* (*is*, *am*, *are*), no additional helping verb is necessary.

Questions:	**Is** the spy story suspenseful?
	Were foreign spies in New York during the 2005 World Summit?
Negatives:	The story **is not** suspenseful.
	Foreign spies **were not** in New York during the event.

A Note about Contractions

In informal writing, it is acceptable to contract negative verb forms. However, you should avoid using contractions in your academic writing.

       does not
The CIA ~~doesn't~~ have enough multilingual interpreters.

 **Use the Correct Question and Negative Forms**

In question and negative forms, always use the base form of the main verb, even when the subject is third-person singular.

            have
Why <u>does</u> the Spy Museum ~~has~~ so many spy gadgets?

            discuss
In 1914, Mata Hari <u>did</u> not ~~discussed~~ her identity.

PRACTICE 6

Write questions for each answer. Remember to add a helping verb (*do*, *does*, or *did*) when necessary.

EXAMPLES:

<u>*Where is the International Spy Museum?*</u>

The International Spy Museum is in Washington.

<u>*What does it contain?*</u>

It contains hundreds of spy gadgets.

1. _____

   The Spy Museum opened in 2002.

2. _____

   The spy gadgets are from nations around the world.

3. _____

   Yes, the museum is open on Sundays.

4. _____

   Yes, the camera has a powerful lens.

5. _____

   Yes, many tourists visit the museum each year.

PRACTICE 7

Combine the words in parentheses to form negatives. Remember to add a helping verb (*do*, *does*, or *did*) when necessary.

EXAMPLE:

Washington's Spy Museum has hundreds of spy gadgets, but it (have, not) _____*does not have*_____ paintings.

1. Washington's International Spy Museum contains many interesting gadgets. For example, on display is a tube of lipstick called "The Kiss of Death." The tube (have, not) _____ an obvious function. It (add, not) _____ color to a person's lips. Instead, the lipstick tube conceals a tiny pistol. In 1965, a female Russian spy carried the pistol in her purse, and the people she met (know, not) _____ about her hidden weapon.

2. The museum also displays interesting spy cameras. The best spy camera, the Minox, (be, not) _____ very large. It has a high-

resolution lens, and it (need, not) _____ to be frequently

reloaded. These days, with microtechnology, cameras and recording devices

(be, not) _____ as large as they used to be. In the 1960s,

recording devices (be, not) _____ very sensitive.

Nowadays, microphones (have, not) _____ to be in

a particular room to pick up a conversation.

3.   Clearly, the Spy Museum is an extremely interesting place. Tourists

(have, not) _____ to spend the entire day at the

museum because it (be, not) _____ a very large place.

> ## Hint   **Use the Base Form After *To***
>
> Remember to use the base form of verbs that follow *to* (infinitive form).
>
> *study*
Greenstein wanted to ~~studied~~ the postcard.

PRACTICE 8

The next selection contains verb tense, spelling, and *past*-versus-*passed* errors.
Correct fifteen errors.

EXAMPLE:

              describe
Many books ~~describes~~ the Navajo code talkers of World War II.

1.   Navajo be an incredibly complex language with complicated syntax

and tonal qualities. It has no alphabet or written forms, and only Navajos

in the American Southwest speaks it. During World War II, Navajos maked

an important contribution to the Allied war effort.

2.   During the war, Japanese and German troops tapped Allied

communication lines and listen to the messages. Japanese code breakers

was particularly capable. They managed to figured out every code that the

Allies came up with. In 1942, the Marines get hundreds of Navajo

volunteers to relayed coded messages about military plans. The Navajos

past messages using their language, and they be very efficient code talkers.

They call fighter planes "hummingbirds" and submarines "iron fish."

3. The Japanese tought that they could figure out the messages. They work hard, but they did not managed to break the Navajo code. After the war ended, the Navajos did not received recognition for their important work as code talkers until 1969.

Avoid Double Negatives

A double negative occurs when a negative word such as *no, nothing, nobody,* or *nowhere* is combined with a negative adverb such as *not, never, rarely,* or *seldom.* The result is a sentence that has a double negative. Such sentences can be confusing because the negative words cancel each other.

The agent <u>didn't</u> accept <u>no</u> money.
(According to this sentence, the agent accepted money.)

How to Correct Double Negatives

There are several ways to correct double negatives.

- Completely remove one of the negative forms.

   accepted no or didn't accept
   The agent ~~didn't accept no~~ money.

- Change *no* to *any (anybody, anything, anywhere).*

   any
   The agent didn't accept ~~no~~ money.

PRACTICE 9

Underline and correct the six errors with double negatives. You can correct each error in more than one way.

EXAMPLE:

had no (or didn't have any)
The spy <u>didn't have no</u> money.

1. Every year, intelligence agencies develop highly sophisticated spy tools. Today, spy planes are lightweight and fly at extremely high altitudes. They don't have no pilots. Instead, ground teams direct the planes using remote control technology. For example, during a 2005 flight over Iraq, the Predator spy drone provided about fifteen hours of surveillance. It didn't make no noise, so people on the ground didn't see or hear nothing. The plane took high-resolution videos. More recently, the Global Hawk flew from the United States to Afghanistan and collected data from a height of

about 65,000 feet. The Global Hawk did not need no refueling during the long journey.

2. Scientists are trying to shrink the size of flying robots. According to the *Washington Post*, federally funded teams are working on remote control insects. However, the CIA did not confirm nothing to the reporters. Intelligence agents do not want nobody to know exactly what they are doing.

REFLECT ON IT

Think about what you have learned in this chapter. If you do not know an answer, review that concept.

1. What are the present and past forms of the verb *be?*

	Present	**Past**
I	_____	_____
he, she, it	_____	_____
you, we, they	_____	_____

2. Write two regular past tense verbs. _____

3. Write two irregular past tense verbs. _____

4. Correct one verb tense error in each of the following sentences.

   a. In 1954, a Russian agent surrender to the United States.

   b. Khokhlov defected because he did not wanted to kill another Russian agent.

   c. Khokhlov past many days and nights hiding in a forest.

   d. The agent owned a cigarette case that be a secret weapon.

   e. The cigarette case fired bullets that was poisonous.

FINAL REVIEW

Correct errors in present and past tense verbs. Also look for a double negative. There are fifteen errors.

EXAMPLE:

think
When people talk about espionage, they generally ~~thinks~~ about secret agents who work for governments.

1.   Industrial espionage occurs when companies spy on each other. It be a major problem. A nation's economic survival depend on its ability to be innovative in the industrial sector. For example, in 1994, a large company develop a new highly efficient engine. It wanted to be the first company to put that engine on the market. That company had to protected its information so that competitors could not put the product out first.

2.   In 2005, Gary Fei Ye and Ming Zhong worked as engineers in Silicon Valley. When they was at their jobs, they done some unethical acts. They easily finded top secret computer chip designs. They brung home the documents, and their employers didn't suspect nothing. Later, Ye and Zhong tried to leave the country. They plan to start their own tech company in China. However, when they be at the San Francisco airport, border guards seen the documents. In a 2008 court case, the two men admitted their guilt.

3.   Governments around the world take industrial espionage seriously. Last year, people in Norway, Israel, and Switzerland was in trouble with the law because they selled company secrets. Today, businesses be more vulnerable than ever.

The Writer's Room

Write about one of the following topics. Check your verb tenses carefully.
1. Have you ever done volunteer work? Explain what you did.
2. Describe an effective election advertisement.

mywritinglab To check your progress in meeting this chapter's objectives, log in to **www.mywritinglab.com**, go to the **Study Plan** tab, click on **The Editing Handbook—Section 3: Problems with Verbs** and choose **Tense** from the list of subtopics. Read and view the resources in the **Review Materials** section, and then complete the **Recall, Apply,** and **Write** sets in the **Activities** section.

Past Participles

Section Theme **POLITICAL INTRIGUE**

In this chapter, you will read about politics and spies.

The Writer's Journal

Do you have a social networking site such as Facebook, Twitter, and so on? Why or why not?

Past Participles

A **past participle** is a verb form, not a verb tense. You cannot use a past participle as the only verb in a sentence; instead, you must use it with a helping verb such as *have, has, had, is, was,* or *were.*

	helping verbs	past participles
Ian Fleming	was	<u>raised</u> in England.
His novels	have	<u>become</u> very popular.

GRAMMAR LINK

For a list of irregular past participles, see Appendix 2.

Regular Verbs

The past tense and the past participle of regular verbs are the same.

Base Form	Past Tense	Past Participle
walk	walked	walked
try	tried	tried

Irregular Verbs

The past tense and the past participle of irregular verbs may be different. For a complete list of irregular past participles, see Appendix 2.

Base Form	Past Tense	Past Participle
begin	began	begun
speak	spoke	spoken

PRACTICE I

Each group of verbs contains one error. Underline the error, and write the correct verb form in the space provided.

EXAMPLE:

Base Form	Past Tense	Past Participle	
lose	<u>losed</u>	lost	*lost*

	Base Form	Past Tense	Past Participle	
1.	cost	cost	costed	_____
2.	come	came	came	_____
3.	build	builded	built	_____
4.	sing	sang	sang	_____
5.	bring	brang	brought	_____
6.	think	thank	thought	_____
7.	choose	choosed	chosen	_____
8.	fall	felt	fallen	_____
9.	feel	felt	fell	_____
10.	blow	blew	blowed	_____
11.	tear	tore	tore	_____
12.	take	taked	taken	_____
13.	bite	bited	bitten	_____
14.	sit	sat	sitten	_____
15.	grow	grew	growed	_____

PRACTICE 2

In the following selection, all irregular past participles are underlined. Correct ten past participle errors.

EXAMPLE:

put

Many parents have <u>putted</u> video cameras in their homes.

CHAPTER 24

1.   Spying on children is not new; in fact, parents have <u>did</u> it for centuries. Parents have <u>read</u> their children's diaries, and some have <u>gone</u> through their children's belongings. However, in recent years, the methods used to spy have <u>became</u> more sophisticated.

2.   According to John Stossel of ABC News, some parents have <u>bought</u> video cameras and miniature tape recorders to spy on their children. For example, in 2002, the Roy family bought a small video camera. It was <u>hided</u> behind a plant in the living room, and their son, Samuel, was not <u>told</u> that the camera was there. One evening, while his parents were out, Samuel was <u>catched</u> on the video camera smoking and drinking with friends. When the boy was <u>shown</u> the tape, he admitted that he had <u>drank</u> the alcohol. The parents insist that they have <u>tought</u> their child a valuable lesson.

3.   Another spy tool can track the speed of a driver. A Miami father, Ed Jarvis, has <u>putted</u> the device in his car so that he can monitor his son's driving. Recently, Ed punished his son, David, when he realized that the boy had <u>broke</u> the law. The device proved that David had <u>drove</u> over the speed limit.

4.   Should parents snoop if their children have <u>maked</u> serious mistakes? Would you spy on your children?

The Present Perfect Tense: *have/has* + Past Participle

Combine *have* or *has* and a past participle to form the **present perfect tense.** You can use this tense in two different circumstances.

- Use the present perfect to show that an action began in the past and continues to the present time. You will often use *since* and *for* with this tense.

PAST   NOW

I **have been** a James Bond fan for five years.

- Use the present perfect to show that one or more completed actions occurred at unspecified past times.

PAST (unspecified past times)   NOW

?   ?   ?   ?

I **have watched** at least four James Bond movies.

 **Hint**   **Use Time Markers**

Time markers are words that indicate when an action occurred.

Simple Past Tense
To refer to a completed incident that occurred at a specific past time, use the following time markers.

yesterday	ago	when I was . . .	last (week, month, year . . .)
in the past	in 2005	during the 1970s	in the early days of . . .

Ian Fleming **wrote** his first novel <u>in 1953</u>.

Present Perfect Tense

- To refer to an action that began in the past and is still continuing, use the following time markers.

since	for (a period of time up to now)	ever
up to now	so far	not . . . yet

Spy films **have been** popular <u>since the 1930s</u>.

- To refer to an action that occurred at unspecified past times, use the following types of time markers

once	twice	several times	lately	recently	many

I **have seen** *The World Is Not Enough* <u>once</u> and *Die Another Day* <u>twice</u>.

Look at the difference between the past and the present perfect tenses.

Simple past: In 1962, Sean Connery <u>appeared</u> in the first James Bond film, *Dr. No.*
(This event occurred at a known past time.)

Present perfect: Many different actors <u>have played</u> James Bond.
(We do not really know when the actors played James Bond.)

James Bond movies <u>have been</u> popular for more than forty years.
(The action began in the past and continues to the present.)

PRACTICE 3

Write the simple past or present perfect form of each verb in parentheses.

EXAMPLE:

For the last six years, my cousin Mike (be) _____*has been*_____ a James Bond fanatic.

1.   Spy fans around the world (watch) _____ James Bond movies since the mid-1960s. Although most people (hear) _____ of James Bond, few people know about the man behind the movies.

2.   Ian Fleming was born in 1906, and his father (be) _____ a successful stockbroker. As a result, Ian (spend) _____ his youth living a high-class lifestyle. In the 1940s, the British Secret Service (draft) _____ Ian Fleming because he could easily mix with upper-class officials.

Daniel Craig, the current James Bond

3.   In 1953, Fleming (use) _____ his experiences to create his first James Bond book. Since then, James Bond (be) _____ extremely popular. Since the first film, the James Bond character (age, never) _____. For more than forty years, beautiful women (try) _____ to seduce him and villains _____ to kill him. Over and over, Bond (escape) _____ danger by using his intelligence, his fast cars, and his secret weapons.

The Past Perfect Tense:
had + Past Participle

The **past perfect tense** indicates that one or more past actions happened before another past action. It is formed with *had* and the past participle.

PAST PERFECT	PAST	NOW
▼	▼	▼

The robbers **had left** when the police arrived.

CHAPTER 24

Notice the differences between the simple past, the present perfect, and the past perfect tenses.

Simple past: Last night I <u>watched</u> a documentary on double agents.
(The action occurred at a known past time.)

Present perfect: I <u>have read</u> many articles about spying.
(The actions occurred at unspecified past times.)

Past perfect: Government officials <u>had suspected</u> the agent for a long time before they arrested him as a spy.
(All of the actions happened in the past, but one action happened before another.)

PRACTICE 4

Underline the correct verb form. You may choose the simple past, the present perfect, or the past perfect tense.

EXAMPLE:

Ben Lee (was / <u>has been</u>) a CIA agent since 2001.

1.   Khaleb and Richard (are / were / have been) friends since they were children. When they (were / had been) eight years old, they (pretended / have pretended) to work for the Central Intelligence Agency. By the age of ten, they (have made / had made) several paper CIA badges.

2.   By the time Richard turned twenty, he (has been / had been) in trouble with the law several times. For example, in 2006, Richard went out with a friend. Richard did not realize that his friend (brought / had brought) some drugs into the car. The police arrested both men and showed them the drugs. Richard truthfully claimed that he (never saw / had never seen) the drugs. He said that someone else (has put / had put) them in the trunk. However,

because Richard was in the car, the officer (charged / had charged) him with possession of narcotics. Now Richard cannot become a CIA agent because he has a criminal record.

3. Khaleb has good grades in college. He (never failed / has never failed) a course in his entire life. Khaleb is also in good physical condition. During his last medical exam, the doctor said that he (never saw / had never seen) such a healthy young man. Furthermore, Kaleb speaks three languages. By the time he was twelve years old, Khaleb (has already learned / had already learned) to speak Spanish and Arabic. Since the summer, the agency (made / has made) several background checks on Khaleb. Up to now, Khaleb (had passed / has passed) all of the tests. Khaleb has a very good chance of becoming a CIA agent.

The Passive Voice: *be* + Past Participle

In sentences with the **passive voice**, the subject receives the action and does not perform the action. Look carefully at the next two sentences.

Active: The diplomat **gave** secret documents to an undercover agent.
(This is active because the subject, *diplomat,* performed the action.)

Passive: Secrets documents **were given** to an undercover agent.
(This is passive because the subject, *documents,* was affected by the action and did not perform the action.)

To form the passive voice, use the appropriate tense of the verb *be* plus the past participle.

Verb Tenses	Active Voice (The subject performs the action.)	Passive Voice: *be* + Past Participle (The subject receives the action.)
Simple present	She writes spy stories.	Spy stories <u>are</u> written (by her).
Present progressive	is writing	<u>are being</u> written
Simple past	wrote	<u>were</u> written
Present perfect	has written	<u>have been</u> written
Future	will write	<u>will be</u> written
Modals	can write	<u>can be</u> written
	could write	<u>could be</u> written
	should write	<u>should be</u> written
	would have written	<u>would have been</u> written

PRACTICE 5

Decide whether each underlined verb is active or passive. Write *A* (for "active") or *P* (for "passive") above each verb.

EXAMPLE:

Many ordinary citizens <u>have been recruited</u> *(P)* as spies even though the work <u>is</u> *(A)* dangerous.

1.   During times of war, armies <u>have used</u> both scouts and spies. Army
scouts <u>can wear</u> their full uniform. They <u>are sent</u> ahead of advancing forces.
Spies, on the other hand, <u>wear</u> disguises and <u>try</u> to blend in with the
regular population.

2.   Spying <u>is</u> much more dangerous than scouting because captured
scouts <u>are treated</u> as prisoners of war. A captured spy, on the other hand,
<u>may be executed</u> immediately. In spite of the obvious dangers, many
people <u>are attracted</u> to the field of espionage because they <u>love</u>
excitement and danger.

> ### Hint   The by ... Phrase
>
> In many passive sentences, it is not necessary to write the *by* ... phrase because the noun performing the action is understood.
>
>   CIA agents are selected according to their abilities.
>   (Adding "by CIA recruiters" after "selected" is not necessary.)

PRACTICE 6

A. Complete the following sentences by changing each italicized verb to the passive form. Do not alter the verb tense. Note: You do not have to include the *by* . . . phrase.

EXAMPLE:

The supervisor *spies* on the workers.

The workers _____are spied on (by the supervisor)._____

1. Sometimes employers *place* spy cameras in their factories.

Sometimes spy cameras _____

_____

2. Last year, Mr. Roy *installed* three surveillance cameras.

   Last year, three surveillance cameras _____

   _____

3. The video cameras *filmed* some sleeping workers.

   Some sleeping workers _____

   _____

4. As a result, the boss *has fired* three technicians.

   As a result, three technicians _____

   _____

5. The workers will file a complaint.

   A complaint _____

   _____

 **Avoid Overusing the Passive Voice**

Generally, use the active voice instead of the passive voice. The active voice is more direct and less wordy than the passive voice. For example, read the next two versions of the same message.

Passive voice: The problem has been rectified by us, and a new order is being prepared for you. You will be contacted by our sales department.

Active voice: We have corrected the problem and are preparing a new order for you. Our sales department will contact you.

In rare cases when you do not know who did the action, the passive voice may be more appropriate.

James Bond's miniature camera was made in Italy.

(You do not know who made the camera.)

PRACTICE 7

Underline examples of the passive voice in the following letter. Then rewrite the letter using the active voice.

Dear Parents,

Security cameras have been installed in our school for several reasons. First, intruders have been seen by students. Also, if fighting is done by students, the scenes will be recorded and the culprits will be caught. In addition, any vandalism to school property can be viewed by our staff. For further information, we can be contacted at any time during school hours.

Sincerely,
Tony Romano, Principal, Rosedale High School

_____

_____

_____

_____

_____

_____

_____

The Past Participle as an Adjective

A past participle can function as an adjective when it appears after a linking verb such as *be* or *feel*. In the example, *excited* modifies *agent*.

The young <u>agent</u> was **excited**.

A past participle can also function as an adjective when it describes or modifies the noun that follows it. In the example, *broken* modifies *promises*.

She was angry about the **broken** <u>promises</u>.

GRAMMAR LINK

For more information about linking verbs, see pages 267–268 in Chapter 16.

> **Hint** ▸ **Be Careful!**
>
> In the passive voice, sometimes the verb *be* is suggested but not written. The following sentence contains the passive voice.
>
>   *that were*
> Many activities done in the 1920s are still common today.

PRACTICE 8

Underline and correct fifteen past participle errors.

EXAMPLE:
                                        convicted
On March 6, 2007, "Scooter" Libby was <u>convict</u> of obstruction of justice.

1.   In 1963, Valerie Plame was borned in Alaska. In the 1980s, she decided to work for the Central Intelligence Agency. She went to Arlington, Virginia, and for six months, she was gave a series of interviews and psychological tests by the CIA. Her friends and neighbors were question. Plame, like all other candidates, was also ask to take a polygraph test. She completed the long hiring process and became a respect government agent. She was thrill with her new job.

2.   In July 2003, after an article was publish in the *Washington Post*, Plame
became well known. The article, wrote by Robert Novak, identified her
as a CIA operative. She was enrage. She had work for the agency for
many years, and she loved her job. However, Plame's husband, Joseph
Wilson, had anger political leaders because he had accuse the Bush
administration of manipulating intelligence reports. Plame's identity
was leak to a *Washington Post* reporter. In January 2006, Valerie Plame
was force to retire because her identity was no longer secret. Her
memoir, *Fair Game*, was release a year later.

REFLECT ON IT

Think about what you have learned in this chapter. If you do not know an answer, review
that concept.

1. Give two circumstances in which you would use the present perfect tense.

_____

_____

2. When do you use the past perfect tense? _____

_____

3. How do you form the passive voice? _____

_____

4. Identify and correct the errors in the following sentences.

a. Robert Ludlum's first book was publish in 1971.

b. By 2000, he had wrote twenty-one spy novels.

c. Millions of people have buyed his novel *The Bourne Identity*.

d. Have you ever saw a movie that was based on a book by Ludlum?

FINAL REVIEW

Part A: Fill in each blank with the appropriate verb tense. The sentence may require the active or passive voice.

EXAMPLE:

Cell phone cameras (be) _____*have been*_____ on the market since 2003.

1.   Since their debut, cell phone cameras (criticize) _____ by those who are worried about privacy issues. For example, in 2003, cell phone cameras (ban) _____ in many health clubs. In January 2004, in the locker room of a European spa, some women (film) _____ by a voyeur. Additionally, since 2003, schoolteachers and others who work with the public (complain) _____ to authorities about the possible misuse of cell phone cameras. For instance, in 2006, a teacher's angry outburst (record) _____ by a student.

2.   On the other hand, since their first appearance, cell phone cameras (help) _____ the police. Since 2003, many crimes (solve) _____ by members of the public. For example, after a 2007 Montreal hockey riot, most of the vandals (catch) _____ because bystanders took cell phone videos. In May 2008, two robbers in Georgia (arrest) _____. Police thanked a teenager who (took) _____ a picture of the robbers' license plate number.

Part B: Underline and correct five past participle errors.

EXAMPLE:
                            used
The photo was <u>use</u> in court.

3.   The cell phone camera has cause a lot of controversy since its appearance. Web sites such as Flickr contain images that were took with the tiny cameras. Many cell phones can also take short videos. Films showing people kissing or yawning have been post on YouTube. Last March, a woman's privacy was not respect when someone put a picture of her online. She forced the Web site to remove the unflattering image.

However, cell phone cameras have also help police solve cases.

Undoubtedly, the little gadget is both a blessing and a curse.

The Writer's Room

Write about one of the following topics. Make sure that verb forms are correct.

1. Define an ideal politician. What characteristics should a great politician have?

2. Why do some parents spy on their children? What are the effects of such spying? Write about the causes and effects of spying on children.

mywritinglab To check your progress in meeting this chapter's objectives, log in to **www.mywritinglab.com**, go to the **Study Plan** tab, click on **The Editing Handbook—Section 3: Problems with Verbs** and choose **Tense and Consistent Verb Tense and Active Voice** from the list of subtopics. Read and view the resources in the **Review Materials** section, and then complete the **Recall, Apply,** and **Write** sets in the **Activities** section.

CHAPTER 25
Other Verb Forms

Section Theme **POLITICAL INTRIGUE**

In this chapter, you will read about political scandals.

The Writer's Journal

In your opinion, is it ethical to use cameras to spy on nannies, babysitters, or other caregivers? Write a paragraph about the issue.

Problems with Progressive Forms (*-ing* Verbs)

Most verbs have progressive tenses. The **progressive tense** indicates that an action is, was, or will be in progress. For example, the present progressive indicates that an action is happening right now or for a temporary period of time.

| **Simple present:** | Detective Jonkala **spies** on cheating spouses everyday. |
| **Present progressive:** | Today, he **is following** Ms. Wang. |

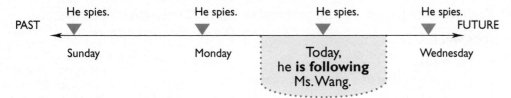

Every day, Detective Jonkala spies on cheating spouses.

PAST
He spies. ▼ Sunday
He spies. ▼ Monday
He spies. ▼ Today, he **is following** Ms. Wang.
He spies. ▼ Wednesday
FUTURE

To form the progressive, use the appropriate tense of the verb *be* with the *-ing* verb.

Present progressive: Right now, Detective Jonkala **is watching** the suspect.

Past progressive: He **was taking** notes when the suspect left the hotel.

Future progressive: Tomorrow, at 6:00 a.m., Natasha **will be following** the suspect.

Present perfect progressive: Detective Jonkala **has been working** for the police since 1994.

Past perfect progressive: Detective Jonkala **had been waiting** in his car when his partner arrived.

Common Errors with the Progressive Form

- Do not use the progressive form when an action happens regularly.

  complains
  Every day he ~~is complaining~~ about his job.

- In the progressive form, use the correct form of the verb *be*.

  is
  Right now the nanny ~~be~~ playing with the children.

- In the progressive form, always include the complete helping verb.

  are *have*
  Right now, the agents examining the photos. They been working for hours.

 **Nonprogressive Verbs**

Some verbs do not take the progressive form because they indicate an ongoing state or a perception rather than a temporary action. Here are some examples of nonprogressive verbs.

Perception Verbs	Preference Verbs	State Verbs	Possession
admire	care*	believe	have*
feel*	desire	know	own
hear	doubt	mean	possess
look*	hate	realize	
see	like	recognize	
seem	love	suppose	
smell*	prefer	think*	
taste*	want	understand	

*The verbs marked with an asterisk have more than one meaning and can also be used in the progressive tense. Compare the next pairs of sentences.

Nonprogressive	**Progressive**
He **has** a video camera. (Expresses ownership)	He **is having** a bad day.
I **think** it is unethical. (Expresses an opinion)	I **am thinking** about you.

PRACTICE 1

Each sentence has errors with progressive forms. Correct each error.

EXAMPLE:

> *have been*
> I <u>been</u> working as a nanny for years.

1. Generally, I am loving my job, but last week something terrible happened.

2. I was watching TV while the baby be sleeping, and I couldn't believe what was on one of the family's videos.

3. When I pressed the "Play" button, I was shocked because I was recognizing myself on the video.

4. The video had been taken months ago while I be reading to the family's children.

5. There is a hidden video camera in the house, and for months the parents been spying on me.

6. I am a good nanny, and every day I am conducting myself professionally.

7. I do not think that families should spy on nannies unless the children been acting upset or the nanny been displaying strange behavior.

8. My employer, a local politician, was not wanting a scandal, so he apologized.

Nonstandard Forms: *gonna, gotta, wanna*

Some people commonly say *I'm gonna*, *I gotta*, or *I wanna*. These are nonstandard forms, and you should not use them in written communication.

- Write *going to* instead of *gonna*.
    > *going to*
    > The nanny is ~~gonna~~ sue her employer.

- Write *have to* instead of *gotta*.
    > *have to*
    > The Smiths ~~gotta~~ go to court to fight the lawsuit.

- Write *want to* instead of *wanna*.
    > *want to*
    > They ~~wanna~~ win their case.

PRACTICE 2

Correct eight incorrect verb tenses or nonstandard verbs.

EXAMPLE:

               want to
Some traitors just <u>wanna</u> earn extra money.

1. From 1976 to 2001, Robert Hanssen worked for the Federal Bureau of Investigation. For fifteen years, while he be doing his day job, he also spying for the Russian government. He regularly passed documents to Russian agents. In 2000, FBI agents realized that Hanssen was a spy.

2. Usually if agents are gonna arrest someone, they gotta have solid evidence. To get that evidence, the FBI promoted Hanssen and placed him under surveillance. Hanssen did not wanna accept the promotion because he would lose access to useful information. However, he had no choice, so he moved to FBI Headquarters. He soon became suspicious. He noticed that his new assistant was watch him closely.

3. By January 2001, Hanssen realized that he was gonna be arrested. Still, he continued working as a spy. On February 18, he placed a white piece of tape on a park sign, which was a signal to his Russian contact. Then, while he was attach a package of documents to the bottom of a wooden footbridge, he was arrested. As agents were handcuffing him, Hanssen asked, "What took you so long?"

Using Gerunds and Infinitives

Sometimes a main verb is followed by another verb. The second verb can be a gerund or an infinitive. A **gerund** is a verb with an *-ing* ending. An **infinitive** consists of *to* and the base form of the verb.

                verb + gerund
Gerund   Hanssen <u>considered **joining**</u> the FBI.

               verb + infinitive
Infinitive   He <u>wanted **to have**</u> a long career.

Do not confuse gerunds with progressive verb forms. Compare the following sentences.

Maria is writing. (The action of writing is in progress right now.)

Some people <u>enjoy</u> **writing**. (Writing is a gerund that follows enjoy.)

Verbs Followed by Gerunds

acknowledge	deny	keep	recall
adore	detest	loathe	recollect
appreciate	discuss	mention	recommend
avoid	dislike	mind	regret
can't help	enjoy	miss	resent
complete	finish	postpone	resist
consider	imagine	practice	risk
delay	involve	quit	tolerate

EXAMPLES:

She would <u>consider</u> **working** for us.

She <u>risks</u> **losing** her job.

Verbs Followed by Infinitives

afford	decide	manage	refuse
agree	demand	mean	seem
appear	deserve	need	swear
arrange	expect	offer	threaten
ask	fail	plan	volunteer
claim	hesitate	prepare	want
compete	hope	pretend	wish
consent	learn	promise	would like

EXAMPLES:

He <u>expected</u> **to keep** his job.

He <u>promised</u> **to be** honest.

Verbs Followed by Gerunds or Infinitives

Some verbs can be followed by either a gerund or infinitive.

begin   continue   like   love   start

Marcus <u>loves</u> **to spy**. Marcus <u>loves</u> **spying**.

 **Using** *Stop*

You can follow *stop* with a gerund or infinitive, but there is a difference in meaning.

Stop + gerund means "to permanently stop doing something."
Hanssen <u>stopped</u> **selling** information to the Soviets.

Stop + infinitive means "to stop an activity to do something else."
The agent was leaving when he <u>stopped</u> **to talk** to an old friend.

PRACTICE 3

Underline the appropriate verb form. Choose the gerund or the infinitive.

EXAMPLE:

The spy's job involved (<u>passing</u> / to pass) information to the Russians.

1.   Robert Hanssen, like many double agents, was a very good liar. Most people can't help (lying / to lie) at one time or another. The psychologist Robert Feldman enjoys (studying / to study) human deception. He says that human beings need (lying / to lie) sometimes. Lying seems (being / to be) a part of human nature.

2.   Feldman conducts experiments to learn how people lie. In one test, he places two strangers in a small room. He asks (videotaping / to videotape) the participants. After ten minutes, he stops (taping / to tape), and then he questions the two people. Usually, the subjects deny (to lie / lying). Then, while watching the video, they stop (fooling / to fool) themselves, and they admit that they have made many inaccurate statements. For instance, in one trial, the male participant falsely claimed (being / to be) a musician, and the female pretended (to like / liking) the same music as the male. They justified (being / to be) inaccurate by saying that their lies were not harmful. It appears that humans simply cannot avoid (lying / to lie) sometimes.

Using Conditional Forms

In **conditional sentences,** there is a condition and a result. There are three types of conditional sentences, and each type has two parts, or clauses. The main clause depends on the condition set in the *if* clause.

First Form: Possible Present or Future

The condition is true or very possible.

If + present tense, . . . future tense . . .

   condition (*if* clause)   result
If you **buy** the book, you **will learn** about satellites.

Second Form: Unlikely Present

The condition is not likely and will probably not happen.

If + past tense, . . . *would* (expresses a condition) . . .

If + past tense, . . . *could* (expresses a possibility) . . .

condition (*if* clause)   result
If I **saw** a UFO, I **would take** a picture of it.

Note: In formal writing, when the condition contains the verb *be*, always use *were* in the *if* clause.

If Jenna **were** a scientist, she would study UFOs.

Third Form: Impossible Past

The condition cannot happen because the event is over.

If + past perfect tense, . . . *would have* (+ past participle) . . .

condition (*if* clause)   result

If aliens **had visited** the earth in 1947, someone **would have photographed** them.

  Be Careful with the Past Conditional

In the third type of conditional sentence, the impossible past, the writer expresses regret about a past event or expresses the wish that a past event had worked out differently. In the *if* part of the sentence, remember to use the past perfect tense.

If + past perfect tense,   . . . *would have* (past participle) . . .

                    had listened
If CIA agents ~~would have listened~~ to the tape, they **would have discovered** the agent's identity.

PRACTICE 4

Fill in the blanks with the past conditional tense.

EXAMPLE:

If the suspect (know) ___had known___ the answer, he (give)

___would have given___ it.

1.   In 2003, America began using torture on suspected terrorists. Matthew

Alexander, a former special intelligence operations officer, wrote a book

called *How to Break a Terrorist*. He believes that torture undermined

America's credibility. In 2003, if the U.S. (refuse) _____

to torture people, terrorists groups (recruit) _____

fewer fighters.

2.   Army Colonel Stuart Herrington conducted interrogations in Iraq, and

he also believes that torture is illegal and immoral. He refused to torture

people. In his opinion, if he (torture) _____ detainees

back in 2003, many of them (lie) _____ to stop the pain.

He believes that torture does not provide credible information. Nine out of

ten people can be persuaded to talk using nonviolent methods. In 2007,

General David Petraeus agreed that Americans must keep "the moral high

ground."

3.   Other government officials support the use of torture. According

to former Vice President Dick Cheney, if interrogators (treat)

_____ detainees kindly during the Bush presidency,

more attacks (happen) _____ on American soil.

What is your opinion about the use of torture?

Nonstandard Forms: *would of, could of, should of*

Some people commonly say *would of, could of,* or *should of.* They may also say *woulda, coulda,* or *shoulda.* These are nonstandard forms, and you should avoid using them in written communication. When you use the past forms of *should, would,* and *could,* always include *have* + the past participle.

  would have
If I had been alive in 1963, I ~~woulda~~ tried to meet President Kennedy.

     should have
Unfortunately, he was assassinated. The president ~~should of~~ traveled in a
bulletproof car.

PRACTICE 5

Underline and correct ten errors in conditional forms or in the past forms of *could*
and *should.*

EXAMPLE:

       have
The government should <u>of</u> interviewed more witnesses.

1.   One of America's most famous spy scandals involved Julius and

Ethel Rosenberg. The New York husband and wife were executed in

1953 for espionage. Some scholars believe that Ethel was innocent,

and the state should not of executed her. Others believe that she

worked with her husband and woulda seen what he was doing.

The Rosenbergs

2. During the trial, Ethel's own brother was the prosecution's primary witness. David Greenglass said that his sister had typed notes containing nuclear secrets. However, in 2001, he changed his story and admitted to lying on the stand to protect himself. If he woulda told the truth, he and his wife woulda had problems. According to Greenglass, he did not realize the government planned to execute his sister. If he would have known that fact, maybe he would not have lie.

3. Morton Sobell was arrested with the Rosenbergs and spent close to eighteen years in prison. During his trial, he admitted that he and Julius Rosenberg had delivered classified documents to the Soviets. In retrospect, he regrets his actions. If he had not helped the Soviets, they would not of built nuclear bombs so quickly. He should of resisted the temptation to work in the spy ring. Then he coulda had a normal life.

4. In 2008, Morton Sobell made an explosive announcement. He said that Ethel Rosenberg was innocent. She was aware of her husband's involvement, but she refused to help him. He shoulda said that during her trial. The truth could have saved Ethel Rosenberg's life.

REFLECT ON IT

Think about what you have learned in this chapter. If you do not know an answer, review that concept.

1. When do you use the progressive form of verbs? _____
    _____

2. Write your own examples of the three types of conditional sentences.
    First form: _____
    _____

Second form: _____

_____

Third form: _____

_____

3. Correct the following sentences by writing the standard form of each nonstandard verb.

a. If you wanna succeed, you gotta work hard.

b. J. Rowen been investigating UFOs since 1978.

c. If Kennedy would have taken another route, maybe he woulda lived.

d. Maybe one day somebody is gonna tell the truth about the Kennedy case.

e. I enjoyed to read a book about the trial.

FINAL REVIEW

Underline and correct twenty errors with verbs. Look for nonstandard verbs and errors with conditionals, gerunds, and progressive forms.

EXAMPLE:
                    have
Chapman should <u>of</u> changed professions.

1.   On a warm June day in 2010, Anna Chapman be sitting in a Manhattan

coffee shop. The twenty-eight-year-old woman was gonna meet up with

a mysterious stranger. While she waiting, she checked her Facebook

account on her iPhone. If you woulda seen her that day, you would of

smiled. She coulda passed for the girl next door. But the perky redhead

was actually an undercover Russian spy.

2.   An FBI agent arrived at the coffee shop and sat at Chapman's table.

He be wearing a wire. He pretended being a Russian consulate employee.

He asked Chapman to deliver a fake passport to another Russian spy, and

she agreed doing it. She shoulda been more careful. Soon after that

meeting, she was arrested along with nine other Russian spies. Of course, they all denied to be part of a spy ring.

3.   The Russian spies could of gone to prison. However, the US and Russia didn't wanna hurt their relationship. High-ranking politicians decided that they gotta make a deal. America returned the ten spies to Russia and were receiving four prisoners in exchange.

4.   The deal, which could of appeared to favor the Russians, was actually better for the Americans. The four prisoners had given extremely important information to western nations. The ten Russians, on the other hand, been producing nothing of value at the time of their arrest. They were called "rank amateurs" by London's *Daily Telegraph* newspaper.

5.   If she hadn't been a spy, Chapman could of had a great life in the United States. People who wanna have a peaceful life gotta stay out of trouble.

The Writer's Room

Write about one of the following topics. Review your verb forms carefully.

1. How would your life have been different if you had lived one hundred years ago? List some ways.

2. Should journalists report on the private lives of politicians? For example, is it important to know if a candidate has committed adultery or has had an addiction to drugs or alcohol? Explain your views.

 **The Writers' Circle** **Collaborative Activity**

Work with a group of two or three other students. Choose a scandal that was in the news. It can be a scandal that happened to a celebrity, politician, sports figure, or business person. Discuss what happened. Then, as a team, write a short paragraph about the scandal. Use the past tense.

After writing the paragraph about the scandal, discuss what you would have done if you had been that person. Then, in a second paragraph, write about what you would have done. Explain why, and give some details.

mywritinglab To check your progress in meeting this chapter's objectives, log in to **www.mywritinglab.com**, go to the **Study Plan** tab, click on **The Editing Handbook—Section 3: Problems with Verbs** and choose **Verbs and Regular and Irregular Verbs** from the list of subtopics. Read and view the resources in the **Review Materials** section, and then complete the **Recall, Apply,** and **Write** sets in the **Activities** section.

READING LINK

Espionage
"How Spies Are Caught" (page 567)
"Why I Worked with La Migra" by Veronica Ortega (page 569)

Subject–Verb Agreement

Section Theme **COLLEGE LIFE**

In this chapter, you will read about topics related to college issues.

The Writer's Journal

In a short paragraph, express your opinion about the extracurricular activities on your campus.

Basic Subject–Verb Agreement Rules

Subject–verb agreement simply means that a subject and verb agree in number. A singular subject needs a singular verb, and a plural subject needs a plural verb.

Singular subject: Mr. Connor **teaches** in a community college.

Plural subject: The students **appreciate** his approach.

Simple Present Tense Agreement

Writers use **simple present tense** to indicate that an action is habitual or factual. Review the following rules for simple present tense agreement.

- When the subject is *he, she, it,* or the equivalent (*Adam, Maria, Florida*), add an *-s* or *-es* ending to the verb. This is also called the **third-person singular form.**

  Singular: Michael **works** in the college bookstore. (one person)

  This neighborhood **needs** a medical clinic. (one place)

  The trophy **belongs** to the best athlete in the college. (one thing)

- When the subject is *I, you, we, they,* or the equivalent (*the Zorns, the mountains, Amber and Tom*) do not add an ending to the verb.

  Plural: College students **have** many options. (more than one person)

  Many colleges **host** political debates. (more than one place)

  The benefits **include** a higher standard of living. (more than one thing)

  For example, review the present tense forms of the verb *help.*

Present Tense of *Help*

	Singular	Plural
First person:	I help	We help
Second person:	You help	You help
Third person:	He help**s**	They help
	She help**s**	
	It help**s**	

PRACTICE I

Write the correct present tense form of each verb in parentheses.

EXAMPLE:

Mila Zahn's family (live) _____*lives*_____ near Hamburg, Germany.

1. Mila Zahn is a German exchange student, and she (study) _____ in an American college.

2. Zahn (see) _____ many glaring cultural differences between Americans and Germans.

3. Many American students (juggle) _____ work and school.

4. For example, Mila's friend Amber (do) _____ not have much money.

5. Amber (work) _____ part time so that she can pay for her studies.

6. However, in Germany, the state (sponsor) _____ all levels of
education, so students (have) _____ no financial pressure.

Troublesome Present Tense Verbs: *be, have, do*

Some present tense verbs are formed in special ways. Review the verbs *be, have,* and *do.*

	Be	**Have**	**Do**
Singular forms			
First person:	I am	I have	I do
Second person:	You are	You have	You do
Third person:	He is	He has	He does
	She is	She has	She does
	It is	It has	It does
Plural forms			
First person:	We are	We have	We do
Second person:	You are	You have	You do
Third person:	They are	They have	They do

> ## *Hint* Use Standard Forms of *Be*
>
> Some people use sentences such as *He be ready* or *She ain't happy.* However, those are nonstandard forms and should not be used in written conversation. Review the following corrections.
>
>   *is*   *is not*
> That man ~~be~~ cool, but he ~~ain't~~ a good candidate for student council president.

PRACTICE 2

In the next selection, each verb is underlined. Correct ten errors in subject–verb agreement or the incorrect use of *ain't.*

EXAMPLE:
                        study
Many exchange students ~~studies~~ in the United States.

1. Emi Kawamura <u>is</u> a Japanese exchange student. According to Emi, some
American students <u>has</u> many misguided ideas about the Japanese. Emi
<u>remind</u> people that she <u>do</u> not <u>fit</u> any stereotype. For example, her math
skills <u>is</u> poor and she rarely <u>uses</u> computers.

2. The educational system in Japan <u>differ</u> from that in the United States.

    Japanese students <u>has</u> a longer school year than American students.

    Japanese college entrance exams <u>is</u> very difficult, and students <u>experience</u>

    high levels of stress. Emi's brother, Jin, <u>attends</u> a private "cramming"

    school called a juku. He <u>have</u> to study six days a week because he <u>hopes</u> to

    get into a good university.

3. Because of complaints from parents and students, Japanese officials <u>wants</u>

    to reform the educational system. One plan <u>is</u> to place less emphasis on

    entrance exams. The current system <u>ain't</u> healthy for students.

Simple Past Tense Agreement

In the past tense, all verbs except *be* have one past form.

Regular:	I called.	He called.	You called.	We called.	They called.
Irregular:	I slept.	He slept.	You slept.	We slept.	They slept.

Exception: *Be*

In the past tense, the only verb requiring subject–verb agreement is the verb *be*, which has two past forms: *was* and *were*.

Was	**Were**
I was	We were
He was	You were
She was	They were
It was	

Present Perfect Tense Agreement

When writing in the present perfect tense, which is formed with *have* or *has* and the past participle, use *has* when the subject is third person singular.

> My college **has** <u>raised</u> tuition fees. Other colleges **have** not <u>raised</u> their fees.

Agreement in Other Tenses

When writing in most other verb tenses, and in modal forms (*can, could, would, may, might,* and so on), use the same form of the verb with every subject.

Future:	I will **work**; she will **work**; they will **work**; you will **work**; we will **work**.
Past perfect:	I had **met**; she had **met**; they had **met**; you had **met**; we had **met**.
Modals:	I can **talk**; she should **talk**; they could **talk**; you might **talk**; we would **talk**.

GRAMMAR LINK

For more information about using the present perfect tense, see Chapter 24.

PRACTICE 3

Correct twelve subject–verb agreement errors among the underlined verbs, and write C above correct verbs.

EXAMPLE:

exists
A problem <u>exist</u> in many colleges and universities.

1. Credit card debt <u>be</u> common on American campuses. Card companies <u>mail</u> applications to students. Today, the average undergraduate <u>have</u> more than $2,000 in credit card debt. Of course, the longer a student <u>takes</u> to pay off a debt, the higher the debt <u>become</u>.

2. Jeremy <u>be</u> a thirty-year-old man who is still paying for the pizza that he ate in college. Ten years ago, Jeremy and his friends <u>was</u> not careful. They <u>were</u> happy to buy food, video games, and clothing with their credit cards. Since then, Jeremy <u>have</u> never <u>managed</u> to pay off the debt. In fact, he still <u>use</u> his Visa card regularly. He <u>want</u> to pay $42, which is the minimum payment. He <u>don't</u> realize that only 89 cents will be applied to his debt. The rest of the money <u>will goes</u> toward late fees and interest fees.

3. Credit card companies <u>charge</u> extremely high fees. When you <u>receives</u> a credit card, you <u>should pays</u> the balance every month. You <u>can avoid</u> interest rates of about 20 percent.

More Than One Subject

There are special agreement rules when there is more than one subject in a sentence.

and

When subjects are joined by *and*, use the plural form of the verb.

> <u>Colleges</u>, <u>universities</u>, and <u>trade schools</u> **prepare** students for the job market.

or, nor

When two subjects are joined by *or* or *nor*, the verb agrees with the subject that is closer to it.

> plural
> Neither Amanda Jackson nor her <u>students</u> **use** the computer lab.

> singular
> Either the students or <u>Amanda</u> **uses** the department's portable laptop computer.

Hint > *As Well As* and *Along With*

The phrases *as well as* and *along with* are not the same as *and*. They do not form a compound subject. The real subject is before the interrupting expression.

<u>Joe</u>, <u>Carlos</u>, and <u>Peter</u> **work** in a career college.

<u>Joe</u>, along with Carlos and Peter, **teaches** business classes.

PRACTICE 4

Circle the correct verb in each sentence. Make sure the verb agrees with the subject.

EXAMPLE:

Colleges and universities (have, has) various interesting programs.

1. Both Theo and Amber (study, studies) nursing.

2. Amber and her mother (live, lives) in Los Angeles.

3. Two buses or a train (transport, transports) Amber to her college campus.

4. Theo and his mother (reside, resides) in a small town outside San Francisco.

5. Neither of the two local colleges nor the university (offer, offers) nursing programs.

6. Every day, Theo, along with his girlfriend Jenna, (travel / travels) to Samuel Merritt College in Oakland.

7. Neither Theo nor his parents (has, have) a lot of money.

8. Each year, either two fast-food restaurants or the local hardware store (sponsor, sponsors) low-income students.

9. Work and careful planning (pay, pays) off for college students.

Special Subject Forms

Some subjects are not easy to identify as singular or plural. Two common types are indefinite pronouns and collective nouns.

Indefinite Pronouns

Indefinite pronouns refer to a general person, place, or thing. Carefully review the following list of indefinite pronouns.

Indefinite Pronouns

Singular	another	each	nobody	other
	anybody	everybody	no one	somebody
	anyone	everyone	nothing	someone
	anything	everything	one	something
Plural	both, few, many, others, several			

Singular Indefinite Pronouns

In the following sentences, the verbs require the third-person singular form because the subjects are singular.

> <u>Everyone</u> **knows** that career colleges offer practical, career-oriented courses.

> <u>Nothing</u> **stops** people from applying to a career college.

You can put one or more singular nouns (joined by *and*) after *each* and *every*. The verb is still singular.

> <u>Each</u> man and woman **knows** the stories about secret societies.

Plural Indefinite Pronouns

Both, *few*, *many*, *others*, and *several* are all plural subjects. The verb is always plural.

> <u>Many</u> **apply** to high-tech programs.

> <u>Others</u> **prefer** to study in the field of health care.

PRACTICE 5

Underline the subjects and circle the correct verbs.

EXAMPLE:

> Many <u>Americans</u> (is /(are)) English instructors in Korea.

1. Min-Jee Park (lives / live) in South Korea. She (is / are) a Korean-American. She, along with her friend Andrea, (teaches / teach) English at a university in Seoul. Both (considers / consider) their jobs to be very satisfying.

2. Koreans (wants / want) to improve their knowledge of English. Many (enrolls / enroll) in language classes while attending university. Korean culture (values / value) social uniformity over individual ability. So universities often (refuses / refuse) to test students for language proficiency. Therefore, Min-Jee (has / have) students of all language levels in her class. All of Min-Jee's students (desires / desire) high grades. Some even (offers / offer) Min-Jee "gifts" for higher marks. This practice is not unusual, but she (refuses / refuse) such presents.

3. Korean students (is / are) very respectful of their instructors. When Min-Jee (walks / walk) past a group of students, everyone (bows / bow) to her. Although Min-Jee is only twenty-five, no one (calls / call) her by her first name. In class, everybody always (listens / listen) to her. Nobody ever

(voices / voice) disagreement with the instructor. Min-Jee sometimes (has / have) difficulty getting her students to debate issues.

4. Neither Min-Jee nor Andrea (wants / want) to return to the United States yet. Both still (has / have) one more year on their teaching contract. They (is / are) becoming used to life in Korea.

Collective Nouns

Collective nouns refer to a group of people or things. These are common collective nouns.

army	class	crowd	group	population
association	club	family	jury	public
audience	committee	gang	mob	society
band	company	government	organization	team

Generally, each group acts as a unit, so you must use the singular form of the verb.

The <u>committee</u> supports the new policies.

If the members of the group act individually, use the plural form of the verb. It is a good idea to use a phrase such as *members of*.

Acceptable: The <u>committee</u> **are** not able to come to an agreement.

Better: The <u>members of the committee</u> **are** not able to come to an agreement.

   **Police Is Plural**

The word *police* is always thought of as a plural noun because the word *officers* is implied but not stated.

The police **have** arrested the Senator.

The police **are** patrolling the neighborhood.

PRACTICE 6

In each sentence, underline the subject and circle the correct verb.

EXAMPLE:

The <u>government</u> (offer / ⟨offers⟩) financial aid for some students.

1. A career college (is / are) a sensible choice for many students wanting practical work skills. Such institutions (offer / offers) a variety of career-

related programs. For example, my college (have / has) programs in high-tech, health care, business, and hospitality.

2. My friend Santosh (studies / study) in the hospitality program. Santosh (was / were) a cook in the army, but now he (want / wants) a career in adventure tourism. The army (provide / provides) financial help to Santosh for his studies. In fact, the military (encourage / encourages) its personnel to continue their education and training. Santosh's family also (give / gives) him encouragement.

3. People (need / needs) social, math, communication, and organizational skills in the hospitality business. Everyone (enter / enters) this field knowing that he or she must be able to get along with people during stressful situations. The industry (is / are) growing, but it (is / are) very important to have the right education. Career colleges (give / gives) students an advantage in this highly competitive market.

CHAPTER 26

Verb Before the Subject

Usually the verb comes after the subject, but in some sentences, the verb comes before the subject. In such cases, you must still ensure that the subject and verb agree.

there or here

When a sentence begins with *there* or *here*, the subject always follows the verb. *There* and *here* are not subjects.

> Here **is** the college course list. There **are** many night courses.

Questions

In questions, word order is usually reversed, and the main or helping verb is placed before the subject. In the following example, the main verb is *be*.

> Where **is** the cafeteria? **Is** the food good?

However, in questions in which the main verb isn't *be*, the subject usually agrees with the helping verb.

> When **does** the library close? **Do** students work there?

PRACTICE 7

Correct any subject–verb agreement errors. If the sentence is correct, write *C* in the blank.

EXAMPLE:

~~Has~~ you ever won a competition?   *Have*

1. There is many athletic scholarships in colleges.   _____

2. Has many students benefited from the scholarships?   _____

3. Does athletes get preferential treatment?   _____

4. Is there a reason to stop giving scholarships to athletes?   _____

5. There is many pressures on student athletes.   _____

6. Why do Wayne Brydon want to play basketball professionally?   _____

7. Do female athletes have the same opportunities?   _____

8. According to Selma Rowen, there have not been enough
   attention given to academically successful students.   _____

9. On the other hand, there is many people who support athletes.   _____

10. In addition to doing their coursework, do college athletes have
    to train for several hours each day?   _____

Interrupting Words and Phrases

Words that come between the subject and the verb may confuse you. In these cases, look for the subject and make sure that the verb agrees with the subject.

      S   interrupting phrase   V

Some <u>rules</u> regarding admission to this college **are** controversial.

      S   prepositional phrase   V

A <u>student</u> in two of my classes **writes** for the college newspaper.

> ### Hint Identify Interrupting Phrases
>
> When you revise your paragraphs, add parentheses around words that separate the subject and the verb. Then you can check to see whether your subjects and verbs agree.
>
>   S   prepositional phrase   V
>
> A <u>student</u> (in two of my classes) **writes** for the college newspaper.
>
> When interrupting phrases contain *of the* or similar words, the subject appears before the phrase.
>
>   S   prepositional phrase   V
>
> <u>One</u> (of my biggest problems) **is** my lack of organization.

CHAPTER 26

PRACTICE 8

Underline the subject in each sentence. Add parentheses around any words that come between each subject and verb. Then circle the correct form of the verb.

EXAMPLE:

One (of the most controversial issues on campus) **is**/are affirmative action.

1. Some colleges in this country **have/has** more relaxed admission standards for students from ethnic minorities. Such colleges, with good reason, **want/wants** to have a vibrant and diverse student population. However, arguing that they have been discriminated against, students from across the nation **have/has** sued their colleges. Judges in many jurisdictions **have/has** had to consider whether affirmative action is unfair.

2. People in favor of affirmative action **have/has** compelling arguments. Historically, some ethnic groups in the United States **has/have** not had access to higher education. Many factors, such as poverty, **contribute/contributes** to the problem. The University of California professor Norman Matloff, in an article for *Asian Week*, **suggest/suggests** that society suffers when there is a large, poorly educated underclass. Additionally, affirmative action **help/helps** create a diverse student body.

3. Opponents of affirmative action **feel/feels** that admissions should be based purely on test scores. Barbara Grutter, a white businesswoman, (was / were) thinking of changing careers. Her application to the University of Michigan's law school (was / were) refused. She (argues / argue) that affirmative action is reverse discrimination. One of her best arguments **is/are** compelling: Grutter, as a forty-year-old single mother, **add/adds** to the university's diversity. On June 23, 2003, a decision about Grutter's affirmative action case **was/were** made. Although justices in the U.S. Supreme Court **were/was** divided, the Court ruled that race can be used as one of the factors in college admissions.

4. For some people, regulations to safeguard affirmative action **help/helps** equalize opportunities in our society. For others, such regulations **is/are** unfair to certain groups. What is your opinion?

Interrupting Words: *who, which, that*

Some sentences include a relative clause beginnning wih the pronoun *who, which,* or *that*. In the relative clause, the verb must agree with the antecedent of *who, which,* or *that*.

In the first example below, the antecedent of *who* is *woman*. In the second example, the antecedent of *that* is *newspapers*. And in the third example, the antecedent of *which* is *article*.

There is a <u>woman</u> in my neighborhood *who* **counsels** students.

Here are some old <u>newspapers</u> *that* **discuss** steroid abuse.

One <u>article</u>, *which* **contains** stories about corruption, is very interesting.

PRACTICE 9

Underline and correct nine subject–verb agreement errors.

EXAMPLE:
                                supports
The candidate who <u>support</u> tax increases is unlikely to win.

1. Students who hope to become politicians usually becomes active in college politics. The experience that they gain help them advance politically. For instance, Chandra Wang, who is in a community college, have a position on the student council. About once a month, she go to council meetings. The Council discusses issues that affects students. In the future, Wang hopes to become a senator.

2. There is many people who wants to enter the political arena. Generally, nobody start at the top. Almost every leader who is successful have a lot of experience.

REFLECT ON IT

Think about what you have learned in this unit. If you do not know an answer, review that concept.

1. When should you add -s or -es to verbs? _____

    _____

2. Look at the following nouns. Circle all the collective nouns.

    family   people   army   committee

    judge   crowd   brothers   audience

3. When do you use *was* and *were*?

Use *was* _____

Use *were* _____

4. Circle and correct any subject–verb agreement errors in the following sentences.

a. There is many colleges in Florida.

b. Yale is a university that have several secret societies.

c. Either the Edwards sisters or Simon have been initiated.

d. One of our cousins go to Yale.

e. There is no hazing rituals on our campus.

FINAL REVIEW

Correct twenty errors in subject–verb agreement.

EXAMPLE:

                                                                  provides
A full-scholarship college in the United States ~~provide~~ students with a wide-ranging education.

1.   Every morning at 7:00 a.m., Conrad Dilbert walk to the outdoor areas on his college campus. He, along with another classmate, weed the flowerbeds. The college provides Conrad with free tuition but expect him to work part time. In fact, everyone who study there works part time.

2.   There is only a few full-scholarship colleges in the United States. Each college committee accept applicants on the basis of financial need and academic standing. Conrad, as well as his classmates, work in the cafeteria, on the grounds, or in the library.

3.   According to *BusinessWeek*, there is many reasons to choose tuition-free colleges. First, the cost of a college or university education have risen in recent years. Many parents find the expense prohibitive. Neither Conrad nor his parents has a lot of money. Furthermore, almost everyone who select such colleges graduate without a lot of student debt. Moreover, these institutions attract students who wants to specialize in subjects such as music or engineering.

4. How do a particular college afford to be tuition free? One of the colleges that recently received publicity are Berea College in Kentucky. The *New York Times* reported that Berea, which were founded more than a century ago, have a very large endowment. The college's billion-dollar fund help it to offer a free education to its students. Nobody pay tuition.

5. Tuition-free colleges help students who cannot afford college fees completes a college education. Such institutions help society.

The Writer's Room

Write about one of the following topics. Make sure that your subjects and verbs agree.

1. Examine this photo. Define a term that relates to the photo. Some ideas might be *debt*, *interest rates*, *reckless spender*, *cheapskate*, *spendthift*, or *credit card junkie*.

2. Should college be free? What could be the advantages or disadvantages of free college?

mywritinglab To check your progress in meeting this chapter's objectives, log in to **www.mywritinglab.com**, go to the **Study Plan** tab, click on **The Editing Handbook—Section 4: Verb Agreement and Consistency** and choose **Subject–Verb Agreement** from the list of subtopics. Read and view the resources in the **Review Materials** section, and then complete the **Recall, Apply,** and **Write** sets in the **Activities** section.

27 Tense Consistency

Section Theme **COLLEGE LIFE**

LEARNING OBJECTIVE

1 Consistent Verb Tense (p. 386)

In this chapter, you will read about people who have made difficult choices.

The Writer's Journal

How do images in the media influence the way that people judge their own bodies? Write a short paragraph about the media and body image.

Consistent Verb Tense

When you write, the verb tense you use gives the reader an idea about the time when the event occurred. A **faulty tense shift** occurs when you shift from one tense to another for no logical reason.

Faulty tense shift:	College reporter Erica Santiago interviewed a protester and <u>asks</u> about his political philosophy.
Correct:	College reporter Erica Santiago interviewed a protester and <u>asked</u> about his political philosophy.

Sometimes the time frame in a text really does change. In those circumstances, you would change the verb tense. The following example accurately shows two different time periods. Notice that certain key words (*during my childhood, today*) indicate what tense the writer should use.

past   present

During my childhood, I <u>ate</u> a lot of fast food. Today, I <u>try</u> to eat a healthy diet.

PRACTICE I

Identify and correct each faulty tense shift. If the sentence is correct, write *C* in the space.

EXAMPLE:

Many adults go back to college and ~~received~~ training in   *receive*
new careers.

1. Career change is a frightening experience for many people
   because they lost the security and familiarity of a job, and
   they have to go back to school to become requalified.   _____

2. Last year, Lee Kim was at a crossroads in his life because he
   is about to change careers.   _____

3. For the previous ten years, Lee had been working as a
   computer service technician for a small company, but a year
   ago, the company downsized, and he lost his job.   _____

4. Suddenly, at the age of thirty-five, Lee is faced with having to
   change careers, and he was scared.   _____

5. Lee met with a career counselor; she advises Lee to check
   out the different programs in various career colleges.   _____

6. Lee researched the courses at different institutions, and he
   finds that the medical laboratories program was a good
   option for him.   _____

7. Now, Lee is enrolled as a student at Holly Fields Career
   College, but he admits that going back to college after many
   years is intimidating.   _____

8. Nowadays, Lee had to budget his money and has to relearn
   how to be a student.   _____

Would and Could

When you tell a story about a past event, use *would* instead of *will*, and use *could* instead of *can*.

could

In 1996, college wrestler Robert Burzak knew that he <u>can</u> bulk up if he used

would

steriods, but he promised his coach that he <u>will</u> not.

PRACTICE 2

Underline and correct ten faulty tense shifts.

EXAMPLE:

broke
Robert began weight training after he <u>breaks</u> his leg.

1.　In 2003, Robert Burzak joined a health club and tries weightlifting. He knew that he can have a sculpted body if he worked out. After a few months of weight training, he starts to get impatient. He wanted to get larger muscles very quickly, so after a training partner told him about steroids, he decides to try them.

2.　Robert started by taking steroids in pill form. Within weeks he noticed a difference. Then he graduated to steroid injections. Others noticed his large muscles, and Robert feels proud of his "six-pack" stomach and his large biceps. He realized that his new look conformed to the images of male beauty seen in the media.

3.　Unfortunately, after Robert began to use steroids, side effects kick in. Robert developed acne on his back and suffered wild mood swings, and he will alternate between violent outbursts and periods of depression. He cannot stop taking the pills because each time he tried to stop, his weight will plummet.

4.　Finally, in 2005, Robert gave up steroids. He knew that the risks to his health outweighed the benefits of having a sculpted body. Furthermore, his girlfriend said that she will leave him if he could not stay off the drugs. Today, Robert is drug free.

REFLECT ON IT

Think about what you have learned in this unit. If you do not know an answer, review that concept.

1.　What is tense inconsistency? _____

_____

2. If you are writing a paragraph about a past event, what word should you use instead of these two?

a. will: _____ b. can: _____

3. Read the following paragraphs and find five tense inconsistencies. Correct the errors.

EXAMPLE: Kaitlin diets because she ~~wanted~~ *wants* to look thinner.

In 2001, college student Amy Heller became severely malnourished. In an attempt to lose weight, Heller ingested diet pills, and she severely restricts her intake of food. When others suggested that she had a problem, Heller will deny it. By July 2004, she weighs only 88 pounds. Heller finally sought treatment, and soon she can eat regular meals.

In 2008, Heller decided to speak about her condition. She went to a treatment center and offers her services. Today, she works with patients who suffer from eating disorders.

FINAL REVIEW

Underline and correct fifteen tense inconsistencies.

EXAMPLE:
The President <u>have</u> *has* many supporters.

1.   During America's 2008 elections, a record number of college students registered and vote. Barack Obama's message resonated with young people, so many are ready to vote for him. Students who cannot go to Washington for Obama's inauguration watched it on television.

2.   In the United States, voting is not compulsory. However, about thirty nations have a voting law. In Greece, Thailand, and Italy, everybody of legal age must vote, but the laws are not strict. During typical elections, officials did not arrest non-voters. Additionally, Mexico and Panama do not enforce the compulsory voting law, so voter turnout remained low.

3.   Many other nations, including Turkey, Uruguay, and Argentina, have very strict voting laws. Officials sometimes punish non-voters with fines or even imprisonment. For example, during Argentina's 2003 election, Ileana Guerera decided that she will not vote in the election because she disapproved of the candidates. She receives a fine, and she had to pay it. Her brother also stayed home on April 27, 2003, but he has a doctor's note. He knew he will not receive a fine. He had a legitimate excuse, so he can stay home that day.

4.   In the early 1920s, many Australian citizens were apathetic, and close to 50 percent do not participate in elections. Then in 1924, government officials passed a law making voting compulsory. In the election of 1925, people rushed to the polling stations and vote. They worried that they can be arrested if they refused to vote. Today, the voter turnout in Australia is about 95 percent.

5.   There are many people who support compulsory voting. They believe that voting was a civic duty. On the other hand, others consider voting a civil right rather than a duty. They regarded compulsory voting laws as an infringement on personal rights. Do you support compulsory voting?

The Writer's Room

Write about one of the following topics. Ensure that your verb tenses are consistent.

1. Describe your college campus. You might describe an interesting building or area of the campus.
2. What is your opinion of compulsory voting? Should everybody have to vote in elections? Explain why or why not.

READING LINK

College Life
"The Case for Affirmative Action" by Dave Malcolm (page 538)
"It's Class, Stupid!" by Richard Rodriguez (page 535)

 **The Writers' Circle**   **Collaborative Activity**

Work with a team of students and create a short survey. Form at least five interesting questions about college life. For example, you can ask about the food services, the course selection, transportation, student fees, extracurricular activities, fashions, student study habits, or any other topic that you can think of.

For each question that you create, include a list of possible choices. It will be much easier to compile your results if all students choose from a selection. Do not give open-ended questions. Finally, if a question asks about student knowledge, give an "I don't know" choice. Otherwise, students may simply make a guess, and that would skew your results.

After you have completed your survey questions, then one team member should remain seated, and the other team members should split up and sit with other groups in the class to ask the questions. After each member has gathered information, the original group should get together and write a summary of the results.

CHAPTER 27

mywritinglab To check your progress in meeting this chapter's objectives, log in to **www.mywritinglab.com**, go to the **Study Plan** tab, click on **The Editing Handbook—Section 4: Verb Agreement and Consistency** and choose **Consistent Verb Tense and Active Voice** from the list of subtopics. Read and view the resources in the **Review Materials** section, and then complete the **Recall, Apply,** and **Write** sets in the **Activities** section.

Nouns, Determiners, and Prepositions

Section Theme **INVENTIONS AND DISCOVERIES**

In this chapter, you will read about topics related to inventions and discoveries.

The Writer's Journal

Think about recent inventions. What is you favorite new gadget? Describe it and explain why you like it.

Singular and Plural Nouns

Nouns are words that refer to people, places, or things. Nouns are divided into common nouns and proper nouns.

- **Common nouns** refer to general people, places, or things and begin with a lowercase letter. For example, *books*, *computer*, and *city* are common nouns.
- **Proper nouns** refer to particular people, places, or things and begin with a capital letter. For example, *Dean Kamen*, *Microsoft*, and *Kitty Hawk* are proper nouns.

Nouns are either singular or plural. A **singular noun** refers to one of something, while a **plural noun** refers to more than one of something. Regular plural nouns end in *-s* or *-es*.

	Singular	**Plural**
People:	inventor	inventors
	writer	writers
Places:	town	towns
	village	villages
Things:	computer	computers
	box	boxes

Hint ▷ **Adding -es**

When a noun ends in s, x, ch, sh, or z, add -es to form the plural.

business/business**es**   tax/tax**es**   church/church**es**

Irregular Plural Nouns

Nouns that do not use *-s* or *-es* in their plural forms are called **irregular nouns.** Here are some common irregular nouns.

Singular	**Plural**	**Singular**	**Plural**
person	people	woman	women
child	children	tooth	teeth
man	men	foot	feet

Some nouns use other rules to form the plural. It is a good idea to memorize both the rules and the exceptions.

- For nouns ending in *f* or *fe*, change the *f* to *v* and add *-es*.

Singular	**Plural**	**Singular**	**Plural**
knife	kni**ves**	thief	thie**ves**
wife	wi**ves**	leaf	lea**ves**

Some exceptions: belief, beliefs; roof, roofs; safe, safes.

- For nouns ending in a consonant + *y*, change the *y* to *i* and add *-es*.

Singular	**Plural**	**Singular**	**Plural**
lady	lad**ies**	baby	bab**ies**
berry	berr**ies**	lottery	lotter**ies**

If a vowel comes before the final *y*, then the word retains the regular plural form.

Singular	**Plural**	**Singular**	**Plural**
day	day**s**	key	key**s**

- Some nouns remain the same in both singular and plural forms.

Singular	**Plural**	**Singular**	**Plural**
fish	fish	deer	deer
moose	moose	sheep	sheep

- Some nouns are thought of as being only plural and therefore have no singular form.

Plural Form with a Plural Verb

clothes	goods	pants	scissors
eyeglasses	proceeds	savings	shorts

Plural Form with a Singular Verb

news	economics	politics	physics

- Some nouns are **compound nouns,** which means that they are made up of two or more words. To form the plural of compound nouns, add -s or -es to the last word of the compound noun.

Singular	**Plural**	**Singular**	**Plural**
bus stop	bus stops	artificial heart	artificial hearts
air conditioner	air conditioners	jet airplane	jet airplanes

In hyphenated compound nouns, if the first word is a noun, add -s to the noun.

Singular	**Plural**	**Singular**	**Plural**
senator-elect	senators-elect	runner-up	runners-up
sister-in-law	sisters-in-law	husband-to-be	husbands-to-be

- Some nouns that are borrowed from Latin or Greek keep the plural form of the original language.

Singular	**Plural**	**Singular**	**Plural**
millennium	millennia	paparazzo	paparazzi
datum	data	phenomenon	phenomena

CHAPTER 28

> **Hint** *Persons* versus *People*
>
> There are two plural forms of *person*. *People* is the most common plural form.
>
> Some people have great ideas. Many people patent their ideas.
>
> *Persons* is used in a legal or official context.
>
> The patent was stolen by persons unknown.

PRACTICE I

Fill in the blanks with either the singular or the plural form of the noun. If the noun does not change, put an X in the space.

EXAMPLES:

Singular	**Plural**
man	*men*
X	goggles

1. person   _____

2. _____   mice

3. brother-in-law   _____

4. lady   _____

5. _____   jeans

6. sheep   _____

7. _____   binoculars

8. _____   shelves

9. _____   sunglasses

10. alarm clock   _____

PRACTICE 2

Correct ten errors in plural noun forms.

1. Many ordinary persons make unplanned inventions. Back in 1905, an eleven-year-old boy named Frank Epperson mixed powdered fruit and water with a stick and accidentally left the drink on his back porch. Overnight, the temperature plummeted. In the morning, he pulled his frozen drink out of his glass and showed it to the other childrens at school. When he was in his twentys, he remembered his invention and patented it. He called his product a "popsicle."

2. In 1869, a wire factory worker named Alan Parkhouse was at a company gathering with several familys. His two sister-in-laws complained about the lack of places to hang their coats. Parkhouse bent a piece of wire into two ovales and created a hook between them, thus inventing the first cloths hanger.

3. In 1853, George Crum, a chef, was cutting potatos when he heard some customers complain about the thickness of his French fries. Then he cut thinner fries, but the two womans still complained. Finally, Crum looked through his selection of knifes and chose the sharpest one. He cut fries that were so thin they could not be eaten with a fork. The potato chip was born!

Key Words for Singular and Plural Nouns

Some key words will help you determine whether a noun is singular or plural.

- Use a singular noun after words such as *a, an, one, each, every,* and *another.*

    As **a** young <u>mother</u>, Dorothy Gerber prepared homemade baby food for her daughter.

    Gerber tried to sell her product to **every** <u>grocery store</u> in her town.

- Use a plural noun after words such as *two, all, both, many, few, several,* and *some.*

    Very **few** <u>companies</u> produced food targeted to children.

    Today, **many** <u>babies</u> eat Gerber's baby food.

 **Using Plural Nouns After *of the***

Use a plural noun after the expressions *one (all, two, each, few, lots, many, most, several) of the . . .*

<u>One of the most</u> useful **items** ever invented is the zipper.

CHAPTER 28

PRACTICE 3

Circle the correct noun in each set of parentheses.

EXAMPLE:

In the future, some of the most useful (invention /(inventions)) will be in the energy sector.

1. Very few (government / governments) would deny that carbon

    reduction is important. Every (year / years), engineers try to come up with

    an automobile (prototype / prototypes) that is fuel efficient and

    economical. Today, many (person / people) discuss electric cars, but did you

    know that such automobiles are not a new (invention / inventions)?

2. In 1897, electric (taxi / taxis) roamed New York's streets. By 1900, 28

    percent of all (car / cars) in the United States were powered by electricity.

    However, during the 1920s, the mass production of combustion (engine /

    engines) wiped out electric vehicles for the next forty years.

3. Then, on October 16, 1973, something happened. All the (member /

    members) of the Organization of the Petroleum Exporting Countries

(OPEC) cut production of oil and announced that they would no longer ship oil to Western nations. One of the (result / results) of the crisis was that people discussed electric cars again. Today, engineers in almost every (nation / nations) want to develop an efficient electric (vehicle / vehicles).

Count Nouns and Noncount Nouns

In English, nouns are grouped into two types: count nouns and noncount nouns. **Count nouns** refer to people or things that you can count, such as *engine, paper,* or *girl.* Count nouns usually can have both a singular and plural form.

> She read a <u>book</u> about inventions. She read five <u>books</u> about inventions.

Noncount nouns refer to people or things that you cannot count because you cannot divide them, such as *electricity* and *music.* Noncount nouns usually have only the singular form.

> The <u>furniture</u> in the inventor's house looked expensive.

> Inventors usually have a lot of specialized <u>equipment</u>.

To express a noncount noun as a count noun, refer to it in terms of types, varieties, or amounts.

> The patent office has **a variety of** <u>furniture</u>.

> My friend works for an entertainment company where he listens to **many styles of** <u>music</u>.

> The clerk at the patent office likes to drink coffee with **four cubes of** <u>sugar</u>.

Here are some common noncount nouns.

Common Noncount Nouns

Categories of Objects		Food	Nature	Substances	
clothing	machinery	bread	air	chalk	fur
equipment	mail	honey	earth	charcoal	hair
furniture	money	meat	electricity	coal	
homework	music	milk	energy	ink	
jewelry	postage	fish	radiation	paint	
luggage	software	rice	water	paper	

Abstract Nouns

advice	evidence	information	progress
attention	effort	knowledge	proof
behavior	health	luck	research
education	help	peace	violence

PRACTICE 4

Change the italicized words to the plural form, if necessary. If a plural form would be incorrect, write *X* in the space. If the word ends in *y*, you may have to change the *y* to *i* for the plural form.

EXAMPLE:

In written communication, there have been many useful *discovery* __ies__ .

1. Early *human*_____ used *substance*_____ such as *charcoal*_____,

   *chalk*_____, and *paint*_____ to write on *wall*_____ and *paper*_____.

   Eventually, a lot of *information*_____ was recorded using ink and a quill.

   Then, in 1884, Lewis Waterman patented one of the most useful

   *invention*_____. Although Waterman's fountain *pen*_____ worked

   reasonably well, they were unreliable, and ink could leak onto

   *clothing*_____ and *furniture*_____.

2. Since the 1930s, a lot of *progress*_____ has been made in written

   communication. In 1938, Ladislo Biro was one of the best-known

   *journalist*_____ in Hungary. He spent a lot of *time*_____ thinking about

   different *type*_____ of writing *tool*_____. Putting quick-drying ink that was

   common in printing *press*_____ together with a small ball bearing, he

   created the first ballpoint pen.

3. These days, *company*_____ do a lot of *research*_____ because they want

   to develop a new, better writing tool. In fact, there are many different

   *kind*_____ of *pen*_____ on the market.

Determiners

Determiners are words that help a reader figure out whether a noun is specific or general.

Arthur Scott used **his** imagination and created **a** new invention, **the** paper towel.

You can use many words from different parts of speech as determiners.

Articles:	a, an, the
Demonstratives:	this, that, these, those, such

Indefinite pronouns:	any, all, both, each, every, either, few, little, many, several
Numbers:	one, two, three
Possessive nouns:	Jack's, the teacher's, a man's
Possessive adjectives:	my, your, his, her, its, our, their, whose

Commonly Confused Determiners

Some determiners can be confusing because you can use them only in specific circumstances. Review this list of some commonly confused determiners.

a, an, the

A and *an* are general determiners, and *the* is a specific determiner.

> general   specific
> I need to find <u>a</u> new **car**. <u>The</u> **cars** in that showroom are expensive.

- Use *a* and *an* before singular count nouns but not before plural or noncount nouns. Use *a* before words that begin with a consonant (*a man*), and use *an* before words that begin with a vowel (*an invention*).

  <u>An</u> ordinary **woman** created <u>a</u> very useful **product.**

  Exceptions:

  > When *u* sounds like *you*, put *a* before it (*a unicycle*, *a university*).
  > When *h* is silent, put *an* before it (*an hour*, *an honest man*).

- Use *the* before nouns that refer to a specific person, place, or thing. Do not use *the* before languages (*he studies Greek*), sports (*we played football*), and most city and country names (*Biro was born in Hungary*).

  In 1885, Karl Benz invented <u>the</u> first **automobile** while living in <u>the</u> **city** of Mannheim, Germany.

many, few, much, little

- Use *many* and *few* with count nouns.

  <u>Many</u> **people** have tried to develop new products, but <u>few</u> **inventions** are really successful.

- Use *much* and *little* with noncount nouns.

  Manu Joshi spent too <u>much</u> **money** on very <u>little</u> **research.**

this, that, these, those

- Use *this* and *these* to refer to things that are physically close to the speaker or at the present time. Use *this* before singular nouns and *these* before plural nouns.

  <u>This</u> **computer** in my purse measures three by five inches. <u>These</u> **days,** computers are very small.

■ Use *that* and *those* to refer to things that are physically distant from the speaker or in the past or future. Use *that* before singular nouns and *those* before plural nouns.

> In the 1950s, computers were invented. In <u>those</u> **years,** computers were very large. In <u>that</u> **building,** there is a very old computer.

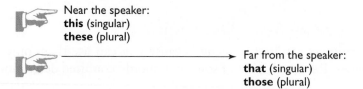

Near the speaker:
this (singular)
these (plural)

Far from the speaker:
that (singular)
those (plural)

PRACTICE 5

Write *a*, *an*, or *the* in the space before each noun. If no determiner is necessary, write *X* in the space.

EXAMPLE:

A modern convenience like ___*a*___ car can make traveling much easier.

CHAPTER 28

1.   Most of us admire _____ beautiful, shiny new automobiles, but we do

not give _____ same admiration to _____ windshield wipers. Indeed, we

take _____ windshield wiper for granted, yet it is _____ extremely

necessary tool when we are driving. In fact, before _____ invention of

_____ windshield wiper, drivers had to stop to clean the front window of

their vehicles.

2.   In 1902, when she was on _____ trip to New York City, Mary

Anderson observed that streetcar drivers had to look through open

windows when they were driving in bad weather. In 1903, she invented

_____ gadget that could clean car windows. Her wipers consisted of

rubber blades on _____ outside of the windshield and _____ handle on

_____ inside of the car. Drivers could turn _____ wipers by turning the

handle.

3.   Anderson received _____ patent for her invention, and by 1916, all

American-made cars had _____ windshield wipers as _____ regular

feature.

PRACTICE 6

Underline the appropriate determiner in parentheses. If the noun does not require a determiner, underline *X*.

EXAMPLE:

Most inventions begin with (X / <u>a</u> / the) great idea.

1.   (This / These) days, (much / many) people want to get rich quickly by

developing (a / the / X) great new product. They also hope to make

(X / the) life easier for others. (Every / Some / X) inventions are extremely

useful, while others are totally absurd.

2.   (Few / Little) inventions are as bizarre as the purse protector. It

requires very (few / little) investment. Attached to the purse is (a / the)

chain and (a / the) metal cuff. A woman can lock (a / the) cuff onto her

wrist. Purse snatchers would never be able to steal (a / the) purse. The

inventor received (a / X) patent in 1989. There were (much / many) other

patents (this / that) year. The purse protector has elicited very (few / little)

interest among consumers.

3.   Although (much / many) absurd inventions never earn a penny, a

(few / little) of them become successful. In 2005, (a / the) cell phone

company in China created a breathalyzer phone. People can program

(a / the) phone to block certain numbers such as that of the boss. If the phone

user is inebriated, he or she cannot dial (that / those) numbers. Although

people in North America do not have (much / many) information about the

phone, it is extremely popular in (the / X) Korea. Over 200,000 people

bought the phones because they wanted to avoid making (a / the / X)

embarrassing phone calls.

4.   (This / That) year, thousands of people will patent their ideas. With a

(few / little) time and (some / many) research, perhaps you can come up

with a great invention.

PRACTICE 7

Correct fifteen errors in singular nouns, plural nouns, and determiners.

EXAMPLE:

One of the most interesting ~~idea~~ *ideas* is a self-cleaning house.

In her autobiography, Agatha Christie wrote that most invention arise from laziness. Peoples invent to save themselves trouble. Christie's comments apply perfectly to Frances Gabe of Newberg, Oregon. Gabe, after a lot of researches, has invented and patented the world's first self-cleaning house. A house will appeal to anyone who hates to clean. On the ceiling of each rooms in Gabe's house, there is a cleaning and drying machines. At the touch of a buttons, each units first sprays soapy water over the room, and then rinses and blow-dries the entire area. The rooms' floors are sloped slightly so that excess waters runs to a drain. The furnitures is made of waterproof material, and there are no carpets. There are not much decorations in the house. In the kitchen, all dish are cleaned, dried, and stored inside dishwasher cupboards. Every sink, tub, and toilets is self-cleaning. Gabe created the designs for the specialized equipments. This days, Gabe actually lives in her patented prototype home.

Prepositions

Prepositions are words that show concepts such as time, place, direction, and manner. They show connections or relationships between ideas.

Scientists made many important discoveries **during** World War II.

American scientists raced **to** build the first atomic bomb.

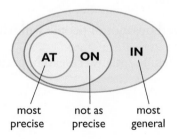

most precise · not as precise · most general

Prepositions	Prepositions of Time	Prepositions of Place
at	at a specific time of day (at 8:30 p.m.) at night at breakfast, lunch, dinner	at an address (at 15 Maple Street) at a specific building (at the hospital)
on	on a day of the week (on Monday) on a specific date (on June 16) on a specific holiday (on Martin Luther King Day) on time (meaning "punctual") on my birthday	on a specific street (on 17th Avenue) on technological devices (on TV, on the radio, on the phone, on the computer) on a planet (on Earth) on top
in	in a year (in 2010) in a month (in July) in the morning, afternoon, evening in the spring, fall, summer, winter	in a city (in Boston) in a country (in Spain) in a continent (in Africa)
from ... to	from one time to another (from 6 a.m. to 8 p.m.)	from one place to another (from Las Vegas to Miami)
for	for a period of time (for six hours)	for a distance (for ten miles)

Commonly Confused Prepositions

to and at

Use *to* after verbs that indicate movement from one place to another.

> Each morning, Albert <u>walks</u> **to** the library, he <u>goes</u> **to** the coffee shop, and he <u>returns</u> **to** his office.

Exception: Do not put *to* directly before *home.*

> Albert returned ~~to~~ home after he won his prize. He didn't go to his friend's home.

Use *at* after verbs that indicate being or remaining in one place (and not moving from one place to another).

> In the afternoon, he <u>stays</u> **at** home. He <u>sits</u> **at** his desk and <u>looks</u> **at** his inventions.

for, during, and since

Use *during* to explain when something happens. Use *for* to explain how long it takes to happen. Use *since* to show when an activity started.

> **During** <u>the month of August</u>, the patent office closes **for** <u>two weeks</u>.

> The inventors of the bomb experimented **for** <u>many years</u> **during** <u>World War II</u>.

> **Since** <u>World War II</u>, many countries have acquired nuclear technology.

PRACTICE 8

Write the correct preposition in each blank. Choose *in, on, at, to, for, during,* or *from.*
If no preposition is necessary, write *X* in the space.

EXAMPLE:

___At___ 5:15 a.m. we heard the news.

1. _____ November 2008, _____ a Friday afternoon _____ 2:00 p.m., Josh
   Freed bought a voice recognition cell phone. The new phones work by
   converting spoken words into a typed message. Then the message gets sent
   _____ an email system.

2. Freed lives _____ Jeanne Mance Street _____ Montreal. Last Friday
   morning, Freed sat _____ his kitchen table. _____ an hour, he relaxed and
   drank a cup of coffee. Then, _____ 10:00 a.m., he spoke into his cell
   phone. He said, "New York Times," and the phone took him _____ the
   correct Web site. He was thrilled with his new gadget.

3. However, some voice recognition systems annoy Freed. One day, he walked
   _____ a store _____ his home. While walking _____ home, he began to
   cough and feel very ill. He decided to call the local hospital, which is
   _____ a street near his home. He asked for the asthma department. The
   voice recognition system kept insisting that he wanted the vaccination
   department. He stayed _____ the phone _____ almost ten minutes, and
   then he finally gave up.

4. Apparently, the new cell phones cannot understand accents. _____ 2008,
   _____ December, many British citizens complained about the iPhone.
   People discussed the issue _____ the radio and _____ television. They
   said that it discriminates against British accents. When some Londoners
   asked for "fish and chips," the iPhone heard "sex on ships."

PRACTICE 9

Underline the correct preposition in the parentheses.

EXAMPLE:

(At / <u>During</u>) the summer of 1976, he lived in Africa.

1. Paintball has been popular (since / for) many years. Charles Gaines first
   had the idea for the game (in / since) 1976. He was in Africa (during / for)
   six weeks. (During / At) his trip, he hunted large animals. A few months

CHAPTER 28

later, (during / on / since) a poker game, he described the excitement of the hunt to his friend, Hayes Noel. They decided to invent a game where people could hunt one another. They could use a gun that shoots balls of paint. They worked on their idea (during / for) the next five years.

2. (During / For) the summer of 1980, paintball became well known. An article about the sport appeared in *Sports Illustrated*. (During / For) three years, the sport grew in popularity, and more companies developed paintball guns. One day (in / on) 1984, Karen Isackson damaged her retina (during / on / since) a game. After that, paintball players decided that they must follow very strict safety rules. Whether the game lasts (during / for) ten minutes or five hours, the players must wear protective goggles and clothing. (Since, For) that time, many people have played the game safely.

Common Prepositional Expressions

Many common expressions contain prepositions. These types of expressions usually convey a particular meaning.

EXAMPLE:

              verb   preposition

    This morning I <u>listened</u> **to** the radio.

Here is a list of common prepositional expressions.

accuse (somebody) of	confronted with	hope for
acquainted with	consist of	hopeful about
add to	count on	innocent of
afraid of	deal with	insist on
agree with	decide on	insulted by
angry about	decide to	interested in
angry with	depend on	introduce to
apologize for	be disappointed about	jealous of
apply for	be disappointed with	keep from
approve of	dream of	located in
argue with	escape from	long for
ask for	excited about	look forward to
associate with	familiar with	opposed to
aware of	feel like	participate in
believe in	fond of	patient with
belong to	forget about	pay attention to
capable of	forgive (someone) for	pay for
care about	friendly with	pray for
care for	good for	prepared for
commit to	grateful for	prepared to
comply with	happy about	prevent (someone) from
concern about	hear about	protect (someone) from

(continued)

proud of	satisfied with	think about
provide (someone) with	scared of	think of
qualify for	search for	tired of
realistic about	similar to	upset about
refer to	specialize in	upset with
related to	stop (something) from	willing to
rely on	succeed in	wish for
rescue from	take advantage of	worry about
responsible for	take care of	
sad about	thank (someone) for	

PRACTICE 10

Write the correct preposition in each blank. Use the preceding list of prepositional expressions to help you.

EXAMPLE:

Many American citizens participated ___in___ the war effort.

1. During World War II, many people believed _____ science. Robert

    Oppenheimer was interested _____ physics. He heard _____ the rise of

    fascism in Germany. He decided _____ become a scientist with the U.S.

    government.

2. Oppenheimer was excited _____ working on atomic bombs for the

    Manhattan Project. Officials searched _____ a secluded location in which

    to develop the bomb and chose a desert area near Los Alamos, New Mexico.

3. When he saw an atomic bomb test, Oppenheimer became afraid _____ the

    bomb's power. Later, when a bomb called Little Boy was dropped on

    Hiroshima, he felt partially responsible _____ changing the world with his

    discovery.

4. After the war, Oppenheimer worried _____ the impact of the atomic bomb.

    He decided that the nuclear arms race was not good _____ society. During

    the 1950s, Oppenheimer was accused _____ having Communist sympathies.

    He was disappointed _____ the government for taking away his security

    clearance. At the end of his career, Oppenheimer took advantage _____ his

    experience with the Manhattan Project and wrote about ethics and morality.

CHAPTER 28

REFLECT ON IT

Think about what you have learned in this chapter. If you do not know an answer, review that concept.

1. Make the following nouns plural.

   a. tooth: _____

   b. backseat driver: _____

   c. bride-to-be: _____

   d. kiss: _____

   e. homework: _____

   f. loaf: _____

2. Correct the errors in the following sentences.

   EXAMPLE: Leonardo da Vinci had ~~much~~ *many* ideas.

   a. He invented much things.

   b. He developed a idea for a parachute.

   c. Da Vinci is one of the most famous artist in the world.

   d. Little of his other works are as famous as the *Mona Lisa*.

FINAL REVIEW

Underline and correct twenty errors in singular or plural forms, determiners, or prepositions.

EXAMPLE:

The invention of the telephone was <u>the</u> *a* great idea.

1. According to Matt Richtel, a *New York Times* journalist, some inventions have complicated historys. In fact, much great idea were preceded by earlier innovations. For instance, Thomas Edison is credited with creating a first sound recording. On February 1878, he patented his sound device. Then on 2008, researchers discovered a recording of an human voice made by a unknown French inventor. The recording had been made seventeen year before Edison's patent was granted.

2. Sometimes two persons have an idea at the same time. In February 14, 1876, Alexander Graham Bell and Elisha Gray filed patents for two separate telephone devices. Bell had been working on his idea during

several years, and he is accepted as the true inventor. However, much years earlier, an Italian immigrant named Antonio Meucci had created his own version of the telephone. At this time, though, Meucci had had very few money, so he could not afford to make a patent application.

3. Sometimes many scientists contribute to new technologys. For example, during the mid-1970s, Dennis Allison depended of computer work for his income. He published a lot of informations about his machines. Also, during that years, Bill Gates and Steve Jobs were working on their products. Because Gates and Jobs were better marketers, their names will be remembered. All of the other who worked on computers will be forgotten.

CHAPTER 28

The Writer's Room

Write about one of the following topics. Then review your nouns, determiners, and prepositions.

1. In the past one hundred years, what events have changed the world? List some events.

2. Think about a recent invention. Contrast peoples' lives before and after that invention.

mywritinglab To check your progress in meeting this chapter's objectives, log in to **www.mywritinglab.com**, go to the **Study Plan** tab, click on **The Editing Handbook—Section 5: More Parts of Speech** and choose **Nouns, Articles, and Prepositions** from the list of subtopics. Read and view the resources in the **Review Materials** section, and then complete the **Recall, Apply, and Write** sets in the **Activities** section.

Pronouns

Section Theme **INVENTIONS AND DISCOVERIES**

In this chapter, you will read about topics related to ancient civilizations.

The Writer's Journal

If you could enter a time machine, which time period would you want to visit? Explain why.

Pronoun Case

Pronouns are words that replace nouns (people, places, or things), other pronouns, and phrases. Use pronouns to avoid repeating nouns.

Hampi was the capital of an ancient Indian kingdom. Today, ~~Hampi~~ *it* is a World Heritage Site.

Pronouns are formed according to the role they play in a sentence. A pronoun can be the subject or object in a sentence, or it can show possession. The next chart shows the three main pronoun cases: subjective, objective, and possessive.

Pronouns

Singular	Subjective	Objective	Possessives	
			Possessive Adjective	**Possessive Pronoun**
1st person	I	me	my	mine
2nd person	you	you	your	yours
3rd person	he, she, it, who, whoever	him, her, it, whom, whomever	his, her, its, whose	his, hers
Plural				
1st person	we	us	our	ours
2nd person	you	you	your	yours
3rd person	they	them	their	theirs

Subjective Case

A **subject** performs an action in a sentence. When a pronoun is the subject of the sentence, use the subjective form of the pronoun.

> **She** has seen many ancient ruins.

> **We** asked questions about Greek mythology.

Objective Case

An **object** of a verb receives an action in a sentence. When a pronoun is the object of a verb in the sentence, use the objective form of the pronoun.

> Rose gave **him** a book about the Ming dynasty.

> My brother told **us** about the documentary.

Possessive Case

A possessive pronoun shows ownership.

- **Possessive adjectives** are always placed before the noun that they modify. In the next sentences, *her* and *their* are possessive adjectives.

  > She finished **her** book about the pyramids, but they did not finish **their** books.

- **Possessive pronouns** replace the possessive adjective and noun. In the next sentence, *her* is a possessive adjective and *theirs* is a possessive pronoun.

  > She finished **her** book about the pyramids, but they did not finish **theirs**.

Problems with Possessive Pronouns

When using the possessive pronouns *hers* and *theirs*, be careful that you do not add an apostrophe before the *s*.

> The archaeology book is ~~her's~~ *hers*. The papyrus map is ~~their's~~ *theirs*.

CHAPTER 29

Some possessive adjectives sound like certain contractions. When using the possessive adjectives *their, your,* and *its,* be careful that you do not confuse them with *they're, you're,* and *it's.*

GRAMMAR LINK

For more information about apostrophes, see Chapter 35.

Their is the possessive adjective.	<u>Their</u> flight to Mexico City was late.
They're is the contraction of *they are.*	<u>They're</u> looking forward to going to Cancun.
Your is the possessive adjective.	<u>Your</u> tour guide has a map of the Tulum Mayan ruins.
You're is the contraction of *you are.*	<u>You're</u> going to enjoy visiting this ancient site.
Its is the possessive adjective.	The Temple of the Frescoes has a beautiful mural on <u>its</u> wall.
It's is the contraction of *it is.*	<u>It's</u> an important piece of Mayan history.

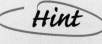 **Hint**   **Choosing *His* or *Her***

To choose the correct possessive adjective, think about the possessor (not the object that is possessed).

- If something belongs to a female, use *her* + noun.

    Cecilia packed <u>her</u> luggage.

- If something belongs to a male, use *his* + noun.

    Tony booked <u>his</u> flight.

PRACTICE I

Underline the correct possessive adjective or possessive pronoun in each set of parentheses.

EXAMPLE:

Historians often cite Greece and (<u>its</u> / it's) ancient monuments as important to the study of Western civilization.

1. Ancient societies revered (their / there) monuments. The Greeks especially loved (their / theirs). Greek philosophers created lists of architectural wonders. They put a variety of items on (their / theirs) lists. Unfortunately, many of the lists have not survived up to (our / ours) time.

2. The oldest surviving list of ancient wonders was written by Antipater of Sidon around 140 BCE. Antipater was a male, and (her / its / his) list mainly consisted of Greek structures. He also listed such structures as the pyramids at Giza and the Lighthouse of Alexandria. Most of the structures are no longer standing. For example, the Lighthouse was destroyed by an earthquake and (it's / its) aftershocks.

3.   My professor, Aspasia Jones, gave a slide show of (her / hers) trip to the pyramids. Many people, of course, have taken photographs of the pyramids, but (her / hers) were particularly interesting. She had permission to go into a chamber closed to the public, and she was able to photograph (it's / its) contents. Her assistant, Milo, used (his / its) new camera to take photos. Would you like to go to Aspasia's next slide show? Could we use (your / your're / yours) car? (My / Mine) is getting repaired. Call me on (my / mine) cell phone.

Pronouns in Comparisons with *than or as*

Avoid making errors in pronoun case when the pronoun follows *than* or *as*. If the pronoun is a subject, use the subjective case, and if the pronoun is an object, use the objective case.

If you use the incorrect case, your sentence may have a meaning that you do not intend it to have. For example, people often follow *than* or *as* with an objective pronoun when they mean to follow it with a subjective pronoun. Look at the differences in the meanings of the next sentences.

objective case

I like ancient history as much as **him.**
(I like ancient history <u>as much as I like him.</u>)

subjective case

I like ancient history as much as **he.**
(I like ancient history <u>as much as he likes ancient history.</u>)

 **Complete the Thought**

If you are unsure which pronoun case to use, test by completing the thought. Look at the following examples.

He likes to visit museums more than **I** (like to visit museums).

He likes to visit museums more than (he likes to visit) **me.**

Pronouns in Prepositional Phrases

In a prepositional phrase, the noun or pronoun that follows the preposition is the object of the preposition. Therefore, always use the objective case of the pronoun after a preposition.

<u>To</u> **her,** learning about history is not important.

<u>Between</u> **you** and **me,** our history class is very interesting.

Pronouns with *and* or *or*

Use the correct case when nouns and pronouns are joined by *and* or *or*. If the pronouns are the subject, use the subjective case. If the pronouns are the object, use the objective case.

Subjective: *He and I*
~~Him and me~~ had to do a presentation on the Incas.

Objective: *him and me*
The instructor asked ~~he and I~~ to present first.

> **Hint**   **Finding the Correct Case**
>
> An easy way to determine whether your case is correct is to say the sentence with just one pronoun.
>
> The librarian asked her and (I, me) to speak quietly.
>
> **Choices:** The librarian asked I . . .   *or*   The librarian asked me . . .
>
> **Correct:** The librarian asked her and <u>me</u> to speak quietly.

PRACTICE 2

Correct any errors with pronoun case. Write *C* in the space if the sentence is correct.

EXAMPLE:
Last summer, my friend and ~~me~~ visited Mexico.   ___*I*___

1. My friend, Maria, is older than me.   _____

2. Maria gave me a book on the Maya civilization because she is as interested in the subject as me.   _____

3. Maria and me took a bus to Chichén Itzá, an ancient site that was built around the middle of the sixth century.   _____

4. At the site, we asked a young man to take a picture of we girls.   _____

5. Maria's camera was newer than mine, so we used her's.   _____

6. The young man, whose name was Karl, climbed with Maria and me to the top of the pyramid.   _____

7. Him and his friend Pedro told us that they were afraid of heights.   _____

8. Between you and I, I was also getting a bit dizzy, so we decided to climb down.   _____

9. Our tour guide told Pedro and me that the Maya abandoned Chichén Itzá in the tenth century.   _____

10. Karl said goodbye to us because him and Pedro had to catch the bus for Belize.   _____

Relative Pronouns (*who, whom, which, that, whose*)

Relative pronouns can join two short sentences. Here is a list of relative pronouns.

who whom which that whose
whoever whomever

- *Who* (or *whoever*) and *whom* (or *whomever*) always refer to people. *Who* is the subject of the clause, and *whom* is the object of the clause.

  Subject: The archeologist **who** specializes in Mayan culture is speaking today.

  Object: The archeologist **whom** you met is my mother.

- *Which* always refers to things.

  The ancient city of Machu Picchu, **which** I have never seen, is located in the Andes.

- *That* refers to things.

  Hiram Bingham wrote a book **that** is about Machu Picchu.

- *Whose* always shows that something belongs to or is connected with someone or something. It usually replaces possessive pronouns such as *his, her,* or *their.* Do not confuse *whose* with *who's,* which means "who is."

  The archaeologist traced the route. His maps were on the table.

  The archaeologist, **whose** maps were on the table, traced the route.

CHAPTER 29

Hint **Choosing Who or Whom**

If you are unsure whether to use *who* or *whom,* test yourself in the following way. Replace *who* or *whom* with another pronoun. If the replacement is a subjective pronoun such as *he* or *she,* use *who.* If the replacement is an objective pronoun such as *her* or *him,* use **whom.**

I know a man **who** works in a museum.
(He works in a museum.)

The man to **whom** you gave your portfolio is the director of the museum.
(You gave your portfolio to him.)

PRACTICE 3

Write the correct relative pronoun in each blank.

EXAMPLE:

The Khmer civilization, _____*which*_____ built the temples of Angkor, lost its power by the fifteenth century.

1. The Hindu temples of Angkor, _____ are magnificent examples of architecture, were built between the ninth and twelfth centuries. The ancient Khmer kings, _____ kingdom was between Cambodia and the Bay of Bengal, commissioned about a hundred temples at the site. King Suryavaram II, _____ was a devout Hindu, built the temples to honor the Hindu god Vishnu. The temple _____ portrays Hindu cosmology is at Angkor Wat.

2. During the powerful reign of the Angkor kings, many people _____ were Vishnu devotees made pilgrimages to the temples. The Angkor kings, for _____ religion was important, preserved these temples for many centuries. The temples were abandoned around 1432 because of political instability.

3. The temples, _____ were very beautiful, were almost forgotten for the next few centuries. Over time, some people, many of _____ were monks, visited the temples. But it was really the French explorer Henri Mouhot _____ popularized the spot for Europeans. Mouhot visited the area _____ the jungle had hidden. On his journey, Mouhot encountered tigers, _____ made his journey difficult.

4. Today, many tourists _____ are interested in ancient monuments visit the site. Looters, _____ steal priceless objects need to be stopped, and temples _____ are world heritage sites need to be protected.

Reflexive Pronouns (*-self / -selves*)

Use **reflexive pronouns** when you want to emphasize that the subject does an action to himself or herself.

I asked **myself** many questions.

History often repeats **itself.**

Do not use reflexive pronouns with the verbs *wash, dress, feed,* and *shave.* However, you can use reflexive pronouns to draw attention to a surprising or an unusual action.

The little boy fed **himself.**
(The boy probably could not feed himself at a previous time.)

The next chart shows subjective pronouns and the reflexive pronouns that relate to them.

Pronouns That End with *-self* or *-selves*		
Singular	**Antecedent**	**Reflexive Pronoun**
1st person	I	myself
2nd person	you	yourself
3rd person	he, she, it	himself, herself, itself
Plural		
1st person	we	ourselves
2nd person	you	yourselves
3rd person	they	themselves

> ## Hint   Common Errors with Reflexive Pronouns
>
> *Hisself* and *theirselves* are not accepted in standard English. These are incorrect ways to say *himself* or *themselves*.
>
>

themselves
>
> The tourists went by ~~theirselves~~ to the museum.
>
>

himself.
>
> Croesus visited the oracle by ~~hisself.~~

PRACTICE 4

Fill in the blanks with the correct reflexive pronouns.

EXAMPLE:

He wanted to explore the forest by ____*himself*____.

1.   Sarah, our guide, hurt _____ by tripping on a tree root. She said to us, "Go to the temple by _____." We climbed the jungle path to the temple by _____.

2.   Matt, a member of our group, thought we were too slow. He ran up the path by _____. I thought to _____ that he would get lost.

3.   He congratulated _____ for finding the temple. Eventually, we also reached the temple and were very pleased with _____.

Pronoun-Antecedent Agreement

Antecedents are words that pronouns have replaced, and they always come before the pronoun. A pronoun must agree with its antecedent, which is the word to which the pronoun refers. Pronouns must agree in person and number with their antecedents.

My instructor went on a vacation to Peru. **He** took **his** family with **him.**
(*My instructor* is the antecedent of *he, his,* and *him.*)

China has many ancient salt mines. **They** date back to the fourth century B.C.E.
(*Salt mines* is the antecedent of *they.*)

Compound Antecedents

Compound antecedents consist of two or more nouns joined by *and* or *or*. When the nouns are joined by *and*, use a plural pronoun to refer to them.

The scholar and her husband brought **their** son to the museum.

When the nouns are joined by *or*, you may need a singular or a plural pronoun. If the antecedents are plural, use a plural pronoun. If both nouns are singular, use a singular pronoun.

Either the men or women completed **their** research first.

Does England or France have **its** own museum of natural history?

Collective Noun Antecedents

Collective nouns refer to a group of people or things. Generally, the noun acts as a unit; therefore, it is singular.

The government tried to implement **its** policies.

> **GRAMMAR LINK**
>
> For a list of collective nouns, see page 379 in Chapter 26.

CHAPTER 29

PRACTICE 5

Fill in the blank spaces with the appropriate pronouns or possessive adjectives.

EXAMPLE:

Since ___*their*___ discovery fifty years ago, the Dead Sea Scrolls have fascinated scholars.

1.   In the middle of the twentieth century, archaeologists heard about a find

that made _____ feel excited. The Dead Sea Scrolls consist of about

one thousand biblical and non-biblical texts. The scientific community was

enthusiastic about the scrolls, and _____ immediate goal was to

authenticate the manuscripts.

2.   In 1947, a Bedouin boy lost _____ goats near the Dead Sea. The

goats had wandered off, and the boy discovered _____ in a cave. The boy threw rocks into the cave to get the goats out. He accidently hit some pottery jars, and _____ broke, exposing the scrolls. In 1948, the boy and _____ mother took the scrolls to an antiquities dealer. The man asked the mother and _____ son about the ownership of the scrolls. They told _____ that the scrolls were _____. The dealer displayed the scrolls, and eventually, he sold _____ to scholars.

3.   Archaeologists found more scrolls in ten other caves and gave _____ to scholars. The manuscripts fade when exposed to air. To prevent damage, scholars have been making digitalized copies of _____. Either Israel or England used _____ specialized X-ray equipment to read the scrolls.

Indefinite Pronouns

Use **indefinite pronouns** when you refer to people or things whose identity is not known or is unimportant. The next chart shows some common singular and plural indefinite pronouns.

Indefinite Pronouns

Singular	another	each	nobody	other
	anybody	everybody	no one	somebody
	anyone	everyone	nothing	someone
	anything	everything	one	something
Plural	both, few, many, others, several			
Either singular or plural	all, any, some, none, more, most, half (and other fractions)			

Singular

When you use a singular indefinite antecedent, also use a singular pronoun to refer to it.

Everybody feels amazed when **he or she** sees China's terracotta army for the first time.

Nobody should forget to visit China's terracotta army in **his or her** lifetime.

Plural

When you use a plural indefinite antecedent, also use a plural pronoun to refer to it.

The two objects are ancient, and both have **their** own intrinsic value.

The world has many illegal excavation sites; there are several operating in China, but **they** cannot be controlled.

Either Singular or Plural

Some indefinite pronouns can be either singular or plural, depending on the noun to which they refer.

Many historians came to the site. <u>All</u> were experts in **their** field.
(*All* refers to historians; therefore, the pronoun is plural.)

We excavated <u>all</u> of the site and **its** artifacts.
(*All* refers to the site; therefore, the pronoun is singular.)

 **Using of the Expressions**

In sentences containing the expression *one of the ...* or *each of the ...* , the subject is the indefinite pronoun *one* or *each*. Therefore, any pronoun referring to that phrase must be singular.

> <u>One</u> of the statues is missing **its** weapon.

> <u>Each</u> of the men has **his** own map.

PRACTICE 6

Identify and correct nine errors in pronoun–antecedent agreement. You may change either the antecedent or the pronoun. If you change any antecedents, make sure that your subjects and verbs agree.

EXAMPLE:

Some of the soldiers had ~~his~~ *their* own swords.

1. In 1974, in Xi'an, China, some local men were digging a well when they made an astounding discovery. One of the men uncovered a clay soldier with their bare hands. Then others, using their shovels, discovered more clay soldiers at the site. Someone rode their bicycle to the local Communist Party headquarters. The worker described what he and the others had found.

2. The local Communist Party organization sent some excavators to the site. When they arrived, everyone expressed shock at the sight before their eyes. They realized that the find was significant. The central government sent a message to the local peasants. Each had to leave their land and move to another location. Nobody was allowed to remain in their home.

3.   Over the next years, specialists excavated the site. They uncovered more than eight thousand terracotta soldiers. The soldiers are life-sized, and many have his own unique physical features. The statues represent every ethnic group in China. Different male artists carved groups of the soldiers. Each engraved their name on the statues.

4.   The clay soldiers have been guarding an ancient emperor for over 2,000 years. Everybody in the all-male army, including generals, officers, cavalry, and archers, had their own life-sized weapon. Today the site is a major tourist attraction in China. Anybody who goes to China on their holiday should try to visit the terracotta army.

 Hint   **Avoid Sexist Language**

Terms like *anybody, somebody, nobody,* and *each* are singular antecedents, so the pronouns that follow those words must be singular. At one time, it was acceptable to use *he* as a general term meaning "all people"; however, today it is more acceptable to use *he or she.*

Sexist:	Everyone had to leave his home.
Solution:	Everyone had to leave his or her home.
Better solution:	The citizens had to leave their homes.

Exception: If you know for certain that the subject is male or female, then use only *he* or only *she.*

PRACTICE 7

Circle the correct pronouns in the following paragraphs.

EXAMPLE:

Some people say that history is not important because (its) it's) information is not relevant to people's everyday lives.

1.   History courses offer information about the past, but many people wonder whether they should spend (his or her, their) time studying the past. In fact, somebody might feel it is more important to think about (his or her, their) future. In other words, some people may not consider history and (it's, its) lessons to be as important as other subjects that are more practical.

2.   In the past, historians and (their, theirs) supporters memorized names and dates. Everybody believed that (his or her, their) knowledge of history indicated a high level of education. Between you and (I, me), I do not think that this reason for studying history is valid. I think that history should be studied for (its, it's) own merits. For example, history tells us about societies and (their, theirs) past behaviors. History informs us about critical moments in the past and (their / theirs) influence on today's lifestyles. Furthermore, history helps us understand more about (yourselves, ourselves).

3.   I like studying history; however, my brother has always liked it far more than (I, me). He became really interested when we were children. (He, Him) and (I, me) used to read stories about World War I. Now my brother is a historian. He is a man (who, whom) believes that everybody should take (his or her, their) history lessons seriously. In fact, my brother met (his, her) future wife in history class. He was sitting by (hisself, himself, herself) when she sat near him. The rest, of course, is history.

Vague Pronouns

Avoid using pronouns that could refer to more than one antecedent.

Vague: Frank asked his friend where <u>his</u> map of ancient Greece was.
        (Whose map is it: Frank's or his friend's?)

Clearer: **Frank** wondered where **his** map of ancient Greece was, so he asked his friend about it.

Avoid using confusing pronouns such as *it* and *they* that have no clear antecedent.

Vague: <u>They</u> say that people should get vaccines before traveling to certain countries.
        (Who are *they*?)

Clearer: **Health authorities** say that people should get vaccines before traveling to certain countries.

Vague: <u>It</u> stated in the magazine that the newly found pyramid belonged to Queen Sesheshet.
        (Who or what is *it*?)

Clearer: **The magazine article** stated that the newly found pyramid belonged to Queen Sesheshet.

This, that, and *which* should refer to a specific antecedent.

Vague: The teacher told us that we should study hard for our history exams because they were going to be difficult. <u>This</u> caused all of us to panic.

(What is *this?* The word(s) that *this* refers to is not explicitly stated; it is only implied.)

Clearer: The teacher told us that we should study hard for our history exams because they were going to be difficult. **This information** caused all of us to panic.

 **Avoid Repeating the Subject**

When you clearly mention a subject, do not repeat the subject in pronoun form.

Egypt's pyramids, ~~they~~ are more than 4,000 years old.

The book ~~it~~ is really interesting.

PRACTICE 8

Each sentence has either a vague pronoun or a repeated subject. Correct the errors. You may need to rewrite some sentences.

EXAMPLE:

The radio reporter announced
~~They said on the radio~~ that archaeologists have discovered a new burial ground along the Yangzte River.

1. Professor Schmitt told Mark that a book about the Great Wall of China is on his desk.

2. They say that the Great Wall is more than 2,000 years old.

3. They built the wall to protect the Chinese empire from northern invasions.

4. This also helped unify China.

5. They say that the emperor Qin Shi Huang ordered the construction of the Great Wall.

6. They persecuted anyone who disagreed with the emperor.

7. The Great Wall it is over 1,500 miles long.

8. They say the only man-made object that can be seen from space is the Great Wall.

CHAPTER 29

Pronoun Shifts

If your writing contains unnecessary shifts in person or number, you may confuse your readers. Carefully edit your writing to ensure that your pronouns are consistent in number and person.

Making Pronouns Consistent in Number

Pronouns and antecedents must agree in **number**. If the antecedent is singular, then the pronoun must be singular. If the antecedent is plural, then the pronoun must be plural.

> singular   *her*
> The **director** of the museum encouraged ~~their~~ employees to be on time.

> plural   *they*
> When **tourists** visit an excavation site, ~~he~~ should be careful not to touch the artifacts.

Making Pronouns Consistent in Person

Person is the writer's perspective. In some writing assignments, you may use first person (*I, we*). For other assignments, especially most college and workplace writing, you may use second person (*you*) or third person (*he, she, it, they*).

When you shift your point of view for no reason, your writing may become unclear, and you may confuse your readers. If you begin writing from one point of view, do not shift unnecessarily to another point of view.

> *we*
> If ~~one~~ considered the expenses involved in visiting another country, **we** would probably never travel.

>   *we*
> **We** visited the pyramids at Teotihuacán, but ~~you~~ could not climb one of them because archeologists were working on it.

 **Avoiding Pronoun Shifts in Paragraphs**

Sometimes it is easier to use pronouns consistently in individual sentences than it is in larger paragraphs or essays. When you write paragraphs and essays, always check that your pronouns agree with your antecedents in person and in number. In the next example, the pronouns are consistent in the first two sentences; however, they shift in person in the third sentence.

> **We** went to Mexico City last year. **We** traveled around on the subway to visit
>
>   *we*
> various archaeological sites. Sometimes the subway was so crowded that ~~you~~
>
> could barely move.

PRACTICE 9

Correct six pronoun shift errors.

EXAMPLE:

I like to visit museums because ~~you~~ *I* see such interesting displays about ancient cultures.

North American native groups left no written records. Scientists believe that by studying human remains, you can obtain information about indigenous history. However, native groups feel that excavation of burial sites is demeaning to one's ancestors. The Dickson Mounds Museum in Illinois exemplifies this controversy. In 1927, an Illinois farmer discovered a Native American burial ground on his land. He dug up the area, and you could see that the site contained ancient artifacts and human skeletons. He built a museum over the site, and thousands of tourists came to see the graves. Scientists also studied the human remains. By the 1970s, many native groups protested such excavations, arguing that their ancestors cannot rest in peace if your bones are on display. By the 1990s, the American government passed a law requiring any federally funded institution to give back their collection to Native American tribes. In 1992, the skeletons were reburied by the Dickson Mounds Museum officials because he wanted to respect native groups.

REFLECT ON IT

Think about what you have learned in this chapter. If you do not know an answer, review that concept.

1. Write a sentence that includes an objective pronoun. _____

   _____

2. When do you use possessive pronouns (*my, mine, his, hers,* etc.)? _____

   _____

3. Circle the best answer: In a sentence, *whom* replaces

   a. the subject.   b. the object

4. What is an antecedent? _____

_____

5. Circle the best answer: Pronouns must agree with their antecedents:

a. only in number.　　　　　　　　b. only in person.

c. both in number and in person.　　d. neither in number nor in person.

FINAL REVIEW

Correct fifteen errors with pronouns in the next paragraphs.

EXAMPLE:

> *A prominent lawyer*
> ~~It~~ says that the dispute between many countries is about cultural
> property rights.

1.　　People learn important things about history by visiting museums

filled with historical artifacts. For example, Britain and France they

have obtained antiquities from countries around the world. The British

government believes in it's right to keep the treasures who are

exhibited in museums. However, countries such as Greece and Egypt

want their treasures back because they view antiquities as a part of

its cultural heritage. Returning antiquities to its native countries is a

complicated issue.

2.　　The removal of artifacts such as mummies has created an ethical

problem for the Egyptian government and their archaeologists. An

interesting science article it says that a lot of information can be acquired

from the scientific study of burial sites. Although some people believe it

is always unethical to dig up the dead, every archaeologist who studies

Egyptian mummies increases their knowledge of ancient Egypt. For

example, centuries ago, the pharaohs believed that they could get to

heaven faster if you were buried with food and treasures for the voyage.

Each pharoah decided for hisself what he would take on his journey to

the afterlife. When a pharaoh died, priests mummified the body and

buried them in the pyramids. Therefore, archaeologists whom have excavated burial sites find not only mummies, but also valuable artworks and other artifacts.

3.   In conclusion, archaeologists are confronted with numerous ethical questions. Specialists debate controversial matters among theirselves. Everyone has their own opinion. My professor is more interested in these issues than me. Because there are no easy answers, these issues will continue to be discussed in the future.

The Writer's Room

Choose one of the following topics. Make sure that pronoun case and pronoun–antecedent agreement is correct.

1. Tell the story about an ideal vacation. Where would you go, and what would you do? Use descriptive language in your writing.

2. How important is history as a school subject? Should history be a compulsory subject?

The Writers' Circle   **Collaborative Activity**

Work with a group of three to five students.

Imagine that you are having a dinner party. You can invite any five people that you want. The guests can be historical figures or living people. As a team, write three sentences about each person and explain who the person is and what he or she will contribute to the party.

CHAPTER 29

READING LINK

Great Discoveries
Reading 14: "The Beeps" by Josh Freed (page 562)
Reading 15: "Gone with the Windows" by Dorothy Nixon (page 564)

mywritinglab   To check your progress in meeting this chapter's objectives, log in to **www.mywritinglab.com**, go to the **Study Plan** tab, click on **The Editing Handbook—Section 5: More Parts of Speech** and choose **Pronouns, Pronoun Antecedent Agreement, Pronoun Reference and Point of View,** and **Pronoun Case** from the list of subtopics. Read and view the resources in the **Review Materials** section, and then complete the **Recall, Apply,** and **Write** sets in the **Activities** section.

Adjectives and Adverbs

Section Theme **HEALTH CARE**

In this chapter, you will read about topics related to health care.

The Writer's Journal

Write a short paragraph describing how people can best protect their health. List several examples in your paragraph.

Adjectives

Adjectives describe nouns (people, places, or things) and pronouns (words that replace nouns). They add information explaining how many, what kind, or which one. They also help you appeal to the senses by describing how things look, smell, feel, taste, and sound.

The **dynamic** <u>doctor</u>, Christiaan Barnard, completed a **complicated** <u>surgery</u>.

He performed the **first heart transplant** <u>operation</u> in 1967.

Placement of Adjectives

You can place adjectives either before a noun or after a linking verb such as *be, look, appear, smell,* or *become.*

Before the noun:	The **young unemployed** man received a scholarship for **medical** school.
After the linking verb:	LV LV He was **shocked**, but he was **happy**.

PRACTICE 1

Underline the adjectives in the next sentences.

EXAMPLE:

About 50 million Americans had no medical insurance in 2009.

1. Self-employed entrepreneurs and small-business owners struggle to get adequate health care.

2. Also, certain groups of elderly Americans cannot afford sufficient, reliable medical treatment.

3. Furthermore, prescription drug costs are higher in the United States than they are in other countries, such as England, Switzerland, Canada, and Sweden.

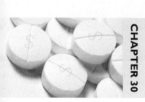

4. Where the average American citizen pays one dollar for a prescription drug, a British citizen pays only sixty-four cents and a Canadian citizen pays only fifty-seven cents.

5. The average annual profit of the top ten drug companies is over three billion dollars.

6. Drug companies argue that they do groundbreaking research on new drugs.

7. In 2010, politicians passed what they hope is decent and fair legislation about health-care issues.

Problems with Adjectives

You can recognize many adjectives by their endings. Be particularly careful when you use the following adjective forms.

CHAPTER 30

Adjectives Ending in *-ful* or *-less*

Some adjectives end in *-ful* or *-less*. Remember that *-ful* ends in one *l* and *-less* ends in double *s*.

> Alexander Fleming, a **skillful** scientist, conducted many **useful** experiments.

> His work appeared in **countless** publications.

Adjectives Ending in *-ed* and *-ing*

Some adjectives look like verbs because they end in *-ing* or *-ed*.

- When the adjective ends in *-ed*, it describes the person's or animal's expression or feeling.

  > The **overworked** and **tired** scientist presented her findings to the public.

- When the adjective ends in *-ing*, it describes the quality of the person or thing.

  > Her **compelling** and **promising** discovery pleased the public.

 **Keep Adjectives in the Singular Form**

Always make an adjective singular, even if the noun following the adjective is plural. In the next example, "year" acts as an adjective.

>   *year*   *other*
> Paul was a nine-~~years~~-old boy when he broke his arm while playing with ~~others~~ children.

CHAPTER 30

PRACTICE 2

Correct eight adjective errors. The adjectives may have the wrong form, or they may be misspelled.

EXAMPLE:

>   *surprising*
> Many ~~surprised~~ medical findings happen by accident.

1. One of the world's amazed scientifics discoveries happened by pure chance. Born in 1881, Alexander Fleming was a tireles medical doctor. He worked in his small London clinic, where he treated famous people for venereal disease. He also conducted many biologicals experiments.

2. One day in 1928, he put some *Staphylococcus* bacteria in a culture dish. Two weeks later, Fleming, who was a carefull researcher, discovered that a clear ring encircled the yellow-green mold on the dish. A mold spore had

flown into the dish from a laboratory on the floor below. At that point,

Fleming made an insightfull observation. He had an astounded revelation.

He realized that the mold somehow stopped the growth of bacteria in the

culture dish.

3.   Fleming named the new product penicillin. During World War II, the

drug saved millions of lives, and it continues to be used today to treat

differents infections.

Adverbs

Adverbs add information to adjectives, verbs, or other adverbs. They give more specific information about how, when, where, and to what extent an action or event occurred.

verb   adverb

Doctors in ancient Rome <u>performed</u> surgeries **skillfully.**

adverb   adverb

These surgeons could remove cataracts **quite** <u>quickly</u>.

adverb   adjective

The ancient Romans were **highly** <u>innovative</u>.

Forms of Adverbs

Adverbs often end in *-ly*. In fact, you can change many adjectives into adverbs by adding *-ly* endings.

- If you add *-ly* to a word that ends in *l*, then your new word will have a double *l*.

scornful + ly

Many ancient Romans viewed surgeons **scornfully.**

- If you add *-ly* to a word that ends in *e*, keep the *e*. Exceptions to this rule are *truly* and *duly*.

extreme + ly

Doctors were **extremely** careful when they operated on patients.

 Some Adverbs and Adjectives Have the Same Form

Some adverbs look exactly like adjectives. The only way to distinguish them from adjectives is to see what they are modifying or describing. The following words can be either adjectives or adverbs.

| early | fast | high | often | right |
| far | hard | late | past | soon |

adjective   adverb

Dr. Greenbay has a **hard** job. She works **hard.**

PRACTICE 3

Circle the correct adjectives or adverbs in each sentence.

EXAMPLE:

In 1980, the World Health Organization (official / officially) stated that it had eradicated smallpox.

1. The worldwide eradication of smallpox was one of the most important accomplishments in modern medicine. Smallpox was a (high / highly) contagious global disease. Throughout history, smallpox epidemics were a (frequent / frequently) occurrence. People who contracted the disease had (painful / painfully) sores. Around 30 percent of smallpox victims suffered (horrible / horribly) deaths. In the Americas, smallpox (severe / severely) weakened native populations.

2. In the mid-twentieth century, in North America and Europe, smallpox outbreaks were (rapid / rapidly) controlled with the use of vaccinations. However, in other parts of the world, the illness occurred (regular / regularly). In the early 1960s, the former Soviet Union proposed a (global / globally) initiative to eliminate smallpox. Health-care workers knew they would have to work (careful / carefully) to help identify regions where the disease still occurred. They (patient / patiently) educated people about the malady and inoculated those at risk. With great effort, the World Health Organization eradicated the (terrible / terribly) disease. Since 1977, there has been no (natural / naturally) recurrence of smallpox anywhere in the world.

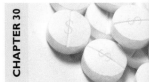

Placement of Frequency Adverbs

Frequency adverbs are words that indicate how often someone performs an action or when an event occurs. Common frequency adverbs are *always, ever, never, often, sometimes,* and *usually*. They can appear at the beginning of sentences, or they can appear in the following locations.

- Place frequency adverbs before regular present tense and past tense verbs.

    Medical doctors **always** recite the Hippocratic oath.

- Place frequency adverbs after all forms of the verb *be (am, is, are, was, were)*.

    My patients are **usually** punctual for appointments.

- Place frequency adverbs after helping verbs.

    I have **never** broken any bone in my body.

PRACTICE 4

Correct seven errors in the placement of frequency adverbs.

EXAMPLE:

often

Chronic pain is ˄ treated ~~often~~ with narcotics.

1. Almost two million Americans are prescribed painkillers every year.

    Patients fail often to recognize that they are addicted to painkillers.

    Doctors label sometimes this problem the "silent addiction."

2. Many patients usually have started taking painkillers after an accident.

    For example, Emma was suffering from chronic back pain. She took

    painkillers to reduce her pain but found soon that she needed a stronger

    dose. So she doubled frequently the dose of her prescription. Her

    personality started to change, and she found that she was critical often of

    people around her. She realized that she was addicted to painkillers and

    spoke to her doctor about her problem. Now she is careful always about

    any medication she takes.

Problems with Adverbs

Use the Correct Form

Many times, people use an adjective instead of an adverb after a verb. Make sure
that you always modify your verbs using an adverb.

really quickly

Ancient Greek medicine advanced ~~real quick~~ after the time of Homer.

slowly

However, patients recovered very ~~slow.~~

PRACTICE 5

Correct eight errors in adjective and adverb forms.

EXAMPLE:

really

Euthanasia is a ~~realy~~ difficult issue.

1. People who oppose the "right-to-die" movement argue that many

    patients who wish for euthanasia may be extremelly depressed. Patients

    may also have incomplete information about other options such as long-

    term care and real effective pain control. Opponents of legal euthanasia also suggest that many desperately people could be coerced into committing euthanasia quick.

2.   People who want to legalize euthanasia strong believe that the quality of a person's life is the most important consideration in the debate. They say that if a patient has become severe disabled as a result of illness, his or her quality of life is drasticaly reduced. They believe that a patient should have the right to die with dignity if he or she chooses. Proponents of euthanasia have real firm beliefs. They think that laws can prevent abuse or coercion of the patient.

Using *Good* and *Well*, *Bad* and *Badly*

Good is an adjective, and *well* is an adverb.

Adjective:	Louis Pasteur had a **good** reputation.
Adverb:	He explained his theories **well**.

  Exception: Use *well* to describe a person's health: I do not feel **well**.

Bad is an adjective, and *badly* is an adverb.

Adjective:	My father has a **bad** cold.
Adverb:	His throat hurts **badly**.

PRACTICE 6

Circle the correct adjectives or adverbs.

EXAMPLE:

Wash your hands (good / ⊙well⊙) before you prepare food.

1. Food poisoning can damage the (good / well) reputations of food companies.

2. Recently, the Bird's Nest Food Company gave the public some (bad / badly) news.

3. After eating the company's hamburgers, many people did not feel (good / well).

4. Many consumers complained of having a (bad / badly) case of indigestion, and they reacted (bad / badly) to the company's news.

5. Fortunately, public health inspectors investigated the case really (good / well).

6. The company workers stated that they had taken (good / well) care when handling the food.

7. The company showed its (good / well) intentions by recalling the food quickly.

8. To avoid food poisoning, authorities warned consumers to cook their food (good / well).

Comparative and Superlative Forms

Use the comparative form to show how two persons, things, or items are different.

Adjectives:	Dr. Jonas Salk was a <u>better</u> researcher than his colleague. Dr. Sabin is <u>more famous</u> for his research on the polio virus than Dr. Enders.
Adverbs:	Dr. Salk published his results <u>more quickly</u> than Dr. Drake. Dr. Salk debated the issue <u>more passionately</u> than his colleague.

Use the **superlative form** to compare three or more items.

Adjectives:	Dr. Salk was the <u>youngest</u> scientist to receive funding for polio research at the University of Michigan. Polio was one of the <u>most destructive</u> diseases of the twentieth century.
Adverbs:	Dr. Parekh talked the <u>most rapidly</u> of all the doctors at the conference. She spoke the <u>most effectively</u> of all of the participants.

CHAPTER 30

How to Write Comparative and Superlative Forms

You can write comparative and superlative forms by remembering a few simple guidelines.

Using -er and -est endings

Add -*er* and -*est* endings to one-syllable adjectives and adverbs.

Adjective or Adverb	Comparative	Superlative
tall	tall**er** than	the tall**est**
hard	hard**er** than	the hard**est**
fast	fast**er** than	the fast**est**

Double the last letter when the adjective ends in one vowel + one consonant.

hot	hot**ter** than	the hot**test**

Using *more* and *the most*

Add *more* and *the most* to adjectives and adverbs of two or more syllables.

Adjective or Adverb	Comparative	Superlative
dangerous	**more** dangerous than	**the most** dangerous
effectively	**more** effectively than	**the most** effectively
nervous	**more** nervous than	**the most** nervous

When a two-syllable adjective ends in *y*, change the *y* to *i* and add *-er* or *-est*.

Adjective	Comparative	Superlative
happy	happ**ier** than	the happ**iest**

Using Irregular Comparative and Superlative Forms

Some adjectives and adverbs have unique comparative and superlative forms. Study this list to remember how to form some of the most common ones.

Adjective or Adverb	Comparative	Superlative
good, well	better than	the best
bad, badly	worse than	the worst
some, much, many	more than	the most
little (a small amount)	less than	the least
far	farther, further	the farthest, the furthest

> **GRAMMAR LINK**
>
> *Farther* indicates a physical distance. *Further* means "additional." For more commonly confused words, see Chapter 33.

PRACTICE 7

Underline the appropriate comparative or superlative form of the words in parentheses.

EXAMPLE:

Some drug ads are (<u>more</u> / most) effective than others.

1. In the past, there was (less / least) drug research than there is today. Anybody could claim to have the (better / best) medicine on the market. For example, in the early twentieth century, one of the (more / most) successful products was Miss Lydia E. Pinkham's Vegetable Compound. The vial, which contained 20 percent alcohol content, promised to cure "female complaints." It had (more / most) alcohol than beer, and it was the (more / most) popular cure of its era.

2. In 1927, the Food and Drug Administration was formed. The FDA's (more / most) important goal was to regulate drug advertising. Companies could no longer say that their products were (better / best) than the competitors' products, and they could not claim that theirs had the (less / least) side effects of all medications.

3. Today, drug companies spend billions on advertising. Critics claim that companies spend (more / most) on convincing consumers to buy their products than they do on testing their products. Those who are against drug advertising say that it makes medications (more / most) expensive than they were before.

4. Companies spend billions convincing consumers that their products are the (more / most) effective on the market. Consumers then pressure their doctors to give them a certain well-known drug, even if there are (better / best) alternative products. On the other hand, advertisements must list side effects, so in some respects, consumers are (better / best) informed than they were in the past.

PRACTICE 8

Complete the sentences by writing either the comparative or superlative form of the word in parentheses.

EXAMPLE:

Some people have (thin) _____*thinner*_____ bones than others.

1. By about age thirty-five, all adults lose some bone mass. Then, as people age, bone deteriorates (rapidly) _____ than before. With osteoporosis, bones become (brittle) _____ than previously. Some people become (short) _____ than they were in their youth because osteoporosis can cause the vertebra in the back to collapse.

2. Osteoporosis is much (common) _____ in women than in men because women have (little) _____ bone mass than men do. In women, the rate of bone loss is (quick) _____ after menopause than it is before menopause.

3.   Some in the medical community say that calcium pills are the

(effective) _____ way to slow the onset of the disease.

Yet women from Asian and African nations who consume very little

calcium have much (low) _____ osteoporosis rates

than American women. Osteoporosis is one of the (little)

_____ understood chronic diseases in the world.

Problems with Comparative and Superlative Forms

Using *more* and *-er*

In the comparative form, never use *more* and *-er* to modify the same word. In the superlative form, never use *most* and *-est* to modify the same word.

> *better*
> Some people thought that Salk's vaccine was ~~more better~~ than Sabin's
> *best*
> vaccine. The polio vaccine was one of the ~~most best~~ discoveries of our
>
> times.

Using *fewer* and *less*

In the comparative form, never use *less* to compare two count nouns. Use *less* to compare two noncount nouns. (Noncount nouns are nouns that cannot be divided, such as *information* and *music*.) Use *fewer* to compare two count nouns.

> *fewer*
> Today, ~~less~~ people get vaccinated than in previous decades because
> *Less*
> some question the safety of certain vaccinations. ~~Fewer~~ information
>
> about vaccines was available in the 1950s than is available today.

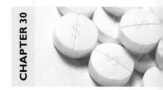

CHAPTER 30

GRAMMAR LINK

For a list of noncount nouns, refer to page 397 in Chapter 28.

 **Using *the* in the Comparative Form**

Although you would usually use *the* in superlative forms, you can use it in some two-part comparatives. In these expressions, the second part is the result of the first part.

    action   result

The more you exercise, the better your health will be.

PRACTICE 9

Correct fifteen adjective and adverb errors.

EXAMPLE:
Americans debate ~~continual~~ *continually* on the ethics of organ transplants.

1. One of the most greatest miracles of modern medicine is organ transplants. Organ transplants save most lives than ever before. With donor organs, many recipients can lead more better lives than previously imagined. However, a public debate about organ transplants is growing rapid.

2. The source of donor organs is a controversial issue. Given the scarcity of organs, some individuals who need transplants quick have obtained organs through unscrupulous methods. For instance, some have bought organs from the most poorest segments of the population in developing countries. Destitute people sometimes sell their organs to rich buyers because they need money real badly.

3. Who should receive an organ transplant? Given the scarcity of supply, should a person who smokes heavy or drinks too much receive a lung or liver transplant? Obviously, the more a person smokes, the worst his or her health will be. Should such people be refused access to organ transplants?

4. In addition, money is an issue in this debate. Hospital administrators are concerned about the high cost of transplants. Less people have adequate medical insurance than ever before. Should those with health insurance be treated more better than those without? According to most experts, the richest a patient is, the best his or her chances are to receive a transplant.

5. Waiting for an organ transplant is one of the worse experiences anyone can go through. Hopefully, in future years, the number of people who sign donor cards will be more higher than it is now.

CHAPTER 30

REFLECT ON IT

Think about what you have learned in this unit. If you do not know an answer, review that concept.

1. What is an adjective? _____

_____

2. What is an adverb? _____

_____

3. Write the correct adjective or adverb in each blank.

a. My doctor treats her patients (good, well) _____. She is one of the (better, best) _____ eye surgeons in Berlin.

b. My brother has (less, fewer) _____ work experience than I do, but he also has (less, fewer) _____ responsibilities.

4. The following sentences contain adjective or adverb errors. Correct each mistake.

a. We had a real nice time at the medical conference.

b. Everyone was dressed casual.

c. My sister changes often her mind about her career.

d. The advancing medical textbook is my sister's.

CHAPTER 30

FINAL REVIEW

Underline and correct twenty errors in adjectives and adverbs.

1.   Health care is one of the most fastest growing fields in the world. In our nation, the aging population is making the demand for nurses more and more intenser. According to *Health Affairs*, an online magazine, there is an acute nursing shortage. Less people enter the nursing profession than in the past. In fact, the number of people in their early twenties entering the nursing profession is at its lower point in forty years. The shortage is worldwide. Canada, England, and many other nations have a more greater shortage than the United States has. As a possible career, more people should consider the nursing profession.

2.   First, nurses have greater responsibility and a more diversely role than most people realize. In states such as California, nurses can write

prescriptions and nurse midwives can deliver babies. Forensic nurses treat traumatizing victims of violent crime. Furthermore, hospitals are not the only places where nurses can work. Nursing jobs are available in walk-in clinics, schools, vacation resorts, and medical equipment firms. Even film studios hire sometimes on-set nurses.

3.   Also, nursing can be an extreme rewarding career. Joan Bowes, a nurse in Oregon, says that she feels as if she is doing something usefull each day. Occasionally, her actions help to save lives. Last month, a young patient who had been injured really bad was admitted to the hospital where Joan works. A few days later, Joan noticed that the patient was unable to move his head as easy as before. She quick alerted a specialist who then diagnosed a meningitis infection. Joan's observation helped to save the patient's life. Joan's husband Keith is a home-care nurse. He is compassionate, and he interacts good with his patients. As one of a growing number of men in the profession, Keith feels that entering nursing was the better decision he has ever made.

4.   Nurses are more better compensated than in the past. In the 1970s, salaries for nurses were much worst than they are today. In fact, nurses were paid the less among health care professionals. Nowadays, because nurses are in such high demand, many hospitals give signing bonuses, decent schedules, and real good salaries.

5.   Potential nurses should enjoy helping people. For those who want to have a rewarding career with decent benefits, nursing is an excellent career choice. The more society appreciates nurses, the best health care will be.

 The Writer's Room

Write about one of the following topics. Underline adjectives and adverbs.

1. What steps can you take to motivate yourself to exercise regularly?

2. What are some possible problems that may occur if euthanasia is legalized in all states?

mywritinglab To check your progress in meeting this chapter's objectives, log in to **www.mywritinglab.com**, go to the **Study Plan** tab, click on **The Editing Handbook—Section 6: Modifiers** and choose **Adjectives and Adverbs** from the list of subtopics. Read and view the resources in the **Review Materials** section, and then complete the **Recall, Apply,** and **Write** sets in the **Activities** section.

CHAPTER 30

Mistakes with Modifiers

Section Theme **HEALTH CARE**

LEARNING OBJECTIVES

1 Misplaced Modifiers (p. 442)
2 Dangling Modifiers (p. 446)

In this chapter, you will read about topics related to alternative medicine.

The Writer's Journal

Have you ever hurt yourself or had an accident? What happened?

Misplaced Modifiers

A **modifier** is a word, phrase, or clause that describes or modifies nouns or verbs in a sentence. For example, *holding the patient's hand* is a modifier. To use a modifier correctly, place it next to the word(s) that you want to modify.

modifier   words that are modified

<u>Holding the patient's hand</u>, **the doctor** explained the procedure.

A **misplaced modifier** is a word, phrase, or clause that is not placed next to the word it modifies. When a modifier is too far from the word that it is describing, then the meaning of the sentence can become confusing or unintentionally funny.

I saw a pamphlet about acupuncture sitting in the doctor's office.
(How could a pamphlet sit in a doctor's office?)

Commonly Misplaced Modifiers

As you read the sample sentences for each type of modifier, notice how the meaning of the sentence changes depending on where the modifier is placed. In the examples, the modifiers are underlined.

Prepositional Phrase Modifiers

A prepositional phrase is made of a preposition and its object.

Confusing:	Cora read an article on acupuncture written by the reporter James Reston <u>in a café.</u> (Who was in the café: James or Cora?)
Clear:	<u>In a café</u>, Cora read an article on acupuncture written by the reporter James Reston.

Present Participle Modifiers

A present participle modifier is a phrase that begins with an *-ing* verb.

Confusing:	James Reston learned about acupuncture <u>touring China.</u> (Can acupuncture tour China?)
Clear:	While <u>touring China</u>, James Reston learned about acupuncture.

Past Participle Modifiers

A past participle modifier is a phrase that begins with a past participle (*walked*, *gone*, *known*, and so on).

Confusing:	<u>Called meridians</u>, acupuncturists claim there are two thousand pathways on the body. (What are called meridians: the acupuncturists or the pathways?)
Clear:	Acupuncturists claim there are two thousand pathways <u>called meridians</u> on the body.

Limiting Modifiers

Limiting modifiers are words such as *almost, nearly, only, merely, just,* and *even.* In the examples, notice how the placement of *almost* changes the meaning.

Almost all of the doctors went to the lecture that disproved acupuncture.
(Some of the doctors did not attend, but most did.)

All of the doctors **almost** went to the lecture that disproved acupuncture.
(The doctors did not go.)

All of the doctors went to the lecture that **almost** disproved acupuncture.
(The lecture did not disprove acupuncture.)

> ## Hint — Other Types of Modifiers
>
> There are many other types of modifiers. For example, some modifiers begin with relative clauses and some are appositives.
>
> **Relative Clause**
>
> | **Confusing:** | The treatments involved acupuncture needles <u>that were expensive</u>. |
> | | (What was expensive: the treatment or the needles?) |
> | **Clear:** | The treatments <u>that were expensive</u> involved acupuncture needles. |
>
> **Appositive**
>
> | **Confusing:** | <u>A very sick man</u>, Monica helped her uncle find a doctor. |
> | | (How could Monica be a very sick man?) |
> | **Clear:** | Monica helped her uncle, <u>a very sick man</u>, find a doctor. |

PRACTICE I

Circle the letter of the correct sentence in each pair. Underline the misplaced modifier in each incorrect sentence.

EXAMPLE:

    a. Simon Weiss learned about acupuncture <u>with enthusiasm</u>.

    ⓑ With enthusiasm, Simon Weiss learned about acupuncture.

1. a. Simon read about acupuncture, which is based on an ancient philosophy.
    b. Based on an ancient philosophy, Simon read about acupuncture.

2. a. By licensed practitioners, many U.S. states allow acupuncture to be performed.
    b. Acupuncture can be performed by licensed practitioners in many U.S. states.

3. a. Only seventeen states allow acupuncturists to practice without medical supervision.
    b. Seventeen states only allow acupuncturists to practice without medical supervision.

4. a. In a hurry, Simon asked for information about acupuncture.
    b. Simon asked for information about acupuncture in a hurry.

5. a. Needing treatment, Mr. Lo examined the patient.
    b. Mr. Lo examined the patient needing treatment.

6. a. Faced with chronic headaches, Mr. Lo was prepared to treat Simon.
    b. Faced with chronic headaches, Simon was prepared to try Mr. Lo's treatment.

7. a. Carefully guiding the needles, Mr. Lo gently pierced Simon's skin.
    b. Carefully guiding the needles, Simon's skin was gently pierced by Mr. Lo.

8. a. Mr. Lo treated Simon wearing a mask
    b. Wearing a mask, Mr. Lo treated Simon.

 **Correcting Misplaced Modifiers**

To correct misplaced modifiers, do the following:

• Identify the modifier.

   The orderly pushed the stretcher <u>in sneakers</u>.

• Identify the word or words that are being modified.

   Who wore sneakers? **The orderly**

• Move the modifier next to the word(s) being modified.

   <u>In sneakers</u>, **the orderly** pushed the stretcher.

PRACTICE 2

Underline the misplaced modifiers in the following sentences. Then, rewrite the sentences. You may have to add or remove words to give the sentence a logical meaning.

EXAMPLE:

   <u>Acting recklessly</u>, the motorcycle was driven too quickly by the young man.

   Acting recklessly, the young man drove the motorcycle too quickly.

1. In a wheelchair, the nurse sat near the patient.

   _____

   _____

2. The patient took the medication with red hair.

   _____

   _____

3. Ross was a teenager with a cast on his leg weighing 120 pounds.

   _____

   _____

4. Not wearing a helmet, the accident could have killed the young man.

   _____

   _____

5. Citing freedom of expression, a fight against helmet laws is being proposed by cycling enthusiasts.

   _____

   _____

6. Scared of having another accident, the motorcycle will not be driven again by Ross.

   _____

   _____

CHAPTER 31

Dangling Modifiers

A **dangling modifier** opens a sentence but does not modify any words in the sentence. It "dangles" or hangs loosely because it is not connected to any other part of the sentence.

To avoid having a dangling modifier, make sure that the modifier and the first noun that follows it have a logical connection.

Confusing:	While talking on a cell phone, the ambulance drove off the road.
	(Can an ambulance talk on a cell phone?)
Clear:	While talking on a cell phone, the ambulance **technician** drove off the road.
Confusing:	To get into medical school, high grades are necessary.
	(Can high grades get into a school?)
Clear:	To get into medical school, **students** need high grades.

PRACTICE 3

Circle the letter of the correct sentence in each pair. Underline the dangling modifier in each incorrect sentence.

EXAMPLE:

    a. <u>Having taken a pill</u>, the results were surprising.

    (b.) Having taken a pill, I was surprised by the results.

1. a. With the patient's budget in mind, the least expensive drugs were prescribed.

    b. With the patient's budget in mind, the doctor prescribed the least expensive drugs.

2. a. Believing in their effects, placebos are often given to patients.

    b. Believing in their effects, Doctor Zimboro sometimes gives placebos to patients.

3. a. After taking a sugar pill, patients often feel relieved.

    b. After taking a sugar pill, there is often a feeling of relief.

4. a. Surprised, the word *placebo* means "to please."

    b. Surprised, I read that the word *placebo* means "to please."

5. a. Thinking about the mind–body relationship, scientist Esther Sternberg conducted an experiment.

    b. Thinking about the mind–body relationship, an experiment was conducted.

6. a. Frustrated, Sternberg's temptation was to give up.

    b. Frustrated, Sternberg was tempted to give up.

CHAPTER 31

7. a. Using laboratory rats, Sternberg discovered a link between the mind and body.

    b. Using laboratory rats, a link was discovered between the mind and body.

8. a. Given an antidepressant, the arthritis disappeared.

    b. Given an antidepressant, some rats no longer had arthritis.

9. a. Excited about her discovery, Sternberg wrote an article for a medical journal.

    b. Excited about her discovery, an article was written for a medical journal.

 **Correcting Dangling Modifiers**

To correct dangling modifiers, do the following:

• Identify the modifier.

> To teach yoga, a flexible body is needed.

• Identify the word or words that are being modified.

> Who needs a flexible body? **The yoga instructor**

• Add the missing subject and, in some cases, also add or remove words so that the sentence makes sense.

> To teach yoga, **the instructor** needs a flexible body.

CHAPTER 31

PRACTICE 4

In each sentence, underline the dangling modifier. Then rewrite each sentence, adding or removing words to provide a logical meaning.

EXAMPLE:

> Worried about their health, laughter yoga is practiced.
>
> *Worried about their health, people practice laughter yoga.*

1. When exercising, getting bored is common.

    _____

    _____

2. Gathering in a park in Mumbai, India, laughter yoga was practiced.

    _____

    _____

3. Muscles are gently stretched while chanting "Haha hoho" in unison.

_____

_____

4. To take a laughter yoga class, 20 dollars is needed.

_____

_____

5. Doing laughter yoga, stress is reduced.

_____

_____

6. When experimenting with laughter yoga, the advice of a professional is helpful.

_____

_____

PRACTICE 5

Some sentences in this practice have dangling or misplaced modifiers. Write *M* next to misplaced modifiers, *D* next to dangling modifiers, and *C* next to correct sentences. If the modifier is misplaced, move it. If the modifier is dangling, add words to make the sentence complete.

EXAMPLE:

people try different therapies.

Hoping to live a long life, ~~different therapies are tried.~~   *D*

1. Called Ayurveda therapy, ancient Indians developed a school

   of medicine.   _____

2. Originally written on palm leaves, researchers found

   2,000-year-old texts.   _____

3. Possibly causing diseases, Ayurvedic medicine teaches about

   an imbalance in mental and physical energies.   _____

4. Ayurvedic medicine is widely followed by people in India.   _____

5. Doing meditation and yoga, essential parts of this alternative

   therapy are learned.   _____

6. Called homeopathy, India has produced a therapy that uses

   plants, animals, and minerals to cure a patient's illness.   _____

CHAPTER 31

7. Later, a German doctor organized the rules of homeopathic

   treatment wearing glasses.   _____

8. In the 1800s, homeopathy became popular in the United States.   _____

9. Feeling skeptical, the merits of homeopathy are questioned.   _____

10. In fact, many conventionally trained doctors do not believe

    in alternative medical therapies.   _____

REFLECT ON IT

Think about what you have learned in this unit. If you do not know an answer, review that concept.

1. What is a misplaced modifier? _____

   _____

2. What is a dangling modifier? _____

   _____

3. What type of modifier error is in each sentence? Write *M* for "misplaced" and *D* for "dangling." Then correct the sentence.

   a. Overeating, a weight problem was developed.

   _____

   b. The doctor examined the X-ray in the lab coat.

   _____

FINAL REVIEW

Underline ten dangling or misplaced modifier errors in the next selection. Then, correct each error. You may need to add or remove words to ensure that the sentence makes sense.

EXAMPLE:

the chiropractor had a surprising result.
Manipulating her neck, ~~a surprising result occurred.~~

1.   There are many fraudulent claims in alternative medicine. In fact,

   feeling desperate, fortunes are spent on suspect therapies. It is difficult for

   members of the public to determine which therapies are valid and which

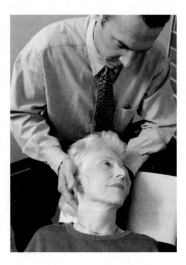

are pure quackery. At an important medical conference, some doctors discussed chiropractic neck treatments eating lunch together.

2.   Based on spinal adjustments, Dr. Daniel Palmer developed a new healing technique. Born in Canada, Palmer did his first treatment in 1895. A janitor complained that he had lost his hearing after straining his back. Manipulating the janitor's neck, the man's hearing was restored. Using the therapy all over America, neck manipulations are actively promoted.

3.   In 2006, a young mother went to see a chiropractor with severe headaches. Misdiagnosing the patient's illness, a mistake was made. Pierrette Parisien died following her neck treatment. The coroner recommended a review of the chiropractic procedures speaking to the media.

4.   Many medical doctors have questioned the safety of neck manipulations. Chiropractors refute the criticism feeling angry. According to Dr. Rick Morris, chiropractors pay low malpractice insurance rates because injuries are so rare. Having confidence in chiropractors, neck manipulations continue to be popular.

CHAPTER 31

The Writer's Room

Write about one of the following topics. Include some modifiers and make sure that your sentences are formed correctly.

1. Have you ever been to an acupuncturist, a massage therapist, a naturopath, a homeopath, or any other alternative healing practitioner? Describe the treatment that you received.

2. Give your opinion about alternative therapies.

The Writers' Circle   Collaborative Activity

Work with a group of students and create an advertisement for an alternative medical treatment. You can even invent a new medical treatment. For example, you can make an advertisement to cure warts, reduce acne, or help back pain.

In your ad, include some adjectives and adverbs. In some of your sentences, include phrases that begin with *who*, *that*, and *which*. When you finish, exchange advertisements with another team. Check that the other team's advertisement contains correct adjectives, adverbs, and modifiers.

mywritinglab   To check your progress in meeting this chapter's objectives, log in to **www.mywritinglab.com**, go to the **Study Plan** tab, click on **The Editing Handbook—Section 6: Modifiers** and choose **Modifiers and Misplaced and Dangling Modifiers** from the list of subtopics. Read and view the resources in the **Review Materials** section, and then complete the **Recall, Apply,** and **Write** sets in the **Activities** section.

READING LINK

Health Care
"Control Your Temper" by Elizabeth Passarella (page 546)
"Don't Worry, Act Happy" by Albert Nerenberg (page 548)
"Musicophilia" by Oliver Sachs (page 551)

CHAPTER 31

Exact Language

Section Theme **THE LEGAL WORLD**

In this chapter, you will read about topics related to property crimes.

The Writer's Journal

Write a paragraph that summarizes the events of a well-known crime. Describe what happened.

Use Specific and Detailed Vocabulary

Great writing evokes an emotional response from the reader. Great writers not only use correct grammatical structures, but they also infuse their writing with precise and vivid details that make their work come alive.

When you proofread your work, revise words that are too vague. **Vague words** lack precision and detail. For example, the words *nice* and *bad* are vague. Readers cannot get a clear picture from them.

Compare the following sets of sentences.

Vague: The movie was bad.

Precise: The predictable film included violent, gory scenes.

Vague: In France, thieves stole some paintings.

Precise: In southern France, armed, masked thieves staged a brazen daylight robbery of paintings by Claude Monet.

Creating Vivid Language

When you choose the precise word, you convey your meaning exactly. Moreover, you can make your writing clearer and more impressive by using specific and detailed vocabulary. To create vivid language, try the following strategies.

- **Modify your nouns.** If your noun is vague, make it more specific by adding one or more adjectives. You could also replace the noun with a more specific term.

    Vague: the man

    Vivid: the shopkeeper   the thin, nervous soldier

- **Modify your verbs.** Use more vivid and precise verbs. You could also add adverbs.

    Vague: walk

    Vivid: saunter   stroll   march briskly

- **Include more details.** Add detailed information to make the sentence more complete.

    Vague: Several signs foretold Caesar's death.

    Precise: Several ominous signs, such as Caesar's horses getting loose and a soothsayer's warning, foretold Caesar's impending murder.

WRITING LINK

You can find more information about appealing to the five senses in Chapter 6, "Description."

> **Hint**   **Use Imagery**
>
> You can make your writing come alive by using **imagery,** which is description using the five senses: sight, sound, smell, touch, and taste. In the examples, the underlined words add details to the sentence and contribute to a more exact description.
>
> Wearing a blond wig, the armed robber smashed the glass display case and pocketed the luxury watches.

PRACTICE I

Replace the familiar words in parentheses with more vivid words or phrases, and add more specific details. Use your dictionary or thesaurus if you need help.

EXAMPLE:

Graffiti artists (write) ___*scrawl words and pictures*___ on walls.

1. Many cities spend a lot of money (cleaning graffiti) _____

   _____

2. (Youths) _____ spray paint on many (places)

   _____

3. They worry about getting caught by (someone) _____

   _____

4. Some cities permit graffiti artists to paint on (certain locations) _____

   _____

5. Sometimes graffiti artists write (bad words) _____

   _____

6. Governments could combat the problem (with many solutions) _____

   _____

7. Some people think graffiti artists should be (treated harshly) _____

   _____

PRACTICE 2

Underline all the words in the paragraph that add vivid details to the description.

EXAMPLE:

The <u>tappity-tap-tap</u> and the <u>thin bell</u> and <u>muffled whir</u> of Effie Perine's typewriting came through the <u>closed</u> door.

Somewhere in a neighboring office a power-driven machine vibrated dully. On Spade's desk a limp cigarette smoldered in a brass tray filled with the remains of limp cigarettes. Ragged gray flakes of cigarette-ash dotted the yellow top of the desk and the green blotter and the papers that were there. A buff-curtained window, eight or ten inches open, let in from the court a current of air faintly scented with ammonia. The ashes on the desk twitched and crawled in the current.

—Dashiell Hammett, *The Maltese Falcon*

Hint   Adding Appositives

An appositive is a word or phrase that gives further information about a noun or pronoun. You can write sentences that are more exact and detailed by adding appositives.

appositive   appositive

Sherlock Holmes, <u>the famous detective</u>, was helped by his friend, <u>Dr. Watson</u>.

Avoid Wordiness and Redundancy

Sometimes students fill their writing assignments with extra words to meet length requirements. However, good ideas can easily get lost in work that is too wordy. Also, if the explanations are unnecessarily long, then writing becomes boring.

To improve your writing style, use only as many words or phrases as you need to fully explain your ideas.

The police department was a <u>distance of two blocks</u> from the municipal library.

(A block is a measure of a distance, so it is unnecessary to repeat that information.)

Correcting Wordiness

You can cut the number of words needed to express an idea by substituting a wordy phrase with a single word. You could also remove the wordy phrase completely.

Because ~~of the fact that~~ the security guard was alone, the thieves easily overwhelmed him.

Some Common Wordy Expressions and Substitutions

Wordy	Better	Wordy	Better
at that point in time	then, at that time	great, few in number	great, few
big, small in size	big, small	in order to	to
in close proximity	close *or* in proximity	in spite of the fact	although, even though
a difficult dilemma	a dilemma	in the final analysis	finally, lastly
due to the fact	because	past history	past *or* history
equally as good as	as good as	period of time	period
exactly the same	the same	personal opinion	opinion
exceptions to the rule	exceptions	reason why is that	because
final completion	end	return again	return
for the purpose of	for	still remain	remain
gave the appearance of	looked like	a true fact	a fact

PRACTICE 3

In the next sentences, cross out all unnecessary words or phrases, or modify any repeated words.

EXAMPLE:

Many

~~A great number of~~ thefts occurred in Beverly Hills, California.

1. In August 2007, five men entered an art museum on the French Riviera for the purpose of stealing paintings.

2. In spite of the fact that there were security guards, the masked thieves managed to take four masterpieces.

3. At that period of time, the thieves stuffed the paintings in bags.

4. In order to escape, the robbers used a motorcycle and a car.

5. The whole entire robbery lasted for ten minutes.

6. The thieves cannot sell their treasures on the open market due to the fact that the Monet and Bruegel paintings are well known.

7. It is a true fact that many paintings are stolen for wealthy private collectors.

8. The paintings still remain missing, and the thieves have not been caught.

9. The FBI estimates that, on a yearly basis, the market for stolen art is $6 billion annually.

Avoid Clichés

Clichés are overused expressions. Because they are overused, they lose their power and become boring. You should avoid using clichés in your writing.

cliché
The defense attorney was <u>fit to be tied</u> when his client confessed.

direct words
extremely upset

CHAPTER 32

Some Common Clichés

a drop in the bucket	break the ice	jump in with both feet
as light as a feather	butter someone up	keep your eyes peeled
as luck would have it	cost an arm and a leg	top dog
axe to grind	drop the ball	under the weather
between a rock and a hard place	easier said than done	work like a dog

Correcting Clichés

When you modify a cliché, you can change it into a direct term. You might also try playing with language to come up with a more interesting description.

Cliché:	She was as busy as a bee.
Direct language:	She was extremely busy.
Interesting description:	She was as busy as an emergency room nurse.

PRACTICE 4

Underline twelve clichéd expressions, and then replace them with fresh or direct language.

EXAMPLE:

Jack Garcia had to ~~keep his eyes peeled~~. *stay alert*

1. Cuban-born Jack Garcia is recognized as the best undercover agent in the FBI's history. During his career, he was a mover and shaker in more than a hundred different operations. For instance, some of Florida's largest drug smugglers are now in the big house thanks to Garcia. The agent's work also led to the arrest of some corrupt Florida police officers. Playing the role of "Big Frankie" or "Big Tony," Garcia would bribe officers. The officers were bent out of shape when they were arrested.

2. Garcia was able to infiltrate New York's Gambino crime family by pretending to be "Jack Falcone." To prepare for his role, Garcia had to jump into Sicilian culture with both feet. For example, he learned about Italian food. He knew he was playing with fire whenever he sat with the crime boss Greg DePalma, and he had to be convincing. If he dropped the ball, he could find himself six feet under.

3. Garcia played DePalma like a fiddle. He constantly buttered up the boss. Also, Garcia provided DePalma with the finer things in life such as jewelry, iPods, and televisions. The FBI agent was so convincing in his role as "Big Jack" that the crime boss offered to promote Garcia in the crime family.

4. Jack Garcia's job was no piece of cake. One day, when Mafia members became suspicious of Garcia, the FBI pulled the plug on the operation. Today, thirty-one members of the Gambino crime family are in jail, and Garcia has retired from the FBI.

Standard English Versus Slang

Most of your instructors will want you to write using **standard American English.** The word *standard* does not imply "better." Standard American English is the common language generally used and expected in schools, businesses, and government institutions in the United States.

Slang is nonstandard language. It is used in informal situations to communicate common cultural knowledge. In any academic or professional context, do not use slang.

Slang:	My friends and I <u>hang</u> together. Last weekend, we watched a movie that was <u>kinda weird but also pretty sweet</u>. It was called *The Untouchables*, and it was about the Mafia during Prohibition.
Standard American English:	My friends and I <u>spend a lot of time</u> together. Last weekend, we watched a movie that was <u>unusual but fascinating</u>. It was called *The Untouchables*, and it was about the Mafia during Prohibition.

 **Hint** **Do Not Use Slang in Academic Writing**

Slang is very informal and should be avoided in academic writing. Keep in mind that slang changes depending on generational, regional, cultural, and historical influences. For example, rather than saying "I have to *leave*," people in one group might say *scram* or *split* while those in another group might say *bail* or *bounce*. Avoid using slang expressions in your writing because they can change very quickly—so quickly, in fact, that you might remark that this textbook's examples of slang are "lame."

PRACTICE 5

Substitute the underlined slang expressions with the best possible choice in standard American English.

EXAMPLE:

Every day, <u>the cops</u> deal with gangs.   *police officers*

1. Gang members can be <u>guys or chicks</u>.   _____

2. Some young people think that gangs are <u>cool</u>.   _____

3. It takes a lot of <u>guts</u> to refuse to join a gang.   _____

4. Someone may join a gang because he or she

   does not want to look <u>like a wimp</u>.   _____

5. Others join gangs because they want to

   earn <u>megabucks</u>.   _____

6. Sometimes people <u>hang</u> with gangs because

   they feel more protected.   _____

7. It is <u>dicey</u> to be in a gang.   _____

8. Police try to <u>keep their cool</u> when they

   deal with gangs.   _____

9. Gang members are often on the lookout

   for <u>narcs</u>.   _____

10. Many gang members end up in <u>the joint</u>.   _____

REFLECT ON IT

Think about what you have learned in this unit. If you do not know an answer, review that concept.

1. What is vivid language? _____

   _____

2. Edit the following sentences for wordiness, clichés, and overused expressions. Modify them to make them more concise.

   a. The suspect lived in close proximity to the bank that he had robbed.

   b. Peter will be in for a rude awakening if he does not study for his law-enforcement exams.

   c. Peter is feeling under the weather today.

3. Edit the following sentences for slang. Replace the slang words with standard American English.

   a. Replacing the contents of a stolen wallet is such a drag.

   b. I read a cool biography about Al Capone.

CHAPTER 32

FINAL REVIEW

Edit the following paragraphs for slang, clichés, and vague language.

Part A

In the next paragraph, four vague words are underlined. Replace these words with specific details to make the paragraph more interesting. Also correct four wordy expressions.

EXAMPLE:

    flamboyant criminal
The <u>man</u> convinced wealthy victims to part with their money.

1.   Christopher Rocancourt is a con artist. Small in size, Rocancourt was the son of an alcoholic house painter and a teenage prostitute. He lived in an orphanage, and then he was adopted at age twelve. Perhaps, as a result of the fact that he grew up in poverty, Rocancourt decided to reinvent himself. In order to fool others, he pretended to be a venture capitalist, the son of a movie director, and a boxing champion. For more than fifteen years, he has managed to steal money from rich <u>people</u> in Hollywood and elsewhere. He says that he simply wanted to have a <u>better</u> life. Rocancourt claims his life has been <u>interesting</u>. At this point in time, <u>he</u> is in prison.

Part B
Replace twelve slang or clichéd expressions.

EXAMPLE:

a skilled manipulator
Christopher Rocancourt is <u>a strange dude.</u>

2.   While in Hollywood, Rocancourt stayed in the Beverly Wilshire Hotel. He managed to pull the wool over many people's eyes. Some actors knew him as Christopher De Laurentiis, the nephew of filmmaker Dino De Laurentiis. To others, he was Christopher de la Renta, nephew of fashion designer Oscar de la Renta. He claimed to be tight with Robert De Niro, Jean-Claude Van Damme, and the Sultan of Brunei. Posing as an investor, he persuaded his wealthy friends to give him tons of dough. Promising to triple or quadruple their money, he easily messed with people's heads. Rocancourt earned millions with his cons. When his wealthy friends learned the truth about him, they were blown away. Today, a lot of his former friends have an axe to grind with Christopher Rocancourt.

3.   Nowadays, the con artist is surprisingly unrepentant. While rapping with a journalist from CBS News, Rocancourt said that he is not a thief. He claims that he simply borrows from friends and then doesn't repay

them. Certainly, he is a slick piece of work who preys on gullible people. Most of his victims wanted to turn a quick buck, and he was happy to let them believe that they could benefit from his financial expertise. Nowadays, those victims are understandably bummed. It will be a cold day in hell before any of the wealthy friends recoup their money. Rocancourt's sweet gig, which included driving Hummers, dating wealthy women, and befriending millionaires, seems to be over.

The Writer's Room

Write about one of the following topics. Make sure that you use exact and concise language.

1. List some steps that parents can take to prevent their children from joining gangs or breaking laws.
2. What are some different categories of crimes? Classify crimes into three different types.

mywritinglab To check your progress in meeting this chapter's objectives, log in to **www.mywritinglab.com**, go to the **Study Plan** tab, click on **The Editing Handbook—Section 7: Word Use and Spelling** and choose **Standard and Non-Standard English** from the list of subtopics. Read and view the resources in the **Review Materials** section, and then complete the **Recall, Apply,** and **Write** sets in the **Activities** section.

CHAPTER 32

CHAPTER 33 Spelling and Commonly Confused Words

Section Theme **THE LEGAL WORLD**

In this chapter, you will read about topics related to crimes and criminals.

The Writer's Journal

What are some reasons that people commit crimes?

Spelling Rules

It is important to spell correctly. Spelling mistakes can detract from good ideas in your work. You can become a better speller if you always proofread your written work and if you check a dictionary for the meaning and spelling of words about which you are unsure. Here are some spelling rules that will help you improve your spelling.

 **Using a Dictionary**

If you are unsure about the spelling or meaning of a word, consult a dictionary. Try to use a recent edition. Also, get to know the features of your dictionary.

Writing *ie* or *ei*

Remember the following rule so that you know when to use *ie* or *ei*. Write *i* before *e*, except after *c* or when *ei* is pronounced *ay*, as in *neighbor* and *weigh*.

i before e:	niece	field	grief	
ei after c:	ceiling	conceive	perceive	
ei pronounced *ay*:	beige	vein	weigh	
Exceptions:	efficient	either	foreigner	height
	leisure	neither	science	seize
	society	species	their	weird

PRACTICE I

Circle the correct spelling of each word.

EXAMPLE:

recieve/receive

1. decieve/deceive
2. foreigner/foriegner
3. friend/freind
4. hieght/height
5. vien/vein

6. science/sceince
7. efficient/efficeint
8. theif/thief
9. deciet/deceit
10. chief/cheif

READING LINK

For more information about using a dictionary, see pages 526–527 in Part V, "Reading Strategies and Selections" (Chapter 38).

Adding Prefixes and Suffixes

A **prefix** is added to the beginning of a word, and it changes the word's meaning. For example, *con-*, *dis-*, *pre-*, *un-*, and *il-* are prefixes. A **suffix** is added to the ending of a word, and it changes the word's tense or meaning. For example, *-ly*, *-ment*, *-ed*, and *-ing* are suffixes.

When you add a prefix to a word, keep the last letter of the prefix and the first letter of the main word.

un + natural = unnatural   dis + satisfaction = dissatisfaction

When you add the suffix *-ly* to words that end in *l*, keep the *l* of the root word. The new word will have two *l*'s.

personal + ly = personally   actual + ly = actually

CHAPTER 33

> ⟨*Hint*⟩ **Words Ending in *-ful***
>
> Although the word *full* ends in two *l*'s, when *-ful* is added to another word as a suffix, it ends in one *l*.
>
> care<u>ful</u>   success<u>ful</u>   hope<u>ful</u>
>
> Notice, however, the unusual spelling when *full* and *fill* are combined: fulfill.

PRACTICE 2

Read the following words and decide if they are correctly spelled. If the word is correct, write *C* in the space provided. If the word is incorrect, write the correct word in the space.

EXAMPLES:

factualy _____*factually*_____   untrue _____*C*_____

1. ilogical _____   6. beautifull _____

2. continually _____   7. iresponsible_____

3. imoral _____   8. unusual _____

4. unecessary _____   9. carefuly _____

5. mispell _____   10. fulfilled _____

Adding *-s* or *-es*

Add *-s* to nouns and to present tense verbs that are third-person singular. However, add *-es* to words in the following situations.

- When words end in *s*, *sh*, *ss*, *ch*, or *x*, add *-es*.

  Noun: church–church**es**   **Verb:** fix–fix**es**

- When words end with the consonant *y*, change the *y* to *i* and add *-es*.

  Noun: berry–berr**ies**   **Verb:** marry–marr**ies**

- When words end in *o*, add *-es* in most cases.

  Noun: hero–hero**es**   **Verb:** do–do**es**

  Exceptions: piano–piano**s**; radio–radio**s**; logo–logo**s**; patio–patio**s**.

- When words end in *f* or *fe*, change the *f* to *v* and add *-es*.

  leaf–lea**ves**   knife–kni**ves**

  Exceptions: belief–belief**s**; roof–roof**s**.

PRACTICE 3

Add *-s* or *-es* to each word and adjust the spelling if necessary. Write the new word in the space provided.

EXAMPLE:

reach   *reaches*

1. hero   _____
2. crutch   _____
3. fix   _____
4. echo   _____
5. carry   _____
6. tomato   _____

7. potato   _____
8. miss   _____
9. fly   _____
10. teach   _____
11. scarf   _____
12. candy   _____

Adding Suffixes to Words Ending in -e

When you add a suffix to a word ending in *e*, make sure that you follow the next rules.

- If the suffix begins with a vowel, drop the *e* on the main word. Some common suffixes beginning with vowels are *-ed*, *-er*, *-est*, *-ing*, *-able*, *-ent*, and *-ist*.

    hope–hop**ing**   encourage–encourag**ing**

    Exceptions: For some words that end in *ge*, keep the *e* and add the suffix.

    courage–courage**ous**   change–change**able**

- If the suffix begins with a consonant, keep the *e*. Some common suffixes beginning with consonants are *-ly*, *-ment*, *-less*, and *-ful*.

    sure–sure**ly**   like–like**ness**

    Exceptions: Some words lose their final *e* when a suffix is added.

    acknowledge–acknowledgment   true–truly
    argue–argument   judgement–judgment

PRACTICE 4

Rewrite each word with the suggested ending.

EXAMPLE:

use + ed   *used*

1. achieve + ment _____
2. strange + est   _____
3. argue + ment   _____
4. love + ing   _____
5. true + ly   _____

6. endorse + ment _____
7. argue + ing   _____
8. nine + ty   _____
9. write + ing   _____
10. change + able _____

Adding Suffixes to Words Ending in -y

When you add a suffix to a word ending in *y*, make sure that you follow the next rules.

- If the word has a consonant before the final *y*, change the *y* to an *i* before adding the suffix.

  beauty–beaut**i**ful   supply–suppl**i**ed

- If the word has a vowel before the final *y*, if the word is a proper name, or if the suffix is *-ing*, do not change the *y* to an *i*.

  day–days   try–trying   the Vronsky family–the Vronskys

Exceptions: Some words do not follow the previous rule.

  day–daily   lay–laid   say–said   pay–paid

PRACTICE 5

Rewrite each word with the suggested ending.

EXAMPLE:

try + ed _____*tried*_____

1. happy + est   _____
2. play + er   _____
3. pretty + er   _____
4. Connolly + s   _____
5. lonely + ness   _____
6. lazy + er   _____
7. envy + able   _____
8. angry + ly   _____
9. day + ly   _____
10. say + ing   _____
11. dirty + est   _____
12. stay + ed   _____

Doubling the Final Consonant

Sometimes when you add a suffix to a word, you must double the final consonant. Remember the next tips.

One-Syllable Words

- Double the final consonant of one-syllable words ending in a consonant–vowel–consonant pattern.

  bat–ba**tt**er   plan–pla**nn**ed   prod–pro**dd**ed

- Do not double the final consonant if the word ends in a vowel and two consonants or if it ends with two vowels and a consonant.

  cool–coolest   park–parking   clean–cleaner

Words of Two or More Syllables

- Double the final consonant of words ending in a stressed consonant–vowel–consonant pattern.

      prefer–preferred   occur–occurred

- If the word ends in a syllable that is not stressed, then do not double the last letter of the word.

      happen–happened   visit–visiting

PRACTICE 6

Rewrite each word with the suggested ending.

EXAMPLES:

	Add -ed			**Add -ing**
stop	*stopped*		try	*trying*

1. slip _____   6. smile _____

2. load _____   7. stay _____

3. mention _____   8. enter _____

4. plan _____   9. begin _____

5. open _____   10. refer _____

PRACTICE 7

Correct twelve spelling mistakes in the next selection.

EXAMPLE:

                    angrily
The parents reacted ~~angryly~~ when they were convicted.

1.   In the United States, every state except New Hampshire has a parental

   responsibility statute. Such laws make parents legaly responsible for their

   children's criminal acts. The first parents who were ever tryed and

   convicted under such laws were from St. Claire Shores, Michigan. In 1995,

   a sixteen-year-old boy commited a series of crimes after he was released

   from juvenile detention. The state questionned why the parents could not

   control their son. The prosecutor was successfull in convicting the parents,

   and the case brought national attention to the issue. Since then, many

CHAPTER 33

parents have been convicted. For example, in one case, a couple's son set the nieghbor's house on fire. The parents had to pay $60,000 to the victim.

2.   Those who are against such laws argue that holding parents responsible definitly does nothing to stop juvenile delinquents from committing crimes. At a certain age, peer groups become more influential than parents. It is unecessary and unfair to force parents to pay for damages. Such laws are ilogical and simply attempt to fix a problem after the fact instead of helping the parents deal with the child before any serious crimes occur.

3.   Some people, argueing for the laws, say parents must be encouraged to take a more active role in their children's lifes. If parents know that they may be charged for their child's actions, they are likly to intervene and try to get their child some help before serious crimes can occur.

Spelling Two-Part Words

Some one-word indefinite pronouns sound as if they should be two separate words, but they are not. Here are some examples of one-word indefinite pronouns.

Words with *any:*	anything, anyone, anybody, anywhere
Words with *some:*	something, someone, somebody, somewhere
Words with *every:*	everything, everyone, everybody, everywhere

> **Hint**   Spelling *another* and *a lot*
>
> **Another is always one word:**   Bonnie committed <u>another</u> crime.
>
> **A lot is always two words:**   She robbed <u>a lot</u> of banks.

PRACTICE 8

Correct ten spelling errors in the next paragraph.

EXAMPLE:

>   *Another*
> ~~An other~~ scandal occurred last year.

Alot of professional athletes have committed criminal acts. Some times the crimes are not serious. For example, Florida State football player Peter Warrick was charged with theft in a designer clothing scheme. Pete Rose is an other athlete who let greed draw him into imoral activities when he bet against his own team. However, some athletes have assaulted, raped, or killed. Ice skater Tonya Harding and her husband hired some body to hit her skating rival in the knee. Boxer Mike Tyson was accused and eventualy convicted of rape, and several professional football players have been charged with murder. Many fans refuse to accept that their heroes have done any thing wrong. Basketball fan Trevor Nixon says, "Any body can make accusations. Unfair attacks on successfull athletes can cause their families much greif." Perhaps the public should accept that athletes are not always heroic.

120 Commonly Misspelled Words

The next list contains some of the most commonly misspelled words in English.

absence	clientele	finally	ninety
absorption	committee	foreign	noticeable
accommodate	comparison	government	occasion
acquaintance	competent	harassment	occurrence
address	conscience	height	opposite
aggressive	conscientious	immediately	outrageous
already	convenient	independent	parallel
aluminum	curriculum	jewelry	performance
analyze	definite	judgment	perseverance
appointment	definitely	laboratory	personality
approximate	desperate	lawyer	physically
argument	developed	ledge	possess
athlete	dilemma	leisure	precious
bargain	disappoint	license	prejudice
beginning	embarrass	loneliness	privilege
behavior	encouragement	maintenance	probably
believable	environment	mathematics	professor
business	especially	medicine	psychology
calendar	exaggerate	millennium	questionnaire
campaign	exercise	minuscule	receive
careful	extraordinarily	mischievous	recommend
ceiling	familiar	mortgage	reference
cemetery	February	necessary	responsible

rhythm	success	truly	woman
schedule	surprise	Tuesday	women
scientific	technique	until	wreckage
separate	thorough	usually	writer
sincerely	tomato	vacuum	writing
spaghetti	tomatoes	Wednesday	written
strength	tomorrow	weird	zealous

> ## Hint — Spelling Strategies
>
> Here are some useful strategies to improve your spelling.
>
> • Keep a record of words that you commonly misspell in your spelling log, which could be in a journal or binder. Have a friend read from your list of misspelled words to give you a spelling quiz. See Appendix 7 for more information about spelling logs.
>
> • Use memory cards or flash cards to help you memorize the spelling of difficult words.
>
> • Write down the spelling of difficult words at least ten times to help you remember how to spell them.

PRACTICE 9

Circle the correctly spelled word in each pair.

EXAMPLE:

 foreigner/foriegner

1. noticable/noticeable
2. echos/echoes
3. writting/writing
4. accommodate/accomodate
5. definitely/definitly
6. running/runing
7. appealled/appealed
8. comittee/committee
9. recommend/recommand

10. absence/absense
11. niece/neice
12. personallity/personality
13. exaggerate/exagerate
14. butterflys/butterflies
15. responsible/responsable
16. efficeint/efficient
17. independent/independant
18. appointment/apointment

PRACTICE 10

Correct twenty spelling mistakes in the next selection.

EXAMPLE:

                      definitely
Forensic television shows ~~definitly~~ influence jurors.

1.   Last Febuary, Ladonna Reed called the police to report a robbery at her

house. The crime scene investigator was very carefull as he dusted for

prints, but Ladonna remained unimpressed with his performance. She was familar with the television show *CSI*, but the investigator did not use tecniques from the show.

2.   Jurors sometimes have unrealistic expectations about forensic science. Police, lawyers, and judges call this phenomenon the "CSI Syndrome." In the *CSI* television shows, investigators use tests that give instant results. While police departments rely on similar tests, it takes time to analyze evidence in a labortory. In addition, jurors who watch shows like *CSI* may think they have a high level of expertise and may prejudice other members of the jury.

3.   The CSI Syndrome has created an unexpected dillemma for police departments and the courts. For example, in June 2005, all three hundred prosecutors from Maricopa County in Arizona filled out a questionaire. Around 38 percent of the prosecutors sincerly believed that they had at least one embarrasing acquittal because of lack of forensic evidence. In such cases, the prosecutors thought that sceintific evidence was unecessary for a conviction. In one case, police officers found a bag with ilegal drugs and a handwriten note. The accused admitted that the drugs were his. However, the jury found him innocent because prosecutors had no DNA or fingerprints from the bag.

4.   Lawyers and judges acknowlege the CSI effect in trials. Lawyers often change opening and closing arguements to prevent juror bias. Judges sometimes recomend to jurors not to rely on television shows as a yardstick for their jugment of the evidence.

> **Hint** **Using a Spelling Checker**
>
> The spelling checker tool on a computer will highlight most misspelled words and provide suggested corrections. However, be aware that a spelling checker's abilities are limited; it cannot verify that you have used commonly confused words accurately. For example, it cannot determine whether you should use *your* or *you're*.
> Because a spelling checker is not 100 percent reliable, remember to proofread for spelling errors before you submit your final work.

Look-Alike and Sound-Alike Words

Sometimes two English words can sound very much alike but have different spellings and different meanings. For example, two commonly confused words are *defiantly*, which means "to resist or challenge something," and *definitely*, which means "finally" or "decisively." Dictionaries will give you the exact meaning of unfamiliar words. Read the next list to get familiar with many commonly confused words.

Word	Meaning	Example
accept	to receive; to admit	The police sergeant accepted an award for outstanding work.
except	excluding; other than	None of his colleagues, except his wife, knew about the award.
affect	to influence	Writer's block affects a person's ability to write.
effect	the result of something	Writer's block can have bad effects on a person's ability to write.
been	past participle of the verb *to be*	Patrick Fitzgerald has been a prosecutor for many years.
being	present progressive form (the *-ing* form) of the verb *to be*	He was being very nice when he signed autographs.
by	preposition meaning *next to*, *on*, or *before*	The defendant sat by her lawyer. By 10:00 a.m., the jury was getting restless. Everyone hoped the case would be over by the weekend.
buy	to purchase	The lawyer will buy a new car with her fees from this case.
complement	to add to; to complete	The car will be a nice complement to her other possessions.
compliment	to say something nice about someone	Chicago's mayor complimented the detectives.
conscience	a personal sense of right and wrong	The robber had no conscience.
conscious	being aware or awake	The robber was conscious of his terrible crime.

Word	Meaning	Example
disinterested	to be impartial	The trial judge was disinterested, favoring neither side.
uninterested	to lack interest in something	The robber looked uninterested when told of his sentence.
elicit	to get or draw out	The police tried to elicit a confession from the gang member.
illicit	illegal; unlawful	The police found evidence of the gang's illicit activities.
everyday	ordinary; common	Crime is an everyday occurrence.
every day	during a single day; each day	The police watch the gang members every day.
imply	to suggest	The reporter implied that the police need more time to investigate.
infer	to conclude	The police inferred from the clues the gang's whereabouts.
imminent	soon to happen	The police stated that an arrest was imminent.
eminent	distinguished; superior	Patrick Fitzgerald is an eminent prosecutor.
its	possessive case of the pronoun *it*	The judge's desk is large, and its legs are ornate.
it's	contraction for *it is*	It's generally known that he is very good at solving crimes.
knew	past tense of *know*	Fitzgerald knew that the newspaper executive was guilty.
new	recent; unused	He had new evidence to present to the court.
know	to have knowledge of	Many people know about Fitzgerald's work.
no	a negative	The police made no arrests.
lose	to misplace or forfeit something	The police did not want to lose track of the stolen money.
loose	too big or baggy; not fixed	Detectives sometimes wear loose clothing as part of their disguises.
loss	a decrease in an amount; a serious blow	The company experienced a serious loss when the money was stolen.
peace	calm sensation; a lack of violence	The two rival gangs finally made peace. They felt a sense of peace when hostilities stopped.
piece	a part of something else; one item in a group of items	The thieves ate a piece of cake to celebrate the successful heist.
personal	private	The criminal has a lot of personal problems.
personnel	employees; staff	The police must hire new personnel.
principal	primary (adj.); director of a school (n.)	The principal detective talked to the principal of our school.
principle	a rule or standard	The police try to follow the principle of law.

(continued)

Word	Meaning	Example
quiet	silent	The thieves remained quiet when arrested.
quite	very	The public is becoming quite angry at the increase in crime.
quit	to stop doing something	The detective sometimes wants to quit the force.
taught	past tense of *teach*	Drake taught a class on criminology.
thought	past tense of *think*	He thought his students were intelligent.
than	word used in comparisons	Fitzgerald is more determined than other prosecutors.
then	at a particular time; after a specific time	Cornwell investigated the case, and then she wrote about it.
that	word used to introduce a clause	She wrote that Walter Sickert was the Ripper.
their	possessive form of *they*	The police officers went to their favorite restaurant.
there	a place	They went there by police van.
they're	contraction of *they are*	They're both interesting people.
through	in one side and out the other; finished	The police cruiser passed through a tunnel. Then they were through for the day.
threw	past tense of *throw*	Somebody threw a rock at the officer's car.
thorough	complete	They did a thorough investigation of the crime scene.
to	indicates direction or movement; part of an infinitive	I want to go to the film.
too	also; very	The robber was too young to be given a prison sentence. Her friend was, too.
two	the number after one	There were two witnesses to the holdup.
where	question word indicating location	The police knew where the diamonds were hidden.
were	past tense of *be*	The diamonds were in a safe place.
we're	contraction of *we are*	We're going to meet the detectives.
write	to draw symbols that represent words	Patricia Cornwell will write about the crime.
right	correct; the opposite of the direction left	The police arrested the right criminal. They found the diamonds in her right pocket.
who's	contraction of *who is*	The police sergeant, who's very well known, spoke to reporters.
whose	pronoun showing ownership	Criminals, whose crimes hurt society, must be punished.

CHAPTER 33

PRACTICE 11

Underline the correct words.

EXAMPLE:

The Stock and Securities (personal / <u>personnel</u>) were shocked to hear about the Ponzi scheme.

1. In December 2008, many wealthy Americans suffered a serious financial (lose / loss).

2. They had (been / being) investing for many years with a well-known financier, Bernard Madoff.

3. Madoff was considered to be an (eminent / imminent) investor.

4. However, he was investing his clients' money in an (elicit / illicit) racket called a Ponzi scheme.

5. Madoff, (who's / whose) reputation is ruined, had used money from later investors to pay off earlier investors, creating an illusion of profit.

6. Madoff's investment scheme crumpled when his clients pulled money out of investment portfolios in an effort (to / too) reduce financial risk.

7. The clients did not (no / know) that he had cheated them out of (their / there) money until they heard the news in the media.

8. Madoff's Ponzi scheme created (quit / quite) a stir when authorities claimed it was the largest fraud in the history of Wall Street.

PRACTICE 12

Correct fifteen errors in the following passages. Look for the commonly confused words that are indicated in parentheses.

EXAMPLE:

>   *too*
> He is ~~to~~ busy these days.

1. (affect, effect; then, that, than)

  In 1995, audiences were fascinated by a celebrity trial than caused a great stir. O.J. Simpson was accused of killing his wife and her friend. Simpson was found not guilty, but the accusation effected his reputation. In 2008, Simpson was involved in another crime. He was first accused of armed robbery, and than he was charged with kidnapping. Simpson claimed than he was trying to get back some stolen sports memorabilia. He was found guilty of the crime. The affect of the verdict on Simpson was enormous. His stature is more tarnished that before.

2. (threw, through, thorough)

In 2006, Paris Hilton was arrested for drunk driving. Police stopped her after she drove her car threw a red light. Thorough a spokesperson, Hilton defended herself. The police made a through investigation of the crime, and the judge put her on probation. However, Hilton did not meet the terms of her probation. In 2007, a judge through the book at her and sentenced her to forty-five days in jail. Later, the sentence was changed to twenty-three days.

3. (lose, loose, loss)

Fans sometimes loose respect for celebrities when the celebrities behave badly. Some fans believe that such loss standards of behavior should not be encouraged. However, many stars think that a lose of reputation is acceptable because they profit from their notoriety.

4. (*who's, whose*)

The public should remember that celebrities who commit crimes are criminals. A person whose famous should not behave criminally. Celebrities who's profession puts them in the public spotlight should be aware of the influence they have, especially on young people.

CHAPTER 33

REFLECT ON IT

Think about what you have learned in this unit. If you do not know an answer, review that concept.

1. a. In a word containing *ie*, when does *i* come before *e*?

_____

b. When does *e* come before *i*?

_____

2. Circle the correctly spelled words. Correct each misspelled word.

realy   finally   unatural   illogical   plentifull

3. Correct eight mistakes in the next passage.

Crimes are quiet a common occurrence in my nieghborhood. The police are planing to increase there surveillance in this area. The public, to, can help. Its important to report any unnusual events. Eventualy, such actions will help lower the crime rate.

FINAL REVIEW

Underline and correct twenty spelling errors and mistakes with commonly confused words in the essay.

EXAMPLE:

Sometimes, laws are unfairly <u>applyed</u>.
applied

1.   Three strikes laws have stired up controversy in the United States. Such laws state that if a person is convicted of two felonys, the felon will recieve a life sentence if convicted of a third crime. The laws aim to make career criminals take responsability for their actions.

2.   The first three strikes law was passed in California in 1994, and it grew out of the public's sense of frustration. The public percieved that there was a steady increase in crime, so the state decided to implement an action plan. Lawmakers excepted the public's viewpoint and designed a law they taught would be tough on criminals. However, the law continus to be debated.

3.   Proponents of this controversial law argue that criminals need a strong deterrent to stop them from doing ilegal activities. In fact, proponents claim that the crime rate has definitly droped since the three strikes law was passed. Moreover, supporters say that other states have passed the same law because it has being so successfull in California.

4.   Critics of this law claim that buy harshly punishing criminals who have committed minor crimes, this law ensures that everybody looses.

Three strikes laws go against the principal of the punishment fitting the crime. Furthermore, opponents argue that the laws should be applyed only to violent felons. Money should not be wasted on jailing those who comit minor offenses such as stealing food or shoplifting. Also, the United States has the highest rate of incarceration in the world. Almost 50 percent of all prisoners worldwide are in our nation's prisons.

5.   Critics forcefuly condemn three strikes laws, argueing that such laws are inhumane, expensive, and unfair. Supporters do not want the laws to be modified. Both sides have valid points of view; therefore, three strikes laws will continue to generate controversy.

The Writer's Room

Write about one of the following topics. Check for spelling errors and verify that you have used the correct word.

1. Do you believe that the three strikes law is fair and effective?
2. Should juveniles who commit serious crimes be treated as harshly as adults?

The Writers' Circle   Collaborative Activity

Work with a partner or a small group of students and compose a paragraph about the qualities of a good comic book hero. In your paragraph, tell a story about a heroic action that the superhero does. Use slang words and clichés in your paragraph. Make sure that your paragraph is double-spaced, and make sure that the writing is clear.

When you have finished your paragraph, exchange sheets with another team of students. Edit the other team's paragraph and imagine that the audience is a college instructor. Change all clichés and slang expressions into standard American English.

READING LINK

The Legal World
"Why I Worked with La Migra" by Veronica Ortega (page 569)
"When the Legal Thing Isn't the Right Thing" by Deborah Mead (page 572)
"Interview with Jimmy Baca" by Elizabeth Farnsworth (page 574)

CHAPTER 33

mywritinglab To check your progress in meeting this chapter's objectives, log in to **www.mywritinglab.com**, go to the **Study Plan** tab, click on **The Editing Handbook—Section 7: Word Use and Spelling** and choose **Spelling and Easily Confused Words** from the list of subtopics. Read and view the resources in the **Review Materials** section, and then complete the **Recall, Apply,** and **Write** sets in the **Activities** section.

Section Theme **THE WORKPLACE**

In this chapter, you will read about business etiquette and wise business decisions.

The Writer's Journal

Have you ever thought about having your own business? What type of business would you like to have? Write a paragraph about owning a business.

What Is a Comma?

A **comma** (,) is a punctuation mark that helps keep distinct ideas separate. There are many ways to use a comma. In this chapter, you will learn some helpful rules about comma usage.

Notice how comma placement changes the meaning of the following sentences. Discuss which animal is having a nap.

The dog bites, the cat runs, and then she has a nap.

The dog bites the cat, runs, and then she has a nap.

Commas in a Series

Use a comma to separate items in a series of three or more items. Remember to put a comma before the final *and* or *or*.

unit 1	,	unit 2	,	and	unit 3
				or	

Houston, Dallas, and Austin have vibrant design industries.

The job search requires courage, perseverance, and energy.

You can network, contact employers directly, or use a placement service.

Hint **Punctuating a Series**

In a series of three or more items, do not place a comma after the last item in the series (unless the series is part of an interrupting phrase).

Her poise, simplicity, and kindness/ impressed us.

Do not use commas to separate items if each item is joined by *and* or *or*.

It is not possible to study <u>and</u> listen to music <u>and</u> have a conversation at the same time.

PRACTICE I

Underline series of items in the next selection. Then add eighteen missing commas where necessary.

EXAMPLE:

Some <u>individuals, small-business owners, and home-based workers design and</u> print their own business cards.

1. Many small companies do not have the money to advertise, so their only means of promoting their product is to hand out cards to friends neighbors and strangers who might be interested in the business. The type of card that people carry depends on the type of business that they have. Photographers pastry chefs artists and musicians often have colors and images on their cards. Doctors lawyers and accountants tend to use simple black-and-white designs printed on good-quality paper.

2. Your business card should transmit more than just your name position telephone number and address. According to consultant Frank Yeoman,

people are attracted to cards that have clear simple and direct messages. At the same time, a business card should stand out in some way, so it is a good idea to think about the color texture and design of the card. The card should be eye-catching.

3.   Yeoman says that you should never put your photo on your business cards unless you are a model or an actor. As trends change, you may be embarrassed to have hundreds of business cards depicting you with an unfashionable hairstyle outdated glasses and an unattractive shirt. You get only one chance to make an impression on new customers, so it is important to put some time effort and planning into your business card design.

Commas After Introductory Words and Phrases

Use a comma after an **introductory word.** The introductory word could be an interjection such as *yes, no,* or *well,* it could be an adverb such as *usually* or *generally,* or it could be a transitional word such as *however* or *therefore.*

> Introductory word(s)   **,**   sentence.

Yes, I will help you complete the order.

Frankly, you should reconsider your customer service promise.

However, the job includes a lot of overtime.

Use a comma to set off **introductory phrases** of two or more words. The phrase could be a transitional expression such as *of course* or *on the contrary,* or it could be a prepositional phrase such as *on a warm summer evening.* The introductory phrase could also be a modifier such as *running out of fuel* or *born in France.*

On the other hand, his career was not going well.

In the middle of the meeting, I received a phone call.

Speaking to the crowd, the manager explained the stock's performance.

PRACTICE 2

Underline each introductory word or phrase. Then add ten missing commas.

EXAMPLE:

In today's job market, people must remain flexible.

CHAPTER 34

1.   For the first time in history workers can expect to outlive the organizations that they work for. For example many financial companies collapsed during the stock market crash of 2008. Additionally many businesses go bankrupt each year.

2.   Furthermore those working in successful companies may see their jobs become obsolete. In fact the majority of the nation's bank tellers were laid off in the 1990s. As a result many people in the banking industry have had to retrain or change jobs.

3.   According to Myriam Goldman the average person should plan for three different careers. Of course some people love their jobs and have no desire to look elsewhere. However even those in secure jobs may get bored and long for a career change down the road. Working in a volatile job market workers should remain open and flexible.

Commas Around Interrupting Words and Phrases

Interrupting words or phrases appear in the middle of sentences. Such interrupters are often asides that interrupt the sentence's flow but do not affect its overall meaning. Some interrupters are *by the way*, *as a matter of fact*, and *for example*. Prepositional phrases can also interrupt sentences.

My sister, for example, has never invested in stocks.
The market, by the way, has been down recently.
My manager, in the middle of a busy day, decided to go to a movie!

CHAPTER 34

 **Using Commas with Appositives**

An appositive gives further information about a noun or pronoun. The appositive can appear at the beginning, in the middle, or at the end of the sentence. Set off appositives with commas.

beginning

A large city in Florida, Miami has a variety of public learning centers.

middle

Dr. Anex, a senior surgeon, recommends the transplant.

end

The office is next to Graham's, a local eatery.

PRACTICE 3

The next sentences contain introductory words and phrases, interrupters, and series of items. Add the missing commas. If the sentence is correct, write *C* in the space provided.

EXAMPLE:

E-mail, voice mail, and cell phones are changing the way that
people do business. _____

1. Jamaal Khabbaz a marketing manager, complains about high-tech

    gadgets in the workplace such as pagers, cell phones and personal

    organizers. _____

2. Many workers in his opinion break rules of basic etiquette. _____

3. He gets annoyed, for example when a lunch meeting is

    interrupted by a ringing cell phone. _____

4. Unfortunately, many people do not consider it rude to answer

    a call in the middle of a meal. _____

5. According to Kabbaz the workplace needs new business

    etiquette rules. _____

6. Electronic mail, a convenient way to send and receive

    messages is not private. _____

7. Without a doubt, it is offensive to read other people's mail. _____

8. Some people, however have no qualms about standing next to

    a computer and reading over the shoulder of an e-mail recipient. _____

9. E-mail junkies, those addicted to electronic messages cause the

    most problems. _____

10. In the middle of a busy day the e-mail addict sends cartoons,

    videos and messages to co-workers. _____

CHAPTER 34

Commas in Compound Sentences

A **compound sentence** contains two or more complete sentences joined by a coordinating conjunction (*for, and, nor, but, or, yet, so*).

> Sentence　　　　　, and　　　　　sentence.

I want a job, **so** I will look in the classified ads.

Some interesting companies are nearby, **and** maybe they are hiring.

PRACTICE 4

Add six commas that are missing from this letter.

EXAMPLE:

I am punctual, and I am hardworking.

Dear Mr. Ruzinka,

On Monster.com, I read that you are looking for a computer technician. I am interested in the job so I have enclosed a résumé highlighting my skills and experience.

I have taken computer technology courses at El Camino College and I completed my program with distinction. I also plan to receive Microsoft certification but I haven't done the final exams. Furthermore, I have worked at a bank and I have experience repairing computers at a local clinic.

I am available for an interview at any time so please do not hesitate to contact me. Thank you for your consideration and I look forward to hearing from you.

Yours sincerely,

Darius George

Darius George

Commas in Complex Sentences

A **complex sentence** contains one or more dependent clauses (or incomplete ideas). When you add a **subordinating conjunction**—a word such as *because, although,* or *unless*—to a clause, you make the clause dependent.

dependent clause　　　　　independent clause

When the stock market opened, he sold his shares.

Use a Comma After a Dependent Clause

If a sentence begins with a dependent clause, place a comma after the clause. Remember that a dependent clause has a subject and a verb, but it cannot stand alone. When the subordinating conjunction comes in the middle of a sentence, it is not necessary to use a comma.

Dependent clause , main clause.

Comma: After the meeting ends, we will go to lunch.

Main clause dependent clause.

No comma: We will go to lunch after the meeting ends.

Use Commas to Set Off Nonrestrictive Clauses

Clauses beginning with *who*, *that*, and *which* can be restrictive or nonrestrictive. A **restrictive clause** contains essential information about the subject. Do not place commas around restrictive clauses.

No commas: The only local company that does computer graphics has no job openings.

(The underlined clause is essential to understand the meaning of the sentence.)

A **nonrestrictive clause** gives nonessential information. In such sentences, the clause gives additional information about the noun but does not restrict or define the noun. Place commas around nonrestrictive clauses.

Commas: Her book, which is in bookstores, is about successful entrepreneurs.

(The underlined clause contains extra information, but if you removed that clause, the sentence would still have a clear meaning.)

 **Which, That, Who**

which
Use commas to set off clauses that begin with *which*.

ImClone, **which** was founded in 1983, creates pharmaceutical products.

that
Do not use commas to set off clauses begining with *that*.

The company **that** Sam Waksal founded creates pharmaceutical products.

who
When a clause begins with *who*, you may or may not need a comma. If the clause contains nonessential information, put commas around it. If the clause is essential to the meaning of the sentence, it does not require commas.

Essential: Many people **who** buy stocks think that they will earn a profit.

Not essential: Domestic guru Martha Stewart, **who** became a multimillionaire, was convicted of obstructing justice in 2004.

PRACTICE 5

Edit the following sentences by adding eighteen missing commas.

EXAMPLE:

The manager, who seems quite nice, asks very probing questions.

1.   When people look for jobs they may encounter several types of interviews. The structured interview which occurs during the screening stage helps a company have a uniform hiring process. The employer, who asks a specific set of questions compares the answers of the candidates.

2.   The open-ended interview which is more relaxed and unstructured allows job seekers to talk freely. If people reveal too much or ramble on they may not be hired. Anyone who wants a job should remember to maintain a business-like demeanor.

3.   During panel interviews a team questions the job-seekers. For instance the supervisor the human resources manager and a coworker may all interact with the candidates. Some companies even have group interviews which are useful for judging people's communication skills.

4.   The worst type of interview is the stress interview. The intense boss, who asks difficult and strange questions often unnerves the candidate. The goal which is not always apparent is to see how people handle demanding situations. Eliza Marcum for example, was asked what type of animal she would like to be. She did not understand the relevance of the question and she responded impatiently. During stress interviews, people who act upset overly nervous, or angry will probably not be hired.

CHAPTER 34

Commas in Business Letters

When you write or type a formal letter, ensure that you use commas correctly.

Addresses

In the address at the top of the letter, insert a comma between the following elements.

- The street name and apartment number
- The city and state or country

Do not put a comma before the zip code.

Dr. Brent Patterson

312 Appleby Road, Suite 112
            ^

Cleveland, OH 45678
         ^

If you include an address inside a complete sentence, use commas to separate the street address from the city and the city from the state or country. If you just write the street address, do not put a comma after it.

Commas: The building at 11 Wall Street, New York, contains the
                                            ^   ^
                Stock Exchange.

No comma: The building at 11 Wall Street contains the New York
                Stock Exchange.

Dates

In the date at the top of the letter, add a comma between the full date and the year. If you just write the month and the year, then no comma is necessary.

May 21, 2006   January 2006
       ^

If you include a date inside a complete sentence, separate the elements of the date with commas.

We visited Washington on Monday, July 26, 2008.
                                ^   ^

 **Hint** ▷ **Writing Numbers**

When writing a date in a letter, it is not necessary to write ordinal numbers such as *first* (1st), *second* (2nd), *third* (3rd), or *fourth* (4th). Instead, just write the number: 1, 2, 3, 4, and so on.

February 24, 2001   October 11, 1966

CHAPTER 34

Salutations

Salutations are formal letter greetings. The form "To Whom It May Concern" is no longer used regularly by North American businesses. The best way to address someone is to use his or her name followed by a comma or a colon. The colon is preferred in business letters.

Dear Ms. Lewin: Dear Sir or Madam: Dear Sarah,

Complimentary Closings

Place a comma after the complimentary closing. Notice that the first word of the closing is capitalized.

Respectfully,   Yours sincerely,   Many thanks,

Sample Letter of Application

You send a sample letter of application to an employer when you apply for a job. Review the parts of the following letter.

CHAPTER 34

Sender's address ➤
(name, phone, and possibly
an e-mail address)

Seamus O'Brien
10 Santa Fe Boulevard
Seattle, WA 90001
(661) 234-5678

Date ➤

September 12, 2010

Recipient's address ➤

Avant Garde Computers
Adelaide and Sinclair Corporation
6116 Greenway Avenue
Seattle, WA 98711

Subject line ➤

Subject: Position of junior programmer

Salutation ➤

Dear Ms. Roebok:

I saw an ad in Saturday's *Seattle Times* stating that you need a junior programmer. I have enclosed a résumé highlighting my skills in this field. I have an aptitude for computers, and, when I was fourteen years old, I created my first game program.

I have just finished a diploma program in computer programming at Marshall College. I took courses in several computer languages. I have also completed a six-week training program, and I have enclosed a letter of reference from the owner of that company.

If you require further information, please contact me. I am available for an interview at any time and could start work immediately. Thank you for your consideration.

Sincerely,

S. O'Brien

Closing (After the closing, ➤
put your handwritten
signature followed by your
typed name.)

Seamus O'Brien

List any documents you ➤
have included.

Enclosures: résumé
               letter of reference

PRACTICE 6

The next letter contains ten errors. Add seven missing commas and remove three unnecessary commas.

Red River Publications

1440 Cliff Street

Austin Texas 76780

April 2 2010

Graham Britt

214 Regents Road,

Austin Texas 77787

Dear Mr. Britt:

On Monday March 12 2010 we received your manuscript. We are pleased to inform you that your article will be published in the May, issue of *Phoenix Magazine*.

Could you please meet with me at our branch office? I will be at 44 Hillside Road, during the last week of the month. We are looking forward to meeting with you.

Yours truly

Terrel Wainwright

Terrel Wainwright

REFLECT ON IT

Think about what you have learned in this unit. If you do not know an answer, review that concept.

1. Explain the rules of comma usage in the following situations.

   a. Series of items: _____

   _____

   b. Introductory words or phrases: _____

   _____

   c. Interrupting phrases: _____

   _____

   d. Compound sentences: _____

   _____

2. What is a nonrestrictive clause? _____

   _____

3. Should you place commas around nonrestrictive clauses? _____ Yes _____ No

4. Write three common closings for a business letter.

_____

_____

FINAL REVIEW

Edit the next essay by adding seventeen missing commas and removing three unnecessary commas.

EXAMPLE:

Entertainers, including comedians, actors and musicians, should consult with a financial advisor.

1.   Horace Madison co-founder of Madison Smallwood Financial Group, manages the careers of top urban rappers, hip-hop artists and blues musicians. Madison, who grew up in Harlem had a middle-class childhood. He heard about many high-profile artists and musicians M. C. Hammer, for example, who ended up going broke. When he began to work on Wall Street, he decided to focus on entertainers, who were at risk of mismanaging their funds.

2.   Madison handles every aspect of his clients' lives. He helps them examine contracts, pay their bills and plan their investment portfolios. After signing million-dollar record deals new artists often want expensive jewelry and cars. They may not realize that they owe the record label for some of the money spent on music videos, marketing and travel. Furthermore new artists also face pressure from family and friends. When friends see the artist in a music video they ask for a handout or a job.

3.   Madison helps artists set up a budget and he carefully monitors what they spend. When someone chooses to waste an outrageous amount on a frivolous luxury item Madison gives that person a "stupid letter." He wants artists to understand, that such spending is against the advice of Madison's firm. In an interview with Mitchell Raphael a journalist with the *National*

Post newspaper Madison gave an anecdote about a female client who wanted to rent a car. A Ferrari which costs $1,400 a day, was her first choice. Madison asked her to sign a stupid letter. The client a rapper changed her mind and decided to rent a Toyota for $300 a day.

4.   Ultimately, excessive spending is not smart. Hip-hop artists must think about their long-term future, because they have a career span of only three or four years. Madison and Smallwood Financial Group have helped OutKast and Usher manage the minefield of fame. Eve, a hip-hop artist has thanked Madison for helping her spend her money wisely.

 The Writer's Room

Write about one of the following topics. Verify that your comma usage is correct.

1. Are you a good money manager? Describe how you handle your finances.
2. Categorize spenders into different types. Give examples for each type.

mywritinglab To check your progress in meeting this chapter's objectives, log in to **www.mywritinglab.com**, go to the **Study Plan** tab, click on **The Editing Handbook—Section 8: Punctuation and Mechanics** and choose **Commas** from the list of subtopics. Read and view the resources in the **Review Materials** section, and then complete the **Recall, Apply,** and **Write** sets in the **Activities** section.

CHAPTER 34

The Apostrophe, Quotation Marks, and Titles

Section Theme **THE WORKPLACE**

In this chapter, you will read about topics related to business success and controversies.

The Writer's Journal

Write about a successful singer. What are some of the person's best songs? Why do you like that singer?

The Apostrophe (')

An **apostrophe** is a punctuation mark showing a contraction or ownership.

> ownership   contraction
> Daymond **John's** business is very successful, and **it's** still growing.

Using Apostrophes in Contractions

To form a **contraction,** join two words into one and add an apostrophe to replace the omitted letter(s).

Apostrophe replaces *o*   is + **not** = isn't
Apostrophe replaces *a*   I + **am** = I'm

Common Contractions

The following are examples of the most common contractions.

- **Join a verb with *not*.** The apostrophe replaces the letter *o* in *not*.

are + not = aren't	have + not = haven't
could + not = couldn't	is + not = isn't
did + not = didn't't	should + not = shouldn't
do + not = don't	was + not = wasn't
does + not = doesn't	were + not = weren't
has + not = hasn't	would + not = wouldn't

Exceptions: will + not = won't, can + not = can't

- **Join a subject and a verb.** Sometimes you must remove several letters to form the contraction.

I + will = I'll	she + will = she'll
I + would = I'd	Tina + is = Tina's
he + is = he's	they + are = they're
he + will = he'll	we + will = we'll
Joe + is = Joe's	who + is = who's
she + has = she's	who + would = who'd

Exception: Do not contract a subject with the past tense of *be*. For example, do not contract *he + was* or *they + were*.

 **Contractions with Two Meanings**

Sometimes one contraction can have two different meanings.

I'd = I had or I would   **he's** = he is or he has

When you read, you should be able to figure out the meaning of the contraction by looking at the words in context.

She's hiring new personnel.   **She's** seen several interesting candidates.
(She is)   (She has)

PRACTICE I

Add nine missing apostrophes to the next selection.

EXAMPLE:

>   *hadn't*
> Many Americans ~~hadnt~~ expected investment banks to collapse in 2008.

1.   In 1850, three German brothers immigrated to America and invested in

cotton in Montgomery, Alabama. After the Civil War, the brothers couldve

stayed in Montgomery, but they took their enterprise to New York. They werent just cotton traders. Theyd also buy and sell other items. Their company got on the New York Stock Exchange and was a successful institution for more than a hundred years. The brothers couldnt have predicted that Lehman Brothers Holdings would be bankrupt by the start of the 21st century.

2. The company finances didnt remain healthy. In 2007, its stock price started to fall. Investors lost confidence in the firm because it had invested in lending mortgages to risky clients. Managers shouldve been more careful. In the summer of 2008, the firm posted huge losses. The American government wasnt willing to lend the corporation money, so the company failed.

3. Politicians criticized the company. Members of Congress felt that the top executives of Lehman Brothers shouldnt have received millions of dollars in bonuses just before the business filed for bankruptcy. When questioned about his performance, CEO Richard Fuld said that hed made the best decisions he could for the company.

PRACTICE 2

Look at each underlined contraction, and then write out the complete word.

EXAMPLE:

They <u>weren't</u> ready to start a business.   *were not*

1. Carol <u>Simon's</u> very happy with her bridal gown company.   _____
2. <u>She's</u> been an entrepreneur for seven years.   _____
3. <u>She's</u> an extremely friendly, ambitious woman.   _____
4. I wish <u>I'd</u> had the same idea as Carol.   _____
5. <u>I'd</u> like to have my own company, too.   _____

Using Apostrophes to Show Ownership

You can also use apostrophes to show ownership. Review the next rules.

Possessive Form of Singular Nouns

Add -'s to a singular noun to indicate ownership, even if the noun ends in *s*.

Daymond's best friends joined his company.

Somebody's house became a factory.

Ross's dad has his own business.

Possessive Form of Plural Nouns

When a plural noun ends in *s*, just add an apostrophe to indicate ownership. Add -*'s* to irregular plural nouns.

Many **companies'** Web sites are down.

The four **friends'** business is very successful.

The **children's** clothing company is expanding.

Possessive Form of Compound Nouns

When two people have joint ownership, add -*'s* to the second name. When two people have separate ownership, add -*'s* to both names.

Joint ownership: Daymond and **Carl's** company is successful.

Separate ownership: **Daymond's** and **Carl's** offices are in different buildings.

PRACTICE 3

Write the singular and plural possessive forms.

EXAMPLE:

	Singular Possessive	**Plural Possessive**
Mr. Cohen	*Mr. Cohen's*	*the Cohens'*
1. client	_____	_____
2. boss	_____	_____
3. secretary	_____	_____
4. Mr. Ness	_____	_____
5. woman	_____	_____
6. salesperson	_____	_____

PRACTICE 4

Write the possessive forms of the following phrases.

EXAMPLE:

the sister of the doctor _____*the doctor's sister*_____

1. the locker of the employee _____

2. the supplies of the employees _____

3. the profits of the company _____

4. the directors of the companies _____

5. the house of Jan and Ted _____

6. the car of Omar and the car of Roy _____

CHAPTER 35

Using Apostrophes in Expressions of Time

When an expression of time (*day, week, month, year*) appears to possess something, use the possessive form of that word.

> **Singular:** The customer won a **year's** supply of paper.

> **Plural:**   Mike Roy gave two **weeks'** notice before he left the company.

When writing the numerals of a decade or century, do not put an apostrophe before the final -*s*.

> In the **1800s,** many immigrants arrived at Ellis Island.

> Many Internet companies failed in the **1990s.**

 **Common Apostrophe Errors**

Do not use apostrophes before the final *s* of a verb.

>   *wants*
> Simon ~~want's~~ to open a franchise.

Do not confuse contractions with possessive pronouns that have a similar sound. For example, the contraction *you're* sounds like the pronoun *your.* Remember that possessive pronouns never have apostrophes.

>   *Its*
> The company is growing. ~~It's~~ slogan is catchy.
>   *theirs.*
> That is my idea. It is not ~~their's.~~

PRACTICE 5

Correct twelve errors with apostrophes.

EXAMPLE:

>   *aren't*   *don't*
> If you ~~arent~~ willing to work hard, ~~dont~~ start your own business.

1. In the late 1970's, when Mike Lazaridis was in high school, he joined a ham radio group. Mikes teacher, the group president, told him that future communications technology would combine computers and wireless systems. Later, after a few year's studying at the University of Waterloo, Mike decided that he would'nt complete his degree. He wanted to run his own business. With some of his parents money, he started his company, Research In Motion (RIM), along with his business partner, Jim Balsillie.

2. The two men never thought that theyd become so successful. Around 1999, RIM developed a wireless device that had multiple functions, such as emailing, text messaging, faxing, and phoning. But designers didnt know

what to call it. Someone thought that the touch buttons resembled the seeds of a berry. The companys managers decided to name it the BlackBerry. Since it's first appearance in the market, the BlackBerrys popularity has remained very high. Even President Barack Obama own's one. In fact, many people joke that theyre addicted to their BlackBerries, and therefore, it has often been called the CrackBerry.

Quotation Marks (" ")

Use **quotation marks** to set off the exact words of a speaker or writer. If the quotation is a complete sentence, there are some standard ways that it should be punctuated.

- Capitalize the first word of the quotation.
- Place quotation marks around the complete quotation.
- Place the end punctuation inside the closing quotation marks.

> . . . declared   ,   "Complete sentence."

Here is an example of a sentence with a quotation.

> Poet William Butler Yeats declared, "Education is not the filling of a pail but the lighting of a fire."

Generally, when using quotations, attach the name of the speaker or writer to the quotation in some way. Review the following rules.

Introductory Phrase

Place a comma after a phrase introducing a quotation.

> . . . says   ,   "_____."

> Malcolm Forbes jokes, "It is unfortunate we can't buy many business executives for what they are worth and sell them for what they think they are worth."

Interrupting Phrase

When a quotation is interrupted, do the following:

- Place a comma after the first part of the quotation.
- Place a comma after the interrupting phrase.

> "_____,"   . . . says,   "_____."

> "I don't know the key to success," Bill Cosby said, "but the key to failure is to try to please everybody."

Ending Phrase

When you place a phrase at the end of a quotation, end the quotation with a comma instead of a period.

> "_____,"   says _____.

> "You're fired," said Donald Trump.

If your quotation ends with other punctuation, put it before the final quotation mark.

"_____?" says _____.

"You can't fire me!" she shouted.

"Why can't I fire you?" he asked.

Introductory Sentence

You can introduce a quotation with a complete sentence. Simply place a colon (:) after the introductory sentence.

He explains his views: "_____."

Albert Highfield explains why businesses fail: "They try to grow too quickly."

Inside a Quotation

If one quotation is inside another quotation, use single quotation marks (' ') around the inside quotation.

"Main quotation, 'Inside quotation.' "

According to Shannon Dowell, "Good parents always say, 'Clean up your own mess.' "

> (Hint) **When the Quotation Is an Incomplete Sentence**
>
> If the quotation is not a complete sentence and you simply integrate it into your sentence, do not capitalize the first word of the quotation.
>
> Sir Francis Bacon once said that an artist's job is to "**d**eepen the mystery."

PRACTICE 6

In each sentence, the quotation is in bold. Add quotation marks and commas or colons. Also capitalize the first word of the quotation if necessary.

EXAMPLE:

Comedian Bob Hope made fun of financial institutions : "A **bank is a place that will lend you money if you can prove that you don't need it.** "

1. According to novelist Lisa Alther **any mother could perform the jobs of several air traffic controllers with ease.**

2. U.S. educator Laurence J. Peter believes that everyone is useful **a miser, for example, makes a wonderful ancestor.**

3. Fred Delaney proclaimed **a celebrity is a person who works hard all his life to become well known, and then wears dark glasses to avoid being recognized.**

4. **In the future, a wall could become a computer screen** according to journalist Kate McNamara.

5. Comedian Mel Brooks believes that humor provides people with a **defense against the universe.**

6. Muhammad Ali describes his profession as a boxer **grass grows, birds fly, waves pound the sand, and I beat people up.**

7. **Success only breeds a new goal** observed actress Bette Davis.

8. **Hard work never killed anybody** declared comedian Edgar Bergen **but why take a chance?**

9. My mother once said **remember the words of humorist Erma Bombeck do not confuse fame with success.**

Punctuation of Titles

When using a title within a sentence, place quotation marks around the title of a short work and italicize the title of a longer work. If your text is handwritten, then underline the titles of long works. Here are some guidelines for both.

Short Works	Long Works
Short story: "The Lottery"	**Novel:** *The Grapes of Wrath*
Web article: "Music Artists Lose Out"	**Web site:** *CNET News.com*
Chapter: Chapter 1, "Exploring"	**Book:** *The Writer's World*
Newspaper article: "Missing in Action"	**Newspaper:** *New York Times*
Magazine article: "Young Entrepreneurs"	**Magazine:** *Forbes*
Essay: "Downsizing"	**Textbook:** *Writing Guidelines*
TV episode: "The Election"	**TV series:** *Prison Break*
Song: "Don't Panic"	**CD:** *Parachutes*
Poem: "Howl"	**Anthology:** *Collected Poems of Beat Writers*
	Movie: *Avatar*

Capitalizing Titles

When you write a title, capitalize the first letter of the first and last words and all the major words.

The Catcher in the Rye   *War and Peace*   "Stairway to Heaven"

Do not capitalize *.com* in a Web address. Also do not capitalize the following words except as the first or last word in a title.

Articles:	a, an, the
Coordinators:	for, and, nor, but, or, yet, so
Prepositions:	by, in, of, off, out, to, up . . .

 **Hint** **Your Own Essay Titles**

When writing the title of your own essay, do not put quotation marks around the title. However, you should capitalize key terms.

A **C**ultural **I**con **I**s **B**orn

PRACTICE 7

A. Add twenty missing capital letters to the titles in the next paragraph.

EXAMPLE:

The magazine *chief executive* featured successful entrepreneurs.

    C   *E*

1.   In recent years, some ambitious, multitalented women have become incredibly successful in different fields. Madonna, for example, has released about ten CDs, including one called *american life*. Her popular songs include "hollywood" and "like a prayer." She has written children's books, such as *the english roses*. She has also appeared in many movies, including *desperately seeking susan* and *swept away*. Critics have not always been kind to the Michigan native. In his article "no madonna is an island," *new york times* film critic A. O. Scott called Madonna a poor actress.

B. Add quotation marks or underline any titles that should be italicized. There are eight titles.

EXAMPLE:

Queen Latifah starred in the 2008 film, <u>The Secret Life of Bees</u>.

2.   Queen Latifah is a versatile performer. She is a rapper, model, and actress. In 1988, Queen Latifah got her big break with the song Princess of the Posse, which became a hit single on her album All Hail the Queen. She received a Grammy for another hit, U.N.I.T.Y. from the CD Black Reign.

In the 1990s, Queen Latifah continued experimenting with her musical style, and she also ventured into acting. From 1993 to 1998, she had a role in a sitcom, Living Single. She also had a part in Spike Lee's hit film Jungle Fever. She became a household name when she received an Oscar for her role as Mama Morton in the film Chicago. Becoming an instant celebrity, she was on the cover of many magazines, including Essence. She continues to achieve great success in her music and acting careers.

Queen Latifah

PRACTICE 8

Correct twelve errors with quotation marks, apostrophes, or capital letters, and underline titles that should be italicized.

EXAMPLE:

Paul Salopek, in an article titled "Children ~~s~~eeking ~~r~~oyalties," denounced the treatment of a South African composer.
<small>S R</small>

1.   Every time a song is placed on a CD or album, the writer receives a royalty. Lee Ann Arbringer, in an article called "How royalties work," says, "currently, the statutory rate is eight cents for each song." To combat illegal file sharing on the Internet, some legal music site's have opened up, but not all artists are happy about it. "I earn almost nothing from the legal file-sharing sites because the users just rent songs", says Jimmy Dee, a guitarist. Roz Hillman, an accountant, agrees, noting that the artist gets "Next to nothing."

2.   Some artists have lost the rights to their own compositions. One of the greatest songs in the last century was written by a nearly unknown South African singer, Solomon Linda. Paul Salopek, of the *Chicago tribune*, wrote about him. In 1939, Linda wrote a song called "Mbube" and sold the rights to Gallo Records for a mere ten shillings, which is less than $2. Since then, Linda song has been rerecorded almost two hundred times, most famously in the 1961 version "The Lion sleeps tonight." The song is on the soundtrack of fifteen movies, including Disney's The Lion King. Solomon Linda died a pauper. "We are sad because he died without praise." said his daughter, Elizabeth.

REFLECT ON IT

Think about what you have learned in this unit. If you do not know an answer, review that concept.

1. In contractions, which letter does the apostrophe replace in the word *not?* ____

2. Write the possessive forms of the following phrases.

   EXAMPLE:
   the wife of my brother: *my brother's wife* _____

   a. the music of Jennifer Lopez: _____
   b. the books of the professor: _____
   c. the house of Rob and Ann: _____
   d. the cases of the lawyers: _____

3. When a sentence ends with a quotation, the period should be
   a. inside the final quotation marks.
   b. outside the final quotation marks.

4. The titles of short works such as essays, articles, and poems should be
   a. underlined or italicized.
   b. set off with quotation marks.

5. The titles of longer works, such as magazines, newspapers, and movies, should be
   a. italicized.
   b. set off with quotation marks.

FINAL REVIEW

Edit the following paragraphs for fifteen errors with apostrophes, quotations, capitalization, and titles. Underline titles that should normally be italicized.

EXAMPLE:

I downloaded Lady ~~GaGas~~ *GaGa's* song "Paparazzi" for only 99 cents.

1. File sharing of music and films has become common in recent year's. A reporter for *Fox news* writes "An estimated 60 million people participate in file-sharing networks." Opinions about file sharing differ greatly.

2. David Charles works in the film industry. He says that video sharing is becoming as common as music downloading. Charles' friend, Melissa Peng, often downloads songs. She says, "students don't want to buy a CD for twenty dollars when there are only one or two songs they like".

CHAPTER 35

3.   There are many court cases about recording companies objections to

illegal downloads. People in the music industry claim theyre losing profits.

In 2007, the Wall Street Journal reported that the record industry lost

20 percent of its CD sales. The Recording Industry Association of

America states its position "If you make unauthorized copies of copyrighted

music recordings, you're stealing." The RIAA has sued many people for

violating copyright laws. However, critics of the music industry object to

such tactics. Mark Fisher is a journalist for the Washington Post. In his

article, "Download uproar: Record Industry Goes After Personal Use,

Fisher writes, "The RIAA's legal crusade against its customers is a classic

example of an old media company clinging to a business model that has

collapsed."

4.   The music and film industries know that consumers will continue to

share files. Consequently, they have developed new schemes to increase

profits. Apple, along with Zune, allows it's customers to download products

for 99 cents. Business student Mitchel Hunt like's the new system: "I can

download the videos I want very cheaply."

The Writer's Room

Write about one of the following topics. Ensure that your punctuation is correct.

1. What is success? Define success and, as a supporting example, describe a successful person whom you know.
2. What reasons do people give for downloading music and films? What are the effects of their actions? Write about the causes and effects of illegal downloading.

CHAPTER 35

mywritinglab To check your progress in meeting this chapter's objectives, log in to **www.mywritinglab.com**, go to the **Study Plan** tab, click on **The Editing Handbook—Section 8: Punctuation and Mechanics** and choose **Apostrophes and Quotation Marks** from the list of subtopics. Read and view the resources in the **Review Materials** section, and then complete the **Recall, Apply,** and **Write** sets in the **Activities** section.

Capitalization and Other Punctuation Marks

Section Theme **THE WORKPLACE**

In this chapter, you will read about topics related to new innovations.

The Writer's Journal

Do you buy products online? Why or why not? Express your opinion about online shopping.

Capitalization

There are many instances in which you must use capital letters. Always capitalize the following words:

- **the pronoun *I* and the first word of every sentence**

  My co-workers and **I** share an office.

- **days of the week, months, and holidays**

    Thursday   June 23   Thanksgiving

    Do not capitalize the seasons: summer, fall, winter, spring.

- **titles of specific institutions, departments, companies, and schools**

    Apple Computer   Department of Finance   Daleview High School

    Do not capitalize general references.

    the company   the department   the school

- **the names of specific places such as buildings, streets, parks, cities, states, countries, continents, and bodies of water**

    Market Street   Times Square   Los Angeles, California
    Brazil   Asia   Lake Erie

    Exception: Do not capitalize general references.

    the street   the state   the lake

- **the names of specific languages, nationalities, tribes, races, and religions**

    Spanish   Mohawk   Buddhist   an Italian restaurant

- **titles of specific individuals**

    General Dewitt   President Abraham Lincoln   Dr. Blain
    Professor Cruz   Prime Minister Gordon Brown   Mrs. Ellen Ross

    Do not capitalize titles if you are referring to the profession in general, or if the title follows the name.

    my doctor   the professors   Diane Feinstein, a senator

- **specific course and program titles**

    Economics 201   Topics in Electrical Engineering   Nursing 402

    Do not capitalize if you refer to a course but do not mention the course title.

    an economics course   an engineering program   a nursing class

- **major words in titles of literary or artistic works**

    Washington Post   *Slumdog Millionaire*   *Lord of the Flies*

- **historical events, eras, and movements**

    World War II   Cubism   the Middle Ages

 **Capitalizing Computer Terms**

Always capitalize software titles, as well as the following computer terms. Also capitalize the word Web in Web site.

Internet   World Wide Web   Microsoft Office

Add fifteen missing capital letters.

EXAMPLE:

> *India*
> Many countries such as ~~india~~ want to manufacture environmentally friendly cars.

1. In recent times, some people have produced interesting inventions including the internet. The magazine *Popular mechanics* reported on a new car. In france, Motor development International has developed a car that runs on compressed air. The car was invented by Guy Negre. He used to be an engineer on the Formula one circuit. The american distribution center is on canaan street in New paltz, New York. In a promotional video, the inventor proudly stated, "i share the same birthday as science fiction writer Jules Verne." Verne predicted that automobiles would run on air.

2. The invention is still being perfected. At Cornell university's Department of Engineering, experts say that such a car design is possible, but it will take some time before consumers can drive the car. Many companies in europe, as well as tata motors of India, have expressed interest in producing the car. But in july 2008, one of Tata's executives said that company engineers are still working on the prototype.

Other Punctuation Marks

Colon (:)

Use a colon for the following purposes.

- To introduce a quotation with a complete sentence

  The writer Oscar Wilde stated his opinion: "All art is quite useless."

- To introduce a series or a list after a complete sentence

  The United States has produced some great writers: Emily Dickinson, F. Scott Fitzgerald, Ernest Hemingway, John Steinbeck, and William Faulkner.

- After the expression *the following*

  Please do the following: read, review, and respond.

- To introduce an explanation or example

  In 1929, investors witnessed a tragedy: the Stock Market Crash.

- To separate the hour and minutes in expressions of time

  The meeting will begin at 11:45.

Hyphen (-)

Use a hyphen in the following situations.

- When you write the complete words for numbers between twenty-one and ninety-nine.

  twenty-six   ninety-nine   seventy-two

- When you use a compound adjective before a noun. The compound adjective must express a single thought.

  No hyphen: The new employee must work under high pressure.

  Hyphen: The new employee has a <u>high-pressure</u> **job.**

  (You cannot say a "high job" or a "pressure job." *High* and *pressure* must go together.)

  No hyphen: Our boss is thirty years old.

  Hyphen: We have a <u>thirty-year-old</u> **boss.**

  (The words *thirty, year,* and *old* express a single thought. You cannot remove one of those words.)

  If the adjectives before a noun function independently, do *not* add hyphens.

  No hyphen: They renovated an old red barn.

  (The two adjectives function separately.)

 **Nonhyphenated Compound Adjectives**

Some compound adjectives never take a hyphen, even when they appear before a noun.

World Wide Web   high school senior   real estate agent

PRACTICE 2

Add eight missing colons and hyphens.

EXAMPLE:

            top-notch
The World Wide Web is a ~~top notch~~ communications system.

1.   Tim Berners-Lee, a respected fifty-five year old man, created the

     World Wide Web while working as a researcher for the European

     Laboratory for Particle Physics. His invention has had long term effects

     in the field of communications.

CHAPTER 36

2.   Born in London, England, Berners-Lee showed an early interest in mathematics. He had many childhood hobbies designing cardboard computers, doing mental mathematical calculations, and experimenting with electronics. Because his parents were interested in computers, Berners-Lee became a computer savvy child.

3.   In 1986, while he was working in Geneva, he had two great ideas designing a software system that linked information on his computer to information on his colleagues' computers, and sharing his program with scientists around the world. Berners-Lee envisioned a web like system of communications links. He named the new system the World Wide Web.

4.   Since 1991, the Internet has become an extremely user friendly research tool. Berners-Lee did not profit monetarily from his creation. In fact, he fights hard to keep it free so that everyone can benefit from it.

Ellipsis Marks (. . .)

You may want to quote key ideas from an author, but you do not always want to quote an entire paragraph. Use ellipsis marks to show that you have omitted information from a quotation.

When you type an ellipsis mark, leave a space before and after each period. If the omitted section includes complete sentences, then add a period after the ellipses. In the next examples, notice how the quotation changes when ellipses are used.

Original Selection

I submit that an individual who breaks a law that conscience tells him is unjust, and who willingly accepts the penalty of imprisonment in order to arouse the conscience of the community over its injustice, is in reality expressing the highest respect for the law.

—Martin Luther King Jr.

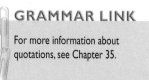

GRAMMAR LINK

For more information about quotations, see Chapter 35.

Quotation with Omissions

I submit that an individual who breaks a law that conscience tells him is unjust . . . is in reality expressing the highest respect for the law.

—Martin Luther King Jr.

PRACTICE 3

Write quotations incorporating material from each of the next passages. Use ellipses to show where you omit words, and remember to keep important information.

1. Normal thoughts of my future (not pertaining to football), friends, family, reputation, moral status, etc., were entirely beyond me.

—From H.D.'s "Dying to Be Bigger"

According to H. D., _____

_____

_____

2. To top it off, our kids are imbued with victimology, which today has become the American way of blame. It is too routine for adults and their kids to explain all their problems as victimization. When a boy in trouble sees himself as a victim, this festers into seething anger. With easy availability of guns, it can explode as murder.

—From Martin Seligman's "The American Way of Blame"

Martin Seligman says, _____

_____

_____

_____

REFLECT ON IT

Think about what you have learned in this unit. If you do not know an answer, review that concept.

1. List five types of words that require capitalization. For instance, the days of the week begin with capital letters.

_____

_____

2. Add hyphens, where necessary, to the following sentences.

He is a twenty five year old man who carries a small red book in his back pocket.

He has a high pressure job, but he remains relaxed at work.

3. Correct the six errors in punctuation and capitalization.

The famous cuban-american actor Andy Garcia was born in havana on april 12, 1956. He has made many films *The Godfather: Part III, Ocean's eleven,* and *The Untouchables.*

FINAL REVIEW

Correct fifteen capitalization and punctuation (colon and hyphen) errors in the next selection.

EXAMPLE:

Facebook developer Mark Zuckerman is a ~~self made~~ *self-made* millionaire.

1. MySpace and facebook have become extremely popular in recent years. Millions of people use such internet sites to reconnect with their long lost friends. Facebook's developer was a twenty-year old Harvard university student. Mark Zuckerberg launched the site in february 2004. The user friendly site fascinated the public. Researchers give three positive outcomes for people using such sites mastering new computer skills, sharing professional information, and increasing social contacts.

2. However, critics complain about privacy issues on these sites. In 2005, two Massachusetts Institute of technology students easily downloaded personal information of around 70,000 Facebook users. In 2008, the BBC program *click* also acquired personal information of Facebook clients.

3. People should be careful when using such sites. Avoid sharing the following your birthday, phone number, school, job, and embarrassing photos. Malicious people often search for such information to steal identities. In addition, around 25 percent of employers say that they check the pages of job applicants. For example, Luther Hudson, of Wayne and smith, a marketing firm, accessed the personal information of an interviewee on friday, august 6, at 220 p.m., about one hour after he had read the applicant's résumé. Hudson saw an embarrassing photo of the candidate mooning her friends. He thought the applicant lacked good judgment and would not fit into the culture of the company.

CHAPTER 36

The Writer's Room

Write about one of the following topics. Ensure that your capitalization and punctuation are correct.

1. Describe your work environment.

2. What types of jobs does society place a high value on? Describe at least three different categories or types of workers who get a lot of respect.

ESSAY LINK

The Workplace
"Aunt Tee" by Maya Angelou (page 554)
"Advertising Appeals" by Michael R. Solomon, Greg W. Marshall, and Elnora W. Stuart (page 557)
"Job Candidates and Facebook" by Wei Du (page 559)

The Writers' Circle **Collaborative Activity**

Work with a partner and think about a job that would interest you. Find a job advertisement from a newspaper, a magazine, or an Internet site. You could refer to one of the following sites.

www.monster.com www.jobs.net www.jobs.org

Compose a letter of application. In the first paragraph, explain what job you want, and tell where you heard about the job. In the second paragraph, briefly detail your qualities and experience. Then, in a third paragraph, explain your availability and how you can be contacted. Ask your partner to help you compose each part of the letter.

Remember to be as direct as possible. After you finish writing, proofread your letter and ensure that you have used correct punctuation and capitalization. Exchange letters with your partner, and proofread your partner's letter.

 mywritinglab To check your progress in meeting this chapter's objectives, log in to **www.mywritinglab.com**, go to the **Study Plan** tab, click on **The Editing Handbook—Section 8: Punctuation and Mechanics** and choose **Capitalization** and **Semicolons, Colons, Dashes, and Parentheses** from the list of subtopics. Read and view the resources in the **Review Materials** section, and then complete the **Recall, Apply,** and **Write** sets in the **Activities** section.

CHAPTER 36

Editing Paragraphs and Essays

EDITING PRACTICE

In this chapter, you will have opportunities to edit different pieces of writing.

After you finish writing the first draft of a paragraph or essay, it is important to edit your work. When you edit, you carefully review your writing to verify that your grammar, punctuation, sentence structure, and capitalization are correct. In this chapter, you can practice editing the types of written pieces that you see every day, including e-mail messages, paragraphs, essays, and business correspondence.

PRACTICE I

Correct 15 errors in the next selection. An editing symbol appears above each error. To understand the meaning of the symbol, refer to the chart on the inside back cover of this book.

1. Sargeant Leung Shiu-yuk's first experience with a <u>chinese</u> ^{cap} triad

    occurred when he was fourteen years old. The young Mr. Leung had an

    <u>arguement</u> ^{sp} with an acquaintance. The <u>classmates</u> ^p father aggressively

    claimed to be a triad member when he <u>comed</u> ^{vt} to see Mr. Leung's father

    about the schoolyard brawl. At that moment, Mr. Leung decided to

    <u>became</u> ^{vt} a policeman to combat organized crime in Hong Kong. Over the

    years, he has become <u>especialy</u> ^{sp} knowledgeable about triad operations. Mr.

    Leung <u>investigate</u> ^{agr} powerful Chinese triads. He is a <u>conscious</u> ^{wc} expert

    witness for the Hong Kong police.

2. Chinese triads <u>been involved</u> ^{vt} in illegal activities in the United States since

    the beginning of the twentieth century. <u>There</u> ^{wc} business includes the drug

    trade, human trafficking, and extortion. Chinese triads also defraud public

    and private <u>institution</u> ^{pl} such as health care, insurance, and investment.

    The triads can manipulate and transfer financial assets across international

    boundaries. Thus, they deceive investors <u>real</u> ^{ad} easily. Triads are <u>responsable</u> ^{sp}

    for much human misery. International police organizations are hopeful

    <u>than</u> ^{wc} they can erase these criminal organizations. Security forces must

    show perseverance to reach <u>his</u> ^{pro} goal.

PRACTICE 2   EDIT AN ESSAY

Correct twenty underlined errors in the next student essay. An editing symbol appears above each error.

Family Dynamics

1   One day, my brothers and <u>me</u> (pro) were discussing our childhood.

We had very distinct viewpoints about our experiences. We realized

that our opinions were <u>influence</u> (vt) by our birth position in the family.

Certainly, birth order has an impact on a person's personality.

2   <u>First time</u> (P) parents, unsure of what to do, <u>tends</u> (agr) to put a lot of

pressure on the firstborn child. Although the oldest child <u>benefited</u> (shift)

from the undivided attention of the parents, he or she also feels

<u>more</u> (ad) stronger pressure than the younger siblings. Oldest children

are most likely to conform to their <u>parents</u> (P) expectations and are

often compliant high achievers. For example, my brother made my

parents proud <u>who became a lawyer</u> (m).

3   Middle children have <u>certains</u> (ad) qualities that <u>sets</u> (agr) them apart.

Immediately, they must fight for their place in the limelight,

especially if they are the same sex <u>than</u> (wc) the eldest child. Middle

children, therefore, tend to learn how to manipulate others to get

what they <u>want, they</u> (ro) sometimes act out to get their parents'

attention. I am a middle child, and I rebelled. Of course, the

wc

attention than I received from my parents were not always

agr

positive, but attention is attention, and I needed it.

ad

4 By the time the youngest child is born, the parents are real

wc

relaxed and have less financial worries. Therefore, they tend to

spoil the baby of the family, letting the youngest get away with

mischief. In my family, my youngest brother did things that I would

wc   *frag*

of been punished for. Including staying out late and taking the car

without permission.

5 Being a parent is time-consuming, heartbreaking, and

//

a reward. Knowing about birth order can help people become

better parents. Nancy Samalin, in her book *Love and Anger: The*

Parental Dilemma, wrote, "Children will observe one another

p

closely and take advantage of any edge they can achieve".

PRACTICE 3 EDIT A PARAGRAPH

There are no editing symbols in the next paragraph. Proofread it as you would your
own writing, and correct fifteen errors.

Identity theft is the ilegal use of someones personal

information. It is a serious crime, in fact, last year there was

over 10 million cases of identity theft in the United States. To

find identities, thieves go threw recycling bins, empty

garbage cans, and stealing mail to obtain somebodys

personal information. Computer hackers can even steal

identities by tapping into personal information that persons keep on their computers. When a criminal has stolen a name, birthplace, address, and social security number, they can take out credit cards in the victim's name. For example, my co-worker, Nick Matsushita. He came home one day and found a large bill from a credit card company. Somebody had use his personal information to apply for credit. Nick and me are good friends, and I know that the identity theft has caused him alot of pain. He says that if he would have known about the way identity thieves work, he would have been more careful with his personal papers. Certainly, victims of identity theft loose time and money trying to fix the problem. To avoid being a victim, be prudent when sharing personal information.

PRACTICE 4   EDIT A WORKPLACE MEMO

Correct eight errors in the next excerpt from a memo.

CHAPTER 37

Re: Summer Vacations

As many of you know, each summers everybody wants to take their vacation at the same time. For this reason, employees are being ask to state your vacation preferences before next friday. Please sign the sheet posted on the bulletin board stating when you wanna take your time off. If you gotta good reason for needing a specific time period, please send Judy or I a memo explaining why.

Michael Rosen

Human Resources Department

PRACTICE 5   EDIT A PARAGRAPH

There are no editing symbols in the next paragraph. Proofread it as you would your own writing, and correct twelve errors.

Physicians overprescribe antibiotics and this practice is having a terrible effect on our health system. First, antibiotics are completely useless against viruses, yet alot of patients ask for and receive it when they have a simple cold. When drugs are overprescribed, some bacterial infections become drugs-resistant. Malaria and tuberculosis for example, are more difficult to treat than they were twenty years ago. The problem is especialy serious in hospitals. According to Dr. Ricki Lewis, antibiotic-resistant infections spread rapidly in a hospital environment. Furthermore, patients who are criticaly ill requires large doses of drugs who cause bacteria to mutate rapidly. We should remember that the body can fight many illnesses on its own. For instance, some common ear infections. Before accepting a prescription, consumers should ask whether antibiotics are necessary. There are problems enough in this world, the population does not need to create new illnesses by overusing antibiotics.

PRACTICE 6

Correct twelve errors in the next essay.

1.   Reid Radnor works for the American military. He, along with his wife, live on the army base in Seoul, South Korea. The base sits in the heart of the city. Everyone think that it looks like a 1950s suburb in america. It has split-level houses, schools, a movie theater, a hotel, and much more.

2.   Reid and his colleagues program computer software for the Army. In Reids office, everybody gets along. Many even socializes outside the office. Reid and his friends often play baseball at the base's baseball diamond. Occasionaly, someone proposes that they watch a movie. Sometimes, either Reid or his friends suggest lunch at the resort hotel. The food. It comes from the United States. In fact, on the base, everything originates in America. Nobody are supposed to feel homesick.

3.   The base is at the center of controversy in Korea, it symbolizes American dominance. Koreans want the military base to move away from Seoul. Some Koreans hope to built a city park on the land. Others wish to construct more housing. The Koreans have mixed feelings about American military presence in they're country.

PRACTICE 7   EDIT A FORMAL LETTER

Correct fifteen errors in the next letter.

Ari Praz

278 First avenue

New York, NY 10009

July 6, 2010

New York Department of Finance

Hearing-by-Mail Unit

P.O. Box 29201

Brooklyn, New York 11202

Subject: Ticket #4089-01411

Attention: Finance Department

I am writing to explain why am I pleading "not guilty" to a parking ticket I recieved on the morning of friday, june 24, 2010. Please read the following explanation and refer to the enclosed documents.

On the evening of june 23, I parked a rented car on the south side of 18th street. I knew I could park there legaly overnight until 8:30 a.m. At approximately 8:15 friday morning, I went to move the car from that parking space. When I arrived, I discovered that the front tire on the passenger side was flat. Unable to change the tire, I went to my apartment a few blocks away to phone the rental companys hotline. I think that I made the call at about 8:30 a.m. On the photocopies of Continentals service records, you will see they dispatched someone at 8:39 a.m. Unfortunately, while I was away from the car making that call, I received a ticket, it was written at 8:40 a.m.

I'm sure you can see why I am pleading "not guilty" to this parking offense. I have every intention of moving the car by the specified time, I was not able to do so until roadside assistance arrived to replace the flat tire.

Yours Truly,

Ari Praz

Ari Praz

Enclosures: 2

PRACTICE 8   EDIT AN ESSAY

Correct twenty errors in the next essay.

1   Sports surround us every day in the papers, on television, and on the radio. Some people criticize our sports-driven culture. Sports critics say that colleges' put young athletes on pedestals and do not emphasize the achievments of students in academic programs. In fact, athletes do not receive enough praise.

2   First, colleges with good sports teams gets a lot of publicity. For example, during the football season, three national television channels covers the games CBS, NBC, and ABC. During the basketball playoffs, March Madness CBS covers the games. The publicity that colleges receive from sports bring more students to the academic programs. Sports help these programs, they do not harm them.

3   In addition, colleges and universities make money from their student athletes. For example, the National Collegiate athletic association (NCAA), the organization devoted to the administration of intercollegiate athletics in the United States, showed $422.2 millions in revenue in its 2002-2003 budget. A large part of this money come from television. Most of the money is redistributed to colleges and universities. Educational institutions use the funds not only for their sports programs but also are giving money to academic programs. Clearly, colleges show good long-term planning when they promote star athletes.

4   Moreover, sports are a motivation for athletes to go to college. Last year, there was about 360,000 student athletes in NCAA-

affiliated colleges. Over 126,000 of thoses athletes received either a partial or a full scholarship. Therefore, they were real motivated. To attend postsecondary institutions.

5   Colleges and universities are right to pay special attention to athletes and sports programs. Because of the extra effort that student athletes must give to suceed, and because of the publicity and money that educational institutions receive from sports programs and their athletes colleges and universities have a serious obligation to encourage there athletes.

mywritinglab   To check your progress in meeting this chapter's objectives, log in to **www.mywritinglab.com**, go to the **Study Plan** tab, click on **The Editing Handbook—Section 9: Editing** and choose **Editing the Paragraph and Editing the Essay** from the list of subtopics. Read and view the resources in the **Review Materials** section, and then complete the **Recall, Apply,** and **Write** sets in the **Activities** section.

CHAPTER 37

Reading Strategies and Selections

In the first part of Chapter 38, you will learn strategies that can help you improve your reading skills. Later in the chapter, you will see a number of thought-provoking essays that present a wide range of viewpoints about topics related to political intrigue, psychology, espionage, great discoveries, college life, health care, the legal world, and the workplace.

As you read each essay, think about how the writer achieves his or her purpose using one or more of these writing patterns:

- **Illustration**
- **Narration**
- **Description**
- **Process**
- **Definition**
- **Classification**
- **Comparison and Contrast**
- **Cause and Effect**
- **Argument**

From Reading to Writing

Aspiring songwriters and musicians study different musical styles to determine which lyrics, notes, rhythms, and so on work well together. In the same way, by reading different pieces of writing, you can observe which elements other writers use and how they use them. Then, you can try applying the same principles to your own writing.

 Reading is to the mind what exercise is to the body. 🟠

—SIR RICHARD STEELE
Irish author

Reading Strategies

When you read, you also develop your writing skills. You expand your vocabulary and learn how other writers develop topics. In addition, you learn to recognize and use different writing patterns. Finally, reading helps you find ideas for your own paragraphs and essays.

The next strategies can help you become a more successful reader and writer. They guide you through the reading process and provide useful tips for getting specific information from a piece of writing.

Previewing

Previewing is like window shopping; it gives you a chance to see what the writer is offering. When you preview, look quickly for visual clues so that you can determine the selection's key points. Review the following:

- Titles or subheadings (if any)
- The first and last sentences of the introduction
- The first sentence of each paragraph

- The concluding sentences of the selection
- Any photos, graphs, or charts

Finding the Main Idea

After you finish previewing, read the selection carefully. Search for the **main idea,** which is the central point that the writer is trying to make. In an essay, the main idea usually appears somewhere in the first few paragraphs in the form of a thesis statement. However, some professional writers build up to the main idea and state it only in the middle or at the end of the essay. Additionally, some professional writers do not state the main idea directly.

 **Making a Statement of the Main Idea**

If a reading does not contain a clear thesis statement, you can determine the main idea by asking yourself *who, what, when, where, why,* and *how* questions. Then, using the answers to those questions, write a statement that sums up the main point of the reading.

Making Inferences

If a professional writer does not state the main idea directly, you must look for clues that will help you **infer** or figure out what the writer means to say. For example, read the next paragraph and try to infer the writer's meaning.

> The band cost about $4,500 for the night. The hall rented for $900, and we figured we got a good deal. We had to decorate it ourselves. There were flowers on every table ($25 for each bouquet), rented china and silverware ($1,850), and tablecloths, tables, and chairs ($900). The catered food worked out to be $40 per person, multiplied by 300. This is not counting the dresses, the tuxedos, the photographer, or the rented limos. Sure, it was a special night. It is too bad the guests of honor split up three months later.

■ PRACTICE I

Read the preceding paragraph. Then answer the following questions.

1. What is the subject of the paragraph? _____

2. What is the writer's relationship to the guests of honor? _____

   _____

3. What is the writer's main point? _____

Finding the Supporting Ideas

Different writers use different types of supporting ideas. They may give steps for a process, use examples to illustrate a point, give reasons for an argument, and so on. Try to identify the author's supporting ideas.

Highlighting and Making Annotations

After you read a long text, you may forget some of the author's ideas. To help you remember and quickly find the important points, you can highlight key ideas and make annotations. An **annotation** is a comment, question, or reaction that you write in the margin of a page.

Each time you read a passage, follow the next steps.

- Look in the introductory and concluding paragraphs. Underline sentences that sum up the main idea. Using your own words, rewrite the main idea in the margin.
- Underline or highlight supporting ideas. You might even number the arguments or ideas. This will allow you to understand the essay's development.
- Circle words that you do not understand.
- Write questions in the margin if you do not understand the author's meaning.
- Write notes beside passages that are interesting or that relate to your own experiences.
- Jot down any ideas that might make interesting writing topics.

Here is an annotated passage from an essay titled "Don't Worry, Act Happy" by Albert Nerenberg.

1   Robert Kall is a Philadelphia-based Positive Psychology conference organizer. While working as a therapist, he tried simple smiling as a way to treat depression. "I would put surface electrodes on the smile muscles in people's faces and, using electromyography, would measure the strength of their smiles," he said. "People who were not depressed had smile muscles that were on average four times stronger than people who were depressed," he said. This amazed him. So he began developing what could only be described as a smiling exercise program. "I would have depressed people pump 'smile' iron," he said. "I would have them do repetitions: three sets of 12 every day." By naturally triggering smiles, the "smilercizers" would seem to drive themselves to happier states.

    — Expert opinion

    — Interesting finding

    — Experiment suggests that happiness can be achieved by smiling

    — I should try it.

    — "smilercizers" —made-up word

2   There's good reason why people resist the Act Happy concept. In primordial situations, fake and phony emotions might suggest a trap or danger. We're naturally suspicious around fake smiles, and forced laughter suggests fraud. We gauge our trust in others by their smiles. A put-on smile may suggest dishonesty and therefore danger, and phony laughter may signal manipulation. However, when using emotions to drive positive states, the dishonesty may not matter.

    — What does "primordial" mean?

    — Reasons humans don't like fake smiles.

    — I don't like fake smiles.

Understanding Difficult Words

When you read, you will sometimes come across unfamiliar words. You can try to guess the word's meaning, or you can circle it and look it up later.

Using Context Clues

Context clues are hints in the text that help define a word. To find a word's meaning, try the following strategies.

- **Look at the word.** Is it a noun, a verb, or an adjective? Sometimes it is easier to understand a word if you know how that word functions in the sentence.

- **Look at surrounding words.** Look at the sentence in which the word appears and try to find a relation between the difficult word and the words that surround it. Maybe there is a **synonym** (a word that means the same thing) or an **antonym** (a word that means the opposite). Maybe other words in the sentence help define the word.

- **Look at surrounding sentences.** Sometimes you can guess the meaning of a difficult word by looking at the sentences, paragraphs, and punctuation surrounding the word. When you use your logic, the meaning becomes clear.

PRACTICE 2

1. Can you easily define the word *affluence?*   Yes   No

2. Can you easily define the word *plagued?*   Yes   No

3. If you do not understand the meanings of those two words, then read them in the context of the next paragraph. You will notice that it is much easier to guess their meanings.

> John Macionis writes in his book, *Sociology,* that until a few centuries ago, the entire world was poor. But some researchers claim that it is **affluence** that demands an explanation. Affluence came within reach of a growing share of people in Western Europe during the late Middle Ages as world trade expanded. Then industrial technology created new wealth and gradually improved the living standard of even the poorest people. Poverty, which had **plagued** humanity throughout history, was finally in decline.

Now write your own definition of the words as they are used in the paragraph.

1. affluence: _____

2. plagued: _____

 **Cognates**

Cognates, or word twins, are English words that may look and sound like words in another language. For example, the English word *responsible* is similar to the Spanish word *responsable,* although the words are spelled differently.

  If English is not your first language, and you read an English word that looks similar to a word in your language, check how it is being used in context. It may, or may not, mean the same thing in English as it means in your language. For example, in English, *assist* means "to help." In Spanish, *assistar* means "to attend." If you are not sure of a word's meaning, consult a dictionary.

Using a Dictionary

If you do not understand the meaning of an unfamiliar word after using context clues, look up the word in a dictionary. A dictionary is useful if you use it correctly. Review the following tips for dictionary usage.

- **Look at the dictionary's frontmatter.** The preface contains explanations about the various symbols and abbreviations.

- **Read all of the definitions listed for the word.** Look for the meaning that best fits the context of your sentence.
- **Look up root words, if necessary.** If the difficult word has a prefix such as *un-* or *anti-*, you may have to look up the root word.

Here is an example of how dictionaries set up their definitions.

Word Division
Your dictionary may use black dots to indicate places for dividing words.

Stress Symbol (′) and Pronunciation
Some dictionaries provide the phonetic pronunciation of words. The stress symbol (′) lets you know which syllable has the highest or loudest sound.

Parts of Speech
The *n* means that deception is a noun. If you don't understand the parts of speech symbol, look in the front or the back of your dictionary for a list of symbols and their meanings.

de•cep′tion / [di-sep′shən] / *n* 1, the act of misleading. 2, a misrepresentation; artiface; fraud.

From *The New American Webster Handy College Dictionary*
(New York: Signet, 2000) 606.

From Reading to Writing

After you finish reading a selection, try these strategies to make sure that you have understood it.

- **Summarize the reading.** When you summarize, you use your own words to write a condensed version of the reading. You leave out all information except the main points.
- **Outline the reading.** An outline is a visual plan of the reading. First, write down the main idea of the essay, and then note the most important idea from each paragraph. Under each idea, include a detail or an example.

Make a Written Response

Your instructor may ask you to write about your reaction to a reading. These are some questions you might ask yourself before you make a written response.

- What is the writer's main point?
- What is the writer's purpose? Is the writer trying to entertain me, persuade me, or inform me?
- Who is the audience? Is the writer directing his or her message at someone like me?
- Do I agree or disagree with the writer's main point?
- What aspects of the topic can I relate to?

After you answer the questions, you will have more ideas to use in your written response.

Reading Selections

Themes: **Popular Culture and College Life**
READING 1

Bound Feet
Jung Chang

Jung Chang was born in Yibin, China, and teaches Oriental and African studies at London University. In the next excerpt from her novel, *Wild Swans, Three Daughters of China*, Chang writes about her grandmother. As you read this descriptive essay, also look for elements of the narration and process writing patterns.

1   My grandmother was a beauty. She had an oval face with rosy cheeks and lustrous skin. Her long, shiny black hair was woven into a thick plait reaching down to her waist. She could be demure when the occasion demanded, which was most of the time, but underneath her composed exterior she was bursting with suppressed energy. She was petite, about five feet three inches, with a slender figure and sloping shoulders, which were considered the ideal.

2   But her greatest assets were her bound feet, called in Chinese "three-inch golden lilies" (*san-tsun-gin-lian*). This meant she walked "like a tender young **willow shoot** in a spring breeze," as Chinese connoisseurs of women traditionally put it. The sight of a woman **teetering** on bound feet was supposed to have an erotic effect on men, partly because her vulnerability induced a feeling of protectiveness in the onlooker.

3   My grandmother's feet had been bound when she was two years old. Her mother, who herself had bound feet, first wound a piece of white cloth about twenty feet long round her feet, bending all the toes except the big toe inward and under the sole. Then she placed a large stone on top to crush the arch. My grandmother screamed in agony and begged her to stop. Her mother had to stick a cloth into her mouth to gag her. My grandmother passed out repeatedly from the pain.

4   The process lasted several years. Even after the bones had been broken, the feet had to be bound day and night in thick cloth because the moment they were released they would try to recover. For years my grandmother lived in relentless, **excruciating** pain. When she pleaded with her mother to untie the bindings, her mother would weep and tell her that unbound feet would ruin her entire life and that she was doing it for her future happiness.

5   In those days, when a woman was married, the first thing the bridegroom's family did was to examine her feet. Large feet, meaning normal feet, were considered to bring shame on the husband's household. The mother-in-law would lift the hem of the bride's long skirt, and if the feet were more than about four inches long, she would throw down the skirt in a demonstrative gesture of **contempt** and stalk off, leaving the bride to the critical gaze of the wedding guests, who would stare at her feet and insultingly mutter their **disdain.** Sometimes a mother would take pity on her daughter and remove the binding cloth, but when the child grew up and had to endure the contempt of her husband's family and the disapproval of society, she would blame her mother for having been too weak.

willow shoot:
the new growth of a willow tree

teetering:
walking unsteadily

excruciating:
extremely painful

contempt:
disapproval

disdain:
disapproval

6 The practice of binding feet was originally introduced about a thousand years ago, allegedly by a concubine of the emperor. Not only was the sight of women hobbling on tiny feet considered erotic, men would also get excited playing with bound feet, which were always hidden in embroidered silk shoes. Women could not remove the binding cloths even when they were adults, as their feet would start growing again. The binding could only be loosened temporarily at night in bed, when they would put on soft-soled shoes. Men rarely saw naked bound feet, which were usually covered in rotting flesh and stank when the bindings were removed. As a child, I can remember my grandmother being in constant pain. When we came home from shopping, the first thing she would do was soak her feet in a bowl of hot water, sighing with relief as she did so. Then she would set about cutting off pieces of dead skin. The pain came not only from the broken bones, but also from her toenails, which grew into the balls of her feet.

7 In fact, my grandmother's feet were bound just at the moment when foot-binding was disappearing for good. By time her sister was born in 1917, the practice had virtually been abandoned, so she escaped the torment. However, when my grandmother was growing up, the prevailing attitude in a small town like Yixian was still that bound feet were essential for a good marriage.

VOCABULARY AND COMPREHENSION

1. Find a word in paragraph 1 that means "modest, quiet, and reserved."

    _____

2. In the past, why were Chinese women's feet bound?

    _____

    _____

    _____

3. Did the author's grandmother choose to have bound feet? Support your answer with evidence from the reading.

    _____

    _____

    _____

4. The author describes the process of binding feet. List the steps in the process.

    _____

    _____

    _____

    _____

CRITICAL THINKING

5. Why would women who had been through the pain of foot-binding subject their daughters to the same torture? Think of some reasons.

    _____

    _____

    _____

    _____

6. Underline some of the most effective images in Chang's narrative.

7. What is the narrator's point of view about her grandmother's bound feet? Look for clues in the text.

_____

_____

_____

Writing Topics

Write about one of the following topics. Remember to explore, develop, and revise and edit your work.

1. This reading describes a painful process that Chinese women went through in the past. Although foot binding seems shocking and distasteful, there are parallels in contemporary society. Explain how people alter their bodies today. Try to use descriptive imagery.

2. Describe an incident from the childhood of your parent or grandparent. Try to use descriptive imagery.

3. Reflect on Thoreau's quotation. Compare and contrast some old fashions that people laugh at and new fashions that they follow.

> *Every generation laughs at the old fashions, but follows religiously the new.*
> —HENRY DAVID THOREAU, AMERICAN AUTHOR

READING 2

Being a Hyphenated American
Zaina Arafat

> Zaina Arafat is a young Arab-American. In the next essay, she reflects on identity and culture. As you read this definition essay, also look for elements of narration and comparison and contrast.

1   During the 1991 Persian Gulf War, I came home from school one day in tears. My classmates had been ridiculing me, and when I told my mother, she went straight to the administration. She said that during this particularly emotional time, they should make extra efforts to prevent discrimination against Arab-American students. They agreed, and assured her that they would. Months later, I came home complaining of the same torment: "They're still calling me fat! Zaina AraFAT!" Right then, my mother realized the teasing had nothing to do with my ethnic background. It was simply kids being kids. As a first-generation Arab-American, my ethnic duality has exposed me to a series of assumptions that stem from both ignorance and fear of the unknown. But these assumptions exist on both sides.

2   My parents moved to the United States from the West Bank a year before I was born. Growing up in the suburbs of Washington, D.C., my family seemed just like everyone else's, with a few variations that most wouldn't have noticed. For example, while my friends' fathers cracked open a bag of chips after work, my dad went straight for pumpkin seeds. My friends' moms drove minivans;

mine, a two-seater. Their parents were big on curfews, grammar, "time outs," and seat belts. Soda was strictly forbidden in their houses, as were Cocoa Puffs for breakfast, and television was allowed only on weekends.

3   I really didn't understand these rules. Since the American tendency toward overparenting contradicted my parents' Mediterranean, **laissez-faire** approach, the structure and what I saw as rigidity that existed in my friends' houses were absent in ours. Rather, our family was informal and spontaneous.

laissez-faire: permissive

4   My friends found much in my life to be confused by, too, such as why my mom and dad called me mom and dad, as is tradition in Arab culture. They wondered why my parents and their friends seemed to be yelling at each other whenever they conversed, why every social gathering inevitably ended with dancing, and why our nicknames were longer than our actual ones: Zanzoon for Zaina; Abu Zooz for my brother, Zaid.

5   As a kid, I was insecure about the nuances that set us apart, especially when friends asked for a bologna sandwich as soon as they saw whatever we were serving. But as I grew older, I began to appreciate my parents' attempt to assimilate while retaining our own traditions. We always had a turkey on Thanksgiving—that it was stuffed with rice and served with **hummus** seemed a fair compromise.

hummus: a spread made with chickpeas, lemon, garlic, and salt, very common in Middle Eastern cooking.

6   I found that while being an Arab-American in the US got better with age, the reverse applied when I visited the Middle East. As a kid, I couldn't wait for these summer excursions. The moment I arrived in Jordan, where my extended family lives, I felt like a celebrity. I was coming from America, and that alone brought me relative fame and adoration. But eventually, things began to change. No longer able to get a free ride because of my American identity, I found there were many unspoken rules that were unfamiliar to me, such as when to put out my hand versus going for the cheek, and if the latter, two kisses or three? Also, no one wears shorts past the age of twelve. (Once on a visit to Bethlehem, my uncle had to trade me his trousers for my cutoffs.)

7   Despite the humbling, awkward moments that accompanied these lessons, I've begun to accept the potential for mistakes as an inevitable cross-cultural byproduct. And in doing so, I've realized that being Arab-American has different meanings, depending on where I am. In the Middle East, it often means having to stress that Americans shouldn't be equated with their country's foreign policy. In the US, it involves explaining that the Islamists shown on television represent a sliver of the Muslim population. It also entails reminding Americans that while **Al Jazeera** may seem oversensationalized, American media seems sanitized to Arabs.

Al Jazeera: a news network based out of Qatar.

8   In many ways, "having a foot in both worlds" means having a full presence in neither. Although the phrase isn't meant to be interpreted literally, after twenty-seven years of balancing between two cultures and continents, I can say with certainty that it's far from figurative. But it's from such a vantage point that stereotypes are abolished. And as I get further away from a cultural identity crisis—and as a Kenyan-American was able to become US president—I realize that having dual ethnicity may be a great thing after all.

Vocabulary and Comprehension

1.   In paragraph 5, what does the word *nuances* mean?
        a. colors   b. problems   c. differences

2. Find a word in paragraph 6 that means the "second of two choices."

_____

3a. Where is the author's family from?

_____

3b. Where do they live presently?

_____

4. What were some cultural differences the author mentions between her "American" friends and her own family? List at least three differences.

_____

_____

_____

_____

CRITICAL THINKING

5. What is the significance of the title?

_____

_____

6. What example does the author use to show that her family tried to integrate into American society?

_____

_____

7. How does the author show that cultural misunderstandings are not just one-sided.

_____

_____

_____

_____

8. How does the author's attitude toward her dual heritage change?

_____

_____

WRITING TOPICS

Write about one of the following topics. Remember to explore, develop, and revise and edit your work.

1. In paragraph 8, the author writes, "'having a foot in both worlds' means having a full presence in neither." Do you agree or disagree with this statement? Give examples to support your ideas.
2. How do you define yourself, as an American or a hyphenated American? Explain your answer.

3.　Reflect on Paz's quote. America promotes itself as a melting pot rather than a mosaic. In your opinion, which idea is better?

❝ *What sets worlds in motion is the interplay of differences, their attraction and repulsions.* ❞
—Octavio Paz,
Mexican writer and diplomat

READING 3

Fads
David A. Locher

David A. Locher is an author and college professor at Missouri Southern State College. The next excerpt about fads is from his book *Collective Behavior*. As you read this classification essay, also look for elements of definition and illustration writing.

1　Fads can take a wide variety of forms. However, almost all fads have a common pattern. They always appear quickly. They seem to come from nowhere and suddenly occupy the attention of virtually everyone. Then, as quickly as they came, they fade from popularity. Most fads can be placed into one of three general categories: activity fads, product fads, and fashion or apparel fads.

2　Activity fads center on some leisure activity like breakdancing or rollerblading. People suddenly feel excited about taking part in an activity that has never seemed appealing before. Prior to the 1950s, nobody felt the urge to stuff themselves into a phone booth with a large number of other people, and few have done it since then. However, it was all the rage for several years in the 1950s. Disco dancing came and (thankfully) went. Manufacturers often capitalize on these fads by producing a range of accessories to go with the activity. Often, music and movies that relate to the activity are rushed into production in an attempt to cash in on the fad before it ends. The song "The Streak," by Ray Stevens, and the film *Wheels* (a skateboarding film) are both good examples of attempts to make money from fad participants.

3　Useful product fads center on the acquisition of products that serve some purpose, however unimportant. In late 1998, "onion-bloom machines" suddenly became popular. Millions of Americans bought this kitchen tool designed to cut a large onion into a ready-to-fry "bloom" similar to the popular fried "onion blooms" served in restaurants. They were advertised on television almost every night. Stores quickly sold out their supply of the devices. The product itself is relatively useful, or at least serves some function. In this case, it makes a kind of variation of onion rings. However, the product is neither particularly necessary nor terribly important. The vast majority of onion-bloom machines are probably gathering dust in kitchen cabinets and closets all over the United States. Like many products at the center of these fads, onion-bloom machines remain on the market, but prices and demand dropped dramatically once the initial excitement wore off and people no longer felt the need for such a product in their lives.

4　Frivolous product fads may be the most interesting of all. People may stand in line for hours, fight with each other, and spend hundreds or thousands of dollars just so they can own something that is useless. The Pet Rock is the ideal example of this type of fad. In late 1975, an entrepreneur marketed a plain rock in a cardboard box called "The Pet Rock" and sold over one million at five dollars each. The Pet Rock was not decorated, nor did it do anything. It was, in fact, an ordinary rock. Today it may seem difficult to understand why one million Americans would pay 5 dollars for a stone, particularly in 1975 when 5 dollars could buy a meal or two tickets to the movies. Such is the nature of useless product fads. They are always difficult to explain or understand after they end.

5   Fashion fads may or may not involve the purchase of a particular item. For example, millions of American women purchased and wore "leg warmers" in the 1980s. These wooly socks without feet were worn over pants or stockings and were used for their look, rather than practical function. Other fashion-related fads may not involve buying anything. In late 1999, at the University of Missouri in Columbia, Missouri, hundreds of young women on campus began wearing their hair loosely gathered into a small ponytail that stuck straight up from the top of their head. The only accessory required was a rubber band. No products were purchased. The rapid adoption of the unflattering look and its relatively rapid disappearance would categorize the hairstyle as a fad.

6   Fads usually seem strange or even ridiculous in hindsight. Looking back, it is hard to believe that hundreds, thousands, or even millions of Americans took part in bizarre fads such as pole sitting, phone booth stuffing, and breakdancing. What drives otherwise normal people to pay money for a rock, to jump from a bridge or crane attached to a bungee cord, or to stand in freezing weather for hours in order to run, push, shove, and fight over a thirty-dollar talking toy? According to Turner and Killian, in their book *Collective Behavior*, there is nothing wrong with the participants in fads. Most of them are ordinary people. It is the situation that is abnormal. Once confusion and uncertainty set in, people can potentially be led into unusual behavior.

VOCABULARY AND COMPREHENSION

1. Find a slang expression in paragraph 2 that means "popular."

    _____

2. How does Locher define a fad?

    _____

    _____

3. Underline the thesis statement in this essay.

4. Locher divides one of the categories mentioned in the thesis statement into two subcategories. What are they?

    _____

5. Give examples of the characteristics of each fad Locher mentions.

    _____

    _____

    _____

    _____

    _____

    _____

CRITICAL THINKING

6. Locher clearly dislikes some of the fads. Which fads does he directly criticize?

   _____

   _____

7. Who benefits the most when a product becomes a fad?

   _____

8. Why do fads disappear?

   _____

   _____

WRITING TOPICS

Write about one of the following topics. Remember to explore, develop, and revise and edit your work.

1. What fads have you followed? Have you bought something silly, joined in an activity that was suddenly popular, or worn your hair in a trendy style? Describe one or more fads that you have followed.
2. Write a classification paragraph or an essay about other types of fads. Make sure the fads are linked by a common classification principle. For example, you might write about types of body improvement fads or types of hair fads, or you might break down fashion fads or activity fads into categories.
3. Reflect on Shaw's quotation. Why do you think some people are motivated to create or follow fads?

> *A fashion is nothing but an induced epidemic.*
> —GEORGE BERNARD SHAW,
> IRISH AUTHOR

READING 4

It's Class, Stupid!

Richard Rodriguez

Richard Rodriguez is a writer and an essayist who published the novel *Days of Obligation*. He also writes for the *Los Angeles Times* and *Harper's*. The next selection is an argument essay about affirmative action that originally appeared in the webzine *Salon.com*. As you read, also look for elements of the comparison and contrast writing pattern.

1   Some weeks ago, a law professor at the University of Texas got in trouble for saying that African Americans and Mexicans are at a disadvantage in higher education because they come from cultures that tolerate failure. Jesse Jackson flew to Austin to deliver a fiery speech; students demanded the professor's **ouster.**

ouster: dismissal

2   It was all typical of the way we have debated affirmative action for years. Both sides ended up arguing about race and ethnicity; both sides ignored the deeper issue of social inequality. Even now, as affirmative action is finished in California and is being challenged in many other states, nobody is really saying what is wrong with affirmative action: It is unfair to poor whites.

3   Americans find it hard to talk about what Europeans more easily call the lower class. We find it easier to sneer at the white poor—the "rednecks," the

du jour:

French term meaning "of the day" or "at the present time"

trailer-park trash. The rural white male is Hollywood's politically correct villain du jour.

4   We seem much more comfortable worrying about race; it's our most important metaphor for social distinction. We talk about the difference between black and white, not the difference between rich and poor. American writers—Richard Wright, James Baldwin, Toni Morrison—are brilliant at describing what it is like to be a racial minority. But America has few writers who describe as well what it is like to be poor. We don't have a writer of the stature of D.H. Lawrence—the son of an English coal miner—who grew up embarrassed by his soft hands. At the University of Texas, it was easier for the Sicilian-born professor Lino Graglia to notice that the students who dropped out of school were Mexican-American or black than to wonder if they might be poor.

5   At the same time, the angry students who accused the law professor of racism never bothered to acknowledge the obvious: Poor students *do* often come from neighborhoods and from families that tolerate failure or at least have learned the wisdom of slight expectations. Education is fine, if it works. I meet young people all the time who want to go to college, but Mama needs her oldest son to start working. It is better to have a dollar-and-cents job working at Safeway or McDonald's than a college diploma that might not guarantee a job.

6   Anyone who has taught poor children knows how hard it is to persuade students not to be afraid of success. There is the boy who is mocked by male classmates for speaking good English. There is the girl who comes from a family where women are not assumed to need, or want, education.

7   We also don't like to admit, though we have argued its merits for twenty years, that the chief beneficiaries of affirmative action—black, brown, female—are primarily middle class. It still doesn't occur to many progressives that affirmative action might be unfair to poor whites. That is because poor whites do not constitute an officially recognized minority group. We don't even notice the presence or, more likely, the absence of the poor white on college campuses. Our only acknowledgment of working-class existence is to wear fashionable working-class denim.

8   A man I know, when he went to Harvard, had only a pair of running shoes to wear and had never owned a tie. He dropped out of Harvard after two years. I suppose some of his teachers imagined it was because he was Hispanic, not that he was dirt poor. The advantage I had, besides my parents, were my Irish nuns—who themselves had grown up working class. They were free of that middle-class fear (typical today in middle-class teachers) of changing students too much. The nuns understood that education is not an exercise in self-esteem. They understood how much education costs, the price the heart pays.

9   Every once in a while, I meet middle-class Americans who were once lower class. They come from inner cities and from West Texas trailer parks. They are successful now beyond their dreams, but bewildered by loss, becoming so different from their parents. If only America would hear their stories, we might, at last, acknowledge social class. And we might know how to proceed, now that affirmative action is dead and so many poor kids remain to be educated.

VOCABULARY AND COMPREHENSION

1.   Find a word in paragraph 6 that means "made fun of."

_____

2. What does the word *constitute* in paragraph 7 mean? Circle the best answer.
    a. govern   b. appoint   c. represent

3. Look in the first two paragraphs and underline the thesis statement.

4. According to the author, what prevents many poor people from attending college? Give at least three reasons.

    _____

    _____

    _____

5. Who benefits the most from affirmative action, according to the author?

    _____

    _____

CRITICAL THINKING

6. Explain why Rodriquez disagrees with affirmative action.

    _____

    _____

    _____

    _____

7. The author compares the English writer D.H. Lawrence with American writers such as Toni Morrison. How is this comparison relevant for this essay?

    _____

    _____

    _____

    _____

8. In paragraph 1, Rodriquez includes an anecdote about a University of Texas law professor. Explain why you think the author agrees or disagrees with the professor.

    _____

    _____

    _____

9. The author writes that his teachers, Irish nuns with working-class backgrounds, "understood how much education costs, the price the heart pays." What does he mean? (Look in paragraphs 8 and 9 for clues.)

    _____

    _____

    _____

    _____

WRITING TOPICS

Write about one of the following topics. Remember to explore, develop, and revise and edit your work.

1. In your employment or education, have you had any positive or negative experiences because of your economic, gender, ethnic, or racial background?
2. Do you agree or disagree with the author's argument? Support your point of view with specific examples.
3. Reflect on Baldwin's quotation. What is his deeper meaning? Do you agree with him? Give examples or anecdotes to support your views.

READING 5

The Case for Affirmative Action
An Open Letter to Five Justices
Dave Malcolm

> Dave Malcolm is a professor in San Diego. In 1995, the following letter was entered into the *Congressional Record* by U.S. Representative Esteban Torres in response to anti–affirmative action decisions by the Supreme Court. As you read this argument essay, also look for elements of illustration, definition, and comparison and contrast.

1   On Monday, June 12, 1995, at 10:50 a.m., I left the office of my cardiologist having just been informed that my aortic valve implant was "leaking" and that replacement surgery would be required within the next three to six months. At 10:55 a.m., on the same date, I heard on my car radio about two new Supreme Court 5-4 decisions, each apparently placing serious additional limitations on programs of affirmative action. I drove homeward, feeling sick at heart—not from feelings of anxiety about my imminent open-heart surgery but from feelings of dismay at the direction in which the country seems to be moving, especially in regard to affirmative action.

2   You see, I know a lot about affirmative action. I count myself an expert on the subject. After all, I have benefited from it all my life. That is because I am white, I am male, I am Anglo, and I am Protestant. We male WASPs have had a great informal affirmative action program going for decades, maybe centuries. I am not speaking only of the way our "old boy networks" help people like me get into the right colleges or get jobs or get promotions. That is only the surface. Underneath, our real affirmative action is much more than just a few direct interventions at key moments in life. The real affirmative action is also indirect and at work twenty-four hours a day, seven days a week, year in and year out. Because it is informal and indirect, we tend to forget or deny just how all-important and pervasive it really is.

3   However, far be it from me to put the direct "old boy" surface stuff down. I was admitted without difficulty to the Ivy League college my father had attended. This was back in the days when the only quotas were quotas to keep certain people out, not to help them get in. There were no limits on reasonably bright kids like me—the admissions people spoke of the children of alumni as "legacies," but whether this was because the college was inheriting us as students or because the college hoped to inherit money from our families, I

was never quite sure. I got a teaching job right out of college in the heart of the Depression—my father was a school superintendent well liked among his colleagues.

4   After World War II, when I became a university professor, I received promotion and tenure in minimum time, more quickly than many of my female colleagues. Of course, the decision makers knew me better; I was part of the monthly poker group and played golf every Friday afternoon. Yes, direct affirmative action—direct preferential treatment because of my gender and my color and good connections—have been good to me.

5   But, like other white males, I have benefited less obviously but far more significantly from indirect preferential treatment. Indirect affirmative action is at work to a greater or lesser degree on behalf of virtually all white males, whether one is aware of it or not. It is what did not happen to me. There were destructive, painful experiences that I did not have to endure. Early in life, I knew that boys were more important than girls and so did the girls. I have never had to worry about whether my skin color was light enough or dark enough.

6   For two of my long-time colleagues and closest personal friends, it has been a very different story. Raymond was the lightest skinned member of his family. He recalls that he was the only one who could get his hair cut downtown—but the family had to drop him off a block away from the barber shop. He once told me that he had probably spent more time worrying about his light skin than any other one thing in life. Would his fellow African Americans think he was black enough? When whites thought he was East Indian or South American, should he let them think so?

7   Maria had the opposite problem. As a child, she was called *la prieta* ("the little dark one"). Even though she knew the **diminutive** was a mark of affection, she still was aware that the label was no compliment. When she became a young woman, well-meaning whites told her, "You don't look Mexican," meaning that she looked more Spanish and hence almost white. The message always hurt deeply not simply because the speakers personally so clearly believed that there was something inferior about being Mexican but also because they had unhesitatingly assumed that she did, too, and hence would consider such a statement to be a compliment.

diminutive: affectionate nickname

8   I have never had to endure "what-is-he-doing-here?" looks any time I walked along a residential street in a suburban area. I have not had to notice white women clutching their purses more tightly when they meet me walking along the street. I have never seen the "For Rent" or "For Sale" signs **figuratively** snatched out of the window as I walked up to the front door. I cannot even begin to imagine the insults, large and small, that send a five- or six-year-old running tearfully home to ask Mommy or Daddy, "Why can't I be white?"

figuratively: symbolically; not literally

9   Out of the dozens of times I have crossed the border from Tijuana to San Diego, the one time I was pulled over to have my car inspected was when returning with my friend, Raymond, and another African American male as passengers. I was furious, but my friends restrained me, assuring me it was no big deal and that it happened to them all the time. That day I got some small sense of the rage and fury and helplessness and frustration that some people experience daily and are forced to smother.

10   I have never been so bombarded by negative messages that I began to internalize them and to suspect they might in part be true. As a professional person, I have never had to carry the burden of knowing that the slightest mispronunciation or grammatical error on my part will be seized upon by

some people as validation of their negative stereotypes, not only about me but also about my people. But entire populations of my potential competitors have labored and are still laboring under disadvantages of this very sort as they compete with me. This is white male "affirmative action" at its most effective—the flip side of destructive life-long bombardment by negative messages.

11   Yes, affirmative action for some folks remains alive and well and unthreatened by court decisions. I ought to know. All my life I have been an indirect beneficiary because indirect affirmative action has been so effective at crippling or eliminating so many of those who might have been my competitors. As a white male, I have never had to compete with them on a level playing field.

12   The promise of the American dream is a society which is color-fair, not color-blind. Formal affirmative action programs play a dual role. They make the playing fields a bit more level, and they remind us that we still have far to go. It is no solution for society to trash its current formal efforts to make opportunity a little more equal as long as so many powerful informal barriers to equality of opportunity still persist. Think about it.

VOCABULARY AND COMPREHENSION

1.   What introduction style does the author use? Circle the best answer.

a. General background   b. Definition
c. Opposing position   d. Anecdote

2.   Using your own words, describe the main idea of this essay.

_____

_____

3.   How has the author benefited from indirect affirmative action? List some examples.

_____

_____

_____

_____

4.   What examples does the author give to illustrate that members of less-favored groups have to live with destructive, painful experiences?

_____

_____

_____

_____

CRITICAL THINKING

5.   Why was Malcolm promoted more quickly than his female colleagues?

_____

_____

6. Explain how a "For Rent" sign could be "figuratively snatched from a window" (paragraph 8).

_____

_____

7. What are Malcolm's main arguments for supporting affirmative action?

_____

_____

_____

_____

_____

8. Who is Dave Malcolm? What have you learned about him after reading this text? List characteristics that describe him, and make some educated guesses about his personality.

_____

_____

_____

_____

_____

_____

WRITING TOPICS

Write about one of the following topics. Remember to explore, develop, and revise and edit your work.

1. Compare Malcolm's view of affirmative action with the view expressed by Richard Rodriguez in the essay titled "It's Class, Stupid!" With whom do you agree, and why?
2. List examples of ways in which people are stereotyped. You can discuss age, appearance, race, and so on.
3. Reflect on Montesquieu's quotation. What is your view about equality? Should laws protect some members of society to ensure equal access to work, education, and housing? Why or why not?

> *All humans are born equal, but they cannot continue in this equality. Society makes them lose it, and they recover it only by the protection of the law.*
> —CHARLES DE MONTESQUIEU, PHILOSOPHER

Themes: Psychology and Health Care

READING 6

Religious Faith Versus Spirituality
Neil Bissoondath

Neil Bissoondath, a journalist and writer, was born in Trinidad and immigrated to Canada. His works include *A Casual Brutality* and *Digging Up the Mountains*. In the next selection, the author contrasts religion and spirituality. As you read this comparison and contrast essay, also look for elements of illustration, description, and argument writing.

1 *Wait till someone you love dies. You'll see. You'll know God exists. You'll want Him to.* The prediction, repeated with minimal variation through the years by believers challenged by my non-belief, was never offered as a promise but as a vague threat, and always with a sense of satisfied superiority, as if the speakers relished the thought that one day I would get my comeuppance. They were, without exception, enthusiastic practitioners of their respective faiths—Roman Catholics, Presbyterians, Hindus, Muslims, God-fearing people all. That was, to me, precisely the problem: Why all this fear?

2 And then one day, without warning, my mother died. Hers was the first death to touch me to the quick. Her cremation was done in the traditional Hindu manner. Under the direction of a **pundit,** my brother and I performed the ceremony, preparing the body with our bare hands, a contact more intimate than we'd ever had when she was alive. As I walked away from her flaming **pyre,** I felt myself soaring with a lightness I'd never known before. I was suddenly freed from days of physical and emotional **lassitude,** and felt my first inkling of the healing power of ritual, the solace that ceremony can bring.

3 Still, despite the pain and the unspeakable sense of loss, the oft-predicted discovery of faith eluded me. I remained, as I do today, a nonbeliever, but I have no doubt that I underwent a deeply spiritual experience. This was when I began to understand that religious faith and spirituality do not necessarily have anything to do with each other—not that they are incompatible but that they are often mutually exclusive.

4 Western civilization has spent two thousand years blurring the distinction between the two, and as we enter the third millennium we are hardly more at peace with ourselves than people were a thousand years ago. Appreciating the distinction could help soothe our anxieties about the days to come.

5 Spirituality is the individual's ability to wonder at, and delight in, the indecipherable, like a baby marveling at the wiggling of its own toes. It is to be at ease with speculation, asking the unanswerable question and accepting that any answer would necessarily be incomplete, even false. It is recognizing that if scientific inquiry has inevitable limits, so too do religious explanations, which base themselves on unquestioning acceptance of the unprovable: Neither can ever fully satisfy.

6 A sense of the spiritual comes from staring deep into the formation of a rose or a hibiscus and being astonished at the intricate delicacy of its symmetry without needing to see behind its perfection of form the fashioning hand of a deity.

7 It comes from watching your child being born and gazing for the first time into those newly opened eyes, from holding that child against your chest and feeling his or her heartbeat melding with yours.

8 It comes from gazing up into the sparkling solitude of a clear midnight sky, secure in the knowledge that, no matter how alone you may feel at moments, the message of the stars appears to be that you most indisputably are not.

9 At such moments, you need no **dogma** to tell you that the world seen or unseen, near or distant, is a wonderful and mysterious place. Spirituality, then, requires neither science nor religion, both of which hunger after answers and reassurance—while the essence of spirituality lies in the opening up of the individual to dazzlement. Spirituality entails no worship.

pundit:
Hindu priest

pyre:
a pile of burning wood used to cremate a dead body

lassitude:
weariness, fatigue

dogma:
a doctrine or set of beliefs unquestionably accepted as true

10   At the very moment of my mother's cremation, her brother, trapped thousands of miles away in England by airline schedules, got out his photographs of her and spread them on his coffee table. He reread her old letters and spent some time meditating on the life that had been lived—his way, at the very moment flames consumed her body, of celebrating the life and saying farewell, his way of engaging with the spiritual.

VOCABULARY AND COMPREHENSION

1.   Circle the best answer: In paragraph 1, *comeuppance* means

   a. rising up.   b. punishment.   c. reward.

2.   Write a synonym for the word *solace* in paragraph 2. _____

3.   How does Bissoondath define spirituality? Give examples from the essay.

   _____

   _____

4.   Why does the author object to believers who try to challenge his nonbelief?

   _____

   _____

CRITICAL THINKING

5.   How does the death of the author's mother change him?

   _____

   _____

6.   Why does the author give a lesser value to science and religion than to spirituality?

   _____

   _____

   _____

   _____

7.   To support his belief in spirituality, why does Bissoondath give the example of his uncle in paragraph 10?

   _____

   _____

   _____

8.   Bissoondath "soared with lightness" during the traditional Hindu ceremony and mentions the "healing power of ritual." Do you believe that such words contradict his strong opinions about religion? Explain your answer.

   _____

   _____

   _____

WRITING TOPICS

Write about one of the following topics. Remember to explore, develop, and revise and edit your work.

1. People cannot learn everything by reading books. Compare and contrast knowledge acquired through books to knowledge acquired through life experiences.
2. Compare and contrast two holidays, ceremonies, or festivals.
3. Reflect on the Hungarian proverb in the margin. What are some reasons that people have for believing in a god or a higher power?

> *The believer is happy; the doubter is wise.*
> —HUNGARIAN PROVERB

READING 7

Dancing with Fear

Bebe Moore Campbell

Bebe Moore Campbell, who passed away in 2006, was a newspaper writer, a commentator for National Public Radio, and a contributing editor for *Essence* magazine. She was also an award-winning novelist whose works include *Your Blues Ain't Like Mine* and *Brothers and Sisters*. In the next selection, the author expresses her thoughts about fear. As you read this definition essay, also look for elements of narration, description, and cause and effect writing.

1   The last day of my first marriage exploded into a final siege of screaming and hollering, doors slamming, and two cars speeding down the driveway, each in search of a demilitarized zone. The silence that followed was the kind that comes when night duty is wide-eyed and **protracted.** I woke up the next morning feeling tired, crazy, and evil. I drank two cups of black coffee and headed off to work because that is what tough sisters do. Little did I know that my weary mind was about to betray me.

protracted:
lasting; drawn out

2   That evening at the Metro station, I boarded the subway for home. Hemmed in by wilted commuters, I began to feel dizzy and uncomfortably light-headed. My heart started racing, perspiration dripped down my face causing my glasses to slide, and I had a hard time breathing. I felt as though I were stuck, trapped by the bogeyman of my worst childhood nightmares. I wanted to flee, but my body was frozen. There was no doubt in my mind that I was going crazy and dying at the same horrible time.

3   Somehow I managed to get off at the next stop, sit down on a bench, and slowly breathe in and out until that rhythm gradually calmed me. Several trains passed me by. When I finally did board one, I was a changed woman: My three-minute ordeal had marked me for life. I was scared as I rode to my destination, gripping a pole so tightly that there were marks on my moist palm. It's going to happen again, my mind told me. And it did.

4   I didn't know it then, but at twenty-seven I'd just had my first panic attack.

5   Panic is to fear what a wildfire is to a match. A panic attack is fear of fear, an irrational, out-of-control emotional response to an original panic that even experts can't pinpoint the source of. Childhood experiences, stress, genetics, caffeine, and insomnia can all play a role in panic disorder. More than the occasional bout of nerves that most people experience, true panic attacks are marked by a predictable pattern of **debilitating fear** and dread in response to specific stimuli, such as crowds, enclosed spaces, and driving on a freeway.

debilitating fear:
fear that is so great one cannot function

6   Ever since my first episode, I have been vulnerable, and not just in subways. I've had panic attacks while at concerts, on street corners, in hotel rooms, and in traffic. Whenever I think I have conquered the feeling, it simply chooses another space. For years, being on airplanes was a trigger. Now elevators are my challenge. In those split seconds when the doors close and the elevator is still, I battle the sensation of being swallowed up and trapped. For a long time, I have tried to shake this affliction and be normal like everybody else. I never dreamed that so many other Americans would become as haunted by the fear of fear as I am.

7   September 11 changed the collective American psyche as much as my first panic attack altered mine. I've spoken with people who admit that they are plagued by nightmares and worry. One New York manager I know had to let go of an employee who, many weeks after the World Trade Center collapsed, was still refusing to return to her Empire State Building office. Another businesswoman told me that the Manhattan apartment building she thought she had sold fell out of **escrow** immediately after the attack. Her prospective buyers admitted that they were too frightened to live in the city.

escrow:
a conditional contract

8   I know the feeling; I avoided subways for months after my first panic attack. And guess what? My fear only increased. In fact, the one guarantee about fear is this: Run from it, and it will find you.

9   You might say that I am a veteran of my own private war against terrorism. Since that long-ago day on the subway, I've learned how to dance with fear, which, in a nation now gripped by it, is a valuable skill. As I watch friends and family grapple with war's new tensions, I am struck by how far I've come. I have by no means conquered the panic that invaded my life all those years ago, but with time and effort I have learned to cope.

VOCABULARY AND COMPREHENSION

1.   What is an *affliction*? Look for context clues in paragraph 6.

   _____

2.   What is the author defining in her essay?

   _____

3.   What are the main symptoms of the author's panic attacks?

   _____

   _____

   _____

4.   In paragraph 5, the author uses an analogy. She compares two unusual things. What is the analogy, and why does she use such an analogy?

   _____

   _____

   _____

5.   Moore Campbell uses descriptive words and phrases that appeal to the senses. Underline at least three examples of descriptive imagery.

CRITICAL THINKING

6. What may have caused the author's first panic attack?

   _____

   _____

7. Why does the author compare her first panic attack with the fear caused by the terrorist attacks of September 11, 2001?

   _____

   _____

   _____

8. In the last paragraph, the author says that she has learned how to "dance with fear." What does she mean?

   _____

   _____

WRITING TOPICS

Write about one of the following topics. Remember to explore, develop, and revise and edit your work.

1. Compare your childhood fears with your adult fears. How are they similar or different? Remember to define your fears.
2. The author says that September 11, 2001, has changed the collective American psyche. Do you agree or disagree? Is the collective fear about terrorism over? Explain your answer and give examples.
3. Reflect on Young's quotation. Then define *courage*. Give examples to support your definition.

> 66 *Courage is one step ahead of fear.* 99
> —COLEMAN YOUNG, POLITICIAN

READING 8

Control Your Temper
Elizabeth Passarella

Elizabeth Passarella is a freelance writer and has written for *At Home Magazine*, *Latina*, and *Allure*. As you read this process essay, look for illustration and cause and effect writing patterns.

1   You don't have to be hot-headed for steam to come out of your ears. Sometimes it seems there are triggers everywhere: the man in your life who always needs help finding his keys, the boss who never notices your hard work, or the telemarketers who call at the worst time. The next thing you know, you've snapped, shed a few tears, or had a full-blown meltdown. So how do you keep your emotions from boiling over? Read on.

2   Mind the clock and calendar. Maybe you lose your temper with your assistant every morning, or you yell at your man if you've had a stressful day at work. Whenever you lose it, take note of the time and day. "When people are tired or stressed, they are more likely not to respond properly," says Hector Machabanski, Ph.D., a clinical psychologist in Chicago. "Do a postmortem

after you lose control. Learning what triggered your emotions gives you tools to manage them." Once you know when your fuses are at their lowest, you can schedule that meeting or date at a time when you tend to be calmer.

3   See the bigger picture. Being overly emotional usually stems from a deeper problem. Knowing the real issue can keep little things from making you crazy. "When you lose it, you are never attacking the real problem," says Carmen Inoa Vazquez, Ph.D., a New York City-based psychologist. Say you have a boss who always points out your mistakes. When you feel yourself ready to start crying or yelling, breathe deeply. Once you've calmed down (deep breaths are an instant emotion controller), think about how you can address the larger issue. You may realize you'll never be able to change your boss's behavior—only your reaction to it. Eventually, you'll learn to shrug him or her off.

4   Give yourself time-outs. Spend time alone, whether it's in the shower, in prayer, or at the gym, and think about why you lost control. Most important, create a strategy of self-control for next time. Maybe you need to hang up on telemarketers rather than argue with them. Or maybe you should get up fifteen minutes earlier so you can enjoy your coffee before you have to deal with the kids, instead of lashing out because they're throwing Cheerios while you're half-dressed for work.

5   Don't beat yourself up about losing control. Being emotional isn't always a bad thing. "We all rage, and we all feel sadness. And some cultures, like ours, are more expressive, more intense. It is acceptable to get excited and to shout," Vazquez says. "But we don't live on an island." In other words, if you hurt another person, you need to think about keeping your emotions in check. But if you just need to have a good cry or freak out a bit, you should. Just put away that glass vase first.

Vocabulary and Comprehension

1.   Find a word in paragraph 1 that means "activators" or "initiators."

     _____

2.   Find an example of slang in paragraph 5 that means "to get upset."

     _____

3.   What does this essay help readers do? Circle the best answer.

     a. complete a process   b. understand a process

4.   This essay does not contain an explicit thesis statement. Using your own words, write a thesis statement for this text.

     _____

     _____

5.   In your own words, list the four steps a person can take to control emotions.

     _____

     _____

     _____

     _____

CRITICAL THINKING

6. What is the author's specific purpose?

_____

7. How does the author add weight to her arguments?

_____

_____

8. In your opinion, how are the suggestions useful or impractical?

_____

_____

_____

WRITING TOPICS

Write about one of the following topics. Remember to explore, develop, and revise and edit your work.

1. Think about a time when you lost your temper. Describe the process that you went through during and after the event.
2. Passarella describes a process for controlling emotional outbursts. Describe a process that people should follow when they feel extremely impatient, nervous, or lonely.
3. Reflect on Queen Elizabeth's quotation. How is it applicable in your life? You might give examples of things that make you feel angry.

> *Anger makes dull men witty, but it keeps them poor.*
> —QUEEN ELIZABETH I, ENGLISH MONARCH

READING 9

Don't Worry, Act Happy
Albert Nerenberg

Albert Nerenberg is a writer, director, and journalist. He has worked on many projects about the power of laughter. In the next essay, Nerenberg reflects on the positive effects of smiling. As you read, notice how the author also uses elements of process and argument.

1 Acting. We usually think about it as the preserve of movie stars and annoying people with fake moustaches and bad accents. But a surging scientific theory says acting could make people happy. The Act Happy theory is that we get happier simply by going through the motions of contentment and joy. The theory arises from a controversial concept, sometimes called the body–mind principle, that emotions can be reverse engineered. It's simple: If we feel good, we may smile. But the surprising part is if we smile, we may feel good.

2 Although the Act Happy idea has been bouncing around for years, all of a sudden there's heat around it. There is increasing evidence that the opposite is true—acting enraged, obsessed, malevolent, or depressed may be bad for you. Actor Leonardo DiCaprio developed obsessive–compulsive disorder while playing Howard Hughes in the blockbuster *The Aviator*. In real life, Hughes had the disorder. Actor David Duchovny, who plays a writer obsessed with sex in the TV series *Californication*, just checked into a sex-addiction clinic. Batman star Christian Bale allegedly assaulted his mother and sister after

completing the violent and brooding *Dark Knight*. Heath Ledger played a tragic and maniacal Joker. Ledger, who had everything going for him, was allegedly clinically depressed. So if people can cultivate rage, depression, and death, can they cultivate joy, hilarity, love, and vitality? If the simple human smile is anything to go by, the answer is yes.

3   Smiling as exercise is both an ancient ritual and a cutting-edge one. A traditional Buddhist adage recommends smiling as the first conscious thing to do each day. Science may concur. Lee Berk, Associate Director of the Center for Neuroimmunology at Loma Linda University in California, was the first to demonstrate that "mirthful emotions" or "mirthful laughter" seem to increase the number of T cells, or immune cells, in the bloodstream.

4   Robert Kall is a Philadelphia-based Positive Psychology conference organizer. While working as a therapist, he tried simple smiling as a way to treat depression. "I would put surface electrodes on the smile muscles in people's faces and, using electromyography, would measure the strength of their smiles," he said. "People who were not depressed had smile muscles that were on average four times stronger than people who were depressed," he said. This amazed him. So he began developing what could only be described as a smiling exercise program. "I would have depressed people pump 'smile' iron," he said. "I would have them do repetitions: three sets of 12 every day." By naturally triggering smiles, the "smilercizers" would seem to drive themselves to happier states.

5   Kall warned people not to look at their reflections. "People are generally so self-critical that if they did the exercise in the mirror, they would focus on their perceived flaws rather than smile," he said. But people had positive feelings after their smiling exercises. And in some cases, patients reported that their depression lifted as a result of the exercise. Kall came out of the experience feeling there was a vast unexplored world out there.

6   There's good reason why people resist the Act Happy concept. In **primordial** situations, fake and phony emotions might suggest a trap or danger. We're naturally suspicious around fake smiles, and forced laughter suggests fraud. We gauge our trust in others by their smiles. A put-on smile may suggest dishonesty and therefore danger, and phony laughter may signal manipulation. However, when using emotions to drive positive states, the dishonesty may not matter.

primordial:
earliest times in the evolution of human beings

7   Smiling exercises might have been unintentionally applied in charm and etiquette schools. A quick poll finds many of these disciplinarian outfits formally include smile work. "We practice smiling over and over again," says Indiana-based Etiquette School owner Robin Thompson and author of *Be the Best You Can Be*. When asked whether she notices an improvement in the kids' moods when they practice smiling, she replied, "Absolutely, they're more up and perky." Tanisha Wright, who runs the Beautiful Beginnings Charm School in New Jersey, said her students would sometimes burst out laughing while exercising their smile.

8   According to Dr. Mark Stibich, a behavior change expert at the University of California, San Diego, smiling not only boosts the immune system and lowers blood pressure, it enhances other people's view of you. The weird thing about practicing positive emotion is that it makes others more apt to reciprocate. This outcome may be smiling's greatest benefit—connection with others. The Act Happy theory is still at the margins of formal science, but people are starting to run with it, probably because it seems to work. In

practice, the fear of phony emotion dissipates quickly and people find they smile and laugh more because they've become good at it.

9   Although it is often viewed with suspicion, acting may just represent a way to expand our emotional range. Acting comes naturally. Kids do it all the time. Since most people can learn to act, perhaps most could learn to Act Happy. If Heath Ledger's tragic torn smile has taught us anything, it may be that you are what you act. So be good to yourself and don't forget to smile.

VOCABULARY AND COMPREHENSION

1.   Find a word in paragraph 5 that means "defects."

     _____

2.   In paragraph 6 what does the word *gauge* mean?

     a. measure   b. develop   c. mistake

3.   Using your own words, describe the Act Happy theory.

     _____

     _____

4.   Why are people so reluctant to act happy if they don't feel happy?

     _____

     _____

5.   What psychological and physical changes does a person experience by acting happy?

     _____

     _____

     _____

6.   What types of support does the author use to prove his thesis?

     _____

     _____

     _____

CRITICAL THINKING

7.   Who would most benefit from trying out the Act Happy theory?

     _____

8.   Why does the author mention actors who portrayed depressed or disagreeable characters?

     _____

     _____

9.   What is significant about the word *Act* in the title of the essay?

     _____

     _____

Writing Topics

Write about one of the following topics. Remember to explore, develop, and revise and edit your work.

1. What makes you happy? Give examples and anecdotes to support your ideas.
2. Look at the photo and reflect on the meaning of happiness. Define happiness and give examples to support your definition.
3. Reflect on Doug Larson's quotation. What is the difference between happiness and contentment? Give examples to support your point.

READING 10

Musicophilia
Oliver Sachs

" The world is full of people looking for spectacular happiness while they snub contentment. "
—Doug Larson,
American author

Dr. Oliver Sachs is professor of neurology and psychiatry at Columbia University. He has written several best-selling books on case studies of people with neurological disorders. His book *Awakenings* (1973) was made into a film in 1990, starring Robin Williams. This excerpt is taken from his book, *Musicophilia*. As you read this narration essay, also look for patterns in cause and effect.

1   Tony Cicoria was forty-two, very fit and robust, a former college football player who had become a well-regarded orthopedic surgeon in a small city in upstate New York. He was at a lakeside pavilion for a family gathering one fall afternoon. It was pleasant and breezy, but he noticed a few storm clouds in the distance; it looked like rain.

2   He went to a pay phone outside the pavilion to make a quick call to his mother (this was in 1994, before the age of cell phones). He still remembers every single second of what happened next: "I was talking to my mother on the phone. There was a little bit of rain; there was thunder in the distance. My mother hung up. The phone was a foot away from where I was standing when I got struck. I remember a flash of light coming out of the phone. It hit me in the face. Next thing I remember, I was flying backwards. Bewildered, I looked around. I saw my own body on the ground. I said to myself, 'I'm dead.'"

3   The police came and wanted to call an ambulance, but Cicoria refused, delirious. They took him home instead, where he called his own doctor, a cardiologist. The cardiologist, when he saw him, thought Cicoria must have had a brief cardiac arrest, but could find nothing amiss with an examination or **EKG.** Cicoria also consulted a neurologist—he was feeling sluggish and having some difficulties with his memory. He found himself forgetting the names of people he knew well. A couple of weeks later, when his energy returned, Dr. Cicoria went back to work. There were still some lingering memory problems—he occasionally forgot the names of rare diseases or surgical procedures—but all his surgical skills were unimpaired. In another two weeks, his memory problems disappeared, and that, he thought, was the end of the matter.

4   What then happened still fills Cicoria with amazement, even now, a dozen years later. Life had returned to normal, seemingly, when "suddenly, over two or three days, there was this insatiable desire to listen to piano music." This was completely out of keeping with anything in his past. He had had a few piano lessons as a boy, he said, "but no real interest." He did not have a piano in his house. What music he did listen to tended to be rock music.

EKG:

electrocardiogram; a device that records electrical activity of the heart

5   With this sudden onset of craving for piano music, he began to buy recordings and became especially enamored of a Vladimir Ashkenazy recording of Chopin favorites—the "Military Polonaise," the "Winter Wind Étude," the "A-flat Polonaise," and the "B-flat Minor Scherzo." "I loved them all," Cicoria said. "I had the desire to play them. I ordered all the sheet music. At this point, one of our babysitters asked if she could store her piano in our house—so now, just when I craved one, a piano arrived, a nice little upright. It suited me fine. I could hardly read the music, could barely play, but I started to teach myself." It had been more than thirty years since the few piano lessons of his boyhood, and his fingers seemed stiff and awkward.

6   And then, on the heels of this sudden desire for piano music, Cicoria started to hear music in his head. "The first time," he said, "it was in a dream. I was in a tux, onstage; I was playing something I had written. I woke up, startled, and the music was still in my head. I jumped out of bed, started trying to write down as much of it as I could remember. But I hardly knew how to notate what I heard." This was not too successful—he had never tried to write or notate music before. But whenever he sat down at the piano to work on the Chopin, his own music "would come and take me over. It had a very powerful presence."

7   Now he had to wrestle not just with learning to play the Chopin, but to give form to the music continually running in his head, to try it out on the piano, and to get it on manuscript paper. "It was a terrible struggle," he said. "I would get up at four in the morning and play till I went to work, and when I got home from work, I was at the piano all evening. My wife was not really pleased. I was possessed."

8   In the third month after being struck by lightning, then, Cicoria—once an easygoing, genial family man, almost indifferent to music—was inspired, even possessed, by music, and scarcely had time for anything else. The music came, often, in "an absolute torrent" of notes with no breaks and no rests between them, and he would have to give it shape and form. Cicoria continued to work on his piano playing and his compositions. He got books on notation, and soon realized that he needed a music teacher. He would travel to concerts by his favorite performers but had nothing to do with musical friends in his own town or musical activities there. This was a solitary pursuit, between himself and his muse.

9   After a few years of practicing and playing, Cicoria took part in a ten-day music retreat for student musicians, gifted amateurs, and young professionals. It was, Cicoria felt, a good time and a good place to make his debut as a musician. He prepared two pieces for his concert: his first love, Chopin's "B-flat Minor Scherzo"; and his own first composition, which he called "Rhapsody, Opus 1." His playing, and his story, electrified everyone at the retreat. Many expressed the fantasy that they, too, might be struck by lightning. He played, said concert pianist Erica VanderLinde Feidner, with "great passion, great brio"—and if not with supernatural genius, at least with creditable skill, an astounding feat for someone with virtually no musical background who had taught himself to play at forty-two.

10   What caused Dr. Cicoria's remarkable access of musicality, his sudden musicophilia? Patients with degeneration of the front parts of the brain, so-called frontotemporal dementia, sometimes develop a startling emergence or release of musical talents and passions as they lose the powers of abstraction and language—but clearly this was not the case with Dr. Cicoria, who was

articulate and highly competent in every way. There was nothing to suggest that Tony Cicoria had had a stroke or experienced any significant brain damage, other than a very transient disturbance to his memory systems for a week or two after the lightning strike.

11   His situation was similar to that of Franco Magnani, the "memory artist." Franco had never thought of being a painter until he experienced a strange crisis or illness—perhaps a form of **temporal lobe epilepsy**—when he was thirty-one. He had nightly dreams of Pontito, the little Tuscan village where he was born; after he woke, these images remained intensely vivid, with a full depth and reality. Franco was consumed by a need to make these images real, to paint them, and so he taught himself to paint, devoting every free minute to producing hundreds of views of Pontito.

temporal lobe epilepsy: seizures produced by abnormal electric discharges in the temporal lobe, which is located in both hemispheres of the brain and is responsible for auditory and memory functions.

12   Why was there such a delay in the development of Cicoria's musicophilia? What was happening in the six or seven weeks that elapsed between his cardiac arrest and the rather sudden eruption of musicality? One has to suspect that Dr. Cicoria's apparent recovery a couple of weeks after these events was not as complete as it seemed. Changes were presumably occurring in the weeks afterwards, when his brain was reorganizing—preparing, as it were, for musicophilia. Many new and far subtler tests of brain function have been developed since Cicoria had his injury in 1994, and he agreed that it would be interesting to investigate this further. But after a moment, he reconsidered, and said that perhaps it was best to let things be. His was a lucky strike, and the music, however it had come, was a blessing, a grace—not to be questioned.

VOCABULARY AND COMPREHENSION

1. Find a word in paragraph 3 that means "remaining."

    _____

2. In paragraph 4, the word *insatiable* means

    a. unsatisfactory   b. unstable   c. uncontrollable

3. In your own words, what happened to Tony Cicoria? Answer *who, what, when, where,* and *how* questions.

    _____

    _____

    _____

    _____

4. Why was it so astounding that Cicoria became a pianist?

    _____

    _____

    _____

5. According to the author, what are some physical causes that may lead someone to become a musicophile?

    _____

    _____

CRITICAL THINKING

6. Did Cicario experience any negative effects because of his *musicophilia*?

_____

_____

_____

7. Who is the audience for this essay?

_____

8. The general purpose of this text is to entertain and inform. What is the specific purpose?

_____

_____

WRITING TOPICS

> *Twiddle enough knobs, and almost anyone can sound good on a record.*
> —JOHN JONES, MUSICIAN

1. Write about a turning point in your life. Narrate what happened.
2. Argue that music or another art form is important in people's lives.
3. Reflect on the quotation. In today's world, how important is raw talent in musical success? Give examples of people who lip sync, etc.

Themes: Great Discoveries and The Workplace
READING 11

Aunt Tee
Maya Angelou

Maya Angelou is a poet, historian, civil rights activist, and writer. In this next essay from her collection *I Wouldn't Take Nothing for My Journey Now*, Angelou writes about an important person in her life. As you read this description essay, also look for elements of narration and comparison and contrast.

1   Aunt Tee was a Los Angeles member of our extended family. She was seventy-nine when I met her, sinewy, strong, and the color of old lemons. She wore her coarse, straight hair, which was slightly streaked with gray, in a long braided rope across the top of her head. With her high cheekbones, old gold skin, and almond eyes, she looked more like an Indian chief than an old black woman. (Aunt Tee described herself and any favored member of her race as Negroes. *Black* was saved for those who had incurred her disapproval.)

2   She had retired and lived alone in a dead, neat ground-floor apartment. Wax flowers and china figurines sat on elaborately embroidered and heavily starched doilies. Sofas and chairs were tautly upholstered. The only thing at ease in Aunt Tee's apartment was Aunt Tee.

3   I used to visit her often and perch on her uncomfortable sofa just to hear her stories. She was proud that after working thirty years as a maid, she spent the next thirty years as a live-in housekeeper, carrying the keys to rich houses and keeping meticulous accounts.

4   "Living in lets the white folks know Negroes are as neat and clean as they are, sometimes more so. And it gives the Negro maid a chance to see white folks ain't no smarter than Negroes. Just luckier. Sometimes."

5   Aunt Tee told me that once she was housekeeper for a couple in Bel Air, California, and lived with them in a fourteen-room ranch house. There was a day maid who cleaned, and a gardener who daily tended the lush gardens. Aunt Tee oversaw the workers. When she began the job, she cooked and served a light breakfast, a good lunch, and a full three- or four-course dinner to her employers and their guests. Aunt Tee said she watched them grow older and leaner. After a few years, they stopped entertaining and ate dinner hardly seeing each other at the table. Finally, they sat in a dry silence as they ate evening meals of soft scrambled eggs, melba toast, and weak tea. Aunt Tee said she saw them growing old but didn't see herself aging at all.

6   She became the social maven. She started "keeping company" (her phrase) with a chauffeur down the street. Her best friend and her friend's husband worked in service only a few blocks away.

7   On Saturdays, Aunt Tee would cook a pot of pigs' feet, a pot of greens, fry chicken, make potato salad, and bake a banana pudding. Then, that evening, her friends—the chauffeur, the other housekeeper, and her husband—would come to Aunt Tee's **commodious** live-in quarters. There the four would eat and drink, play records and dance. As the evening wore on, they would settle down to a serious game of bid whist.

commodious: large; spacious

8   Naturally, during this revelry, jokes were told, fingers were snapped, feet were patted, and there was a great deal of laughter.

9   Aunt Tee said that what occurred during every Saturday party startled her and her friends the first time it happened. They had been playing cards, and Aunt Tee, who had just won the bid, held a handful of trumps. She felt a cool breeze on her back and sat upright and turned around. Her employers had cracked her door open and beckoned to her. Aunt Tee, a little peeved, laid down her cards and went to the door. The couple backed away and asked her to come into the hall, and there they both spoke and won Aunt Tee's sympathy forever.

10   "Theresa, we don't mean to disturb you," the man whispered, "but you all seem to be having such a good time . . ."

11   The woman added, "We hear you and your friends laughing every Saturday night, and we'd just like to watch you. We don't want to bother you. We'll be quiet and just watch."

12   The man said, "If you'll just leave your door ajar, your friends don't need to know. We'll never make a sound." Aunt Tee said she saw no harm in agreeing, and she talked it over with her company. They said it was OK with them, but it was sad that the employers owned the gracious house, the swimming pool, three cars, and numberless palm trees, but had no joy. Aunt Tee told me that laughter and relaxation had left the house; she agreed it was sad.

13   That story has stayed with me for nearly thirty years, and when a tale remains fresh in my mind, it almost always contains a lesson which will benefit me.

14   . . . I draw the picture of the wealthy couple standing in a darkened hallway, peering into a lighted room where black servants were lifting their voices in merriment and comradery, and I realize that living well is an art which can be developed. Of course, you need the basic talents to build upon: They are a love of life and the ability to take great pleasure from small offerings, an assurance that the world owes you nothing, and awareness that every gift is exactly that, a gift. . . . Because of the routines we follow, we often forget that life is an ongoing adventure.

VOCABULARY AND COMPREHENSION

1. What is a *social maven* (paragraph 6)?

   _____

2. What is the meaning of *revelry* in paragraph 8?

   _____

3. Angelou uses descriptive imagery. Descriptive imagery includes active verbs, adjectives, and other words that appeal to the senses (sight, smell, touch, sound, taste). Underline at least six examples of descriptive imagery.

4. Why was it so important for Aunt Tee to be neat and tidy?

   _____

   _____

CRITICAL THINKING

5. Why does Angelou call her aunt's apartment *dead* (paragraph 2)?

   _____

   _____

6. In paragraph 4, Angelou quotes Aunt Tee. Why does the author use the slang word *ain't?*

   _____

   _____

7. What can you infer about the lives of Aunt Tee's wealthy employers? What types of people are they?

   _____

   _____

   _____

8. In paragraph 5, Aunt Tee says that she does not see herself aging. Why does she say this?

   _____

   _____

WRITING TOPICS

Write about one of the following topics. Remember to explore, develop, and revise and edit your work.

1. Write about a time when you saw an event that changed your perception of someone.
2. Angelou tells a story to make a point about living life to the fullest. Write about a moment in time when you felt that you were living life to its fullest. Use descriptive imagery in your writing.
3. Reflect on Rivers' quotation. Do you live in a clean, organized environment or a messy one? Describe a clean or messy room in your home. (You might reread Angelou's depiction of Aunt Tee's home to get some ideas.)

> *I hate housework. You make the beds, you do the dishes, and six months later you have to start all over again.*
> —JOAN RIVERS, ENTERTAINER

READING 12

Advertising Appeals

Michael R. Solomon, Greg W. Marshall, and Elnora W. Stuart

The next essay, which appeared in *Marketing: Real People, Real Choices*, focuses on advertising. As you read this classification essay, also look for the illustration and argument writing patterns.

1   An advertising appeal is the central idea of the ad. Some advertisers use an emotional appeal, complete with dramatic color or powerful images, while others bombard the audience with facts. Some feature sexy people or stern-looking experts—even professors from time to time. Different appeals can work for the same product, from a bland "talking head" to a montage of animated special effects. Although an attention getting way to say something profound about cat food or laundry detergent is more art than science, there are some common appeals that are highly effective.

2   Testimonials are a useful type of endorsement. A celebrity, an expert, or a "man in the street" states the product's effectiveness. The use of celebrity endorsers is a common but expensive strategy. It is particularly effective for mature products that need to differentiate themselves from competitors, such as Coke and Pepsi, which enlist celebrities to tout one cola over another. For example, Michael Jackson and Shakira have been in Pepsi ads, and Bill Cosby and Bill Gates have endorsed Coke. Makeup and perfume companies also hire well-known faces to promote their brands. For instance, Penelope Cruz advertises L'Oreal mascara, and Nicole Kidman promotes Chanel.

3   A slice-of-life format presents a dramatized scene from everyday life. Slice-of-life advertising can be effective for everyday products such as peanut butter and headache remedies that consumers may feel good about if they see "real" people buying and using them. Tide, for instance, regularly depicts ordinary kids playing a rough and tumble game and arriving home covered in dirt and grass stains. Old El Paso shows a family of four sitting around the kitchen table enjoying their tacos.

4   Fear appeal ads highlight the negative consequences of not using a product. Some fear appeal ads focus on physical harm, while others try to create concern for social harm or disapproval. Mouthwash, deodorant, and dandruff shampoo products play on viewers' concerns about social rejection. Also, life insurance companies successfully use fear appeals, as do ads aimed at changing behaviors, such as messages discouraging drug use or encouraging safe sex. Axe, for instance, has a humorous ad depicting a young man with very dirty, messy hair. The young fellow gets ambushed by a group of girls who wash his hair with Axe shampoo. Election campaigns make particular use of fear advertising. For example, during the country's health care debate, many political ads warned about seniors dying and about socialized medicine. Senators regularly warn voters about their opponents' tax plans.

5   Advertising creative types, including art directors, copywriters, photographers, and others, work hard on a "big idea"—a concept that expresses the aspects of the product, service, or organization in a tangible way. The best ads are attention-getting, memorable, and appealing to consumers.

VOCABULARY AND COMPREHENSION

1. Find two words in paragraph 2 that mean the same thing as "promote."

   _____   _____

2. Underline the thesis statement in the essay.

3. What introduction style does the author use? Circle the best answer.
   a. General background
   b. Anecdote
   c. Definition

4. Underline the topic sentence in paragraphs 2 to 4.

5. What is the author's purpose?
   a. to persuade
   b. to inform
   c. to entertain

CRITICAL THINKING

6. Add an appropriate transitional word or phrase to the beginnings of paragraphs 2 to 4. Write your ideas here.

   Para. 2

   _____

   Para. 3

   _____

   Para. 4

   _____

7. Include an additional example of each type of ad. Think about some ads that you have seen.

   testimonial

   _____

   _____

   slice-of-life

   _____

   _____

   fear appeal

   _____

   _____

8. What are ethical problems with fear-appeal ads? Think of examples to support your point.

   _____

   _____

   _____

   _____

9. Which type of advertising is most effective, in your opinion? Which type of ad is least effective? Explain your answers.

_____

_____

_____

_____

_____

WRITING TOPICS

Write about one of the following topics. Remember to explore, develop, and revise and edit your work.

1. Develop another way to classify advertising into at least three categories. List characteristics and examples of each category.
2. Describe a very effective advertising campaign. Include details to support your point.
3. Reflect on Twain's quotation. What products have been elevated into necessities when they are actually quite useless? Have you ever been influenced to buy a useless item because of a really good advertisement? Write about the power of advertising to influence people.

> *Many a small thing has been made large by the right kind of advertising.*
> —MARK TWAIN, WRITER

READING 13

Job Candidates and Facebook
Wei Du

Wei Du is a journalist who has written for MSNBC and CNBC. Currently, he is the Asia reporter for Bloomberg News. In the following essay, he looks at how information on social networking sites can have consequences on people's professional aspirations. As you read the cause and effect essay, also look for elements of narration and argument.

1   Van Allen runs a company that recruits job candidates for hospitals and clinics across the country. With physicians in short supply, he was happy to come across the resumé of a well-qualified young female psychiatrist. As part of his **due diligence** check, Allen looked her up in Facebook, a popular social networking Web site, and found things that made him think twice. "We found pictures of her taking off her shirt at parties," he said, "not just on one occasion, but on another occasion, then another occasion." Concerned about those pictures, he called the candidate and asked for an explanation. She didn't get the job. "Hospitals want doctors with great skills to provide great services to communities," Allen said. "They also don't want patients to say to each other, 'Heard about Dr. Jones? You've got to see those pictures.'" Job candidates who maintain personal sites on Facebook or MySpace are learning—sometimes the hard way—that the image they present to their friends on the Internet may not be best suited for landing the position they're seeking.

2   Although many employers are too old to qualify as members of the Facebook Generation, they're becoming increasingly savvy about using social networking sites in their hiring due diligence. That has both job candidates

due diligence:
reasonable care an employer should take to verify the qualifications of job candidates before offering them employment

and human resources professionals debating the ethics and effectiveness of snooping on the Web for the kind of information that may not come up in a job interview. According to a March survey by Ponemon Institute, a privacy think tank, 35 percent of hiring managers use Google to do online background checks on job candidates, and 23 percent look people up on social networking sites. About one-third of those Web searches lead to rejections, according to the survey.

3   Social networking sites have gained popularity among hiring managers because of the site's convenience and because managers are growing anxious about hiring the right people, researchers say. Big corporations long have retained professional investigators to check job applicants' academic degrees, criminal records, and credit reports. But until now, the cost has deterred the ability of smaller firms to do the same level of checking, said Sue Murphy, a director of National Human Resources Association. For example, new college graduates, the most active social networkers, are most likely to be the target of Web research. "For people new to a field, companies just don't have a lot to look back on," Murphy said. "They can't call up your former boss. They look you up on Facebook."

4   Financial services firms and health care providers are among the biggest users of social networking sites, said Larry Ponemon, founder of the Ponemon Institute. "These industries are stewards of people's property and health, and companies really look for a high level of integrity," he said. Professional services like law and consulting firms are also big users because companies care about how employees present themselves to clients and look for clues in how applicants present themselves online.

5   Risqué pictures are not the only way a job applicant can be tripped up. Pictures of illegal behavior like drug use or heavy alcohol use could disqualify a candidate too. Some also suggest poor writing and bad grammar in Facebook profiles and in blog entries can raise a red flag about communication skills. Derogatory comments or complaints or radical political positions also can draw the scrutiny of a prospective employer.

6   One job applicant indicated in his Facebook profile that he was a leading hacker, and he was applying to be a computer security analyst, said Ponemon. He too didn't get the job. "It's amazing how many things people just put out there," said Murphy of the human resources association. In another high-profile case last spring, a group of law school students found that pictures were taken off their Facebook accounts and reposted onto an online discussion board without their permission. Whoever posted the pictures then invited suggestive comments. The law students tried to have their pictures removed from the discussion board, complaining that they had been shunned in job interviews.

7   "Nothing on the Internet is private. Period," said Michael Fertik, CEO of Reputationdefender.com, a year-old startup offering services to minimize the damage of Web background checks. "People have to understand the standard they will be judged against in hiring. Employers don't have to believe what they see—they only have to decide not to take a chance on you."

VOCABULARY AND COMPREHENSION

1. Find a word in paragraph 5 that means "disrespectful."

   _____

2. In your own words, what is the thesis of this essay?

   _____

   _____

3. What is the percentage of employers who do online background checks on potential employees?

   _____

4. Which professional services are most likely to investigate backgrounds of future employees? Explain your answer.

   _____

   _____

5. List some reasons why an employer may reject a job candidate.

   _____

   _____

   _____

   _____

CRITICAL THINKING

6. Why do young people put potentially embarrassing information on social networking sites such as Facebook?

   _____

   _____

   _____

   _____

7. What sort of information would be considered acceptable on a Facebook page by a future employer?

   _____

8. Explain how the idea of personal privacy has changed from past generations to the present generation?

   _____

   _____

   _____

   _____

   _____

WRITING TOPICS

Write about one of the following topics. Remember to explore, develop, and revise and edit your work.

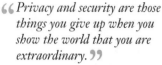

1. Write about new technologies and how they have affected your life.
2. Do people give others too much personal information? Define *oversharing* and give examples from your life.
3. Reflect on Cho's quotation and consider how social networking sites serve to make everybody feel famous in their own social circles.

> *Privacy and security are those things you give up when you show the world that you are extraordinary.*
>
> —MARGARET CHO,
> KOREAN-AMERICAN COMEDIAN

READING 14

The Beeps
Josh Freed

> Josh Freed is an award-winning journalist and documentary film writer. In the following example of an illustration essay, also look for elements of comparison and contrast and cause and effect.

1 Uh-oh. Something in the house is beeping—but what? Is it the stove announcing that dinner is cooked? Or is the dryer proclaiming my clothes are ready? Is the fridge defrosting, the thermostat adjusting, the smoke alarm dying, or is my cell phone dead? I'm living in an electronic jungle, trained to leap at every beep—if I could just figure out which beep it is.

2 I grew up in a time of easier-to-identify sounds, when telephones ding-a-linged, cash registers ka-chinged, and typewriters clacked; when school bells clanged, fire alarms rang, and ambulance sirens wailed—instead of today's digital whooping. Now they are all being replaced by the beep-beeps and bing-bings that are the frantic soundtrack of the 21st century.

3 Many of these high-pitched beeps are strangely hard to locate, even when they are right beside you. I usually fumble around for my cell phone when it rings because I can't figure out which pants pocket it's in—or which pants. Maybe it's lost under the armchair again? Several times a week, a mystery beeping goes off somewhere in our house, and I run around like a lunatic trying to find whatever it is. I listen to our bookshelves, to our laundry piles, and even to the inside of the fridge. But the beeping always stops long before I crack the mystery.

4 Meanwhile, I am bombarded on every side by other urgent electronic sounds. My car beeps constantly, nagging me to put on my seat belt, or turn off the lights, or lock the trunk, or whatever else it's trying to tell me—probably: "Wipe your shoes before you mess up my floor, mister!" My printer beeps identically when it's out of paper, or out of toner, or when something is jammed—but which is it? My microwave beeps all the time, just for fun.

5 Out in the world, elevators and ATM machines beep constantly. TV shows beep when they bleep out swear words. Store machines beep when they swipe your groceries, or you try to swipe theirs without paying. Then there are security beeps: the loud BEEEEP . . . BEEEEP . . . BEEEEP that says you're about to be run down by a city street cleaner that's backing up; the shrill beep-beep-beep-beep that says you have 15 seconds to punch in the house alarm code or an old-fashioned siren will go off alerting a security firm that you are an intruder in your own home. The simple but dreaded beep of an airline security wand means it's time to start your striptease act.

6   Even life itself is measured in beeps. Hospitals are full of machines whose soft beeps indicate you are still alive. "I beep, therefore I am." We are born into the world in a noisy jungle of beeping medical monitors and wires. We will probably leave it the same way—for most of us, the world will end with a beep, not a bang.

7   Who would have guessed the sound of the 21st century would be the cry of the cartoon Road Runner, the fast-stepping bird that was always pursued by Wile E. Coyote, crying beep-beep as it ran? Today we are all Road Runners, frantically beeping as we run for our lives, chased by our own high-speed machines and hectic lifestyles.

8   Beep-beep! Fasten your seat belt. Beep-beep! You have another new email . . . NOW. "BEEP! BEEP! Hello, we value your call, but we can't be bothered to take it now, so please don't speak until the beep." Electronic sounds have become so widespread, ornithologists report many birds are now mimicking our beeps, buzzes, and chirps as part of their mating songs. There are parrots that sound like cell phones, mockingbirds that mimic microwaves, and white-bellied caiques that do perfect car alarms.

9   Will the entire animal kingdom eventually chirp, roar, and growl electronically? Or will a new generation of humans choose more soothing sounds, like a phone ring that sounds exactly like birdsong, instead of vice-versa? Or an alarm clock that sounds like a rooster? Or a cash register that once again makes a genuine ka-ching? Perhaps we will all have truly personalized ring tones made by gentle New Age mechanical voices that show some respect for our space: "Jossshhh . . . This is your sto-o-ove speaking. Dinner is ready whenever you are, but don't rush—I'll keep it warm. Sorry if I disturbed you." "Suu-ssan . . . This is your phone ringing. Suu-ssan. I'm in your brown purse, under your make-up and your dirty gym socks. Will you take the call . . . or should I?" To beep or not to beep? That is the question future generations must face. But for now, I've got to run. That beeping just started again, and I've just figured out what it is: my computer.

VOCABULARY AND COMPREHENSION

1.   Find a word in paragraph 8 that means "imitating."

    _____

2.   Freed states that he is "living in an electronic jungle." What does he mean?

    _____

    _____

3.   The author discusses three main locations where he is bombarded with electronic beeps. List at least three locations and give examples of some noise-making machines in each category.

    _____

    _____

    _____

    _____

4.   How has new office technology affected nature?

    _____

    _____

CRITICAL THINKING

5. Why is the author frustrated with the new technology? Give at least two reasons.

   _____

   _____

   _____

6. What is the tone of the essay? Circle the best answer.

   a. serious   c. humorous
   b. angry   d. neutral

7. The author is indirectly comparing two worlds. What are they?

   _____

   _____

WRITING TOPICS

Write about one of the following topics. Remember to explore, develop, and revise and edit your work.

1. Do you own any gadgets or gizmos? List some gadgets that you own and explain why they are useful.
2. What is your most valuable possession? Give examples of why it is valuable.
3. Reflect on the quotation by Alice Kahn. Does modern technology make life easier or was life better when technology was simpler? Use examples to support your point of view.

66 *For a list of all the ways technology has failed to improve the quality of life, please press three.* 99
—ALICE KAHN,
AMERICAN AUTHOR

READING 15

Gone with the Windows
Dorothy Nixon

Dorothy Nixon, a freelance writer, has written for *Salon.com*, *Chatelaine*, and *Today's Parent* magazine. In the next essay, she compares how information today is stored or lost compared to the past. As you read this comparison and contrast essay, also look for elements of cause and effect and narration.

The other day, I had trouble accessing Photoshop through our home network. The program was on my other computer, so I had to whip downstairs to see what the problem was. I discovered that my back-up computer was in pieces. My eighteen-year-old had pulled its hard-drive apart, no doubt for some mischievous reason, and left the cannibalized carcass to air in the middle of the room.

When I asked, "What's up?" he said he needed a component to be able to play a computer game in his room with his friends—and some other people in Japan. Of course, my son has the most advanced computer in the house, by far. My son also visits all the usual Web sites so popular with teens and gets a lot of viruses on his computer. So he is always "wiping his hard drive," as he puts it.

3   I know this because he and his dad like to discuss such things. (That's definitely a good thing.) I seldom butt in on these conversations, but the other day I overheard a remark that distressed me. My son was oh-so-casually explaining to my husband how he had inadvertently erased all of his photographs from his Grade 11 trip to Europe. The images had evaporated into the ether. All gone. Not to worry, he said, "Lots of other kids still have theirs."

4   Now, he had taken hundreds of pictures of Baroque fountains, messy hotel rooms, and bleary-eyed teens—and shown me the snapshots just once upon his return. I had intended to print out the best ones and mail them to his grandmother. Now she will never see that picture of her grandson Mark with that "gladiator" in front of the Roman Coliseum.

5   Digital technology makes it all just so easy. We can instantly capture our most intimate and spontaneous moments and effortlessly pass these images on to friends and family by e-mail or snail mail or post them on web sites for the entire wired world to see. And, still, my son's record of his once-in-a-lifetime experience is lost forever.

6   I have a different perspective on things: About two years ago, I found some old documents saved by my husband's ancestors from Richmond, Quebec, in a trunk in my father-in-law's basement. There was a direct-mail ad for Crisco Shortening from 1915, when butter was getting costly. I found a National Drug Company promotional brochure with ads for bizarre remedies such as white liniment for ailments like "brain worry" and "fag" (what we might refer to as chronic-fatigue), and impotency.

7   There were family documents, too. Hundreds of letters were tied up in ribbons. Great Uncle Herb's letters reveal he was always in debt. A newspaper clipping described British militant suffragette Barbara Wylie's arrival in Montreal in 1912. Reporters couldn't believe how attractive a feminist could be!

8   I also discovered booklets containing detailed household accounts. For the 1883 marriage, it cost 5 dollars for a lady's ring and 50 cents for a frying pan. In 1884, after the baby's arrival, a toy cost 5 cents, but the doctor's bill was 51 dollars! In 1896, a house built in pseudo-Scottish Baronial style went for 2,712 dollars. Family expenses for the era averaged between 300 and 500 dollars a year. Wood for heating and dentist and medical bills (outside of childbirth) were the big expenses.

9   We're talking a lot of history here, of interest to family as well as to historians. I posted my findings on the Web, and the information has been very well received by the academic community. Some scholars have actually thanked me for making the effort. It was just luck, I tell them, just luck that one day while I was waiting for the washing machine to end its spin cycle, my gaze rested on an old Victorian trunk in a basement where I'd been hundreds of times before. I got curious.

10   Will future amateur historians be as lucky as I was? With all the runaway digital documentation going on in homes today, will today's family history be available or accessible to future inquiring minds like mine? We just recently transferred our baby-videos to CD, but it's possible that in a few years the CD format will be as impenetrable as a **cuneiform tablet**. My son's experience with his high-school pictures suggests that a lot of twenty-first century family history could be, well, gone with the Windows. And that will indeed be ironic—and a great big shame.

cuneiform tablet:
a stone tablet with the earliest known writing system in the world

VOCABULARY AND COMPREHENSION

1. In paragraph 1, what does *cannibalized carcass* refer to?

   _____

2. In paragraph 10, find a word that means "puzzling."

   _____

3. What event happened that made the author think about technology?

   _____

   _____

4. Nixon compares the present with the past. What comparison pattern does she use?

   a. point by point   b. topic by topic

CRITICAL THINKING

5. Nixon actually compares more than the present to the past. List other topics she compares.

   _____

   _____

   _____

   _____

6. Why did the author put the information she found in a trunk on her Web site?

   _____

   _____

7. How does the author see the relationship between history and technology?

   _____

   _____

   _____

WRITING TOPICS

Write about one of the following topics. Remember to explore, develop, and revise and edit your work.

1. Compare one of the following: two decades, two discoveries, or your past to your present.
2. Imagine that you could time-travel to a period in your past. Where would you go and why? Would you change what happened?
3. Reflect on Santayana's quote. Write about an event in history. Narrate what happened.

> *A country without a memory is a country of madmen.*
> —GEORGE SANTAYANA,
> SPANISH PHILOSOPHER AND POET

Themes: **Political Intrique and the Legal World**

READING 16

How Spies Are Caught

> This process essay recounts how spies are caught. As you read the text, also
> look for definition and cause and effect writing patterns.

1   Espionage is a high-risk criminal offense. The traitor must fear arrest
for the rest of his or her life, as the statute of limitations does not apply to
espionage. Former National Security Agency employee Robert Lipka was
arrested in 1996—thirty years after he left NSA and twenty-two years after his
last contact with Soviet intelligence. There are four principal ways by which
spies are detected: Reporting by U.S. sources within the foreign intelligence
service, routine counterintelligence monitoring, a tip from a friend or spouse,
or the traitor's own mistakes.

2   Of the Americans who held a security clearance who have been arrested
for espionage, about half were caught as a result of information provided by a
defector from the foreign intelligence service or an agent or friend within the
foreign service that the spy was working for. People who betray their country
often have little fear of being caught because they think they are smarter than
everyone else. They think they can easily get away with it. However, no matter
how smart or clever a spy may be, he or she has no protection against U.S.
Government sources within the other intelligence service.

3   If the spy is not reported by sources within the other intelligence service,
there is a strong likelihood of detection through routine counterintelligence
operations. Of the cleared Americans arrested for espionage or attempted
espionage during the past twenty years, 26 percent were arrested before they
could do any damage, and 47 percent were caught during their first year of
betrayal. This is not surprising, as counterintelligence agents know many of
the foreign intelligence officers active in the United States and know where
they work, where they live, where they hang out, and how they ply their trade.
Any would-be spy who doesn't know how the counterintelligence system
works is likely to be caught in the counterintelligence web.

4   Espionage usually requires keeping or preparing materials at home,
traveling to signal sites or secret meetings at unusual times and places, a
change in one's financial status with no corresponding change in job income,
and periods of high stress that affect behavior. All of these changes in the
normal pattern of behavior often come to the attention of other people and
must be explained. Other people become suspicious and pass their suspicions
on. This sometimes comes out during the periodic security clearance
reinvestigation.

5   Spying is a lonely business. To explain these changes in behavior, or
because of a need to confide in someone else, spies often confide in a spouse
or try to enlist the help of a friend. The friend or spouse in whom the spy
confides often does not remain a friend or loyal spouse after he or she realizes
what is going on.

6   Most people who betray their country are not thinking rationally, or they
would not be involved in such a self-destructive activity. They are driven, in
large part, by irrational emotional needs to feel important, successful,
powerful, or to get even or to take risks. These emotional needs are out of
control, so the same emotional needs that lead them to betray also cause them

to flaunt their sudden affluence or to brag about their involvement in some mysterious activity. Because they are so mixed up psychologically, they make mistakes that get them caught.

VOCABULARY AND COMPREHENSION QUESTIONS

1. Find a word in paragraph 6 that means "to show off."

   _____

2. What are the four ways in which spies are usually caught?

   _____

   _____

   _____

3. Give an example of the following types of support.

   Statistic: _____

   _____

   Anecdote: _____

4. How might a friend or coworker suspect that someone is a spy?

   _____

   _____

CRITICAL THINKING

5. Give at least three reasons that people betray government secrets.

   _____

   _____

   _____

6. By making inferences, determine some consequences of espionage on the individual spy.

   _____

   _____

   _____

7. In your opinion, how does treachery affect a country?

   _____

   _____

To say 'I accept' in an age like our own is to say that you accept concentration-camps, rubber truncheons, Hitler, Stalin, bombs, airplanes, tinned food, machine guns, putsches, purges, slogans, Bedaux belts, gas-masks, submarines, spies, provocateurs, press-censorship, secret prisons, aspirins, Hollywood films, and political murder.
—GEORGE ORWELL, WRITER

WRITING TOPICS

Write about one of the following topics. Remember to explore, develop, and revise and edit your work.

1. Many people feel insecure in this post-9/11 society. What steps can people take to feel safe in their own homes? Explain.
2. Most people value their privacy. Should government agencies in the United States have the right to spy on citizens by any means?
3. Reflect on Orwell's quotation. Has our age become a time of tyranny or enlightenment? Use examples to support your point of view.

READING 17

Why I Worked with La Migra

Veronica Ortega, as told to Franziska Castillo

Veronica Ortega, who crossed the border illegally as a child, worked as a member of the Army National Guard stopping immigrants from entering the United States illegally. She explains why she's still conflicted over her job. In this narrative essay, also look for comparison and contrast, cause and effect, and argument writing patterns.

1   Back in the 1980s, crossing the border was easy. My mom moved smoothly between our home in Meoqui, Mexico, and the United States a couple of times a year, where she earned a living picking crops and babysitting American kids in New Mexico. We'd stay with my grandma while my mom worked tirelessly to earn a living for us, her three children. While it was hard, we understood that survival meant Mami's feet had to be grounded in both places. Even though none of my relatives had papers, the border was never a deterrent to enter the States. For instance, for a family wedding in New Mexico, we would just pack our good clothes in little plastic baggies and wade across the Rio Grande just in time to join the party. It was a constant *va-y-viene*.

2   I was only ten the day I crossed illegally, but I don't remember being scared. My mom had a cousin who was a retired coyote. He helped my aunt, grandmother, baby brother, and little sister cross over. On the Juárez side of the Rio Grande, he told us to roll up our sleeves and take off our shoes. He had each of us climb onto his shoulders, and he took us one by one across the river. The water was pretty high, up to his neck. But he made us all feel safe.

3   Just a few minutes after being shuttled across the river, we were at a bus stop in El Paso, Texas, headed to meet my mom. It was so simple that the three of us kids imagined we were playing a big game of hide-and-seek. At that age, I just wanted to be with my mom. The boundaries or laws we were breaking never crossed my mind.

4   Ironically, nineteen years later, I ended up back on the border. This time, though, I was on patrol, helping to stop *indocumentados* from coming in. Of course, this was never something I'd planned on doing. After my mom brought us over, she struggled really hard to get us green cards. I learned fluent English, and right out of high school, I joined the Army National Guard. The women in my family have always been very strong, so the military was a natural path for me. For the eleven years I've been serving, the work has been rewarding: At one point, I helped dismantle drug dealers' cars to uncover hidden narcotics. After Hurricane Katrina, I was deployed to New Orleans to help the storm victims.

5   But last June, I was told that my next mission would be working for a few months to support the border patrol in New Mexico as part of Operation Jump Start, a mobilization of about 6,000 National Guardsmen that President George W. Bush was sending to *la frontera* to make it tougher for illegals to slip in. We were going to be stationed in the boiling-hot desert, helping the border patrol with everything from providing food and vehicles to spotting hiding immigrants.

6   My emotions were really mixed. On one hand, I kept thinking, "What if someone had stopped *me* from coming over?" But at the same time, I had signed a contract and felt obligated to fulfill my orders.

va-y-viene:
Spanish words meaning *come and go*

indocumentados:
Spanish word meaning *people without legal immigrant documents*

la frontera:
Spanish words meaning *the US/Mexican border*

7   During the first few weeks, I worked in an office, adding up the number of migrants the border patrol apprehended. I'd force myself not to think about the immigrants as people, but rather as numbers. After work, I'd go home to read books and play with my daughter to keep my mind busy with something else.

8   Then, one night, I was forced to confront the reality of my work. I was sent out to a lookout point as part of an EIT, or Entry Identification Team. EITs, using binoculars, infrared goggles, and cameras, search the desert for migrants. If we saw anything, we were supposed to radio the border patrol and guide them verbally so they could catch the immigrants.

9   A lot of people imagine the National Guard as a group walking up and down the border with M-16s, but actually being part of an EIT is as close as we get to the migrants. During my shift in the tower, everything was quiet. It was a pitch-black night, so I couldn't see anything. Even on the infrared monitor, there were no silhouettes to indicate human activity.

10   But later that night, when I was back on the ground, my partner spotted two groups. I had to radio the ***patrullas*** and explain to them that the UDAs— undocumented aliens—were hiding behind a big mesquite bush.

patrullas: Spanish word meaning *patrols*

11   Turning them in was one of the hardest things I've faced in my life. I knew the migrants were scared and had saved a lot of money to make this trip a reality. Yet there I was, helping to turn them back. And still, I found myself on the radio telling an agent, "Go right. Go left. Now stop—what do you see?" Finally he said, "I see a big bush with a UDA under it," and then we lost communication. I later learned that we helped catch fourteen people that night.

12   At first, I was glad I hadn't seen their faces—I think that would have stuck with me for a long time. But the more I thought about it, the more I began to see a positive side to my role. If we hadn't stopped them right there, they would have had to walk through the desert for three days before reaching a town. People often die out here, and if I prevented their deaths, then I'm proud to have served.

13   Being out here has been an eye-opener for me. I've seen the harsh conditions the migrants face. And I've seen a lot of prejudice among Americans. A lot of times, I end up being the go-between for ***las dos culturas***. Most of the soldiers and agents I've worked with have been really nice and respectful, while others are ignorant. Even some of the Latino soldiers from other states would laugh at the illegals and say, "Oh, they are so stupid. Why can't they just get a job in Mexico?" I had to work hard to stay calm and explain the facts.

las dos culturas: Spanish word meaning *the two cultures*

14   They were usually surprised to hear I crossed the border illegally. I felt proud that my brother, sister, and I are good examples of what former illegals can accomplish; I've earned a college degree in automotive technology, and I'm working on another one in hotel, restaurant, and tourism management. My sister works for the public schools in Las Cruces, New Mexico, and my brother is a nurse.

15   I've had a lot of time to think about the immigration issue. Anti-immigrant groups say illegals take American jobs. But many Americans don't necessarily want to work more than eight hours a day; an illegal will only take eight hours a day *off*. The anti-immigrant groups also say we should seal the border. That's probably impossible; the zone where our unit worked was 54 miles long. The border patrol would need thousands, not hundreds, of agents to spot everyone. And besides, the coyotes will always find other ways to get in.

16   I think the best solution is to improve Mexico's economy. Lots of people, including my aunts and uncles in Chihuahua, don't really want to come north. They don't have a big house, but they know everyone in their village. They share farm machinery. If they need to borrow someone's horse, they can. In the U.S., they would feel lonely and cut off. So if the economy in Mexico got stronger, they'd prefer to stay there. I'm hoping that the new president can make that happen.

17   There's a good chance I'll continue to be in the middle of the immigration issue. I recently signed up for six more years in the Guard, and by the time this article comes out, I'll probably be back out working with the border patrol. Now, the patrol's new Operation Lightning Strike will formally remove all illegal migrants caught for the first time in certain zones, including New Mexico and west Texas. If they are caught entering the country illegally again, they could face jail time. Before, a migrant had to be caught several times and sent back across the border before possibly facing a serious penalty.

18   But, *¿sabes qué?* I believe my work here is important—even helping bust immigrants. If you're smuggling human lives, I'm going to bring you down. And if you're trying to cross the border here in the desert, well, I'm going to save you.

¿sabes qué?:
Spanish question meaning *Do you know what?*

VOCABULARY AND COMPREHENSION

1.   The author uses some Spanish words in this essay. What is her purpose for doing so?

   _____

   _____

   _____

2.   Give an example of how illegal immigrants used to cross the border into the United States when the author was young.

   _____

   _____

   _____

3.   How has the illegal border crossing changed from when the author was a child?

   _____

   _____

   _____

   _____

   _____

4.   Describe the author's job in the National Guard.

   _____

   _____

   _____

   _____

CRITICAL THINKING

5. Why does the author have mixed feelings about her present job with the National Guard?

_____

_____

6. Has the author fulfilled the "American Dream"? Give examples to support your answer.

_____

_____

_____

_____

7. What are some motivations for people to cross the border illegally into the United States from Mexico?

_____

_____

8. What problems might an illegal immigrant face in the United States?

_____

_____

WRITING TOPICS

Write about one of the following topics. Remember to explore, develop, and revise and edit your work.

> 66 *Remember, remember always, that all of us, and you and I especially, are descended from immigrants and revolutionists.* 99
> —FRANKLIN D. ROOSEVELT, AMERICAN PRESIDENT

1. Write about a time when you felt conflicted and had to make a decision. Describe what happened.
2. What are your family roots? Tell a story about an event in your family' history.
3. Reflect on Roosevelt's quotation. Should illegal immigrants be granted amnesty so that they can live and work without fear of deportation? Explain why or why not.

READING 18

When the Legal Thing Isn't the Right Thing
Deborah Mead

> Deborah Mead is a poet and essayist. In the next article, which appeared in the *Christian Science Monitor*, Mead reflects on a moral dilemma. As you read this illustration essay, also look for elements of narration and comparison and contrast.

1   After spending several hours at the mall, I was stuck. Traffic had slowed to a crawl on my side of the Interstate. I was in the right lane, a mile from my exit, and anxious to get home. Apparently other drivers were anxious too, because they were flying past me in the breakdown lane.

2   On most highways, driving on the shoulder is a clear no-no, but on my particular stretch of road, it's a little murkier. The shoulder functions as a travel lane on weekdays from 6 to 10 a.m. and 3 to 7 p.m. But this was 5 p.m. on a Saturday, and by some Cinderella-style governmental magic, the special 55-mile-per-hour lane had officially reverted to its lowly breakdown status.

3   As I watched the smug drivers sail by, my frustration level rising, I tried to reason my way into breaking the law, too. I told myself it's not as if the shoulder is never used as a driving lane. By establishing these windows of travel for the shoulder, the state of Massachusetts recognizes that periods of high traffic call for breaking the normal rules of the road. This was certainly one of those times.

4   I told myself the principle of putting the greater good ahead of my own didn't apply here. It is true that if everyone at a concert stood up to get a better view, all would be worse off, with the same mediocre view but sore feet. But, in this case, if everyone regarded the shoulder as a travel lane, we would all travel **incrementally** faster. If anything, my transgression would benefit society.

incrementally:
increasingly

5   I told myself that I was getting off at the next exit, so in fact the shoulder would just be like a one-mile off-ramp. I would not be merging back into traffic later, and I would not be cutting anyone off. No one would be harmed.

6   I told myself all this—but, still, I couldn't turn onto the shoulder.

7   Unmoved by common sense, I sat in traffic for ten minutes to go that one mile, while other cars continued to whiz by me on the right. There was a time I would have felt morally superior to those selfish people breaking the law. I would have told myself that they had no regard for other people and congratulated myself on being a model citizen.

8   I don't feel that way anymore. Instead, I recognize that I am cowed by authority, particularly when that authority is anonymous, mere words on a sign. Somewhere in my civic upbringing, I confused obedience with goodness.

9   It's too late to reeducate myself now. As much as I reason with myself, and as much as I believe I would be justified in crossing over that solid line, I will bow to rules that make no sense. It is the legal thing to do—it may even be the moral thing to do—but I know it can't be right.

VOCABULARY AND COMPREHENSION

1.   In paragraph 4, find a word that means "a broken rule."

     _____

2.   Where and when does this story take place?

     _____

3.   What moral debate does Mead have with herself?

     _____

     _____

     _____

4.   Write a sentence that sums up the essay's main idea. Use your answers to questions 2 and 3 to form your sentence.

     _____

     _____

     _____

5. Does Mead believe that breaking the law and driving on the shoulder is a good idea? Why or why not?

_____

_____

CRITICAL THINKING

6. How is Mead different from those who drove by her on the shoulder of the road?

_____

_____

_____

7. What does Mead mean when she says that she is "cowed by authority" (paragraph 8)?

_____

_____

8. Mead says that she learned to confuse "obedience" with "goodness." Do you think that these two words mean the same thing? Why or why not?

_____

_____

9. Will Mead change her way of thinking in the future when she is confronted with similar dilemmas?

_____

_____

WRITING TOPICS

Write about one of the following topics. Remember to explore, develop, and revise and edit your work.

1. Mead says, "I learned to confuse obedience with goodness" (paragraph 9). Reflect on the author's words. Explain when obedience may not be a sign of goodness. Use specific examples to support your opinion.
2. Do you believe that people should follow all rules and laws, or do you believe that some rules and laws are made to be broken? Explain your opinion using specific examples of rules and laws.
3. Reflect on Einstein's quotation. Do you agree with Einstein? Explain why we need or do not need laws.

> *Every kind of peaceful cooperation among men is primarily based on mutual trust and only secondarily on institutions such as courts of justice and police.*
> —ALBERT EINSTEIN, PHYSICIST

READING 19

Interview with Jimmy Baca
Elizabeth Farnsworth

Elizabeth Farnsworth, a senior correspondent for the *The NewsHour with Jim Lehrer*, interviewed author and poet Jimmy Santiago Baca. Baca, of Chicano and Apache ancestry, was born in New Mexico. He taught himself to read and write while serving a six-year prison sentence. He has since written a memoir of his childhood called *A Place To Stand*, as well as many award-winning volumes of poetry. In the interview, Baca discusses some pivotal moments in his life.

1   ELIZABETH FARNSWORTH: You tell the story of your childhood. You were deserted by your parents, and your grandparents took care of you for a while. Then you ended up in a orphanage and finally in prison. Tell the specific story of how words and language entered your life and helped save you.

2   JIMMY SANTIAGO BACA: . . . In dark times, it seemed that words were really special to me. We didn't really have a lot of books around the house when I was growing up except the bible. Then, of course, I never had any books until I was in county jail when I took that one book.

3   ELIZABETH FARNSWORTH: Tell us what happened.

4   JIMMY SANTIAGO BACA: Well, I stole the book from the clerk, the desk clerk, and I took it up to my cell. Late at night, I was tearing pages out of it so I could cook up some coffee. The other prisoners were yelling for their coffee. They were wondering why I wasn't coming because I was on time most of the time. As the fire beneath the coffee can was flaring, I caught a couple of words that I recognized phonetically. As I read more and more, I quit tearing the pages out of the book, and I began to read. It was about a man who was walking his dog around a lake. That triggered phenomenal memories in me of my grandfather and the love I had for him and how we went around the pond with our sheep and dog. Incidentally, the man's name that I was reading later on that night, which I fell asleep enunciating, was words—words—**Wordsworth.**

5   ELIZABETH FARNSWORTH: Eventually you had poetry published in *Mother Jones Magazine* even while you were in prison. How did you go from being almost illiterate to that?

6   JIMMY SANTIAGO BACA: It was really funny because I didn't know how to address a letter, and I didn't know people paid for poetry. I was charging people cigarettes and coffees to write letters to their mothers and write letters to their girlfriends and poems and so forth for Mother's Day. A friend of mine came by with a *Mother Jones Magazine* and said, hey, they're buying poems here. I asked how to address a letter. I took my shoebox and grabbed a bunch of poems that I had written on **baby paper.** I sent them to a place called San Francisco—never expecting to hear back from them. When $300 came in, I bought the whole cellblock ice cream that day. Everyone ate ice cream.

7   ELIZABETH FARNSWORTH: Tell us how you love language and why. You've called it almost a physical thing for you.

8   JIMMY SANTIAGO BACA: Oh, I love language. Language, to me, is what sunrise is to the birds. Language, to me, is what water is to a man that just crossed the desert. I remember, as a boy, when grown-ups looked like huge redwood trees in a storm. And the grown-ups in my life were always caught up in dramas. The one thing that they all had in common was they couldn't express that storm inside of themselves. And I was so caught up in that drama that I vowed, one day, I would grasp hold of the power that could evoke their emotions. For me, at least, I wanted to know how to say what was happening to them, and I wanted to name things.

Wordsworth:
William Wordsworth (1770–1850), renowned English Romantic poet

baby paper:
scrap paper

VOCABULARY AND COMPREHENSION

1.   In paragraph 4, what is the meaning of *enunciating?* Try to guess without using a dictionary.

2. What was Baca's life like as a child?

_____

_____

3. How did Baca become interested in reading?

_____

_____

_____

4. Baca describes language metaphorically. A metaphor is a comparison without the word *like* or *as*. Underline two metaphors in paragraph 8.

CRITICAL THINKING

5. Baca compares adults to "huge redwood trees in a storm" (paragraph 8). What does he mean?

_____

_____

6. How does control over language give Baca a sense of empowerment?

_____

_____

_____

_____

7. What lessons can be learned from Baca's life experiences?

_____

_____

WRITING TOPICS

Write about one of the following topics. Remember to explore, develop, and revise and edit your work.

1. What experiences have you had that helped make you the person that you are today?
2. Conduct a short interview with someone whom you think is very interesting. You might choose someone who is much older than you are. Ask questions to discover what major lessons the person has learned in life. Then write about that person.
3. Reflect on Madwed's quotation. Describe ways in which you have invested in yourself.

If you want to be truly successful, invest in yourself.
—SIDNEY MADWED, POET AND MOTIVATIONAL SPEAKER

mywritinglab To check your progress in meeting this chapter's objectives, log in to **www.mywritinglab.com**, go to the **Study Plan** tab, click on **Reading Strategies and Selections** and choose **Critical Thinking: Responding to Text and Visuals** from the list of subtopics. Read and view the resources in the **Review Materials** section, and then complete the **Recall, Apply,** and **Write** sets in the **Activities** section.

Appendix I
Grammar Glossary

The Basic Parts of a Sentence

Parts of Speech	Definition	Some Examples
Adjective	Adds information about the noun	cautious, cold, easy, happy, slow, strange
Adverb	Adds information about the verb, adjective, or other adverb; expresses time, place, and frequency	cautiously, coldly, easily, happily, slowly, strangely, sometimes, usually, never
Conjunctive adverb	Shows a relationship between two ideas	also, consequently, finally, however, furthermore, moreover, therefore, thus
Coordinating conjunction	Connects two ideas of equal importance	for, and, nor, but, or, yet, so
Determiner	Identifies or determines if a noun is specific or general	a, an, the, this, that, these, those, any, all, each, every, many, some
Interjection	A word expressing an emotion	ouch, yikes, oh
Noun	A person, place, or thing	singular: man, dog, person plural: men, dogs, people
Preposition	Shows a relationship between words (source, direction, location, etc.)	at, to, for, from, behind, above
Pronoun	Replaces one or more nouns	he, she, it, us, ours, themselves
Subordinating conjunction	Connects two ideas when one idea is subordinate (or inferior) to the other idea	after, although, because, unless, until
Verb	Expresses an action or state of being	action: run, eat, walk, think linking: is, become, seem

PRACTICE 1

Label each word with one of the following terms.

adjective	noun	verb	adverb
conjunction	preposition	pronoun	interjection

EXAMPLE:

easy   _adjective_

1. human   _____
2. with   _____
3. below   _____
4. herself   _____
5. wow   _____

6. whispered   _____
7. quickly   _____
8. because   _____
9. children   _____
10. they   _____

Types of Clauses and Sentences

Other Key Terms	Definition	Example
clause	An **independent clause** has a subject and verb and expresses a complete idea.	The movie is funny.
	A **dependent clause** has a subject and verb but cannot stand alone. It "depends" on another clause in order to be complete.	although it is violent
phrase	A group of words that is missing a subject, a verb, or both, and is not a complete sentence	in the morning after the storm
simple sentence	One independent clause that expresses a complete idea	The movie is funny.
complex sentence	At least one dependent clause joined with one independent clause	Although the movie is violent, it conveys an important message.
compound sentence	Two or more independent clauses that are joined together	Some movies are funny, and others are deeply moving.
compound-complex sentence	At least two independent clauses joined with at least one dependent clause	Although the movie is violent, it is very entertaining, and it conveys an important message.

PRACTICE 2

Identify the types of sentences. Beside each sentence, write one of the following:

S	simple sentence
C	compound sentence
CX	complex sentence
CCX	compound-complex sentence

1. I took a university course that was very interesting. _____

2. In the course, I read a book about a famous women's rights crusader, and I finished the book in an hour. _____

3. Elizabeth Cady Stanton was born in 1915, and her father was a lawyer, judge, and congressman. _____

4. When Elizabeth was a young girl, she heard about an unfair law. _____

5. The law restricted a woman's right to own property. _____

6. One day, she took a pair of scissors, and she cut out the law from her father's law book. _____

7. She thought that the law would be cancelled. _____

8. Her plan didn't work, of course, but her father had an unusual reaction to her act. _____

9. He put down his pen and looked at Elizabeth. _____

10. With a serious expression on his face, he told Elizabeth that she could change things, and he asked her to think about his words. _____

Appendix 2
Irregular Verbs

Irregular Verbs

Base Form	Simple Past	Past Participle	Base Form	Simple Past	Past Participle
arise	arose	arisen	feel	felt	felt
be	was, were	been	fight	fought	fought
beat	beat	beat, beaten	find	found	found
become	became	become	flee*	fled	fled
begin	began	begun	fly	flew	flown
bend	bent	bent	forbid	forbade	forbidden
bet	bet	bet	forget	forgot	forgotten
bind	bound	bound	forgive	forgave	forgiven
bite	bit	bitten	forsake	forsook	forsaken
bleed	bled	bled	freeze	froze	frozen
blow	blew	blown	get	got	got, gotten
break	broke	broken	give	gave	given
breed	bred	bred	go	went	gone
bring	brought	brought	grind	ground	ground
build	built	built	grow	grew	grown
burst	burst	burst	hang	hung	hung
buy	bought	bought	have	had	had
catch	caught	caught	hear	heard	heard
choose	chose	chosen	hide	hid	hidden
cling	clung	clung	hit	hit	hit
come	came	come	hold	held	held
cost	cost	cost	hurt	hurt	hurt
creep	crept	crept	keep	kept	kept
cut	cut	cut	kneel	knelt	knelt
deal	dealt	dealt	know	knew	known
dig	dug	dug	lay	laid	laid
do	did	done	lead	led	led
draw	drew	drawn	leave	left	left
drink	drank	drunk	lend	lent	lent
drive	drove	driven	let	let	let
eat	ate	eaten	lie*	lay	lain
fall	fell	fallen	light	lit	lit
feed	fed	fed	lose	lost	lost

Lie can mean "to rest in a flat position." When *lie* means "tell a false statement," then it is a regular verb: *lie, lied, lied.*

(continued)

Irregular Verbs (continued)

Base Form	Simple Past	Past Participle	Base Form	Simple Past	Past Participle
make	made	made	speed	sped	sped
mean	meant	meant	spend	spent	spent
meet	met	met	spin	spun	spun
mistake	mistook	mistaken	split	split	split
pay	paid	paid	spread	spread	spread
prove	proved	proved, proven	spring	sprang	sprung
put	put	put	stand	stood	stood
quit	quit	quit	steal	stole	stolen
read	read	read	stick	stuck	stuck
rid	rid	rid	sting	stung	stung
ride	rode	ridden	stink	stank	stunk
ring	rang	rung	strike	struck	struck
rise	rose	risen	swear	swore	sworn
run	ran	run	sweep	swept	swept
say	said	said	swell	swelled	swollen
see	saw	seen	swim	swam	swum
sell	sold	sold	swing	swung	swung
send	sent	sent	take	took	taken
set	set	set	teach	taught	taught
shake	shook	shaken	tear	tore	torn
shine	shone	shone	tell	told	told
shoot	shot	shot	think	thought	thought
show	showed	shown	throw	threw	thrown
shrink	shrank	shrunk	thrust	thrust	thrust
shut	shut	shut	understand	understood	understood
sing	sang	sung	wake	woke	woken
sink	sank	sunk	wear	wore	worn
sit	sat	sat	weep	wept	wept
sleep	slept	slept	win	won	won
slide	slid	slid	wind	wound	wound
slit	slit	slit	withdraw	withdrew	withdrawn
speak	spoke	spoken	write	wrote	written

Appendix 3
A Quick Guide to Verb Tenses

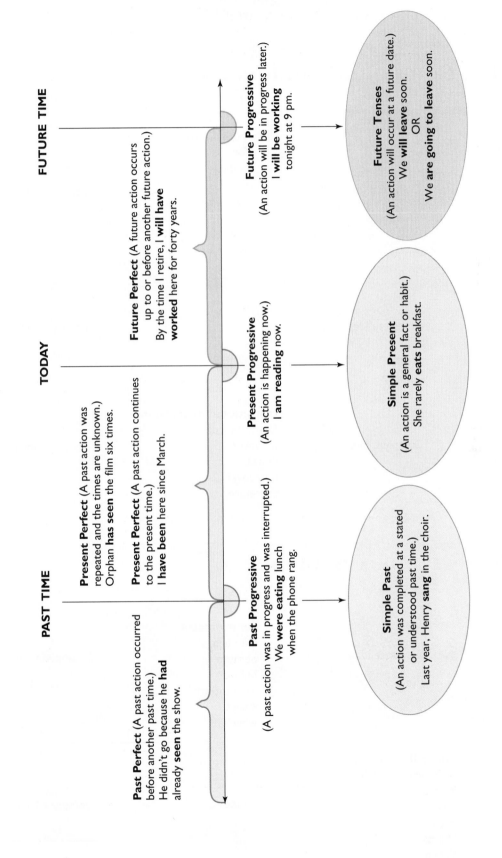

PAST TIME

TODAY

FUTURE TIME

Past Perfect (A past action occurred before another past time.)
He didn't go because he **had** already **seen** the show.

Present Perfect (A past action was repeated and the times are unknown.)
Orphan **has seen** the film six times.

Present Perfect (A past action continues to the present time.)
I **have been** here since March.

Future Perfect (A future action occurs up to or before another future action.)
By the time I retire, I **will have worked** here for forty years.

Future Progressive (An action will be in progress later.)
I **will be working** tonight at 9 pm.

Past Progressive (A past action was in progress and was interrupted.)
We **were eating** lunch when the phone rang.

Present Progressive (An action is happening now.)
I **am reading** now.

Simple Past (An action was completed at a stated or understood past time.)
Last year, Henry **sang** in the choir.

Simple Present (An action is a general fact or habit.)
She rarely **eats** breakfast.

Future Tenses (An action will occur at a future date.)
We **will leave** soon.
OR
We **are going to leave** soon.

Making Compound Sentences

A.

| Complete idea | **, coordinator**
, for
, and
, nor
, but
, or
, yet
, so | complete idea. |

B.

| Complete idea | **;** | complete idea. |

C.

| Complete idea | **; transitional expression,**
; furthermore,
; however,
; in fact,
; moreover,
; therefore, | complete idea. |

Making Complex Sentences

D.

| Complete idea | **subordinator**
although
because
before
even though
unless
when | incomplete idea. |

E.

| **Subordinator**
Although
Because
Before
Even though
Unless
When | incomplete idea | **,** | complete idea. |

Apostrophe (')

Use an apostrophe

- to join a subject and verb together.

    We're late.

- to join an auxiliary with *not*.

    I **can't** come.

- to indicate possession.

    Ross's computer is new.

Comma (,)

Use a comma

- to separate words in a series (more than two things). Place a comma before the final *and*.

    The doctor is kind, considerate, and gentle.

- after an introductory word or phrase.

    In the evenings, Carson volunteered at a hospital.

- around interrupting phrases that give additional information about the subject.

    Alan, an electrician, earns a good salary.

- in compound sentences before the coordinator.

    We worked for hours, and then we rested.

- around relative clauses containing *which*.

    The documents, which are very valuable, are up for auction.

- in quotations, after an introductory phrase or before an ending phrase.

    Picasso said, "Find your passion."

    "Find your passion," Picasso said.

Note: Do not join two complete sentences with a comma!

Colon (:)

Use a colon

- after a complete sentence that introduces a list, or after *the following*.

    The course has the following sections: pregnancy, labor, and lactation.

- after a complete sentence that introduces a quotation.

  Picasso's advice was clear: "Find your passion."

- before an explanation or example.

  Carlos explained what he really needed: a raise.

- to separate the hours and minutes in expressions of time.

  The mall opens at 9:30 a.m.

Semicolon (;)

Use a semicolon to join two independent but related clauses.

  Mahatma Gandhi was a pacifist; he believed in nonviolence.

Quotation Marks (" ")

Use quotation marks around direct speech. When a quotation is a complete sentence, capitalize the first word in the quotation. Place the end punctuation inside the closing quotation marks.

  In his essay, Levi said, "**W**e were interchangeable."

If the end of the quotation is not the end of your sentence, end the quotation with a comma. If your quotation ends with other punctuation, put it inside the closing quotation marks.

  "We were interchangeable," according to Levi.

  "You can't be serious!" she shouted.

  "What did you call me?" he replied.

Integrated Quotations

If you integrate a quotation in a sentence, add quotation marks around the words the speaker quoted.

  Dorothy Nixon calls herself a "terrible mother."

"Inside" Quotations

If one quotation is inside another quotation, add single quotation marks (' ') around the inside quotation.

  Sondra explained, "My mother said, 'Your teacher wants to meet me.'"

Citing Page Numbers

If you are using MLA style, write the page number in parentheses and place it after the quotation. Place the final period *after* the parentheses if the quotation ends the sentence.

  In his essay, Levi says, "We were interchangeable" (4).

Capitalization

Always capitalize

- the pronoun *I* and the first word of every sentence.
- the days of the week, the months, and holidays.

Tuesday   May 22   Labor Day

- the names of specific places, such as buildings, streets, parks, public squares, lakes, rivers, cities, states, and countries.

Kelvin Street   Lake Erie   White Plains, New York

- the names of languages, nationalities, tribes, races, and religions.

Spanish   Mohawk   Buddhist

- the titles of specific individuals.

General Dewitt   Dr. Franklin   Mr. Blain

- the major words in titles of literary or artistic works.

The Great Gatsby   *The Diviners*   *Crime and Punishment*

- the names of historical eras and movements.

World War I   Cubism   the Middle Ages

Punctuating Titles

Place the title of short works in quotation marks. Capitalize the major words. Short works include songs, short stories, newspaper and magazine articles, essays, and poems.

The Beatles' worst song was "Help."

Italicize the title of a longer document. If the title is in handwritten text, underline it. Long works include television series, films, works of art, magazines, books, plays, and newspapers.

Handwritten: We watched the classic movie West Side Story.

Typed: We watched the classic movie *West Side Story*.

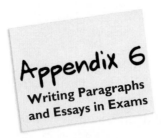

Appendix 6
Writing Paragraphs and Essays in Exams

In many of your courses, you will have to answer exam questions with a paragraph or an essay. Although taking any exam can be stressful, you can reduce exam anxiety and increase your chances of doing well by following some preparation and exam-writing strategies.

Preparing for Exams

Here are some steps you can take to help prepare for exams.

- Before you take an exam, make sure that you know exactly what material you should study. Do not be afraid to ask the instructor for clarification. Also ask what materials you should bring to the exam.
- Review the assigned information, class notes, and the textbook, if any.
- Read and repeat information out loud.
- Take notes about important points.
- Study with a friend.

 **Predict Exam Questions**

An effective study strategy is to predict possible exam questions. Here are some tips:

- Look for important themes in your course outline.
- Study your notes and try to analyze what information is of particular importance.
- Look at your previous exams for the course. Determine whether any questions or subjects are repeated in more than one exam.

After you have looked through the course outline, your notes, and previous exams, write out possible exam questions based on the information that you have collected. Then practice writing the answers to your questions.

Writing Exams

Knowing your material inside and out is a large part of exam writing; however, budgeting your time and knowing how to read exam questions are important, too. When you receive the exam paper, look it over carefully and try these test-taking strategies.

Schedule Your Time

One of the most stressful things about taking an exam is running out of time. Before you write, find out exactly how much time you have. Then, plan how much time you will need to answer the questions. For example, if you have a one-hour exam and you have three questions worth the same point value, try to make sure that you spend no more than twenty minutes on any one question.

Determine Point Values

As soon as you get an exam, scan the questions and determine which questions have a larger point value. For example, you might respond to the questions with the largest point value first, or you might begin with those that you understand well. Then go to the more difficult questions. If you find yourself blocked on a certain answer, do not waste a lot of time on it. Go to another question, and then go back to the first question later.

Carefully Read the Exam Questions

It is important to read exam instructions thoroughly. Follow the next steps.

Identify Key Words and Phrases

When you read an exam question, underline or circle key words and phrases in order to understand exactly what you are supposed to do. In the next example, the underlined words highlight three different tasks.

1. Discuss how each time period differs from the other.

Distinguish between Paleolithic, Mesolithic, and Neolithic. Place these periods in chronological order and describe how the people lived during those times.

2. Organize the essay according to each period's date.

3. Discuss what people did for shelter, food, and leisure activities.

Examine Common Question Words

Exam questions direct you using verbs (action words). This chart gives the most common words that are used in both paragraph- and essay-style questions.

Verb	Meaning
describe discuss review	Examine a subject as thoroughly as possible. Focus on the main points.
narrate trace	Describe the development or progress of something using time order.
evaluate explain your point of view interpret justify take a stand	State your opinion and give reasons to support your opinion. In other words, write an argument paragraph or essay.
analyze criticize classify	Explain something carefully by breaking it down into smaller parts.
enumerate list outline	Go through important facts one by one.
compare contrast distinguish	Discuss important similarities and/or differences.
define explain what is meant by . . .	Give a complete and accurate definition that demonstrates your understanding of the concept.
explain causes	Analyze the reasons for an event.
explain effects	Analyze the consequences or results of an event.

(continued)

Verb	Meaning
explain a process	Explain the steps needed to perform a task.
summarize	Write down the main points from a larger work.
illustrate	Demonstrate your understanding by giving examples.

PRACTICE 1

Determine the main type of response that you would use to answer each essay question.

narrate	explain a process	explain causes/effects	define
argue	classify	compare and contrast	

EXAMPLE:

Discuss the term *affirmative action*.

define

1. Distinguish between the interest rate and the rate of return.

2. Describe what happened during the Tet Offensive.

3. List and describe five types of housing.

4. What steps are required to improve your city's transportation system?

5. List the reasons for global warming.

6. Give a short but thorough description of narcissism.

7. Discuss whether religious symbols should be banned from schools.

Follow the Writing Process

When you answer paragraph or essay exam questions, remember to follow the writing process.

Explore	▪ Jot down any ideas that you think can help you answer the question.
Develop	▪ Use the exam question to guide your topic sentence or thesis statement.
	▪ List supporting ideas. Then organize your ideas and create a paragraph or essay plan.
	▪ Write the paragraph or essay. Use transitions to link your ideas.
Revise and edit	▪ Read over your writing to make sure it makes sense and that your spelling, punctuation, and mechanics are correct.

PRACTICE 2

Choose three topics from Practice 1 and write topic sentences or thesis statements.

EXAMPLE:

Discuss the term *affirmative action*.

Topic sentence or thesis statement: *Affirmative action policies give certain groups in society preferential treatment to correct a history of injustice.*

1. _____

   _____

   _____

2. _____

   _____

   _____

3. _____

   _____

   _____

PRACTICE 3

Read the following test material and answer the questions that follow.

Essay Exam

You will have ninety minutes to complete the following test. Write your answers in the answer booklet.

A. Define the following terms (2 points each).

1. Region
2. Economic geography
3. Territoriality
4. Spatial distribution
5. Gross national product

B. Write an essay response to one of the following questions. Your essay should contain relevant supporting details. (20 points)

6. Define and contrast an open city with a closed city.
7. Discuss industrial location theories in geography, and divide the theories into groups.
8. Explain the steps needed to complete a geographical survey. List the steps in order of importance.

Schedule Your Time and Determine Point Values

1. What is the total point value of the exam? _____

2. How many questions do you have to answer? _____

3. Which part of the exam would you do first? Explain why. _____

_____

_____

4. Schedule your time. How much time would you spend on each part of the exam?

Part A: _____   Part B: _____

Explain your reasoning. _____

_____

_____

Carefully Read the Exam Questions

5. Identify key words in Part B. What important information is in the instructions?

_____

6. What two things must you do in question 6?

a. _____   b. _____

7. What type of essay is required to answer question 7?
   a. Comparison and contrast   b. Classification   c. Process

8. What type of essay is required to answer question 8?
   a. Comparison and contrast   b. Classification   c. Process

Appendix 7
Spelling, Grammar, and Vocabulary Logs

In the first few pages of your writing portfolio or on the next pages, keep spelling, grammar, and vocabulary logs. The goal of keeping spelling and grammar logs is to help you stop repeating the same errors. When you write new assignments, you can consult the lists and hopefully break some ingrained bad habits. The vocabulary log can provide you with interesting new terms that you can incorporate into your writing.

Spelling Log

Every time you misspell a word, record both the mistake and the correction in your spelling log. Then, before you hand in a writing assignment, consult your spelling log. The goal is to stop repeating the same spelling errors.

EXAMPLE:

Incorrect	Correct
realy	rea<u>ll</u>y
exagerated	exa<u>gg</u>erated

Grammar Log

Each time a writing assignment is returned to you, identify one or two repeated errors and add them to your grammar log. Then, before you hand in writing assignments, consult the grammar log in order to avoid making the same errors. For each type of grammar error, you could do the following:

- Identify the assignment and write down the type of error.
- In your own words, write a rule about the error.
- Include an example from your writing assignment.

EXAMPLE: <u>Illustration Paragraph</u>   *(Feb. 12)*   *Run-On*

Do not connect two complete sentences with a comma.

accidents. Other
Bad drivers cause <u>accidents, other</u> drivers do not expect sudden lane changes.

Vocabulary Log

As you use this book, you will learn new vocabulary words. Keep a record of the most interesting and useful vocabulary words and expressions. Write a synonym or definition next to each new word.

EXAMPLE: <u>Exasperating means "annoying."</u>

Spelling Log

Grammar Log

Vocabulary Log

Credits

TEXT:

Page 7: From *Cultural Anthropology*, 10th edition by Carol R. Ember and Melvin Ember. Upper Saddle River, NJ: Prentice Hall, 2002; **p. 7:** Reprinted by permission of Jake Sibley; **p. 19:** Lee Krystek, "Strange Science." Reprinted by permission of The Museum of Unnatural Mystery; **p. 20:** From *Understanding Music*, 3rd edition by Jeremy Yudkin. Upper Saddle River, NJ: Prentice Hall, 2002; **p. 20:** Patricia Chisholm, "The Body Builders." Reprinted with permission of Maclean's Magazine; **p. 20:** From *Criminal Justice Today: An Introductory Text for the Twenty-first Century*, 6th edition by Frank Schmalleger. Upper Saddle River, NJ: Prentice Hall, 2001; **p. 26:** From *The Story of My Life* by Helen Keller, edited by Roger Shattuck. Copyright © 2003 by Roger Shattuck. Used by permission of W.W. Norton & Company, Inc.; **p. 26:** From *Out of Many*, 4th edition, edited by John Mack Faragher et al. Upper Saddle River, NJ: Prentice Hall, 2003; **p. 27:** From *The Great Gatsby* by F. Scott Fitzgerald; **p. 28:** From *1984* by George Orwell; **p. 41:** From *Sociology: A Down-to-Earth Approach: Core Concepts* by James Henslin, © 2009 James Henslin. Reproduced by permission of Pearson Education, Inc.; **p. 65:** From *In the Country of Men* by Hisham Matar. London: Penguin Group (UK) Ltd, 2006; **p. 66:** From *A Short History of Nearly Everything* by Bill Bryson. New York, NY: Broadway Books, a division of Random House, Inc., 2003; **p. 78:** Used by permission of the author; **p. 85:** Used by permission of the author; **p. 91:** From *A Beginner's Guide to the Humanities*, 2nd edition by Philip E. Bishop. Upper Saddle River, NJ: Pearson/Prentice Hall, 2007; **p. 91:** Used by permission of the author; **p. 104:** From *Marketing: Real People, Real Choices*, 4th edition by Michael Solomon. Upper Saddle River, NJ: Pearson Prentice Hall, 2006; **p. 118:** From *Sociology*, 11th edition, by John J. Macionis. Upper Saddle River, NJ: Pearson Prentice Hall, 2007; **p. 126:** Used by permission; **p. 132:** Reprinted by permission of Dorothy Nixon; **p. 133:** From *The Total Package* by Thomas Hine. Boston: Little, Brown and Company, 1995; **pp. 169–170:** Reprinted with permission of Craig Susanowitz; **p. 174:** "Kite Boarding" by Geneviève Leonard. Used by permission of the author; **p. 189:** From *Essentials of Sociology*, 1st edition by Linda L. Lindsey and Stephen Beach. Upper Saddle River, NJ: Pearson Prentice Hall, 2003; **p. 190:** From *Arab Women in the Field* edited by Soraya Altorki and Camillia Fawzi El-Solh. Syracuse, NY: Syracuse University Press, 1988; **p. 190:** From *The Heritage of World Civilizations*, 6th edition by Albert M. Craig, et al. Upper Saddle River, NJ: Prentice Hall, 2003; **p. 191:** From *Anthropology*, 12th edition, by Carole R. Ember, Melvin R. Ember, and Peter N. Peregrine. Upper Saddle River, NJ: Pearson Prentice Hall, 2007; **p. 192:** Reprinted by permission of Dorothy Nixon; **pp. 196–197:** Reprinted with permission of David Raby-Pepin; **pp. 202–203:** From "Regular summer chores pose chemical risks" by Tom Keenan, from *The Calgary Herald*, July 24, 2008. Material reprinted with the express permission of Calgary Herald Group, Inc., a CanWest Partnership; **p. 207:** Reprinted by permission of Jeff Kemp; **pp. 211–212:** Reprinted by permission of Catherine Pigott; **pp. 216–217:** Reprinted by permission of Jake Sibley; **pp. 221–222:** "Homophobia" by Dominic Chartrand. Used by permission of the author; **pp.**

225–226: Damron, W. Stephen, *Introduction to Animal Science: Global, Biological, Social and Industry Perspectives*, 3rd ed., © 2006. Reprinted by permission of Pearson Education, Inc., Upper Saddle River, New Jersey; **pp. 239–240:** Reprinted by permission of Christine Bigras; **p. 249:** From *Crime Scene Analysis: Practical Procedures and Techniques* by Wilson T. Sullivan III. Upper Saddle River, NJ: Pearson Prentice Hall, 2007; **pp. 249–250:** From "The Boys Have Fallen Behind" by Nicholas D. Kristof from *The New York Times*, March 27, 2010; **p. 250:** From "The American Way of Blame" by Martin Seligman from *APA Monitor*, 29(7), p. 2; Washington, D.C., American Psychological Association, July 1998; **pp. 257–258:** Reprinted by permission of Stephanie Samur; **p. 298:** From "The Torchbearer" by Rita Dove, *Time*, June 14, 1999; **p. 528:** "Bound Feet" from *Wild Swans: Three Daughters of China* by Jung Chang, first published by Harper Perennial. Copyright © Jung Chang. Reprinted by permission of Aitken Alexander Associates Ltd, London; **p. 530:** "Being a Hyphenated American" by Zaina Arafat. This article first appeared in *The Christian Science Monitor* (www.csmonitor.com), Feb. 6, 2009. Used by permission of the author; **p. 533:** Locher, David A., *Collective Behavior*, 1st edition, © 2002. Reprinted with permission of Pearson Education, Inc., Upper Saddle River, NJ; **p. 535:** "It's Class, Stupid!" by Richard Rodriguez. Copyright © 1997 by Richard Rodriguez. (Originally appeared in *Salon*, November 10, 1997.) Reprinted by permission of George Borchardt, Inc., on behalf of the author; **p. 541:** Reprinted with permission of CBC.ca; **p. 544:** Reprinted with permission of ELMA, Inc.; **p. 546:** Reprinted with permission from *Latina* Magazine. Article originally appeared in the Mar. 2007 issue. Copyright © Latina Media Ventures; **p. 548:** From "Don't Worry, Act Happy" by Albert Nerenberg, from *The Montreal Gazette*, Oct. 4, 2008. Material reprinted with the express permission of Montreal Gazette Group Inc., a CanWest Partnership; **p. 551:** From *Musicophilia: Tales of Music and the Brain* by Oliver Sacks, copyright © 2007, 2008 by Oliver Sacks. Used by permission of Alfred A. Knopf, a division of Random House, Inc.; **p. 554:** From *Wouldn't Take Nothing for My Journey Now* by Maya Angelou, copyright © 1993 by Maya Angelou. Used by permission of Random House, Inc.; **p. 557:** From *Marketing: Real People, Real Choices*, 4th edition by Michael Solomon. Upper Saddle River, NJ: Pearson Prentice Hall, 2006; **p. 559:** Used with permission of MSNBC from "Job candidates getting tripped up by Facebook" by Wei Du, posted on MSNBC.com, Aug. 14, 2007; permission conveyed through Copyright Clearance Center, Inc.; **p. 562:** "Welcome to the electronic jungle and a life of beeping misery" by Josh Freed, published in *The Montreal Gazette*, Aug. 2, 2008. Used by permission of the author; **p. 564:** "Gone with the Windows" by Dorothy Nixon. Copyright Dorothy Nixon. Reprinted by permission of the author. Dorothy Nixon is the author of the blog "Flo in the City"—a work in progress; **p. 569:** Reprinted with permission from *Latina* Magazine. Article originally appeared in the Oct. 2006 issue. Copyright © Latina Media Ventures; **p. 572:** Reprinted by permission of Deborah Mead; **p. 574:** "Conversation with Jimmy Santiago Baca," The NewsHour with Jim Lehrer, August 9, 2001. © 2001 MacNeil/Lehrer Productions. Used with permission.

PHOTOS:

Page 3: Lynne Gaetz; **p. 8:** ©The New Yorker Collection 1999, Arnie Levin from cartoonbank.com. All Rights Reserved; **p. 14:** Violence Policy Center; **p. 15:** Lynne Gaetz; **p. 34:** © Coco Amardeil / CORBIS All Rights Reserved; **p. 35:** Lynne Gaetz; **p. 36:** Photos.com; **p. 37:** Photos.com; **p. 38:** Photos.com; **p. 39:** Photos.com; **p. 42:** © zxvisual/iStockPhoto; **p. 51:** Tupungato/Big Stock Photo; **p. 56:** Corbis/Thinkstock; Kuzma/Big Stock Photo; Andreas Karelias/iStockphoto.com; Stockbyte/Getty Images—Thinkstock; **p. 60:** Amanda Rohde/iStockphoto.com; **p. 62:** Courtesy Sirchie Fingerprint Laboratories, Youngsville, NC, www.sirchie.com; **p. 69:** Steve Cole/iStockphoto.com; Jermey Edwards/iStockphoto.com; Jost Gantar/iStockphoto.com; **p. 74:** lafoto/Shutterstock; **p. 76:** Digital Vision/Getty Images—Thinkstock; **p. 81:** Polka Dot Images/Getty Images—Thinkstock; Steve Allen /Thinkstock; Jeremy Woodhouse/Thinkstock; **p. 87:** iStockphoto.com; **p. 89:** Getty Images/Thinkstock/Jupiterimages; **p. 95:** JustASC/Big Stock Photo; Prill Mediendesign & Fotografle/iStockphoto.com; jocic/Big Stock Photo; Cornstock/Thinkstock; **p. 100:** Newscom; **p. 102:** Radius Images/Thinkstock; **p. 109:** VikaValter/iStockphoto.com; eholmes5/Big Stock Photo; mifid/Big Stock Photo; **p. 114:** Okea/iStockphoto.com; **p. 116:** JaneB/Big Stock Photo; **p. 123:** ErickN/Big Stock Photo; Vatikaki/Big Stock Photo; C.Miller/Big Stock Photo; **p. 128:** Radka Linkova/Alamy; **p. 130:** hsandler/Big Stock Photo; **p. 137:** Photos 12/Alamy; Aaron Whitney/Shutterstock; Marmion/Big Stock Photo; Purestock/Thinkstock; **p. 143:** Antonio D'Albore/iStockphoto.com; tioloco/iStockphoto.com; **p. 144:** Photos.com; **p. 150:** Jupiterimages/Thinkstock/Getty Images; fintastique/Big Stock Photo; David Woods/Big Stock Photo; **p. 155:** Photo Illustration by Tony Cenicola/The New York Times; **p. 157;** Nancy Ney/Thinkstock; **p. 164:** Duey/Big Stock Photo; pressmaster/Big Stock Photo; Jupiterimages/Thinkstock/Getty Images; **p. 172:** Stuart Westmorland/SuperStock, Inc.; **p. 175:** Dallas and John Heaton/Stock Connection; **p. 197:** Newscom; **p. 198:** David M. Albrecht/Shutterstock; **p. 200:** Jeff Greenberg/PhotoEdit Inc.; **p. 242:** UGUR KOBAN/iStockphoto.com; **p. 248:** Atlantic Feature Syndicate; **p. 262:** andres/Big Stock Photo; **p. 273:** Mike Kemp/Thinkstock; **p. 76:** iStockphoto.com; **p. 285:** Justin Allfree/iStockphoto.com; **p. 294:** Rick Hyman/iStockphoto.com; **p. 297:** Photos.com; **p. 303:** Alex Timaios USA Photography/Alamy Royalty Free; **p. 309:** Colin Anderson/Thinkstock; **p. 317:** Thinkstock; **p. 321:** Thomas Wanstall/The Image Works; **p. 324:** Photos.com/Getty Images—Thinkstock; **p. 333:** Dieter Spannknebel/Thinkstock; **p. 345:** APF Photo/Newscom; **p. 347:** Paul Gilligan/Getty Images, Inc—Artville LLC; **p. 351:** Photos 12/Alamy; **p. 360:** Zhukov Oleg/Shutterstock; **p. 367:** Bettmann/CORBIS; **p. 372:** Joe Sohm/Chromosohm/Stock Connection; **p. 376:** Creatas/Thinkstock; **p. 385:** Victoriya Yatskina/iStockphoto.com; **p. 386:** MARIA TOUTOUDAKI/iStockphoto.com; **p. 392:** Alexey Dudoladov/iStockphoto.com; **p. 409:** Steve Allen/Thinkstock; **p. 413:** Ulrike Welsch/Photo Researchers, Inc.; **p. 415:** Dejan Patic/Thinkstock; **p. 427:** Photos.com; **p. 442:** Yanik Chauvin/iStockphoto.com; **p. 450:** Keith Brofsky/Thinkstock; **p. 452:** James McConnachie © Rough Guides; **p. 462:** Bora Ucak/iStockphoto.com; **p. 479:** Damir Karan/iStockphoto.com; **p. 492:** Mike Kemp/Thinkstock; **p. 501:** Gary Gershoff/Retna Ltd.; **p. 504:** Pavlen/iStockphoto.com; **p. 512:** Big Stock Photo; **p. 523:** Photos.com; **p. 529:** AFP PHOTO/Mark RALSTON/Newscom; **p. 534:** Newscom; **p. 551:** Quavondo/iStockphoto.com; **p. 553:** Courtesy of Franco Magnani, www.francomagnani.com; **p. 562:** Thinkstock/iStockphoto; **p. 564:** Antonis Papantoniou/iStockphoto.com; **p. 570:** Arturo Enriquez/iStockphoto.com.

Index